THE BREAD BOOK

Linda Collister & Anthony Blake

The Lyons Press

TO ALAN AND KYLE

Both metric and imperial quantities are given in the recipes. Use either all metric or all
imperial, as the two are not interchangeable.

The text and recipes of The Bread Book have been revised
and updated especially for this edition.

Published in the US in 2000 by
The Lyons Press
First published in 1993 by
Conran Octopus Ltd

Designer: Paul Welti
Editors: Beverley Le Blanc and Norma MacMillan
Commissioning Editor: Louise Simpson
Editorial Assistant: Jane Chapman
Production: Julia Golding

ISBN 1-58574-057-8
Typeset by Servis Filmsetting Ltd (1993), Peter Howard (1996)
Printed and bound in China

CONTENTS

Introduction 8

BASIC BREADS 12

FLAT BREADS 54

QUICK BREADS 74

FRIED DOUGHS 90

SAVORY BREADS 102

FRUIT AND NUT BREADS 120

CELEBRATION BREADS 138

SOURDOUGH AND RYE BREADS 158

ENRICHED DOUGHS 168

INTRODUCTION

I started making bread after I had lived in Paris for three years. When I returned to London, I was shocked at what I had to pay for the few commercially made breads that I considered worth eating. As I was living on a budget, the only solution was to develop my own recipes to recapture the flavours I had taken for granted in France. That was 12 years ago, and I have made a loaf of bread almost every day since. Bread-making is now part of my life, and bread is an important part of every meal.

Yes, family and work do keep me busy, but baking a loaf a day is not difficult. For our daily needs, I usually bake French Sourdough Loaf (page 162),which allows me great flexibility in preparation and rising times. Also, I frequently make my family Herb Rolls (page 82), which again are neither demanding nor time-consuming. I combine these with a bowl of soup for a nourishing, light meal.

Anthony Blake and I share a passion for well-made bread, but we have come together to work on this book from different backgrounds. I had a classic training as a cook and have worked in Paris and Italy, while Anthony has had a life-long interest in food, which was enriched as he photographed some of the world's greatest chefs at work.

I was helped and inspired in my bread making by Pierre Koffman, chef and owner of La Tante Claire until the 1990s, one of the few restaurants in London awarded three Michelin stars. Pierre is fascinated by bread-making, and in turn fascinates with his knowledge and enthusiasm. His expertise is such that each day he bakes rolls flavored to complement the dishes on offer in the restaurant. Anthony and I both thank him for sharing his wisdom with us.

In the year-and-a-half we traveled about in America, Ireland, Britain, France, Italy and Germany, seeking out both the famous and unsung bread bakers, we met all sorts of bread enthusiasts. They generously shared with us their secrets and tips. We were welcomed by bakers and miller of all ages and experience in a host of private and professional kitchens. Bread-

LEFT
Chef Pierre Koffmann enthusiastically explains
his philosophy of bread-making.

making has introduced us to a warm international community, with each member sharing his or her own way of making a perfect loaf. So many breads, so many recipes!

The first lesson I learned was that you can not make good bread without good flour. It amazes me how many skilled bakers spend time producing impressive-looking loaves that only disappoint on the palate. More often than not this is because they have used mass-produced, bleached, and highly refined flour. Yet, high-quality, flavorful flour is easily available from small, independent millers. Check your local health-food store or see the list of mail-order suppliers on page 187. Once you have started baking with well-produced flours, you will find the flavor and texture of your loaves vastly superior to those made with most ordinary, supermarket flours.

The advantage of stone-ground flours is that they add texture as well as flavor to your breads. The grains are not as finely crushed as they are when mass producers put them through large steel rollers. The traditional, slower method of milling grain between two stone disks does not heat the grains as the modern, rapid techniques do. This means that flour milled in the old-fashioned way retains its good flavor. If the wheat has been organically grown, your loaf will have even more goodness.

The second important lesson of bread-making I have learned is that haste makes waste, not taste. Most bread-baking books instruct you to make the dough with very warm liquid and let it rise in a warm place. A quickly made loaf does have the merit of being homemade but to my mind, it will not have the best flavor or texture.

You will see that most of my recipes are made with cool or lukewarm liquid and then left to rise at cool to normal room temperatures. This is because a slowly risen dough produces a loaf with a fuller flavor. I also prefer this loaf's texture because it is chewier and not filled with air holes. All in all, a slowly risen dough makes a more satisfying loaf than one made with a speedy rising. There is the added advantage that slowly-made bread stays fresher longer.

I am always surprised when people tell me they think bread-making requires great skill. This is not true especially with the basic, everyday loaves; some enriched breads, with their flaky layers, do take a bit of practice. But for the most part, working with yeast doughs is actually simple and straightforward. As long as you do not kill the yeast with too much heat before the loaf is baked, there is very little that can go wrong. Unlike making pastry or cakes, which requires a light touch, kneading dough only requires time and effort. Even a child can successfully knead dough and shape a loaf.

Once you begin baking bread, you will soon discover that you are

Home-baked bread is included in a simple lunch for a farm worker in an oast house in Kent, England. Large, circular oast houses were where hops were traditionally dried after harvesting.

absorbed by the endless variety. Breads come in all shapes and sizes, with different textures and tastes. Remember, too, that simple, basic loaves may be considered peasant food in one part of the world while elsewhere, they are found only on sophisticated gourmet tables.

This book contains my favorite bread recipes, as well as the ones given to Anthony and me by enthusiastic bakers around the world. This is not intended to be an encyclopedia of all the world's bread, or even a technical manual, although, I do, from time to time, illustrate techniques with step-by-step photographs. My hope is that this collection of breads we enjoy eating as well as making will inspire you to bake breads for yourself, your family, and your friends.

BASIC BREADS

It is immensely satisfying to bake an honest, flavorful loaf of bread with a rich, tantalizing aroma. Good, nourishing bread has been held in high esteem since the age of the Pharaohs, and rightly so. The bread you eat today is a slice of social history. The basic ingredients, used by those ancient Egyptians, have remained unchanged – flour, salt, water, and usually leavening – although today we can choose from a dozen different flours, enrich the water with milk, eggs, or fat, and use fresh or dried yeasts, chemical leavening agents, or the natural yeasts produced in a sourdough. Our modern bread can be as fancy or simple, sophisticated or rustic as we choose.

This chapter contains complete instructions and photographs for each stage in the recipe for making a basic loaf of bread. Although bread-making is neither complex nor tricky, you do have to take many variables into account. I bake bread every day, yet I can never be absolutely sure of the result. Much depends on the weather and the kitchen temperature, the kind of flour, the type and age of the yeast, and even the hardness of the water. My aim is that you learn what looks, tastes, smells, and feels right.

OPPOSITE AND ABOVE
Baguettes are a traditional
bread for the French

To the old saying that all you need to make good bread is time, warmth, and love, I would add practice. Once you have mastered a basic recipe – and it will take three or four batches to get the correct feel – you can experiment. Take risks – play around with various shapes, change the flavor and texture of the crumb by mixing flours and grains, or vary the crust with different toppings and glazes. The classic French baguette, for example, has a high proportion of crust to crumb, yet the crust is thin and razor-sharp, the crumb moist and light. You will soon learn that this result is achieved in the shaping, finishing, and baking of the loaf, and that a similar bread dough handled in a different manner is used to make soft, floury baps, a favorite Scottish breakfast roll.

Anthony Blake and I have watched many fine bakers in several countries make bread, and each has a special, individual method. Some bakers start with a "sponge" – yeast, liquid, and some of the flour – while others add all the liquid to the flour at once, and others add all the flour to the liquid. Some bakers swear by ice water; others use quite warm water. Some like hot conditions, while others prefer the refrigerator for the fermentation and rising of the dough. I prefer a loaf made with very little fresh yeast, flavorful flour, cool water, a fair amount of sea salt, and a long rising time in a cool spot. It is this slow fermentation of the dough that produces a well-flavored, chewy, even sturdy loaf that, as it matures, assumes a rich, complex flavor and is slow to stale.

Try the recipes and find what works best for you.

POINTS TO REMEMBER

Before you begin, read these points and The Basic Loaf recipe. These points explain why some of my recipes are made differently than recipes found in other books. For information on the chemistry of bread-making, read Harold McGee's On Food and Cooking: The Science and Lore of the Kitchen (Charles Scribner's Sons, 1984).

– Yeast is an organism that needs moisture, warmth, and sugar or flour to stimulate its growth. As it multiplies, it produces carbon dioxide, which makes dough rise.

– Temperature is crucial to yeast; if the water or liquid you add to it is too hot the yeast will be killed, too cool and its growth will be inhibited – which is actually often desirable if you want a slow rising. According to conventional wisdom, the ideal temperature is between 95°F and 105°F, termed lukewarm.

– The yeast will grow quickly if the dough is left to rise in a warm, draft-free spot. In a cool place, however, the dough will rise more slowly. Therefore rising times can vary from about 1 hour to overnight. I find that the cooler rising temperature gives a better-tasting bread, which is why most of my recipes leave the dough to rise at cool to normal room temperature. Choose a spot which is about 60°F, such as an unheated pantry.

– The quantity of liquid and flour you add varies depending on the flour and conditions, such as the heat and humidity of the kitchen. You may need a little more or a little less than the recipe states to achieve the desired dough consistency. In many recipes I've given a range for the amount of flour.

– To measure flour, scoop a dry-measure cup directly into the bag or canister. Level off the excess. If you prefer to weigh the flour, one cup will weigh 4 ounces (115g).

– I prefer fresh yeast to active dry yeast because it gives loaves a deeper flavor and I find the fresh easier to use. However, most recipes will work with active dry yeast and recipes usually include directions for both types (for detailed instructions; see page 18).

– My recipes call for either flaked (not crystal) sea salt or kosher salt because I prefer the flavor. If you use regular fine table salt, decrease the amount by half.

– Kneading (page 16) is vital for good, even-textured, well-shaped bread. Kneading helps to develop the gluten in the flour, which is necessary to support the carbon dioxide produced by the yeast. Kneading also incorporates air into the dough and ensures that the yeast is evenly distributed throughout so the loaf rises evenly.

– Dough is usually kneaded by hand for 10 minutes, or in a large, stationary mixer using a dough hook. However, I have never found that kneading dough in a food processor does it much good – and, as with all mechanical methods of kneading, it is easy to over-knead, which does more harm than good by breaking down gluten strands.

– The dough should be left to rise covered with a damp linen or cotton (but not terry-cloth) dish towel, or sheet of plastic wrap to prevent a dry crust forming, which can leave hard lumps in the finished loaf. The loaf will be heavy if it is not left to rise for long enough, though over-rising is more of a problem than slight under-rising. If a dough is seriously distended by being left to rise too long, it collapses when baked.

– Punching down the risen dough disperses the gas bubble for uniform texture and crumb.

– I do not usually specify what to use for greasing pans and baking sheets. Some bakers use melted lard, vegetable oil, or non-stick sprays; I prefer melted unsalted butter because doughs do not absorb butter as they do oil, and the loaf is less likely to stick as it bakes.

– Baking in a hot, preheated oven (usually 400°F or higher) kills the yeast quickly (which is what you want to have happen at this point) and prevents over-rising. The hotter the oven, the crisper the crust will be.

– Bread is baked through when it sounds hollow when tapped on the underside. Most breads are turned out of the baking pans onto the wire racks to cool, which prevents the steam from the loaf making the crust soggy underneath.

THE BASIC LOAF

Makes 1 large loaf

3 cups (350g) unbleached white bread
    flour

3 cups (350g) whole-wheat bread flour,
    preferably stone-ground

2 tablespoons (15g) coarse sea salt,
    crushed or ground

1 0.6-oz cake fresh yeast (15g), or 1
    envelope active dry yeast (2½
    teaspoons) plus ½ teaspoon sugar

2 cups (430ml) lukewarm water

extra flour for dusting and sprinkling

a large baking sheet, lightly greased

TO TEST IF THE LOAF IS BAKED
THROUGH, CAREFULLY TURN IT
UPSIDE DOWN AND TAP IT WITH
YOUR KNUCKLES; A THOROUGHLY
BAKED LOAF SOUNDS HOLLOW. IF THE
LOAF SOUNDS DENSE OR HEAVY, BAKE
IT FOR 5 MINUTES LONGER AND TEST
AGAIN. TRANSFER THE BREAD TO A
WIRE RACK TO COOL COMPLETELY.

This is how to make a fine-tasting, good-looking loaf of bread. The combination of white bread flour (preferably stone-ground and unbleached) and whole-wheat (preferably stone-ground) makes a loaf that is easy to work, but with great flavor and a good texture. It is shaped into an oval and simply baked on a cookie sheet, rather than in a loaf pan. Although you may use a loaf pan if you like (see instructions for shaping in A Plain White Loaf, page 24), I find this free-form shape easier and more attractive.

This basic method, which first creates a "sponge," is the same for most yeast doughs. Many of the recipes in this book will refer back to the techniques illustrated and explained below and overleaf. This loaf will keep for up to five days, and can be frozen for one month.

In very cold weather, warming the bowl of flour in a 250°F oven for 5 to 8 minutes, or microwaving on high for ½ to 1½ minutes (be sure to use a microwave-safe bowl), depending upon the amount of flour, helps the yeast start working.

Fresh Yeast Method

Professional bakers use the sponge method shown in steps 1 through 7 on page 16 to test whether the yeast is alive and working — growing and multiplying rapidly — before they add large quantities of flour, which will be wasted if the batter does not become spongy, throw it out and begin again; the yeast is probably too old, or was killed by too hot water.

This sponge technique also has the advantage of lightening the heavier loaves. It is a time-consuming technique, so many experienced home bakers prefer to skip this step, but I think it is a good idea for anyone new to bread-making to use this technique until your knowledge of yeast's characteristics becomes second nature.

The aroma of freshly baked bread will fill the kitchen when the loaf comes out of the oven. This perfectly baked loaf has a good crisp crust and a well-flavored, chewy crumb.

The Basic Loaf
Step-by-Step Directions

MIX TOGETHER THE WHITE FLOUR,
WHOLE-WHEAT FLOUR, AND THE SALT
IN A LARGE BOWL. IN VERY COLD
WEATHER WARM THE BOWL OF FLOUR
(SEE PAGE 15). THIS WILL HELP THE
YEAST START WORKING.

1 CRUMBLE THE CAKE OF FRESH YEAST
INTO A SMALL BOWL WITH YOUR
FINGERS. (IF USING ACTIVE DRY YEAST,
SEE PAGE 18.)

2 MIX ABOUT ¼ CUP OF THE MEASURED
LUKEWARM WATER WITH THE YEAST
UNTIL SMOOTH.

3 MAKE A WELL ABOUT 6 INCHES WIDE
IN THE CENTER OF THE FLOUR. ADD
THE YEAST MIXTURE.

4 POUR THE REST OF THE LUKEWARM
WATER INTO THE WELL.

5 DRAW A LITTLE FLOUR INTO THE WELL
AND MIX THOROUGHLY WITH THE
LIQUID. GRADUALLY MIX IN MORE
FLOUR UNTIL YOU HAVE A THICK,
SMOOTH BATTER IN THE WELL.

6 SPRINKLE THE BATTER WITH A LITTLE
WHITE FLOUR TO PREVENT A SKIN
FROM FORMING.

7 LET THE BATTER STAND FOR ABOUT 20
MINUTES TO SPONGE. IT WILL BECOME
AERATED AND FROTHY AND EXPAND
NEARLY TO FILL THE WELL IN THE
SPONGE.

8 GRADUALLY MIX THE REST OF THE
FLOUR IN THE BOWL INTO THE
BATTER WITH YOUR HANDS.

9 GATHER THE DOUGH INTO A BALL. IT
SHOULD BE FIRM AND LEAVE THE SIDE
OF THE BOWL CLEANLY. IF DRY, ADD
LUKEWARM WATER, 1 TABLESPOON AT
A TIME; IF STICKY, ADD FLOUR, 1
TABLESPOON AT A TIME.

10 TURN DOUGH OUT OF THE BOWL
ONTO A LIGHTLY FLOURED WORK
SURFACE AND KNEAD FOR 10
MINUTES. TO KNEAD, FIRST STRETCH
THE DOUGH AWAY FROM YOU.

11 THEN GATHER THE DOUGH BACK
INTO A BALL.

12 GIVE THE DOUGH A QUARTER TURN, THEN CONTINUE REPEATING THESE THREE MOVEMENTS.

13 AS DOUGH IS KNEADED, IT CHANGES TEXTURE TO BECOME VERY SMOOTH AND ELASTIC. IT LOOKS ALMOST GLOSSY. SHAPE THE DOUGH INTO A SMOOTH BALL.

14 WASH, DRY AND OIL THE BOWL. RETURN DOUGH TO BOWL AND TURN IT OVER SO THE TOP IS OILED TO PREVENT STICKING. COVER THE BOWL WITH A DAMP DISH TOWEL.

15 LET THE DOUGH RISE, OR PROOF, AT ROOM TEMPERATURE (ABOUT 70°F), AWAY FROM DRAFTS, UNTIL DOUBLED IN SIZE, WHICH USUALLY TAKES 1½ TO 2 HOURS.

16 THE DOUGH IS PROPERLY RISEN WHEN YOU CAN PRESS THE TIP OF YOUR FINGER INTO IT AND THE DOUGH DOES NOT SPRING BACK.

17 PUNCH DOWN THE DOUGH WITH YOUR KNUCKLES. THIS BREAKS UP LARGE CARBON DIOXIDE POCKETS AND REDISTRIBUTES THE GAS SO YOU GET AN EVEN-TEXTURED LOAF.

18 TO MAKE A FREE-FORM LOAF, ON A LIGHTLY FLOURED SURFACE, SHAPE THE DOUGH BY GENTLY KNEADING IT INTO AN OVAL 8 x 4 INCHES.

19 WITH THE EDGE OF YOUR HAND, MAKE A DEEP CREASE LENGTHWISE DOWN THE CENTER OF THE DOUGH.

20 ROLL THE SIDES OF THE DOUGH OVER TO MAKE A FAT SAUSAGE-SHAPE. TUCK THE SHORT ENDS UNDER AND PINCH ALL SEAMS TOGETHER TO SEAL THEM.

21 ROLL THE DOUGH OVER ON THE WORK SURFACE SO THE SEAM IS UNDERNEATH AND THE TOP LOOKS SMOOTH AND EVENLY SHAPED. (THE OVAL WILL MEASURE ABOUT 9 x 4 INCHES.)

22 PUT LOAF, SEAM DOWN, ONTO A GREASED BAKING SHEET. MAKE ½-INCH DEEP DIAGONAL SLASHES ON TOP. COVER WITH A DAMP DISH TOWEL; LET RISE UNTIL DOUBLED IN SIZE, 1½ TO 2 HOURS.

Baking Instructions

DURING THE LAST 15 MINUTES OF THE RISING TIME, HEAT THE OVEN TO 425°F. UNCOVER THE LOAF AND SPRINKLE THE TOP WITH ABOUT 1 TABLESPOON OF WHOLE-WHEAT FLOUR. BAKE THE LOAF FOR 15 MINUTES, THEN REDUCE THE OVEN TEMPERATURE TO 375°F AND CONTINUE BAKING FOR ANOTHER 20 TO 30 MINUTES, UNTIL THE LOAF SOUNDS HOLLOW WHEN TAPPED UNDERNEATH (PAGE 15).

Method for Active Dry Yeast

If you are using active dry yeast, it must be reconstituted before it will work. Reconstitute the yeast by sprinkling it over a small bowl containing ¼ cup warm water (105°F to 115°F), or an amount specified in a recipe, and ½ teaspoon granulated sugar.

STIR THE YEAST, SUGAR AND WATER
UNTIL THE YEAST IS DISSOLVED.

YOU SHOULD HAVE A LUMP-FREE
LIQUID. LEAVE IT TO BECOME FOAMY.

This is how reconstituted active dry yeast looks when it is foamy and ready to use. If your yeast does not look like this after 15 minutes, throw it out and begin with another, fresher envelope of yeast. It is a good idea to check the yeast's expiration date before opening.

After 5 to 10 minutes, the mixture should look very foamy. (If after 15 minutes the yeast is not foamy, it is inactive, either because it is too old or because it has been killed by water that was too hot. Throw the mixture out and start again with another, fresher envelope of yeast.) Dry yeast that is near its expiration date or taken from an open container will be slow to work, if it works at all, and the dough may take longer to rise than the times given in specific recipes. Add the foamy yeast mixture to a well in the flour and make the sponge as described in the fresh yeast method. Continue making the dough from step 8 of the fresh yeast method (see page 16).

Using Rapid-rise Dry Yeast

Rapid-rise active dry yeast can be used in all recipes where ordinary active dry yeast is specified. Simply sprinkle the contents of the envelope of yeast directly into the flour with all the other dry ingredients (omitting the sugar for the yeast). Skip the sponging stage, and mix all the liquid into the flour at once to make the dough.

WHAT WENT WRONG? COMMON PROBLEMS IN BREAD-MAKING

CRUST IS SOFT, PALE, AND SOGGY.
– Not baked long enough, or the oven temperature was too low.
– If a loaf does not sound hollow when tapped underneath, return it to the oven for 5–10 minutes longer. To make the crust crisper, place the loaf directly on the oven rack.

LOAF IS CRUMBLY AND DRY.
– Baked for too long, or the oven temperature was too high.
– Too much flour was used in the dough.

LOAF HAS UNINTENDED, LARGE HOLES.
– Over-kneaded in a food processor or electric mixer.
– If made by hand, the dough was under-kneaded (page 16).
– Risen dough was not punched down thoroughly before shaping (page 17).

CRUST IS DETACHED FROM CRUMB.
– Risen dough was not punched down thoroughly before shaping (page 17).
– Dough was not rolled tight enough while being shaped for a loaf pan (page 24).

DOUGH DIDN'T RISE, OR ROSE POORLY.
– Yeast was used past the expiration date on the envelope (page 18).
– Liquids to be mixed with yeast were too hot and killed the yeast. Liquid must be lukewarm (95°F–105°F), which is often described as blood heat or hand-hot.
– Dough was left to rise in a spot that was too hot. This is a particular danger with dough left to rise in a stainless steel bowl, especially when it is placed in an oven with a pilot light or on a stovetop.

BREAD TASTES YEASTY AND DAMP.
– Too much yeast was used. Take particular care measuring fresh yeast.
  Not baked long enough. If the loaf does not sound hollow when unmolded and tapped underneath, bake for 5–10 minutes longer. You can put it directly on the oven rack.

BREAD IS SOGGY, FLAT, AND DENSE.
– Too much liquid was added when making the dough and there was not enough flour to absorb it.
– Dough was not kneaded long enough, nor thoroughly enough (see this page).

LOAF COLLAPSED IN OVEN.
– Dough was left too long during second rising and it became over-risen. Dough should only double in size, or as specified in the recipe.

FREE-FORM LOAVES (Page 17) AND SHAPED LOAVES (Page 26) SPREAD DURING BAKING.
– Dough was too soft or too warm when it was shaped.

LOAF CRACKED ALONG ONE SIDE OR ROSE UNEVENLY.
– Loaf was subjected to uneven heat. It was placed too far to one side, or too near a hot spot in the oven. Check the oven manufacturer's handbook for correct rack and position.
  – If you have an "eccentric" oven, turn loaf regularly while it bakes.
  – Too much dough in the loaf pan, or the pan was too small.

TYPES OF FLOUR

Organic corn ready for grinding at Philipsburg Manor (page 69).

Although wheat flour is the most common variety used for making bread, you should familiarize yourself with the wide range of flours ground from other grains — these are the flours that can vary the flavor and add more texture to your loaves.

Whatever flour you buy, I urge you to search out both the stone-ground and unbleached varieties whenever possible. Your breads will have a deeper, fuller flavor.

In the following glossary, I have included other grain products important to bread-making, as well as flour storage tips (see right).

ALL-PURPOSE FLOUR is a blend of high-gluten hard wheat and low-gluten soft wheat, and is suitable for a wide range of baking needs. The flour is milled from the endosperm of the wheat berry, and contains neither the bran nor the germ. U.S. law requires that any flour not containing the germ of the wheat must have certain nutrients added back in, resulting in a flour labeled "enriched."

BARLEY FLOUR, ground from pearl barley (the grain stripped of husks and germ), imparts to breads a moist, cakelike quality with a malty aftertaste. Low in gluten, it needs to be combined with wheat flour. Adding 10 to 15 percent barley flour to sourdough, rye, and plain whole-wheat doughs makes for especially robust loaves.

BARLEY FLAKES can be cooked as a breakfast cereal or added to wheat flour for bread doughs (see Barley flour above).

BRAN is the outer layer or husk of the wheat berry. It is what gives whole-wheat flour its characteristic color. Unprocessed bran, or miller's bran, is often added to bread doughs, as well as muffin or pancake batters for extra fiber.

BULGHUR (some times spelt bulgur) is wheat berries that have been first steamed, then dried and cracked into either coarse, medium, or fine pieces, the latter often used in bread-making.

UNBLEACHED BREAD FLOUR, or bleached, formulated with practically all hard-wheat flour, has a high proportion of protein to starch. As the dough is kneaded, the protein develops into gluten, the firm, elastic structure that allows breads to rise. Available in whole-wheat or white.

BUCKWHEAT flour does not come from a true cereal but rather from a grass belonging to the sorrel family. The speckled gray-brown flour, ground from the buckwheat groat, has a distinct, slightly bitter flavor, and when mixed with wheat flour produces bread with a pungent, earthy flavor, a soft crust, and a moist, fine crumb. Buckwheat flour is also used in blinis, pancakes, and Japanese soba noodles.

CAKE FLOUR is a fine-textured, soft-wheat flour, with little gluten, and is used where a tender, delicate crumb is desired, as in cakes.

CORNMEAL is ground from dried whole kernels of yellow, white, or blue field corn, and can be milled fine or coarse. Stone-ground is preferable. Degerminated cornmeal has been sieved to remove the germ for longer shelf life. When incorporated into doughs, cornmeal creates a loaf with a grainy, somewhat dry crumb, and a slightly sweet flavor.

COARSE YELLOW CORNMEAL is the key ingredient in the well-known Italian polenta.

CORN FLOUR is finely ground cornmeal from the whole corn kernel and can be mixed with wheat flour for bread-making.

CORNSTARCH is ground from the heart or the endosperm of the corn kernel. Silky in texture, it's used as a thickener and in small quantities, to lighten flour for pastry-making.

MASA HARINA is cornmeal finely ground from white corn kernels that have been soaked in lime water before being dried. It is a major ingredient in tortilla making.

VITAL WHEAT (also known as gluten flour) is made from wheat flour and contains pure gluten, ranging from 70 to 100 percent. Gluten gives bread dough its elasticity and

Fresh stone-ground cornmeal.

allows it to rise. Added to a dough, vital wheat gluten gives it additional resiliency.

MILLET FLOUR is ground from whole millet and is rich in protein, vitamins, and minerals but lacking in gluten. It is used for making flat breads and griddle cakes, and when mixed with wheat flour, produces bread with a buttery, slightly sweet taste, a smooth, thin crust, and a moist, dense crumb.

ROLLED OATS, known commonly as oatmeal, are oat groats that have been hulled, steamed, and flattened into flakes. They can be ground into a coarse meal, or can be added as they are to bread doughs for extra fiber and nutrients.

STEEL-CUT OATS, often called Scotch or Irish oatmeal, are made by cutting the groats (hulled whole oat kernels) into pieces with steel rollers. Used for Scottish Griddle Oatcakes (page 72), they may also be added to bread doughs.

OAT FLOUR, finely ground from oat groats, contains no gluten. When mixed with wheat flour for bread-making, it contributes a firm crust, chewy texture, and a sweet, nutty flavor. Not widely available.

RYE FLAKES are cooked, rolled rye berries (the whole grain), similar to rolled oats. A small amount mixed into bread doughs adds a chewy texture and a slightly tangy flavor.

RYE FOUR adds a distinctive tangy, slightly sour flavor to breads, as well as a chewy texture. Since it contains little gluten, it is usually combined with higher protein flours (usually wheat) to increase elasticity and lighten the dough.

SELF-RISING FLOUR is a blend of all-purpose flour, baking powder, and salt, and is often used in the southern U.S. for corn bread and biscuits.

SEMOLINA FLOUR is finely ground from the endosperm of hard durum wheat. It is not the same as semolina meal which is coarsely ground from spring or winter wheat. Semolina flour adds texture and a strong wheat flavor to breads, and is also used for making pasta.

SOY FLOUR is high in protein and fat, contains no gluten, and is fifteen times richer in calcium and iron than wheat. Ground from toasted soybeans, it is used as a nutrition booster in many foods. For bread-making, a small amount mixed with wheat flour adds a mild almond flavor, a spongy crust, and a moist, fine crumb. Soy flour will cause baked goods to brown faster, so baking times or temperatures may need to be adjusted.

SPELT FLOUR is not a modern hybrid wheat, but rather its ancient ancestor. Although it can be substituted for regular wheat flour in any recipe, the usual rule is to use about 25 percent less liquid since the hydration rate of spelt flour is much higher than wheat. Also, the gluten in spelt flour is fragile, so over-mixing or kneading will produce a flat loaf.

STONE-GROUND flours have a higher nutritional value and better taste than those ground by high-speed steel rollers or hammers. The slow-moving stones crush the grain without tearing the germ and without generating heat that destroys vitamins and enzymes. The texture of stone-ground flour can range from coarse to powdery, depending on the amount of sieving the flour receives at the mill.

WHEAT GERM, the seed or embryo of the wheat kernel or berry, is high in nutrients, especially B vitamins. Its high oil content causes rancidity if it is not refrigerated. Available raw or toasted, wheat germ provides a nutrition boost to baked goods.

WHOLE-WHEAT FLOUR makes excellent breads because of its high gluten content and sweet, nutty taste. It includes the fibrous bran and nutritious germ oil from the wheat kernel or berry.

81% WHOLE-WHEAT FLOUR has had 19% of the husk and bran removed from the wheat berry, leaving only a very small amount of the germ and bran in the flour. This flour is not available retail in the U.S., although some specialty mills may be able to grind it to specification. Whole-wheat flour available in this country is labeled simply whole-wheat and includes all of the bran and germ.

CRACKED WHEAT can be fine, medium, or coarse cut, and is made by cracking the dried wheat berry between rollers. It is an excellent addition to bread doughs.

WHEAT FLAKES are cooked, rolled wheat berries, and can be used in the same way as rolled oats.

FLOUR STORAGE

All flours should be kept in airtight containers, or place the bag of flour in a plastic bag. If you remove the flour from its bag, be sure to label and date the container. All-purpose and white bread flour can be stored at 70°F for up to six months. Any flour, wheat, or otherwise that contains part of the germ from the grain will easily turn rancid because of the oil content. Tightly wrap these flours and refrigerate or freeze for up to three months. Let the flour come to room temperature before using.

TOPPINGS

Dough can be rolled in seeds or nuts after the first shaping and before the second rising, or glazed and then sprinkled with a topping just before baking. Some toppings scorch easily, so be ready to lower the oven temperature or cover the bread with foil after 15 to 20 minutes baking if the top is browning too quickly.

Fried sweet doughs (Page 92) are usually sprinkled with or rolled in confectioners' sugar, granulated or superfine sugar, or a ground cinnamon and sugar mixture after draining on paper towels.

 1 Cornmeal
 2 Wheat flakes
 3 Fresh herbs, such as rosemary
 4 Sunflower seeds
 5 Barley flakes
 6 Sea salt
 7 Sesame seeds
 8 Cracked wheat
 9 Flax seeds
10 Oats
11 Caraway seeds
12 Grated cheese
13 Rye flakes
14 Poppy seeds
15 Plain top

GLAZES

Applied to the dough just before or just after baking, a glaze changes the appearance and taste of the crust, as well as its texture. A good, wide pastry brush (one that doesn't shed) is essential, and two thin coats of glaze give a better result than one thick one.

If you glaze the dough before baking, take care that you do not glue the dough to the rim of the loaf pan or to the baking sheet; this will not only give you a problem when you turn out the baked bread, but will hinder the "spring" as the bread tries to expand in the oven. You will get a cracked or strangely shaped result.

1 Unglazed plain loaf
2 Brushed with 1 egg white beaten with ¼ teaspoon sea salt before baking
3 Dusted with flour before baking
4 Brushed with water before baking
5 Brushed with whole milk before baking
6 Dusted with granulated sugar before baking
7 Brushed with 2 teaspoons sea salt dissolved in 1 cup (230ml) water before baking
8 Brushed with half-and-half before baking
9 Brushed with olive oil after baking
10 Brushed with 1 whole egg beaten with ¼ teaspoon salt before baking
11 Brushed with light or heavy cream before baking
12 Rubbed with a butter wrapper after baking
13 Brushed with 1 egg yolk beaten with a large pinch of sea salt before baking
14 Brushed with olive oil before baking
15 Brushed with a sweet glaze (3 tablespoons granulated sugar dissolved in 3 tablespoons hot milk) after baking

A PLAIN WHITE LOAF

INGREDIENTS

Makes 2 small loaves

6 cups (680g) unbleached white bread
   flour

2 tablespoons (15g) coarse sea salt,
   crushed or ground

1 0.6-oz cake fresh yeast (15g), or 1
   envelope active dry yeast (2½
   teaspoons) plus ½ teaspoon sugar

2 cups (430ml) water from the cold tap

extra flour for dusting

2 loaf pans, about 8½ × 4½ ×
   2¾ inches, lightly greased

This basic recipe for white bread can be used to make puffy loaves, or formed into some traditional English styles of loaves – for example, a large cottage, Coburg, porcupine, or rumpy loaf – or divided into rolls. (See page 26 for shaping breads.) You can also try the toppings and glazes on pages 22 and 23 to alter the taste and appearance of the baked loaf. This loaf will keep for four days and can be frozen for one month.

Make the dough as for The Basic Loaf (page 16) using 5 cups (570g) of the white flour. If the dough is sticky, work in small amounts of the remaining flour. Knead the dough, place it in a clean, lightly greased bowl, turn the dough over so the top is oiled, then cover it with a damp dish towel and let it rise at room temperature, away from drafts. Because of the cool temperature of the water, the dough will take longer to double in size than does the dough for The Basic Loaf – up to 2½ hours.

Punch down the risen dough and turn it out onto a lightly floured work surface. Cut the dough in half. Gently knead the dough, then pat or, with a floured rolling pin, roll it into a rectangle as wide as the pans are long, about ½ inch thick. Beginning with a short side, tightly roll up the pieces of dough, pinching the edges together as you roll, then pinch the seam closed. Tuck the ends under. Place the dough, seam sides down, in the prepared pans. The pans should be half filled.

Cover the pans with damp dish towels and let the doughs rise at room temperature until doubled in size – about 1 hour. (Do not let the doughs overproof and become enormous, however, or they will collapse during baking.) During the last 15 minutes of rising, heat the oven to 450°F.

Uncover the loaves and sprinkle the tops lightly with flour. Using a very sharp knife or razor blade, either make one deep slash lengthwise down the center of the loaves to form a split, or make two diagonal slashes across the tops.

Bake for 15 minutes. Reduce the oven temperature to 400°F. Bake for another 10 to 15 minutes. To test if a loaf is baked, turn it out of the pan and tap it with your knuckles; a thoroughly baked loaf sounds hollow when tapped underneath. Unmold the bread onto wire racks and cool completely.

TO SHAPE THE DOUGH TO FIT THE PAN, ROLL IT UP, PINCHING THE EDGES.

PINCH THE SEAM CLOSED AND TUCK THE ENDS UNDER.

PLACE THE LOAF, SEAM SIDE DOWN, INTO THE PAN. THE PAN SHOULD BE HALF-FULL.

FOR A SPLIT-LOAF SHAPE, MAKE A DEEP SLASH LENGTHWISE DOWN THE CENTER.

OATMEAL ROLLS

INGREDIENTS

Makes 16

2¾ cups (230g) rolled oats

1¾ cups (395ml) milk

1 cup (115g) whole-wheat bread flour,
    preferably stone-ground

1 cup (115g) unbleached white bread
    flour

3½ teaspoons (10g) coarse sea salt,
    crushed or ground

1 0.6-oz cake fresh yeast (15g), or 1
    envelope active dry yeast (2½
    teaspoons) plus ½ teaspoon sugar

2 tablespoons lukewarm water

extra flour for dusting

beaten egg or half-and-half for glazing

extra rolled oats for sprinkling

2 baking sheets, lightly greased

Oats add texture and a distinct mealy taste that you either like or loathe. Oat bread is in vogue on both sides of the Atlantic as I write this, due to the possible connection between a diet high in oat bran and lowered blood cholesterol levels. However, many commercial oat breads taste soapy or cakelike. I suggest you use organic oats for the best flavor. In England, I buy either Jordan's or Mornflake oats.

These rolls are good with soup and are excellent toasted. Eat them the day they're baked, or freeze when cooled. The dough can also be shaped into one medium-size loaf and baked free-form. (For shaping, see The Basic Loaf, page 17.) Allow more time for a single loaf to bake.

Soak the oats in the milk in a large, covered bowl for 2 hours. In a second large bowl, mix together the whole-wheat flour, the white flour, and salt. After the oats have soaked, crumble the fresh yeast into a small bowl and mix with the lukewarm water until smooth. If using dry yeast, mix the granules and the sugar with the lukewarm water, and let stand until foamy, 5 to 10 minutes (see page 18).

Stir the yeast mixture into the soaked oats and stir this mixture into the flour. Mix well to make a soft dough. If the dough is slightly crumbly, add more water, 1 tablespoon at a time, until the dough comes together. If the dough is sticky, gradually knead in more flour, 1 tablespoon at a time, until the dough leaves your hands and the sides of the bowl cleanly. The amount of liquid and flour needed in this recipe varies, depending on the kind of oats and the type of flours you use.

Turn out the dough onto a lightly floured work surface and knead for 10 minutes, or until smooth and elastic. Put the dough into an oiled bowl, and turn the dough over so the top is oiled. Cover with a damp dish towel. Let rise at room temperature, away from drafts, until doubled in size, about 1 hour.

Punch down the risen dough. Turn out the dough onto a lightly floured work surface. Weigh the dough and divide it into sixteen equal pieces, or roll it into a fat rope and cut into sixteen even pieces. Shape each piece into a roll by making a rough ball of dough and cupping your hand over the ball so your fingertips and wrist touch the work surface. Gently rotate your hand so the dough is rolled around and smoothed into a neat roll.

Space the rolls well apart on the prepared baking sheets. Cover lightly with damp dish towels and let rise at room temperature until almost doubled in size, 30 to 45 minutes. During the last 15 minutes of rising, heat the oven to 425°F.

Remove the dish towels. Lightly brush the rolls with the chosen glaze. Sprinkle with oats. Bake the rolls for 20 minutes, or until they are browned and sound hollow when tapped underneath. Transfer to a wire rack and cool completely.

THE OATS WILL LOOK VERY SLOPPY AND SOFT
AFTER THEY HAVE SOAKED IN THE MILK FOR
2 HOURS.

ROTATE YOUR HAND SO THE DOUGH IS ROLLED
AROUND AND SMOOTHED INTO A NEAT ROLL.

TRADITIONAL BRITISH SHAPES

Most of these shapes are typically British and have a long and colorful history. Whenever possible, I'll provide a bit of background material. To make these shapes, use the dough for The Basic Loaf (page 15) or A Plain White Loaf (page 24) and let it rise once, then punch down the dough.

Appealing to the eyes as well as the palate, these homemade breads have been shaped into traditional British-style loaves. The basket includes a Sesame Snail, a Bloomer loaf, two Coburg loaves, and two Porcupine loaves. The round Coburg loaf, baked free-form with a cross cut in the top, was, according to Elizabeth David, originally a four-cornered bread, sometimes called a skull. The porcupine shape is really self-explanatory. The directions for making each shape are explained and illustrated here and on the following two pages.

ROLL OUT THE DOUGH ON A LIGHTLY FLOURED WORK SURFACE WITH A LIGHTLY FLOURED ROLLING PIN TO A RECTANGLE 1 INCH THICK.

Bloomer

Makes one large loaf

Considerable controversy surrounds the origin of this shape, according to the late food writer Elizabeth David. It may have gotten its name because it was baked without a pan, and was thus allowed to "bloom" unhindered in the oven. Another version tells us that the loaf resembled the pantaloons worn by Mrs. Amelia Bloomer, an American, who brought them to England and made them popular as the practical garb for bicycling. Stories aside, the bloomer is shaped into a long, fat loaf with flat ends and deep crosswise slashes on the top.

STARTING FROM A SHORT END, ROLL UP THE DOUGH LIKE A JELLY ROLL, PINCHING IT TOGETHER AFTER EACH ROLL.

Roll out the punched-down dough with a floured rolling pin into a large rectangle, about 1 inch thick. Starting with a short side, tightly roll up the dough like a jelly roll, pinching it together after each roll. Push the ends of the roll of dough toward the center to make a short, thick roll. Pinch the seam to seal and tuck the ends under neatly. These fiddly measures help prevent air pockets from forming in the loaf.

Slide a lightly greased baking sheet under the loaf, cover with a damp dish towel, and let rise at room temperature, away from drafts, until doubled in size, 1 to 1½ hours. During the last 15 minutes of rising, heat the oven to 450°F.

AFTER DUSTING THE LOAF WITH WHITE FLOUR, BRUSH THE SLITS WITH SALT WATER (PAGE 23)

Using a very sharp knife, make six deep slashes across the top of the loaf, being careful not to drag the knife. Dust the loaf with white flour, then brush the slits with salt water (page 23). Bake for 15 minutes. Lower the oven temperature to 400°F and bake for another 25 to 35 minutes, or until the loaf sounds hollow when tapped underneath.

COBURG

MAKE ONE DEEP CUT THROUGH THE MIDDLE, THEN MAKE TWO SHORT CUTS INTO THE CENTER.

OR, USE KITCHEN SCISSORS TO MAKE FOUR DEEP CUTS AT RIGHT ANGLES.

Makes two medium size loaves

On a lightly floured work surface, quickly knead the punched-down dough for a few seconds. Divide the dough in half. Shape each piece into a neat ball. Place each ball on a greased baking sheet. Cover with a damp dish towel and let rise at room temperature, away from drafts, until doubled in size, 1 to 1½ hours.

During the last 15 minutes of rising, heat the oven to 450°F. Using a very sharp knife, slash a deep cross through the top of each ball of dough, making one deep cut through the middle, then two short ones in the center. (Or, using kitchen scissors, make four cuts at right angles.) Brush with salt water (page 23), then dust with flour. Bake for 25 to 30 minutes, or until the loaves sound hollow when tapped underneath. If the loaves are browning too quickly, lower the oven temperature to 400°F.

Porcupine or Rumpy

Makes two medium-size loaves

Shape the punched-down dough into two balls, as for the Coburg (above). Place on greased baking sheets, cover with damp dish towels, and let rise at room temperature, away from drafts, until doubled in size, about 1 to 1½ hours. During the last 15 minutes of rising, heat the oven to 450°F.

Using a very sharp knife, slash the top of the dough several times to make a checkerboard pattern. You could also snip the dough using kitchen scissors. Brush the dough with a glaze (page 23).

Bake for 25 to 30 minutes, or until the loaves sound hollow when tapped underneath. If the loaves brown too quickly, lower the oven temperature to 400°F.

WITH A SHARP KNIFE, SCORE A CHECKERBOARD PATTERN ON TOP OF THE RISEN LOAF.

OR, USE KITCHEN SCISSORS TO MAKE NEAT ROWS OF SNIPS.

SESAME SNAIL

Makes one large loaf

Once again, punch down the risen dough – usually white (page 24) for this loaf, but there is no reason why you cannot use any other shade of dough. With your hands, roll the dough on a lightly floured surface into a rope about 3 inches thick and 25 inches long. Coil the dough into a snail shape, twisting the rope as you lift it, and tuck the ends under. Slide a greased baking sheet under the dough, pressing it back into shape if necessary. Cover with a damp dish towel and let rise, away from drafts, until almost doubled in size, about 1 hour. During the last 15 minutes, heat the oven to 450°F.

Brush the dough with water, then sprinkle with 1 to 2 tablespoons black or white sesame seeds, or a mixture of both. Gently prick the loaf around the sides with a fork. Bake for 15 minutes. Reduce the oven temperature to 400°F. Bake another 25 to 30 minutes, or until the loaf sounds hollow when tapped underneath.

In a North African bakery I found a similar loaf flavored with star anise; it was unusual and very good. To make that version, use a spice mill or clean coffee grinder to grind 2 whole star anise and 1 tablespoon black or white sesame seeds to a fine powder. This should give you a total of 2 tablespoons, which you add to the flour along with the salt. Make the white dough as directed (page 15), then let rise and shape as for the Sesame Snail. After brushing with water and sprinkling with sesame seeds, gently prick the loaf around the sides with a fork, then bake as for the Sesame Snail.

USING YOUR HANDS, ROLL OUT THE DOUGH ON A LIGHTLY FLOURED WORK SURFACE TO A ROPE ABOUT 3 INCHES THICK AND 25 INCHES LONG.

Right COIL THE DOUGH INTO A SNAIL SHAPE, TWISTING THE ROPE AS YOU LIFT IT. TUCK THE ENDS UNDER.

COTTAGE LOAF

Makes 1 large loaf

3 cups (340g) unbleached white bread flour

3 cups (340g) whole-wheat bread flour, preferably stone-ground

2 tablespoons (15g) coarse sea salt, crushed or ground

1 0.6-oz cake fresh yeast (15g), or 1 envelope active dry yeast (2½ teaspoons) plus ½ teaspoon sugar

about 1¾ cups (400ml) water from the cold tap

extra flour for dusting

1 egg, beaten, for glazing

a large baking sheet, lightly greased

SECURE THE BALLS OF DOUGH BY PUSHING TWO FINGERS AND A THUMB THROUGH THE MIDDLE.

CAREFULLY BRUSH THE LOAF WITH THE CHOSEN GLAZE.

SCORE ALL AROUND THE BOTTOM BALL OF DOUGH. REPEAT ALL AROUND THE TOP BALL.

RIGHT Freshly baked cottage loaves at Wreford's Bakery (page 177).

This very distinctive bread is always a round loaf with a smaller ball of dough pressed into the center, like a topknot. For the best taste I like to use a dough with at least 50 percent whole wheat flour, but if you are after a "purer" look, the dough for A Plain White Loaf (page 24) is fine, too.

For the best shape the dough must be quite firm, so be ready to work in a little extra flour if necessary. It is also worth remembering that as the yeast multiplies it produces carbon dioxide and liquid (alcohol), so the dough will become softer after rising. It is best to do the final rising at cool room temperature to preserve the shape.

There are two different methods for assembling this bread. Home bakers tend to fashion the loaf by shaping the dough into two balls, putting the smaller on top, then fixing them together by pushing a finger through the middle of both balls before leaving the loaf to rise. Professional bakers, however, prefer to shape the balls and let them rise separately. They then gently flatten both balls and attach them by pushing two fingers and a thumb joined together through the middle. This technique produces the most reliable shape. Finish the loaf with either an egg glaze or a saltwater glaze (page 23) before baking. This loaf keeps for four days and can be frozen for one month.

Make the dough as for The Basic Loaf (page 16), using the white and whole-wheat flours, salt, yeast, and water. Knead the dough, place in a clean, greased bowl, turn the dough over, then cover it with a damp dish towel and let rise at room temperature, away from drafts, until doubled in size, 1½ to 2 hours.

Punch down the risen dough and turn it out onto a lightly floured work surface. Cut off one-third, then shape both the small and larger pieces of dough into balls. Place the balls well apart on the prepared baking sheet and cover with a damp dish towel. Let rise at room temperature until puffy but not quite doubled in size, usually 30 to 40 minutes. Heat the oven to 450°F.

Gently flatten each ball and put the smaller ball on top of the larger one. Push two fingers and a thumb joined together into the middle of the dough to join the pieces. Let stand for 5 to 10 minutes; if left for much longer, the loaf takes on a "drunken" look.

Brush the loaf with the chosen glaze, then vertically score around the edges of the top and bottom balls with a small sharp knife or razor blade. Bake for 15 minutes. Lower the oven temperature to 400°F. Bake for another 20 to 30 minutes, or until the loaf sounds hollow when tapped underneath. Transfer to a wire rack and cool completely.

BRAIDED LOAF

INGREDIENTS

Makes 1 large loaf

6 cups (680g) unbleached white bread
    flour

1 teaspoon sugar

1 0.6-oz cake fresh yeast (15g), or 1
    envelope active dry yeast (2½
    teaspoons) plus ½ teaspoon sugar

1¾ cups (430ml) lukewarm milk

2 teaspoons salt

2 tablespoons (30g) butter

1 extra large egg, beaten

extra flour for dusting

half-and-half or beaten egg for glazing

2 tablespoons poppy seeds

a large baking sheet, lightly greased

Although you can use a basic all-white dough (page 24) or a dough made with a combination of whole-wheat and white flours (page 15), this slightly richer white dough, made with milk and an egg and sprinkled with poppy seeds, is the one that made my mother's Irish cook Annie famous before the Second World War.

To keep a good, even shape, the dough should not be too soft, and do not be tempted to put the dough to rise in a warm spot. This loaf will stay fresh for two to three days at room temperature, and it can be frozen for one month.

Mix together 1½ cups (170g) of the flour and the sugar in a large bowl. Make a well in the center of the flour and crumble in the fresh yeast. Pour the lukewarm milk over the yeast and mix until combined. If using dry yeast, mix the granules and the additional ½ teaspoon sugar with the milk in a separate bowl and let stand until frothy, 5 to 10 minutes (see page 18). Then pour the yeast mixture into the well in the flour.

Using your hands, work the flour in the bowl into the milk and yeast mixture to make a smooth batter (page 16). Cover with plastic wrap and let stand at room temperature for about 30 minutes until spongy.

Mix most of the remaining flour with the salt in another large bowl. Rub in the butter with your fingertips until the mixture looks like coarse crumbs. Stir the egg into the yeast sponge, then add the sponge to the flour mixture. Mix to form a fairly firm, rather than a soft or sticky, dough, adding as much of the remaining flour as is necessary, about 1 tablespoon at a time.

Turn out the dough onto a lightly floured work surface and punch down with your knuckles. Knead for 10 minutes, until the dough is quite firm, silky-smooth, and elastic. Put the dough into the washed and lightly greased bowl and turn the dough over so the top is oiled. Cover with a damp dish towel and let stand at room temperature, away from drafts, until doubled in size, 1 to 1½ hours.

Punch down the risen dough and turn it out onto the lightly floured work surface. The dough should be quite pliable, but not soft. It should hold its shape well – if not, work

AFTER ABOUT 30 MINUTES THE BATTER WILL
BE SPONGY (FOREGROUND). THEN MIX MOST
OF THE REMAINING FLOUR WITH THE SALT IN
A LARGE BOWL. RUB IN THE BUTTER WITH
YOUR FINGERTIPS.

WHEN THE BUTTER IS RUBBED IN THE FLOUR
MIXTURE WILL LOOK LIKE COARSE CRUMBS.

AFTER THE DOUGH HAS RISEN, TURN IT OUT
OF THE BOWL AND PUNCH IT DOWN.

DIVIDE THE DOUGH INTO THREE EQUAL
PIECES. ROLL EACH PIECE OF DOUGH INTO A
LONG ROPE.

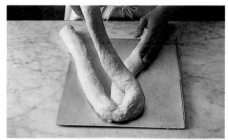

TO BRAID THE DOUGH, ARRANGE THE ROPES
SIDE BY SIDE AND SLIGHTLY APART ON THE
BAKING SHEET. PINCH THE ENDS TOGETHER
FIRMLY. LIFT THE LEFT STRAND OVER THE
CENTER STRAND.

LIFT THE RIGHT STRAND OVER THE NEW
CENTER STRAND.

THEN LIFT THE NEW LEFT STRAND OVER THE
NEW CENTER STRAND. REPEAT THIS PROCESS
UNTIL ALL THE STRANDS ARE BRAIDED.

PINCH THE ENDS TOGETHER TO SEAL THEM.
TUCK UNDER BOTH ENDS FOR A NEAT FINISH.

CAREFULLY BRUSH THE RISEN LOAF WITH
LIGHT OR HEAVY CREAM, HALF-AND-HALF, OR
BEATEN EGG TO GLAZE IT.

in a little more flour. Weigh the dough and divide it into three equal pieces, or roll it into
a fat rope and cut into thirds.

Using your hands, roll each piece into a rope 16 inches long. Lay the three ropes on
the prepared baking sheet, then braid the strands together neatly, but not too tightly.
Take care not to stretch the dough unduly. Tuck the ends under and pinch to seal.

Cover with a damp dish towel and let stand at room temperature until almost doubled
in size, about 1 hour. It is important not to overproof this loaf. During the last 15 minutes
of rising, heat the oven to 450°F.

Carefully brush the loaf with the chosen glaze, then sprinkle with the poppy seeds. Bake
for 15 to 20 minutes or until golden. Reduce the oven temperature to 400°F. Bake for
another 20 minutes, or until the loaf sounds hollow when tapped on the bottom.
Transfer to a wire rack and cool completely.

BAGUETTES

INGREDIENTS

Makes 3 loaves

5 cups (570g) unbleached white bread
    flour, preferably stone-ground

1 cup (110g) cake flour

2 tablespoons (15g) coarse sea salt,
    crushed or ground

1¾ cups (430ml) water from the cold tap

1 0.6-oz cake fresh yeast (15g)

extra flour for dusting

2 teaspoons salt dissolved in 1 cup
    (230ml) water for glazing

a large linen dish towel, floured

a large baking sheet, lightly greased

The traditional French stick loaf — with a shiny crust so crisp it breaks into razor-sharp shards and a fine-tasting, chewy interior with irregular holes — is rapidly disappearing. It is becoming difficult to find even in France, let alone anywhere else. It is also difficult to reproduce at home. In fact, you should probably not attempt this recipe unless you are an experienced bread maker. The best flour for baguettes is French and imported in bulk for bakeries and restaurants, rather than for home bakers. The oven temperature is crucial, too — domestic ovens are rarely hot enough — and, for a crusty crust, jets of steam are also vital. The best homemade loaves are made with a blend of stone-ground unbleached white bread flour and cake flour, and the oven is misted with water during baking.

Chef Pierre Koffmann, from the Michelin three-starred La Tante Claire restaurant in London, taught me how to achieve the correct temperature for the ingredients. He says the room temperature, the flour temperature (usually the same as the room temperature), and the water temperature must all total the number 190. This means if the kitchen is 72°F (a usual kitchen temperature), and the flour the same, the water must be chilled to 46°F. On a warm day it is best to use ice water. Pierre also showed me how to make the dough using what French bakers call the Polish method. The yeast and water mixture is made into a thin batter with an equal quantity of flour. It is then left to rise before continuing with the dough.

You can buy metal baguette pans, but good bakers regard them with contempt: "Avoid the loaf with that pattern of little dots underneath." Large dish towels are cheaper to use and work better for shaping the loaves. It is best to eat these loaves on the day they are made, and they do not freeze well.

Combine 4 cups (455g) bread flour, the cake flour, and the salt in a large bowl. Calculate the room and flour temperatures (see above) and chill the 1¾ cups of water so all the numbers add up to 190. Crumble the fresh yeast into a small bowl. Add 2 tablespoons of the chilled water, stir until smooth, then stir in the remaining water. Put 3 cups of the flour and salt mixture in another large bowl. Make a well in the center of the flour mixture and add the yeast mixture. Gradually work the flour into the liquid, using your hand, to make a sloppy batter (page 16).

Cover with a damp dish towel, or put the bowl into a large plastic bag and tie closed. Let stand for 4 to 5 hours at room temperature, away from drafts. The batter will become frothy, rise up in the bowl, then collapse back down.

Work in the rest of the flour mixture, plus as much of the remaining bread flour (about ¼ cup at a time) as is necessary to form a very soft dough. Turn out the dough onto a lightly floured work surface and knead for 10 minutes, or until the dough becomes firmer and springy, adding more bread flour if needed.

Wash, dry, and oil the bowl. Place the dough in the bowl and turn the dough over so the top is oiled. Cover with a damp dish towel and let rise at cool room temperature until doubled in size, 1½ to 2 hours.

Punch down the dough. Weigh the dough and divide it into three equal pieces, or roll

A sliced baguette, with its soft, irregular crumb, and a country-style loaf ready for the start of a simple meal. Even though the baguette has lost some of its flavor, it still appears on most tables every day in France.

RIGHT pedal power has transported a baguette fresh from the local baker's.

USE YOUR HAND TO MIX THE YEAST MIXTURE AND FLOUR TO MAKE A SLOPPY BATTER.

WHEN LEFT TO RISE, THE BATTER WILL BECOME FROTHY AND RISE UP IN THE BOWL.

AFTER 3 TO 5 HOURS RISING, THE BATTER WILL COLLAPSE BACK DOWN.

WORK IN THE REMAINING FLOUR MIXTURE PLUS THE REMAINING BREAD FLOUR TO FORM A SOFT DOUGH.

KNEAD THE DOUGH ON A LIGHTLY FLOURED WORK SURFACE FOR 10 MINUTES UNTIL IT BECOMES FIRMER AND SPRINGY.

ROLL OUT EACH PIECE OF DOUGH ON A LIGHTLY FLOURED WORK SURFACE INTO A CYLINDER, ABOUT 12 × 3 INCHES.

ARRANGE THE SHAPED LOAVES BETWEEN THE FOLDS OF THE FLOURED DISH TOWEL.

USE THE DISH TOWEL TO HELP ROLL LOAVES ONTO THE LIGHTLY GREASED BAKING SHEET.

USING A SHARP KNIFE, QUICKLY SLASH THE TOP OF EACH LOAF SEVERAL TIMES.

it into a fat rope and cut it into thirds. Roll each piece into a cylinder, about 12 x 3 inches. Fold the floured dish towel lengthwise to make three accordion-like creases or pleats. Arrange the pieces of dough between the folds so the loaves will keep their traditional baguette shape while they rise. Cover with a damp dish towel and let rise at cool room temperature until doubled in size, about 1 hour.

During the last 15 minutes of rising, place the baking sheet on an oven rack in the lowest position and heat the oven to 450°F.

Remove the damp dish towel and roll or lift the loaves onto the prepared baking sheet without crowding. It is best to bake the last loaf after the first two come out of the oven. Using a sharp knife or razor blade, quickly slash the top of each loaf several times, then brush with the salt water glaze.

Put the loaves in the oven, then spray the oven sides and bottom with water. Bake the loaves for 20 minutes, brushing them with salt water and spraying the oven sides and bottom with water after 10 minutes. At the end of 20 minutes, spray the oven again with water and reduce the oven temperature to 400°F.

Bake for another 5 to 10 minutes, until the loaves are crisp and they sound hollow when tapped underneath. Cool the loaves on a wire rack. Increase the oven temperature to 450°F, and bake the third loaf as described.

NOTE: You can use 1 envelope rapid-rise active dry yeast (2½ teaspoons), but I do not recommend using ordinary active dry yeast. Add the rapid-rise yeast to the 3 cups of flour followed by all the chilled water.

BRIDGE ROLLS

INGREDIENTS

Makes 36

6 cups (680g) unbleached white bread
   flour

4 teaspoons sugar

2 tablespoons (15g) coarse sea salt,
   crushed or ground

4 tablespoons (60g) unsalted butter,
   chilled and diced

1 0.6-oz cake fresh yeast (15g), or 1
   envelope active dry yeast (2½
   teaspoons) plus ½ teaspoon sugar

1¾ cups (400ml) lukewarm milk

1 large egg, beaten

extra flour for dusting

extra milk for brushing

2 large baking sheets, lightly greased

These are the small, soft-crusted rolls with a sweetish, light crumb that I remember from children's parties. They are an ideal sandwich roll filled and packed for picnics and lunch boxes. Eat within twenty-four hours of baking or freeze for up to one month.

On a vacation in Maine, I made the rolls a little larger than in this recipe and filled them with the local lobster meat mixed with mayonnaise for "Maine lobster rolls" – sheer heaven!

Put 5 cups (570g) flour, the sugar, and salt in a large bowl. Using your fingertips, rub the butter into the flour until the mixture looks like fine crumbs. Make a well in the center of the flour.

Crumble the fresh yeast into a small bowl. Add 4 tablespoons milk and mix until smooth. If using dry yeast, mix the granules and the additional ½ teaspoon sugar with the milk and let stand until foamy, 5 to 10 minutes (see page 18).

Add the yeast mixture to the well in the flour, then mix in the remaining milk and the beaten egg. Work in the flour that is in the bowl to make a soft, but not sticky dough, adding as much of the remaining flour as is necessary, about ¼ cup at a time.

Turn out the dough onto a well-floured work surface and knead for 10 minutes, or until smooth and elastic. Return the dough to the washed and greased bowl, and turn the dough over so the top is oiled. Cover the bowl with a damp dish towel and let rise at room temperature, away from drafts, until doubled in size, about 2 hours. (It is the milk and slow rising time that gives the rolls a fine, light crumb.)

Punch down the risen dough, roll it into a fat rope, and divide it into thirty-six equal

USING YOUR FINGERTIPS, RUB THE BUTTER INTO THE FLOUR UNTIL THE MIXTURE LOOKS LIKE FINE CRUMBS.

WORK IN THE FLOUR IN THE BOWL TO MAKE A SOFT, BUT NOT STICKY DOUGH, ADDING AS MUCH OF THE REMAINING FLOUR AS NECESSARY.

SHAPE EACH PIECE OF DOUGH INTO AN OVAL BY FIRST ROLLING IT INTO A CYLINDER.

SQUEEZE EACH PIECE WITH THE EDGES OF YOUR HANDS TO MAKE THE ENDS SLIGHTLY POINTED. ARRANGE APART ON THE LIGHTLY GREASED BAKING SHEETS.

LIGHTLY BRUSH THE RISEN ROLLS WITH THE MILK. IT IS BETTER TO BRUSH THE ROLLS LIGHTLY TWICE THAN ONCE HEAVILY.

TRANSFER THE BAKED ROLLS TO WIRE RACKS. COVER WITH DRY DISH TOWELS SO THE CRUSTS REMAIN SOFT. LET THE ROLLS COOL COMPLETELY.

pieces. Shape each piece into an oval by first rolling it on the work surface into a cylinder, then roll the dough on the work surface with both of your hands to make pointed ends. Place the rolls slightly apart on the prepared baking sheets. Cover with damp dish towels and let the rolls rise at room temperature until doubled in size, 30 to 45 minutes. During the last 15 minutes of rising, heat the oven to 450°F.

Lightly brush the rolls with milk. Bake for 5 minutes. Lower the oven temperature to 400°F. Bake for another 5 to 10 minutes, or until the rolls are browned and sound hollow when tapped underneath.

Transfer the rolls to a wire rack. Cover with dry dish towels to keep the crusts soft and let cool completely.

For my wedding reception, I served guests small bridge rolls with a selection of fillings. I think you will find these rolls delicious with any filling you use.

BAPS

INGREDIENTS

Makes 12

6 cups (680g) unbleached white bread
    flour

2 tablespoons (15g) coarse sea salt,
    crushed or ground

¼ cup (60g) lard, diced

1 0.6-oz cake fresh yeast (15g), or
    1 envelope active dry yeast
    (2½ teaspoons)

1 teaspoon sugar

1¾ cups (430ml) mixed lukewarm milk
    and water

extra flour for dusting

extra milk for glazing

2 baking sheets, lightly greased

Traditional Scottish scenes.

RIGHT Flour-topped baps and shiny softies
ready for a traditional Scottish breakfast.

Breakfast and afternoon tea are the best meals of the day in Scotland. Breakfast is my idea of a superb feast, with oatmeal porridge, Loch Fyne kippers, good tea, homemade marmalade, plus floury, white, soft-crusted oval baps, warm from the oven, and *Aberdeen Butteries (page 202).*

When I worked in Scotland, I enjoyed the baps from Leiths in Ballater, Aberdeenshire, and they are still my favorite. The shape, size, and crumb of baps vary from baker to baker in Scotland, but the basic mixture and the techniques are the same. They use equal quantities of milk and water to give a fine, soft crumb, dust the baps with flour, then cover them with a cloth after baking to produce a soft top, rather than a tough or crisp crust. Many bakers add a little lard to the dough, too, to add extra flavor and improve the texture.

For hill walkers and stalkers, baps are wonderful, filled with grilled strips of bacon and a fried egg, then wrapped in plastic wrap or foil, ready for a fresh-air breakfast. Baps should be eaten warm when they are baked, but can be frozen for one month.

Mix 5 cups (570g) of the flour and the salt in a large bowl. Using your fingertips, rub the lard into the flour until the mixture looks like fine crumbs. Make a well in the center of the flour.

Crumble the fresh yeast into a small bowl. Stir in the sugar and 2 tablespoons of the lukewarm milk and water mixture until smooth. If using dry yeast, mix the granules and the sugar with 2 tablespoons of the liquid and let stand until foamy, 5 to 10 minutes (see page 18).

Add the yeast mixture and remaining milk and water to the well and mix in the flour in the bowl to make a very soft dough, adding as much of the remaining flour as is necessary, about ¼ cup at a time. If necessary, add a little more water, but the dough should not stick to your fingers or the sides of the bowl.

Turn out the dough onto a lightly floured work surface and knead for 10 minutes or until it looks and feels smooth and silky, adding a little more flour if necessary to prevent sticking. Put the dough back in the washed and lightly greased bowl, and turn the dough so the top is oiled. Cover with a damp dish towel and let rise, away from drafts, until doubled in size, about 1 hour in a warm kitchen, or 1½ hours at room temperature, or overnight in a cold pantry or the refrigerator.

PAT EACH PIECE OF DOUGH INTO AN OVAL ABOUT 4½ × 3 INCHES. PLACE EACH BAP ON THE BAKING SHEET AS IT IS SHAPED.

SIFT A FINE LAYER OF FLOUR OVER THE BAPS. THEN LET THEM RISE UNTIL DOUBLED IN SIZE, ABOUT 30 MINUTES.

JUST BEFORE BAKING, SIFT A SECOND LAYER OF FLOUR OVER THE BAPS, THEN PRESS YOUR THUMB INTO THE CENTER OF EACH

ABOVE RIGHT A hearty stalker's breakfast of freshly baked bap filled with a fried egg and bacon.

Punch down the risen dough. Turn out the dough onto a lightly floured work surface and knead it for a few seconds.

Weigh the dough and divide it into twelve equal pieces, or roll it into a fat rope and cut it into twelve even pieces. With floured fingers, pat each piece of dough into an oval, about 4½ × 3 inches. Place well apart on the prepared baking sheets. Lightly brush the baps with milk, then sift a fine layer of flour over them. Let rise at room temperature until doubled in size, about 30 minutes, taking care not to let the baps over-proof. While the baps are rising, heat the oven to 425°F.

Sift another fine layer of flour over the baps, then press your thumb into the center of each. This technique makes the surface flattish, rather than domed. Bake immediately for 15 minutes, until golden and cooked underneath. Transfer to wire racks, cover with dry dish towels, and let cool for a few minutes before eating.

VARIATION: SOFTIES OR MORNING ROLLS
Use the same dough as for baps to make the soft rolls known as softies or morning rolls. Shape into smooth rolls by rolling each ball on the work surface under your cupped hand. Then cover and let rise as directed above. Before baking, brush with a little light or heavy cream. Bake in a 425°F oven for 20 minutes, or until golden brown. Brush again with cream after removing from the oven. Transfer to wire racks, cover with dry dish towels, and leave to cool. Serve warm or leave to cool completely.

LIGHTLY BRUSH THE RISEN SOFTIES WITH CREAM JUST BEFORE BAKING.

AS SOON AS THE SOFTIES COME OUT OF THE OVEN, BRUSH AGAIN WITH CREAM.

CORNISH OR DEVONSHIRE SPLITS

INGREDIENTS

Makes 22

6 cups (680g) unbleached white bread
flour

2 tablespoons (15g) coarse sea salt,
crushed or ground

1 0.6-oz cake fresh yeast (15g), or
1 envelope active dry yeast
(2½ teaspoons)

1 teaspoon granulated sugar

1¾ cups (430ml) lukewarm milk

½ cup (110g) unsalted butter, diced

extra flour for dusting

confectioners' sugar for dusting

a large baking sheet, floured

Joe Roskilly drives the family's herd of Jersey
and Guernsey cows to the milking parlor.

In England, these buns, with their soft, sweet crust and light, moist crumb, are eaten warm, split open and spread with clotted cream and treacle, raspberry jam, or golden syrup. The cream and treacle combination, favored by Rachel Roskilly, who makes the best clotted cream I have ever tasted from her Jersey/Guernsey herd at St. Kevern, on The Lizard in Cornwall, is called "thunder and lightning." Clotted cream isn't readily available in the U.S., nor is treacle, but you could make an approximation of this wonderful combination by blending crème fraîche with dark molasses to taste.

Serve splits after they have cooled to warm. Eat within one day or freeze for up to one month.

Mix together the flour and salt in a large bowl. If it is a chilly day, gently warm the flour (page 15). Crumble the fresh yeast into a medium-size bowl. Mix with the sugar and 2 tablespoons of the milk until smooth. If using dry yeast, mix the granules and the sugar with 2 tablespoons of the milk and let stand until foamy, 5 to 10 minutes (see page 18).

Stir the rest of the milk into the yeast mixture, followed by 1½ cups (170g) of the flour, until smooth. Cover with plastic wrap and let stand at room temperature until frothy, about 30 minutes.

Using your fingertips, rub the diced butter into the remaining flour until the mixture looks like fine crumbs. Mix in the frothy yeast sponge to make a soft, but not too sticky, dough. If the dough is dry and crumbly, add a little more milk or water, 1 tablespoon at a time, until the dough comes together. If the dough sticks to your fingers, work in extra flour, 1 tablespoon at a time.

MIX THE BUTTER AND FLOUR MIXTURE WITH THE FROTHY YEAST SPONGE UNTIL THE DOUGH IS SOFT BUT NOT STICKY. IF THE DOUGH STICKS TO YOUR FINGERS, WORK IN ABOUT 1 TABLESPOON FLOUR.

CUP YOUR HANDS OVER A BALL OF DOUGH SO YOUR FINGERTIPS AND WRIST TOUCH THE WORK SURFACE. ROTATE YOUR HAND, SHAPING THE DOUGH INTO A SMOOTH ROLL.

ARRANGE THE ROLLS ON THE FLOURED BAKING SHEET SO THEY ALMOST TOUCH EACH OTHER.

AS SOON AS THE ROLLS COME OUT OF THE OVEN, SIFT CONFECTIONERS' SUGAR OVER THEM. TRANSFER TO WIRE RACKS AND COVER WITH DRY DISH TOWELS. COOL TO WARM.

Rachel Roskilly (left) and an assistant fill pots with rich, thick clotted cream from her family dairy. Rachel's clotted cream is an essential ingredient in local cream teas.

RIGHT A mouth-watering Cornish split filled with Rachel's clotted cream and homemade strawberry jam is a Cornish specialty. Neighboring Devonians also claim this rich treat as their own, calling it a Devonshire split.

Turn out the dough onto a lightly floured work surface and knead for 10 minutes until smooth and elastic. Put the dough into an oiled bowl, and turn the dough over so the top is oiled. Cover with a damp dish towel. Let rise at room temperature, away from drafts, until doubled in size, 1 to 1½ hours.

Punch down the risen dough with your knuckles. Turn out the dough onto a floured surface and knead for about 10 seconds only. Weigh the dough and divide it into twenty-two equal pieces, or roll it into a fat rope and cut it into twenty-two even pieces. Shape each piece into a smooth roll by rolling it on the work surface under your cupped hand. Arrange the rolls on the prepared baking sheets so they almost touch each other. Cover lightly with damp dish towels and let rise at room temperature until almost doubled in size, about 45 minutes. During the last 15 minutes of rising, heat the oven to 425°F. Bake the splits for 15 to 20 minutes, or until golden. Remove the sheets from the oven and immediately sift confectioners' sugar over the splits. Transfer to wire racks and cover with dry dish towels to keep the crusts soft until cooled to lukewarm, then serve.

SPELT BREAD

INGREDIENTS

Makes 2 large loaves

13 cups (1.5kg) spelt flour

2 0.6-oz cakes fresh yeast (30g), or 2
    envelopes active dry yeast (5 teaspoons)
    plus 1 teaspoon sugar

5 cups (1.2 liters) lukewarm water

2½ tablespoons (20g) coarse sea salt,
    crushed or ground

2 tablespoons sunflower or light olive oil

2 tablespoons sunflower seeds for sprinkling
    (optional)

2 loaf pans, about 10 x 5 x 3 inches,
    lightly greased

Michael and Clare Marriage of Doves Farm,
near Hungerford in Oxfordshire, England,
with the organically grown grains they use
for their stone-ground flours.

The flour made from spelt, an ancient wheat grain (page 21), has a distinct, nutty flavor quite different from the wheat flour with which we are familiar. Clare Marriage (left), who has experimented with sacks upon sacks of different flours in more than twenty years of bread making at Doves Farm, is emphatic in her claim that spelt flour "makes the tastiest bread I've ever eaten." It certainly makes a loaf with a nuttier, wheatier taste than most. The flour seems to benefit from the very wet dough of the Grant method (page 44); the flavor develops, and the open texture with plenty of air pockets is very appealing. It also means fewer crumbs when the loaf is sliced.

This recipe is adapted from Clare's Doves Farm Spelt Bread recipe. It tastes best the day after baking and keeps for up to five days. It can also be frozen for one month.

Put the flour into a large bowl and make a well in the center. Crumble the fresh yeast into a medium-size bowl. Pour half the water into the yeast and stir until smooth. If using dry yeast, mix the granules and the sugar with half the water and let stand until foamy, 5 to 10 minutes (see page 18).

Dissolve the salt in the remaining water, then stir in the oil. Pour the yeast mixture into the well in the flour and roughly mix the flour from the bowl into the yeast mixture, using your hand. Add the remaining liquid and mix vigorously with your hand for 5 minutes. Although the dough starts out soft and sticky, it will become smooth and elastic as you work it and will leave the sides of the bowl cleanly. (If not, mix in a little additional flour.) Divide the dough between the two prepared pans. They should be half full. Smooth each top with a damp pastry brush or with moistened fingers, gently easing the dough into the corners. Sprinkle with the sesame seeds, if desired.

Cover each pan with a damp dish towel and let rise at warm room temperature, away from drafts, for 35 to 45 minutes, until the dough rises to just below the top of the pans. During the last 15 minutes of rising, heat the oven to 400°F.

Bake for 45 to 50 minutes, until the loaves sound hollow when unmolded and tapped underneath. The loaves will have flattish tops. Turn them out onto wire racks to cool.

NOTE: This bread can also be baked in four greased 8½ × 4½ × 2¾-inch loaf pans. Baking time will be 30 to 35 minutes.

MIX THE DOUGH FOR 5 MINUTES. IT
WILL BECOME SMOOTH AND ELASTIC.

WHOLE-WHEAT LOAF

Makes 1 large loaf

6 cups (680g) whole-wheat bread flour,
    preferably stone-ground

2 tablespoons (15g) coarse sea salt,
    crushed or ground

1 0.6-oz cake fresh yeast (15g), or
    1 envelope active dry yeast
    (2½ teaspoons) plus ½ teaspoon sugar

1¾ cups (430ml) lukewarm water

2 teaspoons olive oil, vegetable oil, or
    melted butter

extra flour for dusting

a baking sheet, lightly greased

THIS DOUGH WILL BE HEAVY,
SLIPPERY-WET AND DIFFICULT TO
WORK WHEN IT IS FIRST TURNED OUT
FOR KNEADING.

SHAPE THE DOUGH INTO A SMOOTH
BALL. PLACE ON THE LIGHTLY
GREASED BAKING SHEET AND LET RISE
A SECOND TIME AT ROOM
TEMPERATURE UNTIL DOUBLED IN
SIZE, 1½ TO 2 HOURS.

Stone-ground whole-wheat flour makes a very good bread — slightly dense, with plenty of flavor and a chewy crust. You know when you have eaten a slice that you will not feel hungry for a while. This bread is ideal for always-starving teenagers, as it really does fill them up — and healthfully!

This is not, however, a bread for an absolute beginner to try, since whole-wheat flour is difficult to work and knead. But once you get used to the heavy texture, it is not at all scary. If you are new to bread making and want to try a whole-wheat loaf, I suggest you bake The Grant Loaf (page 44) first for a very easy whole-wheat bread. Another alternative is to use The Basic Loaf recipe (page 15) and gradually increase the quantity of stone-ground whole-wheat bread flour each time you make the recipe, simultaneously decreasing the amount of white bread flour, until you are using only whole-wheat flour.

The oil or melted butter makes the loaf less crumbly, and also helps it keep longer. As with many breads in this chapter, this loaf improves on keeping and tastes best the day after it is baked. It can also be frozen for one month.

Prepare the dough as for The Basic Loaf (page 16), using the flour, salt, fresh yeast, and water, and adding the oil or melted butter with the last of the water. If using dry yeast, mix the granules and the sugar with 4 tablespoons of the water and let stand until foamy, 5 to 10 minutes (see page 18). Pour the yeast mixture into the well in the flour.

The dough will seem heavy and slippery-wet at first, but do not be tempted to add more flour at this stage. As you knead the dough and the water is absorbed by the flour, it will gradually become less sticky, although kneading will be hard work at first.

Knead for 10 minutes, until the dough becomes softer and very elastic and pliable, but not sticky or crumbly. If the dough is crumbly, add 1 tablespoon of water at a time, until the dough comes together. If the dough is very sticky after the 10 minutes, knead in additional flour, 1 tablespoon at a time, thoroughly working in each addition before adding more.

Put the dough into a lightly greased bowl and turn the dough over so the top is oiled. Cover with a damp dish towel and let rise at room temperature, away from drafts, until doubled in size, 1½ to 2 hours.

Punch down the dough. Turn out the dough onto a floured work surface and knead for 1 minute, then shape the dough into a ball. Put the ball of dough on the prepared baking sheet and cover with a damp dish towel. Let rise at room temperature until doubled in size, about 1 hour. During the last 15 minutes of rising, heat the oven to 425°F.

Uncover the loaf and snip the top with scissors or slash it with a sharp knife or razor blade to make a cross. Bake the loaf for 15 minutes, until lightly browned. Reduce the oven temperature to 350°F. Bake for another 20 to 25 minutes, until the loaf sounds hollow when tapped underneath. If the loaf sounds dense or heavy, bake it for another 5 minutes, then test again. Transfer the bread to a wire rack to cool completely.

The water-powered Letheringsett Mill supplied local Norfolk communities with freshly ground flour from 1802 until 1944 when it was abandoned and left to deteriorate. It remained unused until 1982 when a conservation trust undertook the repairs and restoration.

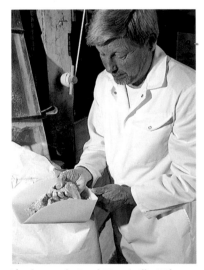

After leaving the Royal Navy, miller Mike Thurlow (above) moved to the mill in 1987 as the tenant-miller and completed the restoration to bring the mill back to working order. The educational demonstrations he gave then for local schoolchildren proved to be a learning experience for him as well because he knew nothing about milling when he first walked into the mill. Today, several London chefs have regular orders for his stone-ground whole-wheat flours.

Local farmers supply many of the grains Mike uses to grind his malted grain and several grades of whole-wheat flours.

MY FAVORITE LOAF

INGREDIENTS

Makes 1 large loaf

1⅓ cups thick wheat flakes

2 cups (230g) whole-wheat bread flour,
    preferably stone-ground

2 cups (230g) unbleached white bread
    flour

2 tablespoons (15g) coarse sea salt,
    crushed or ground

1 0.6-oz cake fresh yeast (15g), or
    1 envelope active dry yeast
    (2½ teaspoons) plus ½ teaspoon sugar

1¾ cups (430ml) lukewarm water

1–2 teaspoons olive oil or melted butter

extra flour for dusting

a loaf pan, about 10 × 5 × 3 inches,
    lightly greased

FOR EXTRA FLAVOR AND TEXTURE,
ADD 2 TABLESPOONS SHELLED
SUNFLOWER SEEDS TO THE FLOURS
AND SALT. ROLL THE DOUGH IN EXTRA
SHELLED SUNFLOWER SEEDS AFTER IT
IS SHAPED.

This is the loaf I come back to time and time again. However much I enjoy making and eating plenty of different styles and types of bread, I find everyone really appreciates the flavor and texture of this loaf. In England, I like to make this bread with a combination of three flours from Letheringsett Mill (left), which miller Mike Thurlow grinds to my specifications. However, the coarse-ground whole-wheat flour he grinds for me is difficult to come by in the States, so I've substituted wheat flakes ground to a medium-coarse meal in a food processor.

Like most whole-wheat breads, this one matures and tastes best one or two days after baking. Store wrapped at room temperature or freeze for up to one month.

Put the wheat flakes and 1 tablespoon of the whole-wheat flour in a food processor. Process 30 to 60 seconds until the flakes are ground to a medium-coarse meal. Put the meal into a large bowl and stir in the remaining whole-wheat flour, the white flour, and the salt. Make a well in the center of the flour mixture.

Crumble the fresh yeast into a small bowl. Add 4 tablespoons of the lukewarm water and stir until smooth. If using dry yeast, mix the granules with the lukewarm water and sugar and let stand until foamy, 5 to 10 minutes (page 18).

Pour the yeast mixture into the well in the flour. Stir the remaining lukewarm water and the oil or butter into the yeast mixture and draw a little of the flour mixture into the well and mix thoroughly. Gradually mix in enough of the flour that is in the bowl to make a smooth, thick batter. Cover the bowl with a damp dish towel and let stand about 20 minutes to form a frothy sponge.

Mix in the remaining flour that is in the bowl, adding as much additional whole-wheat flour as is necessary, about 1 tablespoon at a time, to form a fairly wet dough. Work the dough until it leaves the sides of the bowl cleanly. Then turn it out onto a lightly floured work surface and, with floured hands, knead the dough for 10 minutes. The dough will gradually become firmer and smoother as the water is absorbed by the wheat-flake meal, so don't be tempted to add more flour than is absolutely necessary.

Place the dough in the washed and lightly greased bowl and turn the dough over. Cover and let rise at room temperature until doubled in size, about 2 hours.

Turn out the dough onto a lightly floured work surface and punch it down. Shape it into a loaf to fit the prepared pan (see A Plain White Loaf, page 24). Cover it with a damp dish towel or plastic wrap and let rise until doubled in size, about 1½ hours. During the last 15 minutes of rising, heat the oven to 450°F.

Bake the loaf for 15 minutes. Reduce the oven temperature to 400°F. Bake for another 30 to 35 minutes, or until the loaf sounds hollow when unmolded and tapped underneath. Unmold the loaf onto a wire rack to cool completely.

THE GRANT LOAF

INGREDIENTS

Makes 1 large loaf

6 cups (680g) organic whole-wheat bread
    flour, preferably and stone-ground

1 teaspoon coarse sea salt, crushed or
    ground

2½ cups (570ml) lukewarm water

1 0.6-oz cake fresh yeast (15g) (see
    Notes)

1 teaspoon packed brown sugar or honey

a loaf pan, about 10 × 5 × 3 inches,
    lightly greased and warmed (see Notes)

In 1944, Doris Grant published a simple recipe for a delicious, wholesome bread in her book, Your Daily Bread (Faber & Faber). Ever since, generations of bakers influenced by her have enjoyed making and eating homemade bread. This recipe is the answer to those who claim that bread-making is too difficult or too time-consuming. The dough requires no kneading and has just one short rising period, in the pan. The majority of the bakers I have talked to say they caught the bread-making bug from trying the Grant recipe.

Once again the secret is to start with a good quality stone-ground whole-wheat flour, and to make sure the dough is elastic and slippery when you finish mixing it. The texture of this bread is moist and light, even though it appears quite dense, and the bread keeps well (the taste improves, too). I have halved Mrs. Grant's original quantities and increased the rising time from 20 minutes, as my loaves seem to need 30 to 35 minutes.

Mix 5 cups (570g) of the flour and the salt in a large bowl. In very cold weather, warm the bowl of flour in a 250°F oven for 5 to 8 minutes, or microwave on high for 1 to 1½ minutes. Make a well in the center of the flour.

Put 3 tablespoons of the lukewarm water in a small bowl, crumble in the fresh yeast, and mix until smooth. Stir in the sugar or honey. Let stand for 10 to 15 minutes, until the mixture is thick and frothy.

Pour the yeast mixture and the remaining lukewarm water into the well in the flour. Mix vigorously with your hand for 1 to 2 minutes, working in the flour from the sides to the center, until the dough feels elastic and comes cleanly away from the sides of the bowl. Add as much of the remaining flour as is necessary, about ¼ cup at a time. Doris Grant described the correct texture as "slippery."

Put the dough into the prepared pan and cover with a damp dish towel. Let stand in a warm place for 20 to 35 minutes, until the dough rises to within ½ inch of the top of the pan. While the dough is rising, heat the oven to 400°F.

Bake for 35 to 40 minutes, until the loaf sounds hollow when unmolded and gently tapped underneath. Transfer the bread to a wire rack to cool completely.

NOTES: You can also make this loaf using 1 envelope rapid-rise dry yeast (2½ teaspoons), but I have never been happy with the result when I have used ordinary active dry yeast. For the method, see page 18.

This bread can also be baked in two 8½ × 4½ × 2¾-inch loaf pans. The baking time will be 30 to 35 minutes.

MIX THE WET DOUGH VIGOROUSLY IN THE BOWL FOR 1 TO 2 MINUTES, WORKING IN THE FLOUR FROM THE SIDES TO THE CENTER. CONTINUE MIXING UNTIL THE DOUGH FEELS ELASTIC AND COMES CLEANLY AWAY FROM THE SIDES OF THE BOWL.

Award-winning baker Viola Unruh and her husband, Henry, outside their farmhouse.

VIOLA'S LIGHT WHOLE-WHEAT BREAD

INGREDIENTS

Makes 4 small loaves

3½ cups (800ml) water

2 0.6-oz cakes fresh yeast (30g), or 2
    envelopes active dry yeast (5 teaspoons)

5 tablespoons (60g) sugar

5 tablespoons (70g) vegetable shortening
    or softened butter

2½ tablespoons (20g) coarse sea salt,
    crushed or ground

2¾ cups (310g) whole-wheat bread flour

about 8 cups (900g) unbleached white
    bread flour

3 tablespoons vital wheat gluten

1 large egg, beaten

extra flour for dusting

4 loaf pans, about 8½ × 4½ × 2½
    inches, greased

"Just the kind of bread you like to eat," said one of the judges as Viola Unruh beat two hundred other home bakers to win the 1990 Kansas Festival of Breads Contest, sponsored by the Kansas Wheat Commission.

"My recipe was so simple I never thought I would win against some of the fancier breads," said Viola as she rapidly made yet another batch of four loaves. She swears by vital wheat gluten and Hudson Cream Flour (page 48) to produce a light, fine loaf that looks great. Viola started making bread when she married Henry 45 years ago. The quantity of bread, as well as the quality, is important when you live on a remote corn farm with 3,200 head of cattle in Montezuma, Kansas — and you have to feed your sons and farm workers, who can demolish a batch of bread in just one meal.

This recipe uses the sponging technique, which Viola prefers for all her breads. "You get a better loaf," she says, adding that if you mix and knead bread dough by hand, rather than with a dough hook on a machine, "the texture is much finer."

I have made this bread without the vital wheat gluten, and the recipe still works well. Gluten is found at health-food stores or may be purchased by mail order (see List of Suppliers, page 360). Viola keeps her whole-wheat flour in the freezer to prevent it from becoming rancid in the Kansas heat. This loaf keeps for two days, or it can be frozen for one month.

Warm ½ cup (115ml) of the water to lukewarm. Crumble the fresh yeast into the lukewarm water in a small bowl and stir until smooth. If using dry yeast, mix the granules and the lukewarm water in a small bowl, stir in a teaspoon of the sugar, and let stand until foamy, 5 to 10 minutes (see page 18).

Heat the rest of the water to about 150°F and pour it over the shortening or butter, sugar, and salt in a large bowl. Stir until melted and slightly cooled.

Stir in the whole-wheat flour, followed by about half of the white flour and the vital wheat gluten. Mix thoroughly together. (Viola uses a slotted spoon.) Add the yeast mixture and stir well. Beat in the egg. Beat this sloppy batter for 3 minutes, then cover with plastic wrap and let stand until it becomes spongy, about 10 minutes.

Uncover the sponge and gradually work in some of the remaining white flour, a handful at a time, until the dough is firm enough to turn out onto a lightly floured work surface. Then knead in enough of the remaining flour, very little at a time, until the dough is no longer sticky. Knead the dough for 10 minutes, until it is firm and pliable enough to flop from hand to hand. The exact amount of flour will depend on the flour itself and the temperature in the kitchen. Put the dough back into the bowl (there is no need to oil the bowl). Cover with plastic wrap or a damp dish towel and let rise until doubled in size, about 1 hour in a warm Kansas kitchen. Turn out the risen dough onto a lightly floured work surface. Punch it down and lightly knead, working the dough from hand to hand for 2 to 3 minutes.

Divide the dough into four equal pieces. Shape each piece into a rough ball, then place in the prepared pans. Cover with damp dish towels or plastic wrap and let rest for 10 minutes, which makes the dough easier to shape. Flour the work surface. Remove the dough, one piece at a time, and roll out with a lightly floured rolling pin into a rectangle measuring about 11 x 9 inches, and about ½ inch thick. Starting with a short side, roll up tightly like a jelly roll, then pinch the seam to seal tightly. Return to the loaf pan, seam side down, and tuck the ends under, pinching to seal. Repeat with the remaining dough. Cover the loaves again and let rise until doubled in size, about 45 minutes. During the last 15 minutes of rising, heat the oven to 400°F. Bake the loaves for 10 minutes, then lower the over temperature to 350°F. Bake the loaves for about 25 minutes longer, or until they sound hollow when unmolded and tapped underneath. Turn out the loaves from the pans onto wire racks. Rub the crusts with a butter wrapper and let cool completely.

Viola recommends serving her delicious bread with homemade apricot jam.

LIKE ALL GOOD BAKERS, VIOLA ASSEMBLES AND MEASURES ALL HER INGREDIENTS BEFORE SHE STARTS MIXING. HERE SHE BEATS THE EGG IN A MUG.

SHE POURS HOT WATER OVER VEGETABLE SHORTENING, SUGAR, AND SALT, STIRRING TO MELT THE SHORTENING AND DISSOLVE THE SUGAR.

SHE ADDS THE EGG TO A MIXTURE OF SHORTENING, WATER, SUGAR, YEAST, AND FLOUR. SHE BEATS IT WITH A SLOTTED SPOON TO MAKE A SLOPPY BATTER.

THE BATTER IS COVERED WITH PLASTIC WRAP AND LEFT FOR ABOUT 10 MINUTES UNTIL IT BECOMES SPONGY.

VIOLA THEN USES HER SLOTTED SPOON TO BEAT IN ENOUGH OF THE REMAINING WHITE FLOUR TO MAKE A FIRM DOUGH.

SHE TURNS OUT THE DOUGH ONTO A LIGHTLY FLOURED WORK SURFACE AND KNEADS IT FOR 10 MINUTES, ADDING ADDITIONAL FLOUR, UNTIL THE DOUGH IS NO LONGER STICKY.

AFTER KNEADING, THE DOUGH BECOMES FIRM AND PLIABLE. THE DOUGH IS RETURNED TO THE BOWL, COVERED WITH PLASTIC WRAP, AND LEFT TO RISE.

AFTER THE DOUGH HAS DOUBLED IN SIZE, VIOLA REMOVES THE PLASTIC WRAP, TURNS OUT THE DOUGH AND WORKS IT FROM HAND TO HAND FOR 2 TO 3 MINUTES.

USING A KNIFE, VIOLA CUTS THE DOUGH INTO QUARTERS.

EACH PORTION OF DOUGH IS THEN SHAPED INTO A ROUGH OVAL, PLACED IN THE GREASED PANS AND LEFT TO REST, COVERED, FOR 10 MINUTES.

WORKING WITH ONE PORTION OF DOUGH AT A TIME, VIOLA ROLLS IT OUT TO A RECTANGLE MEASURING ABOUT 11 × 9 INCHES, AND ABOUT ½ INCH THICK.

SHE THEN ROLLS UP THE DOUGH LIKE A JELLY ROLL AND PUTS IT IN THE PAN FOR A SECOND RISING. AFTER THE DOUGH DOUBLES IN SIZE, IT IS PUT IN THE OVEN TO BAKE FOR ABOUT 35 MINUTES, OR UNTIL IT SOUNDS HOLLOW WHEN TAPPED UNDERNEATH.

HUDSON CREAM WHOLE-WHEAT BREAD

Makes 2 large loaves

2 0.6-oz cakes fresh yeast (30g), or 2
    envelopes active dry yeast (5 teaspoons)

1 cup (230ml) lukewarm water

1 cup (230ml) lukewarm milk

⅓ cup (110g) whipped or spun honey

9–10 cups (1–1.1kg) white-wheat or
    whole-wheat bread flour, preferably
    stone-ground

2 large eggs, beaten

2 tablespoons (15g) coarse sea salt,
    crushed or ground

extra flour for dusting

4 tablespoons (60g) butter, lard or
    vegetable shortening, diced

2 loaf pans, about 10 × 5 × 3 inches,
    lightly greased

NOTE: Whipped or spun honey is
solid and nearly white in color. It
is found at most health-food
stores.

Talking to finalists and prize winners of bread-making competitions in the States, I discovered that many swore by Hudson Cream Flour (see List of Suppliers, page 360). One cook in West Virginia who used it for her prize-winning biscuits said, "I want to pass down to my children good morals, good values, and Hudson Cream Flour."

The printed cambric flour bags sold at the mill and by mail order (the flour comes in paper sacks) are sought after for making aprons like the one Viola Unruh is wearing on page 45. Stafford County Flour Mill in Kansas, where this flour is milled, can be seen three miles away from the road, the silos rising from the farmland like a huge block of apartments. Founded in 1905 by a German immigrant, the mill stayed in the same family until 1986; the current president, Al Brensing, has worked there for more than 55 years. The dairy image (the company logo is a Jersey cow) and "cream" brand name refer not to the color of the flour, available bleached or unbleached, but to the very smooth texture, due to the hard red winter wheat from which it is milled. Their organic unbleached flour and white wheat flours (a new type of whole-wheat flour) are slowly finding a market. Look in grocery stores in Pennsylvania, Indiana, Ohio, Kentucky, Tennessee, and West Virginia, as well as in Kansas.

This recipe, using Hudson Cream whole-wheat flour, has won many prizes. A loaf of this bread disappeared very quickly when I took it to a luncheon with friends. It is a moist loaf that keeps well and improves with age. It can be frozen for up to one month.

Crumble the fresh yeast into a large bowl. Add the lukewarm water and stir until dissolved. Stir in the milk and honey. Using your hand or a wooden spoon, beat in 4½ cups (500g) of the flour and the eggs. The original recipe says to beat for one hundred strokes, which takes 2 to 3 minutes. Cover with a damp dish towel and let rest at room temperature until spongy, 20 to 30 minutes. If using dry yeast, mix the granules with half the lukewarm water and half the honey, and let stand until foamy, 5 to 10 minutes (page 18). Add the remaining water and honey, plus the milk, and continue to make a sponge.

Uncover the sponge and mix in the salt, followed by the remaining flour, about ½ cup at a time, until the dough is no longer sticky. The exact amount will depend on the flour you use. Turn out the dough onto a lightly floured work surface and knead for 10 minutes, gradually working in the butter and additional flour, if necessary. When the dough looks and feels smooth and pliable, return it to the washed and lightly greased bowl, and turn the dough over so the top is oiled. Cover with a damp dish towel and let rise at room temperature, away from drafts, until doubled in size, 1 to 1½ hours.

Punch down the risen dough and divide in half. Cover with a damp dish towel and let rest for 10 minutes. Shape the portions into loaves to fit the prepared pans (see A Plain White Loaf, page 24). Cover the pans with damp dish towels and let the dough rise at room temperature until doubled in size, about 1 hour. During the last 15 minutes of rising, heat the oven to 375°F.

Bake the loaves for 10 minutes. Reduce the oven temperature to 350°F. Bake for another 20 to 30 minutes, or until the loaves sound hollow when unmolded and tapped underneath. Turn out the loaves from the pans and transfer to wire racks and cool.

USING YOUR HAND, BEAT HALF THE FLOUR AND
THE EGGS INTO THE YEAST MIXTURE.

CONTINUE ADDING FLOUR UNTIL THE DOUGH
IS NO LONGER STICKY.

MALTED WHEAT LOAF

INGREDIENTS

Makes 1 large loaf

5–6 cups (570–680g) whole-wheat
   bread flour, preferably stone-ground

¾ cup (85g) malted wheat flakes

2 tablespoons (15g) coarse sea salt,
   crushed or ground

1 0.6-oz cake fresh yeast (15g), or
   1 envelope active dry yeast
   (2½ teaspoons) plus ½ teaspoon sugar

1¾ cups (400ml) lukewarm water

1 tablespoon olive oil, vegetable oil or
   melted butter

extra flour for dusting

a loaf pan, about 10 × 5 × 3 inches,
   lightly greased

A combination of whole-wheat flour and malted wheat flakes makes a well-textured loaf with a naturally sweet taste. If you prefer, you could use old-fashioned graham flour instead, or replace one-third of the whole-wheat flour with unbleached white bread flour. Another variation is to shape the dough into a Cottage Loaf (page 29), and to glaze it with beaten egg and sprinkle it with cracked wheat before baking.

This bread makes very good toast, which my family enjoys for breakfast. The loaf will keep for four days and can be frozen for one month.

Make the dough as for The Basic Loaf (page 16), using 5 cups (570g) of the flour, the wheat flakes, salt, yeast, and water, and adding the oil or melted butter with the last of the water. If using dry yeast, mix the granules and the sugar with 2 tablespoons of the water and let stand until foamy, 5 to 10 minutes (see page 18), then pour the yeast mixture into the well in the flour. If the dough is sticky, work in small amounts of the remaining flour. Knead the dough, then place it in a clean, lightly greased bowl. Turn the dough over so the top is oiled, then cover it with a damp dish towel and let it rise at room temperature, away from drafts, until doubled in size, 1¼–1½ hours.

Punch down the risen dough, then turn it out onto a lightly floured work surface. Shape into a loaf to fit the prepared pan (page 24). If you like, make a split loaf shape by cutting a deep slash lengthwise in the top of the loaf using a sharp knife. Cover the pan with a damp dish towel and let the dough rise at room temperature until doubled in size, about 1 hour. During the last 15 minutes of rising, heat the oven to 450°F.

Bake for 15 minutes. Reduce the oven temperature to 400°F and bake for a further 25 to 30 minutes, or until the loaf sounds hollow when unmolded and tapped underneath. Turn out the loaf from the pan and transfer to a wire rack to cool.

It is not surprising that cultures around the world start the day with bread for breakfast. Both whole-wheat and white breads made with enriched flour are an excellent source of niacin, riboflavin, and thiamin, vital vitamins necessary for good health. Breads also contain starch, minerals, and varying amounts of roughage. Serve bread fresh or toasted for breakfast.

GERMAN THREE-GRAIN BREAD

Makes 2 small loaves

Makes 2 small loaves

3 tablespoons (30g) steel-cut oats

4 cups (455g) unbleached white bread
    flour

1⅔ cups (170g) rye flour

3 tablespoons (30g) flax seed

2 tablespoons (15g) coarse sea salt,
    crushed or ground

1¼ cups (280ml) lukewarm water

⅔ cup (140ml) lukewarm milk

1 0.6-oz cake fresh yeast (15g), or 1
    envelope active dry yeast (2½
    teaspoons) plus ½ teaspoon sugar

extra flour for dusting

extra milk for glazing

extra flax seed for sprinkling

a large baking sheet, lightly greased

This is a flavorful loaf made from wheat and rye flours with oats and flax seed, which are available by mail order at health-food stores. They are popular in German baking. This loaf is superb with cured meats, hard cheeses, or smoked fish, and pickles. It tastes best after it has matured for a day and it can be frozen for one month.

Grind the oats in a food processor to the texture of bulgur wheat. In a large, warmed bowl, stir together 3½ cups (400g) white flour, the rye flour, oats, flax seed, and salt. Mix together the water and milk. Put 4 tablespoons of this mixture into a small bowl. Crumble in the fresh yeast and mix until smooth. Add 2 tablespoons of the dry ingredients and stir to make a thick paste. Let stand until frothy and spongy-looking, about 10 minutes. (This won't rise as much as other sponges.) If using dry yeast, mix the granules and the sugar with 4 tablespoons lukewarm liquid and let stand until foamy, 5 to 10 minutes (see page 18).

Make a well in the dry ingredients and add the yeast mixture and the remaining liquid. Mix to form a firm dough, adding as much of the remaining white flour as is necessary, about 1 tablespoon at a time.

Turn out the dough onto a lightly floured work surface and knead thoroughly for 10 minutes, or until smooth and elastic. Put the dough into a lightly oiled bowl and turn the dough over so the top is oiled. Cover with a damp dish towel. Let rise at room temperature, away from drafts, until doubled in size, 2 to 3 hours.

Punch down the risen dough. Shape into 2 small ovals (page 17). Arrange the loaves on the prepared baking sheet. Cover with a damp dish towel and let rise at room temperature until doubled in size, about 1 hour. During the last 15 minutes of rising, heat the oven to 425°F.

Using a sharp knife or a razor blade, make a slash lengthwise down the center of each loaf. Brush with milk to glaze, then sprinkle with the additional flax seed. Bake for 30 to 40 minutes, or until the bread sounds hollow when tapped on the underside. Transfer to a wire rack or two racks to cool completely. Wrap tightly in aluminium foil and let rest at room temperature for one day so the flavors mature.

SPRINKLE FLAX SEED OVER THE
SLASHED LOAVES JUST BEFORE BAKING.

Traditionally dressed Bavarians take a break
from their shopping in a Munich market.
Breads made with rye flour and flax seed are
eaten with full-flavored cured meats and
smoked fish.

There are few days when Kansas home economist Cindy Falk does not bake a loaf of bread for her family. Multi-grain Harvest Bread and Pioneer Bread (page 52) are two of her flavor-packed loaves. Both have the nutritional bonus of being high in protein. Cindy teaches bread-making in local schools, and her children are following in her footsteps. Here her daughter helps her measure water before starting a fresh batch of dough.

MULTI-GRAIN HARVEST BREAD

INGREDIENTS

Makes 4 small loaves

1½ cups (340ml) water

4 tablespoons (60g) butter

2 tablespoons packed dark brown sugar

2 tablespoons molasses

¼ cup (40g) cracked wheat

¾ cup (85g) whole-wheat bread flour, preferably stone-ground

2 tablespoons (20g) nonfat dry milk powder

⅓ cup (40g) soy flour

¼ cup (30g) yellow cornmeal

¼ cup (20g) rolled oats

6 tablespoons (40g) rye flour

6 tablespoons (40g) barley flour or amaranth flour

⅓ cup (40g) oat flour (see introduction)

2 tablespoons (15g) coarse sea salt, crushed or ground

1 0.6-oz cake fresh yeast (15g), or 1 envelope active dry yeast (2½ teaspoons) plus ½ teaspoon granulated sugar

3½–4½ cups (395–500g) unbleached white bread flour

1 large egg, beaten

4 loaf pans, about 7 × 5 × 3 inches, lightly greased

Cindy Falk, a home economist with the Kansas Wheat Commission, lives in Onaga, in northeast Kansas, up toward Nebraska. Her house has wonderful views of the hills and of the fields her husband farms in his spare time. In 1826, Cindy's ancestors came to the States from a dairy farm in Neuchâtel, Switzerland, an area famed for its wine and cheese. This area of Kansas, with its rolling green hills and fields, reminded them of home more than any other part of the state.

Cindy has been making bread since she was eleven years old and has won countless awards at state fairs and national cooking contests, which may not be surprising as her mother is another prize-winning baker. Now Cindy's children win competitions, too. Derek, the fourteen-year-old, cans fruits and vegetables and makes wonderful cakes, while Laura, aged eleven, has won prizes for her Portuguese Sweet Breads (page 138).

This is Cindy's blue-ribbon recipe from the 1992 Kansas State Fair, and it's a flavorful, high-protein loaf. Make the oat flour by processing 5 tablespoons old-fashioned rolled oats in a blender or food processor using the pulse switch until the oats are floury. Eat this blue-ribbon recipe the day it is baked, or the day after; do not refrigerate, or it will go stale more quickly.

Heat together the water, butter, brown sugar, and molasses in a medium-size saucepan over moderate heat for about 2 minutes, stirring frequently, until it is very warm (125°F to 130°F). Stir in the cracked wheat. Remove from the heat and let stand for 5 minutes, stirring occasionally, until the liquid is lukewarm.

In a large bowl, stir together the whole-wheat flour, milk powder, soy flour, cornmeal, rolled oats, rye flour, amaranth or barley flour, oat flour, and salt. (Warm the flours if it is a cold day; see page 15.) Crumble the fresh yeast into a small bowl. Add 2 tablespoons of the lukewarm cracked-wheat mixture and mix until smooth. If using dry yeast, mix the granules and the granulated sugar with 2 tablespoons of the lukewarm cracked-wheat mixture and let stand until foamy, 5 to 10 minutes (see page 18).

Add the yeast mixture and the cracked-wheat mixture to the flours in the bowl along with 3½ cups (395g) of the white flour and beat with your hand or a wooden spoon for

This loaf is excellent for slicing and using for sandwiches.

2 minutes. Add the egg and about ¼ cup of the white flour, then beat for 2 minutes more. Gradually mix in as much of the remaining flour as necessary, about ¼ cup at a time, to make a soft dough that forms a ball and leaves the sides of the bowl cleanly. The exact amount of flour needed will vary depending on the type of flour and the temperature.

Lightly oil your hands and the work surface. Turn out the dough and knead for 10 to 12 minutes until smooth, elastic, but still slightly sticky. The oil stops the dough from sticking as you knead; adding extra flour at this stage would make the loaf tough and dry. Cover the dough with the upturned bowl, or return it to the washed and lightly greased bowl, turn the dough so the top is oiled, and cover with a damp dish towel. Let the dough rise at room temperature, away from drafts, until doubled in size, 1 to 1½ hours.

Punch down the dough and divide into four. Cover with a damp dish towel or plastic wrap and let rest for 10 minutes. On a lightly floured work surface, shape the loaves by rolling each piece with a lightly floured rolling pin from the center onward into a rectangle, about 15 x 7 inches. The dough should be about ¼ inch thick. Starting from a short end, roll up the dough tightly – pushing the dough together and pinching the seams after each roll – so you have a short, fat roll. Seal the ends of the roll with the edge of your hand, pushing down to the counter. Fold the ends under, and pinch to seal.

Put one roll seam side down into each prepared pan to ensure a loaf with an even shape and no large pockets of air or "floating" crust. (Cindy has a quick method for shaping loaves not intended for competitions: Press the lump of punched-down dough into a heavily greased pan. Turn the dough out, then slide it back into the pan so that the side that was underneath is now on top. Cindy covers the second piece of dough with a damp dish towel or plastic wrap while shaping the first to prevent it from drying out.) Cover the pans with damp dish towels or plastic wrap and let the dough rise at room temperature until doubled in size, about 1 hour. During the last 15 minutes of rising, heat the oven to 375°F.

Bake the loaves for 25 to 30 minutes, until they are golden and sound hollow when unmolded and tapped underneath. Transfer the loaves to wire racks and cool completely.

CINDY ROLLS OUT EACH PORTION OF DOUGH, ROLLING FROM THE CENTER OUTWARD INTO A RECTANGLE.

STARTING FROM A SHORT END, SHE THEN ROLLS UP THE DOUGH, SEALING AND PINCHING THE EDGES TOGETHER AFTER EACH ROLL.

PIONEER BREAD

This is Cindy Falk's recipe for "a healthy daily bread dating from Kansas's settler days." Baked in round cake pans, this is a delicious loaf, very nutritious, with a light, but chewy texture. It is best on the day it is baked, or the day after. It toasts and freezes well.

Cindy uses this recipe to teach local schoolchildren just how good homemade bread tastes, as well as to illustrate how American settler history is bound with the land and cultivation. This recipe reflects Kansas's nickname – the

INGREDIENTS

Makes 2 medium loaves

½ cup (65g) yellow cornmeal

¼ cup packed (50g) dark brown sugar

2 tablespoons (15g) coarse sea salt,
    crushed or ground

4 tablespoons vegetable oil

1 cup (230ml) boiling water

2 0.6-oz cakes fresh yeast (30g), or 2
    envelopes active dry yeast (5 teaspoons)
    plus ½ teaspoon granulated sugar

½ cup (115ml) lukewarm water

1 cup (230ml) water from the cold tap

1⅓ cups (165g) whole-wheat bread flour,
    preferably stone-ground

¾ cup (85g) rye flour

5–6 cups (570–680g) unbleached white
    bread flour

extra flour for dusting

3 tablespoons sunflower seeds

extra cornmeal for sprinkling

2 deep 9-inch round cake pans or
    springform cake pans, lightly greased

Sunflower State — as well as its reputation as America's breadbasket.

Cindy also teaches the children how to measure accurately, and sets a timer for the kneading, rising, and baking times.

Combine the cornmeal, brown sugar, salt, oil, and boiling water in a large bowl to soften the cornmeal and dissolve the sugar and salt. The oil prevents the loaf from being crumbly when sliced.

Crumble the fresh yeast into a small bowl and stir in the lukewarm water until smooth. If using dry yeast, mix the granules and the ½ teaspoon granulated sugar with the lukewarm water and let stand until foamy, 5 to 10 minutes (see page 18).

Add the cold tap water to the cornmeal mixture, then add the yeast mixture and stir well. Using your hand or a wooden spoon, beat in the whole-wheat and rye flours, mixing well. Gradually stir in the white flour, a handful at a time, adding just enough to make a dough that is moderately stiff and leaves the sides of the bowl cleanly. (Cindy prefers a dough that is slightly too soft, rather than too stiff, as "you get a nicer bread.")

Turn out the dough onto a lightly floured work surface and knead for at least 10 minutes until smooth and elastic, using only enough additional flour to prevent sticking. (Cindy says she kneads her bread for 25 minutes for competitions, to improve the volume and texture.)

Sprinkle the sunflower seeds over the dough and knead for a couple of minutes to incorporate them evenly throughout the dough.

Put the dough into the washed and lightly greased bowl, turning the dough so the top is oiled. Cover with a damp dish towel or plastic wrap and let rise in a warm place, away from drafts, until doubled in size, about 1 hour.

Punch down the risen dough with your fist. Lightly oil your hands and the work surface to avoid needing extra flour, which can make streaks in the finished loaf. Sprinkle the greased pans with a little extra cornmeal. Turn out the dough and divide it into two equal pieces. Shape each piece into a ball. Then roll it into a pear-shaped oval so one end is narrower than the other.

Put a loaf in each pan, putting the narrow end in first and letting the wider end form the top. Cover with damp dish towels or plastic wrap and let rise at room temperature, away from drafts, until almost doubled in size, about 1 hour. During the last 15 minutes of rising, heat the oven to 375°F.

Using a sharp knife or razor blade, slash the top of each loaf in a star pattern, or use kitchen scissors to snip a star pattern. Bake the loaves for 35 to 45 minutes, or until they are well browned and sound hollow when unmolded and tapped underneath. If the loaves stick to the pans, let them stand for 5 minutes so the steam loosens the bottom, then try again. Transfer the loaves to wire racks and cool completely.

Pioneer Bread has a soft crust and a well-textured crumb. Cindy recommends serving it with a salad and, in fact, she often serves it with her mother's award-winning meatball, pasta, and red pepper salad.

FLAT BREADS

The international collection of breads in this chapter includes the oldest and simplest of all breads to make. Leavened or unleavened, flat breads can be crisp or chewy, plain or rich. They are generally quick to make and cook in minutes, if not seconds, either on top of the stove or in a red-hot oven.

Traditionally cooked on a hot, flat iron plate over a flame, many of these breads have been made for centuries by travelers and nomads, linking the cultures of the world. Pita Bread (page 62) and Lavash (page 63), both from the Middle East, for example, are close cousins of the Naan (page 61) and Chapati (page 56) of India; Branch Bread (page 64) from Scandinavia is a second cousin to Griddle Oatcakes (page 72) of Scotland, Maddybenny Fadge (page 70) of Northern Ireland, and Manx Potato Cakes (page 70).

OPPOSITE *Making an Indian flat bread.* ABOVE *Enjoying a stuffed pita-bread.*

In some cultures in the Middle East, and in parts of Asia, flat breads have the dual purpose of being a basic dietary staple and of replacing plates and silverware, making them essential for every meal. For example, grilled meat kabobs and koftas are enclosed in pita breads so they can be eaten out of hand. Naan and chapatis have been designed to scoop food from the plate to the mouth.

Flat breads cooked on top of the stove traditionally require a griddle, a large, flat cast-iron round pan, al-though you can use a heavy aluminum, or even a nonstick griddle, or a tava, a slightly concave, heavy iron cooking pan used throughout India. (Look for this pan in stores selling Indian foods and cookware.) Even a shallow, cast-iron frying pan works well. Good, heavy-duty baking sheets that will not buckle in extreme heat are essential for flat breads which are to be baked in the oven, such as pitas.

The recipes for Hoe Cakes (page 69), Pita Bread (page 62), Maddybenny Fadge (page 70), and Manx Potato Cakes (page 70) are ideal for new bread makers because they do not require any special equipment or skill. They are also "fun" recipes to make.

One point to remember when making flat breads is to make sure the oven is free from grease and debris before heating it to the maximum setting for pitas and the like. I forgot to check this once and when I opened the door to put in a batch of pitas I was greeted by clouds of smoke.

So if you are as dismayed as I am by the flat breads available in the supermarket, try your hand at the recipes here; I know the results will please.

INDIAN FLAT BREADS

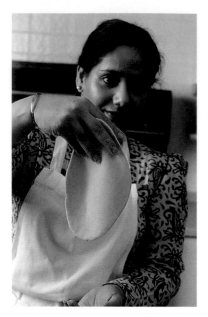

Jagdessh Sohal demonstrates her fail-proof technique for making Indian flat breads.

Whether it is the oval, white naan from the Punjab, the flat, chewy, unleavened chapati, or the flaky, rich paratha of northern India, a flat bread is eaten with every meal in India.

Although I cook a lot of Indian food, I had never thought of making Indian flat breads at home until I met Jagdessh Sohal. Jagdessh was born in Bombay and came to England in 1976, when she married. For the past few years she has been a consultant to Sharwood, a company specializing in Asian foods, making sure their large range of Indian prepared dishes and products is authentic. Jagdessh explained to me that these breads are purposely kept simple in flavor to act as a foil for the rich or spicy dishes in the meal. She also explained which bread to serve with which type of dish; or example, chapatis, pooris, and parathas, are best served with lentil dishes, and naans are best with dry-cooked meat or vegetable dishes, such as tandooris and kebobs. These breads play an important part in the meal, acting as a staple and as a means of scooping up food, often making forks and spoons unnecessary.

To test the heat of a tava, or your frying pan or griddle, before cooking Chapatis (below) and Parathas (page 60), Jagdessh says to sprinkle a good pinch of flour on it. When the tava is the correct temperature, the flour browns in 3 seconds. If it takes longer, the tava is too cool, and if the flour burns instantly, she says to let the tava cool slightly before beginning to cook the breads.

NOTE: The recipes for chapatis, pooris, and parathas call for ghee, a form of clarified butter, although clarified butter or melted unsalted butter can be substituted. Ghee is the fat used most often in Indian cooking. It has a high smoking point, which makes it ideal for sautéing and frying. The distinct, almost caramelized, flavor (a bit like unsweetened, condensed milk) is produced as the butter simmers and the water evaporates. It can be purchased in food shops specializing in Indian foods, or it's easy to prepare at home. To make ghee, melt 2 cups (230g) of unsalted butter in a small saucepan over low heat. Simmer for about 15 minutes, or until the white milk solids on the bottom of the pan turn golden. Watch carefully for the color change. The simmering time will depend on the amount of water in the butter. Once the particles have turned golden, strain the mixture through a strainer lined with cheesecloth. Let the ghee cool, then pour it into a jar with a tight-fitting lid. Refrigerate it for up to six months or freeze it for up to a year.

CHAPATIS

INGREDIENTS

Makes 8

2¼ cups (255g) sifted whole-wheat
    pastry flour

⅔–¾ cup (165ml) water

1 teaspoon salt

extra flour for shaping

ghee (see above), clarified butter or melted
    butter for brushing

a tava, large cast-iron frying pan, or heavy
    griddle

These are flat, unleavened disks made with atta, a very fine whole-wheat flour available in Indian stores. As an alternative, Jagdessh suggests using the whole-wheat flour sold for making pastry, with the coarser bits of bran sifted out, and I find this works just as well. She makes ten to fifteen chapatis every night for dinner, cooking them on an ungreased tava, a concave iron pan, on top of the stove. My cast-iron frying pan makes a good substitute, as does a griddle. Jagdessh also uses a special rolling pin that is thicker in the middle, but a regular one works just fine. Eat chapatis warm.

Put the flour in a medium-size bowl. Add 3 tablespoons of the water and roughly mix together, then add the salt. Mix briefly, then add a further 4 tablespoons water. Mix with your fingertips or a spoon, until the flakes of dough start to come together. Gradually work in additional water, about 1 tablespoon at a time, to make a very sticky dough. Jagdessh's method is to pour the water into her cupped hand, sprinkling it over the dry dough at the side of the bowl and working it in, discarding any excess water. After you've made this dough several times, you will be able to master her traditional technique.

Using unfloured knuckles, knead the dough in the bowl very thoroughly. When the dough feels firm and elastic, but still slightly sticky, cover the bowl with a dish towel and let stand for 5 to 10 minutes. The dough should become firmer and no longer sticky.

Put a little flour in a shallow dish. Using floured fingers, pull off egg-size pieces of dough. Between your floured palms, roll each piece of dough into a ball. Flatten each ball into a disk with a lump in the middle by rotating the dough between the palm of one hand and the fingers of the other hand. Use your fingers to press and gently pull out the rim, turning the dough to make a circle. The disk will be about 2½ to 3 inches in diameter.

Press the disk into the dish of flour to lightly coat it on both sides. Then roll it out with a rolling pin into a circle about 7 inches across and ⅛ inch thick. (Jagdessh likes to stretch the dough more by flipping it from hand to hand.)

Heat the tava, frying pan, or griddle over moderately high heat until very hot, but do not add any oil or the kitchen will fill with smoke. When the pan is the proper temperature, a pinch of flour sprinkled into the pan will brown in 3 seconds. Cook a chapati in the pan for about 30 seconds, or until the color of the upper surface changes. Using your fingers or a thin-bladed metal spatula, flip the chapati over so the speckled, cooked surface is on top. Cook for about 30 seconds longer. Flip it over again and use a dry dish towel to press down the edges of the chapati as it rises and puffs up, so the bread cooks evenly. Flip the chapati again and repeat with the other side. Lift out of the pan, place on a clean dish towel, and lightly brush the top with ghee, clarified butter, or melted unsalted butter. As you cook them, keep the chapatis hot on a baking sheet in a 250°F oven, loosely covered with foil. Serve hot.

JAGDESSH USES HER FINGERS TO MIX TOGETHER THE FLOUR AND 3 TABLESPOONS WATER.

SHE SPRINKLES EXTRA WATER THROUGH HER CUPPED HANDS INTO THE DOUGH IF IT IS DRY.

THE FLAKES OF DOUGH COME TOGETHER AS IT IS MIXED.

USING UNFLOURED KNUCKLES, SHE KNEADS THE DOUGH IN THE BOWL.

USING FLOURED FINGERS, JAGDESSH PULLS OFF EGG-SIZE PIECES OF DOUGH.

SHE SHAPES EACH PIECE OF DOUGH INTO A BALL BY ROLLING IT BETWEEN HER FLOURED PALMS.

OPPOSITE

No Indian meal is complete without a selection of flat breads to accompany the exotically spiced dishes. In Indian homes, the breads are often used for scooping up foods, removing the need for forks and spoons. When Indian food is served in Western homes or in restaurants, however, it is usually eaten with silverware. This meal includes naan (foreground), as well as chapatis (middle), and parathas (background).

TO SHAPE A CHAPATI, JAGDESSH ROTATES A BALL OF DOUGH BETWEEN HER PALM AND FINGERS.

SHE THEN USES HER FINGERS TO PRESS AND GENTLY PULL OUT THE RIM, TURNING THE DOUGH TO MAKE A CIRCLE.

USING AN INDIAN-STYLE ROLLING PIN, SHE ROLLS THE FLOURED DOUGH INTO A 7-INCH CIRCLE.

SHE THEN FLIPS THE CIRCLE FROM HAND TO HAND SEVERAL TIMES TO STRETCH THE DOUGH.

SHE USES HER FINGERS TO FLIP THE CHAPATI OVER AFTER IT HAS COOKED FOR 30 SECONDS.

USING A FOLDED DISH TOWEL, JAGDESSH PRESSES DOWN ON THE PUFFED AREAS OF THE CHAPATI SO IT COOKS EVENLY.

POORIS

INGREDIENTS

Makes 8

1 recipe Chapati dough (page 56)
additional flour for shaping
vegetable oil for frying

a heavy, deep, 10-inch frying pan

These use the same dough as chapatis, but they are smaller and puffed up like pillows because they are cooked in hot fat rather than in a dry pan. For a lighter dough, use half unbleached all-purpose flour and half sifted whole-wheat pastry flour. Some cooks also like to add 1–2 tablespoons of ghee (page 56) to the dough for extra richness.

Prepare the dough and shape and roll it as for Chapatis, making the circles only 5 inches in diameter. Heat about 1 inch of oil in the frying pan over moderately high heat until it reaches 375°F. Add one poori to the oil. At first it will sink to the bottom of the pan, then it will float and begin to puff up. Turn it over using two slotted spoons or a large skimmer and a metal spoon. Spoon some oil over the top, then turn it over again. It will puff up more after turning. This whole cooking process will take about 1½ minutes. The poori will puff up like an overstuffed pillow and be very lightly speckled with brown.

Using the two spoons, lift the poori from the oil and let it drain a second or so over the pan, then transfer to paper towels to drain completely. Repeat with the remaining pooris. Serve each poori immediately after it is fried and drained.

PARATHAS

Makes 8
1 recipe Chapati dough (page 56)
additional flour for shaping
ghee (page 56), clarified butter, or melted
    unsalted butter

a tava, a cast-iron frying pan, or a heavy
    griddle

A cooked paratha contains crisp layers of rich
dough.

Parathas are made in a similar way to chapatis, with the same dough, but they are flakier and richer. The chapati dough is brushed with ghee, folded several times, and cooked with more ghee on a tava, or frying pan, or a griddle to make a crisp, rich, flaky bread. Serve parathas as soon as possible after cooking.

Prepare and divide the dough as for Chapatis. Roll each piece of dough into a ball. Press the ball of dough in a small bowl of flour, turning it over so it is lightly dusted on all sides. Roll out the dough into a circle, about 6 inches across.

Lightly brush about 2 teaspoons ghee, clarified butter, or melted unsalted butter over each circle of dough. Fold each into thirds like an envelope – top third down and bottom third up. Fold the ends in to make a square package of dough. Dip all sides of the dough in the flour. Roll out the package with a rolling pin, turning the dough to make a 7-inch square about ⅛ inch thick. It is traditional to flip the square from hand to hand a couple of times to stretch the dough.

Heat a tava, frying pan, or griddle until very hot, but do not add any oil. When the tava, frying pan, or griddle is the proper temperature, a pinch of flour sprinkled into the pan will brown in 30 seconds. Cook the paratha in the hot pan for 30 seconds. Flip it over and cook the second side about 30 seconds. Turn the paratha over again and brush the top with ghee, clarified butter, or melted unsalted butter. Turn the paratha over and brush the other side as before. The cooked paratha should be crisp, speckled with brown patches, and slightly puffy. As you cook them, keep the parathas warm on a platter or baking sheet in a single layer, uncovered, in a 250°F oven.

TO DEVELOP THE FLAKY LAYERS, JAGDESSH FOLDS THE DOUGH LIKE AN ENVELOPE. SHE THEN FOLDS THE ENDS IN TO MAKE A SQUARE PACKAGE OF DOUGH.

SHE DIPS ALL SIDES OF THE DOUGH INTO FLOUR BEFORE SHE ROLLS IT OUT.

SHE FLIPS THE DOUGH BETWEEN HER HANDS SEVERAL TIMES TO STRETCH IT.

SHE SPREADS MELTED GHEE ON EACH SIDE OF THE PARATHA AS IT COOKS. YOU CAN ALSO USE MELTED CLARIFIED BUTTER OR REGULAR BUTTER. IT IS THE EXTRA FAT THAT GIVES THE PARATHA ITS RICHNESS.

NAAN

INGREDIENTS

Makes 8
1 ⅔ cups (250g) self-rising flour
2 tablespoons plain yogurt
1 teaspoon salt

about ½ cup (115ml) lukewarm water

Naan is a Punjabi leavened bread made with white flour and yogurt, which ferments the dough and adds flavor. Jagdessh prefers to use the chemical leavening agents in self-rising flour, rather than yeast, to raise this bread.

These breads are traditionally baked in a clay oven sunk into the ground, called a tandoor, few Indian homes — let alone houses in England or the U.S. — possess a tandoor, so Jagdessh cooks her naan under a very hot broiler. Other home cooks use heated baking sheets in an oven heated on the maximum setting, but Jagdessh says her method works best — and I can vouch that the results are excellent. Jagdessh also makes flavored naan. She rolls out the dough and brushes it lightly with melted ghee (page 56) as below. Then she presses cumin or sesame seeds or a little minced onion into the dough before broiling.

Serve naan warm.

Combine the flour, yogurt, and salt in a large bowl. Add the lukewarm water, 1 tablespoon at a time, working it into the flour mixture with your fingers and bringing the flakes of dough together. Add just enough water to make a soft, slightly sticky dough.

Knead the dough roughly in the bowl for a couple of seconds, then cover with a damp dish towel and let stand in a warm spot so the dough ferments, about 1 hour. During the last 15 minutes of standing time, heat the broiler and broiler pan.

Flour your fingers and pull off a piece of dough about the size of an egg. Between your palms, form the dough into a ball, then roll it out with a rolling pin on an unfloured work surface into an oval 8 to 9 inches long and about ⅓ inch thick. Repeat with the remaining dough to make eight naan.

Put one naan on the hot broiler pan and broil, about 3 to 4 inches from the source of heat, until it puffs up and is speckled with brown spots. Naan cook very quickly, in about 30 seconds, so watch it constantly. Turn it over and cook the second side. Repeat with the remaining seven naan.

JAGDESSH ADDS WATER THROUGH HER FINGERS UNTIL THE DOUGH IS SOFT AND SLIGHTLY STICKY.

USING FLOURED FINGERS, SHE PULLS OFF EGG-SIZE PIECES OF DOUGH.

SHE ROLLS OUT EACH BALL OF DOUGH INTO AN OVAL, 8 TO 9 INCHES LONG.

SHE BROILS THE NAAN FOR ABOUT 30 SECONDS ON EACH SIDE UNTIL IT IS PUFFED AND SPECKLED WITH BROWN. IT IS THEN READY TO SERVE.

Middle Eastern Breads

Claudia Roden, who has written the definitive book on Middle Eastern food, *A New Book of Middle Eastern Food* (Viking, 1986), says that for some in the Middle East, bread, more than any other food, is considered a direct gift from God. Middle Eastern and Indian flat breads must be first cousins, as there are so many similarities. The crackerlike lavash, although leavened with yeast, is cooked rapidly on a very hot, ungreased pan, as are chapatis. Pita bread, also made with yeast, is like naan — thin, soft, and flat — and it is cooked rapidly, in the oven, where it puffs up spectacularly. Like Indian breads, lavash and pitas are used for scooping up dips and sauces. Pitas, which have an inside "pocket," can also be stuffed with meat, kabobs, vegetables, or felafel.

PITA BREAD

INGREDIENTS

Makes 12

1 0.6-oz cake fresh yeast (15g), or
   1 envelope active dry yeast
   (2½ teaspoons) plus ½ teaspoon sugar
1¼ cups (280ml) lukewarm water
1 tablespoon olive oil
about 4 cups (455g) unbleached white
   bread flour
1 teaspoon salt
extra flour for dusting

several heavy baking sheets

Pita bread, the daily bread of the Middle East, should not be flabby or leathery, as are many commercial versions. If your pitas are tough, replace half of the bread flour with unbleached all-purpose flour to reduce the gluten content. This will make the flour mixture softer and the baked pitas more tender. Cool pitas for at least 10 minutes before eating, or cool them completely and store in plastic bags or freeze.

Crumble the fresh yeast into a large bowl. Mix in 4 tablespoons lukewarm water until smooth. If using dry yeast, mix the granules and the sugar with the lukewarm water and let stand until foamy, 5 to 10 minutes (page 18). Stir the remaining lukewarm water and the olive oil into the yeast mixture.

Add a handful of the flour and the salt to the yeast mixture in the large bowl, beating with your hand to make a smooth batter. Add enough of the remaining flour, a handful at a time, to make a soft dough. As you begin to add the flour, first beat the batter with your hand or a wooden spoon; as the dough becomes firmer, vigorously knead in the flour with lightly floured hands, working in the bowl. The dough should eventually become soft and not sticky. Turn out the dough onto a lightly floured work surface and let it rest for about 5 minutes.

Knead the dough with lightly floured hands until it becomes smooth, silky, shiny, and firm, but still elastic, adding more flour as needed. (My Turkish friend Zeynep says it should feel like a baby's bottom.) Wash and dry the bowl and oil it. Put the dough in the bowl and turn the dough over so the top is oiled. Cover with a damp dish towel. Let the dough rise at room temperature until doubled in size, about 1½ hours.

Punch down the dough, and turn it out onto a lightly floured work surface. Weigh the dough and divide it into twelve equal pieces, or roll it into a fat rope and cut it into twelfths. Roll each piece between your palms into a rough ball. Smooth the balls by bringing the sides down underneath the ball and pinching them together. Place the balls

A PITA BREAD BEGINS TO PUFF UP AFTER IT HAS BEEN IN THE OVEN FOR 1 MINUTE.

AFTER 2 MINUTES IT PUFFS EVEN MORE.

on the work surface, cover with a dry dish towel or sheet of plastic wrap, and let rest for 10 minutes. This helps the dough to relax, making it easier to roll out.

Using a very lightly floured rolling pin, roll out each ball on a very lightly floured work surface into a round, about 6 inches across and ¼ inch thick. (If they are too thin they will become crisp, like crackers, when baked.) Rolling them out takes a bit of practice because the dough will spring back. Lay the dough rounds on floured dish towels or a floured baking sheet and let rise at room temperature until doubled in size, about 30 minutes. During the last 15 minutes of standing, heat the oven to 500°F. Place a baking sheet on each shelf of the oven to heat up. (Nonstick ones work well, as do well-seasoned old baking sheets. If you have only newer ones, they may need to be very lightly greased.)

Wearing very thick oven mitts, transfer a round to each very hot baking sheet and lightly mist or sprinkle it with water to keep it pale. Bake for 2 minutes, without opening the door. After checking that it hasn't browned too much, bake for another minute or so (depending on how hot your oven gets) until the pita is firm, yet still pale. If the pita starts to brown before it is firm, lower the oven temperature slightly. Transfer the pitas to a wire rack and let stand until just warm. Then cover with a dry dish towel or plastic wrap to keep the crust soft. Bake the remaining rounds in the same way.

INGREDIENTS

Makes about 15

1 cup (110g) whole-wheat pastry flour, preferably stone-ground

3 cups (340g) unbleached white bread flour

1 teaspoon salt

1 0.6-oz cake fresh yeast (15g), or
    1 envelope active dry yeast
    (2½ teaspoons) plus ½ teaspoon sugar

about 1¼ cups (280ml) lukewarm water

extra flour for dusting

a griddle or cast-iron frying pan

LAVASH

This bread is rolled so thin it cooks rapidly to make a bubbly, crisp cracker. If it puffs up like pita or naan, roll the circles thinner (let rest for 10 minutes first). Serve the same day, with mezze (appetizers), such as baba ghanoush, stuffed grape leaves, hummus, taramasalata, and tabbouleh.

Stir together the flours and salt in a large bowl. Make a well in the center of the flour mixture. Crumble the fresh yeast into another bowl and stir in half of the lukewarm water until smooth. If using dry yeast, mix the granules and the ½ teaspoon sugar with the lukewarm water and let stand until foamy, 5–10 minutes (page 18). Add the yeast mixture to the well in the flour. Stir in the flour from the bowl with your hand or a wooden spoon to make a soft, but not sticky dough. If the dough is dry and crumbly, add as much of the remaining water as needed, one tablespoon at a time.

Turn out the dough onto a lightly floured work surface and knead for about 5 minutes until smooth. Put the dough back into the bowl, cover with a damp dish towel and let rise at room temperature, away from drafts, until doubled in size – about 1 hour. Punch down the dough and turn out onto a floured work surface. Weigh the dough and divide into 15 equal egg-size pieces, or roll it into a fat rope and divide into 15 pieces. Shape into smooth balls as for Pita Bread (left), cover with a dry dish towel or sheet of plastic wrap and let rise for 30 minutes.

Working with one ball at a time, roll out each as thinly as possible on a very lightly floured surface to make an almost translucent round, about 5 inches across, using as little flour as possible. Heat the griddle or frying pan until very hot. Gently dust off any excess flour (the flour will scorch in the pan, causing black specks – you may need to wipe out the pan after cooking each). Cook the round for about 1 minute, then flip it over and briefly cook the other side (30 seconds at the most) – the bread should be lightly browned on top of the bubbles which have formed. Remove with a spatula to a wire rack to cool. Cook the remaining dough in the same way, rolling out the next one as soon as the previous one has been removed from the griddle to cool. If your griddle is large enough, you can cook two breads at once. Cool in single layers on wire racks.

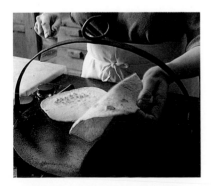

REMOVE EACH LAVASH FROM THE GRIDDLE WHEN THE TOPS OF THE BUBBLES ARE LIGHTLY BROWNED.

BRANCH BREAD

INGREDIENTS

Makes 12

1 cup (110g) rye flour

1 cup (110g) whole-wheat bread flour,
    preferably stone-ground

2½ cups (340g) unbleached all-purpose
    flour

1½ teaspoons salt

½ teaspoon sugar

1¼ cups (280ml) milk

2 tablespoons (30g) unsalted butter

extra flour for dusting

coarse sea salt for sprinkling

2 baking sheets, lightly greased

USING A SHARP KNIFE, CUT A SERIES
OF CHEVRONS IN THE DOUGH.

I have my friend Stephen Pouncey to thank for this Icelandic recipe, which he gleaned and translated on a deer-stalking trip in Sweden. Branch bread is a crispbread — made without yeast, and designed to keep. If you are in a hurry, however, choose another recipe, as these take some time to roll and bake. When rolling out the dough, it should be as thin as a flower petal.

Branch bread is good to serve with soups, pâtés and dips. It is also excellent for feeding to teething babies (without the salt topping). After cooling, store carefully in an airtight container because these are very fragile. They will keep for up to one month.

Mix together the flours, salt, and sugar in a large bowl. Make a well in the center.

Heat the milk in a small saucepan over moderately low heat until small bubbles appear around the edges. Remove the milk from the heat and stir in the butter. When the butter has melted, pour the hot liquid into the well in the flour mixture. Stir the flours into the liquid using a wooden spoon. As soon as the dough becomes cool enough to handle, work it into a smooth dough with your hands, pressing the dough together to eliminate any lumps, as if making shortbread, rather than kneading it.

Turn out the dough onto a lightly floured work surface and cover with the upturned bowl; the dough should still be warm. Let the dough rest for 30 minutes. Heat the oven to 425°F.

Divide the dough into twelve equal pieces. Roll out each piece as thinly as possible into a round. Using a 9- to 9½-inch dinner plate as a guide, trim the dough; discard the scraps. Using a sharp knife, cut a series of chevrons in the dough: once baked these will make a spruce tree design. Transfer one round to each prepared baking sheet, lifting it carefully, or sliding the baking sheet underneath.

Brush the dough very lightly with water and sprinkle with coarse salt to taste. Bake two breads at a time until lightly browned and crisp, 8 to 10 minutes. Keep your eye on them, as they bake very quickly. Transfer the breads to wire racks to cool completely. Repeat with the remaining dough.

During the baking, the chevrons in branch
bread open out to look like the branches of a
spruce tree.

Quaintly old-fashioned, toasted crumpets
remain a favorite afternoon teatime treat.
Serve them with hot with good-quality butter.

INGREDIENTS

Makes about 18

2 cups (230g) unbleached white bread
   flour

1⅔ cups (230g) unbleached all-purpose
   flour

¾ teaspoon cream of tartar

1 0.6-oz cake fresh yeast (15g), or
   1 envelope active dry yeast (2½
   teaspoons) plus ½ teaspoon sugar

2¼ cups (510ml) lukewarm water

3½ teaspoons (10g) coarse sea salt,
   crushed or ground

½ teaspoon baking soda

⅔ cup (140ml) lukewarm milk

a griddle or cast-iron frying pan
4 crumpet rings, about 3½ inches
   diameter, greased

CRUMPETS OR "LES ÉPONGES"

Well-made crumpets — light, with large air holes, and very tasty — are absolutely scrumptious. The rubbery commercial ones I have found in England are travesties best avoided. In the States, English muffins resemble crumpets more than they do our English muffins, but crumpets have a moist, almost damp crumb. Crumpets are eaten whole, not split in two, either hot from the griddle or toasted, and spread with butter. Do not stint on the butter. Crumpets also freeze well, and you can toast them straight from the freezer. Les éponges is what a young French friend calls these crumpets, and the name has stuck.

Fellow food writer Elaine Hallgarten gave me a copy of The Modern Baker Confectioner and Caterer, by Master Baker John Kirkland, published in 1907, and his advice and recipe remain invaluable. I have found the combination of flours in this recipe works well.

Sift together the flours and cream of tartar into a large bowl. Crumble the fresh yeast into a medium-size bowl. Mix in the lukewarm water until smooth. If using dry yeast, mix the granules and the sugar with ¾ cup (170ml) lukewarm water and let stand until foamy, 5 to 10 minutes (page 18). Stir in the remaining lukewarm water.

Mix the yeast mixture into the flour to make a very thick, but smooth batter, beating vigorously with your hand or a wooden spoon for 2 minutes. Cover the bowl with plastic wrap and let stand in a warm spot until the batter rises and then falls, about 1 hour.

Add the salt and beat the batter for about 1 minute. Then cover the bowl and let stand in a warm spot for 15 to 20 minutes, so the batter can "rest."

Dissolve the baking soda in the lukewarm milk. Then gently stir it into the batter. The batter should not be too stiff or your crumpets will be "blind" — without holes — so it is best to test one before cooking the whole batch.

Heat an ungreased, very clean griddle or frying pan over moderately low heat for about 3 minutes until very hot. Put a well-greased crumpet ring on the griddle. Spoon or pour ⅓ cup of the batter into the ring. The amount of batter will depend on the size of your crumpet ring.

As soon as the batter is poured into the ring, it should begin to form holes. If holes do not form, add a little more lukewarm water, a tablespoon at a time, to the batter in the bowl and try again. If the batter is too thin and runs out under the ring, gently work in a little more all-purpose flour and try again. Once the batter is the proper consistency, continue with the remaining batter, cooking the crumpets in batches, three or four at a time. As soon as the top surface is set and covered with holes, 7 to 8 minutes, the crumpet is ready to flip over.

To flip the crumpet, remove the ring with a towel or tongs, then turn the crumpet carefully with a spatula. The top, cooked side should be chestnut brown. Cook the second, holey side of the crumpet for 2 to 3 minutes, or until pale golden. The crumpet should be about ¾ inch thick. Remove the crumpet from the griddle. Grease the crumpet rings well after each use.

BEAT THE BATTER VIGOROUSLY WITH YOUR HAND UNTIL IT IS THICK AND SMOOTH.

GENTLY STIR IN THE MILK MIXTURE.

SPOON OR POUR ABOUT ⅓ CUP BATTER INTO EACH GREASED CRUMPET RING.

USING A DISH TOWEL, EASE OFF THE RING WHEN THE UPPER SURFACE IS HOLEY.

USING A SPATULA, FLIP THE UNMOLDED CRUMPET OVER AND COOK FOR 2 TO 3 MINUTES LONGER. THE HOLEY SIDE SHOULD BE PALE GOLDEN.

A cozy afternoon tea with homemade muffins (front) and crumpets in front of a roaring fire is just the thing to brighten up a damp, cold British winter's day.

A plate of freshly made pikelets is kept warm next to the fire. Pikelets are the northern cousins of crumpets, traditionally made in Derbyshire, Yorkshire, and Lancashire. They are cooked on a griddle like crumpets, but without the restraining rings. As a result, they look like small, thin pancakes.

To make pikelets, use the ingredients for Crumpets (page 65), but increase the amount of milk to 1¼ cups (280ml). Make the batter the same way, then drop 2 tablespoons batter in pools directly onto a hot, ungreased griddle or cast-iron frying pan. Cook for about 3 minutes on each side. This should yield about 30 pikelets.

ENGLISH MUFFINS

Early in the 20th century, Master Baker John Kirkland (page 65) wrote that these muffins are different in almost every respect from crumpets: "Muffins are thick, extremely lightly fermented dough cakes, not holey or tough, three inches across and almost two inches thick." He recommends using flour with a moderately strong gluten level for best results, and I find that this mixture of flours works well.

The dough is very soft indeed, and that, along with the three risings, gives these muffins their lightness. They are nothing like the rubbery raisin and bran ones sold commercially, or the really disappointing "sourdough English muffins" I came across in New England supermarkets. To American tastes, these will not be what is usually expected in an English muffin; English muffins in the States are more like our crumpets. But please do try this recipe; it's not at all difficult and the results are truly delicious.

Makes 8

3 cups (340g) unbleached white bread
   flour

¾ cup (110g) unbleached all-purpose
   flour

3½ teaspoons (10g) coarse sea salt,
   crushed or ground

1 0.6-oz cake fresh yeast (15g), or
   1 envelope active dry yeast
   (2½ teaspoons)

½ teaspoon sugar

1 cup (230ml) lukewarm water

⅔ cup (140ml) lukewarm milk

extra flour for dusting

rice flour, cornstarch or cornmeal for
   dusting

2 or 4 baking sheets

a griddle or cast-iron frying pan

The "proper" way to eat English muffins is to open them slightly with a fork at the middle joint, toast them on both sides, and then tear them open with the fork and spread thickly with butter. Store them wrapped at room temperature or freeze them.

Mix the flours with the salt in a large bowl and warm the bowl of flour (page 15). This will help the yeast start working and give the muffins their light texture.

Crumble the fresh yeast into a small bowl. Mix in the sugar and half of the lukewarm water until smooth. If using dry yeast, mix the granules and the sugar with half of the lukewarm water and let stand until foamy, 5 to 10 minutes (page 18).

Make a well in the warmed flour. Add the yeast mixture, the remaining lukewarm water, and the milk and mix with your hand to make a very soft, slightly sticky dough. Turn out the dough onto a lightly floured work surface and knead with floured hands for 10 minutes until the dough is soft, elastic, smooth, and no longer sticky. Shape the dough into a ball.

Return the dough to the bowl. Cover with a damp dish towel. Let rise in a warm spot, away from drafts, until doubled in size, about 1 hour.

Punch down the dough and turn it out onto a lightly floured surface. Knead it again for 5 minutes. John Kirkland recommends dipping your hands in a little lukewarm water for this stage. Return the dough to the bowl and cover again. Let rest for 30 minutes.

Divide the dough into eight pieces. According to John Kirkland, "The usual method is to squeeze the dough through a ring made by the thumb and forefinger of one floured hand," and this is the method I use. Squeeze off the ball of dough and drop it onto a baking sheet well dusted with rice flour, cornstarch, or cornmeal. Sprinkle the dough with more rice flour, cornstarch, or cornmeal. Cover the tray of muffins with another baking tray, then a damp dish towel. Let rise in a warm spot for 30 minutes.

Heat an ungreased griddle or frying pan about 2 minutes over moderate heat until moderately hot. With a metal spatula, invert the muffins, three at a time, onto the hot griddle. Cook about 12 minutes or until the undersides are golden brown. Turn the muffins over and cook 10 to 12 minutes longer, or until the second side is browned and the sides of the muffins spring back when pressed. Transfer the muffins to a warm serving platter and wrap with a dry dish towel to keep warm. Wipe out the griddle or pan with a cloth and continue cooking the remaining muffins.

USE YOUR HANDS TO MIX A VERY SOFT,
SLIGHTLY STICKY DOUGH.

DIVIDE THE DOUGH INTO BALLS BY SQUEEZING
IT THROUGH YOUR THUMB AND FOREFINGER.

COVER THE DOUGH WITH A BAKING SHEET,
THEN A TOWEL AND LET RISE.

USING A SPATULA, FLIP OVER EACH MUFFIN SO
BOTH SIDES ARE GOLDEN BROWN.

HOE CAKES

"Do not think of making this recipe unless you have good bacon fat," says Caroll Boltin, adamantly. "They will be tasteless." She has spent many years researching the American pioneers and their early settlements in New York State's Hudson Valley.

 "This was a fast way to have bread in colonial times. It was cheap, easy, and quick, and everyone had bacon fat in the larder." The simple, gritty cornmeal batter was cooked over the open fire in a flat garden hoe — hence the name — and eaten immediately with soup or a vegetable stew.

 This is Caroll's recipe, which she often makes at Philipsburg Manor, a historic restoration in North

The water-powered mill at Philipsburg Manor (right), on the Pocantico River at North Tarrytown, New York, has been grinding and selling cornmeal since early in the 18th century. Here, miller Peter Curtis employs a traditional grinding method similar to those used by the Manor's earliest millers.

INGREDIENTS

Makes about 12

1¾ cups stone-ground yellow cornmeal
½ teaspoon salt
about ⅔ cup (140ml) boiling water
bacon fat for cooking

a heavy cast-iron frying pan

Tarrytown, New York, to illustrate what 17th-century life was like. To cook the cakes, wealthier settlers would have used a spider, a kettle with built-in legs that sat in the fireplace, but a heavy cast iron frying pan on the stove top works just as well for the modern cook.

 Be sure to eat these cakes while they're still hot; they do not keep well.

Mix together the cornmeal and salt in a small bowl, then stir in enough of the boiling water to make a sloppy batter that barely holds its shape. Let stand for 5 minutes.

 Heat a frying pan on the stove over moderately high heat or over the glowing embers of a fire — there should be no flames — until hot, about 2 minutes.

 Add plenty of bacon fat or vegetable oil to the hot pan so it is about ¼ inch deep. Heat the fat about 2 to 3 minutes until the surface is rippling and a small bit of the batter bubbles as soon as it is dropped into the fat. Drop the batter by generous tablespoons into the pan. Do not crowd the pan; the cakes should be cooked in batches. Cook the cakes until the undersides are golden and crisp, 1 to 2 minutes. Flip the cakes over with two slotted spatulas and cook the other side 1 to 2 minutes until browned and crisp. Transfer to paper towels to drain. Adjust the heat as necessary to maintain the temperature of the fat, and continue to cook the remaining cakes.

NOTE: You'll need about ⅔ cup of bacon fat to cook these in, about the amount rendered from 1 pound (455g) of bacon.

MADDYBENNY FADGE

INGREDIENTS

Makes 18

2 cups (455g) cooked mashed potatoes

2 tablespoons (30g) unsalted butter, diced

½ teaspoon salt

about ¾ cup (110g) unbleached all-purpose flour

extra flour for dusting

bacon fat or vegetable oil for frying

a griddle or heavy cast-iron frying pan

ROLL OUT THE DOUGH ON A LIGHTLY FLOURED WORK SURFACE, THEN CUT IT INTO TRIANGLES OR SQUARES.

RIGHT

A sizzling farmhouse breakfast of fadge, crisp bacon, mushrooms, and a sunny-side-up egg.

This recipe comes from Rosemary White, of Maddybenny Farm, Portrush, Northern Ireland. I met her when she won the Great Irish Breakfast award for her farmhouse bed and breakfast a few years ago; the judge had said, "Her breakfast was magnificent, and the presentation faultless." To win the prize, Rosemary prepared her famous Ulster Fry — lean, crisp bacon, meaty sausages, mushrooms, apple rings, and eggs accompanied by fadge, the local potato cakes, and her Maddybenny Wheaten Bread (page 81). The secret of a good breakfast, Rosemary says, is freshness. "I never start to cook for my guests in the morning until I see the whites of their eyes." Serve fadge hot.

Put the mashed potatoes in a large bowl. Add the butter and salt. Knead in the flour, adding just enough to bind the potatoes, making a soft, but not sticky dough. Too much flour will make the dough tough. Cover and chill for several hours or overnight.

Roll out the dough with a lightly floured rolling pin on a lightly floured work surface to a ¼ inch thickness. Cut into triangles or squares. Heat a griddle or cast-iron frying pan over moderately high heat. Add a little bacon fat or oil to the griddle, just enough to prevent the fadge from sticking. Cook the fadge in batches until brown on one side, about 1 minute. Turn the fadge over and cook the second side until brown. Keep warm in a 250°F oven while cooking the remainder. Add more fat to the griddle as needed.

NOTE: The exact amount of flour needed for this recipe and Manx Potato Cakes (below) depends on the consistency of the mashed potatoes. The dough should be soft, but not sticky. Do not mash the potatoes or make the dough in a food processor — the machine will make the results gluey and disgusting.

MANX POTATO CAKES

INGREDIENTS

Makes about 9

2 cups (455g) cooked mashed potatoes

2 tablespoons (30g) unsalted butter

½ teaspoon salt, or to taste

plenty of black pepper

1 large egg, beaten

¼ cup (30g) shredded aged Cheddar cheese

about ¾ cup (110g) self-rising flour

bacon fat or vegetable oil for frying

My Manx grandmother (from the Isle of Man), who prided herself on keeping a good table and larder, made these potato cakes for high tea to go with ham and poached eggs. These are richer than Maddybenny Fadge (above). Eat immediately after cooking.

Prepare the dough as for Maddybenny Fadge (above), adding the black pepper, egg, and cheese to the potatoes with the salt and butter. There is no need to chill this dough.

Pull off nine egg-size pieces of dough and roll them between your palms, flouring your hands to prevent sticking, if necessary. Flatten the dough balls to make thin cakes, about 3 inches across and ¼ inch thick.

Heat a griddle or cast-iron frying pan over moderately high heat. Add a little bacon fat or oil to the griddle, just enough to prevent the cakes from sticking. Fry the cakes in batches until golden brown, crispy, and slightly puffed, about 3 minutes. Turn the potato cakes over with a metal spatula and cook the second side about 3 minutes longer, until crisp. Add more fat to the griddle as needed.

BLINIS

Blinis are light, crumbly, flavorful, yeast-leavened pancakes. Their intense, slightly bitter taste comes from the speckled gray-brown buckwheat flour. Traditionally, blinis should be eaten with sour cream or melted butter and Beluga or pressed caviar, but these days lumpfish roe, salmon caviar, chopped hard-boiled egg, and/or smoked fish are more usual — and easier on the budget. Eat these while still warm.

Crumble the fresh yeast into a large bowl. Mix in the sugar and 4 tablespoons lukewarm water until smooth. If using dry yeast, mix the granules and the sugar with ¼ cup of the lukewarm water and let stand until foamy, 5 to 10 minutes (page 18).

Whisk the remaining lukewarm water and the egg yolk into the yeast mixture. Whisk in the flour and salt to make a very thick batter. Cover with a damp dish towel. Let rise in a warm place, away from drafts, until doubled in volume, 1½ to 2 hours.

Whisk in the lukewarm milk to make a batter the consistency of thick heavy cream. Cover again and let stand in a warm place until small bubbles appear on the surface, about 1 hour. Beat the egg white in a small bowl with an electric mixer until it forms stiff peaks, then gently fold it into the batter with a rubber spatula.

Heat a crêpe pan, frying pan, or griddle pan over moderate heat until moderately hot, 1½ to 2 minutes or until your palm held 1½ inches above the pan feels warm after 15 seconds. Swirl 1 teaspoon of the butter into the pan. When the butter has melted, spoon a scant ¼ cup of batter into the pan and gently spread the batter with the back of a spoon to make a 4-inch pancake. Cook until the edges of the blini have set and small bubbles form on the surface, 2 to 3 minutes. Turn the blini over with a spatula and cook the second side for about 2 minutes, or until dry and the top springs back when pressed lightly in the center with your fingertips. Keep warm in a 300°F oven, uncovered, in a single layer, while cooking the remaining batter. Add more butter to the pan as needed.

INGREDIENTS

Makes about 12 blinis
1 0.6-oz cake fresh yeast (15g), or
    1 envelope active dry yeast
    (2½ teaspoons)
1 teaspoon sugar
¾ cup (170ml) lukewarm water
1 large egg, separated
1¼ cups (140g) buckwheat flour
1 teaspoon salt
¾ cup (170ml) lukewarm milk
butter or lard for frying

a heavy frying pan, crêpe pan, or griddle

WHISK THE BATTER UNTIL IT IS VERY THICK.

WHISK IN THE LUKEWARM MILK. THE BATTER SHOULD BE THE CONSISTENCY OF HEAVY CREAM.

COOK EACH BLINI UNTIL THE UPPER SURFACE HAS SET, 2 TO 3 MINUTES, THEN TURN THE BLINI OVER WITH A SPATULA AND COOK THE SECOND SIDE ABOUT 2 MINUTES. CONTINUE UNTIL ALL BLINIS ARE COOKED.

GRIDDLE OATCAKES

INGREDIENTS

Makes about 12 oatcakes

1⅓ cups (230g) steel-cut oats

½ teaspoon salt

2 tablespoons (30g) meat drippings, bacon fat, or lard, melted

6–8 tablespoons (85–115ml) boiling water

flour for rolling and cutting

a griddle or large cast-iron frying pan

2 jelly-roll pans fitted with wire racks

Scottish oatcakes are thin, crumbly, brittle-crisp biscuits made from oats ground into a meal (not a flour), salt, good, flavorful meat drippings or bacon fat, and hot water. As there is no leavening, the lightness comes from the steam produced during cooking. The shortness and the taste depend on the fat used — bacon fat adds a good flavor.

Oatcake expert F. Marian McNeill declared, in The Scots Kitchen (Edinburgh: Blackie, 1929), "Oatcakes are especially good with herring, sardines, cheese, buttermilk, or broth, or spread with butter and marmalade to complete the breakfast." That is surely true, but today you are more likely to see oatcakes in the Scottish Highlands served at tea time with butter, homemade raspberry jam, or a heather honey. In fancy restaurants Scottish soft cheeses are sometimes offered with oatcakes, although these are rarely homemade.

Medium-ground steel-cut oats are commonly used in the Highlands for oatcakes. In the States, the steel-cut oats sold are usually the coarse-ground type. Even the oats labeled fine-ground are coarser than Scottish medium-ground oats, so I've found it necessary to grind the oats briefly in a food processor to obtain the proper texture. This takes just a minute or so, though.

Triangular curly-edged oatcakes are cooked on a griddle, while a circular variety is baked in the oven.

You need to be careful when making oatcakes because they are likely to become crumbly as you roll them out. If this happens, you can add a few drops of hot water, or gently warm the dough in a very low oven if it has stiffened. According to Master Baker John Kirkland (page 65), "The springing effects [the expansion of the dough when baked] in their turn are modified for good or evil according to the manner in which the dough has been manipulated. If properly handled, the dough will be short and plump. If badly treated, [it will be] thin and hard."

Put the oats in a food processor and grind until they turn to a coarse meal, like the texture of fine bulgur wheat. Mix together the oats and salt in a medium-size bowl. Stir in the melted drippings, bacon fat, or lard with a metal spatula. Mix in 5 tablespoons of the boiling water, then add additional water as needed until the mixture binds together. It should be firm, not too sticky, and not crumbly. Gently knead for a few seconds to bring together into a dough.

Divide the dough in half. Quickly roll out the first half on a very lightly floured work surface using a lightly floured rolling pin, to a round about 10 inches across and ¼ inch thick. Use your fingers to press in and reform the edges if they start to crack or crumble. Cut the round into 6 triangles. Repeat with the other portion of dough. Let the dough triangles dry, uncovered, for 20 minutes.

Heat the oven to 300°F. Heat a griddle or frying pan over moderately low heat for about 3 minutes, until moderately hot; your palm will feel warm when held 1½ inches above the griddle after about 30 seconds. To speed up the cooking process you can use two griddles or frying pans, or a griddle and a frying pan — whatever you have — if you like. Do not grease the griddle.

USING A SHARP KNIFE, CUT THE ROLLED-OUT DOUGH INTO SIX TRIANGLES

COOK THE TRIANGLES UNTIL THE EDGES START TO CURL UPWARD.

Cook the triangles in batches, about three at a time, spaced apart, on the griddle, until they curl upward, 5 to 6 minutes. Turn them over with a metal spatula and cook the second side for about 4 to 5 minutes, until they become paler in color and are firm. Transfer to the wire racks on the jelly-roll pans in single layers. When all the oatcakes are cooked, place the jelly-roll pans with the oatcakes in the oven to dry out for about 20 minutes. (Catherine Brown, an authority on Scottish cooking, says that to remove excess moisture, oatcakes used to be dried in a special toaster in front of the fire.) Remove the oatcakes from the oven and take the racks off the pans. Let them cool completely and then store them in airtight containers.

PUPUSAS

Anà Sylvia Landeverde, a young professional cook from El Savador, showed Anthony Blake and me how to make her country's national dish of cornmeal griddle cakes, which are flavored with cheese and topped with chili-pickled cabbage and carrots. They were delicious, and were scoffed down as they came off the griddle.

Prepare the pickled topping at least 2 hours before you plan to eat. Mix all the topping ingredients together, then cover and let stand at room temperature for 2 hours. Stir well before using.

To prepare the griddle cakes, mix together the masa harina, salt, lime juice, and enough water to make a stiff, clammy dough. Work it together lightly with your fingertips until you have a smooth ball. If the dough is crumbly, add 1 tablespoon water; if it is sticky, work in a little more masa harina. Cover the dough and let stand for 30 minutes.

Weigh the dough and divide into eight equal pieces. Take one piece and slap it palm to palm to make a fairly thick cake about 3 inches in diameter and about 1 inch thick.

Place 1 tablespoon of the cheese in the center of each cake, pressing it firmly. Pinch the edges of the dough together over the cheese, then roll it in your hands so the cheese is securely enclosed. Using your hands, flatten the ball to make a rough disk 5 inches across and about ¼ inch thick, patting it and turning it with your palms, trying to make sure the cheese doesn't break through the dough. Keep shaped pupusas covered with plastic wrap while you repeat the process with the remaining dough.

Heat the oven to 250°F to keep the cooked pupusas warm on a platter, uncovered, while the others cook. (These take a few minutes to cook, so to speed up the process you can use two griddles or two frying pans, thus cooking four pupusas at once.)

Heat the griddle or pan over moderately high heat about 3 minutes, until moderately hot. Lightly brush the griddle with oil. Cook the griddle cakes, two at a time if they fit in your griddle or pan, turning them frequently, reducing the heat if necessary, until the cheese melts and they are speckled with brown and slightly puffy, about 5 minutes. Brush the griddle or pan with oil as needed. When they are all cooked, top with the pickled vegetables and serve immediately.

INGREDIENTS

Makes 8

2 cups (230g) masa harina (tortilla flour)

½ teaspoon salt

3 tablespoons fresh lime juice

½–¾ cup (115-170ml) water from the cold tap

¾ cup (85g) shredded aged Cheddar cheese

TOPPING:

2½ cups (230g) finely shredded white cabbage

1 cup (110g) finely shredded carrots

a little ground black pepper, to taste

1 teaspoon salt

½ cup (110ml) white wine vinegar

1 tablespoon chopped fresh oregano

½–1 teaspoon chopped fresh hot chili pepper, to taste

a heavy cast-iron frying pan or griddle

A ready-to-eat pupusa with the pickled vegetable topping.

ANÀ PUTS THE SHREDDED CHEESE IN THE CENTER OF THE THICK DOUGH CAKE.

ANÀ TRANSFERS THE HOT PUPUSA TO A PLATE.

QUICK BREADS

The varied breads in this chapter are called quick breads because the batters are simply mixed and then baked. No lengthy kneading or rising periods are necessary, so you can have freshly baked bread in a short time. They are all made without yeast, relying instead on chemical leavening agents (baking soda and baking powder), which rapidly produce bubbles of gas when they come in contact with moisture and warmth.

To leaven a dough or batter, baking soda, an alkali, must be combined with a slightly acidic dry ingredient like cream of tartar, or with an acidic liquid like buttermilk, sour milk, or a milk and yogurt mixture. Baking soda is also used when doughs contain brown sugar, molasses, any form of citrus, sour cream, or dried fruit. Baking powder is a ready-mixed combination of alkali and acid leavening agents. The gases that baking

powder and baking soda to rise, although with not yeast. Once mixed, the shaped or spooned into the prolonged kneading with in the flour should not be softer flours – all-purpose or flour with baking powder used instead of strong, The finished dough should while the leaveners are

Most of these breads cook will find they have a denser and they stale more quickly. butter or oil, eggs, or longer-keeping loaf. savory breads to accompany picnics, have in the kitchen

OPPOSITE *A morning's baking.*
ABOVE *A bemused lad at afternoon tea.*

produce help the dough quite the same effect as dough or batter is quickly pan. There is no need for these breads, as the gluten developed; for this reason, self-rising flour (all-purpose and salt added) – are high-gluten bread flours. be baked immediately, still active.

fairly rapidly, and you texture than yeast breads Enriching the dough with fruit helps to produce a These are sweet and meals, take along on for ready snacks or serve

with a cup of tea to revive sagging spirits late in the afternoon. Fresh Soda Bread (page 90) is a real morning treat, and Blueberry Muffins Hertz (page 78) are always welcomed for breakfast, as a snack, or in packed lunches. I often include Bacon Loaf (page 82) when I am planning the menu for a party, as it is good to serve with a selection of cheeses.

On chilly winter days, try the Herb Rolls (page 84) with steaming vegetable soups. The flavor of the fresh herbs and mild cream cheese makes this a great combination, which my family always enjoys.

NOTE: Adding extra baking powder or baking soda will not improve the texture. Rather, it will add a nasty chemical tang to the finished result, and the combination of bleached flour and too much of a leavening agent can often produce a chlorine aftertaste.

BLUEBERRY MUFFINS HERTZ

Makes 12

1 cup (140g) unbleached all-purpose flour

1 cup (140g) whole-wheat flour,
    preferably stone-ground

7 tablespoons (85g) sugar

1 tablespoon baking powder

a large pinch of salt

1¼ cups (280ml) milk

¼ cup (60ml) soy oil

1 extra large egg, beaten

2 teaspoons lemon juice

1¼ cups (140g) fresh or frozen blueberries

a 12-cup muffin pan, well greased or lined
    with paper muffin cases

OPPOSITE *A selection of sweet quick breads. Left to right (front): Tina's Breakfast Loaf, Date and Apple Loaf (page 83), and Smithy Loaf (page 81). On tray: Gingerbread (page 80) and Blueberry Muffins Hertz.*

American muffins bear no resemblance to English muffins; they are made with all-purpose flour and baking powder rather than from a yeast batter, and are baked in muffin pans instead of being cooked on a griddle. They look, and can taste, rather like cupcakes, or what we Brits call "fairy cakes," though they are less sweet, and have a moist, spongy crumb and a light texture. The best homemade muffins are a world away from the sawdust-dry, dense commercial variety, and wild blueberry muffins are the best of all.

My husband's mother, Annette Hertz, welcomed me into the family as only an all-American mother can. She enthusiastically introduced me to Maine's finest bounty — fresh seafood, rich ice cream, and the exquisite-tasting wild blueberries that she uses to make muffins for her grandchildren. This is her recipe, using a mixture of all-purpose and whole-wheat flours. (Annette uses a 50/50 flour blend that she buys from her supermarket.)

Maine wild blueberries are small, about the size of fresh currants, intensely flavored, and slightly tart, with more depth of taste than the fatter, cultivated ones. As fresh blueberries are only available for a few weeks, you can use frozen blueberries, straight from the freezer, out of season. The blueberries can also be replaced with fresh red currants, cranberries, huckleberries, pitted cherries, blackberries, diced apple, or dried fruits and nuts.

You can also experiment with spices — try cinnamon, nutmeg, pumpkin-pie spice, or add a bit of grated fresh lemon or orange rind. Or try one of the freshly ground spice mixtures on page 150. The oil can be replaced with an equal quantity of melted unsalted butter for a richer taste. Muffins should be eaten warm from the oven, or at least on the day of baking. They can also be frozen for one month.

Heat the oven to 400°F. Mix together the flours, sugar, baking powder, and salt in a large bowl. Whisk together the milk, oil, egg, and lemon juice in a medium-size bowl. Stir the milk mixture into the dry ingredients until almost combined. Quickly but gently fold in the blueberries with a rubber spatula; the mixture should still look lumpy. Overmixing will make the muffins tough. Spoon the batter into the prepared muffin pan, filling each two-thirds full.

Bake the muffins for 20 to 25 minutes, or until they have a distinct cracked peak in the middle and are golden brown and firm to the touch. A wooden pick inserted in the center of a muffin should come out clean. If the muffins seem slightly wet or soft, bake a few minutes longer. Cool the muffins in the pan for about 1 minute. Turn them out on to a wire rack to cool for a few minutes.

Blueberry Muffins Hertz are delicious served warm.

TINA'S BREAKFAST LOAF

INGREDIENTS

Makes 1 large loaf

½ cup (110g) unsalted butter, softened

¾ cup packed (170g) dark brown sugar

1⅔ cups (255g) unbleached all-purpose
  flour

2 teaspoons baking soda

a pinch of salt

1 cup + 2 tablespoons (260ml) sour
  cream

1 large egg

TOPPING:

3 tablespoons packed light brown sugar

2 teaspoons ground cinnamon

½ cup (60g) roughly chopped walnuts

a loaf pan, about 10 × 5 × 3 inches,
  lightly greased and bottom lined with
  waxed paper

This recipe dates back to the late seventies, when I was working in Paris. It comes from Tina Ujlaki, now the food editor of Food & Wine magazine in New York City, who used to make this simple and satisfying cake as an antidote to all the elaborate, rich French pâtisserie we consumed while we were there. This cake is a favorite of Tina's family. I enjoy serving it warm for breakfast with freshly brewed coffee.

Heat the oven to 350°F. Mix all the topping ingredients in a small bowl with your fingertips until blended.

To make the cake: Beat together the butter and sugar with an electric mixer at high speed, or with a spoon, until the mixture is pale yellow and fluffy. Sift together the flour, baking soda, and salt on to a sheet of waxed paper. Whisk together the sour cream and eggs in a small bowl. Add the flour mixture and the sour cream mixture to the butter and sugar and mix on low speed, or stir just until the batter is thoroughly combined. The batter will be quite soft.

Spoon half the batter into the prepared pan. Sprinkle half of the topping over the batter. Spoon the remaining batter into the pan. Evenly sprinkle the remaining topping over the batter and press it lightly into the surface.

Bake the cake for 45 to 55 minutes, or until it is lightly browned and a wooden pick inserted in the center comes out clean. Cool the cake in the pan on a wire rack for about 5 minutes.

Carefully turn the cake out of the pan, remove the waxed paper from the bottom, and put upright on a serving platter. Then cut into slices and serve warm.

GINGERBREAD

Makes 1 large loaf

1⅔ cups (230g) unbleached self-rising
    flour

1 teaspoon baking soda

1 tablespoon ground ginger

1 teaspoon ground cinnamon

1 teaspoon pumpkin-pie spice

½ cup (110g) unsalted butter, chilled and
    diced

⅓ cup (110g) dark unsulfured molasses

⅓ cup (110g) golden syrup (see Note)

½ cup + 2 tablespoons packed (110g)
    light brown sugar

1¼ cups (280ml) milk

1 extra large egg, beaten

a loaf pan, about 10 × 5 × 3 inches,
    greased and bottom lined with waxed
    paper

In my time as a pastry chef I have made many gingerbreads, but this is the most wonderful, sticky, spicy gingerbread I've ever tasted. It is dark, moist, well-spiced, not particularly sweet, and the flavor is unhampered by fruit or nuts. For the best flavor, let the gingerbread age a couple of days before eating. Enjoy it thickly sliced, with butter or slices of cheese.

Heat the oven to 350°F. Sift the flour, baking soda, and spices into a large bowl. Rub in the butter with your fingertips until the mixture looks like fine crumbs. In a small saucepan, heat the molasses with the syrup until melted, then let cool to lukewarm. Meanwhile, in another small pan, dissolve the sugar in the milk over a low heat, stirring. Whisk the milk into the flour mixture, then whisk in the molasses mixture followed by the egg. When thoroughly combined, you should have a thin batter.

Pour the batter into the prepared pan. Bake for 50 to 60 minutes, or until a skewer inserted off center comes out clean. (As the gingerbread bakes it will bubble up and rise, then fall, leaving a large, moist depression.) Let cool completely in the pan. Turn the cake out of the pan and remove the paper. Wrap the cake in waxed paper and then in foil.

NOTE: Golden syrup is found in jars or cans in most gourmet shops or better supermarkets.

WHISK THE BATTER UNTIL IT IS SMOOTH. IT SHOULD BE FAIRLY THIN.

BAKE UNTIL A SKEWER INSERTED OFF CENTER COMES OUT CLEAN.

Homemade gingerbread is an old-fashioned treat that still has great appeal. The flavor will be at its best if you bake this a couple of days before serving.

SMITHY LOAF

I'm not sure where this recipe came from originally, but it was given to me by Malcolm Appleby, who is a distinguished silversmith — hence the loaf's name. Malcolm lives in Scotland, in what was once a railway station. This recipe reminds me of the teas he serves on his station platform in sight of his herb garden and the "bulb" garden (made from colored lights). Malcolm has the most marvelous sense of humor, and I always smile when I make this good loaf. Eat this bread the day after it's made, sliced and buttered.

Heat the oven to 350°F. Bring the 1 cup of water to a boil in a large saucepan. Add the raisins, butter, sugar, pumpkin-pie spice, baking soda, and salt. Lower the heat and simmer gently for 5 minutes, stirring occasionally to combine the ingredients, until the raisins have plumped and the butter is melted. Let the mixture cool slightly. Stir in the flour and baking powder until well combined, then stir in the beaten eggs. Scrape the batter into the prepared pan and smooth the surface.

Bake the loaf for 40 to 50 minutes, or until a wooden pick inserted in the center comes out clean. Completely cool the loaf in the pan on a wire rack. Then turn it out and wrap with waxed paper and then foil.

INGREDIENTS

Makes 1 medium loaf

1 cup + 2 tablespoons (260ml) water
2 cups (340g) golden raisins
½ cup (110g) unsalted butter
½ cup + 2 tablespoons packed (110g) light brown sugar
2 teaspoons pumpkin-pie spice
1 teaspoon baking soda
a pinch of salt
1⅔ cups (230g) unbleached all-purpose flour
1 teaspoon baking powder
2 large eggs, beaten

a loaf pan, about 7 × 5 × 3 inches, greased and bottom lined with waxed paper

Maddybenny Wheaten Bread

STIR IN THE FLOUR AND BAKING POWDER UNTIL WELL COMBINED.

SCRAPE THE BATTER INTO THE PREPARED LOAF PAN.

MADDYBENNY WHEATEN BREAD

Another of Rosemary White's delicious and easy recipes from Northern Ireland (see her recipe for fadge on page 70). Here, four loaves are baked in one pan and then broken apart after baking. Any spare loaves can be frozen, well wrapped, for up to one month.

INGREDIENTS

Makes 1 medium loaf
6 cups (680g) whole-wheat bread flour, preferably stone-ground
1 tablespoon baking soda
1 tablespoon sugar
2 teaspoons salt
3–3¾ cups (710–850ml) buttermilk
extra flour for dusting

a baking pan, about 13 × 9 inches, greased

Heat the oven to 425°F. Stir together the flour, baking soda, sugar, and salt in a large mixing bowl. Make a well in the center. Add 3 cups (710ml) of the buttermilk. Using a metal spatula, mix the flour into the buttermilk to form a soft, but not sticky dough. Depending on the flour, you may need to add more buttermilk, 1 tablespoon at a time.

As soon as the dough comes together, turn it out on to a lightly floured work surface. With lightly floured hands, knead the dough gently for a few seconds, just until the dough looks even and has no floury patches. It still should look quite lumpy. Place the dough in the prepared pan and, with lightly floured hands, press it gently into the corners. Cut a deep cross on top with a sharp knife to score four equal rectangular sections. Bake the bread for 35 to 45 minutes, or until it has a firm, brown crust.

Turn out the bread on to a wire rack. Cover it with a clean dish towel, tucking the ends of the towel under the bread loosely. Let it cool to warm, if you wish, or cool it completely. Cut or break into four loaves.

A selection of savory quick breads. Left to right: Beer Bread (opposite), Herb Rolls (page 84), Bacon Loaf, and Maddybenny Wheaten Bread (page 81).

INGREDIENTS

Makes 1 large loaf

4 oz (110g) thick-sliced bacon, diced (about 1 cup)

2½ cups (340g) unbleached all-purpose flour

2 teaspoons baking powder

freshly ground black pepper, to taste

a large pinch of salt

¾ cup (170g) unsalted butter, chilled and diced

4 oz (110g) thickly sliced lean ham, diced (about 1 cup)

4 large eggs, beaten

a loaf pan, about 10 × 5 × 3 inches, greased

BACON LOAF

This richly flavored loaf smells so tantalizing in the oven, it's difficult to wait until it is cool enough to slice. Although the recipe comes from an American relative in Boston, I like to make it with thickly sliced smoked English bacon and a thick slice of good ham. In the States, if you can't get English bacon, use thick-sliced double-smoked bacon, available from a good butcher or gourmet foods store. This loaf is best on the day it is made.

Heat the oven to 350°F. Put the bacon into a cold frying pan and fry over moderately high heat for 5 minutes, stirring frequently, until crisp. Remove from the heat.

Sift together the flour, baking powder, pepper, and salt into a large bowl. Rub in the butter until the mixture looks like fine crumbs. Make a well in the center.

Stir the bacon and the bacon fat into the flour mixture. Add the ham and eggs, and stir to form a stiff batter. Spoon the batter into the prepared pan and smooth the surface. Bake the loaf for 45 to 55 minutes, or until it is lightly browned and a wooden pick inserted into the center comes out clean. Let cool in the pan on a wire rack for 5 minutes. Turn out the loaf on to the rack. Eat warm or let cool completely.

STIR IN THE CRISP BACON, HAM, AND EGGS TO MAKE A STIFF BATTER.

SPOON THE STIFF BATTER INTO THE PREPARED LOAF PAN.

DATE AND APPLE LOAF

INGREDIENTS

Makes 1 small loaf

½ cup (110g) unsalted butter, softened

½ cup + 2 tablespoons packed (110g)
   light brown sugar

2 large eggs, beaten

¾ cup (110g) unbleached self-rising flour

¾ cup (110g) whole-wheat flour,
   preferably stone-ground

1 cup (110g) chopped walnuts

¾ cup (110g) chopped pitted dates

¾ cup (110g) peeled and grated apple

about 2 tablespoons milk

a loaf pan, about 7 × 5 × 3 inches,
   greased and bottom lined with waxed
   paper

Use a well-flavored, tart apple for this slightly sweet loaf. In England I like this best made with Bramley cooking apples. In the States I suggest using Rhode Island greenings, Jonathans, Ida Reds, or a good, firm Granny Smith apple. The quantity of milk needed will depend on the flour you choose. This bread is tasty sliced and spread with butter or cheese.

Heat the oven to 350°F.

Beat together the butter and sugar in a large bowl with an electric mixer at high speed, or with a spoon, until light and fluffy. Beat in the eggs one at a time. With mixer on low speed, stir in the flours, walnuts, dates, and apples. Stir in enough milk to make a batter that clings to a wooden spoon, but falls when the spoon is tapped. Spoon the batter into the prepared pan.

Bake the loaf for 1 to 1¼ hours, or until a wooden pick inserted in the center comes out clean. Cool the loaf in the pan on a wire rack for 10 minutes. Then turn out the loaf on to a wire rack, remove the waxed paper from the bottom, and cool completely.

Make Date and Apple Loaf (above) in the fall when apples are at their best.

BEER BREAD

INGREDIENTS

Makes 1 small loaf

3¼ cups (455g) whole-wheat flour,
   preferably stone-ground

1 tablespoon baking powder

½ teaspoon salt

1 teaspoon honey

1½ cups (340ml) full-flavored dark ale

a loaf pan, about 7 × 5 × 3 inches, well
   greased

A very quick loaf, this takes just over an hour from start to finish. Eat it with a good aged cheese, such as Cheddar, or with a soup. I prefer to use very coarse Irish wheaten flour, which I am able to buy in Ireland (it isn't available anywhere else), but regular whole-wheat flour, or whole-wheat pastry flour will work fine too. Your choice depends on how coarse or fine textured you like your bread.

This bread is a British favorite, but it may not be to everyone's taste. If your family or friends are not fond of beer, you should probably choose another recipe. Eat this loaf the day you make it, or toast it later. It can also be frozen for one month.

Heat the oven to 350°F. Mix together the whole-wheat flour, baking powder, and salt in a large mixing bowl. Stir in the honey and ale to make a heavy, wet dough.

Spoon the dough into the prepared pan and smooth the surface.

Bake the bread for 40 to 50 minutes, or until golden brown and a pick inserted in the center comes out clean. Turn out on to a wire rack and let cool completely.

HERB ROLLS

INGREDIENTS

Makes 8

3¼ cups (455g) unbleached self-rising
   flour

1 teaspoon salt

freshly ground black pepper, to taste

1 cup (230g) cottage cheese

1 large egg

2 tablespoons chopped fresh herbs, such as
   chives, parsley, and thyme

about 1 cup (230ml) milk

extra flour for dusting

extra milk for brushing

a baking sheet, greased

Fresh herbs are vital for this recipe — dried herbs simply won't do. The rolls look rough and craggy, which is part of their charm. The flavor goes well with winter vegetable soups, as well as with salads. Eat these warm with butter. The rolls can be kept in a plastic bag for a day, and they freeze well for up to one month.

Heat the oven to 350°F. Sift together the flour, salt, and pepper into a large bowl.

Put the cottage cheese, egg, and herbs into a blender or food processor. Process until smooth. If you don't have a blender or food processor, finely mince the herbs, then combine with the cottage cheese and egg in a bowl and whisk until well blended and as smooth as possible.

Stir the cheese mixture into the flour using a metal spatula. Add just enough of the milk to make a soft but not sticky dough.

Turn the dough out on to a lightly floured work surface and lightly knead four to six times until it is fairly smooth. Divide the dough into eight equal pieces. Gently shape each piece into a rough ball. Arrange them spaced apart on the prepared baking sheet. Brush the rolls with milk. Bake for about 25 minutes, or until they turn golden brown and sound hollow when tapped underneath. Transfer to a wire rack to cool slightly.

Lovage, tansy, bee balm, and summer savory are among the more unusual aromatic herbs and plants, dating from the 17th century, flourishing in the kitchen garden of Philipsburg Manor (page 69). The combination of chives, parsley, and thyme in the ingredients for Herb Rolls (above) makes the most of readily available herbs, but it is only a suggestion. Use any mix of herbs you like, as long as they are fresh. Oregano or marjoram would be lovely instead of thyme, and you could use basil leaves in place of the parsley.

When Europeans arrived in New England in the 17th century, corn was growing in abundance, and they soon adapted many Native American recipes for cooking and baking the indigenous crop. Ever since, cornmeal has been a staple in American kitchens and corn bread, in numerous regional guises, is popular all across the country.

My selection of cornmeal recipes (right) includes Corn Dabs (below), a colonial recipe baked in corn-stick pans, and in individual antique rectangular molds with crisp bacon pieces added, and Corn Bread (page 86).

For the best cornmeal, search out small local mills who stone grind the corn. Buy it in small quantities and, for freshness, keep it in the refrigerator or freezer.

Freshly baked corn bread is on the menu at Windham Hill Inn, in West Townshend, Vermont.

CORN DABS

This recipe is an authentic heirloom from colonial America, and may be a surprise to modern tastes. Although the corn dabs look like corn sticks, they are much denser and coarser, and they will not rise because they do not use any leavening.

"Leavening agents did not arrive until 1820," explains food historian Caroll Boltin (page 69). "White flour was scarce, so the cornmeal used alone would give a gritty texture." However, the dabs remain moist and creamy on the inside, thanks to the addition of sour cream — an example of the Dutch settlers' influence in New York State's Hudson Valley.

These plain and simple dabs were eaten with rich oyster or clam stews and fish soups — a good combination. They are a nice change from today's more usual, sweeter baked cornmeal muffins and breads. Eat them while they're still warm.

Heat the oven to 425°F.

INGREDIENTS

Makes 7

¾ cup (170ml) boiling water

1 cup #aa 2 tablespoons (140g) yellow
    cornmeal

¼ cup (60ml) sour cream

1 large egg, beaten

1 tablespoon melted bacon fat or butter

¼ teaspoon salt (optional)

plenty of extra bacon fat for greasing pan

a cast-iron corn-stick pan, greased

Pour the boiling water over the cornmeal in a large bowl. Mix well with a fork. Then add the sour cream. Mix thoroughly and let stand for 10 minutes to soften the cornmeal. Put the corn-stick pan on a baking sheet and place in the oven to heat up for 10 to 15 minutes, until pan is just smoking.

Stir the egg, bacon fat or butter, and salt into the batter. Stir in the crumbled bacon too, if you wish. Pour the batter into a large glass measuring cup for easier handling.

Open the oven door and pull the rack with the corn-stick pan on it toward you. Generously brush the melted bacon fat or butter into the hot corn-stick pan. Return it to the oven for a couple of minutes to heat the fat. Pour the batter into the molds to almost full – the batter should sizzle when it hits the very hot fat. Bake the dabs for 15 minutes, or until crusty and golden and just slightly puffed, and the edges pull away from the pan; a wooden pick inserted in the center should come out clean. Turn out the dabs immediately.

NOTE: Three strips of bacon will render enough fat for the recipe and for greasing the pan; you can also crumble the cooked bacon and add it to the batter for more flavor in the dabs.

CORN BREAD

INGREDIENTS

Makes 9 squares

1 cup (140g) unbleached all-purpose flour

1 cup #aa 2 tablespoons (140g) yellow
    cornmeal

¼ cup (50g) sugar

4 teaspoons baking powder

½ teaspoon salt

1 cup (230ml) milk

2 large eggs, beaten

1 tablespoon melted butter

1 teaspoon caraway seeds

an 8-inch square cake pan, greased

This is Caroll Boltin's favorite recipe for corn bread. "The caraway seeds are an authentic colonial addition," says Caroll, who has researched American settlers (see page 69). "It reflects the Dutch influence on cooking here in the Hudson Valley of New York State."

Heat the oven to 375°F.

Stir together the flour, cornmeal, sugar, baking powder, and salt in a large bowl. Add the milk, eggs, and melted butter and stir well to make a smooth batter. Stir in the caraway seeds. Scrape the batter into the prepared pan and smooth the surface.

Bake the bread for 20 to 25 minutes, or until the corn bread is golden, firm to the touch, and has shrunk from the corners of the pan, and a wooden pick inserted in the center comes out clean. Cool the corn bread on a wire rack for 10 minutes, then turn it out on to a platter. Serve warm, cut into squares.

NOTE: If you prefer to make corn muffins, bake the batter in a twelve-cup muffin pan, greased or lined with paper or foil liners.

CAROLL BEATS CARAWAY SEEDS INTO
THE CORN BREAD BATTER.

SHE SCRAPES THE BATTER INTO THE
PREPARED CAKE PAN. THE CORN BREAD
IS THEN READY TO BE BAKED.

PHOEBE LETT'S TREACLE BREAD

Makes 2 small loaves

4¾ cups (680g) whole-wheat flour,
    preferably stone-ground

1⅔ cups unbleached all-purpose flour

1 tablespoon raw brown sugar, such as
    Demerara

2 teaspoons salt

2 teaspoons baking soda

1½ teaspoons ground ginger

4 tablespoons (60g) butter, well chilled
    and diced

3–3¼ cups (690–710ml) buttermilk

3 tablespoons dark unsulfured molasses

1 large egg, beaten

extra flour for shaping

sesame seeds for sprinkling (optional)

2 loaf pans, about 7 × 5 × 3 inches, or
    8-inch layer cake pans, greased and
    bottom lined with waxed paper

I love making this simple and well-flavored Irish loaf — it smells wonderful, and has become a picnic favorite. This recipe is a specialty of Phoebe Lett, who lives in Enniscorthy, County Wexford, in Ireland. Phoebe and her husband Bill are tremendous hosts; after spending five minutes with them you feel you've known them a lifetime.

A restaurant in Wexford serves an excellent first course — triangles of this warm treacle bread with Cashel Blue cheese (an Irish blue cheese) melted on top, surrounded by a good salad with a nicely tart dressing. Or simply eat this bread sliced, with butter and cheese.

Since treacle isn't widely available in the U.S., I've adapted this recipe to use dark unsulfured molasses, but you can use treacle instead.

Heat the oven to 400°F.

Stir together the flours, sugar, salt, baking soda, and ginger in a large bowl. Rub in the butter with your fingertips, or cut in with a pastry blender, until the mixture looks like fine crumbs.

Whisk together 3 cups (690ml) buttermilk, the molasses, and egg in a medium-size bowl. Quickly stir the buttermilk mixture into the dry ingredients using a wooden spoon. The dough should be heavy and slightly sticky; if there are dry crumbs, add a little more buttermilk, one tablespoon at a time.

Flour your hands and gently knead the dough in the mixing bowl until it comes together — a few seconds only. It will still look rough and lumpy. Divide the dough in half and shape each half into an oval (or a round, if using round pans). Put one piece into each pan and press the dough into the corners. Sprinkle the tops with the sesame seeds if you wish, and press them firmly into the loaves so they don't fall off when the loaves are turned out.

Bake the loaves for 10 minutes, then reduce the oven temperature to 350°F and bake for another 35 to 40 minutes. (Cover the loaves loosely with a sheet of foil if they brown too quickly.) When they are done, the loaves will have a crunchy crust and be well-risen; when tapped underneath, they will sound hollow.

Turn the loaves out, remove the waxed paper from the bottoms, and cool completely on wire racks. Wrap in waxed paper and then foil, and keep at room temperature for a day before slicing. The extra loaf can be frozen up to one month.

THE DOUGH SHOULD REMAIN ROUGH AND LUMPY AFTER IT HAS BEEN GENTLY KNEADED. DIVIDE IT IN HALF, SHAPE INTO OVALS AND PLACE IN THE PANS.

Treacle bread is best simply served with butter, as here, or with cheese. Sesame seeds add extra texture.

BASIC BROWN BREAD

TOP
John Doyle (right) discusses the day's events on the farm with his nephew, while Mary's bread bakes in the cast-iron pot. Extra ashes have been placed on top of the pot so the bread bakes evenly.
ABOVE
After about 40 minutes, Mary removes the perfectly baked bread.

Phoebe Lette (page 87) insisted we visit Mary Curtis, whom she calls "a true country woman — her bread is supreme." Mary and her husband farm at Bree in Country Wexford, Ireland. In 1989 she won the Farmers Journal Farm Woman of the Year award in an impressive competition that involved cooking an entire meal in front of an audience, making an evening gown (not in public), and changing the wheel on a farm vehicle against the clock. With four grown-up children who still come home each weekend, the Curtises "go through a lot of bread," and Mary bakes three loaves at a time to make the best use of her forty-year-old, oil-fired Rayburn oven.

"No two days will I make the same bread — I'll add sesame, poppy, or caraway seeds, or thyme and sage to go with soups,' she says. Mary grows her own vegetables and herbs, and uses the full-fat unpasteurized milk from her own cows to make buttermilk. When it comes to flour she prefers Odlums cream flour ("cream" meaning unbleached) and Abbey stone-ground wholemeal (whole-wheat) flour, which she calls "good and coarse."

To bake a batch of brown bread in the traditional way — in a cast-iron pot suspended over the red embers of an open fire — Mary walked across a couple of fields, over a stile, and under a barbed-wire fence to visit her next-door neighbors, Pat and John Doyle, farming brothers well into their eighties. The open-fire method was regularly used in rural areas of Ireland for baking until the 1950s and, as Mary has discovered, it bakes wonderful, slightly smoky bread; the closed pot traps the steam inside to produce a softer than usual crust.

The Doyles prepared the fire a good hour before the bread was put in to bake, so the flames had died down and the embers glowed red. Then they suspended a massive, solid iron pot on a chain from a swing arm and heated it until moderately hot.

"To test the pot, sprinkle a little flour inside. It should change color slowly," she says. "If it turns black instantly, swing the pot away from the fire for a few minutes." Mary placed her shaped brown loaf into the pot, covered the pot with its heavy lid, then heaped hot ashes on top of the lid so the loaf would cook evenly.

After 40 minutes spent chatting about old times on the farm, she checked on the bread's progress — it looked wonderful. The cooked loaf was wrapped in a cloth to soften the crust, left to cool, then eagerly devoured.

Here is Mary's recipe for brown bread, adapted for more modern kitchens. This loaf is best eaten within twenty-four hours.

INGREDIENTS

Makes 1 medium loaf

2½ cups (340g) whole-wheat flour,
   preferably stone-ground

¾ cup (110g) unbleached all-purpose
   flour

½ cup (30g) wheat bran

2½ tablespoons (15g) wheat germ

1 teaspoon baking soda

1 teaspoon salt

2 tablespoons (30g) butter or margarine,
   chilled and diced

1¼–1¾ cups (280–430ml) buttermilk

extra flour for dusting

a large baking sheet, well floured

Heat the oven to 425°F. Mix together the flours, bran, wheat germ, baking soda, and salt in a large bowl. Rub in the margarine or butter using your fingertips, lifting the mixture high above the bowl to aerate the dough, until it looks like fine crumbs.

Stir in enough of the buttermilk to make a stiff dough; it will look a bit rough. Turn the dough out on to a well-floured work surface and quickly knead it with the heel of your hand, pushing the dough from the middle out and then pulling it back. Use your other hand to rotate the dough as you knead it. As soon as the dough looks smooth, shape it into a flat disk. Place the loaf on the prepared baking sheet. Sprinkle with flour and cut a deep cross in the loaf. Bake the bread for 35 to 45 minutes, or until the loaf is crusty, browned, and sounds hollow when tapped underneath. Transfer to a wire rack and cool completely.

NOTE: Mary Curtis gave me an old recipe for buttermilk from the days when every farm made its own buttermilk and butter. You need to start a buttermilk "plant," which will ferment milk. Cream 2 0.6-oz cakes fresh yeast (30g) with 2½ tablespoons (30g) sugar in a large bowl until smooth. Gradually stir in 5 cups (1.15 liters) lukewarm milk. Cover the bowl with a dish towel and let stand for a couple of days at room temperature. The mixture should smell and taste like buttermilk. Line a strainer with a double thickness of cheesecloth and strain the mixture. Refrigerate the buttermilk, and it is ready to use. (It will keep for one day, covered.) The residue in the cheesecloth can be used to make the next batch of buttermilk. Rinse the residue in the cheesecloth with lukewarm water, then put it into a clean container, preferably one scalded in boiling water. Add a generous teaspoon of sugar, mix, add the milk, and proceed as before.

USING HER FINGERTIPS, MARY RUBS IN THE MARGARINE.

ALL THE INGREDIENTS ARE STIRRED TO MAKE A STIFF DOUGH.

USING THE HEEL OF HER HAND, MARY KNEADS THE DOUGH.

SHE PATS THE LOAVES INTO FLAT DISKS.

PROUD MARY'S LOAVES ARE READY FOR THE OVEN.

SHE TESTS A LOAF BY TAPPING IT ON THE BOTTOM.

SODA BREAD

INGREDIENTS

Makes 4 large triangles

3¼ cups (455g) unbleached self-rising flour, white or whole-wheat

1 teaspoon sugar

1 teaspoon salt

2 tablespoons (30g) butter, well chilled and diced

about 1½ cups (340ml) buttermilk

fat or oil for cooking

a large, heavy cast-iron frying pan with a lid or baking sheet to cover

This is Mary Curtis's recipe for soda bread, the traditional bread of Ireland, which is quickly made from self-rising flour and buttermilk and cooked on top of the stove in a heavy cast-iron frying pan. "It's a quick way to have fresh bread, and it's good and puffy and fluffy," says Mary. Make sure the pan is large enough to turn the bread with ease — otherwise cook it in two batches or use two frying pans. Eat this bread while it's still warm.

Heat the pan over moderately low heat while you make the dough. Sift together the flour, sugar, and salt into a large bowl. Rub in the butter with your fingertips or cut in with a pastry blender, lifting the mixture a few inches above the bowl and letting it fall to aerate the dough, until the mixture looks like fine crumbs. Stir in enough buttermilk to just moisten the dry ingredients and to make a soft, light, and fluffy dough; don't overwork the dough. Quickly turn it out on to a floured surface and knead four to five times until the dough comes together and forms a smooth ball. Pat out to a disk about 1 inch thick. Cut the disk in quarters.

Lightly brush the pan with oil. Put the bread into the heated pan, cover, and cook over moderately low heat for 15 to 20 minutes, turning the triangles over two or three times so they cook evenly. The finished bread should be golden brown and well risen. Remove the bread from the pan, transfer to a wire rack, and wrap with a dry dish towel until ready to serve.

MARY RUBS IN THE BUTTER, LIFTING THE FLOUR MIXTURE *ABOVE THE BOWL.*

USING FLOURED FINGERS, SHE PATS THE DOUGH INTO *A FLAT DISK.*

USING *A SHARP KNIFE,* SHE CUTS THE DOUGH INTO QUARTERS.

THE DOUGH QUARTERS ARE COVERED WHILE THEY COOK.

AFTER 5 MINUTES' COOKING, MARY FLIPS OVER THE QUARTERS TO ENSURE EVEN COOKING.

SHE PLACES THE COOKED BREAD ONTO *A WIRE RACK.*

OPPOSITE

Soda bread from a local bakery, along with cheese, farmhouse butter, and a fruit tart, made a simple, impromptu picnic when Anthony and I were in Co. Cork, Ireland.

FRIED DOUGHS

"Where can you find a really good doughnut these days?" lamented an elderly friend as she recalled her favorite childhood treat. A good doughnut is light, flavorful, and made from kneaded dough, perhaps filled with plenty of proper fruit jam, cooked in lard or a good vegetable oil, then coated in crunchy white sugar. Such doughnuts may no longer be easy to find commercially, but they are not at all difficult to make.

I'm quite conservative about what I eat for breakfast and was about to help myself to a bowl of granola at the Windham Hill Inn in West Townshend, Vermont, when innkeeper Linda Busteed appeared with a plate of freshly cooked doughnuts. My in-laws jumped for joy. "Positively the finest you'll ever taste," they said, being long-term fans of Windham Hill's cooking. They were right (see Megan's Potato Doughnuts, page 98),

but they didn't guess the (mashed potatoes). doughs originated as the last bread dough. The pieces cut, or filled with fruit or as a treat for the children, or cooked breakfast, as Lois For Ina McNeil (page 102), part of the early fall of Native Americans). the U.S. to cook sweet and quantities for these events, larly for her family. Lois Wheat Grebble (page 101) is powder dry bread (through way), but Lois' dough is Doughnuts and fried the brioche-like Fancy Ring

OPPOSITE *Freshly made doughnuts, New Orleans style.* ABOVE *Doughnuts frying.*

secret of their lightness Doughnuts and fried scraps of a big batch of would be sweetened and jam, and then fried – either as a necessity for a quickly Keller explains (page 101). fry breads are an essential powwows (large gatherings Although she travels all over savory fry breads in huge she still makes them regu- Keller's German Whole- similar to Ina's baking- handled in a very different formed into twisted strips. doughs can be rich, such as Doughnuts (page 97) or

the Dutch Oliebollen (page 100), or quick and simple, like The Fry-Bread Queen's Fry Bread. But either way, homemade doughnuts are a treat indeed.

TIPS FOR FRYING DOUGHS

– Use good quality, fresh vegetable oil (lard or solid white vegetable shortening can also be used), cool the oil, and strain it after each use through a coffee filter or strainer lined with white paper towels. If necessary, skim the oil with a skimmer or a long-handled, fine strainer between batches of doughnuts to remove any charred crumbs, which will ruin both the taste and appearance of your doughnuts.

– To avoid accidents, don't fill the pan more than one-third full with oil – it will bubble up when you add the doughnuts. Keep the lid close by to cover the fat should it ever catch fire, and never leave the pan unattended.

– For the best results, the oil should have reached the correct temperature – 350°F on a frying or candy thermometer. Many electric fryers have a built-in thermostat. To test the temperature if you don't have a thermometer, drop a cube of bread in the oil. It should brown in 40 seconds at that heat. If the oil is too cool, the doughnut will sink to the bottom, absorb the oil, and become greasy. If the oil is too hot, the outsides will be hard and overcooked while the centers are still raw.

– Fry the doughnuts (which should be at room temperature) a few pieces at a time – don't crowd the pan.

– Turn the doughnuts over frequently with a skimmer or slotted spoon so they cook and brown evenly. Adjust the heat under the oil and test its temperature between batches; reheat it, if necessary.

– Remove the doughnuts with a fry basket or a slotted spoon, a skimmer, or a pair of long-handled tongs, then drain on plenty of paper towels. Eat as soon as possible – they don't keep and can't be frozen.

JAM DOUGHNUTS

INGREDIENTS

Makes about 12

4–4½ cups (455–510g) unbleached
   white bread flour

1 teaspoon salt

1 0.6-oz cake fresh yeast (15g), or

1 envelope active dry yeast (2½ teaspoons)

3 tablespoons (40g) sugar

1 cup (230ml) lukewarm milk

2 large eggs, beaten

2 tablespoons (30g) butter, melted and
   cooled

extra flour for dusting

about ¼ cup raspberry or strawberry jam

oil for deep-frying

extra sugar for sprinkling

a 2½-inch round biscuit or cookie cutter

a pastry brush

1–2 large baking sheets, lightly floured

a deep-fat fryer or large Dutch oven

I like homemade raspberry or strawberry jam in the center of my doughnut, but a nice tart apricot conserve, chunky, dark marmalade, or even a little mincemeat left from Christmas can be substituted. This dough is flavorful and very light. The secret to making these doughnuts is to seal the cut circles of dough thoroughly so the filling doesn't leak out during cooking. Eat the same day for best texture and taste.

Mix together 4 cups (455g) flour and the salt in a large bowl. Make a well in the center of the flour. Crumble the fresh yeast into the well. Add the sugar and 2 tablespoons of the lukewarm milk. Mix until the liquid is smooth. Add the remaining milk to the well. If using dry yeast, mix the granules with 2 tablespoons of the lukewarm milk and 2

SPOON ABOUT 1 TEASPOON OF JAM IN THE CENTER OF ONE DOUGH ROUND.

COVER WITH A SECOND DOUGH ROUND AND PRESS AND PINCH THE EDGES TOGETHER TO SEAL THOROUGHLY.

THE FILLED DOUGHNUT SHOULD BE SEALED ALL AROUND SO JAM DOESN'T LEAK OUT DURING FRYING.

LIFT THE DOUGHNUTS OUT OF THE HOT OIL WHEN THEY ARE WELL BROWNED AND PUFFED.

Made with flavorful and very light dough, these jam-filled doughnuts will be popular with children and adults. For extra sweetness, you can gently roll the doughnuts in granulated sugar, coating both sides, instead of just sprinkling the tops.

tablespoons sugar in a small bowl and let stand until foamy, 5 to 10 minutes (page 18). Add the yeast mixture to the well in the flour along with the remaining milk and sugar.

Add the eggs and butter to the well. Mix these liquid ingredients together. Work in the flour to make a soft, but not sticky dough. If there are crumbs of dry dough, add a little extra milk, 1 tablespoon at a time. If the dough sticks to your fingers, work in extra flour, 1 tablespoon at a time.

Turn out the dough onto a lightly floured surface and knead until smooth and elastic, about 10 minutes, adding a little more flour as needed to prevent sticking. Clean and dry the bowl and oil it lightly. Put the ball of dough back into the bowl and turn it over. Cover and let rise, until doubled in size, about 2 hours.

Punch down the risen dough. Turn out onto a lightly floured surface and knead for a few seconds. With a lightly floured rolling pin, gradually roll out the dough to about ½ inch thick. When rolling out the dough, let it rest periodically to relax the dough.

Cut out rounds with the floured biscuit or cookie cutter. Re-roll the scraps and cut; you should have about 24 rounds.

Spoon about 1 teaspoon of jam in the center of one round. Brush the edges with a little water. Cover with a second round and press and pinch the edges together to seal thoroughly. Repeat with the remaining dough. Place on lightly floured baking sheets, spacing them apart, and cover lightly with a dry dish towel. Let rise at warm room temperature, away from drafts, until almost doubled in size, about 20 minutes.

Meanwhile, pour the oil into the deep-fat fryer or Dutch oven to a depth of about 3 inches. Slowly heat until the oil registers 350°F on a frying thermometer (see page 93). Lower three doughnuts into the hot oil with a slotted spoon. Fry the doughnuts, turning them frequently, until well browned and puffed, about 10 minutes. Lift out the doughnuts and drain on paper towels. Fry the remaining doughnuts in batches. While still warm, sprinkle the doughnuts with granulated sugar. Let cool.

ONTARIO APPLE DOUGHNUTS

On a trip to Canada a few years ago, I had the chance to visit the vast apple orchards in Ontario's Norfolk County. I wanted to visit Mrs. Judson's apple doughnut shop, and indeed drove by it many times, but tight schedules frustrated me. Eventually a kindly apple grower provided a breakfast of Mrs. Judson's just-fried apple doughnuts. They were simply delicious, and I've tried to reproduce the recipe. They are excellent for dessert served hot with a sauce made from puréed fresh, canned, or cooked dried apricots.

Prepare the Jam Doughnut dough through the first rising. While the dough is rising, peel, core, and thickly slice the apple. Place in a small saucepan with the water, cover, and cook very slowly, stirring occasionally, until the apple is very soft. Add granulated sugar to taste, and small amounts of any of the optional flavoring ingredients.

Punch down the dough, transfer to a lightly floured work surface, and knead for a few seconds. Gradually roll out the dough with a rolling pin to a large rectangle, about ½ inch thick, letting the dough rest periodically. With a floured knife, cut the dough into 3-inch squares. Re-roll the scraps and cut into squares. Place 1 teaspoon of the apple filling into the center of each square. Brush the edges lightly with water. Fold each square in half diagonally over the filling to form a triangle. Seal by pressing and pinching the edges together. Place the triangles, spaced apart, on lightly floured baking sheets. Let rise, uncovered, at warm room temperature, away from drafts, until almost doubled in size, 20 to 30 minutes.

Meanwhile, pour the oil into the deep-fat fryer or Dutch oven to a depth of about 3 inches. Slowly heat over moderate heat until the oil registers 350°F on a frying thermometer (see page 93).

Place three dough triangles in the fry basket and lower into the hot oil, or slip them, one at a time, into the oil with a slotted spoon. Do not crowd the pan. Fry the doughnuts, turning them often so they brown evenly, until nicely puffed and golden, about 5 minutes. Lift out the doughnuts with the fry basket or slotted spoon and place on paper towels to drain. While still warm, sprinkle the doughnuts with cinnamon-sugar. Fry the remaining doughnuts in batches. Eat the same day.

INGREDIENTS

Makes about 14

1 batch Jam Doughnuts dough (page 94)

1 large Granny Smith apple

1 tablespoon water

sugar to taste

ground cinnamon, grated lemon or orange rind, golden raisins, or chopped walnuts or pecans (optional)

oil for deep-frying

ground cinnamon mixed with sugar for sprinkling

1–2 baking sheets, lightly floured

a deep-fat fryer or large Dutch oven

For a delicious dessert, serve these apple doughnuts while they are still warm with apricot purée and crème fraîche.

PLACE ONE TEASPOON OF THE APPLE FILLING IN THE CENTER OF EACH DOUGH SQUARE.

FOLD EACH SQUARE OVER THE FILLING TO FORM A TRIANGLE.

WORK THE BUTTER INTO THE DOUGH,
SQUEEZING THE TWO TOGETHER
UNTIL THOROUGHLY COMBINED

RIGHT *Fancy Ring Doughnut*

INGREDIENTS

Makes 18

4 cups (455g) unbleached white bread
    flour

1 teaspoon salt

1 0.6-oz cake fresh yeast (15g), or
    1 envelope active dry yeast
    (2½ teaspoons)

¾ cup (170ml) milk, at room
    temperature

5 tablespoons (60g) granulated sugar

4 large eggs, at room temperature, beaten

½ cup (110g) butter, at room
    temperature

extra flour for dusting

oil for deep-frying

confectioners' sugar for sprinkling

a 3-inch doughnut cutter, or a 3-inch
    round biscuit or cookie cutter and a ½-
    inch round cutter

1–2 large baking sheets, lightly floured

a deep-fat fryer or large Dutch oven

FANCY RING DOUGHNUT

The dough here is very rich — it's a type of brioche — and it makes the lightest, finest-textured doughnuts. After chilling and shaping the dough, gently bring it back to warm room temperature before frying to avoid a heavy, soggy result. Eat these the day they are made.

Stir together the flour and salt in a large bowl. Crumble the fresh yeast into a small bowl. Stir in 2 tablespoons of the milk until smooth. If using dry yeast, mix the granules with 2 tablespoons of the milk and ½ teaspoon of sugar in a small bowl and let stand until foamy, 5 to 10 minutes (page 18).

Mix the sugar into the flour mixture. Make a well in the center of the flour and pour in the yeast mixture, the remaining milk, and the beaten eggs. Using your hand, combine all the ingredients in the well, then gradually work in the flour from the bowl to make a smooth batter. Beat the batter with your hand, pulling and stretching it, for about 10 minutes. The dough will be very sticky at this stage. Cover the bowl with a damp dish towel and let stand at room temperature, away from drafts, until doubled in size, about 1½ hours.

Punch down the dough with floured knuckles. Keeping the mixture in the bowl, work the butter into the dough, squeezing the two together until thoroughly combined. The dough should look smooth and glossy, with no streaks, and should be somewhat sticky.

Cover the bowl with a damp dish towel and refrigerate for at least 4 hours or until doubled in size (the dough can be left in the refrigerator overnight at this point).

Punch down the dough — it should be quite firm. Turn out the dough onto a floured work surface. Roll out the dough with a floured rolling pin to a circle about 1 inch thick. Using the floured doughnut cutter or the large floured biscuit or cookie cutter, stamp out circles. If using the biscuit or cookie cutter, use the smaller cutter to stamp out a round in the center of each. Re-roll the scraps and centers and cut: you should have about 18 rings. Place the rings, spaced apart, on floured baking sheets. Let rise, uncovered, away from drafts, until they have doubled in size and warmed to room temperature, 30 minutes to 1 hour.

Meanwhile, pour the oil into the deep-fat fryer or Dutch oven to a depth of about 3 inches. Slowly heat until the oil registers 350°F on a frying thermometer. Lower about three rings of dough into the hot oil. Fry the doughnuts, stirring from time to time and turning the rings, for about 5 minutes, or until golden brown. Lift the doughnuts out with the fry basket or slotted spoon and drain on paper towels. Cook the remaining doughnuts in batches. Sprinkle the doughnuts, while still warm, with the confectioners' sugar. Let cool.

MEGAN'S POTATO DOUGHNUTS

These are the best doughnuts I've ever tasted. Last summer my in-laws introduced me to the beautiful Windham Hill Inn, in West Townshend, Vermont, during their annual visit to the Marlboro music festival. These were so wonderful I asked innkeeper Linda Busteed for the secret. "Potatoes and spice, and Megan," she replied giving the credit to her assistant, Megan McCooey. Eat these the day you make them.

INGREDIENTS

Makes 14

1 cup (230g) freshly cooked mashed
    potatoes

3¼–4 cups (455–570g) unbleached all-
    purpose flour

1 cup (200g) granulated sugar

1 tablespoon baking powder

½ teaspoon grated nutmeg

½ teaspoon ground ginger

3 tablespoons (40g) butter, softened and
    cut into small pieces

2 large eggs, beaten

1 cup (230ml) milk

a few drops of vanilla extract

extra flour for dusting

oil for deep-frying

confectioners' sugar for sifting

a 3-inch doughnut cutter, or a 3-inch
    round biscuit or cookie cutter and a ½-
    inch cutter

a deep-fat fryer or large Dutch oven

Put the potatoes into a large bowl (they should be free of lumps and at room temperature). Add 3¼ cups (455g) of the flour, the sugar, baking powder, and spices. Add the butter, eggs, milk, and vanilla, and mix thoroughly to make a soft, biscuit-like dough. If necessary, add more flour, 1 tablespoon at a time, until the dough holds together.

Turn out the dough onto a floured work surface. Knead for about 1 minute, or until just smooth. Roll out the dough with a floured rolling pin to an 8-inch circle about 1 inch thick. Cut out rounds using the floured doughnut cutter or the larger floured biscuit or cookie cutter. If using the biscuit or cookie cutter, stamp out the center of each round – to make a ring – using the floured smaller cutter. Re-roll the trimmings and cut out more rings. If you wish, the center rounds can also be fried.

Pour the oil into the deep-fat fryer or Dutch oven to a depth of about 3 inches. Slowly heat over moderate heat until the oil registers 350°F on a frying thermometer (see page 93). Place about three rings of dough in a fry basket and lower the basket into the hot oil, or slip the rings, one at a time, into the hot oil with a slotted spoon. Don't overcrowd the pan. Fry the rings, turning frequently so they brown evenly, for about 8 minutes, or until puffy and golden brown. Lift the rings out with the fry basket or slotted spoon and place on paper towels to drain. Sift confectioners' sugar over the doughnuts, and let cool. Fry the remaining doughnuts in batches.

Serve these spicy doughnuts and the fried centers with freshly brewed coffee.

Innkeeper and cook Linda Busteed rises early each morning to prepare freshly baked goods for her guests. These light potato doughnuts are served at least once a week. Here she is cutting out a batch in her sunny kitchen.

Gnocci fritti are best served warm sprinkled with freshly grated Parmesan cheese.

GNOCCI FRITTI

This is a savory fried dough from Italy. The dough is cut into squares, which puff up to resemble pillows as they cook. Gnocci fritti are eaten warm, dusted with Parmesan cheese, accompanied by thin slices of good prosciutto. This recipe will serve eight or ten as a first course. These take some time to fry, about 30 minutes, so you may want to invite guests into the kitchen to eat them freshly cooked.

INGREDIENTS

Makes about 32

5 cups (570g) unbleached white bread
   flour

1 teaspoon salt

1 0.6-oz cake fresh yeast (15g), or
   1 envelope active dry yeast
   (2½ teaspoons) plus ½ teaspoon sugar

1¼ cups (280ml) mixed lukewarm milk
   and water

1 tablespoon olive oil

extra flour for dusting

oil for deep-frying

freshly grated Parmesan cheese or coarse sea
   salt for sprinkling

a deep-fat fryer or large Dutch oven

Mix together the flour and salt in a large bowl. Make a well in the center of the flour. Crumble the fresh yeast into a small bowl. Stir in 2 tablespoons of the warm liquid until smooth. Then stir in the rest of the liquid and the olive oil. If using dry yeast, mix the granules with 2 tablespoons of the warm liquid and the sugar and let stand until foamy, 5 to 10 minutes (page 18). Stir in the rest of the warm liquid and the olive oil.

Add the yeast mixture to the well in the flour. Mix in the flour from the bowl to make a fairly firm dough. If necessary, add a little more warm water, 1 tablespoon at a time, if the dough seems dry and won't come together.

Turn out the dough onto a lightly floured work surface and knead for 5 minutes. The dough should be glossy and elastic. Cover the ball of dough with the upturned bowl and let stand at room temperature for 30 minutes. The dough will rise slightly and become quite pliable. Punch down the dough with floured knuckles. With a lightly floured rolling pin, roll out the dough on a lightly floured work surface to about ¼ inch thick.

With a floured, large, sharp knife, cut the dough into 2-inch squares. Re-roll and cut the scraps, or fry the odd-shaped pieces. Cover the dough squares with dry dish towels so they don't form a hard crust.

Pour the oil into the deep-fat fryer or Dutch oven to a depth of about 3 inches. Slowly heat over moderate heat until the oil registers about 350°F on a frying thermometer (see page 93). In the time this takes, the dough will have risen slightly. Place about four squares of dough in the fry basket and lower the basket into the hot oil, or slip them, one at a time, into the hot oil with a slotted spoon. Don't overcrowd the pan. Fry the dough squares, turning them frequently, until they are puffed and evenly golden brown, about 4 minutes. Lift out the squares with the fry basket or slotted spoon and place on paper towels to drain. Keep warm on a baking sheet in a 250°F oven. Fry the remaining squares in batches. Arrange the warm squares on a serving dish. Sprinkle with Parmesan cheese or salt and serve immediately with prosciutto.

Enjoy oliebollens Dutch style as a snack. The dough is very rich, so they also make a delicious dessert if served with a scoop of vanilla ice cream.

OLIEBOLLEN

INGREDIENTS

Makes 14

2½ cups (280g) unbleached white bread flour

½ teaspoon salt

1 0.6-oz cake fresh yeast (15g), or
   1 envelope active dry yeast
   (2½ teaspoons)

2 teaspoons sugar

1¼ cups (280ml) lukewarm milk

finely grated rind and juice of ½ lemon

⅓ cup (60g) currants

⅓ cup (60g) raisins

1 Golden Delicious apple

extra flour for dusting

oil for deep-frying

extra sugar for rolling

2 baking sheets, lightly floured

a deep-fat fryer or large Dutch oven

These Dutch doughnuts are very light and moist, and are flavored with plenty of dried fruit, chopped apple, and lemon. The cooked puffy doughnuts are rolled in sugar while still hot.

Mix the flour and salt in a large bowl. Make a well in the center of the flour. Crumble the fresh yeast into a small bowl. Stir in the sugar and half the lukewarm milk until smooth. If using dry yeast, mix the granules with the sugar and half the lukewarm milk and let stand until foamy, 5 to 10 minutes (page 18). Pour the yeast mixture into the well. Mix in a little of the flour in the bowl to make a thin batter. Cover the bowl with a dry dish towel or plastic wrap and let stand until spongy, about 20 minutes (page 16).

Add the remaining milk and the lemon rind and juice to the well and mix thoroughly with the yeast mixture. Gradually work in the remaining flour in the bowl with your hands to make a very soft, quite sticky dough.

Knead the dough very thoroughly in the bowl by slapping it up and down with your hand for 10 minutes. It should stiffen somewhat, yet still be a bit sticky, and come away in one piece from the side of the bowl.

Sprinkle the currants and raisins over the dough. Quickly peel, core, and dice the apple into ¼-inch pieces (you should have about 1 cup). Sprinkle over the dough. Work the dried fruit and apple into the dough by gently squeezing the mixture through your fingers until the fruits are evenly distributed, but not crushed. Cover the bowl with a damp dish towel. Let rise at room temperature, away from drafts, until doubled in size, about 1 to 1½ hours. Meanwhile, pour the oil into the deep-fat fryer or Dutch oven to a depth of about 3 inches. Slowly heat the oil over moderate heat until it registers 350°F on a frying thermometer (see page 93). Punch down the dough with floured knuckles. Using an ice cream scoop, scoop up a rough ball of dough and drop it into the hot oil. Add three more balls of dough to the pan and fry, turning them over occasionally, until golden brown and puffed up, 7 to 8 minutes. Keep the remaining dough covered while these fry. Lift the doughnuts out with the fry basket or a slotted spoon and place on paper towels to drain. While still warm, roll the doughnuts in sugar to coat and let cool. Fry the remaining dough in batches. Eat the doughnuts the day they are made.

WHOLE-WHEAT GREBBLE

INGREDIENTS

Makes 22

1⅓ 0.6-oz cakes fresh yeast (20g), or
    1½ envelopes active dry yeast
    (3¾ teaspoons)

½ cup (110ml) lukewarm water

¼ cup packed (50g) light brown sugar or
    2½ tablespoons honey

about 5¼ cups (600g) whole-wheat bread
    flour, preferably stone-ground

½ teaspoon baking soda

1½ cups (340g) cottage cheese

2 large eggs, beaten

2 tablespoons (30g) butter, melted

2 teaspoons salt

extra flour for dusting

oil for deep-frying

confectioners' sugar for sprinkling

a deep-fat fryer or large Dutch oven

This German recipe has been passed down to Lois Keller through her husband Jerry's family. Its origins lie in the ingenuity of farmers' wives, she explained. "They used to mix up their bread dough at night, wrap the warmed bowl in blankets — don't forget, this was before central heating and winter nights were very cold — and leave the dough to rise overnight. In the morning, they could fry the dough quickly in lard to make a good, fresh breakfast." The Keller family lives near Ellis in west-central Kansas on a 5,000 acre farm of mixed crops — wheat, corn, and beans — and "nodding donkeys" (oil wells). Lois is an amazing woman. She works in the fields all day drilling oil or driving the combine, then cooks a massive meal for everyone. After dinner, she is still hard at work. "Some people knit in the evening, but I hand-clean some of our wheat." Lois grinds the wheat in a machine that resembles a huge coffee grinder, making it as coarse or as fine as she likes. It takes 3 or 4 minutes to grind 1½ pounds of wheat kernels, which is enough for a loaf of bread. This dough can also be shaped and made into light, slightly sweet rolls (for shaping and baking instructions, see Oatmeal Rolls, page 25).

Crumble the yeast into a small bowl. Stir in the warm water and the sugar or honey until smooth. If using dry yeast, sprinkle the granules over the warm water. Stir in the sugar or honey and let stand until foamy, 5 to 10 minutes (page 18).

Mix together half the flour with the baking soda, making a well in the center. Blend the cottage cheese, eggs, butter, and salt until smooth. Pour this mixture into the well. Add the yeast mixture to the food processor or blender and process briefly. Tip this into the well and mix together, working in the flour from the sides until the dough comes together and is soft, but not sticky.

Turn it out onto a floured surface. Flour your hands and knead the dough for 10 minutes until it is firm, smooth, and elastic, only adding extra flour to prevent it from sticking. Put the ball of dough back into the washed, dried, and oiled bowl and turn it over. Cover with a damp dish towel and let stand at warm room temperature, away from drafts, until doubled in size, about 1 hour.

Pour the oil into the deep-fat fryer or Dutch oven to a depth of about 3 inches. Slowly heat over moderate heat until the oil registers 350°F on a frying thermometer (page 93).

Punch down the dough and divide into twenty-two pieces. Using a floured rolling pin, roll each piece into an oval about ¼ inch thick. Cut a slit lengthwise down the center of each dough oval, cutting almost to the edges. Shape the ovals by twisting the ends of each in opposite directions. Place about three dough twists in a fry basket and lower the basket into the hot oil. Fry the grebbles, turning constantly, for about 2 minutes, or until puffed, golden brown, and crispy. Lift out the grebbles with the fry basket and drain on paper towels. Eat immediately dusted with confectioners' sugar.

BELOW RIGHT Grebbles can be sprinkled with confectioners' sugar just before serving.

LOIS TWISTS EACH END OF THE OVAL IN THE OPPOSITE DIRECTION.

THE FRY-BREAD QUEEN'S FRY BREAD

Makes about 20 large diamonds

4 cups (680g) unbleached all-purpose
   flour

scant 1 cup (100g) dry milk powder

½ cup (100g) sugar

3 tablespoons baking powder

2 teaspoons salt

1¼–1½ cups (280–340ml) water from
   the cold tap

extra flour for dusting

oil for deep-frying

a deep-fat fryer or large Dutch oven

Ina McNeil is the great-granddaughter of Chief Sitting Bull of Little Bighorn fame. She is also known as the "fry-bread queen" because of her cooking at huge powwows and feasts.

On the Sioux reservation where Ina was born, along the North/South Dakota border, women compete to make the best fry bread for powwows. The meetings are large, and making enough fry bread can involve using up to 35 pounds of flour. "This recipe is very quick," Ina says. "My mother says that the mood you are in will determine how your fry bread will turn out. So be happy and people will enjoy your bread and be happy, too."

Ina grew up watching her mother and grandmother make fry bread, so she learned to cook by sight and touch, rather than by using exact measurements. The secret of a good fry bread, she says, is not to overwork the dough when you knead it. Make sure it feels elastic and springy.

Mix the flour, powdered milk, sugar, baking powder, and salt in a large bowl. Make a well in the center. Add 1¼ cups (280ml) water to the well. Gradually mix in the flour in the bowl with your hand to make a soft biscuit-like dough. It should not be dry or stiff. If the dough seems sticky, add flour, 1 tablespoon at a time. If too dry, add water, 1 tablespoon at a time.

Pour oil into the deep-fat fryer or Dutch oven to a depth of about 3 inches. Slowly heat over moderate heat until the oil registers 350°F on a frying thermometer (see page 93).

Turn out the dough onto a lightly floured work surface. Roll with a lightly floured rolling pin or pat out the dough to a large rectangle, about ¼ inch thick. With a floured, sharp knife, cut the dough into 4- to 5-inch triangles or diamond shapes. Re-roll the scraps and cut. Cut a slit along the center of each piece with a small knife, cutting through the dough and almost to the edges, to help the middle cook at the same rate as the edges. Shake or brush off the excess flour.

Place a couple of triangles of dough in the fry basket and lower the basket into the hot oil, or drop the dough one piece at a time into the oil with a slotted spoon, without crowding the pan.

Fry the pieces of bread, turning them so they cook evenly, until they puff and are browned, about 2 minutes. Lift the pieces out with the fry basket or slotted spoon and place on paper towels to drain. Eat while still warm.

INA DROPS A DOUGH TRIANGLE INTO THE HOT OIL TO FRY.

BEFORE STARTING TO FRY, INA TESTS THE OIL'S TEMPERATURE BY DROPPING IN A SMALL PIECE OF DOUGH. "IT SHOULD PUFF UP AND RISE TO THE SURFACE IMMEDIATELY," SHE SAYS.

Right DRAIN FRY BREAD ON PAPER TOWELS AS SOON AS IT IS REMOVED FROM THE HOT OIL.

YEAST FRY BREAD WITH RAISINS

INGREDIENTS

Makes about 20

1 0.6-oz cake fresh yeast (15g), or
    1 envelope active dry yeast
    (2½ teaspoons)
2½ tablespoons (30g) granulated sugar
2 cups (455ml) lukewarm water
1 large egg, beaten
2 tablespoons vegetable oil
2 teaspoons salt
3 tablespoons (30g) raisins
6½ cups (750g) unbleached white bread
    flour
extra flour for dusting
oil for deep-frying
confectioners' sugar for sprinkling

a deep-fat fryer or large Dutch oven

Ina McNeil (opposite) adds raisins to this yeast dough and fries it as a favorite snack for her grandchildren.

When I visited Ina with Anthony Blake she made this fry bread (without raisins and confectioners' sugar). We ate it like a taco, filled with chili-spiced meat, bean sauce, lettuce, tomatoes, grated cheese, and salsa. How we feasted! As Ina explained, "You are not invited to a Native American's home unless they can feed you."

Crumble the fresh yeast into a large bowl. Whisk in the sugar and lukewarm water until smooth. Let stand 15 minutes, until foamy. If using dry yeast, mix the granules with the sugar and water and let stand until foamy, 5–10 minutes (page 18).

Whisk the egg, oil, and salt into the yeast mixture. Stir in the raisins. Stir in half the flour to make a sloppy batter. Work in enough of the remaining flour to make a soft, sticky dough.

Turn out the dough onto a lightly floured surface. Knead for 5 minutes, until smooth and elastic, using the heel of your hand to stretch out the dough. Shape it into a ball. Wash, dry, and oil the bowl. Put the dough in the bowl, and turn it over so the top is oiled. Cover with a dish towel and let rise at room temperature, away from drafts, until doubled in size, about 1 hour.

Punch down the dough in the bowl, then shape it into a ball again. Cover and let rise again at room temperature, away from drafts, until doubled in size, about 1 hour.

Pour enough oil into the deep-fat fryer or Dutch oven to reach to a depth of about 3 inches. Slowly heat over moderate heat until the oil registers 350°F on a frying thermometer (page 93).

Punch down the dough. With floured hands, pinch off an egg-size piece of dough. Flatten into a disk, then toss it from hand to hand, pulling it out into a round the size of a bread plate. (Ina shapes and fries the dough one piece at a time.) Place the dough into a fry basket and lower the basket into the oil, or slip the round into the oil with a slotted spoon. Fry the round about 1 minute on each side, turning it over with a slotted spoon. It should puff up instantly. Remove from the oil and drain on paper towels. Sprinkle with confectioners' sugar and eat immediately.

SAVORY BREADS

For far too long even good restaurants served bland and boring bread. If you were lucky, the melba toast might be nicely browned and crisp. Bread was necessary, but not important enough to merit a special baker or source. Now top chef-owners vie to offer the biggest choice of savory breads, presenting customers with ever-expanding breadbaskets and even loaded carts to confuse indecisive diners.

The selection of savory breads you can make is virtually endless, requiring only a good basic dough and some imagination. Kneading fruity, slightly peppery extra-virgin olive oil into a plain white dough and letting it rise slowly produces a flavorful, mellow loaf with a light, open texture and a thin, tearable crust (see Pugliese, page 106). Working olives – black, green, or those stuffed with anchovies, almonds, or pimientos – into a

OPPOSITE Italian Pugliese
ABOVE Outdoor Italian
bread oven.

dough makes a bread that is particularly good to eat with Mediterranean dishes, or to use for sandwiches. A fabu- lous tomato bread can be made with sun-dried toma- toes, or sun-dried tomato purée. However, avoid using ordinary tomato paste, which tends to make a pretty loaf, but one that lacks flavor or is too sweet. Adding smoked tomatoes to bread is the latest fashion – very esoteric. You can make powerfully flavored savory loaves simply by spreading a basic dough with sliced yellow or red onions that have been sautéed until soft in olive oil and seasoned with plenty of fresh thyme. Then you roll up the dough like a jelly- roll, enclosing the onions as a filling. Another idea is to twist pieces of dough around while roasted garlic cloves to make savory rolls. Pesto sauce made from fresh basil in season, cilantro, crisp cracklings left from a pork roast, or cracked black peppercorns can also be used as flavorings for wonderful savory breads. Serve a thick slice with a bowl of soup for a satisfying, nourishing meal.

In this chapter, I use enriched brioche dough – often thought of as only a breakfast bread – to make a flavorful cheese loaf (see Brioche de Gannat, page 113) and as a rich and spectacular bread casing for a whole Brie (see Alyson Cook's Brie en Brioche, page 115). This may be served warm with a salad for a main course, or as part of a buffet spread.

Pissaladière (page 115), Flamiche aux Maroilles (page 120), Tarte Flambée (page 116), and Focaccia (page 110) are made from flattened doughs that act as plates, or trays, for a topping or filling. The crust can be thin, crisp, and crunchy, or soft, deep, and chewy. Scattered on top of or pushed into the dough are herbs, salt, and cheese, or an elaborately rich mixture, such as ratatouille.

Any of these doughs will lend itself to endless experimentation, though I am not a fan of too-trendy combinations, like tandoori pizza or Caribbean pizza, topped with pineapple and ham.

PUGLIESE

Makes 1 very large loaf

13 cups (1.5kg) unbleached white bread
    flour

3½ tablespoons (30g) coarse sea salt,
    crushed or ground

2 0.6-oz cakes fresh yeast (30g), or 2
    envelopes active dry yeast (5 teaspoons)

1 teaspoon sugar

3¾–4½ cups (850–990ml) lukewarm
    water

⅔ cup (140ml) extra virgin olive oil

extra flour for dusting

a large baking sheet, floured

*A Tuscan hillside covered with olive trees. It
is the fruity taste of golden-green extra-
virgin and virgin olive oils from this part of
Italy that flavors many Italian breads. If you
buy a good-quality oil, you will be rewarded
with authentic-tasting breads. It is not worth
using a cheaper substitute.*

*This soft-crumbed yet chewy, white olive-oil bread with a pale, thin crust is based on one I tasted in Puglia, Italy.
Store this bread, wrapped, at room temperature for two to three days.*

Mix together the flour and salt in a large mixing bowl. Make a well in the center of the
flour. Crumble the fresh yeast into a small bowl. Stir in the sugar and 3 tablespoons of
the lukewarm water until smooth. Let stand for 5 minutes, or until it starts to become
foamy. If using dry yeast, mix the granules and the sugar with 3 tablespoons of the
lukewarm water and let stand until foamy, 5 to 10 minutes (page 18).

Pour the yeast mixture into the well in the flour, adding most of the remaining
lukewarm water. Roughly mix in the flour from the bowl with your hand or a wooden
spoon. Then mix in the olive oil and continue mixing until the dough comes together. If
the dough remains dry and crumbly, gradually add the remaining water, 1–2 tablespoons
at a time, as necessary; the dough should be soft, but not sticky, and should hold its
shape. Turn out the dough on to a lightly floured work surface. Knead for 10 minutes
until it becomes very smooth and elastic.

Shape the dough into a ball. Wash, dry, and oil the bowl. Return the dough to the
bowl, and turn the dough over so the top is oiled. Cover with a damp dish towel and let
rise at cool to normal room temperature, away from drafts, until the dough has doubled
in size, 3½ to 4 hours (this will depend on the temperature of the room and the dough).
Gently turn out the dough on to the prepared baking sheet, without punching it down.
Gently pull out the sides of the dough, then tuck them underneath to make a neat, pillow-
like round loaf. Do this several times, but do not knead the dough, punch it down, or
turn it over.

Cover the dough with a damp dish towel and let rise, away from drafts, until almost
doubled in size, 1 to 1½ hours. During the last fifteen minutes of rising, heat the oven to
450F. Lightly dust the loaf with flour. Bake the bread for 12 minutes. Then lower the
oven temperature to 375F and bake for 25 to 35 minutes longer, or until the loaf is nicely
browned and sounds hollow when tapped underneath. Transfer the loaf to a wire rack
and cool completely.

VARIATIONS: PUGLIESE WITH TOMATOES AND BASIL Chop the contents of one 8-
ounce (230g) jar well-drained sun-dried tomatoes packed in olive oil. Chop enough
fresh basil to yield ½ cup. Knead the tomatoes and basil into the dough when it is smooth
and elastic, just before the first rising. Proceed with the recipe as above.

PUGLIESE WITH OLIVES Roughly chop 6 to 9 ounces (170–255g) pitted black or
green olives, or stuffed green olives; the more you use, the more pronounced the flavor
will be. Knead the olives into the dough when it is smooth and elastic, just before the first
rising. Proceed with the recipe as above.

TUCK THE SIDES UNDERNEATH TO MAKE A
TIDY, PILLOW-LIKE ROUND.

SOFT-CRUMBED PUGLIESE IS DELICIOUS EATEN
FRESH SOON AFTER BAKING.

Fresh basil, juicy, sun-ripened tomatoes, and mozzarella cheese are the natural partners for freshly baked ciabatta.

CIABATTA

INGREDIENTS

Makes 2 loaves

6 cups (680g) unbleached white bread flour

2 0.6-oz cakes fresh yeast (30g)

2 cups (430ml) water from the cold tap

⅔ cup (140ml) extra virgin olive oil

2 tablespoons (15g) coarse sea salt, crushed or ground

extra flour for sprinkling and dusting

2 baking sheets, heavily floured

TIP *A PORTION OF DOUGH ONTO EACH PREPARED BAKING SHEET TO FORM ROUGH-LOOKING RECTANGULAR LOAVES, ABOUT 1 INCH THICK. YOU MAY HAVE TO USE A SPATULA TO NUDGE THE DOUGH INTO SHAPE.*

This Italian loaf comes from the area around Lake Como in the north, and it is supposed to resemble a slipper. In any case, it is free-form — simply poured out of the bowl in which it has risen on to the baking sheet in a rough and ready rectangular loaf. It has large holes, and a soft but chewy, floury crust. I find that many commercial loaves taste of stale olive oil or lack the pungency of good extra-virgin oil.

Finding a good recipe for this bread was difficult, and I made about thirty before I was happy with the results. Taking advice from chef Pierre Koffmann, I adapted his baguette recipe (page 32), adding a good quantity olive oil to the dough, and altering the final consistency. As with the baguettes, it is not easy to achieve a perfect result the first time, even though the final loaf should taste very good. I have not had good results with either regular or rapid-rise active dry yeast, so I have only included instructions for using fresh yeast.

Put 4 cups (455g) flour into a large bowl. Make a well in the center of the flour. Crumble the fresh yeast into a small bowl. Stir in ½ cup (110ml) of the water until smooth. Pour the yeast mixture into the well in the flour. Then add the remaining water to the well and mix. Mix the flour from the bowl into the yeast mixture in the well with your hand or a wooden spoon to make a very sticky batterlike dough. Using your hand, beat the mixture for 5 minutes until very elastic. Cover the bowl with a damp dish towel and let rise at room temperature, away from drafts, for 4 hours. The dough will rise up enormously, so check that it does not stick to the dish towel.

Punch down the dough. Add the oil and salt to the dough and mix briefly with your hand. Then gradually work the rest of the flour into the dough with your hand to make a soft, quite sticky dough. When the dough is smooth and the flour has been thoroughly combined, cover the bowl with a damp dish towel and let rise at room temperature, away from drafts, until doubled in size, about 1 hour.

Using a very sharp knife, divide the dough in half, disturbing the dough as little as possible. Do not punch it down or try to knead or shape the dough at all. Tip a portion of dough on to each prepared baking sheet, nudging it with a spatula, to form two rough looking rectangular loaves, about 1 inch thick. Sprinkle the loaves with flour and let rise, uncovered, at room temperature, away from drafts, until doubled in size, 45 minutes to 1 hour. During the last 15 minutes of rising, heat the oven to 425F.

Bake the loaves for about 35 minutes, or until they are browned and sound hollow when tapped underneath. Transfer the loaves to wire racks to cool. They are best eaten warm and fresh, or they can be frozen for up to one week.

GRISSINI

INGREDIENTS

Makes about 46

3 cups (340g) whole-wheat bread flour,
    preferably stone-ground

1 cup (115g) unbleached white bread
    flour

2 teaspoons salt, or more to taste

1 0.6-oz cake fresh yeast (15g), or
    1 envelope active dry yeast
    (2½ teaspoons) plus ½ teaspoon sugar

1 cup (230ml) lukewarm water

¼ cup (60ml) olive oil

extra flour for dusting

2 large baking sheets, lightly greased

Napoleon was so fond of what he called *les petits bâtons* that he had them sent daily by post to his court. These thin, crunchy breadsticks are made from a simple yeast dough enriched with a little olive oil or lard. In England, I prefer making grissini with 85 percent brown flour, a whole-wheat flour that has had some of the wheat germ removed; it produces a texture somewhere between white and whole-wheat flour. This flour is not available in the States, so I've used a combination of flours. You can vary the proportions to your taste. Children particularly like the Parmesan variation. Another idea is to sprinkle the dough with sesame seeds, poppy seeds, or coarse sea salt before baking.

Once you get the hang of making grissini, the thin strips of dough can be rapidly rolled, pulled, and stretched by hand to form sticks. The distinctly nonuniform look of the finished result is very appealing. These go well with soups, salads, and antipasti, as well as dips, and are a wonderful replacement for the often-dreadful party nibbles. Store them in an airtight tin.

Mix together the whole-wheat flour, the white flour, and salt in a large bowl and make a well in the center. Crumble the fresh yeast into a small bowl and stir in half the water until smooth. If using dry yeast, mix the granules and the sugar with half the water and let stand until foamy, 5 to 10 minutes (see page 18).

Add the yeast mixture to the well in the flour and mix in enough of the flour in the bowl to make a thick batter. Let stand for 20 minutes to sponge (page 16). Add the remaining water and the oil and mix to form a fairly firm dough. If the dough is sticky, work in small amounts of the remaining whole-wheat flour.

Turn out the dough on to a lightly floured work surface and knead for 10 minutes, or until it is smooth and elastic.

Return the dough to the washed and greased bowl and turn the dough over so the top is oiled. Cover with a damp dish towel and let rise at room temperature, away from drafts, until just doubled in size, about 1 hour. It is better to slightly underproof this

ROLL OUT THE DOUGH ON A LIGHTLY FLOURED WORK SURFACE TO A RECTANGLE ABOUT ¼ INCH THICK.

CUT THE RECTANGLE IN HALF LENGTHWISE, THEN SLICE EACH RECTANGLE CROSSWISE INTO STRIPS ½ INCH WIDE.

USING YOUR HANDS, ROLL OUT AND STRETCH EACH STRIP UNTIL IT IS ABOUT 10 INCHES LONG. PLACE ON THE LIGHTLY GREASED BAKING SHEETS.

HALFWAY THROUGH THE BAKING TIME, TURN THE GRISSINI OVER SO THEY BROWN EVENLY.

dough than to overproof it. During the last 15 minutes of rising, heat the oven to 450F.

Punch down the risen dough. Roll it out on a lightly floured work surface with a lightly floured rolling pin to a large rectangle about ¼ inch thick.

Using a sharp knife, cut the rectangle in half lengthwise to make two long, narrow rectangles. Slice each rectangle crosswise into strips ½ inch wide. Using your hands, roll and stretch each strip until it is about 10 inches long. Place on the prepared baking sheets. Work as quickly as possible, as the grissini should be baked as soon as they are shaped. Do not give the dough a second rising.

Bake the grissini for 12 to 20 minutes, depending on how crispy you like them. Turn them over halfway through baking so they brown evenly. Transfer the grissini to wire racks to cool completely.

VARIATIONS: PARMESAN GRISSINI Add ½ cup (60g) freshly grated Parmesan cheese to the flour with the salt. Then proceed with the recipe.

TOMATO GRISSINI Add 2 tablespoons drained and chopped oil-packed sun-dried tomatoes to the kneaded dough before letting it rise.

Serve grissini for nibbling with pre-dinner drinks or as part of a first course. Ideal accompaniments include fruity black olives and rich unsalted butter.

FOCACCIA

INGREDIENTS

Makes 1 large loaf

1 0.6-oz cake fresh yeast (15g), or
   1 envelope active dry yeast
   (2½ teaspoons) plus ½ teaspoon sugar
1¼ cups (280ml) water from the cold tap
6–7 tablespoons extra virgin olive oil
about 4½ cups (500g) unbleached white
   bread flour
2 teaspoons salt
extra flour for dusting
2 teaspoons coarse sea salt for sprinkling

a large roasting pan, about 10 × 14
   inches, greased

DIMPLE THE DOUGH BY PRESSING
YOUR FINGERTIPS INTO IT FIRMLY SO
IT IS MARKED WITH INDENTATIONS
ABOUT ½-INCH DEEP.

*A simple loaf of focaccia can turn into a feast
when served as an antipasto with Italian
salami, a bowl of homemade Italian vinegar-
and-olive-oil dressing, and additional coarse
salt to sprinkle over the bread. To serve
Italian style, dip hunks of the bread in the
dressing or into fruity olive oil. A carafe of
crisp, dry Italian wine is all that is needed to
complete the feast. The focaccia dough also
makes a good base for a deep-crust pizza, but
if you use it for pizza, do not dimple the
dough or give it the third rising.*

*This version of focaccia, flavored with olive oil and salt, comes from Genoa, Italy. Although it is made in a
roasting pan, you can shape the dough into one or two rounds and bake them on jelly-roll pans. The crumb is
open, light, and moist, and the crust thin and full of flavor — never soggy and rubbery, or too crisp and dry. The
thickness and flavorings are determined by the baker or the region.*

Enjoy this bread on picnics, with salads and cold meats, or as a snack.

Crumble the fresh yeast into a large bowl. Stir in ½ cup of the water until smooth. Then
stir in the remaining ½ cup water and 3 tablespoons of the oil. If using dry yeast, heat
half of the water to lukewarm. Mix the yeast granules and the ½ teaspoon sugar with the
lukewarm water and let stand until foamy, 5 to 10 minutes (page 18). Stir in the
remaining water and 3 tablespoons oil.

With your hand or a wooden spoon, beat half the flour and the 2 teaspoons salt into
the yeast mixture. Work in enough of the remaining flour to make a very soft, but not
sticky dough. Turn out the dough on to a floured work surface and knead for 10 minutes
until very smooth and silky. Wash, dry, and oil the bowl. Return the dough to the bowl,
and turn the dough so the top is oiled. Cover and let rise at room temperature, away from
drafts, until doubled in size, about 2 hours.

Punch down the dough. Turn out the dough on to a lightly floured work surface and
roll it out with a lightly floured rolling pin to a rectangle the same size as your roasting
pan. Lift the dough into the pan and pat it into the corners. Cover with a damp dish towel
and let rise at room temperature, away from drafts, until not quite doubled in size, 45 to
60 minutes. Dimple the dough by pressing your fingertips into it firmly so it is marked
with indentations about ½ inch deep. Cover and let rise at room temperature until
doubled in size, 1 to 1½ hours. During the last 15 minutes, heat the oven to 425F.

Drizzle the remaining olive oil over the dough so the dimples are filled, then sprinkle
with the coarse salt. Put the focaccia in the oven, then spray the oven sides and bottom
with water (avoiding the light bulb). This helps produce a good, moist bread. Bake for 5
minutes, then spray the oven sides and bottom again. Bake about 20 minutes longer until
the focaccia is golden brown. Lift the focaccia on to a wire rack and eat while still warm.

A selection of olive-oil flavored breads is an essential part of most Italian family feasts.

VARIATIONS: CHOPPED OLIVE FOCACCIA Work ⅔ cup (85g) chopped pitted black oil-cured or Kalamata olives into the dough toward the end of the kneading time. Proceed as opposite, dimpling the dough and letting it rise. Drizzle with the oil, but omit the salt topping. Bake as opposite.

ROSEMARY FOCACCIA Add 1 tablespoon chopped fresh rosemary leaves to the dough with the last handful of flour. Then proceed with the kneading and rising. After you have dimpled the dough and it has risen, press small sprigs of fresh rosemary into the dough every 2 to 3 inches. Drizzle with the oil, but omit the salt topping, and bake as opposite. This smells heavenly as it bakes.

ROSEMARY-GARLIC FOCACCIA Prepare the dough as opposite, then dimple. Slice several garlic cloves into slivers. Press the garlic slivers into the dough. Cover and let rise as opposite. Press a few small sprigs of fresh rosemary into the dough. Drizzle with the oil, sprinkle with the salt topping, and bake as opposite.

RED-ONION FOCACCIA Prepare the dough as opposite, then dimple it and let it rise as directed opposite. Slice 2 small red onions into thin rings. Scatter the onion rings over the risen dough, then drizzle with the oil and sprinkle with the salt topping. Bake as opposite.

CHEDDAR CHEESE AND ONION LOAF

INGREDIENTS

Makes 1 large loaf

6 cups (680g) unbleached white bread flour

2 tablespoons (15g) coarse sea salt, crushed or ground

1 teaspoon mustard powder

1 0.6-oz cake fresh yeast (15g), or
    1 envelope active dry yeast
    (2½ teaspoons) plus ½ teaspoon sugar

2 cups (420ml) water from the cold tap

extra flour for dusting

milk for glazing

FILLING AND TOPPING:

1 cup (110g) shredded aged Cheddar cheese

⅔ cup (85g) diced aged Cheddar cheese

1 medium onion, finely chopped

2 tablespoons vegetable oil

1 small onion, sliced in rings, for topping the loaf

a loaf pan, about 10 × 5 × 3 inches, greased

Made to eat warm or toasted with soups and salads, this bread is not for the faint hearted. For a really full flavor, use a nutty, well-aged Cheddar cheese and strong onions; they will mellow and blend with the other ingredients during baking. It is important to roll up the dough tightly (page 26) to avoid gaps in the baked loaf.

Mix together the flour, salt, and mustard in a large bowl. Make a well in the center of the flour. Crumble the fresh yeast into a small bowl. Stir in half of the water until smooth. If using dry yeast, heat half of the water to lukewarm. Mix the yeast granules and the ½ teaspoon sugar to the lukewarm water and let stand until foamy, 5 to 10 minutes (page 18).

Pour the yeast mixture into the well in the flour. Mix enough of the flour from the bowl into the yeast mixture with your hand or a wooden spoon to make a thin, smooth batter. Sprinkle the batter with a little flour to prevent a skin forming. Cover the bowl with a damp dish towel and let stand until spongy and foamy, about 20 minutes.

Add the remaining water to the foamy batter and mix together. Gradually work in the flour from the bowl with your hand to make a soft, but not sticky dough. Turn out the dough on to a floured work surface and knead for 10 minutes, until smooth and elastic. Wash, dry, and oil the bowl. Return the dough to the bowl, and turn the dough over so the top is oiled. Cover with a damp dish towel and let rise at cool to normal room temperature, away from drafts, until doubled in size, about 2 hours.

Meanwhile, combine ¾ cup (85g) of the shredded cheese with all the diced cheese; the variety of textures makes the filling more interesting. Sauté the chopped onion in the oil over low heat until it is soft and begins to turn golden, 10 to 12 minutes. Let cool.

Punch down the dough and turn it out on to a floured work surface. Roll out the dough with a floured rolling pin into a 10 × 15-inch rectangle. Sprinkle the cheese mixture over the dough, leaving a ½-inch border at all edges. Top with the sautéed onion. Roll up

Full, robust flavors characterize Roquefort and Walnut Loaf (left) and Cheddar Cheese and Onion Loaf. If you prefer, add a slightly nutty taste and more texture to either loaf by using 4 cups (455g) whole-wheat bread flour and 2 cups (230g) unbleached white bread flour, rather than all white flour as in the recipe. You can also substitute pecans for the walnuts.

tightly from a short side like a jelly-roll to make a loaf 10 inches long. Place the loaf, seam side down, into the prepared pan, tucking under the ends so it fits. Cover and let rise at room temperature, away from drafts, until doubled in size, about 1 to 2 hours. During the last 15 minutes of rising, heat the oven to 400F. Brush the loaf with a little milk, then sprinkle with the remaining shredded cheese. Bake the loaf for 20 minutes. While the loaf is baking, blanch the onion rings in a pan of boiling water for 1 minute, then drain. Arrange the blanched onion rings on top of the loaf and bake 20 to 25 minutes longer until the loaf sounds hollow when unmolded and tapped underneath. Turn out the loaf on to a wire rack to cool completely.

ROQUEFORT AND WALNUT LOAF

INGREDIENTS

Makes 1 large loaf
1 batch dough for Cheddar Cheese and
   Onion Loaf (page 111)
5 oz (140g) Roquefort cheese
1 cup (110g) coarsely chopped walnuts
milk for glazing

a loaf pan, about 10 × 5 × 3 inches,
   greased

A good spinach salad, with young, tender leaves, fried bacon lardons (thick, matchstick-size strips of bacon), and a hot piquant dressing made by deglazing the bacon pan with vinegar, is the ideal accompaniment to this bread. Any well-made blue cheese — by which I mean one that tastes more of creamy, ripe, buttery blue cheese than of salt — can be substituted for the ewes' milk Roquefort. When buying cheese, always ask for a taste.

Prepare the dough with the flour, salt, mustard powder, yeast, and water. Cover and let rise, away from drafts, until doubled in size, about 2 hours.

Turn out the dough on to a floured work surface. Roll out the dough with a floured rolling pin into a 10 × 15-inch rectangle. Crumble the Roquefort cheese over the dough, leaving a ½-inch border all around. Top with the walnuts.

Then roll up the dough from a short side like a jelly roll. Place the loaf, seam side down, in the prepared loaf pan, tucking under the ends. Cover and let rise at room temperature until doubled in size, 1 to 2 hours. During the last 15 minutes of rising, heat the oven to 400F. Brush the loaf with a little milk. Bake the loaf for 40 to 50 minutes, or until the loaf sounds hollow when unmolded and tapped underneath. Turn out the loaf on to a wire rack to cool completely.

BRIOCHE DE GANNAT

INGREDIENTS

Makes 1 large loaf

2½ cups (280g) unbleached white bread
    flour

1 teaspoon salt

freshly ground black pepper

1 0.6-oz cake fresh yeast (15g), or
    1 envelope active dry yeast
    (2½ teaspoons) plus ½ teaspoon sugar

½ cup (115ml) lukewarm milk

2 eggs

4 tablespoons (60g) unsalted butter,
    melted

extra flour for dusting

1 cup (110g) shredded Cantal or Gruyère
    cheese

1 egg beaten with ½ teaspoon salt for
    glazing

a loaf pan, about 7 × 5 × 3 inches,
    greased

This cheese brioche comes from the small town of Gannat in the Auvergne region of France, where flavorful Cantal cheese is made. The brioche dough in this recipe is not as complicated or as rich in eggs and butter as the dough for Michel Roux's Brioche (page 203); the richness here comes from the cheese. This brioche is light in texture, and I think it is best eaten on the day it is baked. Otherwise, this loaf tastes good toasted. I serve it with cheese and salads, or slice it and melt cheese on top. I've adapted this recipe from French Regional Cooking, by Anne Willan (Morrow, 1979).

Mix together the flour, the salt, and pepper from several turns of the peppermill in a large bowl. Make a well in the center of the flour.

Crumble the fresh yeast into a small bowl. Whisk in the lukewarm milk until smooth. Whisk in the eggs just to break them up, then whisk in the butter. If using dry yeast, mix the granules and the ½ teaspoon sugar with the lukewarm milk and let stand until foamy, 5 to 10 minutes (page 18). Whisk the eggs and butter into the yeast mixture.

Pour the yeast mixture into the well in the flour. Gradually work the flour from the bowl into the liquid with your hand or a wooden spoon to make a soft, but not sticky dough, adding a little more flour as needed, 1 tablespoon at a time, to prevent the dough sticking to your fingers.

Turn out the dough on to a lightly floured work surface and knead for 10 minutes until smooth and elastic. Wash, dry, and oil the bowl.

Return the dough to the bowl, and turn the dough over so the top is oiled. Cover with a damp dish towel and let rise at cool to normal temperature, away from drafts, until doubled in size, 1½ to 2 hours.

Punch down the risen dough. Turn out the dough on to a lightly floured work surface and gently knead in the shredded cheese, reserving 2 tablespoons for sprinkling on top of the loaf just before baking. Shape the dough into a loaf to fit the loaf pan (page 24). Put the dough, seam side down, into the prepared pan, pinching and tucking under the ends so it fits. Then cover with a damp dish towel and let rise at room temperature, away from drafts, until it rises to the top of the pan, 1 to 1½ hours. During the last 15 minutes of rising, heat the oven to 400F.

Gently brush the dough with the egg glaze, taking care not to "glue" the dough to the sides of the pan. Then sprinkle with the reserved 2 tablespoons of cheese. Bake the bread for 35 to 45 minutes, or until the loaf is golden brown and sounds hollow when unmolded and tapped underneath. Turn out the brioche on to a wire rack to cool completely.

THE GLAZED LOAF IS TOPPED WITH THE
RESERVED CHEESE.

THE BRIOCHE DOUGH BAKES INTO A SOFT,
DELICATE CRUMB.

PROVENÇAL VEGETABLE TARTS

INGREDIENTS

Makes 2 tarts; each serves 6 to 8

3½ cups (395g) unbleached white bread
   flour

2 teaspoons salt

1 0.6-oz cake fresh yeast (15g), or
   1 envelope active dry yeast
   (2½ teaspoons) plus ½ teaspoon sugar

scant 1 cup (200ml) lukewarm milk

2 large eggs, beaten

4 tablespoons (60g) unsalted butter,
   softened

2 tablespoons chopped mixed fresh herbs,
   such as parsley, basil, thyme,
   rosemary, and oregano

extra flour for dusting

RATATOUILLE FILLING:

3 tablespoons extra virgin olive oil

1 small onion, chopped

3 cloves garlic, chopped

1 red bell pepper, seeded and diced

5 plum tomatoes, peeled, seeded, and diced

1 small eggplant, cut into thick matchstick
   strips

2 zucchini, cut into thick matchstick strips

1 teaspoon chopped fresh thyme

salt and freshly ground black pepper

2 oz (60g) Gruyère cheese, thinly sliced

2 large eggs, beaten

⅔ cup (140ml) heavy cream

2 deep 8- to 9-inch quiche pans or
   springform pans, lightly greased

I adore ratatouille, whether served hot with roast lamb or cold as a salad. It also makes a substantial filling for these crisp, rich, herby, bread-crust tarts, which I serve warm with a big green salad for a summer lunch.

To make the bread crust: Mix together the flour and salt in a medium-size bowl. Make a well in the center of the flour. Crumble the fresh yeast into a small bowl. Whisk in the lukewarm milk until smooth. If using dry yeast, mix the granules and the ½ teaspoon sugar with 4 tablespoons lukewarm milk and let stand until foamy, 5 to 10 minutes (page 18). Add the remaining milk. Whisk the eggs into the yeast mixture until well blended.

Pour the yeast mixture into the well in the flour. Work in the flour from the bowl, beating to make a smooth, soft, and slightly sticky dough. Knead the dough by pulling it up with your fingers and pushing it down in the bowl with the heel of your hand until very smooth and elastic, about 5 minutes. Beat in the butter and herbs until the dough is smooth, with no streaks of butter or herbs. Shape into a ball. Wash, dry, and oil the bowl. Return the dough to the bowl, and turn the dough over so the top is oiled. Cover and let rise at cool to normal room temperature until doubled in size, about 2 hours.

Meanwhile, make the filling. Heat the oil in a large, deep skillet. Add the onion and garlic and cook until tender but not browned, 7 to 10 minutes. Add the red pepper and cook, stirring frequently, for 5 minutes. Stir in the tomatoes, eggplant, zucchini, thyme, and salt and pepper to taste. Cook, stirring occasionally, about 10 minutes, or until the vegetables are tender but not mushy. Adjust the seasoning, and let cool.

Punch down the dough. Turn out the dough on to a floured work surface and divide into two equal portions. Roll out each portion with a floured rolling pin into an 11-inch round. Put one round into one of the pans, lining the base and sides by pressing the dough with your knuckles and fingers; the dough should be even with the top of the quiche pan, and it will extend up the side of a springform pan about 1 inch. Cover the dough with half of the cheese. Then fill with half the ratatouille. Line and fill the second pan with the remaining dough, cheese, and ratatouille.

Beat the eggs with the cream and a little salt and pepper to taste. Pour this mixture over the ratatouille in each pan, dividing equally, and using a fork to ease the vegetables apart; do not puncture the dough. Let stand, uncovered, away from drafts, until the dough starts to rise, about 15 minutes. Meanwhile, heat the oven to 400F. Bake the tarts for 30 to 35 minutes, or until they are golden brown and the fillings are set. Serve warm.

The ratatouille filling in this tart captures the sun-drenched flavors of the South of France. Juicy-ripe tomatoes, red bell peppers, eggplant, and zucchini, along with plenty of garlic, olive oil, and thyme combine to evoke images of summer along the Mediterranean. This tart is best served warm, so if you bake it in advance, reheat it in a 350F oven for 15–20 minutes.

RIGHT
The bottom round of dough should be six inches larger than the cheese.

FAR RIGHT
After Alyson wraps the cheese with the dough, she brushes it with the egg glaze. Serve this the day it is baked, ideally with a selection of salads. The brioche dough, however, can be made and the recipe assembled the night before you plan to serve this loaf, then covered with plastic wrap and chilled overnight. Remove from the refrigerator, unwrap, and cover with a dry dish towel. Let the brioche rise at normal to room temperature until the dough puffs up, as directed. (This can take up to four hours.) Then bake it as described in the recipe.

INGREDIENTS

Makes 1 very large loaf

1 0.6-oz cake fresh yeast (15g), or
   1 envelope active dry yeast
   (2½ teaspoons) plus ½ teaspoon sugar

5 tablespoons (70ml) lukewarm milk

2 tablespoons (15g) coarse sea salt,
   crushed or ground

4½ cups (500g) unbleached white bread
   flour

6 large eggs, beaten

1 cup #aa 2 tablespoons (250g) unsalted
   butter, softened

2 teaspoons sugar

extra flour for dusting

a 2-lb (900g) whole Brie cheese, 8 to 9
   inches in diameter

1 jar (about 12 oz/340g) spiced apricot
   chutney or mango chutney

1 egg beaten with ¼ teaspoon salt for
   glazing

a baking sheet lined with parchment paper

ALYSON COOK'S BRIE EN BRIOCHE

I will be honest. The main point of the trip Anthony Blake and I took to California was to see my best friend Alyson, who comes from Somerset, England. We met many years ago at The Cordon Bleu, in London. She now owns a classy catering business in Los Angeles and is cooking for Hollywood legends who like to dine at home in style. This is one of Alyson's most-frequently requested dishes. It is ideal for parties.

Make the brioche dough as for Michel Roux's Brioche (page 203), using the proportions listed here. Add the yeast mixture to the flour, then beat in the eggs and knead the dough; finally, work in the butter and sugar mixture. Chill the dough after the first rising until it is firm but not hard, 3 to 5 hours. Turn out the dough on to a lightly floured work surface. Cut off one-quarter of the dough and cover with a damp dish towel.

Measure the cheese, then roll out the large piece of dough with a lightly floured rolling pin into a round, about 8 inches larger than the cheese, and about ½ inch thick. Spread the chutney evenly over the top of the cheese. Gently place the cheese upside-down in the center of the dough circle. Trim the edges of the dough, if necessary, to neaten it. Roll out the reserved dough into a circle ½ inch larger than the cheese.

Lightly brush the top of the cheese with the egg glaze. Bring the dough up around the sides of the cheese, in toward the center, leaving some of the cheese exposed in the middle, and pressing gently so the dough adheres to the cheese. Brush the top of the dough with the egg glaze. Place the other dough round on top of the cheese and gently pat the dough to seal it.

Lightly flour your hands and turn the wrapped cheese upside-down on to the prepared baking sheet. If necessary, gently mold the sides into an even shape with your hands.

Lightly score the top in a diamond or checkered pattern with the tip of a sharp knife. Let rise, uncovered, at room temperature, away from drafts, until the dough puffs up, 30 to 45 minutes. During the last 15 minutes of rising time, heat the oven to 375F. Slide another baking sheet under the first to insulate the bottom so the brioche doesn't scorch.

Bake the brioche for 35 minutes, or until puffed and golden brown. Brush with the remaining egg glaze and bake 10 minutes longer. (Alyson says this gives a better finish than glazing before baking.) Transfer to a wire rack to cool completely.

TARTE FLAMBÉE

INGREDIENTS

Makes 2 thin tarts; each serves 2–3

4 cups (455g) unbleached white bread flour

1½ teaspoons salt

1 0.6-oz cake fresh yeast (15g), or

1 envelope active dry yeast (2½ teaspoons) plus ½ teaspoon sugar

1¼ cups (280ml) water from the cold tap

1 teaspoon vegetable oil or melted butter

extra flour for dusting

TOPPING:

8 oz (230g) slab bacon

1¼ cups (280ml) crème fraîche, or ⅔ cup (140ml) each sour cream and heavy cream

2 onions, very thinly sliced

freshly ground black pepper

2 baking sheets or jelly-roll pans, lightly greased

Matchsticks of bacon, called lardons, and crème fraîche are combined with very thinly sliced onions to make the traditional topping for this rich, crisp Alsatian tart. Take care to slice the onions as thinly as possible, or they will still taste raw after the short baking time. I suggest you use the thin slicing blade of a food processor, or a mandolin.

Tarte flambée, with a wafer-thin, crunchy crust and a rich, but simple, shallow topping of crème fraîche, thinly sliced onions, and bacon slivers, can be found in almost every café-bar and restaurant in the Alsace region of France. It makes a good, inexpensive snack or ample first course.

In Riquewihr, Anthony Blake and I found the A la Fontaine restaurant, where bakers cooked these tarts to order in an outside oven situated right in the midst of the diners. The oven, built in typical Alsace style, is long, thin, and fired by logs underneath. The wood fire gives the tarts a smoky taste and a crisp crust – and it cooks the dough rapidly. The baker transferred each baked tart from the oven to the logs underneath to "flambé" it for a few seconds before serving.

Thanks to Patricia Well's invaluable book, The Food Lover's Guide to France (Workman, 1987), we also visited the Ferme Auberge, in Weiterswiller. You can eat tarte flambée to your heart's content at this working farm and inn, where owner Simone Bloch bakes the tarts in her 45-year-old oven. Shaped like a metal coffin, 1 foot deep and 8 feet long, the oven stands on a brick platform in her small kitchen. I watched as she rapidly assembled tarts measuring 12 × 18 inches. She also adds cheese or mushrooms on request. The day we were there, tarte flambée was the only item on the menu, and nobody complained as more and more tarts kept appearing at the tables. Folding up the tarts in local fashion and eating with our fingers, Anthony and I managed three between us.

To make the crust: Mix together the flour and salt in a large bowl. Make a well in the center of the flour. Crumble the fresh yeast into a small bowl. Stir in the water until smooth.

If using dry yeast, heat ½ cup (110ml) of the water to lukewarm. Mix the granules and the ½ teaspoon sugar with the lukewarm water and let stand until foamy, 5 to 10 minutes (page 18). Mix in the remaining water.

Pour the yeast mixture into the well in the flour. Stir in the oil or melted butter. Mix enough of the flour from the bowl into the yeast mixture with your fingers or a wooden spoon to make a thin, smooth batter. Sprinkle the batter with a little flour to prevent a skin forming. Cover the bowl with a dish towel and let the batter stand until spongy and foamy, about 20 minutes.

Work the rest of the flour from the bowl into the batter with your hands or a wooden spoon to make a soft, not sticky dough. Turn out the dough on to a lightly floured work surface and knead for 10 minutes until smooth and elastic. Wash, dry, and oil the bowl. Return the dough to the bowl, and turn the dough over so the top is oiled. Cover with a damp dish towel and let rise at room temperature, away from drafts, until doubled in size, 1½ to 2 hours. During the last 15 minutes of rising, heat the oven to 450F and prepare the topping.

Cut the bacon into thick matchstick shapes, called lardons, discarding any rind. If using sour cream and heavy cream, mix them together.

Punch down the risen dough. Turn it out on to a lightly floured work surface and divide into two equal portions. Roll out half the dough with a lightly floured rolling pin to a very thin rectangle the same size as your baking sheet or jelly-roll pan.

Roll the dough up on the rolling pin and unroll on to the prepared baking sheets or jelly-roll pans to cover it completely. Do not worry if the dough stretches and flops over the edges, because they will be folded in before baking. Repeat with the second piece of dough on the second prepared baking sheet or pan.

Spread one sheet of dough with half of the crème fraîche or the cream mixture. Sprinkle with half of the sliced onions and half of the bacon; season with plenty of pepper, to taste. Fold over the edges to make a ½-inch border. Repeat the process with the second sheet of dough.

Bake the tarts for 12 to 15 minutes, or until the tarts are golden and the bases crisp. Eat immediately.

PISSALADIÈRE

Makes 1 large pissaladière; serves 6–8

2¼ cups (255g) unbleached white bread flour

1½ teaspoons salt

1 0.6-oz cake fresh yeast (15g), or
   1 envelope active dry yeast
   (2½ teaspoons) plus ½ teaspoon sugar

½ cup #aa 2 tablespoons (130ml) lukewarm milk

2 large eggs, beaten

7 tablespoons (100g) unsalted butter, softened

extra flour for dusting

FILLING:

2½ 2-oz cans anchovy fillets packed in oil, drained

¼ cup (60ml) milk

14½-oz can plum tomatoes, drained

2 tablespoons tomato paste

2 tablespoons olive oil

2 cloves garlic, or to taste

1 tablespoon chopped fresh oregano

salt and freshly ground black pepper

sugar

lemon juice

about ½ cup (90g) pitted black olives

extra olive oil for brushing

a baking sheet or jelly-roll pan, about
   12 × 8 × 1 inch, greased

This is another recipe from my friend Alyson Cook (page 115). She says she likes to use a brioche dough for pissaladières because it is moister and richer than a plain white dough. She varies the topping, sprinkling capers over the traditional anchovies and tomatoes, or spreading lightly sautéed sliced onions on the dough before adding the tomato topping. Sometimes she replaces the oregano with fresh basil and then garnishes with fresh basil leaves. The black olives can be replaced with garlic slices.

To make the crust: Mix together the flour and salt in a large bowl. Make a well in the center of the flour. Crumble the fresh yeast into a small bowl. Stir in the lukewarm milk until smooth. If using dry yeast, mix the granules and the ½ teaspoon sugar with the lukewarm milk and let stand until foamy, 5 to 10 minutes (page 18).

Pour the yeast mixture into the well in the flour. Add the beaten eggs, mixing with your fingers or a small whisk to combine the ingredients. Gradually work in the flour from the bowl with your hands or a wooden spoon to make a very soft and quite sticky dough. Knead the dough by lifting it with one hand and slapping it against the sides of the bowl. Work in the softened butter by beating and slapping the dough up and down with your hand. Cover with a damp dish towel and let rise at room temperature, away from drafts, until doubled in size, 1½ to 2 hours.

Punch down the risen dough with your knuckles. Cover with a dish towel and chill until firm, but not hard, 4 to 5 hours.

Meanwhile, prepare the topping: Soak the anchovies in the milk for 15 to 20 minutes to remove some of the excess salt. Drain the anchovies and discard the milk. Purée the plum tomatoes in a blender or food processor with the tomato paste, olive oil, garlic cloves, and oregano leaves. Or, you may chop the plum tomatoes, garlic cloves, and oregano leaves by hand and stir in the tomato paste and olive oil. Season to taste with salt and pepper, sugar, and lemon juice. Heat the oven to 400F.

Turn out the dough on to a lightly floured work surface and roll out with a lightly floured rolling pin into a 12 × 8-inch rectangle, or a rectangle to fill the baking pan you are using. Roll up the dough on the rolling pin and transfer to the prepared baking pan. Press it on to the bottom of the pan and into the corners, squeezing out any bubbles of air trapped between the pan and dough. Spoon the tomato mixture over the dough and spread evenly, leaving a ½-inch border at all edges.

Arrange the drained anchovies in a criss-cross pattern over the top. Put an olive in the center of each diamond.

Bake the pissaladière for 20 to 25 minutes, or until the crust is golden brown and crisp. Remove from the oven and brush the rim of the crust with olive oil. Drizzle a little olive oil over the topping as well. Then cool to warm, cut into squares, and serve.

PRESS THE DOUGH INTO THE BOTTOM AND CORNERS OF THE PAN.

ANCHOVIES AND BLACK OLIVES ARE THE TRADITIONAL TOPPING FOR THIS PIZZA-LIKE FLAT TART.

Leek Tart (left) and Flamiche aux Maroilles
are both made with a rich brioche dough
crust, which makes an interesting change
from more familiar piecrust.

FLAMICHE AUX MAROILLES

This is a savory cheese tart with a brioche crust. The ideal cheese for this is Maroilles, a strong, pungent, soft cheese with a brown rind that has been washed in beer as the cheese ripens. It is named after the town of Maroilles, in northern France, where it is made. However, Maroilles is next to impossible to find in the States, as it is almost never exported beyond the Continent. Edward Edleman, of the Ideal Cheese Shop, in New York City, suggested the following substitutes, in order of preference: Chaumes, Alsatian Muenster, Pont l'Evêque, Saint-Nectaire, Danish Esrom, or Appenzeller. Cooked leeks or onions may be used as substitutes for the cheese filling (see the subsequent recipe), but I prefer the version made with cheese. Serve flamiche warm from the oven, with a green salad.

INGREDIENTS

Makes 1 large tart; serves 6–8
1 batch Pissaladière dough (page 117)
FILLING:
8 oz (230g) Maroilles cheese (see
    introduction), rind removed and then
    thinly sliced
½ cup #aa 2 tablespoons (130ml) crème
    fraîche or heavy cream
1 large egg
1 large egg yolk
¼ teaspoon freshly grated nutmeg
salt and freshly ground black pepper

a deep 9- to 9½-inch quiche pan,
    springform pan or deep-dish pie plate,
    greased

Prepare the dough as for the Pissaladière. Cover with a damp dish towel and let rise at room temperature, away from drafts, until doubled in size, 1½ to 2 hours. Punch down, cover again, and chill until firm, but not hard, 4 to 5 hours.

Turn out the dough on to a lightly floured work surface. Roll with a lightly floured rolling pin into a 12-inch round. Wrap the dough around the rolling pin and lift it over the prepared quiche pan or pie plate. Gradually unroll the dough so it is draped over the pan, then press it gently with your fingers on to the bottom and up the sides to evenly line the pan; do not stretch the dough. Trim off any excess dough to make a neat crust.

Arrange the cheese in an even layer over the bottom of the dough. In a medium-size bowl, beat together the crème fraîche or cream with the egg and egg yolk, nutmeg, and plenty of black pepper and a little salt to taste, just until combined. Pour this mixture over the cheese. Let the tart rise at warm room temperature (75F), away from drafts, until it is puffy and the rim is almost doubled in size, 30 to 45 minutes. During the last 15 minutes of rising, heat the oven to 400F.

Bake the tart for 40 to 50 minutes, or until the filling is set and the crust is golden brown and crisp.

LEEK TART

INGREDIENTS

Makes 1 large tart; serves 6–8

1 batch Pissaladière dough (page 117)

FILLING:

2 lb (900g) leeks, trimmed

4 tablespoons (60g) butter

salt and freshly ground black pepper

½ cup #aa 2 tablespoons (130ml) crème fraîche or heavy cream

1 large egg

1 large egg yolk

a deep 9- to 9½-inch quiche pan or deep-dish pie pan, buttered

Prepare the dough as for Pissaladière (page 117). Cover with a damp dish towel and let rise at room temperature, away from drafts, until doubled in size, 1½ to 2 hours. Punch down the dough. Cover again and chill until firm, but not hard, 4 to 5 hours.

Meanwhile, prepare the filling. Halve lengthwise and thoroughly rinse the leeks of sand and grit. Drain them well, then thinly slice. Melt the butter in a large, heavy-bottomed frying pan with lid. Add the leeks and salt and pepper to taste, and stir. Cover with a disk of buttered parchment paper and the pan's lid and cook slowly until the leeks are very tender, but not browned, about 25 minutes. Let cool. Heat the oven to 400F. Turn out the dough on to a lightly floured work surface. Roll with a lightly floured rolling pin into a 12-inch round. Line the quiche pan or pie plate as for Flamiche aux Maroilles. Beat together the crème fraîche or cream, egg, and egg yolk in a medium-size bowl until just combined. Season lightly with salt and pepper. Spoon the leeks into the dough crust, then pour over the cream mixture. Let rise as Flamiche aux Maroilles. Heat the oven to 400F. Bake the tart for 40 to 50 minutes, or until the filling is set and the crust is golden brown and crisp. Serve warm.

ETHIOPIAN SPICE BREAD

INGREDIENTS

Makes 1 large loaf

6 tablespoons (85g) butter

2 tablespoons minced onion

1 clove garlic, minced

1½ tablespoons ground coriander

1 tablespoon ground fenugreek

1½ tablespoons sweet paprika

½ teaspoon freshly ground black pepper

½ teaspoon ground cinnamon

¼ teaspoon cayenne

a large pinch of freshly grated nutmeg

a large pinch of ground cloves

6 cups (680g) unbleached white bread flour

2 teaspoons salt

1 0.6-oz cake fresh yeast (15g), or 1 envelope active dry yeast (2½ teaspoons)

1½ cups #aa 2 tablespoons (370ml) lukewarm water

2½ tablespoons packed (30g) light brown sugar

extra flour for dusting

1 tablespoon (15g) butter, melted, for glazing

a baking sheet, lightly greased

I found this recipe in The Independent, a British newspaper, and have made it regularly ever since. It was attributed to Dr. Fiona Pharoah, and my thanks go to her and Kumud, who gave it to her. I have altered the recipe amounts and method slightly, but the basic recipe is the same. The texture is light, the color inside is golden, and the flavor is mild, yet intriguing, developing to its best after 24 hours. Everyone likes this!

Melt the butter in a small saucepan. Add the onion, garlic, and spices and cook over low heat, stirring constantly, for 2 minutes until the spices are fragrant and lose their raw taste. Remove from the heat and let cool slightly.

Meanwhile, mix together the flour and salt in a large bowl. Make a well in the center of the flour. Crumble the fresh yeast into a small bowl. Stir in the water until smooth, then stir in the sugar. If using dry yeast, mix the granules and 1 teaspoon of the sugar with ½ cup (110ml) of the water and let stand until foamy, 5 to 10 minutes (page 18). Add the remaining sugar and water.

Pour the yeast mixture into the well in the flour, followed by the spice and onion mixture. Mix enough flour from the bowl into the yeast mixture to make a medium-thick batter. Sprinkle the batter with a little flour to prevent a skin forming. Cover the bowl and let stand until the batter becomes spongy and foamy, about 20 minutes.

Work the rest of the flour from the bowl into the batter to make a fairly firm dough. Turn out the dough on to a lightly floured work surface and knead for 10 minutes until smooth and elastic, adding a little extra flour if the dough is sticky.

Return the dough to the bowl. Cover and let rise at room temperature, away from drafts, until doubled in size, about 2 hours. Punch down the dough. Break off a large walnut-size piece of dough and reserve. Turn out the dough on to a floured work surface and shape into a free form loaf as for The Basic Loaf (page 17). Put the loaf on the prepared baking sheet. With a sharp knife, lightly score a cross on top of the loaf. Place the small nut of dough in the center of the cross. Cover and let rise at room temperature, away from drafts, until doubled in size, about 1 hour. During the last 15 minutes of rising, heat the oven to 375F. Bake for 40 to 50 minutes, or until the loaf is browned and sounds hollow when tapped underneath. Transfer to a wire rack. Brush with the melted butter and let cool.

BAGELS

INGREDIENTS

Makes 20

4 cups (455g) unbleached white bread
    flour

2 teaspoons salt

1 0.6-oz cake fresh yeast (15g), or
    1 envelope active dry yeast
    (2½ teaspoons)

1 cup (230ml) mixed milk and water, at
    room temperature

1 teaspoon sugar

2 tablespoons (30g) butter, melted, or
    vegetable oil

1 large egg, separated

extra flour for dusting

sesame seeds or poppy seeds for sprinkling
    (optional)

3 baking sheets, greased

a steamer pot with a lid, or a large deep
    skillet, a wire rack and aluminum foil

The popularity of the bagel — literally, "a roll with a hole" — has spread from Jewish communities to the wide world. A bagel was just a bagel to me until I realized I had married into a family of American East Coast bagel mavens. Yet they particularly love those made by a man called Noah in, of all places, Berkeley, California. "Noah's bagels have Yiddish in their souls," I was told. "There's nothing like them in Brooklyn."

Noah Alper bakes 250,000 bagels a week in the college town of Berkeley, and I met with him in his College Avenue shop. He defined the archetypical bagel for me. "It's important that it's big, crusty on the outside, chewy inside, tasty, and with plenty of seeds. Of course you don't have to be Jewish to know what a good bagel tastes like." I've adapted his recipe to make bagels that are smaller than what is usually encountered, because that is what I prefer.

Bagels were first made centuries ago in Poland. Badly made, a bagel will be rubbery, heavy, and soggy. The best ones, like Noah's, are finished by hand. The added toppings can be poppy seeds, sesame seeds, onions, caraway seeds, salt, or, as a California curiosity, sunflower seeds.

Eat bagels sliced and plain, toasted and buttered, spread with a schmear (a liberal coating) of cream cheese, or with cream cheese and lox or smoked salmon, onions, and pickles. These bagels are best eaten as soon as possible after baking; otherwise cool, wrap in freezer bags, and freeze for up to one month. Remove from the bags and reheat straight from the freezer on the oven racks in a 350F oven for about 10 minutes before serving.

Mix together 3½ cups (400g) of the flour and the salt in a large bowl. Make a well in the center of the flour. Crumble the fresh yeast into a small bowl. Whisk in the milk mixture until smooth. Stir in the sugar. If using dry yeast, heat ½ cup (110ml) of the milk mixture to lukewarm. Mix the yeast granules and the sugar with the lukewarm liquid and let stand until foamy, 5 to 10 minutes (page 18). Stir in the remaining liquid.

Pour the yeast mixture into the well in the flour, followed by the melted butter or vegetable oil. Lightly beat the egg white until frothy, then add to the well and mix with a small whisk until thoroughly combined. Gradually work in the flour from the bowl with your hand or a wooden spoon to make a soft and pliable dough. Turn out dough on to a lightly floured work surface. Cover with the upturned bowl and let stand for 5 minutes.

Then knead for 10 minutes until the dough is smooth and elastic, adding the remaining flour as needed, 1 tablespoon at a time, to prevent sticking. Wash, dry, and oil the bowl

Noah Alper's bagel shop in Berkeley, California. Noah's method of bagel making — he steams his bagels before baking them, instead of poaching them — has caused something of a controversy among the bagel lovers of the Bay Area. Among his faithful followers, "super onion," with onion in the dough and sprinkled on top, is his best-seller.

A sumptuous brunch of fresh bagels with smoked salmon, cream cheese with snipped fresh chives, and just-brewed coffee.

Return the dough to the bowl, and turn the dough over so the top is oiled. Cover with a damp dish towel and let rise at room temperature, away from drafts, until doubled in size, 1½ to 2 hours.

Punch down the dough. Weigh the dough and divide it into twenty equal portions, or roll it into a 20-inch rope and cut into twenty 1-inch pieces. Using your hands, and only flouring them and the work surface if it is necessary to prevent the dough from sticking, roll each piece into a sausage about 6 inches long. Taper the ends, then join them securely together using a little cold water to make a neat ring. Arrange the bagels, well apart, on the prepared baking sheets. Cover with dry dish towels and let rise at room temperature, away from drafts, until almost doubled in size, about 45 minutes. During the last 15 minutes of rising, heat the oven to 400F.

Bring some water to a boil in the bottom of a steamer pot or half fill a large, deep skillet with water and bring to a boil. Reduce the heat so the water is simmering. Place the steamer rack or wire rack over the simmering water. Arrange three or four bagels at a time, spaced apart, on the steamer rack or wire rack and cover with the steamer lid or a dome-shaped piece of aluminum foil; keep the remaining bagels covered. Steam for 1 minute.

Transfer the bagels to the greased baking sheet. If you prefer, the bagels can be poached, three at a time, for 30 seconds each.

Beat the egg yolk with 2 teaspoons cold water. Brush the steamed or poached bagels with the egg glaze. Leave plain, or sprinkle with sesame or poppy seeds. Bake the bagels for 20 to 25 minutes, or until they are golden brown and puffed up. Transfer to wire racks to cool.

FRUIT AND NUT BREADS

When I was four years old, I was so proud of my new green gingham uniform dress I refused to take it off at the end of my first day at school, despite a large sticky patch on the back of my skirt. During the school break we had been given a glass of milk and a buttered currant bun with a sticky, shiny glaze. My new little friends told me the only way to eat the bun – which I had never seen the likes of – was to sit on it, then cram the squashed mass into my mouth in one go. I did not think of the consequences, but ate the bun as instructed. What fun – what a good bun! It came from the Victoria Bakery in Barnet High Street, in north London, a bakery renowned for its fruit and nut breads, spicy buns, and hot cross buns. This unfortunate introduction to sweet fruit breads did not deter my enthusiasm for them. I have been collecting the best recipes for years.

land are among the breads generations of home bakers have served at teatime, instead of

For centuries, breads were held in high esteem, cakes we eat today. They currants, or other dried prunes, peaches, and pears, and nuts. The large breads yeast that was a by-product chemical leavening agents Today, it is almost as if we once again sweet fruited ever, some consider them a high calorie content from in the dried fruit) and the

OPPOSITE and ABOVE
Sandra's Saffron Buns

made from soft, rich doughs and took the place of the were flavored with raisins, fruits, such as apricots, and sometimes with spice were leavened with the from brewing ale until became generally available. have come full cycle, and breads are in fashion; how-luxurious treat due to the the sugar (both refined and fat they contain.

In this chapter, I want to introduce you to traditional fruit and nut breads. The London (page 131), Bara Wales, and the similar Barm

pass on my enthusiasm and and modern varieties of famous Chelsea Buns of Brith (page 129) from Brack (page 128) from Ire-

a cake. More modern fruit and nut breads include Viola's Caramel Cinnamon Rolls (page 127) from America, the attractive Peach Couronne (page 134), and the light Hazelnut, Apricot, and Honey Loaf (page 133). If all these seem too sweet, try the Walnut Bread (page 136), which is excellent with a good farmhouse cheese.

These breads are easy to make and do not require much skill, so they're ideal for introducing children to bread-making. You will find that homemade fruit and nut breads, including the ever-popular sticky buns, are light, moist, and full of flavor. They really are worth making, because many of the commercial varieties have become dense, flavorless, and far too sweet.

SANDRA'S SAFFRON BUNS

INGREDIENTS

Makes 14

1 teaspoon saffron strands

2 tablespoons lukewarm water

4 cups (455g) unbleached white bread
flour

½ teaspoon salt

7 tablespoons (85g) granulated sugar

1¼ cups (200g) mixed dried fruit such as
dark and golden raisins and currants

2½ tablespoons (30g) chopped mixed
candied citrus peel

1½ cups (170g) unsalted butter, chilled
and diced

2 0.6-oz cakes fresh yeast (30g), or 2
envelopes active dry yeast (5 teaspoons)

¾ cup (170ml) lukewarm milk

2 tablespoons (30g) butter, melted

2½ tablespoons (30g) coarse granulated
sugar or raw brown sugar such as
Demerara

2 baking sheets, well greased

Quite by chance, Anthony Blake and I booked a fortnight's bed and breakfast stay at the house of one of Cornwall's finest bakers, named Sandra. She was apparently tireless, and relentlessly cheerful. No matter what time we looked into her kitchen, there she was baking, weighing warmed flour, rinsing dried fruit, kneading large balls of dough, and constantly checking the color of the loaves in the oven. Every day Sandra started at 5 A.M., finishing well after midnight, baking batch after batch of pungent saffron buns, which are her specialty, along with a few dozen pasties, and her standard white and whole-wheat loaves. We returned late after a day of photography to discover that, although Sandra had had a massive and shiny new oven installed after breakfast, she had not missed a beat with her baking.

Saffron is used a good deal in Cornish baking, despite the fact that the local saying "as dear as saffron" is all too apt. Good saffron is fabulously expensive because each saffron crocus produces only three stamens, which have to be laboriously plucked out with tweezers, and 4,000 stamens weigh only one ounce. Although nearly all our saffron now comes from Spain, until a hundred years ago it was grown extensively in England around the towns of Saffron Walden, in Essex, and Stratton, in Cornwall. For centuries, this expensive flavoring was used to make breads and cakes look and taste wonderfully rich. The best saffron buns, like these, are generously flecked with saffron filaments. As this dough is enriched with a fair quantity of butter, it takes quite a bit of time to rise, but the result is light textured, fine crumbed, rich, and highly aromatic. Eat the buns within two days of baking, spread with butter. These buns do not freeze well.

Put the saffron strands onto a heatproof saucer or in a small ovenproof skillet and toast in a 350°F oven for 10 to 15 minutes, or until their color darkens. Soak the saffron strands in the lukewarm water in a cup for at least 1 hour – it is best if you can leave it overnight.

Stir together the flour and salt in a large bowl. Stir in all but 1 teaspoon of the granulated sugar, all the dried fruit, and the mixed candied citrus peel. Rub in the butter with your fingertips until the mixture resembles fine crumbs.

Make a well in the center of the flour. Crumble the fresh yeast into a small bowl. Stir in the reserved 1 teaspoon sugar and half of the lukewarm milk. Let the yeast mixture stand for about 5 minutes, or until it starts to become foamy. If using dry yeast, mix the granules and the reserved 1 teaspoon sugar with half the lukewarm milk and let stand until foamy, 5 to 10 minutes (page 18).

Pour the saffron, its soaking liquid, and the yeast mixture into the well in the flour,

Golden yellow and studded with dark and golden raisins and currants, these saffron-flavored buns are best spread with creamy, unsalted butter or with cream cheese. The dough can also be shaped into one large loaf, which is ideal for slicing and toasting.

Above
SHAPE EACH PIECE OF DOUGH INTO A
NEAT BUN BY ROLLING IT BETWEEN
YOUR FLOURED PALMS.

Top
KNEAD THE DOUGH IN THE BOWL
UNTIL IT IS VERY SMOOTH AND
ELASTIC. PULL OFF FOURTEEN PIECES
OF DOUGH.

adding most of the remaining lukewarm milk. Using your hand, mix the flour mixture from the bowl into the liquid in the well until the dough comes together. If the dough is dry and crumbly, gradually add more lukewarm milk, 1 tablespoon at a time; the dough should be soft, but not sticky. Knead the dough in the bowl for 10 minutes, working it thoroughly against the side of the bowl, until it is very smooth and elastic. Cover with a damp dish towel and let rise, away from drafts, until doubled in size. This heavy dough is slow to rise and can take as long as overnight in a cool room, or 3 to 4 hours in a warm kitchen.

Punch down the dough. Using lightly floured hands, one at a time, pull off fourteen equal-size pieces of dough and roll each between your palms to form neat buns. Or, roll the dough into a fat rope and cut into fourteen equal pieces. Using floured hands, shape each portion into a bun. Put on the prepared baking sheets, spaced well apart. Cover with a damp towel and let rise at warm room temperature (about 75°F) until doubled in size, about 2 hours. During the last 15 minutes of rising, heat the oven to 375°F.

Bake the buns for 15 minutes. Then lower the oven temperature to 350°F and bake for 5 minutes longer, or until the buns sound hollow when tapped underneath. Brush the hot buns with melted butter and sprinkle with coarse sugar. Then bake for 3 minutes longer. Transfer to wire racks to cool completely.

NOTE. You can also make a saffron loaf, instead of buns. After the first rising, shape the dough into a loaf (page 24) and put it, seam side down, into a well-greased 10 × 5 × 3-inch loaf pan. Let rise as above, then bake in a 375°F oven 40 minutes. Lower the oven temperature to 350°F and bake for 15 to 20 minutes longer, or until the loaf sounds hollow when unmolded and tapped underneath. Brush with melted butter and sprinkle with the coarse sugar. Then bake 3 minutes longer. Unmold onto a wire rack to cool.

GENTLY WORK THE CANDIED FRUIT
AND ALMONDS INTO THE SOFT, RICH
DOUGH

ABOVE RIGHT
Serve slices of sugar-crusted pougno for a
delicious breakfast.

INGREDIENTS

Makes 1 small loaf

2 cups (230g) unbleached white bread
    flour

½ teaspoon salt

1 0.6-oz cake fresh yeast (15g), or
    1 envelope active dry yeast
    (2½ teaspoons)

2½ tablespoons (30g) sugar

2 tablespoons lukewarm milk

3 large eggs, beaten

extra flour for dusting

4 tablespoons (60g) butter, softened and
    diced

finely grated rind of 1 lemon and 1 orange

¾ cup (110g) finely chopped mixed
    candied fruits (see introduction)

½ cup (60g) roughly chopped blanched
    almonds

sugar for dredging

a baking sheet, greased

POUGNO

This bread, generously studded with fruits confits, or candied fruits — also called glacé or crystallized fruit — comes from the Provence region of southern France. The region is justly famous for preserving whole fruit, such as strawberries, mandarins, figs, tiny whole pineapples, and greengage plums, by cooking them in a concentrated sugar syrup. Pieces of fruit, such as pineapple rings, lemon and orange slices, and melon and pumpkin chunks, are also preserved in sugar. The confits are sold in the region's best grocers and confiseurs, and used for making cakes, breads, and pastries, as well as being eaten with a knife and fork at the end of a festive meal, usually Christmas.

Quality candied fruits are expensive because the preserving process is time-consuming and often done by hand. For the best flavor, do not used candied citrus peel from the supermarket. If you cannot get good candied fruit, use dark or golden raisins instead. In Provence, pougno is eaten for breakfast with bowls of very milky, strong coffee. It is best eaten within four days of baking, and can be frozen for up to one month.

Stir together the flour and salt in a warmed medium-size bowl and make a well in the center of the flour. Crumble the fresh yeast into a small bowl. Stir in the sugar and lukewarm milk until smooth. Let the yeast mixture stand for about 5 minutes, or until it starts to become foamy. If using dry yeast, mix the granules and the sugar with the lukewarm milk and let stand until foamy, 5 to 10 minutes (page 18).

Pour the eggs and the yeast mixture into the well in the flour. Mix in the flour from the bowl with your hand or a wooden spoon to make a soft dough. Turn out onto a lightly floured surface and knead for 10 minutes, or until it becomes smooth, shiny, and elastic.

Using your hand, with fingertips splayed, gently beat the butter into the dough until incorporated. Add the grated lemon and orange rinds, working in the same way.

Shape the dough into a ball. Wash, dry, and oil the bowl. Return the dough to the bowl, and turn the dough over so the top is oiled. Cover with a damp dish towel and let rise at room temperature, away from drafts, until doubled in size, about 2 hours.

Punch down the dough, then turn out onto a lightly floured surface. Gently work in the candied fruit and almonds until thoroughly incorporated. Shape the dough into a disk about 1½ inches thick and put it on the prepared baking sheet. Cover lightly with a damp dish towel and let rise at room temperature (about 75°F) until doubled in size, about 1 hour. During the last 15 minutes of rising, heat the oven to 375°F. Bake the loaf for 15 to 20 minutes, or until it is golden and sounds hollow when tapped underneath. Dredge in the sugar, then transfer to a wire rack to cool completely.

VIOLA'S CARAMEL CINNAMON ROLLS

Makes 15

1 0.6-oz cake fresh yeast (15g), or
   1 envelope active dry yeast
   (2½ teaspoons)

½ cup (115ml) lukewarm water

¼ cup (50g) #aa 1 teaspoon granulated
   sugar

4 tablespoons (60g) butter, diced

¾ teaspoon salt

1¼ cups (280ml) hot water (about
   150°F)

about 6 cups (680g) unbleached white
   bread flour

1½ tablespoons vital wheat gluten
   (optional)

1 large egg, beaten

extra flour for dusting

FILLING:

6 tablespoons (85g) butter, softened

7 tablespoons packed (85g) dark brown
   sugar

1 tablespoon ground cinnamon, or to taste

CARAMEL TOPPING:

1 cup packed (200g) dark brown sugar

½ cup (115ml) heavy cream

a roasting pan, about 13 × 9 inches, well
   greased

a baking sheet, lightly greased

INVERT THE ROLLS ONTO A BAKING
SHEET AND PULL APART TO SERVE.

The lightest, moistest, and gooiest sticky buns ever! Viola Unruh (page 45) says the secret to these rolls is to let the sweet, rich, and airy dough rise three times. This old-fashioned American prairie kitchen recipe, her husband Henry's favorite, is an absolute treasure. The vital wheat gluten Viola includes in every batch is unobtainable in Great Britain, yet may be purchased at health-food stores or by mail order in the States (page 360). However, the results are just as enjoyable when the dough is made without it. In England I use good-quality unrefined Barbados muscovado sugar, but dark brown sugar works well, too. This recipe makes plenty of caramel topping. When the rolls have cooled, store them, well wrapped, at room temperature, and eat them within two days.

To make the dough: Crumble the fresh yeast into a small bowl. Stir in the lukewarm water and the 1 teaspoon granulated sugar until smooth. Let the yeast mixture stand for 5 to 10 minutes, or until it starts to become foamy.

If using dry yeast, mix the granules and the 1 teaspoon sugar with the lukewarm water and let stand until foamy, 5 to 10 minutes (page 18).

Meanwhile, put the butter, the remaining granulated sugar, and the salt into a large bowl. Pour in the hot water and stir until the butter melts. Add 2 cups (230g) of the flour and the vital wheat gluten, if using, and beat together well with a wooden spoon until the mixture is very smooth. Pour in the yeast mixture and the egg and beat for 1 minute until well blended. Cover with a damp dish towel and let rest for 10 minutes.

Working in the bowl, gradually knead in 2 cups (230g) of the remaining flour to make a soft dough. Turn out the dough onto a lightly floured work surface and knead for 10 minutes, gradually working in as much of the remaining flour as is necessary, a handful at a time, to make a soft, but not sticky dough. Wash, dry, and oil the bowl.

Return the dough to the bowl, and turn the dough over to oil the top. Cover with a damp dish towel and let rise at room temperature, away from drafts, until doubled in size, about 1 hour. Punch down the dough. Leave the dough in the bowl, cover again and let rise again at warm room temperature (about 75°F) until almost doubled in size, about 1 hour.

Punch down the dough. Turn out onto a lightly floured work surface and knead for 1 minute. Cover with an upturned bowl and let rest for 10 minutes.

Meanwhile, make the filling: Beat the butter with the dark brown sugar and cinnamon in a medium-size bowl with a spoon or electric mixer until light and fluffy.

Roll out the dough on a lightly floured work surface with a lightly floured rolling pin into a 15 × 10-inch rectangle. Gently spread the filling over the rectangle, trying not to stretch the dough, spreading all the way to the edges. Then roll up tightly from a long side, like a jelly-roll. Cut the roll into fifteen even slices, each about 1 inch thick. Arrange the slices, with a cut side down, in the prepared baking pan, with the sides just touching. Cover with a damp dish towel and let rise at room temperature until doubled in size, about 45 minutes. (If the temperature is too warm, the filling will ooze out.) During the last 15 minutes of rising, heat the oven to 350°F.

Bake the rolls for 30 to 35 minutes, or until they are well risen and golden brown. (Viola recommends that you do not bake them too near the bottom of the oven.)

Meanwhile, make the caramel topping: Whisk the dark brown sugar and cream together in a small bowl until no lumps remain. Turn out the buns in one piece onto the baking sheet.

Pour the caramel topping into the baking pan. Tilt the pan so the topping covers the bottom evenly. Then slide the buns, upside-down, back into the pan on top of the caramel mixture. Return to the oven and bake 10 minutes longer. Remove from the oven and let the buns cool in the pan for 6 minutes. Invert the pan onto a baking sheet, so the caramel sauce is on top of the rolls. Pull the rolls apart to serve.

BARM BRACK

INGREDIENTS

Makes 1 loaf

4 cups (455g) unbleached white bread
    flour

1 teaspoon ground cinnamon

1 teaspoon pumpkin-pie spice

1 teaspoon salt

6 tablespoons (85g) butter, diced

7 tablespoons packed (85g) light brown
    sugar or granulated sugar

1 0.6-oz cake fresh yeast (15g), or
    1 envelope active dry yeast
    (2½ teaspoons)

½ cup (115ml) lukewarm milk

2 large eggs, beaten

extra flour for dusting

2 cups (280g) currants

1 tablespoon granulated sugar dissolved in
    2 tablespoons boiling water for glazing

an 8-inch round, deep cake pan, greased

This spicy loaf, dotted with currants, is from Ireland, where it was originally baked in a cast-iron pot suspended over a fire. Although now baked in conventional ovens, the bread is still made in a traditional round shape rather than as a loaf. The word "barm" in the name comes from the liquid ale yeast that was used to raise the dough before blocks of compressed yeast made bread-making easier.

Barm brack is a close cousin to bara brith (opposite), but it is sweeter and more cake-like. It keeps, well wrapped, for four or five days, or can be frozen for up to one month.

Put the flour, cinnamon, pumpkin-pie spice, and salt into a large bowl. Rub the butter into the flour with your fingertips until the mixture resembles fine crumbs. Stir in the sugar (reserve 1 teaspoon if using dry yeast). Make a well in the center of the flour mixture.

Crumble the fresh yeast into a small bowl. Stir in the lukewarm milk until smooth. If using dry yeast, mix the granules and the reserved 1 teaspoon sugar with the lukewarm milk and let stand until foamy, 5 to 10 minutes (page 18). Add the eggs to the yeast mixture and stir to mix. Pour the mixture into the well in the flour. Gradually work the flour from the bowl into the yeast and egg mixture to make a soft but not sticky dough. If the dough is dry and crumbly, add more milk or water, 1 tablespoon at a time. If the dough sticks to your fingers, add more flour, 1 tablespoon at a time.

Turn out the dough onto a lightly floured work surface and knead for about 10 minutes, until smooth and elastic. Gradually knead in the currants until evenly distributed, 4 to 5 minutes. Return the dough to the bowl (there is no need to oil the bowl for this recipe). Cover with a damp dish towel and let rise at room temperature, away from drafts, until doubled in size, 2 to 2½ hours.

Punch down the dough. Turn it out onto a floured surface and shape the soft dough into a round to fit the pan. Put the round into the prepared pan. Cover with a damp dish towel and let rise at room temperature, away from drafts, until doubled in size, 1 to 1½ hours. During the last 15 minutes, heat the oven to 400°F.

Bake the loaf for 50 to 60 minutes, or until it is browned and sounds hollow when unmolded and tapped underneath. If the loaf is browning too much during baking, cover loosely with butter wrappers or a sheet of foil.

Remove from the oven and brush with the hot, sweet glaze. Return to the oven for 2 minutes longer. Turn out onto a wire rack, glazed side up, and let cool completely.

ABOVE
Rich with currants, barm brack is served in Ireland for afternoon tea. It is just as delicious with a cup of coffee for a mid-morning snack.

RIGHT
Rural Ireland, where you can still see milk being transported by horse and cart, has a rich baking heritage. Accomplished home bakers keep traditional recipes alive, of which barm brack remains one of the most popular. More variations include golden raisins and candied citrus peel; if you wish, replace some of the currants with a tablespoon or two of diced candied peel.

A farmhouse afternoon tea: Teacakes For Toasting (page 130), Bara Brith, and Barm Brack (opposite).

BARA BRITH

INGREDIENTS

Makes 1 large loaf

1⅓ cups (230g) mixed dried fruit, such as dark and golden raisins, currants, and chopped candied citrus peel

1½ cups (340ml) strong hot tea

4 cups (455g) unbleached white bread flour

5 tablespoons packed (60g) light brown sugar

1 teaspoon salt

½ teaspoon pumpkin-pie spice

1 0.6-oz cake fresh yeast (15g), or 1 envelope active dry yeast (2½ teaspoons)

about 2 tablespoons lukewarm milk

4 tablespoons (60g) butter, melted and cooled

a loaf pan, about 10 × 5 × 3 inches, greased

The name of this speckled loaf from Wales means currant bread. I've also added dark and golden raisins and a bit of candied citrus peel for extra flavor. To avoid over-baking the loaf, be sure to check it after 30 minutes.

Put the mixed dried fruit and candied citrus peel into a medium-size bowl. Add the hot tea and stir well. Cover with plastic wrap and let soak overnight at room temperature.

The next day, place the flour, brown sugar (reserve 1 teaspoon if using dry yeast), the salt, and the spice into a large bowl. Rub the brown sugar into the flour with your fingers to break up any lumps and to mix the ingredients. Make a well in the center of the flour mixture.

Crumble the fresh yeast into a small bowl. Stir in the lukewarm milk until smooth. If using dry yeast, mix the granules and the reserved 1 teaspoon brown sugar with the lukewarm milk and let stand until foamy, 5 to 10 minutes (page 18). Pour the yeast mixture into the well in the flour. Add the melted butter and the fruit mixture with all the soaking liquid and stir with a wooden spoon to mix with the yeast mixture. Mix the flour from the bowl into the yeast and fruit mixture to make a soft dough. If the dough is dry and crumbly, add a little more milk, 1 tablespoon at a time. If the dough sticks to your fingers, add more flour, 1 tablespoon at a time.

Gently knead the dough in the bowl for 5 minutes, or until the fruit is evenly distributed and the dough is elastic; it will be quite soft. Turn out the dough onto a sheet of waxed paper and wash, dry, and oil the mixing bowl. Return the dough to the bowl, and turn the dough over so the top is oiled. Cover with a damp dish towel and let rise at room temperature, away from drafts, until doubled in size, 1½ to 2 hours.

Punch down the dough. Turn out the dough onto a floured surface and shape into a loaf to fit the prepared pan (page 24). Put the loaf, seam side down, into the pan. Cover with a damp towel and let rise at room temperature, away from drafts, until doubled in size, 1 to 1½ hours. During the last 15 minutes, heat the oven to 400°F. Bake the loaf for 30 to 40 minutes, or until it sounds hollow when unmolded and tapped underneath. If the loaf is browning too quickly during baking, cover it loosely with foil. Turn the loaf out of the pan onto a wire rack to cool.

Right
REMOVE THE TEACAKES FROM THE
OVEN WHEN THEY ARE GOLDEN
BROWN AND PUFFED UP.
Far right
SERVE TOASTED TEACAKES SPREAD
WITH BUTTER. TO TOAST THEM UNDER
A HOT BROILER, TOAST THE TOP AND
THE BOTTOM. SPLIT THE TEACAKES IN
HALF AND TOAST THE CUT SURFACES.

TEACAKES FOR TOASTING

INGREDIENTS

Makes 8

⅓ cup (60g) currants

2½ tablespoons (30g) chopped mixed
    candied citrus peel

⅔ cup (140ml) strong hot tea

about ⅔ cup (140ml) milk

1 0.6-oz cake fresh yeast (15g), or
    1 envelope active dry yeast
    (2½ teaspoons)

2½ tablespoons (30g) sugar

4 cups (455g) unbleached white bread
    flour

1 teaspoon salt

4 tablespoons (60g) lard or butter, chilled
    and diced

extra flour for dusting

milk for brushing

2 baking sheets, greased

My mother, like her mother before her, comes into her own at teatime. She possesses a china cupboard stacked from floor to ceiling with exquisite tea services, including some porcelain so eggshell-thin it is almost transparent; she enjoys using it, despite the hazards. Each day, teatime is an important ritual, even if it is "just family."

My American husband is greatly amused by the quaintness of this almost bygone English custom, although he has succumbed to its soothing comforts — even if he does insist on black coffee, instead of tea.

The best way to toast teacakes is under a very hot broiler, or over the red-hot embers of an open fire. These teacakes stale quickly so eat within one day, or you can keep for two days if you plan to toast them. They can also be frozen for up to one month. Thaw at room temperature before toasting.

Put the currants and candied citrus peel into a small bowl. Pour in the hot tea, stir well, and let steep for 1 hour. Drain the fruit in a strainer set over a measuring cup. Add enough milk to the tea soaking liquid to make 1¼ cups (280ml).

Crumble the fresh yeast into a small bowl. Stir in the tea mixture until smooth. If using dry yeast, note the amount of tea soaking liquid left after the fruit is strained. Reserve the tea. Measure an amount of milk that when added to the tea will total 1¼ cups (280ml) of liquid. Heat the measured amount of milk in a small saucepan to lukewarm. Mix the dry yeast granules and 1 tablespoon of the granulated sugar with the lukewarm milk and let stand until foamy, 5 to 10 minutes (page 18). Then stir in the tea soaking liquid.

Mix together the flour and salt in a large bowl. Rub in the lard or butter with your fingertips until the mixture resembles fine crumbs. Stir in the sugar (the remaining 1 tablespoon if using the dry yeast) and the soaked currants and candied citrus peel. Make a well in the center of the flour mixture.

Pour the yeast mixture into the well. Mix the flour from the bowl into the liquid in the well with your hand or a wooden spoon to make a soft dough. Turn out the dough onto a lightly floured work surface and knead for 10 minutes until smooth and elastic.

Return the dough to the bowl. (There is no need to oil the bowl.) Cover with a damp dish towel and let rise at room temperature, away from drafts, until doubled in size, 1½ to 2½ hours, depending on the weather and the temperature of the room.

Gently punch down the dough. Turn out the dough onto a lightly floured work surface. Weigh the dough and divide it into eight equal pieces, or roll it into a fat rope and cut it into eight equal pieces. Shape each portion into a neat roll (see Oatmeal Rolls, page 25). Flatten each roll so it is about 5 inches wide and ¾ inch thick. Arrange the teacakes on the prepared baking sheets, spaced well apart. Cover loosely with a damp dish towel and let rise at room temperature until almost doubled in size, about 45 minutes. During the last 15 minutes of rising, heat the oven to 400°F.

Glaze the teacakes with milk. Bake them for about 20 minutes until they are golden brown and puffed up.

Transfer to wire racks. Lightly dust each teacake with flour, then cover loosely with dry dish towels to keep the crusts soft. Let them cool completely.

CHELSEA BUNS

INGREDIENTS

Makes 9

4 cups (455g) unbleached white bread
 flour

1 teaspoon salt

3 tablespoons (40g) granulated sugar

1 0.6-oz cake fresh yeast (15g), or
 1 envelope active dry yeast
 (2½ teaspoons)

¾ cup (170ml) lukewarm milk

1 extra large egg, beaten

4 tablespoons (60g) butter, melted

extra flour for dusting

FILLING:

3 tablespoons (40g) butter, melted

⅓ cup packed (70g) light or dark brown
 sugar

1 cup (140g) mixed dried fruit, such as
 dark and light raisins, currants, and
 mixed candied citrus peel

STICKY GLAZE:

7 tablespoons packed (85g) light brown
 sugar

4 tablespoons (60g) butter

¼ cup (60ml) milk

2 tablespoons honey

an 8- to 9-inch square cake pan about
 1½ inches deep, greased

For about a hundred years, until its demise in 1839, the Chelsea Bun House was famous for its spicy, sugary, sticky buns. Situated in Bunhouse Place, off Pimlico Road, in London, the bakery was hugely fashionable, the place to be seen standing in line to buy a Chelsea bun. The owners also claimed to have invented the hot cross bun. In fact, the bakery's hot cross buns were in such demand that one Good Friday, thousands of people, including King George III, thronged down Ebury Street toward the shop. Eat these within two days of baking.

To make the dough: Mix together the flour, salt, and half the sugar in a large bowl. Make a well in the center of the flour mixture. Crumble the fresh yeast into a small bowl. Stir in the remaining sugar and the lukewarm milk until smooth. If using dry yeast, mix the granules and the sugar with the lukewarm milk and let stand until foamy, 5 to 10 minutes (page 18).

Pour the yeast mixture into the well in the flour and mix enough flour from the bowl into the liquid with your hand or a wooden spoon to make a thick batter. Let stand until spongy, about 10 minutes. Beat the egg and melted butter into the spongy mixture with your hand or a small whisk. Gradually work in the flour from the bowl to make a soft, but not sticky dough. If the dough is dry, add water or milk, 1 tablespoon at a time.

Turn out the dough onto a lightly floured work surface and knead for 10 minutes until very smooth, elastic, and satiny. Wash, dry, and oil the bowl. Return the dough to the bowl, and turn the dough over so the top is oiled. Cover with a damp dish towel and let rise at room temperature, away from drafts, until doubled in size, about 1½ hours.

Punch down the dough. Turn out the dough onto a floured work surface and roll out with a floured rolling pin into a 16 × 9-inch rectangle, with a long side facing you.

For the filling: Brush the dough with the melted butter. Then sprinkle with the sugar, followed by the mixed dried fruit and the candied citrus peel, leaving a ½-inch border all around the edge. Starting from the long side, roll up the dough fairly tightly, like a jelly roll. Cut the roll into nine even pieces and arrange them, cut side down, in the prepared pan, touching but not squashed together. Cover the pan with a damp dish towel and let rise at room temperature, away from drafts, until almost doubled in size, 30 to 40 minutes. During the last 15 minutes of rising, heat the oven to 400°F.

To make the sticky glaze: Combine the brown sugar, butter, milk, and honey in a small saucepan and heat over moderately low heat, stirring frequently, until the butter melts and the sugar dissolves. Bring to the boil, then simmer for 1 minute. Pour the glaze over the risen buns. Bake the buns for 25 to 30 minutes, or until golden brown.

Cool in the pan for about 10 minutes, or until the topping is firm, but not set. Then transfer the buns to a wire rack set over a sheet of foil and let cool. If the topping is left too long and welds onto the pan, put the pan back in the oven until the topping softens again. Pull or tear the buns apart when they have cooled.

POUR THE STICKY GLAZE OVER THE RISEN
BUNS, THEN BAKE.

COOL THE BUNS ON A WIRE RACK, THEN PULL
OR TEAR APART TO SERVE.

GERMAN PEAR LOAF

INGREDIENTS

Makes 1 loaf

1 cup (170g) chopped dried pears
⅓ cup (60g) chopped dried figs
⅓ cup (60g) chopped pitted prunes
⅔ cup (140ml) apple or prune juice
⅔ cup (140ml) water from the cold tap
3½ cups (395g) unbleached white bread
   flour
⅔ cup (60g) rye flour
7 tablespoons packed (85g) light brown
   sugar
1 teaspoon salt
1 0.6-oz cake fresh yeast (15g), or
   1 envelope active dry yeast
   (2½ teaspoons)
2 tablespoons lukewarm water
grated rind of 1 lemon
1 cup (110g) mixed chopped blanched
   almonds and hazelnuts
extra flour for dusting

a baking sheet, greased

A loaf packed with dried fruit and nuts, but not as rich, heavy, or moist as the densely fruited Hutzelbrot from Nuremberg (page 151). This is traditionally served with a glass of kirsch or fruit liqueur, but is equally good with coffee for breakfast. Eat within one week of baking, or freeze for up to one month.

Mix together the pears, figs, and prunes in a medium-size bowl. Add the apple or prune juice and cold water and stir well. Cover with plastic wrap and let soak overnight.

The next day, drain the fruit in a strainer set over a bowl. Put the fruit into a small bowl and cover with cling film. Set the fruit and the soaking liquid aside.

Put the white flour, rye flour, sugar (if using dry yeast, reserve 1 teaspoon of the sugar), and salt into a large bowl. Rub the ingredients together with your fingertips to break up any lumps of brown sugar and to combine the ingredients. Make a well in the center of the flour mixture.

Crumble the fresh yeast into a small bowl. Stir in the 2 tablespoons lukewarm water until smooth. If using dry yeast, mix the granules and the reserved 1 teaspoon sugar with the lukewarm water and let stand until foamy, 5 to 10 minutes (page 18).

Pour the yeast mixture and the reserved fruit soaking liquid into the well in the flour. Mix in the flour from the bowl with your hand or a wooden spoon to make a soft but not sticky dough. If the dough seems too wet and sticky, add more white flour, 1 tablespoon at a time. If the dough is dry, add more water, 1 tablespoon at a time.

Turn out the dough onto a lightly floured work surface and knead for 10 minutes or until smooth and elastic. Return the dough to the bowl. (There is no need to oil the bowl.) Cover with a damp dish towel and let rise at room temperature, away from drafts, until doubled in size, about 1½ hours.

Punch down the dough. Turn out onto a lightly floured surface and press out into a rough rectangle. Sprinkle the soaked fruit, lemon rind, and nuts over the dough, then gently knead until they are evenly distributed, about 5 minutes. Shape the dough into an oval loaf (see The Basic Loaf, page 17) about 10 inches long. Place the loaf, seam side down, on the prepared baking sheet. Cover with a damp dish towel and let rise at room temperature, away from drafts, until it again doubles in size, 1–1½ hours. During the last 15 minutes of rising, heat the oven to 350°F.

Bake the loaf for 1–1¼ hours, or until it is golden brown and sounds hollow when tapped underneath. Transfer to a wire rack to cool completely.

HAZELNUT, APRICOT, AND HONEY LOAF

INGREDIENTS

Makes 2 small loaves

1 0.6-oz cake fresh yeast (15g), or
   1 envelope active dry yeast
   (2½ teaspoons)

⅔ cup (140ml) lukewarm milk

1 tablespoon well-flavored honey

¾ cup (110g) roughly chopped dried
   apricots

⅔ cup (140ml) boiling water

4 cups (455g) unbleached white bread
   flour

¾ cup (85g) toasted and halved hazelnuts

1 teaspoon salt

2 tablespoons hazelnut oil, or 2 tablespoons
   (30g) butter, melted

extra flour for dusting

⅔ cup (60g) rye flour

2 loaf pans, about 7 × 5 × 3 inches,
   greased

This recipe uses hazelnut oil, more expected on salads than in breads, along with a flavorful honey, such as orange blossom, heather, or wildflower. I was given this recipe by Shaun Hill of Gidleigh Park, in Devon, England. Eat this loaf within three days, or toast and serve with butter or cheese. It can be frozen for one month.

Crumble the fresh yeast into a small bowl. Stir in the lukewarm milk and honey until smooth. Let the yeast mixture stand 5 to 10 minutes, or until it starts to become foamy. If using dry yeast, mix the granules with the lukewarm milk and the honey and let stand until foamy, 5 to 10 minutes (page 18). Meanwhile, put the apricots into a small bowl. Pour in the boiling water and let soak for about 10 minutes, or until the fruit has plumped up and the water cooled to lukewarm. Mix together 3½ cups (400g) flour, the hazelnuts, and the salt in a large bowl and make a well in the center.

Pour the yeast mixture into the well in the flour mixture, followed by the hazelnut oil or melted butter, and the apricots and their soaking liquid. Mix together all the ingredients in the well with your hand or a wooden spoon. Then gradually work the flour from the bowl in to the liquid in the well to make a soft, but not sticky dough. If the dough sticks to your fingers, work in the rest of the flour, as needed, 1 tablespoon at a time.

Turn out the dough onto a lightly floured work surface and knead for 10 minutes until smooth and fairly firm. Return the dough to the bowl (there is no need to oil the bowl). Cover with a damp dish towel and let rise at room temperature, away from drafts, until doubled in size, 1½ to 2 hours.

Punch down the dough. Turn it out onto a surface covered with the rye flour. Divide it in half. Knead each portion in the rye flour for 1 minute, then shape into a loaf to fit one of the pans (see A Plain White Loaf, page 24). Put a loaf, seam side down, into each prepared pan. Cover with a damp dish towel and let rise at room temperature until almost doubled in size, about 45 minutes. During the last 15 minutes of rising, heat the oven to 425°F.

Bake the loaves for 35 to 40 minutes, or until they are golden brown and sound hollow

LET THE LOAVES RISE IN THE PAN UNTIL ALMOST DOUBLED IN SIZE.

This twisted ring with its unusual fruit and nut filling can be served as a coffee cake, or as a winter dessert. It is especially good with pouring cream, or vanilla-scented, lightly whipped heavy cream. The intricate-looking shape is surprisingly easy to make, but you should allow yourself plenty of time for your first attempt.

when unmolded and tapped underneath. Turn out onto a wire rack to cool completely.

PEACH COURONNE

Dried peaches plus raisins and walnuts make a deliciously tart filling for this pretty ring. The dried peaches can be replaced by an equal quantity of dried apricots, if you wish. Serve the couronne warm as a dessert, with cream if you like, or at teatime. Eat within one day, or freeze for only one week.

Place the peaches in a small bowl. Pour in the orange juice and let soak overnight.

To prepare the dough: Mix the flour and salt in a medium-size bowl. Rub in the butter until the mixture resembles fine crumbs. Make a well in the center of the flour mixture. Crumble the fresh yeast into a small bowl. Stir in the lukewarm milk until smooth. If using dry yeast, mix the granules and the ½ teaspoon sugar with the lukewarm milk and let stand until foamy, 5 to 10 minutes (page 18). Mix the egg into the yeast mixture.

Pour the yeast mixture and the egg into the well. With your hand, gradually work the

INGREDIENTS

Makes 1 large ring

¾ cup (110g) chopped dried peaches

⅔ cup (140ml) orange juice

2 cups (230g) unbleached white bread flour

½ teaspoon salt

3 tablespoons (40g) butter, chilled and diced

⅔ 0.6-oz cake fresh yeast (10g), or ⅔ envelope active dry yeast (2 teaspoons) plus ½ teaspoon granulated sugar

5 tablespoons (70ml) lukewarm milk

1 large egg, beaten

extra flour for dusting

2 tablespoons granulated sugar

2 tablespoons cold milk (optional)

FILLING:

6 tablespoons (85g) butter, softened

5 tablespoons packed (60g) light brown sugar

3½ tablespoons (30g) unbleached all-purpose flour

⅓ cup (60g) walnut pieces

6½ tablespoons (60g) raisins

grated rind of 1 orange

a baking sheet, greased

flour from the bowl into the liquid to make a soft, but not sticky dough. Turn out the dough onto a floured work surface and knead for 10 minutes until smooth, elastic, and satiny.

Shape the dough into a ball. Return it to the bowl. Cover with a damp dish towel and let rise at room temperature, away from drafts, until doubled in size, about 1 hour.

Meanwhile, prepare the filling: Drain the peaches, reserving the soaking liquid. Beat the butter and brown sugar in a medium-size bowl with an electric mixer on medium-high speed until fluffy. On low speed, beat in the flour, then the walnuts, raisins, orange rind, and peaches. Or, stir them in with a wooden spoon.

Punch down the dough. Turn out the dough onto a floured work surface and with a floured rolling pin roll out into a 12 × 9-inch rectangle. Spread the filling evenly over the dough. Roll the dough up fairly tightly from a long side, like a jelly roll. Gently roll the dough back and forth, stretching it, until it is 20 inches long.

Carefully cut the dough in half lengthwise. Working with the cut sides facing up, twist the halves together. Lift gently onto the prepared baking sheet and shape the twisted roll into a neat ring, twisting and pinching the ends together to close the ring. Cover loosely with a damp dish towel and let rise at room temperature, away from drafts, until doubled in size, about 1 hour. During the last 15 minutes of rising, heat the oven to 400°F.

Bake the ring for 20 to 25 minutes, or until firm and golden. Stir the sugar with the cold milk or 2 tablespoons of the reserved peach soaking liquid in a small saucepan and bring to a boil, stirring to dissolve the sugar. Remove the couronne from the oven and immediately brush with the hot glaze. Slide onto a wire rack to cool.

SPREAD THE FILLING EVENLY OVER THE DOUGH. ROLL UP THE DOUGH FROM A LONG SIDE, AS FOR A JELLY ROLL.

USING A VERY SHARP KNIFE, CAREFULLY CUT THE DOUGH IN HALF LENGTHWISE.

WORKING WITH THE CUT SIDES FACING UP, TWIST THE TWO HALVES TOGETHER.

BRING THE ENDS OF THE DOUGH TOGETHER TO CLOSE THE RING. PINCH THEM TO SEAL.

LOIS'S FRUIT SLICE

INGREDIENTS

Makes 2 large fruit slices

1 0.6-oz cake fresh yeast (15g), or
    1 envelope active dry yeast
    (2½ teaspoons)

½ cup (100g) #aa 2 teaspoons sugar

¾ cup (170ml) lukewarm water

1 cup (230ml) heavy cream

1 teaspoon salt

2 large eggs, beaten

2 tablespoons (30g) butter, melted

about 6 cups (680g) unbleached white
    bread flour

extra flour for dusting

FILLING:

1½ lb (680g) prune plums, halved and
    pitted, or 1¼ lb (570g) fresh berries,
    such as blueberries, blackberries,
    raspberries, and pitted sour cherries

1½ tablespoons cornstarch or 2 tablespoons
    tapioca

about 1½ cups (300g) sugar

CRUMBLE TOPPING:

¾ cup (110g) unbleached all-purpose
    flour

½ cup #aa 2 tablespoons (130g) sugar

½ cup (110g) butter, at room
    temperature

2 baking sheets with edges or jelly-roll
    pans, about 14 × 8 inches, greased

Lois Keller with a freshly baked fruit slice.

Here is another recipe from Lois Keller (page 103), who lives in the heart of America — indeed, she is almost exactly at America's center, if you fold the map in fourths. This recipe, from her husband's German family, uses white flour, and is one of the few recipes Lois makes with refined flour. (She prefers to grind her own flour from whole wheat kernels.) Lois likes to use the wild berries that grow around her farm, or the German purple-blue plums she also grows, which are packed with flavor. You may use the European type of plums called prune plums. Prune plums are small, dark purple, and usually freestone plums with pointed, not rounded, ends. Grown in California, the Pacific Northwest, Michigan, and New York State, they become available in August. This coffee cake is eaten with coffee for breakfast or mid-afternoon tea. It is best eaten within two days of baking.

To prepare the dough: Crumble the fresh yeast into a large bowl. Stir in the 2 teaspoons sugar and the lukewarm water until smooth. If using dry yeast, mix the granules and the 2 teaspoons sugar with the lukewarm water and let stand until foamy, 5 to 10 minutes (page 18). In a medium-size bowl, whisk the cream with the remaining sugar and the salt just until mixed. Whisk in the eggs and melted butter until well blended.

Add 1½ cups (170g) flour to the yeast mixture and mix in with your hand. Stir in the cream mixture. Then work in enough of the remaining flour to make a very soft dough. If the dough seems too sticky, work in a little extra flour, 1 tablespoon at a time. If the dough is dry and crumbly, work in a little extra water, 1 tablespoon at a time. Turn out the dough onto a lightly floured work surface and knead with floured hands for 10 minutes to form a smooth and satiny ball. The dough should be soft rather than dry or tough. Return the dough to the bowl. Cover with a damp dish towel and let rise at room temperature, away from drafts, until doubled in size, about 1 hour. During the last 15 minutes of rising, heat the oven to 350°F.

Meanwhile, prepare the filling. Mix together the plums, berries, or cherries, the cornstarch or tapioca, and sugar to taste in a large bowl. (If the fruit is very sweet you'll need less sugar than listed.) Cover and let stand while the dough is rising.

To prepare the crumble topping: Mix together the flour and sugar in a medium-size bowl. Using a fork, work in the butter to make coarse crumbs. Set aside.

Punch down the dough. Turn out the dough onto a floured surface and knead for 30 seconds. Divide the dough in half. Roll out each portion on a floured work surface with a floured rolling pin into a rectangle about ¼ inch thick, the same size as the prepared baking sheets or jelly-roll pans. Roll up the dough loosely on the rolling pin and unroll onto the sheets or pans, patting the dough with your hands into the corners, forming a slight rim on all sides. Spoon half the fruit filling evenly over each piece of dough. If using plums, arrange them cut-side up on the dough. Sprinkle half of the crumble topping evenly over each coffee cake. Bake the cakes for 30 to 35 minutes, or until the base is golden and firm. Serve warm with cream.

WALNUT BREAD

Toasting the walnut halves until lightly browned gives this loaf a dense, nutty flavor. Some bakers also add a tablespoon or two of walnut oil or melted butter with the last of the water. Eat this loaf within three days of baking, or freeze for up to one month.

Stir together the whole-wheat and white flours and the salt in a large bowl and make a well in the center. Crumble the fresh yeast into a small bowl. Stir in half of the lukewarm water and the honey until smooth. If using dry yeast, mix the granules and the honey with half of the lukewarm water and let stand until foamy, 5 to 10 minutes (page 18).

Walnut Bread variations in this photo include sliced Raisin Bread.

INGREDIENTS

Makes 2 medium loaves

4 cups (455g) whole-wheat bread flour,
   preferably stone-ground

2 cups (230g) unbleached white bread
   flour

2½ teaspoons salt

1 0.6-oz cake fresh yeast (15g), or
   1 envelope active dry yeast
   (2½ teaspoons)

2 cups (460ml) lukewarm water

1½ tablespoons well-flavored honey

1 tablespoon walnut oil or melted butter
   (optional)

extra flour for dusting

2½ cups (230g) walnut halves, toasted,
   cooled and roughly chopped

1 or 2 baking sheets, greased

Pour the yeast mixture into the well in the flour. Mix in enough flour from the bowl with your hand to make a thick batter. Let stand until spongy, 10 to 15 minutes.

If necessary, reheat the remaining water to lukewarm. Pour the water into the sponge, along with the oil or melted butter, if using. With your hand or a wooden spoon, gradually work the flour from the bowl into the sponge to make a soft, but not sticky dough. If the dough sticks to your fingers, work in a little extra flour, 1 tablespoon at a time. If the dough is dry and crumbly, work in a little extra water, 1 tablespoon at a time. Turn out the dough onto a lightly floured work surface and knead for 10 minutes until smooth and elastic. Gently knead the walnuts into the dough until they are evenly distributed, about 2 minutes. Wash, dry, and oil the bowl.

Shape the dough into a ball. Return the dough to the bowl, and turn the dough over so the top is oiled. Cover with a damp dish towel and let rise at room temperature, away from drafts, until doubled in size, about 2 hours.

Punch down the dough. Turn it out onto a floured surface and knead gently for 1 minute. Divide in half. Shape each half into a neat ball and place on the prepared baking sheet(s). Cover with a damp dish towel and let rise at room temperature, away from drafts, until doubled in size, about 1½ hours. During the last 15 minutes of rising, heat the oven to 425°F. Cut three shallow slashes in the top of each loaf. Bake the loaves for 15 minutes. Then lower the oven temperature to 375°F and bake for 20 to 30 minutes longer, or until the loaves sound hollow when tapped underneath. Cool on wire racks.

VARIATIONS: PECAN BREAD Use 3 cups (340g) each whole-wheat bread flour (preferably stone-ground) and unbleached white bread flour and prepare the dough as for the Walnut Bread. Replace the walnuts with an equal amount of coarsely chopped, untoasted pecans.

MIXED NUT BREAD Prepare the dough as for the Walnut Bread. Replace the walnuts with 2½ cups (280g) coarsely chopped, toasted mixed nuts, such as walnuts, skinned hazelnuts, pecans, and/or macadamia nuts.

RAISIN BREAD Prepare the dough as for the Walnut Bread, replacing up to 1 cup (110g) of the whole-wheat flour with rye flour, if you wish. Replace the walnuts with 1½ cups (225g) raisins.

FRUIT AND NUT BREAD Prepare the dough as for the Walnut Bread. Replace the walnuts with 1½ cups (225g) dark or golden raisins and 1½ cups (170g) coarsely chopped toasted walnuts.

CINDY'S PORTUGUESE SWEET BREADS

INGREDIENTS

Makes 2 loaves

⅓ cup (40g) currants

1 tablespoon orange juice, rum, Madeira, sherry, or hot water

2 0.6-oz cakes fresh yeast (30g), or 2 envelopes active dry yeast (5 teaspoons)

1¼ cups (280ml) lukewarm water

¾ cup (150g) granulated sugar

¼ cup (30g) dry milk powder

7–8 cups (795–900g) unbleached white bread flour

3 large eggs, beaten

½ cup (110g) unsalted butter, softened

1 teaspoon salt

extra flour for dusting

1 egg beaten with a pinch of salt for glazing

Demerara or granulated sugar for sprinkling

a 9-inch round deep cake tin, greased

a large baking sheet

Called pao doce in Portuguese, this recipe makes two loaves, one with currants and braided, and the other shaped like a small snail, called caracois.

Cindy Falk (page 52) was given this recipe by a colleague in the Kansas Wheat Commission, and now her eleven-year-old daughter Laura uses it to win baking competitions. Laura makes the neatest braid I have ever seen. To ensure a good shape to your loaf, do not let the shaped dough over-rise or leave it in too warm a place to rise.

Eat this bread sliced and buttered within two days of baking. If you do not plan to eat both loaves, wrap and freeze one loaf for up to two months.

Put the currants in a small bowl. Add the 1 tablespoon of the liquid of your choice and let stand for 1 hour, or until the currants are softened.

Crumble the fresh yeast into the bowl of an electric mixer fitted with a dough hook, or into a large bowl. Mix in 4 tablespoons lukewarm water and 1 teaspoon of the granulated sugar until smooth. Let stand about 5 minutes, or until it starts to become foamy. If using dry yeast, mix the granules and 1 teaspoon of the granulated sugar with 4 tablespoons lukewarm water and let stand until foamy, 5 to 10 minutes (page 18). Add the rest of the water and sugar, the milk powder, and 3 cups (340g) of the flour. Beat on medium speed with a dough hook for 2 minutes, or with your hand or a wooden spoon for 4 minutes, until it is a smooth, thick batter.

With the mixer on low speed, gradually add the eggs, the butter, and the salt and mix until thoroughly combined, or mix in the ingredients with your hand or a wooden spoon. Add enough of the rest of the flour, a handful at a time, to make a soft, but not sticky dough that gathers in a ball around the dough hook or comes together and leaves the sides of the bowl cleanly. Knead the dough on slow speed for 5 minutes until it is smooth and feels "as silky as a baby's behind," as Cindy says. Or, turn out the dough onto a floured work surface and knead for about 10 minutes until smooth and soft.

Wash, dry, and oil the bowl. Return the dough to the bowl, and turn the dough over so the top is oiled. Place the bowl in a large greased plastic bag and tie closed, or cover the bowl with a damp dish towel, and let rise at room temperature, away from drafts, until doubled in size, about 2 hours.

Punch down the dough. Turn it out onto a lightly floured work surface and divide into two equal portions. With lightly floured hands, knead the softened currants and any soaking liquid that has not been absorbed into one portion of the dough. Cover both portions of dough with a damp dish towel and let rest at room temperature, away from drafts, for 20 minutes.

Shape the plain portion of dough into the snail loaf: Roll out the dough with your lightly floured hands into a rope 25 inches long and 1½ inches thick. Coil the rope in the

LET THE BRAIDED LOAF RISE AT ROOM TEMPERATURE, AWAY FROM DRAFTS, UNTIL DOUBLED IN SIZE, ABOUT 1 HOUR.

*TO MAKE CINDY'S SPECIAL BRAID,
ARRANGE TWO OF THE DOUGH ROPES
IN A CROSS ON THE PREPARED BAKING
SHEET. PLACE THE THIRD ROPE
STRAIGHT THROUGH THE MIDDLE, TO
MAKE A STAR SHAPE. BEGIN BRAIDING,
FOLLOWING THE DIRECTIONS IN THE
NOTE (BELOW RIGHT).*

TOP
*A selection of breads baked by Cindy Falk
(page 52), including the highly glazed
Portuguese Sweet Breads shaped into a long
braid and as a snail. Other loaves include her
Multi-grain Harvest Bread (page 51), which
was baked in a loaf pan, and two round
Pioneer Breads (page 52). For this
photograph, Cindy slashed the Pioneer Breads
with a checkerboard design, rather than the
star shape suggested in the recipe.*

prepared cake pan, starting in the center and twisting the dough as you coil it around to form a snail shape, and tuck the ends under. Place the pan in a large greased plastic bag and tie closed, or cover with a damp dish towel, and let rise at room temperature, away from drafts, until doubled in size, about 1 hour.

After you've shaped the snail loaf, make the braided loaf. On a lightly floured work surface, divide the currant dough into three equal pieces. Roll out each piece of dough with floured hands into a 16-inch-long rope. Lay the three ropes side-by-side on the prepared baking sheet, then braid the strands together neatly, but not too tightly. (See page 31 and the Note.) Tuck the ends under and pinch to seal. Cover with a damp dish towel and let rise at room temperature, away from drafts, until doubled in size, about 1 hour. During the last 15 minutes of rising, heat the oven to 350°F.

When each loaf has doubled in size, brush with the egg glaze, taking care not to let it dribble down the sides or "glue" the dough to the pan or baking sheet. Sprinkle each with the coarse sugar. The snail loaf will probably be ready to bake before the braid, depending on how warm your kitchen is and how quickly you formed the braid. Slide another baking sheet under the sheet holding the braid to prevent the bottom of the loaf from browning. Put each loaf into the oven when it is ready; the baking times will overlap. Bake each loaf for 30 to 40 minutes, or until it is golden brown and sounds hollow when tapped underneath. Cover the loaves with foil during baking if they appear to be browning too quickly. Transfer to wire racks to cool completely.

NOTE: Another way to braid the loaf is to arrange two of the ropes in a cross shape on the prepared baking sheet. Place the third rope straight through the middle, to make a star shape. Braid the three ropes racing toward you, then turn the baking sheet around and braid the three other ends. This gives a slightly more unusual shape to the loaf. Pinch the ends together and tuck under to give a neat shape.

CELEBRATION BREADS

These elaborate, lightly textured, and richly flavored breads are intended to be a contrast to everyday breads. They often take a special place of pride on tables around the world during Christmas, Easter, the Jewish Sabbath, and Christian harvest celebrations. Made with generous quantities of expensive butter and eggs, these loaves are flavored with spices, honey, candied fruit peels, dried fruits, and nuts. You could be forgiven for thinking the loaves in this chapter are more like cakes than breads.

Yet it is not just the taste that lets you know these breads are out of the ordinary. They look special. Alice's Christmas Loaf (page 158) from Czechoslovakia and the Jewish challahs (page 168) are lovingly braided, using up to nine strands of dough to create intricate patterns. The Alsatian Kugelhopf (page 152), and the Italian Panettone (page 155) are baked in molds that instantly herald a celebration. My husband says my towering Panettone reminds him of a monument. (The Leaning Tower of Pisa, perhaps?) Fluted kugelhopf molds are so attractive that they often double as kitchen decorations in Alsace.

OPPOSITE
A Bulgarian farmer's harvest loaf.
ABOVE An altar harvest loaf.

Even the more familiar English Hot Cross Buns (page 160) are finished with a flour and water paste to make them special for Good Friday observances. Loaves shaped to look like sheaves of wheat (page 164) have been made by generations of British country bakers to mark a successful harvest. Served at harvest suppers held in church halls, this decorative loaf came to symbolize the end of hard labor for farm workers and a time of plenty for most farms. This custom is still followed throughout Europe, as you can see from the decorated round loaf proudly displayed by the jovial Bulgarian farmer (opposite). That loaf was made by the local bakery to celebrate a bountiful wine harvest. You can make such a loaf to eat at a Thanksgiving meal; or, bake it for much longer in a very low oven to create an attractive, nonedible decoration (page 165).

Some of the loaves in this chapter can be very time-consuming to make, so if you want to make a celebration bread in a hurry, I suggest you try Bishops Bread (page 160). This is a quick bread as it is not yeast-raised and therefore has no lengthy rising times.

If you do have some free time to spare, however, I hope you will try one of the more elaborately braided loaves, or the Harvest Wheat Sheaf (page 164). These are delicious breads, and not as difficult to make as they look, although they do require time and patience, especially for the first attempt. Anyone who does not feel confident at braiding dough should try Caroll's Twisted Ring (page 170). Strips of the dough are simply braided together, then the loaf is baked in a tube pan so it does not lose its shape.

SPICE MIXTURES

Like many good bakers, Brigitte prefers the pungency of freshly ground spices. Here she crushes cardamom seeds to add a subtle, yet distinctive, flavor to the stollens.

Fragrant spices are important ingredients in these recipes. And if, like me, you have tired of the blandness of commercial ground mixed spices, you will take great pleasure in making your own blends.

Even in 1907, Master Baker John Kirkland (page 65) was writing about the importance of "giving your spice mixture special considerations." His formula was 6 tablespoons (30g) each of ground coriander, ground cinnamon, and ground ginger; 2 tablespoons plus 2 teaspoons (15g) freshly grated nutmeg; and 2 tablespoons (10g) ground white peppercorns or ground allspice.

More recently, Elizabeth David suggested grinding together 1 large nutmeg, 1 tablespoon white peppercorns or whole allspice, 30 whole cloves, a 2-inch piece of dried gingerroot, and a little cumin seed.

You will notice that both these combinations make a small quantity. I suggest you make up a batch when you need it, rather than storing a large amount.

BRESLAU STOLLEN

INGREDIENTS

Makes 1 large loaf

9 cups (1kg) unbleached white bread flour

2 tablespoons (15g) coarse sea salt, crushed or ground

7 0.6-oz cakes fresh yeast (100g), or 7 envelopes active dry yeast (scant 6 tablespoons)

1 cup (200g) granulated sugar

about ½ cup #aa 3 tablespoons (155ml) lukewarm milk

1½ cups (230g) whole blanched almonds, chopped finely or roughly

3⅓ cups (500g) raisins

½ cups (250g) chopped mixed candied citrus peel

1 cup (150g) currants

grated rind of 2 large lemons

½ teaspoon ground cardamom

½ teaspoon freshly grated nutmeg

2 cups (1lb/455g) unsalted butter, soft but not melted

4 extra large eggs, beaten

extra flour for dusting

about 3 cups (1½ lb/680g) unsalted butter for brushing

confectioners' sugar for sprinkling

a large baking sheet, greased

Breslau, in Silesia, formerly part of Germany but now in Poland, is where my friend Brigitte Friis's mother came from. Brigitte's mother always made these extravagant weihnachtsstollens several weeks before Christmas. The cardamom is an inspired touch. Liberal applications of melted butter brushed over the stollens after baking are traditional – the stollens absorb the butter, resulting in a moist, ultrarich, cakelike taste and texture.

Sift the flour and salt into a very large bowl. Make a well in the center of the flour. Crumble the fresh yeast into a medium-size bowl. Stir in 1 tablespoon of the sugar and the lukewarm milk until smooth. If using dry yeast, mix the granules and 1 tablespoon of the sugar with the lukewarm milk and let stand until foamy, 5 to 10 minutes (page 18).

Pour the yeast mixture into the well. Work in a little of the flour into the yeast mixture to make a thick batter. Sprinkle with a little flour to prevent a skin forming. Cover with a dry dish towel and let stand in a warm place (about 75°F) for 15 to 20 minutes until spongy.

In a medium-size bowl, mix the almonds, raisins, candied citrus peel, currants, and the lemon rind. Add 2 tablespoons of the flour from the other bowl and toss to coat. Stir in the spices.

Mix the remaining sugar into the sponge. Add the butter and mix it with the sponge and the flour in the bowl by gently turning the mixture over with your hand until the flour is almost worked in. Gradually add the eggs and work the mixture with your hand until it forms a soft dough that holds its shape. If the dough is too sticky, add flour, 1 tablespoon at a time. If the dough is too dry, add milk, 1 tablespoon at a time.

Turn out the dough onto a well-floured work surface and "knead until it begins to show bubbles," says Brigitte. Large bubbles or blisters should appear after 10 minutes. Re-flour the work surfaces as necessary. The dough will become firmer and more pliable and you should be able to feel the bubbles.

Pat out the dough into a large rectangle about 1-inch thick, with a long side facing you. Spread the fruit and nut mixture along the center of the dough. Fold in the two long edges so they meet in the center. Fold in the short ends. Then, working from the right-hand side, fold the dough over to make a small package. Continue folding the dough over and over on itself, pressing down very lightly with your hand and giving the dough a

BRIGITTE FOLDS DOWN THE TOP
THIRD OF THE DOUGH TO MAKE A
THREE-LAYER RECTANGULAR DOUGH
SANDWICH.

AFTER THE DOUGH HAS RISEN THE
SECOND TIME, IT WILL BE DOUBLE IN
SIZE AND BE READY TO BAKE.

*Fruity and spicy, this butter-rich stollen is
ideal for holiday entertaining.*
*For easier mixing and kneading, you can
transfer the flour mixture to a stationary
mixer fitted with a dough hook before you
add the eggs. Add the eggs, then knead on low
speed for 5 to 10 minutes, until the dough
becomes firm and pliable.*

quarter turn after each folding. Do not worry if the odd piece of fruit escapes; just put it back as make the next fold.

Brigitte incorporates the fruit this way, instead of kneading it into the dough. It takes at least 5 minutes and must be done gently. The dough should not be streaky or sticky, and it will be very soft. Shape the dough into a ball and dust lightly with flour. Return the dough to the bowl if it is large enough, or leave the dough on the floured surface. Cover it with dry dish towels. Let rise at warm room temperature (about 75°F), away from drafts, until doubled in size, about 2 hours.

Turn out the dough onto the floured surface (if it is in the bowl). Punch down the dough. You should hear the air being expelled as you do this. Knead it for 1 minute. Pat out the dough with lightly floured hands to a large rectangle about ½-inch thick, with a long side facing you. Fold the bottom third of the dough up and fold the top third down, to make a long, narrow rectangle with three layers. Pat to round the corners for a neat shape. Slide a second baking sheet under the prepared baking sheet to prevent the stollen from browning too much on the base. Transfer the stollen to the baking sheet. Cover with a dry dish towel and let rise at warm room temperature (75°F), away from drafts, until doubled in size, about 2 hours. During the last 15 minutes of rising, heat the oven to 350°F.

Place the stollen, on the doubled baking sheets, on an oven rack set in the middle position. Bake for 1¾ to 2 hours, or until golden brown and firm, and a skewer inserted into the center comes out clean. If the stollen appears to be browning too quickly during baking, cover with butter wrappers or parchment paper.

Melt 1 cup (230g) of the butter. As soon as the stollen comes out of the oven, brush or smear the butter over the loaf. It should gradually absorb all this butter. Transfer to a wire rack and let cool completely. When cool, wrap in waxed paper and then foil and leave at room temperature.

The next day, heat the oven to 350°F. Unwrap the stollen and place on a baking tray. Warm in the oven for 10 minutes. Melt ¾ cup (170g) of the remaining butter. Remove the stollen from the oven and brush with melted butter until the loaf will not absorb any more. Transfer to a wire rack to cool completely, then wrap in waxed paper and foil again.

Repeat this procedure for the next two days, using the rest of the butter. When the stollen has cooled after the final buttering, sift a thick layer of confectioners' sugar over the top. It is traditionally wrapped in cellophane and tied with a red ribbon, but waxed paper and foil will do. Keep the stollen in a cool place, but not the refrigerator, for at least two weeks and up to six weeks, before serving.

KUGELHOPF

INGREDIENTS

Makes 1 large loaf

about 2 tablespoons (30g) unsalted butter, very soft, for greasing

⅔ cup (60g) sliced almonds

3½ cups (395g) unbleached white bread flour

½ teaspoon salt

1 0.6-oz cake fresh yeast (15g), or 1 envelope active dry yeast (2½ teaspoons)

5 tablespoons (60g) granulated sugar

1 cup (230ml) lukewarm milk

3 large eggs, beaten

grated rind of 1 lemon

6–10 tablespoons (85–140g) unsalted butter, softened, to taste

¾ cup (110g) mixed dark and golden raisins

confectioners' sugar for dusting

a 9- to 10-inch kugelhopf mold

Jugelhopfs are easy t identify with their distinctive shapes.

These pretty, almond-topped, fluted loaves can be found in Austria and Germany, as well as in Alsace, France, where the recipe originated. Clarisse Deiss, whose husband Jean-Michel makes the most exquisite wines at Bergheim, in Alsace, became both my culinary guide to the region and wine tutor.

Kugelhopf is the region's traditional celebration cake, baked for weddings, baptisms, wine harvests, and Christmas. The dough is similar to that used for brioche, but the kugelhopf is studded with fruit and sometimes flavored with lemon rind. At Easter, the sweet dough is baked in the shape of a fish or a lamb, and its richness depends on how much butter is included. "If you buy a kugelhopf, always go to a pâtisserie, rather than a boulangerie, because it will contain more butter," Clarisse advised.

The traditional, high-fluted mold is made of earthenware with a hole in the center, which allows the heat to penetrate to the middle of the dough for more even and thorough baking. Molds that are highly decorated on the outside are used for kitchen ornaments when not being used in the oven. Indeed, an elaborate mold was once an essential part of a woman's trousseau. On the wedding day, the bride would be given the family kugelhopf recipe by her mother.

I bought a selection of earthenware molds, some unglazed and plain on the outside, at Ribeauvillé, France, from a shop within sight of the town's famous local attraction — nesting storks. I should add that an equally important event is the town's kugelhopf festival, held each June. Although the earthenware molds are perhaps the prettiest, nonstick, glass, and metal heatproof molds can also be used. But remember, metal molds bake the quickest — a kugelhopf made in an earthenware mold will take about 10 minutes longer to bake than one made in a metal mold. This will keep for up to one week if tightly wrapped in foil, or it can be frozen for one month.

Thickly coat the mold with the 2 tablespoons butter. Evenly line the mold with the almonds by pressing them against the base and sides so they stick. Chill the mold while preparing the dough.

Mix together the flour and salt in a medium-size bowl and make a well in the center. Crumble the fresh yeast into a small bowl. Stir in the sugar and the lukewarm milk until smooth. If using dry yeast, mix the granules and ½ teaspoon of the sugar with half of the lukewarm milk and let stand until foamy, 5 to 10 minutes (page 18). Stir in the

remaining sugar and lukewarm milk.

Pour the yeast mixture into the well in the flour. With your hands, work enough flour from the bowl into the yeast mixture to make a thick batter. Cover with a damp dish towel and let stand at room temperature until spongy, about 30 minutes (page 16).

Add the eggs and lemon rind to the sponge in the well and mix together with a small whisk or your hand. Gradually mix the flour from the bowl into the sponge with your hand to make a very soft and sticky dough. Beat the dough in the bowl with your hand, slapping it up and down, for 5 minutes, or until it becomes firmer, smooth, very elastic, and glossy.

Beat in the butter, beating the dough until the butter is evenly incorporated. Gently mix in the fruit with your hand until evenly incorporated.

Carefully spoon the dough into the chilled mold without dislodging the almonds. The mold should be half full. Cover with a damp dish towel and let rise at warm room temperature (about 75°F), away from drafts, until the dough has almost doubled in size and has risen to about 1 inch below the mold's rim, 40 to 50 minutes. During the last 15 minutes of rising, heat the oven to 400°F.

Bake the kugelhopf for 40 to 50 minutes, or until the loaf is golden brown and a skewer inserted in the center comes out clean. Cover the loaf loosely with butter wrappers or parchment paper if it appears to be browning too quickly during baking. Cool the loaf in the mold for 5 minutes. Then carefully turn it out onto a wire rack to cool completely. To serve, dust with confectioners' sugar by sifting it over the cake. Offer slices of kugelhopf with a glass of Alsatian wine, such as a Tokay Pinot Gris.

SAVORY KUGELHOPF

Clarisse Deiss (opposite) also makes kugelhopfs without the sugar and dried fruit, using bacon or ham instead. The region of Alsace is renowned for cured pork, and one of Alsace's famous dishes, choucroute garni, is rich with smoked or salted pork, bacon, and meaty sausages.

This savory kugelhopf is served in Alsace with an aperitif such as a glass of Riesling or Gewurztraminer before dinner. Eat this loaf within three days of baking.

Thickly coat the mold with the 2 tablespoons butter. Evenly line the inside of the mold with the walnuts, pressing the pieces against the base and sides so they stick. Chill the mold while preparing the dough.

Prepare the dough as for the Kugelhopf (opposite), using the flour, salt, pepper (adding the pepper to the flour), yeast, milk, eggs, and butter.

If using dry yeast, mix the granules and the ½ teaspoon granulated sugar with ½ cup of the lukewarm milk and let stand until foamy, 5 to 10 minutes (page 18). Stir in the remaining lukewarm milk.

Meanwhile, while the dough is "sponging," fry the bacon (if using it) in a medium-size skillet over medium heat until crisp, but not too brown. Remove the bacon pieces with a slotted spoon to paper towels to drain well and cool. Fold in the bacon or ham after beating the butter into the dough.

Carefully spoon the dough into the mold without dislodging the walnuts. Cover with a damp dish towel and let rise at warm room temperature (about 75°F) until the dough has almost doubled in size and has risen to about 1 inch below the mold's rim, 40 to 50 minutes.

During the last 15 minutes or rising, heat the oven to 400°F. Bake as for the Kugelhopf (opposite), but omit the dusting of confectioners' sugar. Cool the loaf in the mold for 5 minutes. Then carefully turn it out onto a wire rack to cool completely.

The best of Alsace – a glass of Jean-Michel Deiss' finest, crisp white wine, a kugelhopf, and a thick, moist pear loaf, another regional specialty. (This one is darker than my recipe for pear loaf on page 132.) The kugelhopf was baked by Clarisse Deiss. She used an old family recipe and baked it in the unglazed, earthenware mold she was given on her wedding day as tradition dictates.

INGREDIENTS

Makes 1 large loaf

about 2 tablespoons (30g) unsalted butter, very soft, for greasing

⅔ cup (60g) walnut halves

3½ cups (395g) unbleached white bread flour

1 teaspoon salt

freshly ground black pepper

1 0.6-oz cake fresh yeast (15g), or
   1 envelope active dry yeast
   (2½ teaspoons) plus ½ teaspoon sugar

1 cup (230ml) lukewarm milk

3 large eggs, beaten

6–10 tablespoons (85–140g) unsalted butter, softened, to taste

4 oz (110g) thick-sliced bacon or cooked full-flavored ham such as York, Westphalian, or Smithfield, diced

a 9- to 10-inch kugelhopf mold

Twinkling lights and traditional decorations herald the start of the Christmas season in Nuremberg's Christkindelmarkt. Shoppers buy slices of spicy hutzelbrot to nibble as they brows for gifts, or they purchase whole loaves to share with family and friends.

HUTZELBROT

This Bavarian Christmas bread is packed with dried fruits and nuts. It is sold in the traditional Advent markets held in town squares throughout southern Germany.

The oldest of these markets is the Nuremberg Christkindelmarkt. It is held from the Friday before the beginning of Advent until Christmas Eve. The market — with food, toys, and decorations — began about 1639. With row upon row of red-and-white striped stalls, all iced with snow, the market is decorated with tiny white lights, fir tree garlands, and Christmas motifs.

The chilly air is laced with enticing smells — frying sausages, hot spicy gluhwein, caramelized almonds, and roasting chestnuts. Rich and fruity hutzelbrots are sold by the slice, so even their fragrant aroma adds to the atmosphere. Eat this bread sliced and buttered, toasted, or with honey.

Mix together the pears, prunes, figs, dark and golden raisins, dates, kirsch or brandy, and lemon rind in a large bowl. Pour in enough of the boiling water to cover the fruit. Stir well, cover, and let soak overnight.

INGREDIENTS

Makes 2 loaves

1⅔ cups (230g) chopped dried pears

1 cup (200g) chopped pitted prunes

⅔ cup (85g) chopped dried figs

¾ cup (120g) mixed dark and golden
  raisins

¼ cup (30g) chopped dried pitted dates

2 tablespoons kirsch or brandy

grated rind of ½ lemon

about ¾ cup (170ml) boiling water

about 3½ cups (400g) unbleached white
  bread flour

1 teaspoon ground cinnamon

½ teaspoon salt

a large pinch each ground cloves and
  aniseed

1 0.6-oz cake fresh yeast (15g), or
  1 envelope active dry yeast
  (2½ teaspoons)

about 1¼ cups (280ml) lukewarm water

2 tablespoons packed light brown sugar

1 tablespoon honey

extra flour for dusting

6 tablespoons (60g) whole blanched
  almonds, lightly toasted and chopped

⅓ cup (60g) hazelnuts, lightly toasted,
  skinned, and chopped

⅔ cup (60g) sliced almonds for decorating
  (optional)

a large baking sheet, greased

The next day, drain the fruit, reserving any liquid, although most should have been absorbed. Set the fruit aside, covered.

Sift together the flour, cinnamon, salt, cloves, and aniseed in a large bowl. Make a well in the center of the flour mixture. Crumble the fresh yeast into a small bowl. Mix together the fruit soaking liquid, if any, and enough lukewarm water to measure 1¼ cups (280ml). If necessary, heat the fruit liquid mixture in a small saucepan until lukewarm. Stir the brown sugar and the fruit liquid mixture into the yeast until smooth. If using dry yeast, mix the granules and the brown sugar with the lukewarm fruit liquid mixture and let stand until foamy, 5 to 10 minutes (page 18).

Pour the yeast mixture into the well in the flour along with the honey. Mix these ingredients together briefly with a small whisk or your hands. Then mix the flour from the bowl into the yeast mixture with your hand or a wooden spoon to make a soft, but not sticky dough. If the dough is too sticky, work in a little extra flour, 1 tablespoon at a time. If the dough is dry and crumbly, work in a little extra water, 1 tablespoon at a time.

Turn out the dough onto a lightly floured work surface and knead for 10 minutes until smooth and elastic. Return the dough to the bowl (no need to wash or oil the bowl). Cover with a damp dish towel and let rise at room temperature, away from drafts, until doubled in size, about 1½ hours.

Punch down the dough. Turn out the dough onto a lightly floured work surface. Sprinkle the soaked fruit and chopped almonds and hazelnuts over the dough and gently knead for 2 to 3 minutes until they are evenly distributed. Divide the dough into two equal portions and shape each portion into an oval (see The Basic Loaf, page 15–17) Arrange the loaves on the prepared baking sheet. Cover with a damp dish towel and let rise at room temperature, away from drafts, until doubled in size, about 1½ hours. During the last 15 minutes of rising, heat the oven to 400°F.

To decorate the loaves, if you wish, gently press the sliced almonds lightly on the surface. Bake the loaves for 30 to 40 minutes, or until they are golden brown and sound hollow when tapped underneath. Loosely cover the loaves with butter wrappers or parchment paper if they are browning too quickly during baking. Transfer the loaves to wire racks to cool completely. Wrap the cooled loaves in waxed paper and overwrap in foil and keep at room temperature for at least 2 hours, or up to 1 week, before slicing. This helps the flavor to develop. After slicing, it stays fresh for five days.

PANETTONE

You can find panettone — prettily wrapped in cellophane, tied and hung by ribbons — in every Italian delicatessen in England (as well as in the States) as Christmas approaches. It is a specialty of Milan, where bakers vie to make the tallest, lightest, most delicate butter-rich loaf.

Since the classic tall, cylindrical panettone molds are difficult to find, some bakers use large 2-pound coffee cans. I prefer to use a 6-inch-round cake pan that has sides 3 inches high. I extend the pan about 4 inches upward by wrapping it on the outside with a stiff collar made of doubled heavy-duty foil that I secure with a paper clip, and on the inside with a sheet of buttered parchment paper, as if lining a soufflé dish.

For the best results, buy large pieces of candied orange and lemon peel and chop them yourself, as the flavor is much fresher than the ready-chopped variety from supermarkets.

Valentina Harris, the Italian food writer, once served me an excellent festive pudding made with panettone. She sliced off the domed top of the panettone, hollowed out the center slightly, filled it with a warm zabaglione, and replaced the top. You can also eat this loaf simply sliced into wedges like a cake within a week of baking. For the first couple of days after it is baked, this panettone will be moister than those bought from the bakery.

Mix together 2½ cups (280g) flour and the salt in a medium-size bowl and make a well

INGREDIENTS

Makes 1 loaf

about 3 cups (355g) unbleached white
    bread flour

½ teaspoon salt

1 0.6-oz cake fresh yeast (15g), or
    1 envelope active dry yeast
    (2½ teaspoons)

3 tablespoons lukewarm water

⅓ cup (70g) sugar

2 extra large eggs, beaten

2 extra large egg yolks

grated rind of 1 lemon

a few drops of vanilla extract

¾ cup (170g) unsalted butter, softened

extra flour for dusting

⅔ cup (85g) golden raisins

⅓ cup (60g) finely chopped candied orange
    and lemon peel

about 3 tablespoons (40g) butter for
    finishing

a panettone mold, greased, or a 6-inch
    round, deep cake pan, prepared with foil
    and parchment paper (see introduction)

*At holiday times, a buttery, fruit-studded
panettone makes a lovely gift, especially when
wrapped in cellophane and festooned with
ribbons.*

in the center of the flour mixture. Crumble the fresh yeast into a small bowl. Stir in the lukewarm water until smooth. If using dry yeast, mix the granules and ½ teaspoon of the granulated sugar with the lukewarm water and let stand until foamy, 5 to 10 minutes (page 18).

Pour the yeast mixture into the well in the flour. Add the sugar and beaten whole eggs to the well. Mix together these ingredients in the well with a small whisk or your hand. Then, with your hand or a wooden spoon, mix enough flour from the bowl into the mixture in the well to make a thick batter. Sprinkle the top with a little of the flour to prevent a skin forming. Let stand at room temperature, away from drafts, until spongy, 45 minutes to 1 hour (page 16).

Add the egg yolks, lemon rind, and vanilla extract to the sponge. Mix together these ingredients in the well. With your hand, gradually beat the remaining flour from the bowl into the sponge to make a soft and very sticky dough. Again using your hand, gradually beat the softened butter into the dough until thoroughly incorporated.

Turn out the dough onto a lightly floured work surface and knead, working in the remaining flour, for 10 minutes, or until soft, satiny, and pliable.

Return the dough to the bowl (no need to wash and oil the bowl). Cover with a damp dish towel and let rise at room temperature, away from drafts, until almost doubled in size, 2 to 2½ hours.

Punch down the dough. Cover with a damp dish towel and let rise again at room temperature, away from drafts, until doubled in size, 1 to 1½ hours.

Punch down the dough. Turn out onto a lightly floured work surface. Toss the golden raisins and chopped candied citrus peel with 1 teaspoon flour in a small bowl to prevent them from sticking together. Sprinkle the raisins and peel over the dough and gently knead in with lightly floured hands until the fruit is evenly distributed, 2 to 3 minutes.

Shape the dough into a ball and drop it into the prepared panettone mold or the lined cake pan. Using the tip of a long, sharp knife, score a cross in the top of the dough.

Cover with a damp dish towel and let rise at room temperature, away from drafts, until doubled in size, about 1 hour.

During the last 15 minutes of rising, heat the oven to 400·F.

Melt 2 tablespoons of the remaining butter in a small saucepan. Brush the top of the panettone with some of the melted butter. Put the third tablespoon of butter in the center of the cross.

Bake the panettone for 10 to 12 minutes, or until it begins to color. Then brush the top again with the rest of the melted butter. Lower the oven temperature to 350°F and bake for 30 to 40 minutes longer, or until the loaf is golden brown and a skewer inserted in the center comes out clean.

Remove the panettone from the oven. It will be fragile, so stand the mold on a wire rack for 5 minutes while the loaf firms up. Gently unmold the loaf and place it on its side on the wire rack to cool completely.

PLACE REMAINING BUTTER IN THE CENTER OF THE CROSS.

WHEN THE TOP BEGINS TO BROWN, BRUSH AGAIN WITH BUTTER.

I suggest using a mild-flavored olive oil for these decorative Provençal breads, rather than the heavier, fruity extra-virgin oil I more often use in breads. I think it is vital to use good-quality candied orange peel from gourmet shops or by mail order (page 360). It comes in large pieces and has more flavor than the ready-chopped variety from supermarkets. You can chop the peel as finely as you like. To keep it from sticking to the knife, sprinkle the peel with a little flour before you start.

FOUGASSES

INGREDIENTS

Makes 8 small loaves

6 cups (680g) unbleached white bread flour
¾ cup (170g) sugar
1½ teaspoons salt
1 0.6-oz cake fresh yeast (15g), or
    1 envelope active dry yeast
    (2½ teaspoons) plus ½ teaspoon sugar
about 6 tablespoons (85ml) lukewarm water
2 large eggs, beaten
6 tablespoons (85ml) mild olive oil
grated rind and juice of 1 large orange
1 tablespoon orange flower water
¾ cup (85g) chopped candied orange peel
extra flour for dusting
extra oil for brushing

several baking sheets, greased

This flat-bread recipe comes from Provence, where you find the best candied oranges and orange flower water. Fougasse usually forms the central part of the thirteen desserts (symbolizing the twelve disciples and Christ) that are served for the Christmas Eve meal in Provence. The meal usually begins with fish and vegetable dishes followed by a salad. Then come the thirteen desserts, which include a selection of nougats, raisins, dried figs, glacé fruits, and fresh fruits, such as figs, grapes, apples, clementines, and pears. All these are accompanied by a dessert wine.

Use a mild olive oil in this bread, and good-quality candied orange peel from a gourmet shop (you can buy the orange flower water there, too). Eat the fougasses the day they are baked.

Mix the flour, sugar, and salt in a large bowl and make a well in the center. Crumble the fresh yeast into a small bowl. Stir in the lukewarm water until smooth. If using dry yeast, mix the granules and the ½ teaspoon sugar with the lukewarm water and let stand until foamy, 5 to 10 minutes (page 18). Pour the yeast mixture into the well in the flour. Mix enough flour from the bowl into the liquid with your hand to make a thick batter. Let stand until spongy, about 10 minutes (page 16).

Meanwhile, whisk the eggs, oil, the orange rind and juice, and orange flower water in a medium-size bowl. Add to the sponge in the well and mix together with your hand. Gradually work in the flour from the bowl to make a soft, but not sticky dough. If the dough is dry, add extra water, 1 tablespoon at a time. If the dough sticks to your fingers, add extra flour, 1 tablespoon at a time.

Turn out the dough onto a lightly floured work surface and knead for 10 minutes until smooth and elastic. Wash, dry, and oil the bowl. Return the dough to the bowl, and turn it over to oil the top. Cover with a damp dish towel and let rise at room temperature, away from drafts, until doubled in size, about 1½ to 2 hours.

Punch down the dough. Turn it onto a floured surface and knead in the candied orange peel until distributed, about 5 minutes. Divide the dough into eight equal pieces. Roll out each piece to a ½-inch thick oval that is 9 inches long and about 6 inches wide. Cut eight or nine slits in the top, in a herringbone design. Arrange the fougasses, spaced well apart, on the prepared baking sheets. Lightly cover with a damp dish towel and let rise until almost doubled in size, about 1 hour. During the last 15 minutes of rising, heat the oven to 400°F. Lightly brush the fougasses with olive oil. Place each baking sheet on another sheet to prevent the bottoms from burning. Bake for 15 to 20 minutes, or until the fougasses are golden brown and sound hollow when tapped on the bottom.

Transfer to wire racks to cool completely.

CUT EIGHT OR NINE SLITS IN EACH TOP, IN A HERRINGBONE DESIGN

Nine strands of dough are braided together to make this elaborate, almond-studded loaf. Using a freshly ground spice mixture (page 148), instead of pumpkin-pie spice, adds a fresh flavor.

If you don't have time to make the braid, shape the dough into rolls instead. It will make about 25 rolls; follow shaping instructions for Oatmeal Rolls, page 25. Brush the shaped rolls with egg glaze, top each with a halved almond, let rise, uncovered, at cool room temperature until almost doubled in size, 30–45 minutes. Gently glaze again, then bake at 375°F for about 25 minutes, or until the rolls are golden brown and sound hollow when tapped underneath. Cool on wire racks.

ALICE'S CHRISTMAS LOAF

INGREDIENTS

Makes 1 large loaf

2 cups (230g) whole-wheat bread flour, preferably stone-ground

1 0.6-oz cake fresh yeast (15g), or
   1 envelope active dry yeast
   (2½ teaspoons)

1 tablespoon packed light brown sugar

1½ cups (280ml) lukewarm milk or water, or a mixture of the two

4 cups (455g) unbleached white bread flour, preferably stone-ground

½ cup + 2 tablespoons (110g) granulated sugar

½ cup (110g) unsalted butter, diced

1 teaspoon each ground cinnamon and pumpkin-pie spice, or to taste

grated rind of 1 lemon

2 large eggs, beaten

extra flour for dusting

¾ cup (110g) mixed dark and golden raisins

1 egg beaten with a pinch of salt for glazing

about ⅔ cup (85g) sliced or halved almonds for decorating

a baking sheet lined with parchment paper

thin bamboo skewers

While Anthony Blake and I were visiting Mary Curtis in Ireland (page 88), she took us to meet her friends Gerry and Alice Turner. While Gerry makes wonderful sourdough bread for everyday (page 182), Alice bakes for special occasions with family recipes, including this elaborate Czech loaf with nine strands of dough braided together. Her trick of securing the shape of the braid with bamboo skewers while it rises should be useful to anyone new to shaping dough braids. Look for the skewers in Asian shops. Eat this loaf within four days.

Put the whole-wheat flour into a medium-size bowl and make a well in the center. Crumble the fresh yeast into a small bowl. Stir in the brown sugar and the lukewarm liquid until smooth. If using dry yeast, mix the granules and the brown sugar with half of the lukewarm liquid and let stand until foamy, 5 to 10 minutes (page 18). Stir in the remaining lukewarm liquid. Pour the yeast mixture into the flour. Work the flour from the bowl into the yeast mixture to make a thick batter. Cover with a damp towel and let stand at room temperature, away from drafts, until spongy, about 1 hour.

Mix together the white flour and granulated sugar in a large bowl. Rub in the butter with your fingertips until the mixture looks like fine crumbs. Stir in the cinnamon, pumpkin-pie spice, and the lemon rind. Make a well in the flour mixture. Add the eggs. Then pour in the sponge. Mix the ingredients in the well with a small whisk. Then, with your hand, mix the flour from the bowl into the yeast mixture to make a soft, but not sticky dough. If the dough is dry and crumbly, add milk, 1 tablespoon at a time. If the dough is too sticky, add flour, 1 tablespoon at a time.

Turn out the dough onto a floured surface and knead for 10 minutes until firm, pliable, and smooth. Return to the bowl. Cover with a damp dish towel and let rest at room temperature for 30 minutes.

Turn out the dough onto a floured surface. Roll out the dough, rolling away from you with a floured rolling pin, into a rectangle, about 1½ inches thick, with a short side facing you. Sprinkle one-third of the raisins over the dough, leaving a ½-inch border at the edges. Fold up the bottom third of the dough, then fold down the top third to make a three-layer dough sandwich, as for the Aberdeen Butteries (page 202). Give it a quarter turn to the left so the completely enclosed side is to your left. Roll out to a rectangle again. Sprinkle with another one-third of the raisins, and proceed as above. Repeat the process to incorporate the remaining raisins. Knead the dough just enough to form a ball. Be careful not to overwork the dough. Return the dough to the bowl and cover. Let rise at cool room temperature until doubled in size, 3 to 8 hours.

Punch down the dough. Roll it into a fat rope and cut it into nine pieces. To make the elaborate braid, first make a four-strand braid.

To make a four-strand braid: With floured hands, roll out four pieces of dough into ropes 14 inches long and 1 inch thick. Pinch the ends together firmly at one end. Arrange the four strands side by side and slightly apart, with the unattached ends facing you. Move the strand on the far left under the two strands to its right. Twist the same strand over the last strand it went under, which was originally the third strand from the left. Move the strand on the far right under the twisted two strands in the center. Twist the same strand over the last strand it went under; it then becomes the third strand from the left.

Repeat this process until all the strands are braided. Pinch the ends together. Transfer the braid to the prepared baking sheet and tuck under the ends for a neat finish. Using the edge of your hand, make an indentation lengthwise down the center of the braid.

To make a three-strand braid: Roll out three of the remaining portions of dough into 16-inch-long ropes. Braid the three strands together as for the Braided Loaf (page 31). Carefully place the three-strand braid in the indentation on top of the four-strand braid. Tuck the top ends under the bottom braid for a neat finish. Using the edge of your hand, make an indentation lengthwise down the center of this braid.

Knead the remaining two pieces of dough together with your hands and roll out into a 20-inch-long rope. Place the index finger of your left hand in the center of the rope and press down to hold the rope. Fold the dough over your finger, then wind the two pieces of the strand together to make a twisted rope. Place this in the indentation on top of the assembled braid and tuck the loose ends of the twisted rope under itself.

Pat the loaf to make a neat, high, slim loaf. Insert bamboo skewers near each end and the center. Brush with the egg glaze. Decorate liberally with the almonds, pressing them into the surface. Let rise, uncovered, at cool room temperature until almost doubled in size, 30 minutes to 1 hour. Take care not to over-rise the dough. During the last 15 minutes, heat the oven to 425°F. Brush the loaf with the egg glaze. Bake the loaf for 10 minutes. Lower the temperature to 375°F and bake for 25 to 35 minutes, or until it is firm and golden brown, and sounds hollow when tapped underneath. If the loaf seems to be browning too quickly during baking, cover with butter wrappers or parchment paper. Transfer to a wire rack to cool. Carefully remove the skewers.

TO TOP THE LOAF, ALICE WINDS THE TWO STRANDS OF DOUGH AROUND HER FINGER TO MAKE A TWISTED ROPE.

SHE GENTLY PLACES THE TWIST ON TOP OF THE ASSEMBLED BRAID.

ALICE BRUSHES THE LOAF A SECOND TIME WITH THE EGG GLAZE. THE SKEWERS HELP THE LOAF KEEP ITS SHAPE WHILE BAKING.

*SPOON THE BRANDY OVER THE
FRESHLY BAKED LOAF*

RIGHT
*For easy entertaining over the Christmas
holidays, make this fruit and nut loaf and
serve it with liqueur or brandy.*

BISHOPS BREAD

A friend in Australia sent me this recipe for a Christmas ring loaf, which seemed most peculiar at first glance. Almost solid with fruit and nuts, the loaf is held together with a little batterlike dough, and after baking is soused in brandy. Because it does not contain yeast and is not decorated or iced, it is a very quick recipe to make – which really is welcome with all the last-minute rush surrounding Christmas.

INGREDIENTS

Makes 1 loaf

6 oz (170g) candied pineapple

⅓ cup (60g) candied cherries

⅓ cup (60g) crystallized ginger

1¼ cups (170g) raisins

2 cups (230g) unbleached white bread
    flour

⅔ cup (60g) walnut halves

⅓ cup (60g) pecan halves

⅓ cup (60g) whole blanched almonds

⅓ cup (60g) Brazil nuts

1 teaspoon baking powder

¼ teaspoon salt

2 extra large eggs

5 tablespoons packed (60g) light brown
    sugar

¼ cup (60ml) brandy

a jelly-roll pan

a deep 8-inch round cake pan, greased and
    bottom lined with waxed paper

a 15-oz empty can, label removed and can
    cleaned, well greased on the outside

Heat the oven to 400°F. To prepare the fruit and nuts: Rinse the pineapple, candied cherries, and ginger in a strainer with hot water. Drain, and then dry well on paper towels. If necessary, cut the pineapple and ginger into small chunks. Halve the cherries. Mix the pineapple, cherries, and ginger with the raisins in a medium-size bowl. Then toss with 1 tablespoon of the flour to coat the fruit.

Spread the nuts in an even layer on the jelly-roll pan. Toast in the oven for about 10 minutes, or until very lightly browned, stirring occasionally. Let the nuts cool, but do not chop them. Lower the oven temperature to 300°F.

Stir together the remaining flour, baking powder, and salt in a large bowl. Add the fruit mixture and cooled nuts and mix together well. Put the eggs and sugar in another large bowl and beat with an electric mixer on medium speed until pale and thick. By hand, stir in the flour mixture until well blended. You will have a stiff mixture of fruit and nuts bound together by a little batter. Position the well-greased can in the middle of the prepared cake pan. Spoon the batter into the cake pan around the can and smooth the surface with the back of the spoon.

Bake the bread for 1¼ hours, or until the loaf is firm and golden brown. Remove from the oven and immediately spoon the brandy evenly over the bread. Let the bread cool in the pan on a wire rack. Then turn out the bread. Store at room temperature, wrapped in waxed paper and overwrapped in foil. Eat within a week.

HOT CROSS BUNS

Betty Charlton, who gave me this recipe, lives near Norwich, in Norfolk, England. She is a great baker of yeast doughs and makes the best hot cross buns, according to Joy Skipper, who has assisted Anthony Blake and me with this book. Joy has diligently tasted every bread described in the recipes.

INGREDIENTS

Makes 24

8 cups (900g) unbleached white bread
 flour

½ cup + 1 tablespoon (110g) sugar, or
 to taste

2½ teaspoons pumpkin-pie spice, or to
 taste

1 teaspoon salt

1½ cups (230g) mixed dried fruit, such
 as dark and golden raisins, currants,
 and chopped mixed candied citrus peel

2 0.6-oz cakes fresh yeast (30g), or 2
 envelopes active dry yeast (5 teaspoons)

2 cups (460ml) lukewarm water

¾ cup (85g) nonfat dry milk powder

½ cup (110g) butter or margarine,
 softened

2 large eggs, beaten

extra flour for dusting

1 large egg beaten with 1 tablespoon milk
 for glazing

TOPPING:

¼ cup (35g) all-purpose flour

1 tablespoon sugar

¼ cup (60ml) water

1 or 2 baking sheets, greased

Betty likes to use all unbleached white bread flour from her local mill, Reads. You can, however, replace a portion of the white flour with stone-ground whole-wheat bread flour. These buns are very moist and light, packed with fruit and spice. They are delicious freshly baked on Good Friday, and are equally good for the rest of the Easter weekend when split, toasted, and buttered. If you do not eat all the buns within three days, they will freeze for up to one month. The hot cross buns I tasted in the States were sweeter and less spicy than the British ones, so add more sugar or spice if you prefer.

Heat the oven to its lowest setting. Mix together the flour, sugar (reserving 1 teaspoon if using dry yeast), spice, salt, mixed dried fruit, and candied citrus peel in a large bowl. Make a well in the center of the flour mixture. Put the bowl in the oven for 5 to 8 minutes to warm the ingredients while you prepare the yeast.

Crumble the fresh yeast into a medium-size bowl. Stir in the lukewarm water and nonfat dry milk powder until smooth. If using dry yeast, mix the granules and the reserved 1 teaspoon granulated sugar with ½ cup (110ml) lukewarm water and let stand until foamy, 5 to 10 minutes (page 18). Stir in the milk powder and the remaining lukewarm water. Then stir in the butter or margarine until melted.

Pour the yeast mixture into the well in the warmed flour mixture. Add the eggs to the well and blend together with the yeast mixture with a small whisk or your hands. With your hand or a wooden spoon, gradually work the flour from the bowl into the yeast mixture to make very soft, but not sticky dough. If the dough is dry and crumbly, work in water, 1 tablespoon at a time. If too sticky, work in flour, 1 tablespoon at a time.

Turn out the dough onto a floured surface and knead for 10 minutes, or until smooth and elastic. Return the dough to the bowl. Cover with a damp dish towel and let rise at warm room temperature (about 75°F) until doubled in size, 30 minutes to 1 hour.

Punch down the dough. Turn out onto a lightly floured surface and knead gently for 5 minutes until very smooth and elastic. Weigh the dough and divide it into twenty-four equal portions, or roll it into a fat rope and cut it into twenty-four pieces. Shape each portion into a neat roll (see Oatmeal Rolls, page 25). Arrange fairly close together, but not touching, on the prepared baking sheet. Cover with a damp dish towel and let rise at warm room temperatures until the buns have almost doubled in size and have joined together, 30 to 45 minutes. During the last 15 minutes of rising, heat the oven to 500°F.

While the buns are rising, make the topping: In a small bowl, mix the flour and sugar with enough of the water to make a thick, smooth paste. Spoon the paste into a small pastry bag fitted with a narrow, plain tip. With the back of a table knife, make an indentation about ¼-inch deep in the shape of a cross on the top of each bun. Brush the buns with the egg glaze. Pipe a cross of the flour paste over the indentation on each bun.

Put the buns in the oven, then immediately lower the oven temperature to 400°F and bake for 15 to 20 minutes, or until the buns are nicely golden brown. Transfer the buns to a wire rack to cool. When completely cool, pull the buns apart.

BETTY PIPES THE FLOUR PASTE OVER
THE INDENTATION ON TOP OF EACH
BUN.

*Spicy and fruity hot cross buns are
traditionally baked on Good Friday
throughout the Christian world.*

HARVEST WHEAT SHEAF

INGREDIENTS

Makes 1 large loaf

12 cups (1.35kg) unbleached white bread
   flour

2½ tablespoons (20g) coarse sea salt,
   crushed or ground

2 teaspoons sugar

1 0.6-oz cake fresh yeast (15g), or
   1 envelope active dry yeast
   (2½ teaspoons)

about 3 cups (690ml) lukewarm water

extra flour for dusting

1 large egg beaten with a pinch of salt for
   glazing

a very large baking sheet (see
   introduction), greased

In autumn, fresh vegetables replace the more traditional flower decorations in Anglican churches throughout Britain to celebrate the harvest festivals. After the service of thanksgiving, many congregations enjoy a meal in the church hall, which can include a decorated loaf of bread, such as this wheat sheaf.

"Toward the end of September or the beginning of October each year, bakers, especially in the southern parts of England, are frequently asked to supply large loaves as ornamental as the baker can make them for harvest festivals in churches," wrote Master Baker John Kirkland in 1907 (page 65). For him, a convenient size was a loaf made of an incredible 26 to 28 pounds of dough. And although he says an ordinary bread dough made a little firmer by adding less liquid will do, this lightly yeasted dough works better. This is a scaled-down version of his recipe to make a wheat sheaf about 17 × 13 inches.

You will need a kitchen scale to make this recipe. If you don't have a scale already, this provides a very good reason to purchase this very useful piece of kitchen equipment.

Mix together the flour, salt, and sugar (if using dry yeast, reserve ½ teaspoon of the sugar) in a very large bowl. Make a well in the center of the flour mixture. Crumble the fresh yeast into a small bowl. Stir in ¾ cup (170ml) of the lukewarm water until smooth. If using dry yeast, mix the granules and the reserved ½ teaspoon sugar with ¾ cup (170ml) of the lukewarm water and let stand until foamy, 5 to 10 minutes (page 18).

Pour the yeast mixture into the well in the flour. Add almost all the remaining lukewarm water and mix well. With your hand or a wooden spoon, work the flour from the bowl into the yeast mixture in the well to make a soft dough. (John Kirkland said it should not be sticky or dry). If the dough is dry and crumbly, work in more of the water, 1 tablespoon at a time. If the dough is too sticky, work in extra flour, 1 tablespoon at a time.

Turn the dough onto a lightly floured work surface and knead for 10 minutes, or until very elastic.

Wash, dry, and oil the bowl. Return the dough to the bowl and turn the dough over so the top is oiled. Cover with a damp dish towel and let rise at room temperature, away from drafts, until doubled in size, about 2 hours.

Punch down the dough. Turn it out onto a floured surface and knead for 2 minutes to work out the air bubbles. Cover with the upturned bowl and let rest for 10 minutes.

To shape the wheat sheaf: Cut off 10 ounces (280g) of the dough. Cover the remaining dough with a damp dish towel (see Note). Roll out the cut-off piece of dough on a lightly floured work surface with a lightly floured rolling pin into a 10 × 6-inch rectangle to form the base for the wheat stalks, patting the dough as necessary to keep the shape. Center a short side of the rectangle on a short side of the prepared baking sheet, so the dough is almost touching one edge of the sheet. (The space should be equal at both long sides, and there should be empty space above the sheaf.)

Roll or pat out 12 ounces (340g) of the remaining dough into a crescent shape with rounded ends, 11 inches wide across the crescent and longer than the rectangle. Position the crescent on top of the rectangle so it looks like a very large mushroom. Prick the dough all over with a fork and brush with water to prevent a crust forming.

To make the wheat stalks: Divide 14 ounces (395g) of the remaining dough into thirty equal pieces, by weight. Roll each piece on a floured surface with your hands into a thin rope about 10 inches long. Twist or braid three ropes together to make the sheaf band. Set this aside. Lay the remaining twenty-seven "stalks" side-by-side along the length of the stalk base, covering it, to create the sheaf. Place the twisted sheaf band across the center of the sheaf, curving it slightly. Do not press the band down onto the sheaf. Tuck the ends under the sheaf.

Set aside 1 ounce (30g) of the remaining dough to make the mouse. Weigh the remaining dough and divide into five equal portions. Divide each fifth into twenty equal pieces by weight, for a total of one hundred pieces. These will form the ears of wheat. Roll each piece with your hand on the floured work surface into a fat, oval-shaped roll. Pinch each roll at one end to make a point and round it at the other end. Using a small

POSITION THE DOUGH CRESCENT OVER THE
TOP OF THE STALK BASE AND PRICK THE
DOUGH ALL OVER WITH A FORK.

TWIST THREE DOUGH ROPES TOGETHER TO
MAKE THE SHEAF BAND.

ARRANGE THE WHEAT STALKS ON THE BASE.
PLACE THE TWISTED SHEAF BAND ACROSS THE
CENTER OF THE STALKS, CURVING THE BAND
SLIGHTLY.

SNIP ANGLED SHALLOW CUTS DOWN THE
CENTER OF EACH EAR. THEN SNIP ALONG
EACH SIDE, ANGLING THE CUTS IN THE SAME
DIRECTION.

ARRANGE THE EARS, A FEW AT A TIME, CLOSE
TOGETHER BUT NOT TOUCHING ALONG THE
TOP OF THE CRESCENT.

SHAPE THE DOUGH MOUSE, THEN POSITION IT
ON THE STALKS AS IF IT IS CLIMBING UP THE
SHEAF.

*This decorative loaf looks attractive
hanging on a kitchen wall, or makes a
wonderful housewarming gift for a special
friend. If you want to use the wheat sheaf
purely for decoration, bake it an extra 6
hours at 250°F.*

pair of kitchen scissors, snip angled, shallow cuts down the center of each ear (without
cutting all the way through), working from the rounded end to the pointed end. Then
make shallow cuts down each side of the first snips, positioning these cuts between the
cuts of the center row.

Arrange the ears close together, but not touching, along the edges of the crescent. The
next row should be arranged between these ears, leaving about 1½ inches of the first row
exposed. Do not arrange the ears too regularly, and leave one or two to droop slightly.
Repeat until the crescent center has been filled and all the wheat ears used.

Shape the remaining 1 ounce (30g) dough into an egg-shaped mouse with a pointed
nose and a long, thin tail.

Using small scissors, cut two small flaps toward the pointed end, then lift them up and
forward to resemble ears. Make two small holes for the eyes.

Brush the underside with water and place it on the stalks as if it is climbing up the sheaf.

Heat the oven to 425°F.

Carefully brush the wheat sheaf with the egg glaze. Then prick "in a good many
places," according to Kirkland, with the tip of a pointed knife to prevent the loaf from
cracking during baking. The knife holes should be made vertically, following the pattern
of the stalks and ears, so there are no visible cuts.

Bake the bread for 15 minutes. Brush with more glaze. Then lower the oven
temperature to 325°F and continue baking for 25 minutes longer, or until the loaf is
golden brown and very firm.

Let the loaf cool completely on the baking sheet.

NOTE: If your kitchen is warm, it is best to keep the portions of dough you are not using
in the refrigerator, tightly covered with plastic wrap. If the dough rises too fast, the sheaf
will lose its crisp shape.

CHALLAH

Challah is the Jewish white egg bread which is often braided into an elaborate loaf. It is regarded as an essential symbol for celebrating the Sabbath on Friday night. The word challah means dough offering in Hebrew. Its meaning dates back from the Temple period, about 380 BC, when a portion of the dough from the Sabbath loaf, generally made with finely-milled flour, rather than the coarse, everyday variety, was given to the temple priests. After the Temple was destroyed in 70 AD, Jews continued this practice symbolically, by throwing a small piece of the challah dough into the fire to burn while a blessing is recited.

Ashkenazi Jews, originally from central and Eastern Europe, often have two symbolic loaves of challah on their Sabbath dinner table. The loaves are covered with a special embroidered cloth, called a challah cover.

The elaborately braided challah, sometimes made with up to twelve strands of dough, was first baked by Central European Jews during the Middle Ages. This special, sweeter loaf was in complete contrast with the coarse, dark, slightly bitter bread eaten during the rest of the week. At the beginning of a Sabbath meal, the challah is blessed. Then, in some traditions, pieces are broken off, dipped in salt, and tossed unceremoniously to the diners, rather than being passed around, to symbolize the gift of bread from God.

Sephardic Jews, originally from Spain, Portugal, North Africa, and the Middle East, do not necessarily bake a special Sabbath loaf. Instead they use two of their everyday breads, such as pitas, or other flat breads. The breads are covered and placed on the Sabbath table to be blessed, and then sometimes broken and dipped in salt.

The symbolic challah made for Rosh Hashana, the Jewish New Year, is circular, or crown-shaped. It signifies peace, unity, and the creation of the Universe. In some communities, for Chanukah, the challah is shaped like a menorah, a seven-branched candle holder. Ukranian Jews may often bake three different shaped challahs: a bird-shaped challah for Yom Kippur, the Jewish day of Atonement; a spiral loaf for Rosh Hashana; and a key-shaped loaf for the Sabbath after Passover.

Some challahs are made with dark or golden raisins, nuts, and saffron, or other spices, depending on the traditions of the community.

The characteristic dark, shiny, reddish-brown color of the commercial varieties is achieved by glazing the loaf with egg yolk tinted with a few drops of red or yellow food coloring.

BRAIDED CHALLAH

INGREDIENTS

Makes 1 loaf

¼ teaspoon saffron strands

1 cup (230ml) boiling water

1 0.6-oz cake fresh yeast (15g), or
   1 envelope active dry yeast
   (2¼ teaspoons)

2 tablespoons honey

about 6 cups (680g) unbleached white
   bread flour

2 teaspoons salt

3 large eggs, beaten

6 tablespoons (85g) unsalted butter,
   melted and cooled

extra flour for dusting

1 egg yolk beaten with a pinch of salt for
   glazing

2 baking sheets, one of them greased

This honey-sweetened, saffron-gold, rich dough can be braided into a twist using up to twelve strands, but I am giving only some of the simpler examples in this section. If you are attempting to shape a braid for the first time, you might like to try this tip from Alice Turner (page 158): Insert 10- to 12-inch thin bamboo skewers through the braided strands while the loaf is rising, to help retain the shape.

Traditional challah dough has three risings, but should never be left in too warm a place, or it will become too soft to shape. Glazing the braid twice with egg yolk gives a deeper-colored finish to the loaf. Eat the challah within three days, or freeze for up to one month.

Crumble the saffron strands into a small bowl. Pour in the boiling water and let stand to infuse until the water cools to lukewarm. Crumble the fresh yeast into a small bowl. Stir in the lukewarm saffron mixture and the honey until smooth. If using dry yeast, mix the granules and the honey with the lukewarm saffron mixture and let stand until foamy, 5 to 10 minutes (page 18).

Stir together the flour and salt in a large bowl and make a well in the center of the flour mixture. Pour the yeast mixture into the well in the flour, followed by the beaten eggs and melted butter. Mix together the ingredients in the well with a small whisk or your hand. Then, with your hand or a wooden spoon, gradually mix the flour from the bowl into the ingredients in the well to form a soft, but not sticky dough. If the dough is too sticky, add a little extra flour, 1 tablespoon at a time. If the dough is dry and crumbly, add a little extra lukewarm water. 1 tablespoon at a time.

TUCK THE ENDS OF THE BRAID UNDER
FOR A NEAT FINISH.

Right
BAKE THE CHALLAH FOR 10 MINUTES.
THEN REMOVE IT FROM THE OVEN
AND BRUSH A SECOND TIME WITH THE
EGG AND SALT GLAZE.

Turn out the dough onto a lightly floured work surface. Knead for 10 minutes until smooth and elastic. Wash, dry, and oil the bowl. Return the dough to the bowl, and turn the dough over so the top is oiled. Cover with a damp dish towel and let rise at room temperature, away from drafts, until doubled in size, about 1½ hours.

Punch down the dough in the bowl. Cover with a damp dish towel and let rise again at room temperature, away from drafts, until doubled in size, about 45 minutes.

Punch down the dough. Turn out the dough onto a very lightly floured work surface. Knead for about 1 minute until the dough is smooth and elastic. Cover the dough with the upturned bowl and let rest for 5 minutes.

To shape a two-strand twist, divide the dough into two equal portions. Using your hands, roll each portion into a 15-inch-long rope about 2 inches thick. Pinch the ropes together firmly at one end. Wind the two ropes together to make a neat twist. Pinch the ends together. Transfer to the prepared baking sheet and tuck the ends under to give a neat shape.

To shape a three-strand braid, see Braided Loaf (page 31).

To shape a four-strand braid, divide the dough into four equal portions. Using your hands, roll each portion into a 13-inch-long rope about 1 inch thick. Pinch the ropes together firmly at one end.

Arrange the four strands side by side and slightly apart, with the unattached ends facing you. Move the strand on the far left under the two strands to its right. Twist the same strand over the last strand it went under, which was originally the third strand from the left. Move the strand on the far right under the twisted two strands in the center. Twist the same strand over the last strand it went under; it then becomes the third strand from the left. Repeat this process until all the strands are braided. Pinch the ends together. Transfer to the prepared baking sheet and tuck under the ends for a neat finish.

To make a double braid, using nine strands, see Alice's Christmas Loaf (page 158).

Cover the shaped challah loosely with a damp dish towel and let rise at room temperature, away from drafts, until doubled in size, 45 minutes to 1 hour. During the last 15 minutes of rising, heat the oven to 425°F.

Slide the second baking sheet under the first to prevent the bottom of the challah from overbrowning. Gently brush the risen challah with the egg glaze. Bake for 10 minutes. Remove from the oven and glaze it again. Return the loaf to the oven, lower the oven temperature to 375°F, and bake for 20 to 35 minutes longer, with the thicker, more complicated braids taking the longer time, until the loaf is a good golden brown and sounds hollow when tapped underneath. If the loaf is browning too quickly, cover loosely with a sheet of foil. Transfer to a wire rack to cool completely.

NOTE: For its second rising, the dough can also be left overnight in the refrigerator.

CAROLL'S TWISTED RING

INGREDIENTS

Makes 1 loaf

about 6 cups (680g) unbleached white bread flour

2 tablespoons sugar

2 teaspoons salt

1 0.6-oz cake fresh yeast (15g), or 1 envelope active dry yeast (2½ teaspoons)

1 cup (230ml) lukewarm water

6 tablespoons (85g) unsalted butter, melted and cooled

3 large eggs, beaten

1 large egg, separated

extra flour for dusting

1 teaspoon poppy seeds for sprinkling

a 9-inch tube pan, greased

Caroll Boltin (page 69) uses her challah dough to make a braided ring loaf for family celebrations. But I enjoy this loaf for everyday eating with soup or cheese, especially a mature, runny Milleen from Veronica Steele's dairy in Ireland. Caroll recommends using this rich bread for French toast, or pain perdu. Eat within three days, or use for toast.

Stir together 1½ cups (170g) flour, the sugar (reserve ½ teaspoon of the sugar if using dry yeast), and the salt in the bowl of a heavy-duty stationary electric mixer fixed with a dough hook. Crumble the fresh yeast into a small bowl. Stir in the lukewarm water until smooth. If using dry yeast, mix the granules and the reserved ½ teaspoon sugar with half of the lukewarm water and let stand until foamy, 5 to 10 minutes (page 18). Stir in the remaining lukewarm water.

Pour the yeast mixture and the melted butter into the flour mixture. Beat on medium speed for 2 minutes. Add the 3 whole eggs and the egg white. Beat on high speed for 2 minutes, or until the dough is very smooth. Gradually add enough of the remaining flour, with the machine on low speed, to make a soft, but not sticky dough that gathers into a ball around the dough hook and leaves the sides of the bowl cleanly. Knead the dough with the dough hook at medium speed for 10 minutes, or until the dough is satiny-smooth and elastic. If the dough is too sticky, add a little extra flour, 1 tablespoon at a time. If the dough is dry and crumbly, add a little extra water, 1 tablespoon at a time.

If you prefer, you can prepare the dough by hand: Mix together 1½ cups (170g) of the flour, the sugar, and the salt in a large bowl. Make a well in the center of the flour. Prepare the yeast mixture as above, using fresh or dry yeast. Pour the yeast mixture and the melted butter into the well in the flour. With your hand or a wooden spoon, gradually work the flour from the bowl into the liquid. Then beat the batter vigorously with your hand for 2 minutes. Add the 3 whole eggs and the egg white and beat with your hand for 4 minutes. Gradually mix in enough of the remaining flour to make a soft, but not sticky dough. Turn out the dough onto a lightly floured work surface and knead for 10 minutes until satiny-smooth and elastic.

CAROLL BRAIDS THE THREE FLAT STRIPS OF DOUGH TOGETHER.

AFTER THE DOUGH IS BRAIDED, CAROLL WILL PUT IT IN THE TUBE PAN.

This ring loaf is easier to shape than more elaborately braided challas, yet it's attractive enough to make any celebration more special. Here Caroll has displayed her loaf with an arrangement of vegetables, a bowl of apples, and an old-fashioned, wooden candelabra.

Put the dough into a lightly oiled bowl, and turn the dough over so the top is oiled. Cover with a damp dish towel and let rise at room temperature, away from drafts, until doubled in size, 1 to 1½ hours.

Punch down the dough. Turn out the dough onto a lightly floured work surface. With lightly floured knuckles, pat the dough out into a 22 × 10-inch rectangle, about 1 inch thick. (You may also roll out the dough with a lightly floured rolling pin.) Cut the rectangle lengthwise into four strips, unequal in width: three strips 3 inches wide, and one strip 1 inch wide.

Pinch the three wide strips together at one end. Braid as for the Braided Loaf (page 31) to make a flat, braided rope 18 to 20 inches long. Arrange the dough in the prepared ring mold, pinching the two ends together. Use the remaining narrow strip of dough to wrap like a strap around the point where the two ends meet and tuck underneath, so the loaf is an even thickness all the way around.

Beat the reserved egg yolk with 1 teaspoon water to make a glaze. Brush over the loaf, making sure not to glue the loaf to the mold. Sprinkle the top of the loaf evenly with the poppy seeds.

Cover with a damp dish towel and let rise at room temperature, away from drafts, until doubled in size, about 1 hour. Check from time to time to make sure the dough is not sticking to the cloth. During the last 15 minutes of rising, heat the oven to 400°F.

Bake the loaf for 10 minutes. Then lower the oven temperature to 350°F and bake 40 minutes longer, or until the loaf is golden brown and a skewer inserted in the center comes out clean.

Let the bread cool in the pan for a couple of minutes. Then carefully turn out onto a wire rack to cool completely.

SOURDOUGH AND RYE BREADS

One of the joys of baking bread is the miracle of yeast. Yeast is a living thing, needing food, some warmth, and pampering to survive – and to perform its job, which is to make a dough rise. What sets sourdough breads apart from other yeast breads is that much of their rising power comes from the wild yeasts that are naturally present in the air, rather than from commercial yeast.

Sourdoughs are not the types of bread that can be made quickly. A starter can take up to three days to ferment. And once the starter is made, the dough can take as long as ten days to ferment, as in the German Friendship Cake (page 176). The rising times are often lengthy as well. Leaving the doughs for an extra hour or so will not cause them to over-rise, as is the case with most other doughs. This suits me. I like being able to shape a dough that has risen overnight while I boil the kettle for tea at breakfast, knowing that when I finish working in the evening, the dough will be ready for the oven.

all or part rye flour, a dark Rye breads are made with in Northern, Middle, and gray flour, commonly used which has a distinctly tangy Eastern European baking, This taste is enhanced and and slightly acidic taste. is combined with a sour- heightened when the flour dough starter.

Unlike wheat flours, rye flour contains very little gluten so doughs made exclusively iwth rye flour are heavy and sticky, and do not rise much. Conse- quently, rye-flour doughs are often lightened, and the gluten boosted by the addi- tion of unbleached white bread flour or stone-ground whole-wheat flour. These combinations make the dough easier to work, but more importantly, I feel the taste is improved. It is worth searching out good, coarse, stone-ground rye flour from

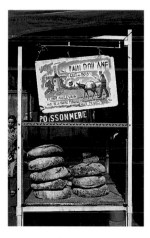

OPPOSITE Lionel Poilâne with his sourdough loaves. ABOVE Poilâne bread for sale in Paris.

local mills, health-food stores, or through mail order (see page 360).

For a basic, heavy rye loaf, combine three parts rye flour to one part wheat flour. A light rye loaf is made with the reverse proportions: one part rye flour to three parts wheat flour. Anthony Blake bakes a loaf of rye bread to perfection every day. He uses equal proportions of rye flour, coarse stone-ground whole-wheat flour, and unbleached white bread flour. Gerry's Sourdough Rye Bread (page 182) also uses this combination of flours, but his recipe begins with a sourdough starter.

Some rye bread recipes, such as Scandinavian Rye Bread (page 187) include buttermilk to provide an extra tang. Molasses is used to impart color and an intense flavor to breads like the Pumpernickel Loaf (page 183).

The flavor of sourdough bread becomes distinctly tangy the longer it is left to rise at a cool temperature. The sourness also depends on the pungency of the starter.

Jeffrey Hamelman, of Hamelman's Bakery, in Brattleboro, Vermont, bakes the best sourdough bread I have tasted outside Europe. He makes 500 loaves of bread each day, and considers delicious, well-flavored sourdough bread to be the highest expression of a baker's skill.

"You learn by your mistakes. There are not any shortcuts to wonderful sourdough," he says. "The important thing to remember is that the dough is alive. The baker performs alchemy, and if he or she is successful the yeast becomes exuberant and more lively. If the baker does not supply the yeast's needs, it will be crippled."

Each afternoon before Jeffrey leaves his bakery, he combines a new batch of dough with a starter and leaves it to ferment for 16 hours. He then adds flour and water at regular intervals until the dough is finally baked 24 hours after it was first mixed. Just like home bakers, Jeffrey has to take account of weather conditions when he prepares his dough. In Vermont, the weather can change dramatically and the winters are very cold; the summers extremely hot.

Sourdough breads are slow to stale, and, as they mature, the flavors mellow and blend. Most sourdough breads will stay fresh for up to a week.

TIPS FOR MAKING SOURDOUGH BREADS

– Flexibility is a key factor when making sourdough breads. The rising times can be variable and unpredictable and, unfortunately, there are times when a dough fails to thrive for no apparent reason. When this happens, you have to accept defeat. Throw away the dough and begin again. Flour and liquid quantities are never precise (as with most yeast breads) because of everyday variations in temperature and humidity and the quality of the flour. Work by feel, and treat the recipes as guides, adding the amounts of ingredients you feel the dough requires.

– There are certain signs that let you know that your starter has "died," is weak, or has gone off. If a starter smells bad, rather than sour, or if it has patches of mold throw it away. Check that it is "alive" by looking for bubbles on the surface and a distinct yeasty, or sour, smell. You will notice that the mixture gradually turns gray as it ferments – this is a good sign. A failed starter will produce a flat, dense loaf. If this happens your starter is not active; you must use a fresh starter for the next loaf.

– Do not use bleached flours. The best starters are made with unbleached, stone-ground flours in which yeasts thrive. The chemical treatment used to bleach flour seems to hinder the development of the starter and – even worse – it may produce a chlorine taste.

– Do not add salt to a starter mixture because it will inhibit the development of the yeast.

– I think a kitchen counter is the best location in the house to leave a starter while it is developing. The kitchen is often warmer than other rooms, and because it is the place where food is prepared, there seem to be more yeasts in the air. The best sourdough breads I have ever made were ones at Anthony Blake's studio, after a week of food photography.

– Do not cover the starter mixture, or the sponge, with plastic wrap, foil, or a lid. Use a damp thin dish towel, to provide a warm, moist environment which will attract the yeasts naturally present in the air and encourage them to multiply.

– When you are leaving a starter to ferment over several days, be sure to re-dampen the towel at least once a day.

– Starters develop at different rates depending on the season and the weather. You will find starters and doughs tend to develop most quickly in hot and humid conditions.

– In my recipes I specify how long you can keep a starter before you have to use it in another loaf. If, however, there is not an instruction in a recipe or you want to keep a portion of the dough to use as a starter for the next loaf for more than three days, you must "feed" it. Add ½ cup (110ml) water from the cold tap and enough flour to make a soft dough every four days. Store the dough in a covered container in the refrigerator or in a cool pantry. Do not keep the starter longer than two weeks.

GERMAN FRIENDSHIP CAKE

I had heard a lot about friendship cakes, a sourdough loaf made from a starter that has been passed from friend to friend, but I had never tasted one until recently. One day, friend and fellow cookery writer Elaine Hallgarten arrived on my doorstep with a container of starter and some instructions that had been given to her. You certainly know who your friends are when you start making this recipe! Coincidentally, a letter from my mother-in-law in America containing a recipe for Amish friendship bread arrived in the next post. It was identical!

This loaf is delicious and simple to make, more like a crumb cake than a bread, but it does take ten days – once you've made the starter. I discovered it is a good idea to write down the date of Day 1, or you might lose your place in the recipe. After ten days, you will have enough starter to give two portions away and keep two portions for yourself: one to bake immediately and one to refrigerate. You cannot use active dry yeast to make this recipe; it simply doesn't work. Eat the bread within three days after baking, or freeze for up to one month.

INGREDIENTS

Makes 1 large loaf
STARTER:

2 cups (280g) unbleached all-purpose
    flour

1 0.6-oz cake fresh yeast (15g)

2 cups (455ml) water

FOR DAY 1 AND DAY 5:

1 cup (200g) granulated sugar

1 cup (140g) unbleached all-purpose flour

1 cup (230ml) milk

FOR FINISHING LOAF:

2 cups (280g) unbleached all-purpose
    flour

1 cup (200g) granulated sugar

3 Granny Smith apples, peeled, cored, and
    diced

½ cup (85g) golden raisins

½ cup (110ml) vegetable oil

2 large eggs, beaten

½ cup (60g) chopped walnuts or pecans

2 teaspoons ground cinnamon

2 teaspoons baking powder

½ teaspoon salt

a few drops of vanilla extract

TOPPING:

½ cup packed (100g) light brown sugar

7 tablespoons (100g) unsalted butter,
    melted and cooled

a baking pan or roasting pan, about
    9 × 13 inches, well greased

The first time I made this fruit-filled
sourdough loaf, I gave a portion of the starter
to Joy Skipper, who has assisted on this book,
and she has made a new loaf every ten days
since then. She has also passed on portions of
her starter to friends and neighbors in the
small Norfolk village where she lives, and the
starter is now making its way around
Britain.

  "Most sourdoughs are too sour to my
taste," she says, "but this is delicious."

  Joy has also experimented with different
flavorings for this loaf, and recommends
replacing the golden raisins and apples with
finely grated orange rind and prunes.

To make the starter: Put the flour in a large nonmetallic bowl and make a well in the center of the flour. Crumble the fresh yeast into the well in the flour. Then pour the water into the well and stir with a wooden spoon or your hand until the mixture is smooth. Stir the flour from the bowl into the yeast mixture to make a sticky batter.

Cover with a damp dish towel and let stand on the kitchen table or counter, at room temperature, away from drafts, so the batter absorbs the natural yeasts in the air. Stir the batter once a day for each of the next three days and re-dampen the dish towel if it gets dry. The starter is ready to use when it is gray and foamy.

DAY 1	Stir the starter you have made, or the starter you have been given. Add the sugar, flour, and milk to the starter in the bowl. Stir well, cover with a damp dish towel, and let stand overnight at room temperature, away from drafts.
DAY 2	Stir the starter well and re-cover with a damp dish towel.
DAYS 3 and 4	Do nothing. If the dish towel is dry, re-dampen it.
DAY 5	Stir the starter well and add the sugar, flour, and milk. Stir well again, cover with a damp dish towel, and let stand overnight at room temperature, away from drafts.
DAY 6	Stir the starter well and re-cover with a damp dish towel.
DAYS 7, 8 and 9	Do nothing. Re-dampen the dish towel if it is dry.
DAY 10	Stir the starter well and divide the mixture into four equal portions. Give two portions to friends with instructions, keep one portion for your next batch (see below), and use one portion to make the loaf.

To make the dough: Heat the oven to 350°F. Place one reserved portion of the starter in a very large mixing bowl. Add the flour, sugar, apples, golden raisins, oil, eggs, nuts, cinnamon, baking powder, salt, and vanilla to the starter. Mix with your hand or a wooden spoon. When all the ingredients are thoroughly combined, place the dough in the prepared pan and smooth the surface.

For topping: Sprinkle the top of the loaf with the brown sugar, then drizzle with the butter. Bake the loaf for 30 to 40 minutes, or until a wooden skewer inserted in the center comes out clean. Turn out onto a wire rack to cool completely.

TO KEEP A STARTER FOR THE NEXT BATCH: Add 1 teaspoon of granulated sugar to the portion of starter you are going to keep for your next loaf. Stir well, then store in a covered container in the refrigerator for up to one week. To make a fresh cake, begin at Day 1, using this starter.

FRENCH SOURDOUGH LOAF

INGREDIENTS

Makes 1 large loaf
STARTER:
2 cups (230g) whole-wheat bread flour,
    preferably stone-ground
about 1 cup (230ml) lukewarm water
SPONGE:
⅔ cup (140ml) lukewarm water
2 cups (230g) unbleached white bread
    flour
DOUGH:
¼ cup (55ml) lukewarm water
2¼ tablespoons (20g) coarse sea salt,
    crushed or ground
about 2 cups (230g) unbleached white
    bread flour
extra flour for dusting
a round wicker basket, about 9 inches wide
    and 4 inches deep, lined with a heavy
    floured dry dish towel

a baking sheet, heavily floured, or a loaf
    pan, about 10 × 5 × 3 inches, greased

This is my version of the delicious, thick-crusted, chewy loaf made popular by the Poilâne family in Paris. The huge loaves from their bakery in the rue du Cherche-Midi are baked in old, wood-fired ovens, which gives them a delicious, smoky flavor. The sourdough tang in this loaf is quite strong, and may not be to all tastes.

You can vary the flour in this recipe using any combination, including a little rye flour. The loaf is an excellent keeper, tasting better as it matures, and it is best thinly sliced. The first two or three batches will taste good, but will not rise as well as later batches when the starter is established. Eat within one week.

To make the starter: Mix together the flour and enough of the lukewarm water in a small bowl to make a very thick batter. Cover with a damp dish towel and let stand at room temperature, away from drafts, for three days, so it absorbs the yeasts in the air. (Re-dampen the dish towel when necessary.) After three days, the starter should be smelly, gray, and only slightly bubbly.

To make the sponge: Pour the starter into a large bowl. Then add the lukewarm water, stirring to dissolve any lumps in the starter. Add the white bread flour. Beat with your hand or a wooden spoon for about 1 minute to make a thick batter. Cover with a damp dish towel and let stand at room temperature, away from drafts, for 24 to 36 hours, or until it is spongy and slightly bubbly. (Re-dampen the dish towel when necessary.) The longer you leave the sponge, the more pronounced the sour taste will be.

To make the dough: Stir down the sponge. Beat in the lukewarm water and the salt. Then mix in enough white bread flour, about one handful at a time, to make a soft, but not sticky dough.

Turn out the dough onto a lightly floured work surface and knead for 10 minutes until firm, smooth, and elastic, adding more flour as needed. Return the dough to the bowl (no need to wash and oil the bowl). Cover with a damp dish towel and let rise at room temperature, away from drafts, until almost doubled in size, 8 to 12 hours.

Punch down the dough. Cut off 6 to 8 ounces of the dough (about 1 cup) and set aside for making the next starter (see below). Shape the rest of the dough into a ball and put into the cloth-lined basket, if using, or onto the prepared baking sheet. (The basket gives the loaf a nice round shape.) Or shape into a loaf to fit the prepared pan (see A Plain White Loaf, page 24). Cover with a damp dish towel and let rise at room temperature, away from drafts, until almost doubled in size, about 8 hours. Subsequent batches may take less time to rise.

To bake: Heat the oven to 425°F. If you used the basket, invert the loaf from the basket onto the prepared baking sheet. Using a sharp knife or a razor blade, slash the top of the loaf four times, or make two diagonal slashes across the top if you are baking the loaf in a pan. Sprinkle with a little white flour. Bake the loaf for 20 minutes. Then lower the oven temperature to 375°F and bake for 35 to 55 minutes longer, or until the loaf sounds hollow when tapped underneath. Transfer the loaf to a wire rack and cool completely.

TO KEEP A STARTER FOR THE NEXT BATCH: Put the reserved 6- to 8-ounce (about 1-cup) portion of dough into a greased plastic bag and store in the refrigerator for up to three days. Or place the dough in a small bowl, covered with a damp dish towel, and let stand at room temperature, away from drafts, for up to two days. (To keep the starter longer, see page 176.) To use for making a loaf, start at the sponging stage in the above recipe, and beat in a little extra lukewarm water to make a thick batter. Proceed with the recipe.

TO MAKE THE STARTER: STIR TOGETHER THE WHOLE-WHEAT BREAD FLOUR AND ABOUT 1 CUP LUKEWARM WATER TO MAKE A VERY THICK BATTER.

AFTER THREE DAYS, THE STARTER SHOULD BE SMELLY, GRAY, AND SLIGHTLY BUBBLY.

WHEN THE DOUGH HAS RISEN TO DOUBLE IN SIZE, HAVE READY THE BASKET WITH THE FLOURED CLOTH.

RESERVE 6 TO 8 OUNCES DOUGH FOR THE NEXT STARTER. SHAPE THE REST OF THE DOUGH INTO A BALL AND PUT IT INTO THE CLOTH-LINED BASKET.

AFTER THE DOUGH HAS RISEN AT NORMAL ROOM TEMPERATURE FOR ABOUT 8 HOURS IT WILL HAVE DOUBLED IN SIZE.

SLASH THE TOP OF THE LOAF FOUR TIMES, THEN SPRINKLE WITH FLOUR.

Gerry turns out his dough onto a floured surface for kneading.

INGREDIENTS

Makes 1 large loaf
STARTER:
2 cups (230g) rye flour
about 1¼ cups (280ml) lukewarm water
SPONGE:
1¼ cups (280ml) lukewarm water
about 2½ cups (280g) rye flour
DOUGH:
1 tablespoon salt
1–2 teaspoons ground caraway seeds, or to taste
2 tablespoons sunflower oil
2 cups (230g) whole-wheat bread flour, preferably stone-ground
2 cups (230g) rye flour
about 2 cups (230g) unbleached white bread flour
extra flour for dusting

a large, oval or round cast-iron casserole with lid, or an ovenproof enamel Dutch oven, greased

GERRY'S SOURDOUGH RYE BREAD

"For me, the only bread worth eating is sourdough. Everything else tastes like cake," says Gerry Turner of Bree, County Wexford, in Ireland. Gerry started baking his own bread in 1981, when he moved to Ireland. He had lived in Prague, where he met his charming wife Alice (page 158), and where he developed a liking for rye bread, particularly the sourdough variety.

"I invented a loaf to satisfy our tastes. It was trial and error for many weeks," he says. Part of his technique is to bake the loaf in a covered cast-iron casserole.

Gerry saves a quarter of his prepared dough to use as the starter for the next loaf. His dough is uniquely flavored with ground caraway seeds. A mortar and pestle, a clean coffee grinder, or a spice grinder will do the job nicely.

To make the starter: Mix the flour and water in a large bowl to make a stiff batter. Cover with a damp dish towel and let stand at room temperature, away from drafts, for four days to absorb the natural yeasts in the air. Re-dampen the towel as necessary. After four days, the batter should be very gray and foamy. (Gerry says you need strong nerves, and a good sense of smell is a disadvantage, as the batter will smell dreadful.)

To make the sponge: Stir down the starter in the bowl with a wooden spoon or your hand. Then add the lukewarm water, stirring to dissolve any lumps in the starter. Add enough rye flour to make a very thick, sticky batter – the exact quantity will vary depending on your flour. Sprinkle the surface of the batter with a little more rye flour to prevent a crust from forming. Cover with a damp dish towel and let stand in a cool place, away from drafts, until smelly and bubbly, about 18 hours.

To make the dough: Sprinkle the salt, ground caraway seeds, and sunflower oil evenly onto the sponge. Mix to make a very sloppy batter. Mix in the whole-wheat flour, then the rye flour. Mix in enough of the white bread flour, a handful at a time, to make a soft, but not sticky dough. Turn out the dough onto a floured surface and knead for 10 minutes, or until firm and elastic, adding extra white flour as needed. Cut off one-quarter of the dough and set aside for making the next starter (see below).

Shape the larger piece of dough into an oval or a round to fit the prepared casserole. Put the dough into the casserole and sprinkle with a little rye flour. Cover with the lid and let rise at room temperature, away from drafts, until doubled in size, 1 to 4 hours, depending on the vigor of your dough and the room temperature. When ready to bake, heat the oven to 400°F. Bake the loaf in the casserole, covered, for 50 to 70 minutes, or

164

until the loaf sounds hollow when unmolded and tapped underneath. Turn the loaf out of the casserole onto a wire rack to cool.

TO KEEP A STARTER FOR THE NEXT BATCH: Grease the inside of a plastic bag. Put the reserved piece of dough in the bag and store in the refrigerator for up to three days to use for the next batch. (To keep the starter longer, see page 176.) To prepare the sponge: Put the reserved dough into a large bowl and pour in enough lukewarm water to cover. Let stand for 5 minutes. Then mix the water and dough together with your hands, squeezing the dough between your fingers. Beat in enough rye flour with your hand to make a very thick batter. Sprinkle the surface of the batter with a little rye flour to prevent a crust from forming. Cover with a damp dish towel and let stand in a cool place, away from drafts, until smelly and bubbly, about 18 hours. Proceed with the recipe.

PUMPERNICKEL LOAF

INGREDIENTS

Makes 2 small loaves

2½ cups (280g) rye flour, preferably coarsely stone-ground

1¼ cups (140g) unbleached white bread flour

1¼ cups (140g) whole-wheat bread flour, preferably stone-ground

2 teaspoons salt

1 0.6-oz cake fresh yeast (15g), or 1 envelope active dry yeast (2½ teaspoons)

1½ cups (340ml) lukewarm water

1 tablespoon packed light brown sugar

¼ cup (85g) unsulfured molasses

1 tablespoon vegetable oil, or 1 tablespoon butter, melted and cooled

extra flour for dusting

1 tablespoon potato starch

2 tablespoons boiling water

2 loaf pans, about 7 × 5 × 3 inches, greased

You cannot buy pumpernickel flour because it does not exist. Pumpernickel bread is actually made of a mixture of several flours, always including a high proportion of rye flour. The dark color of this dense, tasty bread is usually achieved both by tinting the dough with coffee, molasses, cocoa, or even liquid gravy browning and by long, slow baking. The loaf includes only a small amount of molasses, so it is lighter in color than breads made commercially. If you like a tangier-tasting loaf, replace some of the milk with an equal quantity of buttermilk. For a slightly sweeter taste, add ½ cup (85g) raisins to the dough before shaping it into loaves. Across northern Europe, pumpernickel is enjoyed with cured or smoked fish or meats, cheese, and soups.

Mix together the flours and salt in a large bowl and make a well in the center of the flour mixture. Crumble the fresh yeast into a small bowl. Stir in the lukewarm water until smooth. If using dry yeast, mix the granules and the 1 tablespoon brown sugar with half of the lukewarm water and let stand until foamy, 5 to 10 minutes (page 18). Stir in the remaining lukewarm water.

Pour the yeast mixture into the well in the flour. Add the sugar, molasses, and oil or melted butter to the well in the flour and mix these ingredients together with a small whisk or your hand. Mix the flour from the bowl into the liquid in the well with your hand or a wooden spoon to make a soft and slightly sticky dough. It will be difficult to work. Turn out the dough onto a lightly floured work surface and knead for 10 minutes until the dough becomes firm, smooth, and elastic. If necessary, add a little more rye and whole-wheat flours to prevent sticking. The dough will feel heavier than a non-rye dough. Return the dough to the bowl. Cover with a damp dish towel, and let rise at room temperature, away from drafts, until doubled in size, 2 to 3 hours.

Punch down the dough. Turn out the dough onto a lightly floured work surface and knead for 1 minute until it feels elastic. Divide the dough into two equal portions. Shape each into a loaf to fit the prepared pans (see A Plain White Loaf, page 24). Put the shaped dough, seam side down, into the prepared pans. Cover with a damp dish towel and let rise at room temperature, away from drafts, until doubled in size, 1½ to 2 hours. During the last 15 minutes of rising, heat the oven to 400°F.

Whisk together the potato starch and boiling water in a small bowl until smooth. Gently brush the risen loaves with the potato starch glaze. Bake the bread for 35 to 40 minutes, or until it is dark brown and sounds hollow when unmolded and tapped underneath. Turn out onto a wire rack to cool completely. Wrap in waxed paper, overwrap with foil, and keep at room temperature for at least one day or up to one week before slicing thinly.

ONION AND CARAWAY RYE BREAD

OPPOSITE
Use slices of Scandinavian Rye Bread to make
colorful open-face sandwiches.

INGREDIENTS

Makes 1 large loaf

2½ cups (230g) rye flour

about 3 cups (340g) unbleached white
    bread flour

1 tablespoon caraway seeds, or to taste

2 teaspoons salt

1 0.6-oz cake fresh yeast (15g)

1 teaspoon dark brown sugar

1½ cups (340ml) mixed lukewarm milk
    and water

1 medium onion, minced

2 tablespoons vegetable oil

extra flour for dusting

extra caraway seeds for sprinkling

a loaf pan, about 10 × 5 × 3 inches,
    greased

Extremely good with pickled, cured, and smoked fish, this light rye loaf tastes best one or two days after it has been baked. Replace the caraway seeds with toasted cumin seeds for a spicier, more fragrant loaf. This bread is best made with fresh yeast, so I have not given any instructions using dry yeast. Eat within four days of baking.

Mix together the flours, caraway seeds, and salt in a large bowl and make a well in the center. Crumble the fresh yeast into a small bowl. Stir in the brown sugar and the lukewarm milk and water until smooth.

Pour the yeast mixture into the well in the flour. With your hand or a wooden spoon, mix enough of the flour from the bowl into the yeast mixture in the well to make a thick batter. Cover with a damp dish towel and let stand at room temperature, away from drafts, until spongy, about 20 minutes (page 16). Meanwhile, sauté the onion slowly in the oil in a skillet until softened, but not browned, about 10 minutes. Let cool.

Add the cooled onion and any remaining oil in the skillet to the sponge in the well and mix together with your hand or a wooden spoon. Gradually mix the flour from the bowl into the sponge with your hand or a wooden spoon to make a soft, but not sticky dough.

Turn out the dough onto a lightly floured surface and knead for 10 minutes until firm, smooth, and elastic. Return the dough to the bowl. Cover with a damp dish towel and let rise at room temperature, away from drafts, until doubled in size, 2 to 3 hours.

Punch down the dough. Turn it out onto a floured surface and shape into a loaf to fit the prepared pan (see A Plain White Loaf, page 24). Place the dough, seam side down, in the pan. Cover with a damp towel and let rise at room temperature, away from drafts, until doubled in size, 1½ to 2 hours. During the last 15 minutes, heat the oven to 375°F. Gently brush the loaf with water. Sprinkle the top with caraway seeds.

Bake the loaf for 35 to 45 minutes, or until the loaf sounds hollow when unmolded and tapped underneath. Transfer to a wire rack to cool completely.

ADD THE COOLED ONION AND ANY
REMAINING OIL TO THE SPONGE.

SPRINKLE THE TOP WITH CARAWAY
SEEDS JUST BEFORE BAKING.

INGREDIENTS

Makes 1 loaf

1½ cups (170g) unbleached white bread
     flour

3⅓ cups (370g) rye flour, preferably
     stone-ground

2 teaspoons salt

2 tablespoons (30g) unsalted butter

1 0.6-oz cake fresh yeast (15g), or
     1 envelope active dry yeast
     (2½ teaspoons) plus ½ teaspoon sugar

⅔ cup (140ml) lukewarm milk

⅔ cup (140ml) buttermilk

1 tablespoon barley malt extract

1 tablespoon black treacle or unsulfured
     molasses

extra flour for dusting

a baking sheet, greased

SCANDINAVIAN RYE BREAD

Buttermilk and a high proportion of rye flour to white bread flour makes this bread the strongest tasting and most densely textured in this chapter. The dough is quite sticky to work and it will feel heavier than even an all-whole-wheat dough — but it is worth the effort. Barley malt extract is found at well-stocked health-food stores.

Wrap the loaf in waxed paper and keep for one day after baking. It will stay fresh for five days, or can be frozen for up to one month.

Mix together the flours and salt in a large bowl. Rub in the butter with your fingertips until the mixture looks like fine crumbs. Make a well in the center of the flour. Crumble the fresh yeast into a small bowl. Stir in the lukewarm milk until smooth. If using dry yeast, mix the granules and the ½ teaspoon sugar with the lukewarm milk and let stand until foamy, 5 to 10 minute (page 18).

Pour the yeast mixture into the well. Add the buttermilk, barley malt extract, and black treacle or molasses and mix these ingredients together. Mix the flour from the bowl into the liquid in the well with your hand or a wooden spoon to make a soft and sticky dough. If the dough is dry and crumbly, add a little more buttermilk, 1 tablespoon at a time. If the dough is too wet, add a little more white flour, 1 tablespoon at a time.

Turn out the dough onto a floured surface and knead for 10 minutes until firm, elastic, and smooth. Return the dough to the bowl. Cover with a damp dish towel and let rise at room temperature, away from drafts, until doubled in size, about 2 hours.

Punch down the dough. Turn out the dough onto a lightly floured work surface and shape into an oval loaf (see The Basic Loaf, page 17). Place the loaf on the prepared baking sheet. Using a sharp knife or a razor blade, slash the loaf down the center. Cover with a damp dish towel and let rise at room temperature, away from drafts, until doubled in size, about 1½ hours. During the last 15 minutes of rising, heat the oven to 400°F. Bake the loaf for 35 to 45 minutes, or until it sounds hollow when tapped underneath. Transfer to a wire rack to cool completely.

ENRICHED DOUGHS

Rich, rich, rich. These are extravagant recipes, where white yeast dough is transformed into luxurious pâtisserie by adding what appear to be extravagant quantities of butter, eggs, or cream. Technique is all-important in working with these doughs – pastry chefs may practice for years before they are satisfied. Equally important are the ingredients. Because of the large amounts of butter, lard, or cream incorporated into these doughs, they must be of the very best quality and really fresh, untainted by "refrigerator smells" or exposure to air. I think firm, pale, and creamy-tasting unsalted butter, or "sweet" butter is best for enriching doughs. Unsalted butter from the French regions of Normandy or Brittany is particularly prized by European pastry chefs. In the States, look for unsalted butter graded AA; it will have the best flavor. Buy butter from a store

store with a high turnover. margarine for butter or cream, because the results not totally inedible. Whole- itself to these recipes either. such a high proportion of proportion to the flour than wise to let the doughs rise warm room temperature too hot, the fat will melt soggy, heavy dough will doughs such as the one chilled before shaping, brioche dough, are so soft give them shape. The ings in these recipes help to textures: Aberdeen Butteries Croissants (page 192), and

OPPOSITE Michel Roux and croissants. ABOVE A basket of freshly baked enriched breads.

Never try to substitute coffee lightener for heavy will be disappointing, if wheat flour does not lend As these doughs contain fat, they have more yeast in usual to help them rise. It is fairly slowly at normal to because, if the room is and ooze out, and a be your result. Some soft for croissants, need to be while others, such as they also need a mold to numerous fairly slow ris- give the breads their fine (page 202), Michel Roux's Danish Pastries (page 195)

are made like puff pastry, with crisp, flaky layers that should not be damp or doughy; Michel Roux's Brioche (page 203) has an even, fine crumb; Sally Lunns (page 200) have a delicate texture similar to a rich sponge cake, while Rum Babas (page 206) and Savarin (page 207) develop a honeycomb structure, like a bath sponge, ready to absorb plenty of flavored syrup. Lardy Cake (page 199) is a rich, sweet cake with layers of flaky dough.

These recipes do take a lot of time and need a bit of practice, but the results are always worth eating and will provide you with a tremendous sense of achievement. You, too, can make croissants like Michel Roux!

MICHEL ROUX'S CROISSANTS

INGREDIENTS

Makes 16–18

3 tablespoons (40g) sugar

1 tablespoon (10g) coarse sea salt, crushed or ground

1 cup + 6 tablespoons (310ml) chilled water

1 0.6-oz cake fresh yeast (15g), or 1 envelope active dry yeast (2½ teaspoons) plus ½ teaspoon sugar

¼ cup (30g) dry milk powder

4½ cups (500g) unbleached white bread flour

1 cup + 5 tablespoons (300g) unsalted butter

extra flour for dusting

1 egg yolk beaten with 1 tablespoon milk for glazing

a triangular template, 7 × 7 × 6 inches

2 baking sheets that will fit in your refrigerator, lightly greased

A Meilleur Ouvrier de France, 1976, Pâtissier-Confiseur, Michel Roux is one of France's finest pastry chefs. He is also the owner of a Michelin three-star restaurant in England, the Waterside Inn, at Bray-on-Thames.

As you might suspect, Michel is a perfectionist who cares passionately about his work. He spent many hours developing this exquisite croissant recipe so it can be made at home without specialized pastry training or equipment. Making successful croissants is a challenge for even the most experienced home baker, so remember Michel's warning that "only practice makes perfect," and take it from me that it is worth the effort required to make these. You will not find a better recipe anywhere.

If you want to have freshly baked croissants for breakfast, cover the shaped and glazed dough with plastic wrap and let it rise very slowly overnight in the refrigerator. (The croissants should slowly double in size.) In the morning, let the dough stand at room temperature for about 30 minutes, then glaze again and bake. If the refrigerator is very cold, the croissants may not rise sufficiently overnight. In that case you will have to leave them at room temperature longer, until they are doubled in size.

Croissants are best eaten warm, soon after baking, or at least on the day they are baked. If that is not possible, however, croissants and Petits Pains au Chocolat (page 195) freeze well for up to two weeks. After baking, while they are still warm, place them in freezer bags and freeze immediately. To use, remove them from the bags and place them, still frozen, on a baking sheet. Bake at 500ºF for 5 minutes, or until warmed through.

You can also freeze unbaked croissants for up to one week. Place the shaped croissants on a baking sheet as described below. Before glazing them and leaving them to rise, cover the baking sheet well with plastic wrap or a plastic bag and freeze. Then let them thaw in the refrigerator overnight, or at room temperature for 4 to 6 hours. When thawed, glaze and leave to rise until doubled in size. Glaze again and bake as in the recipe.

Dissolve the sugar and salt in ½ cup (110ml) of the cold water. Crumble the fresh yeast into a small bowl. Stir in the remaining water until smooth, then beat in the milk powder. If using dry yeast, heat the remaining water to lukewarm. Mix the yeast granules and the

MICHEL HAS ROLLED OUT THE DOUGH, LEAVING A ROUGH, 5-INCH SQUARE IN THE CENTER.

HE WRAPS THE DOUGH OVER THE BUTTER SO IT IS COMPLETELY ENCLOSED.

TO BEGIN FOLDING, HE TURNS THE DOUGH ON A LONG SIDE. HE THEN FOLDS THE RIGHT THIRD OVER INTO THE CENTER.

MICHEL THEN FOLDS OVER THE LEFT THIRD. THE COMPLETELY ENCLOSED SIDE OF THE DOUGH IS ON HIS LEFT.

AFTER THE THIRD CHILLING, HE ROLLS THE DOUGH INTO A 16 #AA 30-INCH RECTANGLE.

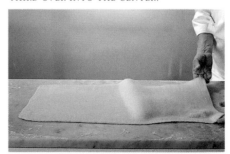

TO AERATE THE DOUGH, HE GENTLY LIFTS AND FLAPS IT AGAINST THE WORK SURFACE.

AFTER TRIMMING THE EDGES, MICHEL CUTS THE DOUGH LENGTHWISE INTO TWO STRIPS.

USING A LIGHTLY FLOURED KNIFE, HE CUTS EACH STRIP INTO EIGHT OR NINE TRIANGLES.

TO SHAPE A CROISSANT, MICHEL GENTLY STRETCHES OUT THE TWO SHORTER POINTS OF THE TRIANGLE.

STARTING FROM THE WIDE EDGE, HE ROLLS THE DOUGH TOWARD THE POINT. HE SHAPES IT INTO A CRESCENT AND PUTS IT ON A BAKING SHEET.

THE CROISSANTS THAT WILL BE CLOSEST TO THE OVEN'S HOT SPOTS ARE ARRANGED SO THE TIPS POINT TO THE CENTER OF THE

BAKED CROISSANTS WILL BE WELL RISEN AND GOLDEN BROWN. MICHEL COOLS THEM ON A WIRE RACK.

½ teaspoon sugar with the lukewarm water and let stand until foamy, 5 to 10 minutes (page 18). Beat in the milk powder.

Put the flour in the bowl of a heavy-duty stationary electric mixer. Using the dough hook and beating at low speed, beat in the sugar-salt liquid, then beat in the yeast mixture. Stop beating as soon as the ingredients are well mixed and the dough comes away from the sides of the bowl, which should not take longer than 1½ minutes. The dough will be soft and sticky, and it is important not to overwork the dough at this stage. Or, combine the flour, sugar-salt liquid, and the yeast mixture in a large bowl and beat with a wooden spoon until the dough is soft and sticky and comes away from the sides of the bowl, which should not take longer than 3 minutes.

Cover the dough with a damp dish towel and let rise in a warm place (about 75°F, but not more than 86F), away from drafts, until doubled in size, about 30 minutes.

Punch down the dough by quickly flipping it over in the bowl with your fingers to release the carbon-dioxide gases. Do not knead or overwork the dough, or the croissants will be heavy. Cover with plastic wrap and refrigerate for 6 to 8 hours, or until the dough slowly doubles in size. If the dough rises again after an hour, punch it down as above, re-cover, and return to the refrigerator.

If using sticks of butter, shape them into a 5-inch square by cutting the sticks in half lengthwise, arranging the pieces side by side, and mashing them together with your fingertips. Otherwise, using a rolling pin, gently roll and shape the butter into a 5-inch square. The butter must be firm, but still quite pliable, and about the same temperature as the dough when they are combined. If necessary, pound the butter between two sheets of waxed paper with a rolling pin to make it more pliable, or chill until it is firmer.

Punch down the dough. Turn it out onto a lightly floured work surface and shape it into a ball. Using a sharp knife, cut a cross in the top of the dough. Roll out the dough with a lightly floured rolling pin in four places, giving the dough a quarter turn to the left after each roll, making a rough circle with a thick, rough 5-inch square of dough in the center. Brush off any excess flour.

A French-style breakfast of freshly baked croissants and pains au chocolat. In France, butter-rich croissants are sometimes not shaped into crescents, but left straight like these. This custom developed after World War II when butter was in short supply and bakers were forced to make croissants with margarine instead. Shoppers were then able to tell at a glance what they were buying because a crescent shape indicated margarine had been used.

Put the butter on the rough square of dough. Fold the dough over the butter, tucking in the edges and making sure the butter is completely enclosed so it does not ooze out during the following rolling and folding processes.

Roll out the dough, rolling away from you, on a lightly floured surface with a floured rolling pin, into a 16 × 27-inch rectangle. Turn the dough rectangle so a long side faces you. Brush off any excess flour. Fold over the right third of the dough, then fold over the left third on top of the right third to make a three-layer dough sandwich with the completely enclosed side on your left. Use the rolling pin to seal the top, bottom, and right edges by pressing down on them. Wrap the dough in plastic wrap and chill for at least 20 minutes but no more than 45 minutes. Repeat the rolling, folding, and chilling twice more, turning the dough a quarter turn to the left so the enclosed side is on the bottom before each roll. Dust off excess flour.

After the third chilling, roll out the dough with a lightly floured rolling pin into a 16 × 30-inch rectangle, flouring the work surface very lightly as you roll.

Gently lift the dough and flap it against the work surface twice to aerate it and prevent shrinkage during baking, taking care not to spoil the shape of the rectangle. Using a large, lightly floured knife, trim the edges of the dough rectangle to neaten it, then cut the dough lengthwise into two equal strips. You can use a ruler as a guide if you like. Do not re-roll the trimmings – just bake as they are to enjoy as nibbles.

Lay the short side of the triangular template along one long edge of the dough and mark the outline with the back of the knife. Continue this way, using both pieces of dough, until you have marked out a total of sixteen to eighteen triangles. Then cut out the dough triangles. Marking out the triangles first helps prevent mistakes. If you feel confident, cut out the triangles without using the template, as Michel Roux does.

Arrange the triangles on the prepared baking sheets. Cover tightly with plastic wrap and refrigerate for a few moments: If the dough becomes too warm, it may soften and crack while the croissants are being shaped.

Place one dough triangle at a time on the floured work surface with the longest point toward you. (Keep the rest refrigerated.) Gently stretch out the two shorter points. Then, starting from the edge opposite the long point, roll up the triangle toward you; use one hand to roll the dough and the other to gently pull the long point. Make sure that this pointed end is in the center and tucked underneath it, so it will not rise up during baking.

As soon as the croissant is shaped, place it on a lightly greased baking sheet, turning the ends in the same direction in which you rolled the dough to make a curved crescent shape. Space the croissants about 2 inches apart. If your oven has a "hot spot," such as the back, arrange the row of croissants closest to it with the tips pointing towards the center of the sheet or the tips may dry out and burn.

Lightly brush the croissants with the egg glaze, brushing upward from the inside of the crescent, so the layers of dough do not stick together and prevent the croissant from rising properly during baking. Let the croissants rise, uncovered, in a warm (about 75°F), humid place, away from drafts, until doubled in size, 1 to 2 hours. During the last 15 minutes of rising, heat the oven to 450°F.

Very lightly brush the croissants in the same direction again with the egg glaze. Then bake for 15 minutes until golden brown, well risen, and slightly crisp. Lower the oven temperature to 400°F if the croissants are browning too quickly. Transfer them immediately to wire racks to cool, making sure they are not touching.

VARIATION: PETITS PAINS AU CHOCOLATE Croissant dough is also used to make these classic French breakfast rolls, which have a rich, dark chocolate filling. When you are in France, look out for the long, thin bars of couverture chocolate traditionally used for making these. Otherwise, use a good-quality semisweet chocolate.

After the third rolling, folding, and chilling, roll out the dough as for the croissants. Cut the dough into 6 x 4-inch rectangles. Place one or two thin squares of semisweet chocolate on one short end. Fold over the dough loosely to make a small, flattish cylinder. Arrange on a lightly greased baking sheet. Glaze with egg glaze. Let rise, uncovered, then glaze again, and bake as for Michel Roux's Croissants (above). Do not re-roll the trimmings – just bake them as they are to enjoy as nibbles.

DANISH PASTRIES

In Denmark, these crisp and flaky filled sweet pastries are called Vienna bread, or wienerbrot. This is because the method of interleaving yeast-bread dough with butter was brought to Denmark about 150 years ago by Austrian pastry chefs, who, in turn, had learned the technique from Turkish bakers working in Vienna. It was the Danes who added the sweet fillings to the pastries. The three fillings given here are the ones I like best, and you'll need to make all three to fill the four different Danish pastry shapes this recipe makes. If you prefer, you can create your own fillings: Try using a good conserve or jam; sweetened ground walnuts; almond paste; or cottage or farmers' cheese flavored with grated lemon rind and sugar. Vary the fillings and shapes to suit your fancy.

Whatever the filling, the baked pastries should be crisp, light, and flaky, not spongy or cake-like. After the dough has been rolled out, folded, and chilled three times, it can be wrapped well and left in the refrigerator for one day, or frozen for up to two weeks. These are best eaten on the day they are baked.

Golden Danish pastries shaped into twists, windmills, pinwheels, and envelopes.

INGREDIENTS

Makes about 28

4 cups (455g) unbleached white bread
flour

1 teaspoon salt

1 0.6-oz cake fresh yeast (15g), or
1 envelope active dry yeast
(2½ teaspoons) plus ½ teaspoon sugar

¾ cup (170ml) lukewarm water

4 tablespoons (60g) lard, vegetable
shortening, or unsalted butter, chilled
and diced

2 large eggs, beaten

extra flour for dusting

1¼ cups (280g) unsalted butter

Almond Filling (page 176)

Vanilla Cream Filling (page 176)

1 egg, beaten, for glazing

Apricot Filling (page 176)

sliced almonds

Glacé Icing (page 176)

apricot jam, warmed and strained
(optional)

4 baking sheets, greased

Stir together the flour and salt in a large bowl. Crumble the fresh yeast into a small bowl. Stir in the lukewarm water until smooth. If using dry yeast, mix the granules and the ½ teaspoon sugar with the water and let stand until foamy, 5 to 10 minutes (page 18).

Rub the lard, shortening, or butter into the flour with your fingertips until the mixture looks like fine crumbs, lifting your hand well above the bowl to toss and aerate the mixture. Make a well in the center of the flour. Add the yeast mixture to the well. Then mix the eggs into the yeast mixture in the well. Work in the flour from the bowl with your hand or a wooden spoon to make a soft, but not sticky dough. Turn out the dough onto a lightly floured work surface and gently knead for 2 minutes only. Wash and dry the bowl and oil it lightly. Return the dough to the bowl and turn the dough over so the top is oiled. Cover the bowl with a damp dish towel. Let the dough rise at room temperature, away from drafts, until doubled in size, about 1 hour.

Punch down the dough in the bowl. Cover with plastic wrap and chill in the refrigerator for 2 to 4 hours until firmer and chilled, but not hard.

If using sticks of butter, shape them into a 5-inch square by cutting the sticks in half lengthwise, arranging the pieces side by side, and mashing them together with your fingertips. Otherwise, using a rolling pin, roll and shape the butter into a 5-inch square. The butter must be quite firm, but still pliable, and about the same temperature as the dough when they are combined. If necessary, pound the butter between two sheets of waxed paper with a rolling pin to make it more pliable, or chill until it is firmer.

Turn out the dough onto a lightly floured work surface and shape it into a ball. Using a sharp knife, mark four evenly spaced points around the center, stopping about 1½ inches from the center. Roll out the four sections of dough with a lightly floured rolling pin, giving the dough a quarter turn after each roll and leaving a thick, rough 5-inch square of dough in the center. Brush off any excess flour.

Put the butter on top of the rough square of dough. Fold the dough over the butter, tucking in the edges and making sure the butter is completely enclosed so it does not ooze out during the following rolling and folding processes.

Roll out the dough, rolling away from you, on a lightly floured surface with a lightly

FOR THE ENVELOPES, SPOON VANILLA CREAM FILLING IN THE CENTER OF EACH SQUARE.

BRING THE CORNERS UP OVER THE FILLING TO MEET IN THE CENTER. PINCH THE ENDS TOGETHER FIRMLY.

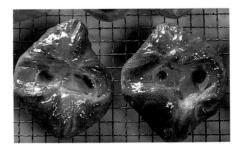

THE BAKED ENVELOPES WILL HAVE A SHINY FINISH IF THEY ARE GLAZED WITH APRICOT JAM.

FOR THE TWISTS, CUT THE FILLED, FOLDED DOUGH INTO NINE STRIPS.

TO SHAPE THEM, TWIST EACH STRIP FIRMLY, TURNING THE ENDS IN OPPOSITE DIRECTIONS.

LET THE TWISTS RISE UNTIL ALMOST DOUBLED IN SIZE. THEN BRUSH WITH THE BEATEN EGG GLAZE.

TO SHAPE PINWHEELS, ROLL UP THE FILLED DOUGH FROM A LONG SIDE, LIKE A JELLY ROLL.

USING A LIGHTLY FLOURED KNIFE, CUT THE ROLL INTO ELEVEN EVEN SLICES. ARRANGE ON A BAKING SHEET.

AFTER THE DOUGH HAS RISEN, BRUSH WITH THE EGG GLAZE AND SPRINKLE WITH SLICED ALMONDS.

BRUSH THE EDGES OF THE FILLED WINDMILLS LIGHTLY WITH BEATEN EGG GLAZE.

FOLD EVERY OTHER CORNER INTO THE CENTER. TWIST THE ENDS TOGETHER FIRMLY.

ARRANGE ON A BAKING SHEET, THEN LET THEM RISE UNTIL THEY ARE ALMOST DOUBLED IN SIZE.

floured rolling pin, into an 18 × 6-inch rectangle, with a short edge facing you. Brush off any excess flour from the dough's surface. Fold up the bottom third of the dough, then fold down the top third to make a three layer dough sandwich that is 6 inches square with the completely enclosed side at the top. Use the rolling pin to seal the side and bottom edges. Wrap in plastic wrap and chill for 15 minutes. Repeat the rolling, folding, and chilling processes twice more. Each time, roll out the dough with the completely enclosed or folded side on your left.

Divide the dough into four equal portions. Then shape and fill the pastries, covering and chilling the portions you are not working with. Here are the shapes and fillings I used for the photographs.

To shape pinwheels, roll out one portion of the dough with a rolling pin to a 9 x 6-inch rectangle, with a long side facing you. Spread evenly with the Almond Filling, leaving a ½-inch border at the edges. Then roll up loosely from the long side, like a jelly roll. Using a lightly floured knife, cut into eleven even slices. Arrange with a cut side up on a greased baking sheet and cover with plastic wrap. Let rise at warm room temperature (about 75°F), away from drafts, until almost doubled in size, 45 minutes to 1 hour.

To shape the envelopes, roll out one portion of the dough with a rolling pin into an 8-inch square. With a lightly floured knife, cut into four equal squares. Put one-quarter of the Vanilla Cream Filling in the center of each square. Brush the corners with a little of the beaten egg glaze, then bring the corners over the filling to meet in the center. Pinch together firmly with your fingers to seal and enclose the filling. Arrange on a greased baking sheet and cover with plastic wrap. Let rise at warm room temperature (about 75°F), away from drafts, until almost doubled in size, 45 minutes to 1 hour.

To shape windmills, roll out one portion of the dough with a rolling pin to an 8-inch square. Cut into four equal squares. Using half the Apricot Filling, put 1 heaping teaspoonful in the center of each square. With a lightly floured knife, make a cut diagonally from each corner to within ½ inch of the center. Brush the edges with a little of the beaten egg glaze. Fold every other corner into the center and twist them together firmly to seal and partially enclose the filling. Arrange on a greased baking sheet and cover with plastic wrap. Let rise at warm room temperature (about 75°F), away from drafts, until almost doubled in size, 45 minutes to 1 hour.

To shape twists, roll out one portion of the dough with a rolling pin to a 9 × 6-inch rectangle. Spread evenly with the other half of the Apricot Filling, leaving a ½-inch border at the edges. Fold the dough in half lengthwise. With a lightly floured knife, cut crosswise into nine equal strips. Twist each strip firmly (some filling may ooze out), then arrange on a greased baking sheet. Cover with plastic wrap. Let rise at warm room temperature (about 75°F), away from drafts, until doubled in size, 45 minutes to 1 hour.

During the last 15 minutes of rising, heat the oven to 425°F. Lightly brush each pastry with the egg glaze, avoiding the cut edges. Sprinkle the pinwheels and twists with sliced almonds. Bake for 10 to 12 minutes, or until well risen and golden. Transfer to a wire rack to cool. You can leave them plain, or brush with a thin layer of strained, warm apricot jam and/or drizzle with Glacé Icing.

Almond Filling

Whisk 1 large egg white in a bowl until stiff peaks form. Fold in 2½ tablespoons (30g) sugar, ½ cup (40g) ground almonds, and 1 tablespoon kirsch or light rum, or a few drops of almond extract. Cover and refrigerate for up to one day until ready to use. Makes enough to fill eleven pinwheels, or four envelopes, or four windmills, or nine twists.

Vanilla Cream Filling

Heat ⅔ cup (140ml) half-and-half with half a split vanilla bean in a small heavy saucepan until scalding (bubbles will appear around the edges). Remove from the heat, cover, and let infuse for 15 minutes. Meanwhile, beat together 1 large egg yolk with 1 tablespoon granulated sugar and 1 tablespoon unbleached all-purpose flour in a small bowl until very thick and almost paste-like. Remove the vanilla bean from the half-and-half, scrape the seeds with the tip of a small knife into the half-and-half, and discard the bean. Whisk the warm half-and-half into the egg mixture. Rinse and dry the saucepan. Return the mixture to the saucepan and simmer over low heat, stirring constantly, until thick enough to coat the back of the spoon. Do not let the mixture boil. Scrape it into a small bowl and cover the surface with plastic wrap to prevent a skin forming. Let cool. Refrigerate for up to one day. Makes enough to fill four windmills or four envelopes; do not use for pinwheels or twists.

After the pastries have cooled, you can drizzle them with Glacé Icing, if you like. Here I am decorating baked pinwheels.

Apricot Filling

Drain a 14-oz can of apricots and purée the fruit in a blender or food processor. Put the purée in a small, heavy saucepan and simmer over medium heat until very thick, stirring frequently to prevent scorching. Let cool. Beat together 2 tablespoons (30g) softened unsalted butter, 2½ tablespoons (30g) sugar, and 1 teaspoon ground cinnamon in a small bowl until soft and smooth. Then beat in the purée. Add a few drops of lemon juice and extra cinnamon to taste, if you wish. Cover and refrigerate for up to one day until ready to use. Makes enough to fill eight windmills or eight envelopes; or eighteen twists; or four windmills and four envelopes and nine twists.

Glacé Icing

Mix 3 tablespoons sifted confectioners' sugar with 1 teaspoon warm water in a small bowl to make a smooth icing that leaves a trail when you lift the spoon. Makes enough to decorate eleven pinwheel Danish pastries.

An old-fashioned, British teatime favorite, yeasted Lardy Cakes are utterly delicious. The outside is crisp, crunchy, and slightly caramelized, while the layered inside is moist and flaky without being too sweet or heavy.

LARDY CAKES

INGREDIENTS

Makes 2 loaves

4½ cups (500g) unbleached white bread flour

1 tablespoon (10g) coarse sea salt, crushed or ground

1 0.6-oz cake fresh yeast (15g), or
  1 envelope active dry yeast
  (2½ teaspoons)

1 cup + 3 tablespoons (240g) sugar

1 cup (230ml) lukewarm milk

1 large egg, beaten

extra flour for dusting

1 cup (230g) lard, or ½ cup (110g) butter and ½ cup (110g) lard, at room temperature and diced

1½ cups (230g) mixed golden raisins and currants

2 deep 8-inch round cake pans or springform pans, greased

In the North of England, a good pinch of mixed sweet spice (akin to pumpkin-pie spice in the U.S.) is often added to this dough. In the West Country (the region in southwestern England that includes the counties of Devon, Somerset, and Cornwall), recipes insist on using good pork lard, a holdover from when lardy cake was a luxury saved for feasts, harvest suppers, and farm celebrations. Along with some bakers, I prefer to use half butter and half lard for a lighter texture and richer taste. The calories, however, remain the same.

For many years, I regularly bought lardy cakes from Wreford's, a small, old-fashioned bakery situated right on highway A303 near West Camel in Somerset. Just before their baker Chris Wreford retired, he showed me how to make his especially delicious lardies. This is his recipe, as he learned it from his father.

The cakes should be eaten within two days of baking, but are best warm from the oven, served thickly sliced. Lardy cake is also good toasted, and if you do not eat the second cake right away, it can be frozen, tightly wrapped in plastic wrap or a freezer bag, for up to one month. Thaw at room temperature for 4 to 6 hours, then unwrap, place on a baking sheet, and warm thoroughly in a 350°F oven for 10 minutes.

Mix together the flour and salt in a medium-size bowl. Make a well in the center of the flour. Crumble the fresh yeast into a small bowl. Stir in 1 teaspoon of the sugar and the lukewarm milk until smooth. If using dry yeast, mix the granules and the 1 teaspoon sugar with the lukewarm milk and let stand until foamy, 5 to 10 minutes (page 18). Add the yeast mixture to the well in the flour. Work in just enough of the flour from the bowl with a small whisk or a spoon to make a thin, smooth batter. Sprinkle the batter with a little of the flour to prevent a skin forming. Cover the bowl with a dish towel and let stand at room temperature until the batter becomes spongy and frothy, 20 to 30 minutes.

Add the eggs to the batter. Then gradually work in the remaining flour from the bowl with your hands or a wooden spoon to make a soft, but not sticky dough.

Turn out the dough onto a lightly floured work surface and knead for 10 minutes until smooth and elastic. Wash, dry, and lightly oil the bowl. Put the dough back into the bowl, then turn the dough over so the top is oiled. Cover with a dry dish towel and let rise at room temperature, away from drafts, until doubled in size, 1 to 1½ hours.

Punch down the dough and turn out onto a lightly floured work surface. Divide the dough into two equal pieces; cover one piece and set aside. Divide the lard (or the butter and lard mixture), the remaining sugar, and the dried fruit into two equal batches.

Roll out the uncovered piece of dough on a lightly floured surface with a lightly floured rolling pin into a 10 × 6-inch rectangle, with a short side facing you. Dot the top two-thirds of the dough rectangle with one-third of the first batch of lard, leaving a 1-inch border at the edges of the dough. Sprinkle with one-third of the first batch of sugar and one-third of the first batch of dried fruit. Fold up the uncovered bottom third of the dough over half the filling. Then fold down the top third of the dough to make a three-layer dough sandwich. Use the rolling pin to seal side and bottom edges. Give the dough a quarter turn to the left, so the completely enclosed side is on your left. Then repeat the whole procedure twice more, to make a total of three rollings, fillings, and foldings. Make sure to give the dough a quarter turn to the left each time.

Let the dough rest, uncovered, at room temperature for 5 to 10 minutes. Meanwhile, roll, fill, and fold the second piece of dough the same way, using the remaining batch of lard, sugar, and dried fruit.

Roll out each piece of dough on a lightly floured surface with a lightly floured rolling pin into an 8-inch square. Put a piece of dough into each prepared cake or springform pan, tucking under the corners, so the dough roughly fits the pan. Cover each pan with a damp dish towel and let rise at room temperature, away from drafts, until the dough has almost doubled in size and expanded to fit the pans, 45 minutes to 1 hour. During the last 15 minutes of rising, heat the oven to 425°F.

Just before baking, using the tip of a sharp knife or a razor blade, score the surface of each cake in a criss-cross pattern. Place each cake pan on a jelly-roll pan to catch any fat that may run out of the pans. Bake the cakes for 25 to 30 minutes until golden brown and crisp. Lower the oven temperature to 375°F if the cakes are browning too quickly. Unmold the cakes onto the jelly-roll pans, leaving them upside down. Bake for 5 minutes longer so the fat seeps downward and the bases (which are now on the top) have a chance to get crispy. Turn out onto wire racks to cool.

AFTER FOLDING UP THE BOTTOM THIRD OF THE DOUGH OVER HALF THE FILLING, FOLD DOWN THE TOP THIRD TO MAKE A THREE-LAYER DOUGH SANDWICH.

SALLY LUNNS

INGREDIENTS

Makes 2 cakes

a large pinch of saffron threads

¼ cup (60ml) milk

4½ cups (500g) unbleached white bread flour

2 teaspoons salt

1 0.6-oz cake fresh yeast (15g), or
    1 envelope active dry yeast
    (2½ teaspoons)

1 teaspoon sugar

1 cup (230ml) heavy cream

4 large eggs

3 tablespoons sugar dissolved in 3 tablespoons boiling milk for glazing

clotted cream, lightly whipped cream, or unsalted butter for serving

2 deep 6-inch round cake pans (see Note), or 6-inch copper saucepans, well greased

This very rich, sponge-like cake is similar to the kugelhopf of Alsace (page 152). The dough is so soft it is worked in the bowl and must be baked in a deep pan, as it will not hold a shape.

Who or what was Sally Lunn? All sorts of tales surround the origin of the cake – that Sally Lunn sold cakes along the fashionable streets of Bath, England, in the 18th century; that she was a Bath pastry chef with a shop in Lilliput Alley; or that Sally Lunn is a corruption of "Soleil Lune," the French sun-and-moon cake, a yellow layer cake filled with white clotted cream. There are many versions of the recipe as well, all claiming authenticity. Some enrich the dough with eggs and melted butter, others add milk too, and some use cream. Saffron, the West Country's favorite spice, is often added, and Elizabeth David recommends grated lemon rind or ground mixed sweet spice in her recipe.

This is my favorite recipe for Sally Lunn. In the 18th century, 5-inch cakes were popular, but the larger pans I use in this recipe are easier to come by nowadays. Slices of this are delicious toasted. If you prefer, you may freeze the second cake. Before splitting and filling it, wrap the cooled cake well in plastic wrap and then in foil, or place it in a freezer bag. The cake will keep in the freezer for up to one month. Thaw, wrapped, at room temperature for 4 to 6 hours. Then unwrap, place on a baking sheet, and heat for 5 minutes in a 350°F oven. When the cake is warm, split and fill it as described.

Crumble the saffron into a small bowl. Heat the milk in a small saucepan until scalding (bubbles will appear around the edge). Then pour it onto the saffron, stir, and let stand to infuse until the milk is lukewarm.

Mix together the flour and salt in a large bowl. Crumble the fresh yeast into the saffron liquid. Then stir in the sugar until smooth. If using dry yeast, mix the granules and the sugar with the lukewarm milk mixture and let stand until foamy, 5 to 10 minutes (page

18). Make a well in the center of the flour. Add the yeast mixture to the well. Mix in enough flour from the bowl with your hand or a wooden spoon to make a thick, smooth batter. Sprinkle the batter with a little flour to prevent a skin forming. Cover the bowl with a damp dish towel and let the batter sponge and become frothy, about 15 minutes.

Whisk the cream and eggs together in a medium-size bowl, then add to the well in the flour. With a small whisk or a spoon, blend the cream and egg mixture into the yeast mixture. When thoroughly combined, gradually work in the flour from the bowl to make a very soft, sticky dough. Using your fingers, work the dough in the bowl for 5 minutes, or until it is glossy, smooth, elastic, and no longer sticks to your fingers.

Divide the dough in half. With lightly floured hands, shape each portion into a ball and place one in each of the prepared cake pans or saucepans. Cover them with damp dish towels and let rise at room temperature, away from drafts, until doubled in size, 1½ to 2 hours. During the last 15 minutes of rising, heat the oven to 400°F.

Bake the cakes for about 25 minutes until golden brown and firm. Cover the cakes with a piece of foil or parchment paper if they brown too quickly while baking. When turned out, a completely baked cake will sound hollow if tapped underneath. Turn out the cakes onto a wire rack, and immediately brush with the hot sweet glaze. Let stand until warm, then slice each cake horizontally into three layers. Spread each layer with clotted cream, whipped cream, or good unsalted butter and reassemble. Eat immediately.

NOTE: The 6 inch cake pans called for in this recipe may be purchased at cookware or specialty bakeware stores that sell supplies for making wedding cakes, or by mail order. See List of Suppliers (page 360).

With its rich, sponge-like texture, Sally Lunn can be served plain, or sliced into layers and filled with clotted cream or whipped cream. A more simple presentation would be to spread unsalted butter between the layers.

A delicious Scottish breakfast of warm butteries served with homemade preserves and a pot of tea.

ABERDEEN BUTTERIES

INGREDIENTS

Makes 20

6 cups (680g) unbleached white bread
   flour

2 tablespoons (15g) coarse sea salt,
   crushed or ground

1 0.6-oz cake fresh yeast (15g), or
   1 envelope active dry yeast (2½
   teaspoons) plus ½ teaspoon sugar

2 cups (430ml) lukewarm water

1 tablespoon sugar

extra flour for dusting

¾ cup (170g) butter, at room
   temperature

¾ cup (170g) lard, at room temperature

a 3-inch round or oval biscuit or cookie
   cutter

2-3 baking sheets, lightly floured

These Scottish pastries are delicious served warm for breakfast, with unsalted butter and orange marmalade. All the bakers in Aberdeenshire aim to make pastries that are crisp, flaky, and rich.

Stir together the flour and salt in a large bowl. Crumble the fresh yeast into a small bowl. Stir in the lukewarm water and sugar until smooth. If using dry yeast, mix the granules and the sugar with the lukewarm water and let stand until foamy, 5 to 10 minutes (page 18). Make a well in the center of the flour. Add the yeast mixture to the well. Work in the flour from the bowl and mix to make a soft, but not sticky dough.

Turn out the dough onto a lightly floured work surface and knead for 10 minutes, or so until the dough is smooth and elastic. Wash and dry the bowl. Return the dough to the bowl. Cover the bowl with a damp dish towel and let rise at room temperature, away from drafts, until doubled in size, 1½ hours.

In a small bowl, mash together the butter and lard. Then divide it into three batches. Punch down the dough. Roll out the dough, rolling away from you, on a lightly floured surface with a lightly floured rolling pin, to an 18 x 6-inch rectangle, with a short side facing you. Dot the top two-thirds of the dough rectangle with one batch of the butter and lard mixture, leaving a ½-inch border at the edges. Fold the uncovered bottom third of the rectangle up over half the fat, then fold the top third of the rectangle down to make a three-layer dough sandwich about 6 inches square, with the completely enclosed side at the top. Seal the side and bottom edges by pressing down with a rolling pin. Wrap the dough in plastic wrap and refrigerate for 30 minutes. Repeat the rolling, filling, folding, and chilling processes twice more. Each time, roll out the dough with the completely enclosed side to your left. After the last folding, tightly cover the dough. Then, for easiest handling, chill at least a day, or overnight, before cutting.

Roll out the dough to a circle about ¾ inch thick. Leave to rest, uncovered, for 5 minutes. Brush off the excess flour. Using a floured biscuit or cookie cutter, stamp out about twenty rounds or ovals. Place the cutouts, upside down and apart, on the prepared baking sheets. Cover with plastic wrap. Let stand until slightly risen, about 20 minutes. Meanwhile, heat the oven to 400°F. Bake them for 20 to 25 minutes, or until golden brown and crisp. Transfer to wire racks.

MICHEL ROUX'S BRIOCHE

INGREDIENTS

Makes 1 large brioche

1 0.6-oz cake fresh yeast (15g), or
  1 envelope active dry yeast
  (2½ teaspoons) plus ½ teaspoon sugar

5 tablespoons (70ml) lukewarm milk

2 tablespoons (15g) coarse sea salt,
  crushed or ground

4½ cups (500g) unbleached white bread
  flour

6 large eggs, beaten

1½ cups #aa 1 tablespoon (355g)
  unsalted butter, softened

2½ tablespoons (30g) sugar

extra flour for dusting

1 egg yolk lightly beaten with 1 tablespoon
  milk for glazing

a large brioche mold, 9½ inches wide at
  the top and 4½ inches across the base,
  greased, or a 7-inch round copper
  saucepan, greased

"The perfect golden brioche has a delicious rich, buttery flavor, yet it does not leave a trace of butter on your fingers or an aftertaste on the palate," says Michel Roux (page 192).

He likes to use 355g of butter to 500g of flour when he makes brioche; pastry chefs vary the quantity from 110g of butter right up to an extravagant 500g of butter without altering the quantity of flour, but these variations depend on how the brioche is to be used. The most common proportion is half the amount of butter to flour. But remember, the best, freshest unsalted butter is vital for good flavor, whatever quantity of butter you use.

The fine, sponge cake-like crumb of a brioche is achieved through three risings, two at normal room temperature and one in the refrigerator. (If the rising is done at two warm a temperature, the butter will melt and ooze out of the dough.) The soft, rich dough is then chilled before it is shaped, so the dough is firm enough to maintain its distinctive top-heavy shape.

Although brioches are usually eaten warm with butter and preserves for breakfast, firmer, plainer doughs are used for savory dishes such as Alyson Cook's Brie en Brioche (page 115), or for sweeter pastries such as the Fancy Ring Doughnuts (page 97). Richer brioches can be hollowed out and filled with sautéed wild mushrooms or seafood in a spicy or creamy sauce.

Michel Roux says, "For a real treat, cut the brioche into slices, sprinkle with confectioners' sugar, and glaze under a very hot broiler. Serve the slices by themselves for breakfast or, as a monstrous indulgence, warm, with chocolate mousse." He adds that brioche looks very impressive if braided or formed into a crown shape.

Brioche dough can be frozen, wrapped in a freezer bag, after it has risen and been punched down, but before it is shaped. To use, let the dough thaw gradually in the refrigerator for 4 to 5 hours, then proceed with the recipe.

Crumble the fresh yeast into the bowl of a large stationary electric mixer fitter with a dough hook or a large bowl, if mixing by hand. Stir in the lukewarm milk and salt until smooth. If using dry yeast, mix the granules and the ½ teaspoon sugar with the lukewarm milk and let stand until foamy, 5 to 10 minutes (page 18). Stir in the salt.

Add the flour and eggs to the yeast mixture and beat with the dough hook to form a

USING HIS FINGERS, MICHEL FORMS A DEEP INDENTATION IN THE LARGE PIECE OF DOUGH IN THE BRIOCHE MOLD.

THE INDENTATION SHOULD EXTEND ALMOST TO THE BOTTOM OF THE MOLD.

HE ROLLS THE SMALLER PIECE OF DOUGH INTO AN ELONGATED PEAR SHAPE.

HE GLAZES THE TOP OF THE RISEN BRIOCHE.

AFTER THE DOUGH HAS RISEN, USING SCISSORS THAT HAVE BEEN DIPPED IN COLD WATER, MICHEL SNIPS ALL AROUND THE EDGE.

WHEN UNMOLDED, BRIOCHES AND MINI BRIOCHE HAVE DISTINCTIVE SHAPES.

soft dough. Then knead the dough with the dough hook until it is smooth and elastic, about 10 minutes. Or, if mixing by hand, stir the flour and eggs into the yeast mixture. With a sturdy wooden spoon or your hand, beat until the dough is smooth and elastic, about 20 minutes.

Beat together the softened butter and sugar in a medium-size bowl until light and fluffy. Beating at low speed, add the butter mixture to the dough, a little at a time, making sure it is completely incorporated after each addition. If you are working by hand, or if the dough feels stiff and it takes a long time to add the butter with the mixer, squeezer the butter mixture into the dough with your hands. Then, continue beating with the dough hook for about 5 minutes, or by hand for 15 minutes, until the dough is perfectly smooth, glossy, shiny, and fairly elastic.

Cover the bowl with a damp dish towel. Let the dough rise at room temperature, away from drafts, until doubled in size, 1¾ to 2 hours.

Punch down the dough by flipping it over quickly with your fingertips not more than two or three times. Return the dough to the bowl. Cover with a damp dish towel and refrigerate for several hours, but not more than 24 hours.

Turn out the dough onto a lightly floured work surface and shape it into a large ball. To make the brioche in a mold, cut off one-third of the dough to make the topknot. Shape the larger piece of dough into a ball and place it in the prepared mold. Form a deep indentation in the center with your fingers, almost down to the bottom of the mold. With your palm held at an angle against the work surface, roll the smaller piece of dough into an elongated pear shape with a narrow neck.

Using lightly floured fingertips, gently press the narrow neck well down into the hole in the center of the large ball.

If you are using the saucepan, line it with a sheet of buttered parchment paper twice the height of the pan. Shape all the dough into a ball, then place in the pan. The brioche will bake into a tall, cylinder shape.

Lightly brush the top of the brioche with egg glaze, working from the outside inward. Take care not to let any glaze run into the crack between the main body of the dough and the topknot, or onto the edges of the mold, because it will prevent the dough from rising properly. Cover with plastic wrap.

Let the dough rise at room temperature, away from drafts, until almost doubled in size, 1½ to 2 hours; it may take an hour or so longer if the dough has been chilled 24 hours. During the last 15 minutes of rising, heat the oven to 425°F.

Glaze the brioche again. Using scissors dipped in cold water, snip all around the edges so the dough doesn't stick to the pan to help it rise properly in the oven. Bake for 40 to 45 minutes, or until the brioche is golden brown and sounds hollow when tapped underneath. If the brioche is browning too quickly, cover loosely with foil. Carefully unmold the brioche and transfer to a wire rack to cool.

VARIATION: MINI BRIOCHES You can use the same dough to make individual, mini brioches. Lightly butter twenty small brioche molds measuring 3¼ inches wide at the top and 1½ inches wide at the base (5 fluid ounce capacity). Weigh the dough and divide it into twenty equal pieces, or roll it into a fat rope and cut it into twenty equal pieces. Shape as for the large brioche, above. Glaze, cover with plastic wrap, and let rise at room temperature, away from drafts, until doubled in size, about 1 hour. Glaze again. Bake in a 425°F oven for about 8 minutes, or until the brioches are golden brown and sound hollow when tapped underneath. Cool on a wire rack.

BABAS AND SAVARINS

A very light, yeasty dough that produces a holey crumb is used to make babas and savarins because it soaks up sugar syrup like a bath sponge. The final result is a thoroughly sodden, cake-like dessert that is, nevertheless, light in texture, never heavy.

Babas are said to have been "invented" in the mid-17th century by Duke Stanislas of Lorraine, who dunked his stale kugelhopf in a rum syrup. He was so taken by his creation, according to the legend, he named it after Ali Baba, his favorite character in A Tale of a Thousand and One Nights. Dome-topped babas are usually baked in individual bucket-shaped baba or dariole molds, then soaked in syrup flavored with rum, although you can use other liqueurs. Kirsch is delicious, especially if you slice strawberries into the reserved syrup to serve with the babas.

Savarins, on the other hand, are ring shaped, large or small. They are made without the currants that are generally included in babas, although the savarin dough is often flavored with other fruit additions, such as grated lemon or orange rind or chopped candied fruit, which are added after the butter is incorporated. The soaking syrup is enhanced with grated lemon or orange rind; spices, such as cinnamon or cardamom; or liqueurs, such as kirsch, rum, Grand Marnier, Cointreau, or Cognac.

A savarin is especially delicious served with a filling in the center of the ring. Try sweetened, vanilla-flavored whipped cream, fruit salad, or poached fruit. Savarins are usually decorated with candied cherries and angelica that has been cut into leaves, but I prefer to do without these ornamental extras.

Correct rising is vital when you make babas and savarins. Not enough time and the dough will be heavy; too much time and the dough will run over the top of the mold during baking. Also, make sure the dough rises in a spot that is warm, but not hot.

Babas and savarins keep well, tightly wrapped, for up to 24 hours. They can also be baked and stored in an airtight container for two or three days, or wrapped and frozen for one month. If frozen, unwrap them, place them still frozen on baking sheets, and reheat in a 350°F oven for 10 to 12 minutes for babas, 15 to 20 minutes for savarins. Baste them with hot syrup shortly before serving.

Saturated with a lemon- or orange-flavored sugar syrup and filled with fresh fruit, a savarin makes a dessert that is as impressive looking as it is delicious. It is ideal to serve for a dinner party. I have filled this one with fresh strawberries and oranges but you can use any fruit.

JUST BEFORE SERVING, SPOON THE
RUM OVER EACH BABA.

RUM BABAS

This recipe is adapted from one taught at L'Ecole de Cuisine La Varenne, which is based at the Château du Fey, in France's Burgundy region.

INGREDIENTS

Makes 8

4 cups (230g) unbleached white bread
    flour

1 teaspoon salt

1½ tablespoons sugar

1 0.6-oz cake fresh yeast (15g), or
    1 envelope active dry yeast
    (2½ teaspoons) plus ½ teaspoon sugar

3 tablespoons lukewarm milk

3 large eggs, beaten

¼ cup (60ml) dark rum

3 tablespoons water

½ cup (70g) currants

½ cup (110g) unsalted butter, softened

SYRUP:

2½ cups (500g) sugar

1 quart (1 liter) water

6 tablespoons dark rum

8 baba molds of 8½ fl oz (245ml)
    capacity

Stir together the flour, salt, and sugar in a large bowl. Crumble the fresh yeast into a small bowl. Stir in the lukewarm milk until smooth. If using dry yeast, mix the granules and the ½ teaspoon sugar with the lukewarm milk and let stand until foamy, 5 to 10 minutes (page 18). Make a well in the center of the flour. Add the yeast mixture to the well. Then mix the eggs into the yeast mixture. Using your hand, work in the flour from the bowl to make a smooth, very thick batter-like dough.

Knead the dough in the bowl by beating it with your hand. Tilt the bowl slightly and, using your hand like a spoon with fingers together and palm upward, lift the dough and throw it back into the bowl with a slapping motion. Continue kneading for 5 minutes, or until the dough becomes very elastic, smooth, and slightly stiffer.

Cover the bowl with a damp dish towel. Let rise in a warm place (about 75°F), away from drafts, until doubled in size, 45 minutes to 1 hour. Meanwhile, warm the rum and water in a small saucepan. Add the currants and let them soak. Butter the molds and chill them in the freezer for 10 minutes. Butter them again. This double buttering helps prevent the soft, rich dough from sticking; the butter sets and does not get absorbed by the dough as it rises. If the kitchen is very hot and the butter starts to melt, put the molds in the refrigerator; otherwise, leave them at room temperature.

Punch down the risen dough in the bowl. Using your hand as before, gradually beat in the softened butter until the dough, like a very thick batter, is smooth and even, not streaky. Drain the currants and work them into the dough.

Drop the dough from an ungreased metal spoon into the molds, filling each one-third full. Arrange the molds on a baking sheet and cover with a damp dish towel. Let rise at warm room temperature (about 75°F), away from drafts, until the dough rises almost to the top of the molds, 30 to 50 minutes. Check to make sure the dough is not sticking to the cloth. During the last 15 minutes of rising, heat the oven to 400°F.

Bake the babas on the baking sheet for about 20 to 30 minutes, or until they are golden brown and begin to shrink from the sides of the molds. Unmold them onto a wire rack and let cool.

To make the syrup, stir together the sugar and water in a medium-size saucepan over low heat until the sugar is dissolved. Bring to a boil and let boil for 2 to 3 minutes, or until the syrup becomes clear.

Remove the pan from the heat. Add the babas, one or two at a time, to the very hot syrup. Using a large slotted spoon, gently turn them over several times to make sure they absorb as much syrup as possible; they will swell and become very shiny. Using the slotted spoon, carefully lift the babas out of the syrup and onto a plate. Soak the remaining babas. Reserve the remaining syrup. Just before serving, sprinkle the babas with the rum. Add any remaining rum to the reserved syrup and serve separately for spooning over the babas.

VARIATIONS: MINI RUM BABAS Grease about sixteen small baba molds or 4½ fl oz (125ml) capacity, dariole molds, or muffin pans. Make the baba batter as above. Butter and fill the molds as above. Cover with a damp dish towel. Let rise at warm room temperature (about 75°F), away from drafts, until the dough has risen almost to the top of the molds, 20 to 45 minutes. Bake in a 400°F oven for 18 to 20 minutes. Then cool and soak with the syrup and sprinkle with the rum as described above.

GRAND BABA In Alsace and Lorraine, whole giant babas are served at parties or celebration meals. Make the baba batter as above, but let it rise in a well-buttered 9-inch kugelhopf mold and then bake in a 400°F oven for 40 to 45 minutes. Cool and soak with the syrup and sprinkle with the rum as described above.

SAVARIN

Make the Rum Baba batter as opposite, omitting the currants and their rum soak. Butter a large 5-cup (1.15 liter) ring or savarin mold or two smaller 1½-cup (340ml) ring molds, as described in the baba recipe. Fill the mold or molds one-third full with the batter. Let rise at warm room temperature, away from drafts, for 30 to 50 minutes, or until the dough is almost to the top of the mold. Bake in a 400°F oven for 20 to 25 minutes until it is golden and shrinks from the sides of the mold. Unmold it onto a wire rack.

Make the sugar syrup as for Rum Baba (opposite) in a large, shallow pan, adding the finely grated rind and juice of 1 large lemon when the syrup is removed from the heat. If the savarin fits, place it in the very hot syrup in the pan and spoon the syrup over it until it is saturated. If the savarin is too big for the pan, put it on a wire rack set over a jelly-roll pan and spoon the hot syrup over it, reheating any syrup that drips onto the pan and spooning it over the savarin, until all the syrup is absorbed. The savarin will swell and look very shiny.

Just before serving, sprinkle 3 to 4 tablespoons amber or dark rum over the savarin. Fill the center with whipped cream that has been sweetened to taste and flavored with vanilla, or with fresh fruit salad.

THE DOUGH WILL RISE ALMOST TO THE TOP OF THE MOLD.

SPOON THE HOT SYRUP OVER THE FRESHLY BAKED SAVARIN.

EQUIPMENT

BRIDGE KITCHENWARE
214 E. 52nd Street
New York, NY 10022
800-274-3435
Professional bakeware,
cookware, tools.
Catalog available.

BROADWAY PANHANDLER
520 Broadway
New York, NY 10012
212-966-3434
Bakeware, cookware, tools.

DEAN & DELUCCA, INC.
MAIL ORDER DEPARTMENT
560 Broadway
New York, NY 10012
800-221-7714
Specialty bakeware, including
brioche pans, cookware, tools.
Catalog avaliable.

KING ARTHUR® FLOUR
BAKER'S CATALOG
P.O. Box 876
Norwich, Vermont 05055
800-827-6836
Specialty bakeware and tools.
Catalog available.

KITCHEN KRAFTS
P.O. Box 805
Mount Laurel, NJ 08054
800-776-0575
Specialty bakeware.
Catalog available.

LA CUISINE
323 Cameron Street
Alexandria, VA 22314
800-521-1176
Cookware and bakeware; baking
ingredients.
Catalog available.

MAID OF SCANDINAVIA
3244 Raleigh Avenue
Minneapolis, MN 55416
800-328-6722
Specialty bakeware and tools.
Catalog available.

WILLIAMS-SONOMA
P.O. Box 7456
San Francisco, CA 94120-7456
800-541-2233
Bakeware, cookware, tools.
Catalog available.

ZABAR'S
2245 Broadway
New York City, NY 10024
212-496-1234
Bakeware, cookware, tools.
Catalog available.

FLOURS AND GRAINS

BRUMWELL MILLING
328 East Second Street
Sumner, LA 50674
319-578-8106
Stone-ground certified organic
bread flour, rye and spelt flours,
cornmeal.
Price list available.

BUTTE CREEK MILL
P.O. Box 561
Eagle Point, OR 97524
503-826-3531
Stone-ground bread flour, pastry
flour, buckwheat flour,
cornmeal.
Price list available.

GRAY'S GRIST MILL
P.O. Box 422
Adamsville, RI 02801
508-636-6075
Stone-ground certified organic
bread flour, rye and spelt flours,
stone-ground cornmeal.
Price list available.

THE GREAT VALLEY MILLS
R.D. 3, Country Line Road
Box 1111
Barto, PA 19504
800-688-6455
Stone-ground bread flour, pastry
flour, rye and semolina flour,
steel-cut oats.
Catalog available.

KING ARTHUR® FLOUR
BAKER'S CATALOG
(see EQUIPMENT)
Stone-ground bread flour, pastry
flour, white whole-wheat flour,
amaranth, barley, semolina, and
spelt flours, cornmeal, vital
wheat gluten, cracked wheat,
wheat flakes.

NEW HOPE MILLS
R.R. 2, P.O. Box 269A
Moravia, NY 13118
315-497-0783
Stone-ground bread flour,
buckwheat, rye, and spelt flours,
vital wheat gluten, cornmeal.
Catalog available.

PETE'S SPICE AND
EVERYTHING NICE
174 First Avenue
New York, NY 10009
212-254-8773
Bread flour, pastry flour,
buckwheat, rye, semolina, and
spelt flours, cornmeal.
Catalog available.

SHILOH FARMS INC.
P.O. Box 97
Sulphur Springs, AR 72768
800-362-6832, for the West and the
Midwest on the East Coast.

GARDEN SPOT
438 White Oak Road
New Holland, PA 17557
800-829-5100
Certified organic, stone-ground
bread flour, and spelt flour.

STAFFORD COUNTY FLOUR
MILLS Co.
P.O. Box 7
Hudson, KS 67545
316-458-4121
Hudson Cream unbleached
white and whole-wheat flours.

WAR EAGLE MILL
Route 5, Box 411
Rogers, AR 72756
501-789-5343
Certified organic, stone-ground
bread flour, buckwheat and rye
flours, cornmeal.
Catalog available.

DRIED AND CANDIED FRUIT AND CITRUS PEELS

DEAN & DELUCCA, INC.
(see EQUIPMENT)
Dried and candied fruit, candied
citrus peels, in season.

PETE'S SPICE AND
EVERYTHING NICE
(see FLOURS AND GRAINS)
Dried and candied fruit, candied
citrus peel.

TIMBER CREST FARMS
4791 Dry Creek Road
Healdsburg, CA 95448
707-433-8251
Certified organic, no-sulphur-
added dried apples, apricots,
peaches, pears, prunes, raisins.
Catalog available.

ACKNOWLEDGEMENTS

Linda Collister and Anthony Blake would like to
thank the following people and companies:

IN THE UNITED STATES: Noah Alper, Linda and
Ken Busteed, Alyson Cook, Cindy Falk, Betty and Abe
Groff, Jeffrey Hamelman, Lucinda Hampton
(Pennysylvania Dutch Visitors Bureau), Dottie and Andy
Hess, Hayely Matson, Ina McNeil, Dee Dee and Jack
Meyer, Will and Annette Hertz, Jim Friedlander, Lois and
Ezia Lamdin, Caroll Bolton, and at Young's Pecans,
Florence, South Carolina, James Swink, Susan Stephenson,
Helen Watts, Diane Dorsey, Shawn Price, Mac
Davenport, Henry Unruh, Rosemary Underdahl and
Barbara Walker.

IN FRANCE: Kate and John Barber, Jean-Jacques
Bernachon, Jean-Pierre St Martin, Clarisse and Jean
Michel Deiss and Lionel Poilâne.

IN GREAT BRITAIN: Joy Skipper, Beverley LeBlanc,
Janet Bligh, Sandra Bosuston, Betty Charlton, Julia
Royden-Cooper, Elaine Hallgarten, Randolph Hodgson of
Neals Yard Dairy, Pierre Koffman, Barbara Levy, Norma
MacMillan, Joy Portch, Rachel Roskilly, Michel Roux,
Louise Simpson, Jagdeesh Sohal, Anna Rollo and Cosmo
Sterk, Mike Thurlow of Letheringsett, Jonathan Topps,
Paul Welti, Sharon Turner and Yvonne Jenkins, Stephen
Bull, Marc and Max Renzland, Brigitte Friis, Zeynep
Stromfelt, Katie Stewart, Sallie Morris, Alan Hertz,
Michael Sealey, Rena Salaman, Betty Charlton, Jean

Bush, Alice Portnoy at Neff and Sheila Rossen.
IN IRELAND: Mary Curtis, Phoebe and Bill Lett,
Veronica Steele of Milleens Dairy and Alice and
Gerry Turner.
IN GERMANY: Nurnberg Tourist Office
FOR PHOTOGRAPHY: Uli Hinter at Leica Cameras.
FOR CROCKERY AND CUTLERY: Villeroy and
Boch; for equipment: The Kitchenware Company; for
kitchen appliances; Neff. Braun, Kenwood, Magimix.

The authors also wish to express their appreciation to the
Bulgarian Wine and Tourist Agency, Kansas Wheat
Commission, Nuremberg Tourist Office, Sharwoods and
Trustees Philipsburg Manor.

INDEX

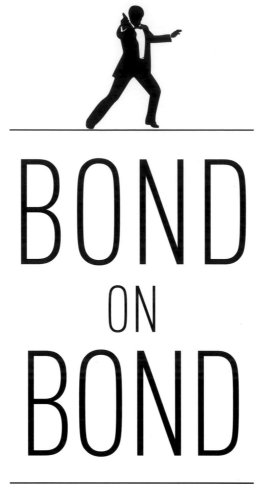

BOND
ON
BOND

Reflections on 50 Years of James Bond Movies

ROGER MOORE

with Gareth Owen

LYONS PRESS
Guilford, Connecticut

An imprint of Globe Pequot Press

For my favourite Bond girl – Kristina

First published in Great Britain in 2012 by
Michael O'Mara Books Limited

This Lyons Press edition first published in 2012

Lyons Press is an imprint of Globe Pequot Press.

Library of Congress Cataloging in Publication Data is available on file.

ISBN 978-0-7627-8281-9

Papers used by Michael O'Mara Books Limited are natural,
recyclable products made from wood grown in sustainable forests.
The manufacturing processes conform to the environmental regulations of
the country of origin.

Designed and typeset by Design 23

1 2 3 4 5 6 7 8 9 10

Printed and bound in China

CONTENTS

INTRODUCTION

The year 2012 not only witnesses the release of the twenty-third James Bond film in the shape of *Skyfall*, but it also marks fifty years since our intrepid hero first burst onto cinema screens in *Dr. No*.

We've seen six incarnations of Jim Bond – whose name his creator Ian Fleming borrowed from the author of a book entitled *Birds of the West Indies* – in the official Eon-produced series of films: Sean Connery, George Lazenby, Timothy Dalton, Pierce Brosnan, Daniel Craig and ... erm ... oh yes, me!

It has been suggested that over half the world's population

BELOW: The scene in which the infamous line, 'Bond, James Bond', is first delivered by Sean in *Dr. No*.

has seen at least one of the films in what has become the world's longest-running movie franchise; and a series in which 007 has got to know over fifty-five 'Bond girls', has fought over 130 villains and *femme fatales*, has knocked-back numerous vodka martinis, has driven five different models of Aston Martin, has visited over fifty different countries and has been armed with over one hundred gadgets and guns – a few of which he even returned intact.

The escapism, entertainment, fun, beauty and thrills that so encapsulate each and every film were set down by the blueprint designed by producers Albert R. 'Cubby' Broccoli and Harry Saltzman, who helmed the early movies together before Cubby took the reins alone in 1977; which he in turn then handed over to his daughter Barbara and stepson Michael in 1995.

The combined box office of the first twenty-two films has exceeded $5 billion and while the *Harry Potter* and *Star Wars*

ABOVE: *Goldfinger* was the first Bond film to have a premiere, which was held at the Odeon Leicester Square. The crowds went crazy and had to be held back by the police.

ABOVE: *Octopussy* proved to be another crowd puller.

films may come close, they have enjoyed more limited theatrical life spans whereas Bond is very much set to continue indefinitely and – who knows – maybe he too will even get a 3D retro-makeover?

It isn't just about cinema, either. I'm often told by people, friends and fans, how they regarded it as a big occasion when a Bond film first came on TV, in the dark ages before DVDs and online streaming, that is, and I'm proud to say that when, on Christmas Day in 1980, *The Man With The Golden Gun* premiered, it attracted (and has since held the record of) the largest ever audience of any Bond film on the box. In fact all the 007 films, not just mine, regularly attracted huge audiences on broadcast, which, incidentally, the networks usually reserved for Bank Holidays and Christmas. Coupled with those screenings, the wide and affordable introduction of VHS (remember that?)

and DVD opened up an even bigger market for the films, and brought with them new audiences to the continuing franchise.

There is certainly a huge loyalty in the world of 007 fans; fans who not only collect the films, but also the memorabilia, the books (such as this one, dear reader) and posters; they also anticipate news of upcoming adventures, with huge excitement, on the multitude of fan sites and forums in which they scrutinise, analyze and dissect every little detail. Of course, many on these forums insist I'm their favourite Bond, but modesty prevents me complimenting their amazingly good taste!

Although 2012 marks a golden anniversary for the series, it also marks a ruby anniversary for me. You see, in October 1972 I reported for duty as the third actor to play James Bond on screen for Eon Productions. Can it really be forty years ago? Back then I could leap out of a chair without fear of my knees cracking; could chew on a toffee without fear of losing a filling, or worse still a tooth; could admire my long flowing locks of hair; and as I swooned in front of the mirror, proudly admire my bronzed, slim torso. Ah yes, with a flex of my toned muscles and a twitch of the old eyebrow I set pulses racing across the world, they say.

These days it's my pacemaker that keeps my pulse racing and as for my other above mentioned attributes … well, I still have my memories.

When I was invited by my publisher to take a look at the Bond films from my own fairly unique perspective (well, unique in that there are only six of us) of being James Bond on the big screen, it seemed rather a taxing demand for someone who has only appeared in seven of the films, and who is not necessarily an avid repeat viewer of the others. However, by calling on a few friendships and with the guidance of one or two people, I have attempted to fill up the spaces between some lovely photos with interesting words, thoughts and memories. What I can't remember, I'll just have to make up.

BELOW: A typical day in the Moore household. It's a hard life, but someone's got to do it.

BOND
ON
BEGINNINGS

BOND ON BEGINNINGS

As I write I am sitting in Monte Carlo with my wife Kristina. The sweltering sun is beating down upon us as we sip our early-morning coffee, slip on our dark glasses and watch the millionaires – and billionaires – passing by in their designer clothes, their fast cars and on their yachts, while their luscious lady friends, all potential Bond girls, are busy sunning themselves on the terraces at the Monte Carlo Beach Club. It is a very 'Bondian' setting in which to write a book, though I feel I should start by confessing it wasn't until 1962 that I first heard mention of James Bond – some eight or nine years after Ian Fleming had started writing his hugely popular books – but they, and he, had somehow passed me by.

PREVIOUS PAGES: Bonded by success: Harry Saltzman (right), Ian Fleming and Cubby Broccoli pose for a photo after signing their agreement to produce the first James Bond film in 1962.

LEFT: The birth of an icon: a very early publicity shot of Sean Connery as 007.

WILL HE, WON'T HE?

Following a spell in Hollywood, where two studio contracts were swiftly followed by a plane ticket home, in 1960 I wound up in Rome, making a couple of what you might call 'miracle-movies'. That is to say, it was a miracle if anyone got to see them.

My agent, Dennis Van Thal, called while I was in Venice gorging my face on a favourite dish of black pasta, flavoured with a little garlic, shallots and with a decent handful of prosciutto, all complemented by a glass of Pinot Grigio on the terrace of the Gritti Palace Hotel, which itself sits on the banks of the picturesque Grand Canal. Very Flemingesque, eh?

Dennis had received an offer from British television mogul Lew Grade for me to play Simon Templar in a television series of *The Saint*. I was immediately and greatly interested because I knew those books and had, in fact, at one point made an – unsuccessful – approach to their author, Leslie Charteris, to buy the rights.

To cut a long story short, I accepted the contract and found myself back in England with a regular salary jingling away in my pocket.

A little financial security is always a good thing for an insecure actor, and with it I soon began behaving in a Bond-like fashion by

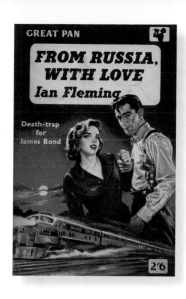

ABOVE: It had to start somewhere! A few covers of Ian Fleming's books, which I'm assured all sell for more than 2 shillings and 6 pence these days. Interesting that I'm on the cover of *Dr. No* – even though a well known Scottish actor was in the film.

visiting the tables of the gaming houses in London's Curzon Street. It was there I first met two larger-than-life, and obviously affluent, American gentlemen who introduced themselves as producers Harry Saltzman (a Canadian) and Cubby Broccoli (an American of Italian descent). Over the ensuing months we exchanged a fair amount of casino money across the table, but moreover developed a close friendship, which lasted the rest of their lives.

They were then just setting out on producing a series of films about 'James Bond'. That was the very first time I'd heard the name.

RIGHT: Photocall on the roof of London's Dorchester Hotel, announcing me as the new James Bond with director Guy Hamilton on the left, Cubby Broccoli in the middle and Harry Saltzman on the right. Note how Harry's looking at my hair, wondering how many inches I should lose.

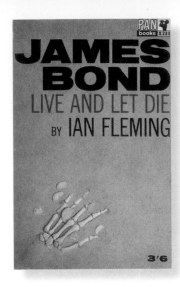
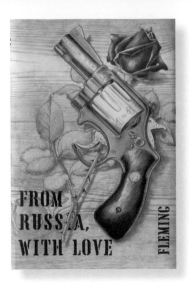

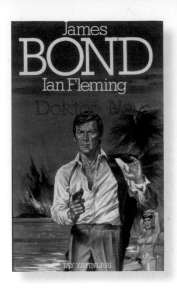

Cubby and Harry told me about agent 007 and invited me to the first screening of *Dr. No* and, later, all the other Sean Connery Bond films, at their Mayfair headquarters, Eon Productions in South Audley Street. I was greatly enlightened, entertained and captivated by the good Commander and his amazing exploits.

The Saint, meanwhile, happily ran and ran. In fact I clocked up 118 episodes over seven years. It was towards the end of the penultimate series in 1967–8 that the idea of me playing Jimmy Bond was first mooted. Sean Connery had completed *You Only*

BELOW: I was big in Birmingham. A ticket stub for a first-night screening.

15

ABOVE: With my dear friend Lew Grade, who told me that playing Bond would ruin my career.

RIGHT: I was expected to do everything! On location for *The Man With The Golden Gun.*

Live Twice and stated that it was to be his last. Keen to keep the franchise afloat, the producers started thinking about recasting. They must have heard I worked cheap.

Producer Harry Saltzman called. 'Let's talk about you doing Bond.'

Producers, writers and agents' discussions commenced around an adventure set in Cambodia. Unfortunately, very soon afterwards all hell broke loose in that country and the production was shelved. With uncertainty about what might happen, and with the prospect of another – financially appealing – series of *The Saint* looming, I returned to film what would be my last season of the show.

Keen to get back into movies, I simultaneously began developing a couple of projects with my *Saint* producing partner Bob Baker, one of which – *Crossplot* – we filmed with funding from United Artists, the backers of the Bond movies. I then became an actor-for-hire

in *The Man Who Haunted Himself* for Bryan Forbes at EMI, before teaming up with Bob Baker again to star in, occasionally direct, and produce a TV series called *The Persuaders!*. Oh, and thanks to my friendship with Cary Grant I also took up an executive position at Brut Films to oversee a few rather successful productions, including the Oscar-winning *A Touch Of Class*.

Life was pretty good, and very busy. Cubby and Harry were busy doing their thing too, and while we stayed in touch, when they regrouped I became 'unavailable' due to my own filming commitments, and so they made Jimmy Bond an Australian, albeit for one adventure only.

Only after Sean returned for – and said 'never again' following – *Diamonds Are Forever*, in 1971, was I brought back into the frame and, happily, I was between acting gigs.

'Are you alone?' Harry asked when he called me long distance at my Denham home (my phone number, oddly enough, was Denham 2007). 'You mustn't talk about this,' he added, 'but Cubby

agrees with my thinking in terms of you for the next Bond.'

I didn't say anything to anyone. Once bitten, twice shy.

Contracts were drawn up and duly signed. It was a few weeks before Harry called again, to say he and Cubby felt I was 'too fat' and my hair was 'too long'. I said I'd get a haircut and take the weight off.

I told my dear friend Lew Grade (who along with *The Saint* also bankrolled *The Persuaders!*) that I was to be the next 007. With tears welling in his eyes, he shook his head and said, 'Roger, don't do it. It'll ruin your career!'

'What career?' I hear you say.

There is always a huge challenge associated with taking over a role from another actor, particularly when he has enjoyed great success in said role. I knew I'd face comparisons and wondered if I'd even be accepted by audiences. However, I consoled myself by thinking about the hundreds of actors who have all played Hamlet. Besides, if it didn't work out I could always go back to modelling sweaters and gorging myself on more Flemingesque lunches in Venice, while letting my hair grow down my back.

BELOW: It's not every day my getting a haircut made the newspapers.

SQUARE CUT

For 007, the old 'short back and sides' is a must

Studio barber giving Moore the treatment

By IAN CHRISTIE

THERE is more to being James Bond than just signing a fat contract, thwarting the villains and accepting the advances of ravishing girls. In a sense it is like joining the Army.

For Roger Moore, who takes over the role in the next Bond adventure, "Live And Let Die," was given the order by producer Harry Saltzman: "Get your hair cut!"

was not the approved hair-style.

Said Harry Saltzman: "After all, he is not just a civilian, he is Commander Bond."

Image

Co-producer Cubby Broccoli commented: "We think Bond looks more masculine with his hair cut to a reasonable length.

"This is the image we have built up over the years and it is one we wish to keep. Basically Bond is a square."

FINDING THE KEY

At the outset, I knew I would have to be tougher than the other screen heroes I had played: Beau Maverick, Ivanhoe, Simon Templar and Brett Sinclair. However, having known many soldiers and servicemen, I didn't necessarily believe that Bond was a man who enjoyed killing. He'd have to be rather sadistic to get a kick out of it. In fact, when I re-read the Fleming novels there was a line that stated, 'Bond did not particularly enjoy killing'. And that was the key to my interpretation of the role: I wouldn't enjoy killing, but I'd do it professionally, quickly and accurately.

What else? Well, Fleming made it clear Bond enjoyed the finer things in life from food, drink, cars and travel to, ahem, women. That's not a bad job description, is it?

But what of Bond the man? Ian Fleming gave very little away about the character until he penned an obituary for Bond. Had the author not been persuaded otherwise by his publisher, the obituary would have come a lot sooner than it actually did. After just four books, feeling he'd done his duty and his adventures had run their course, Fleming grew tired of his hero, much as Arthur Conan Doyle had done with Sherlock Holmes. He fully intended to have Bond murdered at the end of *From Russia With Love*. Thankfully, he was talked out of it and continued the series. The memorial piece was reserved until *You Only Live Twice* was published (six novels later) – and was written by 007's boss, M.

'Commander James Bond, CMG, RNVR,' it started, referring to Bond's naval service and his being a Companion in the Order of St Michael and St George, 'was born to Andrew Bond, of Glencoe, Scotland, and Monique Delacroix, from the Canton de Vaud, in south west Switzerland.'

Andrew Bond was a foreign representative of the Vickers armaments firm, and Jimmy travelled with his parents wherever their work took them. When Jimmy was but a mere eleven years of age, both parents were killed in a climbing accident in the Aiguilles Rouges, France.

Jimmy was an orphan. Poor Jimmy.

Bond's early education was undertaken abroad and so he became fluent in both French and German. After his parents' deaths, young Jim went to live with his aunt, Miss Charmian Bond, in Pett Bottom, a hamlet near Canterbury, Kent.

Then, Fleming revealed, aged twelve our young hero was entered at Eton College, but after a year there was 'some alleged trouble with one of the boys' maids' and he was transferred to Fettes College in Edinburgh, where he took part in wrestling, founded a judo class and graduated early at the age of seventeen.

As for me, at seventeen I'd left school, been fired from my first

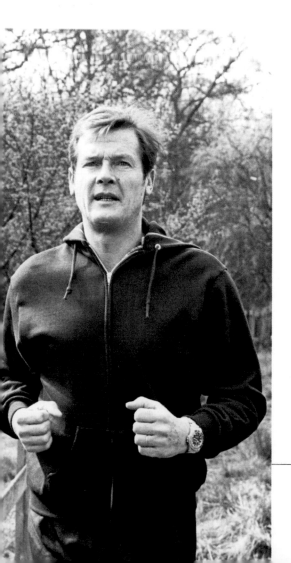

BELOW: Having lost some hair, I was now trying to get fit and lose some weight – at my family home in Denham.

job (not through problems with any maids, I might add) and was wondering what I would do with my future. Unlike Jimmy, I was not recruited by the special branch of the Royal Navy Volunteer Reserve, nor, a few years later, was I approached by MI6.

Thankfully, the obituary was a ruse to put off Jimmy's pursuers. He wasn't dead, but it proved a helpful ploy in the adventure. It also proved helpful to us readers in stitching together a backcloth to the character. I've never been guilty of method acting – or even acting, if you want to argue a point – but doing this bit of background reading in *You Only Live Twice* gave me a few ideas about the character and why he was who he was. But throughout I kept thinking about that line 'James Bond did not particularly enjoy killing'. That was the key.

BRITISH NAVAL COMMANDER MURDERED

In the early hours of this morning, in an Hong Kong Hotel bedroom, was discovered the body of the British Naval Commander James Bond.

The body was discovered by two Police Inspectors of the Hong Kong Police Force, who answered an emergency call from a near-by bar. The gunfire was heard by people in the street below, and the police were on the scene within minutes.

As yet there has been no arrest made, but the police are working on a definite clue. Foul play is suspected and the question is being asked what a high ranking naval officer was doing in such a notorious district.

ABOVE: Bond's demise was reported in *You Only Live Twice* on the front page of a newspaper.

THE BOND PHENOMENON

Sean Connery had enjoyed huge success as the first filmic Bond. When *Dr. No* first hit the screens in 1962, in my humble opinion, where leading heroic parts were concerned, Sean changed everything. The world of Bond blew a hurricane breath of fresh air into the adventure-movie genre with its larger-than-life villains, even more evil than Satan himself; drop-dead-gorgeous girls who in fact did often drop dead if they found their way to Bond's bed in the first half-hour of the film; hugely glamorous locations and sets; and a hero who was impeccably turned out, with the best taste in everything and the enviable ability to disrobe a leading lady in the flick of a camera shutter.

In an era when travel was the reserve of the rich, post-war rationing and rebuilding was still a vivid memory, and fine living

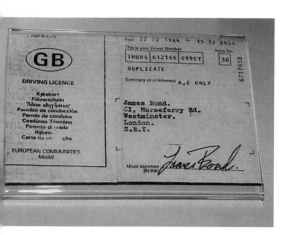

ABOVE: Although relatively few details are known about Jimmy's home life, he did have a driving licence for one of the films. Westminster? Hmmm. I thought he lived in Chelsea.

consisted of a night out at the pictures followed by a fish-and-chip supper, James Bond offered something exciting – something previously unimaginable. Bond swiftly became a phenomenon.

But, as with all success stories, it very nearly wasn't.

Harry Saltzman had an option on the books, which was fast running out. Columbia Pictures had turned it down, as had other potential backers. It was through partnering with Cubby Broccoli, and Cubby's friendship with Arthur Krim at United Artists, that the series was eventually launched.

A deal was struck with Krim and the fact that Cubby was able to loan Harry the airfare to get to New York and sign the deal saw the making not only of a great franchise, but also of a brilliant Scottish actor's career, as well as fairly regular employment not only for Bonds but the villainous characters, glamorous girls, extras willing to fall off bridges and stuntmen keen to be hurled into the air by explosions and dive into shark-infested pools. The screenplay was co-written by Richard Maibaum, who went on to collaborate on twelve more of Jim's adventures.

It is well documented that the first James Bond film was given a $1 million budget – and even for 1962, that was considered tight. Thankfully, it increased exponentially film by film, not least to accommodate my fee …The future of the franchise was very squarely dropped at my feet in 1972. I was to be the first English actor to play 007, and quite possibly the last if I ballsed it up.

THE SAME, BUT DIFFERENT ...

So how do you follow someone as hugely popular as Sean? I hear you ask. Well, I was conscious I should at least not speak with a Scottish accent, and after discussions with director Guy Hamilton it was decided I would never order a vodka Martini, neither shaken nor stirred, nor would I drive an Aston Martin. They were too closely associated with Sean. I had to be the same, but different.

Of course, I watched Sean's films again, and while not speaking directly with him about the part – after all, would I have called Larry Olivier and asked him about playing Hamlet had I been offered it? – being a friend of his I knew why he quit the role, and remember his declaring he'd 'created a monster'. Sean wanted to distance himself from 007 and the associated hysteria and potential typecasting, to tackle other acting roles. I, on the other hand, was just grateful for a job.

Oh, and I should not forget George Lazenby, who had one shot at playing Jim in *On Her Majesty's Secret Service* in 1969. By his own admission George was not an actor. He was a car salesman who began modelling and then slid sideways into acting work. His good looks and ability to throw a punch, coupled with his arrogance, secured him the part. I got to know him later on and, with hindsight, he admitted he had made a huge mistake in not signing on for seven movies, as originally offered, and parachuting out after just one on the advice of his friend-cum-manager Ronan O'Rahilly, who stated, 'Bond is Connery's gig. Make one and get out.' The irony is, George is probably never going to be able to shake Bond off.

My friend Peter Hunt directed *On Her Majesty's Secret Service* and, while very pleased with how it turned out, did confide in me that he'd had many problems with his lead actor's behaviour; presumably not helped by Harry Saltzman saying, 'You are now a star, George. Behave like one.' Stories became legendary of George sending back the studio car in the mornings because he didn't like the colour, demanding a car to take him the fifty yards from his dressing room to the Pinewood restaurant, and of eating garlic ahead of a love scene.

As had become the tradition, Cubby and Harry invited me to Eon's HQ in South Audley Street to watch the first screening of *On Her Majesty's Secret Service*. I guess there were thirty or forty other people there, one being Bob Goldstein, who then headed up 20th Century Fox. He stood up at the end of the film, leaned over to Cubby and said in his gruff voice, 'You should have killed him and saved the girl!'

In October 1972, I picked up my script, turned to page one and, heeding the advice of The Master, Noël Coward, prepared to 'learn the lines and don't bump into the furniture'. I guess I did something right, as, from then until we wrapped on my seventh Bond adventure thirteen years later, people went to see the films and kept me gainfully employed.

When I handed in my licence to kill I was constantly asked who should replace me. No! I lie. I was asked that question after about my third film, which, of course, gives an insecure actor a great feeling of being wanted. In fact, I did make a number of suggestions to Cubby – always names of really bad actors so I looked good by comparison. In the end, I was forced to abandon that idea as I couldn't find any actors worse than me.

BELOW: Ready for action in *Live And Let Die*, my first outing as Jimmy Bond.

ALBERT R. 'CUBBY' BROCCOLI CBE

I could write a whole book on Cubby alone. He was a big man in both life and charm. A kind, caring and fun person, Cubby would always listen to ideas and suggestions from any member of the crew – he might not necessarily agree, but he listened – and that was a quality that endeared him to everyone. He was known universally as Cubby, from studio heads to the tea lady. There were no pretentions or nasty sides to Cubby. Sure, he could be tough in business, but his heart was a big one and his loyalty unswerving.

Cubby had read Ian Fleming's books and thought they would make terrific films, but on enquiring about the rights discovered that a Canadian producer named Harry Saltzman had an option on them, which is how the duo got together in the first place. From there, a production company named Eon was formed, and the rest is history.

Cubby's enthusiasm for Bond never diminished. He loved making the films, and took great pride in showing every dollar of the budget up on the big screen. But that was never enough for the press: they always asked Cubby if he ever wished he'd won an Oscar.

'The only award I need is green with Washington's head on it,' he replied, referring, of course, to dollar bills at the box office. A successful movie was bigger than any trophy to Cubby. However, in 1982 the issue was addressed by the American Academy, when they bestowed their highest honour – the Irving G. Thalberg Award – on my friend. They asked me to present it to him on the night, and I remember Dana, his wonderful wife, looking rather worried that I might say something silly and fool around on this very prestigious night. Me? Would I?

After *Octopussy*, I resigned myself to thoughts of retirement. There are only so many stunts an ageing actor can tackle, and only so many young girls he can kiss without looking like a perverted

grandfather. However, I was persuaded back by Cubby for *A View To A Kill*. A year later and with rumours of a new Bond script being finalized, I decided I really couldn't go on to an eighth. I sat down with Cubby, who had obviously had similar thoughts, and it really became a mutual decision over lunch that I would step down. There were no tantrums, no attempted negotiations. It was all extremely amicable.

My friendship with Cubby outlived my time as Bond, and he told me of his thoughts of casting Pierce Brosnan in the role of 007. I said it was a terrific idea, as Pierce was an actor not unlike myself in style and looks. When that didn't quite work out because of contractual complications, Cubby told me he was signing Timothy Dalton for three films, and I wished them both great success.

The next time I met up with Pierce and Timothy was in 1995, at the memorial service for Cubby at London's Odeon Leicester Square. When I last saw him in California we laughed and joked about the times we'd shared, but, alas, Cubby was suffering ill health and was never able to return to the set of a Bond film, which I know he so looked forward to doing. I miss him greatly.

BOND
ON
VILLAINS

BOND ON VILLAINS

PREVIOUS PAGES: Evil Hugo Drax with manservant Chang in *Moonraker*. Although French, Drax did so enjoy taking afternoon tea in his château.

They're a jolly bunch of people, all loved by their mothers and all with a sick plan to take over the world or dominate it in one form or another. From the feared head and members of SPECTRE to international drug barons, deadly assassins, warped idealists and terrorists ... from the sublime to the ridiculous and back. They are all Bond villains.

In truth, I always wanted to play a Bond villain as they invariably have the best dialogue – describing their complex, evil and very sinister schemes to do away with Jimmy Bond – whereas 007 just walks around saying his name and ordering Martinis. The villains aren't on set every day, either, which means I'd have had a few days off here and there!

OPPOSITE LEFT: It all started with Dr. No, as played by Joseph Wiseman. I wouldn't advise you to shake hands with him, as he has cold hands *and* a cold heart.

BELOW: Get a grip, man! Dr. No's metal hands couldn't do much to save his slippery descent into hell.

THE SPECTRE OF EVIL

In several of the books and early films it is the aforementioned SPECTRE – the **SP**ecial **E**xecutive for **C**ounter-intelligence, **T**errorism, **R**evenge and **E**xtortion – with which Jimmy is most concerned. Its evil head, Ernst Stavro Blofeld, is not aligned to any nation or political ideology, aside from his own unhinged ones.

SPECTRE arose from the need to create a politically neutral enemy for Bond. In 1959, with the Cold War at its height, Ian Fleming, Jack Whittingham and Kevin McClory were writing a screenplay on which the novel *Thunderball* was later based. However, Fleming thought that the Cold War could end in the two years it would take to produce the film, which would make the film feel like 'old news' even before release. So they decided instead to create SPECTRE, the dastardly twenty-one members of which are drawn from six of the world's greatest criminal organizations – the Gestapo, the Russian counter-intelligence agency SMERSH, President Tito's legendary secret police, the Mafia, Corsican

ABOVE: Lotte Lenya (Rosa Klebb) and Robert Shaw (Red Grant) in the Pinewood gardens, which you can see out of my office window.

hoodlums from the Unione Corse, and a Turkish drug-smuggling operation.

SPECTRE's main aim is to spark conflict between the superpowers – the Soviet Union and the United States – in the hope that this conflict will make them vulnerable enough for SPECTRE to snatch their power. In *From Russia With Love*, Blofeld likens SPECTRE's *modus operandi* to the three Siamese fighting fish he keeps in an aquarium, noting how one fish refrains from attacking the other two until their fight is first concluded. Then, the waiting fish attacks the weakened victor and kills it much more easily.

But it was not all plain sailing for SPECTRE, as it and its characters became the centre of long and bitter litigation between Kevin McClory and Ian Fleming. When plans were abandoned to film the story written by Fleming, McClory and Whittingham, Fleming later published it as the novel *Thunderball*. A court case ensued and, in 1963, Fleming settled out of court with McClory. However, McClory secured the film rights to *Thunderball*, although literary rights remained with Fleming.

After the 1963 settlement, Eon Productions made a separate agreement with McClory to adapt *Thunderball* into the fourth official James Bond film, while stipulating that McClory would not be allowed to make further adaptations for at least ten years – perhaps thinking that by then 007 would have run out of steam? After several failed attempts to re-make *Thunderball*, in 1983 McClory finally succeeded to produce *Never Say Never Again*.

Never one to leave the stage quietly, McClory later contested the filmic ownership of James Bond himself, and threatened to make other 007 films based on earlier script ideas he'd penned. After another court case, in 2001 the UK courts awarded Eon Productions the exclusive film rights to the character James Bond. However, until his death in 2006, McClory continued to claim that SPECTRE and its evil head were his inventions – even launching a legal action when he heard that Karl Stromberg was to be a member of SPECTRE in *The Spy Who Loved Me*. The use of the organization was avoided by Eon from then on.

THE CHANGING FACE OF BLOFELD

Super-villain Blofeld first featured on screen – albeit not in camera shot – in *From Russia With Love*, although identified by name only in the closing credits of the film. Anthony Dawson supplied his body, Eric Pohlmann his voice. The gimmick was repeated in *Thunderball* but when *You Only Live Twice* commenced filming, Jim was to meet Blofeld in person. At last, we were going to see him!

Czech actor Jan Werich was cast as SPECTRE's 'Number 1' but both producer Cubby Broccoli and director Lewis Gilbert were anxious when he arrived at Pinewood at the start of the shoot, feeling that Werich resembled a 'poor, benevolent Santa Claus' rather than an arch villain. Lewis started filming but within a few days it became apparent

ABOVE: Jan Werich filmed only a few scenes as Blofeld in *You Only Live Twice* before departing the production ...

LEFT: ... in favour of the more menacing Donald Pleasence.

ABOVE: But in *On Her Majesty's Secret Service* Blofeld had another look, and came in the shape of Telly Savalas.

that Werich simply wasn't menacing enough. So they recast the role with Donald Pleasence.

'They had already started work on the film,' Donald Pleasence revealed, 'and the Blofeld character was still open. They said they wanted me to read the script and create a character totally different to anything that had been done before, and I think we achieved that.'

He experimented for about a week at Pinewood with humps, lame hands and a beard – not all at once, mind you – before it was decided the now-distinctive scar would best convey the character's almost Himmler-esque quality of villainy (and, as Donald played Himmler on film, that was a good analogy of mine, I reckon). Thus one of the screen's most memorable villains was born.

On the swift re-casting, actor Burt Kwouk, who played SPECTRE's 'Number 3' in the movie recalled, 'One day we were filming with Werich in the control booth, and then the next day I turned around and there was a different actor sitting in Blofeld's chair.'

Whoever was in Blofeld's chair, one somewhat unexpected – and unfortunate – occurrence came as a result of all the explosions on set: Blofeld's trademark white Persian cat didn't take too well

to them, and frequently relieved itself on its master!

Two years later, in *On Her Majesty's Secret Service*, the feared head of SPECTRE returned in the guise of Telly Savalas. Given there was much more physicality involved in this movie – including skiing – director Peter Hunt didn't feel the more diminutive Pleasence would be convincing as an athletic Blofeld. So he turned to Greek-born Savalas. Blofeld escapes – as he does in earlier films – but not before he and his sidekick Irma Bunt murder Bond's new bride, Tracy. Understandably, Jim sets out on revenge and, in *Diamonds Are Forever*, tracks down his old nemesis – this time played by Charles Gray.

When George Lazenby was cast as 007, and thoughts were turned to introducing the different-looking character, Cubby had a dream about an opening scene where Jim comes out of a plastic-surgery operation. In the end, it was agreed they should just introduce a new actor and not really point it out, however, Cubby's dream proved useful in explaining a different-looking Blofeld (and his doubles).

Charles Gray's Blofeld was much lighter in style and tone – even appearing in drag at one point – which probably wouldn't have suited Telly Savalas. Again, Blofeld eludes capture, but, thanks to the ongoing legal battle with Kevin McClory, doesn't return to the series for a full ten years, and then isn't actually referred to as Blofeld: John Hollis supplied his body and Robert Rietty his voice in the pre-title sequence of *For Your Eyes Only*. I ended up dropping him down an industrial chimney. Did he survive? Who knows?

BELOW: In *Diamonds Are Forever*, having undergone plastic surgery, Blofeld has yet another face – this one looking suspiciously like Charles Gray.

SO MANY FOES

ABOVE: Oddjob's custom-made steel-brimmed hat.

BELOW: Rosa Klebb's poison-tipped shoe and the design sketch by Pinewood effects engineer Bert Luxford.

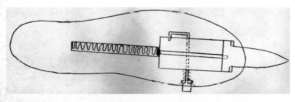

Aside from the esteemed Number 1, SPECTRE has offered up many foes to Jimbo. There was of course crazed genius Dr. Julius No, as played by Joseph Wiseman, and as with all great Bond villains he has a physical anomaly: in developing nuclear energy for no-good uses, he lost his hands and they were replaced by a metallic pair. The good doctor actually met his maker after being lowered into his own reactor coolant and, being unable to grip anything with his metal hands, it was good night Vienna.

When casting ideas for *Dr. No* were first mooted, Ian Fleming suggested his friend Noël Coward to play the villainous doctor. A telegram was sent to the Master, which he answered with, 'Dr. No? No! No! No!' Harry Saltzman is said to have then chosen Wiseman because of his performance in a dark 1951 movie called *Detective Story*.

Ken Adam's futuristic set of No's base – and Ken's sets are always a major contribution to the nutcase megalomaniac villain's thoughts of superiority – featured a huge aquarium in the background of the dining room. It was described as being constructed from convex glass to give the impression of a ten-times magnification, making 'minnows look like whales'. A classic touch was added on set when a reproduction of a Goya painting of the Duke of Wellington, which had actually been stolen in 1961, was placed on an easel next to the stairs Bond stops to look as he passes it. Thankfully, the real portrait was recovered in 1965.

Rosa Klebb, as played by Lotte Lenya, was also known as 'Number 3' in SPECTRE ranking. A thoroughly unpleasant lady with a penchant for peculiar shoes, in *From Russia With Love* we learn that Klebb secretly defected from SMERSH and used her former rank to deceive and recruit Tatiana Romanova, who in turn assisted the British in acquiring a Russian Lektor decoding device. By sending in Red Grant (Robert Shaw) to kill Bond, the Lektor would then fall into the hands of SPECTRE, or so she reckoned.

Grant is first introduced to audiences in the pre-title sequence – the premiere in the series – stalking a 007 lookalike around SPECTRE Island. It was inspired by the film *L'année dernière à Marienbad*, which had a lush garden setting, complete with eerie statues to stalk amongst. Director Terence Young dressed the gardens at Pinewood Studios and introduced a few false hedgerows to achieve a similar setting.

When Red Grant later gave himself away as an imposter to Bond on board the Orient Express by not knowing his wine, one of the classic Bond fights ensued. Set in the confines of a train

carriage, although the fight took just a few minutes of screen time, it took weeks of rehearsal.

And then there was Auric Goldfinger as played by German actor Gert Fröbe. He wasn't a member of SPECTRE, though I'm sure they'd have welcomed him. His plan was simple, and known as Operation Grandslam: amass huge wealth through gold bullion, and then increase its value tenfold by setting off a nuclear device inside the US gold depository, Fort Knox, rendering it untouchable.

Auric Goldfinger was named after Ian Fleming's neighbour, Ernő Goldfinger, a rather eminent architect and furniture designer.

ABOVE: Goldfinger was the first villain to lend his name to a Bond film title. German-born Gert Fröbe played the titular character, and his Korean Man Friday (Oddjob) was played by Harold Sakata.

It was said that some of his less endearing character traits were borrowed from him too. When the book was published in 1959, Ernő Goldfinger was unhappy and consulted his lawyers, prompting Fleming to suggest renaming the character 'Goldprick', but Goldfinger eventually settled out of court in return for his legal costs, six copies of the novel and an agreement that the character's first name 'Auric' would always be used.

In both the novel and film, Goldfinger is aided in his crimes by his manservant, Oddjob, a mute, monstrously strong Korean who ruthlessly eliminates any threat to his employer's affairs. Another notable feature was Oddjob's rather unusual taste in headgear.

When Jim's captured by Goldfinger, we really do fear for his life. He's laid out, spread-eagled on a table, hands and feet secured, with a powerful laser rising between his legs.

ABOVE AND BELOW:
Goldfinger's lethal laser, seen here on set and in the Pinewood workshop, was not really able to cut through metal. Its beam was added in to the film later, optically.

Bond: 'Do you expect me to talk?'
Goldfinger: 'No, Mr Bond. I expect you to die.'
Ah, classic lines.

In fact, the laser beam was added optically later on and the cutting effect was achieved by F/X engineer Bert Luxford lying underneath the aforementioned table, on his back, with a blowtorch. He slowly cut up towards Sean's groin – having only a chalked line to tell him where he should stop. Sean was, understandably, rather anxious.

LIP SYNCH

Gert Fröbe was cast after he impressed the producers and director Guy Hamilton as paedophile killer Schrott in the German/Swiss version of *The Pledge*. They asked his agent if he spoke English, and the reply came back, 'Of course he does'. When Fröbe arrived at Pinewood to start shooting, he walked over to Guy Hamilton and said, 'How do you do? I am very pleased to be here.'

Guy asked if his hotel was OK. 'How do you do?' Gert replied. 'I am very pleased to be here.' It soon became evident their lead villain

spoke no English whatsoever!

Undaunted, Guy suggested they could dub him later, and asked Gert to speak the lines phonetically. In order to maintain a believable delivery pace, Guy asked him to speak very quickly rather than think about the words too much. In rushes the next day, the two producers couldn't believe what they were seeing and hearing. It was total babble. Guy told them not to worry, and drafted in Michael Collins to provide the English voice, and his delivery matched the lip movement of Gert Fröbe brilliantly well.

Emilio Largo was a force to be reckoned with as 'Number 2' in *Thunderball*. Italian actor Adolfo Celi played the villainous Largo, who used his talents well as head of extortion operations at SPECTRE. Fleming described Largo as a 'ruthless Neapolitan black marketeer and fence who moved to riskier and more profitable ventures on the international crime scene', and his black eye patch gave him a certain evil *je ne sais quoi*. Adolfo also had quite a strong accent and his voice was dubbed by Robert Reitty.

Blaxploitation movies were fast becoming popular in 1970s cinema, and screenwriter Tom Mankiewicz thought it would be very daring to use black villains in *Live And Let Die*, especially with the Black Panthers and other racial movements being very active. The 'swinging sixties' had romanticized the use of soft drugs, but in the early 1970s it was taken a step further by drug barons and counterculture. This all combined for an exciting plot in which Jimmy Bond tackled the drug barons head on, or at least Harlem drug lord Mr Big, whose plan was to distribute the world's largest cache of heroin, free of charge, on the open market. It would drive other drug cartels out of business, increase the number of addicts, and give Mr Big and his alter ego, poppy-farming Dr Kananga, a monopoly.

As director Guy Hamilton was a jazz fan, he suggested filming in New Orleans and decided to use an opulent New Orleans jazz funeral as the starting point in the film, and as a cover to enable the villainous Mr Big to make a few agents disappear. Then, while searching for Kananga's island retreat (in Jamaica), the crew

ABOVE: Emilio Largo (Adolfo Celi) was SPECTRE Number 2 in *Thunderball*. A nasty piece of work if ever there was one.

ABOVE: Maybe a spoonful of sugar would have persuaded Mr Big (Yaphet Kotto) to swallow this deadly pill?

discovered a crocodile farm owned by a certain Dr. Kananga (after passing a sign warning that 'trespassers will be eaten'). The farm was incorporated into the script and that inspired Mankiewicz to name Mr Big's alter ego after the owner.

Yaphet Kotto was cast as Kananga/Mr Big, the first (and to date only) African American villain in a 007 adventure.

GOLDEN MOMENTS

For my second outing, my old pal – and Ian Fleming's cousin, as it happened – Christopher Lee was cast as my opponent, Francisco Scaramanga, aka *The Man With The Golden Gun*. Christopher and I had worked together on a film called *Trottie True* right back in 1949 when I was starting out, and then again in an episode of the TV series *Ivanhoe* in the 1950s.

On *The Man With The Golden Gun* I used to tease Christopher mercilessly about his role as Dracula and, just before the director

LEFT: Nick Nack (Hervé Villechaize) was the diminutive hired help of Scaramanga, and as this photo indicates, he was quite a ladies' man.

BELOW: In *The Man With The Golden Gun* I faced up to my old friend Christopher Lee.

RIGHT: A rather provocative poster image for the film, featuring Christopher Lee's hand.

BELOW: Remember the bullet with 007 on that arrived in M's office? Well, it was a custom-made, 4.2-millimetre, golden (23-carat gold with traces of nickel) dum-dum bullet.

called 'Action', I would lean over and say, 'Go on, Chris, make your eyes go red!'

Then there was the time we first entered the mouth of the cave on James Bond Island, which was replicated back at Pinewood as Scaramanga's HQ. A mass of bats flew out towards us. Without flinching, Christopher held up his hand and said, 'Not now, Stanislav!'

He looked sheepishly at me and said, 'You're going to use that against me, aren't you?'

Me? As if!

Scaramanga is assisted by the diminutive Nick Nack, as played by Hervé Villechaize. Dear Hervé was a fun character – and sex

mad! I asked him how many girls he'd had while we were shooting in Hong Kong.

'Forty-five,' he replied in his squeaky French voice.

'Ah!' I said. 'But it doesn't count if you paid them.'

'Even when I offer to pay sometimes they refuse me,' he added sadly.

He trotted up to Maud Adams in the lobby of the Peninsula Hotel in Hong Kong one morning, tugged on her knee-length skirt and looked up to say, 'Maud, tonight I am going to creep into your room, climb under the duvet and make mad passionate love to you.'

Unfazed, Maud replied, 'If I find out you have, I'll be very cross.'

Poor Hervé.

Karl Stromberg was very nearly a member of SPECTRE, as I mentioned earlier. However, his bizarre undersea ideology was enough to make him a stand-alone villain, especially with his quirky webbed fingers. Curt Jurgens played Stromberg, and we became great friends. He introduced me to Gstaad, and when I realized I'd have to find a home outside of the crippling UK tax regime, he offered my family and me his chalet in the Swiss resort to see if we'd like the town. We did, and moved there.

THE TALLER THEY COME ...

Every good villain has a good henchman, of course. The most memorable of all has to be Jaws, as played by my good friend Richard Kiel.

Richard, who stands seven foot two and a half inches tall, was cast after script supervisor June 'Randy' Randall saw him in an episode of the US TV series *Barbary Coast*. She knew the team was looking for a very tall actor – and they didn't come much taller than Richard.

When we filmed the scenes among the ruined Karnak temples in Egypt, Lewis Gilbert told Richard that for one shot he needed to be up in the scaffolding, high above Jimmy Bond. Richard went pale, and said he suffered with vertigo. 'Hey, I don't even like being this tall!' he exclaimed.

Faced with what seemed an insurmountable problem, my stunt double, Martin Grace, said he'd impersonate Richard, and used

ABOVE: Richard Kiel as Jaws was voted the best Bond villain in a recent poll.

BELOW: His teeth could munch through solid cables – if he'd had his Weetabix.

pieces of orange peel wrapped in tin foil for Jaws' 'metal' teeth. As it turned out, Martin mimicked Richard's every move so well that when Richard's mother saw it she asked him how on earth – with his fear of heights – he managed to film that sequence. She wouldn't believe it wasn't him.

Of course, Jaws got his name from the ominous, glinting steel teeth he wore. Poor devil, they were so uncomfortable to wear – Richard could only keep them in for about half a minute at a time. The comical expressions he had to convey were quite the opposite of what he was feeling, with an overwhelming urge to gag!

Jaws' popularity stemmed from the humour Richard injected into the character, and we all agreed he made a superb villain. In the script, he died at the end of *The Spy Who Loved Me*; however, Cubby felt it could be worth saving him, and the scene

was re-written. Jaws didn't drown, but popped up in the ocean and started swimming. That raised a round of applause at the premiere – especially from the youngsters.

He did of course return, in *Moonraker*, as did Hervé Villechaize ... for a set visit. Our unit publicist thought he'd spotted a photo opportunity and asked if they'd pose together, as 'little and large' villains. Richard quite rightly said, 'I don't do freak photos.'

BELOW: Arriving on the *Moonraker* publicity trail – me and my two mates, Michael Lonsdale and Richard Kiel.

TO SPACE AND BEYOND!

Moonraker was filmed in Paris as an Anglo-French co-production under the 1965–79 film treaty. France had much more favourable taxation laws for the creative industries, and that was a great lure to Cubby in setting up the film there, but part of their qualifying criteria was that the lead villain had to be French. Hugo Drax was going to be played by James Mason, who coincidentally I worked with later that year in *North Sea Hijack*; I admired him greatly and thought it terrific casting. However, because of the qualifying criteria, bilingual Frenchman Michael Lonsdale was accordingly offered the part, and made a wonderfully underplayed yet menacing Drax. He became the first Bond villain to take a giant step for mankind, and perished in space.

Of course, once you've been to space, there isn't a lot further you can go with a Bond villain, and so it was decided to bring the next film, *For Your Eyes Only*, and its protagonists back to earth. The only problem, for Jim, is that he couldn't really be sure who the bad guy was: Kristatos (Julian Glover) or Columbo (Topol)?

It really is a much more grounded story, with the villains being the good old, dependable Russians – keen to get their hands on the British ATAC device. The Soviets were at it again in *Octopussy,* too. Crazed General Orlov (Steven Berkoff) thought he could make the West

disarm by setting off a nuclear device inside an American airbase in West Germany. He and Kamal Khan (Louis Jourdan) used the Octopussy Circus as a front for their dastardly plans.

By the time of my swansong, *A View To A Kill*, technology was becoming the world's major boom industry, and accordingly became the subject for our original screenplay. Our villain, Max Zorin, played by Christopher Walken, was the product of nasty Nazi medical experimentation during World War II, in which pregnant women were injected with massive quantities of steroids in an attempt to create 'super-children'. Most of the pregnancies failed, but the few that did survive went on to become extraordinarily intelligent individuals – but with a taste for world domination and more than a streak of ruthlessness.

My only sadness with this film was the sheer amount of violence, gunfire and explosions, killing scores of innocent Zorin employees in the finale. It seemed a little over the top in my mind, and not quite in the Bond tradition.

With détente and a warming Cold War, the Russians obviously couldn't be Bond's enemy for much longer, but in *The Living Daylights* General Koskov, played by Dutch actor Jeroen Krabbé, played on the thawing relations to draw Britain into a double-crossing plot, which would help him eliminate the head of the KGB and leave the way clear to take over.

A complete change of tone was ushered in with Franz Sanchez in *Licence To Kill*: he ran a drug cartel from South America to Asia. Played by Robert Davi, Sanchez had an interesting choice of pet in a large green iguana that wore a rather fetching diamond collar. I found the iguana quite diverting, but the story was one of personal revenge for the murder of Felix Leiter's new wife, Della, and, for me, it became far too dark in style and content.

It was interesting, therefore, to see that the next Bond villain – in *GoldenEye* in 1995 – was intent on taking over control of the aforenamed satellite and using it for personal profit – back to the good old baddies! Formerly known as 'Agent 006', Alex Trevelyan, played by Sean Bean, was a contemporary of Jim's from MI6. Apparently, Sean Bean had been considered for the role of Jimbo at one point, but became a baddie instead. That's what happens, you see.

TOP TO BOTTOM: Louis Jourdan was Kamal Khan in *Octopussy*.

Christopher Walken as Max Zorin in *A View To A Kill*.

Sean Bean played Alec Trevelyan in *GoldenEye*.

Robert Davi played drug baron Franz Sanchez in *Licence To Kill*.

Of course, many Bond villains are modelled on real people, or should I say real circumstances in which they could exist.

❦ Take Elliott Carver (Jonathan Pryce, above right) in *Tomorrow Never Dies*: a global media magnate who wanted to expand his empire by any means, and in particular into China. Who does that remind you of?

❦ Oil is a massive player in the world energy stakes. Control the pipelines, you control the wealth. Elektra King (Sophie Marceau, right) thought it acceptable to destroy Istanbul and thus control the Bosphorus oil supplies in *The World Is Not Enough*. That's not nice.

❦ Satellites orbit our earth, and control all manner of things. Control one of them with a powerful death ray attached, and the world would be in trouble – as Gustav Graves (Toby Stephens, right) realized in *Die Another Day*.

❦ But who finances the crooks and their schemes? One such person is LeChiffre, the terrorists' banker. Only thing is, he needed to turn a profit on investments left in his care, and made unwise decisions. He had to win it back in a high-stakes poker game to prevent the mysterious head of Quantum, Mr White (Jesper Christensen, right), from becoming upset in *Casino Royale*.

❦ Mr White and Quantum are also behind Dominic Greene's (Mathieu Amalric, right) attempts to control water in Bolivia – or at least I think that was the plot – in *Quantum Of Solace*. Mr Greene didn't survive, but Mr White is still out there. I just hope I don't bump into him!

BOND
ON
GIRLS

JAMES BOND 007
CONTRE "Dr. NO"
(Dr. NO)

BOND ON GIRLS

How does one describe a 'Bond girl'? Bond girls are considered to be 'ubiquitous symbols of glamour and sophistication', according to Robert A. Caplen in his book *Shaken & Stirred: The Feminism of James Bond*, that is. Bond girls are certainly bewitching, beguiling and memorable but they are not always necessarily *just* the victims of Bond's charm: many villainesses, allies and co-workers are given the moniker too, as is my wife Kristina – my favourite Bond girl of all.

In Fleming's books, Bond girls always seemed to be in their mid-twenties, a decade or so younger than Jim, though in *Goldfinger* Fleming wrote that Bond suspected Pussy Galore was in her early thirties. An older woman? Perish that thought!

LEFT: Ursula Andress was voted 'Best Bond Girl of All Time' by readers of one national newspaper in 2008. She also received a Golden Globe as 'New Star of the Year' for her role in *Dr. No*.

BELOW: Eunice Gayson was the very first Bond girl. Her famous red dress was in fact a last-minute change, and as it wasn't made to measure, she had to use a few strategically placed clothes pegs to hold it together!

BEAUTY IS IN THE EYE …

Needless to say, all Bond girls are very beautiful, more often than not sporting a light sun tan, and with their eyes and mouths widely spaced – or so wrote Ian Fleming. Their eyes, by the way, are usually blue, but in *Diamonds Are Forever* Tiffany Case's are chatoyant – 'varying with the light from grey to grey-blue' – while in *Goldfinger* Pussy Galore has deep-violet eyes, the only truly violet eyes Bond had ever seen.

Yes, they all usually have exotic-sounding names too. In addition to the aforementioned, we have Suki, Vesper, Honey, Tatiana, Solitaire, Chew Me, Bibi, Octopussy, Mayday, Kara, Lupe, Paris and Elektra. Suggestive, sexy and very, very Bondian.

Fleming indicated that most of the Bond girls were sexually experienced by the time they met 007, which is probably just as well. However, not all of their experiences had been positive, with histories of sexual violence often a contributory factor in alienating them from men – until Jim arrived on the scene. Jim, meanwhile, I should add, lost his virginity on his first visit to Paris when he was sweet sixteen.

Though this darker backcloth to the characters is largely absent from the films, many Bond girls do face some abuse on screen – Domino (Claudine Auger) at the hands of Largo's cigarette and ice in *Thunderball*; Andrea Anders (Maud Adams) in *The Man With The Golden Gun* is hurt by the dastardly Francisco Scaramanga; Lupe Lamora (Talisa Soto) in *Licence To Kill* is whipped by Franz Sanchez … perhaps these events were behind their determination to resist Bond at first?

But Jimmy's charms win through … even in the case of lesbian Pussy Galore when, in bed, Bond says, 'They told me you only liked women,' and she tellingly replies it was because 'I never met a man before.'

You have to laugh. To think Bond could turn a gay woman is quite comical. But then again, Judi Dench's M did describe Jim as being 'a sexist, misogynist dinosaur. A relic of the Cold War…' in *GoldenEye*, so he'd probably like to think he could.

BELOW: Margaret Nolan played Dink in *Goldfinger*. A well-rounded role!

ABOVE: Put 'em up! Honor Blackman (centre) with Shirley Eaton (left) and Tania Mallett inside the Fort Knox set on *Goldfinger*.

Cubby Broccoli admitted that Honor Blackman had been cast on the back of her success in *The Avengers*, despite the fact that the American audience had never even seen the programme. He said, 'The Brits would love her because they knew her as Mrs Gale, the Yanks would like her because she was so good, it was a perfect combination.'

One time I was doing an interview with Jimmy Tarbuck on *Sunday Night at the London Palladium* and Tarbuck said:

'You're the Saint, Sean Connery is Bond, Patrick McGoohan is Danger Man and Patrick MacNee is in *The Avengers* ... do you ever meet up?'

I said, 'Yeah, sure.'

'Do you go out together?'

'Yeah,' I said.

'Pussy Galore?'

'Well, we don't go looking for it ...' I replied.

I'm still not sure how we got away with it!

BEWARE NUMBER ONE

Bond rarely limits himself to just one conquest per film. The pattern established by Cubby and Harry – and still honoured to this day – usually sees anyone sleeping with Bond in the first reel bumped off before the end of the second. So beware young actresses.

Roald Dahl summed it up best when he spoke about being contracted to write the screenplay for *You Only Live Twice* (1967): '"You put in three girls," the producers said, "girl number one is pro-Bond. She stays around roughly for the first reel of the picture, then she is bumped off by the enemy, preferably in Bond's arms.

'"Girl number two is anti-Bond and usually captures him, and he has to save himself by knocking her out with his sexual charm and power. She gets killed in an original (usually grisly) fashion mid-way through the film. The third girl will manage to survive to the end of the film."'

To date, only two Bond girls have actually turned the formula around and captured Bond's heart – though neither lived very long, proving you can't tamper with the recipe too much. In *On Her Majesty's Secret Service*, Tracy di Vicenzo (Diana Rigg) married Bond, though she was shot dead soon after the ceremony by Irma Bunt and Ernst Stavro Blofeld. The second to wed was Vesper Lynd (Eva Green) in *Casino Royale*. Bond professes his love for her and resigns from MI6 in order that they can have a normal life together. Later, he learns she was actually a double agent working for his enemies at Quantum (in the film) – the enemy organization ostensibly kidnapped her former lover and was blackmailing her to secure her cooperation. She died by drowning in a lift in a building under renovation. Realizing his betrayal and loss in equal measure, Bond confirmed, 'The bitch is dead' – one of the most intense lines of all Fleming's novels, which was also used in the film.

FAQS

Among the most frequently asked questions I am asked in interviews (and I assume this is true of any other retired 007) is, 'Who is your favourite Bond girl?'

'Oh! How original!' I exclaim. 'No one has ever asked me that before.'

I never give an answer as I think it is terribly unfair to name one co-star as being any better than another; you immediately upset someone. 'What was wrong with me?' they cry out.

Avoiding naming names also allows me to talk about some leading ladies without actually identifying them, though if I drop the odd hint, you might put two and two together.

In the 1960s, while playing Simon Templar, I was being interviewed by a television station and the journalist started off with, 'You've played Ivanhoe, Maverick and now the Saint … you must have got through a lot of leading ladies in your time.'

'You can't say that!' I cried.

My interrogator didn't seem to realize what he was saying. He re-phrased it and said virtually the same thing again. I cringe whenever I see the clip.

Normally when you have a scene involving kissing a lady (or I guess a man if you fancy it), you never actually go in for the kiss during rehearsal as it tends to smudge make-up and ruffle hair. You just go through the motions, move in close, say 'and they kiss' and get on with the rest of the scene. In *The Spy Who Loved Me* I rehearsed one such scene with an Italian actress, and it all seemed to go rather well. Lewis Gilbert leaned over and said, 'Can we have a sample of the kiss, dear?'

Suddenly from across the stage floor, this long snake-like tongue shot at me at the speed of light, worked its way around my teeth like dental floss and plunged deep into my throat. I was quite taken aback.

There is certainly no romance in a love scene, save that for the dressing room, if you're lucky – and if your wife ever walks in on you, heed the advice of Burt

LEFT TOP: Sean and Martine Beswicke in *Thunderball*. Martine also appeared in the gypsy fight sequence in *From Russia With Love*.

LEFT BELOW: Mollie Peters played Patricia in *Thunderball*, and helped soothe Jim's stress.

BELOW: The happiest days of Bond's life. Mr and Mrs James Bond in *On Her Majesty's Secret Service*.

Lancaster as relayed to me by Tony Curtis: 'Just continue, and when you get home, explain they have people that look like you on the film.'

Far from being a romantic moment of intimacy shared by two people, a film love scene is often witnessed by fifty or sixty crew members, many being hairy-arsed technicians in the rafters clenching fists and shouting, 'Go on, Rog! Give her one for us!' It does rather put one off one's stride. And if there's mention on the call sheet of a love scene, or one of at least partial nudity, it always amazes me how the crew size swells and we tend to inherit workers from adjacent stages and productions.

ABOVE: My good friend Jill St John, Mrs Robert Wagner these days, showing that diamonds are a girl's best friend in 1971.

RIGHT: My first leading lady, Jane Seymour. In the casting session, she removed her hat, shook her head, and let her long hair fall out. There was no question of anyone else after that.

54

WHO WILL IT BE?

There is always a huge interest in who is going to be cast as the next Bond girl, not least among the crew, and inevitably there is a press conference to introduce her. She then has a few minutes to talk about being 'different from the normal Bond girls' by 'being independent, tough, intelligent and a new type of girl'. They all say it.

Many girls, particularly in the early films, were cast because of their ravishing good looks. There's nothing wrong with that, and I'm no sexist either, let me add. If they happened to have rather large busts, that certainly sealed their involvement as far as Cubby was concerned. He was what you'd call 'a boob man'. Though he also once remarked, on set, while looking at one of the lovely beauties wandering about, that she had a 'particularly lovely derrière'. The lady seemingly also had particularly good hearing, as she turned, pounced and told Cubby he was a 'sexist, misogynist swine' and went into a long diatribe about how women have been kept down over the centuries by men like him, and how women are actually better than men, and how dare he treat her like a bimbo.

Another time we incurred the wrath of one of our leading ladies was when Lewis Gilbert offered me a little direction: 'Roger, when you come in and she sees you ...'

'She! *She*?' exclaimed the intelligent, tough, independent beauty. 'I have a name and it is ******!' and she spelled it out in a very loud voice.

'I wasn't talking to you, dear, I was talking to *him*,' Lewis replied rather nonchalantly.

On another occasion, when giving direction to the same lady, Lewis suggested, 'You come in here, and follow him over there.'

'Why do I always have to follow *him*?' she asked.

'Because, dear, he is f***ing James Bond!' Lewis helpfully replied.

To be perfectly honest, ladies cast in a Bond film were

ABOVE: His and Hers outfits came as standard on this set. Lois Chiles as Dr Holly Goodhead. In explaining away her character's name to her father she said, 'I'm a doctor, with a very good head on my shoulders.' Well, what else would it mean?

primarily signed because of their beauty, charm, charisma and, oh yes, a little acting ability helped too. It's no great secret that Nikki Van Der Zyl dubbed many of the voices in the sixties films, because their accents were considered a little too heavy, but their outstanding beauty made them much sought-after individuals.

Not all were very experienced in screen acting technique, and I recall all too well a sequence when cigarette smoke (or actually a stun gas) had to be blown into my face. For smoke, talcum powder was substituted, and instead of blowing it slightly to the side of my face the lady in question blew it straight into my eye – not just in one take, but in four. It wasn't one of my favourite days.

Just ahead of a rather large set piece, involving big explosions, another leading lady wondered why my make-up man had presented me with a set of earplugs.

BOND ON GIRLS

I explained the noise would be rather deafening. 'Oh well, that won't bother me as I'll stand near you.' I had to explain that it was *me* they were trying to kill.

Towards the end of my tenure, I believe I was extraordinarily patient and good-willed with two leading ladies who became obsessive about dashing back to their handbags after every take to re-apply lipstick and face powder. I'd wait and wait for them to reappear with another layer, say a line and then disappear again. This went on incessantly and wasted so much time. When they weren't looking, I decided to take the lipsticks out of the bags, and built a little pile of them, along with powder puffs and mirrors, but the ladies never really noticed as, without flinching, they dipped their hand in to their bottomless bags to produce yet another one. Heaven only knows how many sets they owned.

The character of Goodnight appears in Ian Fleming's books *On Her Majesty's Secret Service* and *You Only Live Twice* as Bond's secretary, before becoming a fully-fledged Bond girl in *The Man With The Golden Gun*. Britt Ekland was a great fan of the books and lobbied the producers to cast her in the role. Then, as is often the way in this business, she read an article saying Swedish actress Maud Adams had been confirmed as the next Bond girl. Her heart sank. Of course, she then received a call to say she had got the part after all, Maud was playing the villain's girlfriend, Andrea Anders.

On James Bond Island the crew rigged up explosions for the finale of the movie, when Scaramanga's HQ goes up in smoke. Everything was carefully timed for us to run from A to B as the explosions went off. Rather worryingly, the cameras were set up offshore on boats.

Guy Hamilton called 'Action!' and I ran. But Britt hesitated for a moment. I was faced with a split-second decision: carry on running, or be the gallant hero and go back for her. I turned around, grabbed and pulled her forward, towards me. I then felt all the tiny hairs on her back singe after the first explosion. I'm such a hero.

Barbara Bach, former model and

LEFT: The lovely Cassandra Harris played Countess Lisl. She was joined by her young husband for the premiere. Cubby thought he could be a candidate for Bond …

BOTTOM LEFT: If you're going to fool around in a wardrobe, I suggest you do it with the delectable Madeline Smith.

BELOW: My Swedish friend Britt Ekland. *Bon appétit*, and Goodnight.

wife-to-be of Ringo Starr, was quite a different Bond girl in that she was the Soviet oppo of Jim. As agent Triple X she perhaps had the most prominent starring role since Diana Rigg in *On Her Majesty's Secret Service*.

Cubby was under huge pressure to get everything right on this film, and I know he had spent a long time looking for the perfect girl. He answered the question of why Barbara Bach with his usual aplomb: 'There isn't an actress today, with the possible exception of Barbra Streisand, who can open a film. We explored a certain lady in Hollywood who commands a $500,000 fee and that blew her right out of the box for me because she'd contribute no more than Barbara Bach.'

I used to pull her leg, of course, dubbing her Barbara-Back-to-Front, and in Luxor when we left for the location each morning we'd always pass hundreds of black-burka-clad women.

'The nuns are out early again,' I said, rather lightheartedly.

'Oh, are they all Catholics here?' she asked earnestly.

She and Ringo are now neighbours of mine in Monaco, and we still see each other from time to time.

A ONE-WOMAN BOND

In my final outing, I was joined by Mary Stavin, Fiona Fullerton, Tanya Roberts and Grace Jones.

A day in a hot tub with Fiona could never be considered 'work' really, could it? And floating away on board a submarine with Mary Stavin must be many men's dream. As to the others, I'll leave it there, I think.

Post-me, in the mid-1980s, HIV/AIDS was becoming a major issue in the world and Bond writers felt that Timothy Dalton's new 007 should not be as promiscuous as my 007. He therefore became a one-woman Bond with Maryam d'Abo's Kara Milovy

LEFT: Another obligatory posse. Do I complain?

FAR LEFT: Maud Adams as *Octopussy*.

BELOW FAR LEFT: She who shall remain nameless.

BELOW LEFT: 'Would you like it harder, Miss Fullerton?' – the massage I meant! A de-briefing scene from *A View To A Kill*.

BELOW RIGHT: In *Quantum Of Solace* Olga Kurylenko provided Bond's back-up girl, Camille.

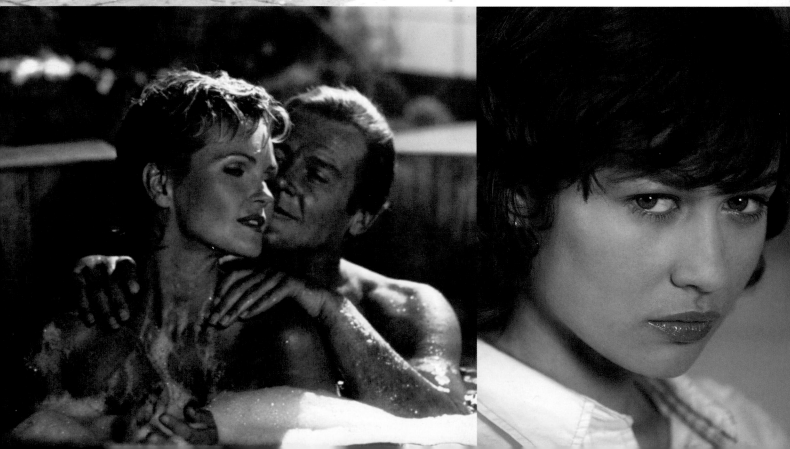

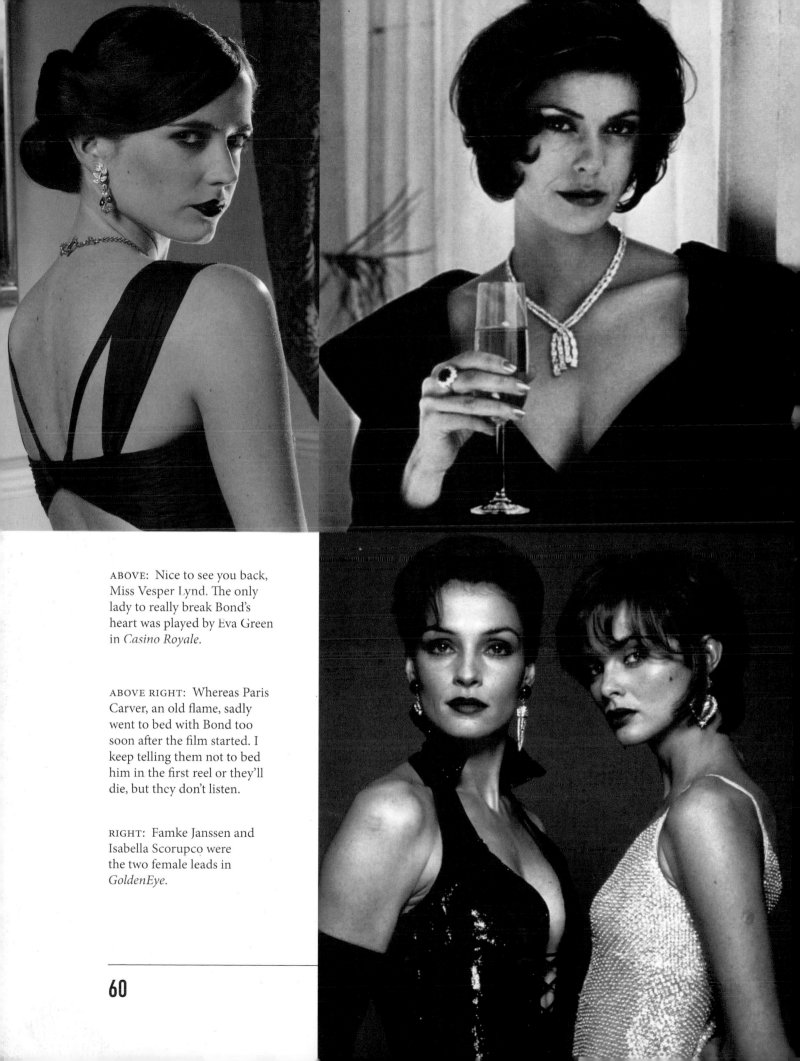

ABOVE: Nice to see you back, Miss Vesper Lynd. The only lady to really break Bond's heart was played by Eva Green in *Casino Royale*.

ABOVE RIGHT: Whereas Paris Carver, an old flame, sadly went to bed with Bond too soon after the film started. I keep telling them not to bed him in the first reel or they'll die, but they don't listen.

RIGHT: Famke Janssen and Isabella Scorupco were the two female leads in *GoldenEye*.

60

in *The Living Daylights* but stepped up a gear in *Licence To Kill* with two romantic interests, Carey Lowell and Talisa Soto.

When Pierce came along, the team took the decision to introduce a few more well-known actresses to the franchise, such as Teri Hatcher, Michelle Yeoh, Denise Richards and Halle Berry – who won her Oscar mid-production on *Die Another Day* for the movie *Monster's Ball*. In a nod to *Dr. No,* Halle emerged from the ocean in a sexy bikini in the film's only main location; the majority of filming was studio-bound. She proved such a popular character that producers felt a *Jinx* spin-off movie would be a sure-fire hit. Neil Purvis and Robert Wade were engaged to write a script; Stephen Frears was reportedly keen to direct and all looked set ... until MGM got nervous about the budget, and felt they'd rather have another Bond film than risk launching a new franchise. MGM cited 'creative differences'.

With Daniel Craig came Eva Green as Vesper Lynd. The character's name, incidentally, is a pun on West Berlin, signifying Vesper's divided loyalties as a double agent under Soviet control. Eva became the fifth French actress to be cast as a Bond girl. Following in her footsteps was Ukrainian-born Olga Kurylenko in *Quantum Of Solace* as Camille, with a backstory of child abuse akin to Ian Fleming's original flawed heroines.

BELOW: A more feisty Bond girl came in the shape of Pam Bouvier in *Licence To Kill,* played by Carey Lowell.

FAR RIGHT: The twentieth Bond film, in the fortieth year, paid homage to some of the earlier films, most notable here with Halle Berry re-creating Ursula Andress's famous scene in *Dr. No*.

RIGHT: Maryam d'Abo was the only Bond girl in *The Living Daylights*, when worries about HIV/AIDS were at their height.

BELOW: Christmas Jones was played by Denise Williams, and in her case proved Christmas came more than once a year.

Moneypenny

The lovely Lois Maxwell was a Canadian actress whom I first met way back during my time at RADA. We often appeared in the same student plays.

In 1962 Lois contacted her old friend director Terence Young and asked if there might be a part for her in his next film, as her husband had recently suffered a heart attack and they desperately needed the income. Terence said there were two possible parts: Sylvia Trench, Bond's love interest; or Miss Moneypenny. Lois read the script and didn't much care for the Sylvia Trench role, as it featured a scantily dressed scene with 007, so she opted for Moneypenny and received £200 for two days' work.

Alongside her role in the Bond movies, Lois appeared with me in an episode of *The Saint* and *The Persuaders!* before we resumed our on-stage association when I took on the role of Jimmy Bond.

It's interesting to note that despite her worldwide fame, Lois's total screen time as Moneypenny in her fourteen films was less than twenty minutes, and she spoke fewer

LEFT: The one and only Lois Maxwell in the role she loved.
ABOVE: Samantha Bond (no relation) played Moneypenny in all the Pierce Brosnan films.
ABOVE RIGHT: Pamela Salem was Sean Connery's choice for the role in *Never Say Never Again*.
ABOVE, FAR RIGHT: Caroline Bliss was a two-time Moneypenny for a two-time Bond, Timothy Dalton. She had a penchant for Barry Manilow records!
RIGHT: Two of a kind, Lois with Desmond Llewelyn – how I miss them both.

than 200 words. That's the power of Bond for you.

It was a huge shock to hear of Lois's death in 2007. She was always fun, wonderful company to be in and was absolutely perfect casting. Towards the end of my tenure as Jimbo, Lois said to Cubby that she would like to see Moneypenny become the new M. Cubby smiled and said, 'I don't think we can have a female head of the Secret Service.'

It was a great pity that after I moved out of Bond they didn't take her on to continue in the Timothy Dalton films, but I guess a younger Bond flirting with an older Moneypenny wasn't to be.

Other Miss Moneypennys include Caroline Bliss, Samantha Bond and – in the unofficial *Never Say Never Again* – Pamela Salem. Call me old-fashioned if you will, but there'll only ever be one Miss Moneypenny for me.

BOND
ON
GADGETS

BOND ON GADGETS

Almost every Bond film features a trip into Q-Branch, an underground Aladdin's cave-like bunker beneath the power desks of MI6, where a group of boffins led by their Quartermaster feverishly develop and invent wonderful gadgets, gizmos and accoutrements for the field operatives of Her Majesty's Secret Service. It's unclear just how many of these devices are ever returned; certainly if Jim is a yardstick then very few come back intact.

FINDING Q

While being one of the most well known and favourite of the returning characters, Q's origins are not terribly clear. There is a reference to Q in Chapter 3 of Fleming's *Casino Royale*. M says to Bond, 'Go over a few days before the big game starts and get your hand in. Have a talk to Q about rooms and trains, and any equipment you want.'

Q-Branch features occasionally in the novels, supplying Bond with equipment and gadgets, but it is said by scholars that the true origin of the Q character lies in the first film, *Dr. No*. The secret service armourer, Major Boothroyd, replaces Jim's Beretta with a new Walther PPK. There is no direct reference to Boothroyd being associated with Q Branch, though the character was based on a real person who advised Fleming on changing Bond's weapon, Major Geoffrey Boothroyd.

In the next film, Desmond Llewelyn's character is referred to as the 'Equipments Officer', when he supplies Jim with his new attaché case, although he is credited as Boothroyd in the closing titles. Of course, forever after we knew him as Q, which to my mind is far less confusing.

PREVIOUS PAGES: We must get them in the shops for Christmas, Q.

LEFT: One of my first 007 gadgets. A radio transmitter housed in a hairbrush.

BELOW: The famous Walther PPK as presented to Jim by 'The Armourer' in *Dr. No*. The PPK was used in most of the films up to *Tomorrow Never Dies*, and then made a welcome return in *Quantum Of Solace*.

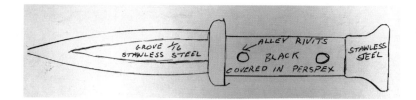

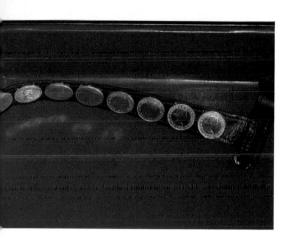

ABOVE: The first real gadget was the attaché case in *From Russia With Love*. It included twenty gold sovereigns, a throwing knife (this original design is by Pinewood effects engineer Bert Luxford), a tear gas canister and hidden ammunition.

RIGHT: The miniature spy camera from *On Her Majesty's Secret Service*, that Jim used to photograph Blofeld's Angels of Death.

Desmond Llewelyn played Q from 1963 to 1999 in a total of seventeen films. On screen, he was the gadget master who invented wonderful, never-before-seen devices, whereas off screen Desmond was a complete technophobe who struggled even to operate his own video recorder.

Desmond was not in *Dr. No*; that was Peter Burton. However, when Burton proved unavailable for *From Russia With Love,* Terence Young cast Desmond after remembering him from a few years earlier in a film called *They Were Not Divided*.

When Desmond arrived on set Terence asked him how he was going to play the character. 'As an English civil servant,' Desmond replied.

'No, you're a Welshman. Play it as a Welshman,' said Terence.

Desmond argued that a Welsh accent wouldn't carry the air of authority he felt the character should have. Nevertheless, he did as his director asked and put on a very broad Welsh accent.

'Well, look-see, I have this smashing case for you ... press this 'ere button and out pops a lovely knife ...'

'No, you're quite right,' said Terence. 'Play it as you thought.'

On the next film, *Goldfinger*, the character was really rounded out. Guy Hamilton told me that when Sean entered Q-Branch, Desmond stood up to greet him.

'No! No! No!' said Guy. 'You hate this man. He destroys everything you ever give him. You have nothing but contempt for him! Don't stand up to greet him.'

From then on, Q treated Bond with a circumspect irritation and established that wonderful love–hate relationship that lasted throughout the series.

Q's appearance in a Bond film was always highly anticipated, so you can imagine my disappointment when he wasn't in *Live And Let Die*. Apparently, it was decided that Bond was relying a little too much on gadgets, and Q would therefore be dropped.

However, there was such an outcry after the film's release that Q was immediately written back into the next film.

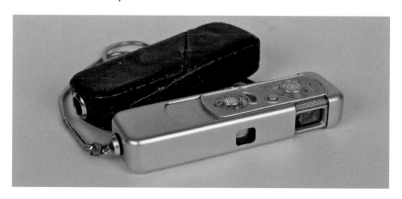

ABOVE AND LEFT: In Japan, Tiger Tanaka demonstrated the rocket-firing cigarette to Bond. They say smoking kills ...

LEFT: In *Goldfinger*, early GPS-style technology was employed in these two tracking devices. One was affixed to Auric Goldfinger's car while the other, smaller, device was hidden in Jim's shoe.

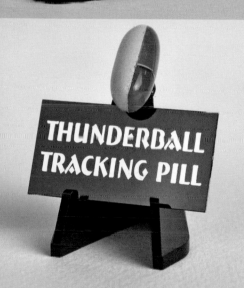

THUNDERBALL TRACKING PILL

ROMEO Y JULIETA

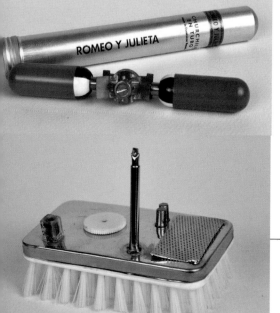

EVIL PERSONIFIED (ME, THAT IS)

Desmond always struggled to learn his dialogue, as after all, it was usually quite technical. I, being a caring and kind performer, noticed this early on in our working relationship and decided to take full, evil advantage of it.

Lewis Gilbert, who had directed *You Only Live Twice*, told me how Desmond complained about having to wear shorts in the movie. He didn't particularly like exposing his legs to the elements, and so whenever Desmond was in earshot I'd say quietly to Lewis, 'Oh, do you think it would work better if Q were to wear shorts in this sequence?'

'Eh? What?' said a worried Desmond.

'Yes, good idea, Rog!' Lewis replied. 'And perhaps in the next sequence too?'

Then I was particularly evil in rewriting his dialogue with the script supervisor, June Randall, and handing it to director John Glen to give to Desmond when he arrived at the studio. My rewrite was, of course, the biggest load of gibberish you can imagine. Desmond had already struggled to learn his lines and went into a blind panic when he was handed new pages so soon before being called on set. Of course, when he was called and saw me slowly shaking with stifled laughter, the penny dropped, as did a few choice words.

Sometimes we had 'idiot boards' on set, with his technical dialogue written in large text. As he glanced up to remind himself of the next line, the cards were peeled back one after the other. I helpfully rewrote some of those too. I like being helpful.

Desmond was always keen that his part be extended, and it finally was in *Licence To Kill* in 1989, but in an early draft of *The Man With The Golden Gun* by Tom Mankiewicz, he very nearly has an extra scene with me as Bond at Hong Kong airport. In the draft, Q tried to persuade 007 to take a gadget-laden camera with him on his trip. It featured gas ejection, which, by selecting various shutter speeds, instantly solidified anything in its path. Bond said something like, 'Most ingenious, but I'm sure there's one thing this contraption can't do ... take a photo.' Q castigated him for being facetious before adding, 'Yes you're right, but I'm working on it ...'

It was quite comical. Perhaps too comical? It was cut. After all, Q is quick to remind us, 'I never joke about my work, 007'.

A TASTE OF THINGS TO COME

While many of Q's gadgets – highly charged magnetic watches, remote-control cars, a signature gun, underwater cameras, wrist-triggered dart guns, GPS tracking devices, fake fingerprints and acid pens – seemed outlandish and improbable, Desmond always maintained that they were 'prototypes' and forerunners of things that did eventually make it into commercial production. In fact, so sought-after were some, that the highest powers in the land weren't averse to phoning through to the Bond production office for insights into their design. In 1965 the Royal Corps of Engineers, having seen *Thunderball*, asked the then art department draftsman Peter Lamont, 'How long can a man use your underwater breather device for?'

His answer was, 'How long can you hold your breath?'

Although more often than not exasperated, Q has always shown a warm and fatherly concern for 007's welfare, such as at Bond's wedding in *On Her Majesty's Secret Service*, when he pulled Jim to one side, to say that if there was ever anything Jim needed … oh and the occasion, at the behest of Miss Moneypenny, when Q secretly sneaked gadgets out of MI6 to help Bond survive his vendetta against the drug tyrant Sanchez in *Licence To Kill*. When he arrived, posing as Bond's uncle, he flatly told a dismissive 007, 'If it hadn't been for Q-Branch, you'd have been dead long ago.'

How true.

In 1999, aged eighty-five, Desmond voiced his concern that he may not be around for many more films. He asked the writers to pave the way for a new Q. In what was to be his last movie, *The World Is Not Enough*, Desmond's Q talks of his plan to retire and go fishing. A crestfallen Bond says, 'You're not planning on retiring any time soon, are you?'

FAR LEFT AND LEFT: Beware of pickpockets … or should that be, beware pickpocketers. A finger trap slipped in the inside jacket pocket gives any hoodlum in search of your gun a nasty snap.

MIDDLE LEFT: The bug detector, used by Bond in his Istanbul hotel room. Walls have ears, you know.

LEFT: The Nikon underwater camera – a prototype for future technology, as were many of the early Q-Branch gadgets – was first seen in *Thunderball*.

LEFT: In *Thunderball*, Jim was issued with another tracking device, but this one used (harmless) radioactivity principles and took the form of an everyday pill.

LEFT: The underwater breather, which as well as appearing in *Thunderball*, made a return in *Die Another Day*. The air supply lasts for as long as you can hold your breath!

LEFT: The radio transmitter hairbrush was very neat.

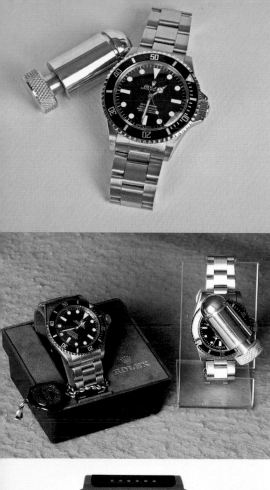

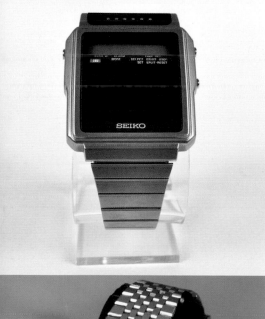

Q: 'I've always tried to teach you two things: First, never let them see you bleed.'

Bond: 'And the second?'

Q: 'Always have an escape plan.'

He is then lowered out of view.

When in 1998 Desmond asked me to pen a Foreword for his autobiography, simply entitled, *Q*, I wrote one of the things I missed most after leaving Bond was him. That was absolutely true. He bore my childish pranks so patiently and, being gadget mad (as my wife will attest), I used to love playing with all the gizmos in Q-Branch.

I was watching Sky news on Sunday 19 December 1999, when I heard the awful news that Desmond had been involved in a car accident. He was returning home to Bexhill from a book signing. He died from his injuries. I was devastated.

A few months later, I attended his memorial service in London and spoke of the gentle gentleman who, despite having hands the size of spades and a total incomprehension of what he was talking about, always managed to explain and demonstrate his devices with great skill and endear himself to millions of fans across the world.

With the reboot of the Bond series in 2006's *Casino Royale* and its successor, *Quantum Of Solace*, the character of Q did not appear, though gadgets were still very much in evidence.

Other actors to have played Q on film include John Cleese in

Die Another Day, Geoffrey Bayldon in 1967's *Casino Royale* and Alec McCowen in *Never Say Never Again*, with that wonderful line on Jim's return to Q-Branch, 'Good to see you, Mr Bond. Things have been awfully dull around here without you. I hope we're going to see some gratuitous sex and violence …'

GUNS 'N' AMMO

Think of 007 and you conjure up images of girls, gadgets and … guns. Yes, Jim's firearms have played as important a part of his adventures as anything else, and though he has carried many, in the films at least, there has always been one constant in his chamois leather holster – the Walther PPK.

However, the Beretta was the gun Fleming's literary Bond carried. It was described, by firearm enthusiast Geoffrey Boothroyd in a letter to Fleming, as 'a lady's gun, and not a very nice lady at that'. He suggested it had little stopping power and that Bond would be much better served with a revolver such as the Smith & Wesson Centennial Airweight. Fleming thanked Boothroyd for his letter and said he felt Bond ought to have an automatic instead of a revolver, though agreed the Beretta 418 lacked power.

LEFT: Ah, my favourite gadget – the magnetic Rolex. Ideal for deflecting bullets, attracting gas pellets or for unzipping ladies' dresses.

LEFT: Seiko took over as the official Bond watch suppliers in *The Man With The Golden Gun*.

LEFT: A couple of years on, and Seiko were still supplying 007 with their latest watch. It was waterproof.

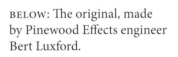

BELOW: Sometimes the Bond baddies have gadgets too. In *The Man With The Golden Gun* it came in the shape of … yes, you've guessed it, a golden gun. The gun comprised everyday items such as a pen, a cufflink and a cigarette case.

BELOW: The original, made by Pinewood Effects engineer Bert Luxford.

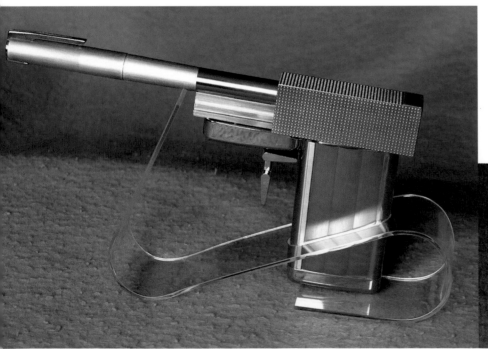

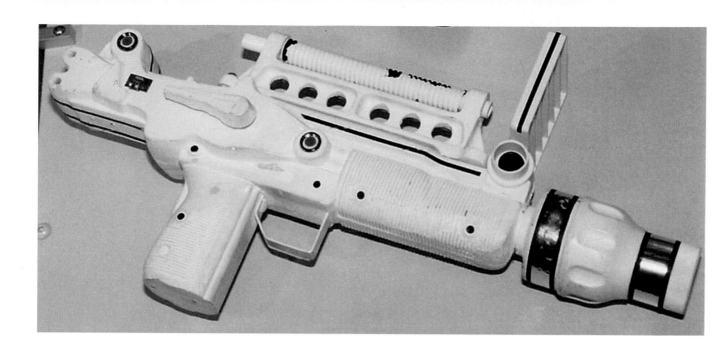

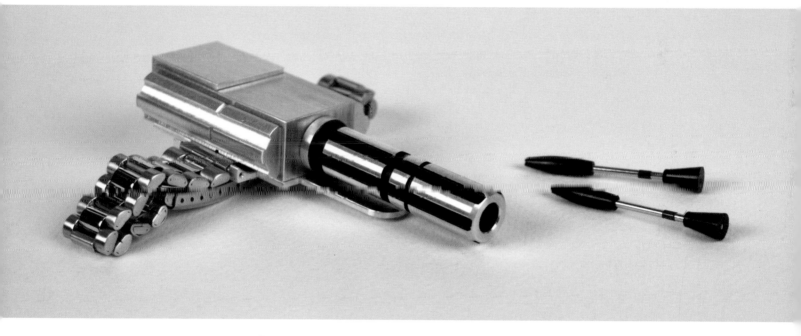

TOP: One of the laser guns we used in our space-fight finale in *Moonraker*.

ABOVE: A handy wrist dart gun, as described by Q in *Moonraker*. Another 'must' for Christmas.

RIGHT: Bond was issued with a new gun in *Tomorrow Never Dies*, a Walther P99, which he kept for the next few adventures.

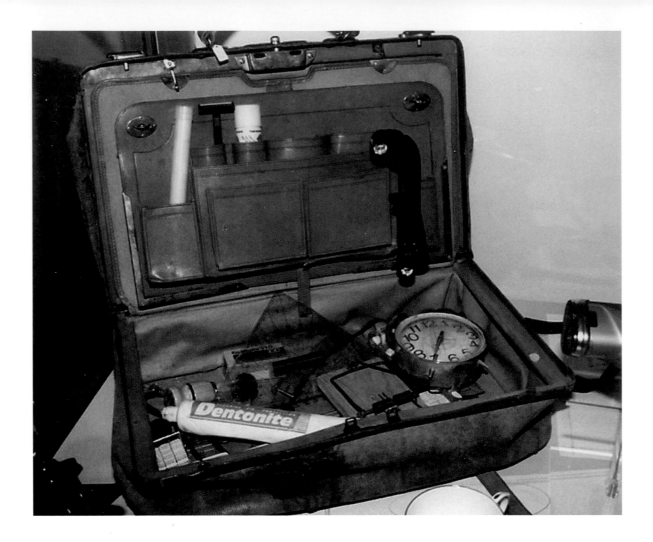

ABOVE: Everything for the traveller abroad – Q's deadly travel kit includes an alarm clock (guaranteed never to awaken the user) and Dentonite toothpaste, the latest in plastic explosive.

In *Dr. No* Jimmy was hauled in to M's office, where we learned he had carried a Beretta for ten years but, on one assignment, the said pistol – with the suppressor attached – snagged in his waistband. He was hospitalized for six months.

Boothroyd recommended the Walther PPK 7.65 mm as being the best choice for an automatic, with ammunition available everywhere. In thanks to Boothroyd, Fleming later called his armourer Major Boothroyd.

The Walther PPK was presented to Jim in *Dr. No* and was said to have an impact like 'a brick through a plate-glass window'. I used a PPK in all my films, though it fell out of favour with the real Secret Service when, on 20 March 1974, an attempt was made to kidnap HRH Princess Anne. The police officer protecting the princess was carrying a Walther PPK and it jammed. The gun was subsequently withdrawn from use.

In the Pierce Brosnan films the PPK was updated with a Walther P99, but they reverted to a PPK again with Daniel Craig in *Quantum Of Solace*. Whenever I had to fire the PPK, I used to anticipate the 'bang' and blink. The director would call for us to go again, because I often blinked and winced several seconds before I pulled the trigger. Such a coward.

ABOVE: A rocket-firing plaster cast. Only Q could come up with such a novelty!

TOP RIGHT: A new Ericsson mobile phone did everything from remotely driving a car to ... making a phone call in *Tomorrow Never Dies*.

BOTTOM RIGHT: Desmond Llewelyn posing as a car rental salesman at Hamburg Airport in *Tomorrow Never Dies*. He had a hard time persuading Pierce Brosnan's Jimmy Bond to take out accident insurance!

EXPLOSIVE FUN

The first real Bond gadget was of course the attaché case in *From Russia With Love*. It contained:

An AR-7 .22 survival rifle with infrared telescope
50 Gold Sovereigns
A tear gas canister disguised as talcum powder
Ammunition for rifle
A throwing knife

But should you ever find yourself issued with one, be sure to turn the catches the correct way when opening, or else the tear gas canister will explode in your face.

Terence Young and Peter Hunt decided to have a bit of fun with this element of the case when some United Artists executives were visiting Pinewood. They ran the first couple of reels of the movie, and when it reached the scene where Bond opens the attaché case, Peter cut to the huge explosion from the end of *Dr.*

No and ran the closing titles. The End.

Although he and Terence collapsed in hysterics, the UA execs were not particularly amused. But that was the type of fun you could have on a Bond movie.

In *Goldfinger* a brilliant set of homing beacons was presented to Jim. The first, larger, one was attached to the villain's vehicle and its early GPS-type technology used to locate his Swiss base. The second, smaller one, concealed in Jim's shoe, allowed MI6 to track him. It really was a prototype of GPS as we know it today – and very useful for the likes of jealous wives.

Q came up with some jolly ideas in *Thunderball* – the first time he was sent on location, incidentally, but Desmond couldn't sun himself in the Bahamas for continuity reasons – including the Bell Rocket Belt, which was used to propel Bond into the air when escaping Jacques Bouvar; then there was the Underwater Jet Pack used during the final undersea battle. Most usefully, there was an underwater camera capable of taking eight shots in darkness using an infrared film. We take that sort of thing for granted these days, but back then it was revolutionary.

While in Japan, Jim took full advantage of visiting their version of Q-Branch in *You Only Live Twice*. He marvelled at the mini-rocket cigarette Tiger Tanaka demonstrated – capable of shooting a jet-powered dart accurately up to thirty yards – and quipped, 'This cigarette can really save your life.'

Then there was dear Little Nellie: the Wallis WA-116 Series 1 autogyro, assembled (and disassembled) to fit into several suitcases. Nellie is armed with rocket launchers, air mines, machine guns, rear-mounted flame-throwers and infrared-guided AA smart missiles. The idea for her inclusion came one morning when Ken Adam heard a radio interview with Nellie's inventor, Wing Commander Ken Wallis, saying he'd relish the chance to pit his little autogyro against 'the big boys'. She certainly did him proud in the movie.

When Sean departed the series and George Lazenby stepped in there was a distinct lack of gadgets. Okay, there was radioactive lint, a safe cracker and a prototype Xerox machine, but not much else to excite us technical geeks. Bond was to rely more on his wits than Q-Branch. Wits are good, but gadgets are fun, and thankfully more were in evidence when Sean returned for *Diamonds Are Forever*, which featured the pickpocket's hated snap trap; a fake fingerprint to trick Tiffany Case into believing 007 is Peter Franks; and a voice changer that Blofeld uses to fool employees into thinking he is Willard Whyte and, subsequently, Q uses to fool Blofeld.

The most profitable of all gadgets, however, was a little ring that prompted every fruit machine to pay out a jackpot. Desmond said he collected up hundreds of dollars' worth of coins from the machines when the scene was completed, and decided rather than take them home he'd feed them back in to win an even bigger jackpot. Alas, the F/X guys had long gone home and the magic ring was of no use ... he lost the lot!

LEFT: A handy set of folding pocket binoculars.

BELOW LEFT: In order to identify a few people in *A View To A Kill*, Jim is issued with a miniature camera cunningly hidden in his signet ring.

BELOW: One of Q's new toys in *A View To A Kill* was a remote-controlled surveillance device called SNOOPER.

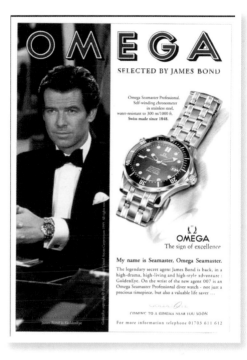

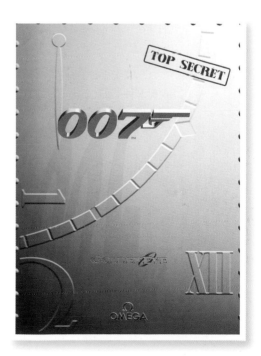

TIME TO PLAY

But more lovely toys were to come when yours truly stepped into the role in 1973. Apart from the Bug Sweeper, a Clothing Brush Communicator, a Shark gun that fired special highly pressurized air pellets and a genuine 'Felix Lighter' radio transmitter/receiver, there was a brilliant state-of-the-art Pulsar watch that illuminated to show the digital clock face.

There was also a lovely Rolex Submariner given to Bond by Moneypenny, after being repaired by Q. This was no ordinary watch. It featured a powerful electromagnet that was said to be able to deflect a bullet. More importantly, it could be used to unzip a lady's dress. I was ever so disappointed when the F/X boys said it didn't really work, and that Derek Meddings would instead have his hand up Maddy Smith's skirt, pulling the zip down using a piece of wire. Lucky old Derek. Constant retakes did mean I got to spend the whole day with dear Maddy, perfecting my technique. Ah, if only I could find a working prototype of that watch today … I could give Maddy a call to see if she fancied re-enacting the scene. The Submariner also featured a spinning bezel that acted as a rotating saw, enabling Jim to cut his rope restraints and escape a pool full of man-eating sharks and then go on and rescue Solitaire.

Did I ever get to keep any of the gadgets, is something I'm often asked. Alas no, they were whisked from set as soon as filming ended for the day. Shame, as I could earn a nice pension on eBay.

In my second outing, it was the villainous Francisco Scaramanga who had the great gadgets. His legendary Golden Gun was assembled from a pen (the barrel) inserted into a cigarette case (the firing chamber), a cigarette lighter (the handle), and a cufflink (the trigger). This gun is limited to just one golden bullet, which are all handcrafted by speciality munitions manufacturer Lazar – they are all 4.2 mm (an unusual size) and made of twenty-three-carat gold. The bullets flatten upon impact.

In *The Spy Who Loved Me* I of course had the wonderful Lotus Esprit and all its gadgets, but in addition was issued with a handy ski-pole cum-gun, modified to fire .30-calibre rounds from a four-shot magazine in the handle. I saw Michael Billington off with that.

Then there was a Seiko Quartz watch. It was the second film to feature the brand after a major tie-in for *The Man With The Golden Gun*, but this was the first film in which it had a purpose – a ticker-tape pager that allowed MI6 to send important messages to Jim. The Seiko was back in *Moonraker*, though this time with

the added bonus of a high explosive charge and remote detonator incorporated. It accompanied the wrist dart gun, capable of firing both cyanide-coated and armour-piercing darts. Jim used that to save himself from an out-of-control centrifuge simulator and then kill Hugo Drax. It's never a good idea to get into an out-of-control centrifuge simulator without one, let me tell you.

I was also armed with a safe-cracking device concealed within a cigarette case; a mini-camera imprinted with 007; and a laser gun. Oh, and I stole a poison pen from CIA agent Holly Goodhead's toys. Bond used this particular gadget to dispose of Drax's pet python. I think when you have to act alongside a twelve-foot-long rubber snake – and try to appear more animated than it – you know you've cracked this acting lark.

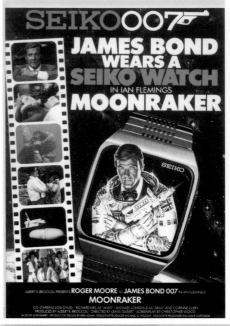

FABERGÉ EGGS TO FAKE CROCS

My trusty Seiko survived to accompany me in *For Your Eyes Only*, where it received digital message read-outs and operated as a two-way radio/transmitter for voice communications, much to the Prime Minister's surprise.

The main object of the film's story was to locate and retrieve the Automatic Targeting Attack Communicator (ATAC), which had been lost when the British spy ship *St Georges* was sunk. This device controlled all of Britain's Polaris nuclear submarines and

TOP: Seiko were with us again on this one.

ABOVE: My flexible friend. Handy for opening any lock, and paying for lunch, too.

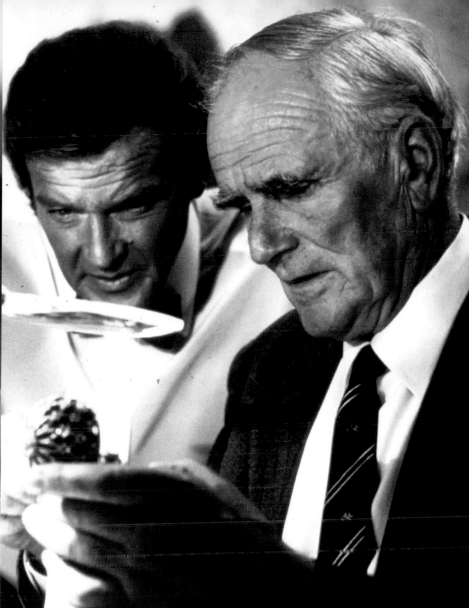

ABOVE AND RIGHT: In *Octopussy*, Q fixed a listening and homing device inside the Fabergé egg.

could either render them inoperative or coordinate them against major Western cities or, heaven forbid, against Britain herself. In its pursuit I helped Q load up the Identigraph device to assemble a photo of our suspect by selecting characteristics from a variety of lists including hair colour, hairstyle, nose form, style of eyeglasses etc. Poor Desmond Llewelyn had terrible trouble setting up the machine and remembering his complicated lines, so I took over the technical end and it worked rather well.

When *Octopussy* came around, the Seiko graduated to containing a universal radio direction finder, working in conjunction with a listening device inside Bond's fountain pen and the fake Fabergé egg. I also employed loaded backgammon dice – though not in my games with Cubby – and a Mont Blanc fountain pen that contained a mixture of nitric and hydrochloric acids. Have you seen the price of refills for those things?

BOND ON GADGETS

One of the fun gadgets – or is it a mode of transport? – was the 'fake crocodile', actually a miniature motorboat used to get Jimmy to Octopussy's Island. I bravely climbed into it for the close-ups, but allowed Paul Weston to drive it in the scene, just in case a *real* frisky crocodile wandered into shot. That might have been tricky!

In my last outing as Jim I was armed with all manner of useful gizmos. There were polarizing sunglasses that let Jim see clearly through tinted glass; a ring containing a miniature camera; a billfold that used ultraviolet light to read previously written material by picking up the indentations of pen marks on paper; a bug detector contained within an electric razor; a credit card for popping open locked windows; a tracking device to locate a stolen microchip buried in the snow; and, of course, SNOOPER – one of Q's surveillance inventions in the form of a small, animal-like remote-controlled camera that can transmit audio/video.

ABOVE: An innocent-looking pair of CK glasses. But touch a switch and it sets off a detonator in Jim's P99 gun.

BELOW: This innocent-looking electric shaver is actually a sophisticated bug detector in *A View To A Kill*.

GADGET HEAVEN

After my tenure as 007 ended, Q stayed on to look after Timothy Dalton and Pierce Brosnan. Their haul of gadgets was ever impressive and ingenious. In *The Living Daylights* Q produced a Philips Keychain, which had become widely popular in locating lost keys. However, Q's contained some non-standard extras, including a capsule of stun gas, activated by the first bars of 'Rule, Britannia', and an explosive charge set off by a wolf whistle! The keychain also featured a lock-pick, effective on ninety per cent of the world's locks …

In his second film with Timothy Dalton, Q found himself in the field and carried a bag of everyday travel items including

ABOVE: Q with my successor, Timothy Dalton, who was receiving a briefing on the key finder, which was operated by a whistle.

RIGHT: Of course there were toy guns produced to tie in with the films. They came in all shapes and sizes.

Dentonite Toothpaste – actually plastic explosive with the detonator disguised as a packet of cigarettes. There was also a wonderful gun that could be programmed to fire for only one person, and an exploding alarm clock – guaranteed never to wake up anyone who uses it.

When Pierce donned the famous tuxedo it was accompanied by a leather belt that concealed a piton capable of firing up to seventy-five feet of high-tensile wire, that could take the weight of an average person. Then there was a Parker pen for his top pocket that contained a class-four grenade. A new wristwatch in the shape of Omega Seamaster Professional – with laser cutter and remote detonator – completed the ensemble.

When *Tomorrow Never Dies* came around, the burgeoning mobile-phone market was tapped and Ericsson supplied a concept model loaded with a variety of features, including a 20,000-volt stun gun, and a nifty fingerprint analyser. The best feature in my view was the remote control for Jimmy's BMW – a masterpiece that no agent should be without.

With the fortieth anniversary of the films in 2002, the producers decided it was time to pay homage to some of the gadgets laid up in storage from the previous twenty films and have Bond wander around them, picking up a wristwatch (with explosive detonator and laser cutter) and a ring that can shatter bulletproof glass.

Since *Casino Royale* in 2006, the character of Q and his lab have been absent from the films. While Bond is still outfitted with a number of gadgets, they seem less futuristic and awe-inspiring and are based on technology already commercially available rather than Q's flights of fancy. The cellphones are smarter – the one in *Quantum Of Solace* had an identification imager that could compile a composite facial image. I wonder if that was on contract or pay-as-you-go?

One thing that is constant is Jimmy's love of a good watch – and let's face it, it's his watch that has got him out of several nasty situations. I used to wear an Omega all the time, and still do wear my limited-edition Submariner on occasion, but my main timepiece is a Breitling, which I used in a commercial for the Hanson Trust in Ireland. After the third and last day of filming, I asked my son Christian (who was assistant director) to take it back to the production office.

'No, keep it, it's yours,' he said. There was no way I was going to pinch a £5,000 watch!

'No,' he said, 'Kristina saw you admiring it and has bought it for you.'

My wife also bought me a Piaget watch, which I use when in formalwear as it's very lightweight and thin. My wife, as well as having great taste, is also very generous.

ABOVE AND BELOW: Omega remained Jimbo's watch of choice throughout Pierce's tenure – and still features with Daniel in the role.

BOND
ON
CARS

BOND ON CARS

PREVIOUS PAGES: Daniel Craig continues to be a safe driver and I believe he took out accidental damage insurance in case of a dent or scratch.

As well as gadgets, of course, Q has supplied 007 with cars for many decades now. Jimmy has driven his fair share of models: Bentley … Ford … GM … Aston Martin … Mercedes-Benz … BMW … Lotus … Rolls-Royce … Citröen … Renault. All were internationally recognized makers of motorcars and all have benefited hugely from the exposure.

PETROL HEADS UNITE!

BELOW: It wasn't really until *Goldfinger* that the 'Bond car' really grabbed people's imagination. The Aston Martin DB5 featured a wealth of optional extras.

It was a different story when I was making a TV series called *The Saint*. We thought it would be rather good if Simon Templar drove a British Jaguar car and our production manager, Johnny Goodman, duly approached them about a twenty-six-part primetime TV show. 'Oh, and we need three … next week.'

They shrugged their shoulders in a rather pompous way. 'Think of the publicity!' Johnny exclaimed. They told Johnny they

LEFT: The gear knob triggered an ejector seat, there was an early GPS tracking monitor, weapons tray, front-firing machine guns, mud slick, rear bulletproof screen and more.

RIGHT: Oh yes, it also had revolving number plates inspired by director Guy Hamilton getting fed up of receiving parking tickets in London.

BELOW: The Bond DB5 even had its own specification booklet.

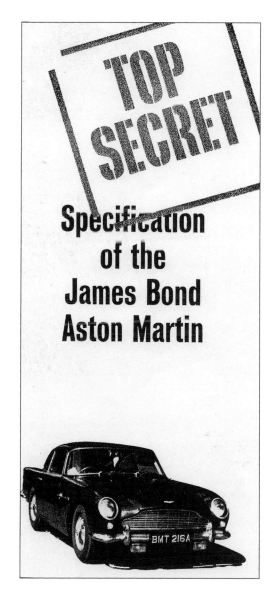

TOP SECRET

Specification of the James Bond Aston Martin

had order books bulging and a waiting list they couldn't fulfil as it was ... 'Why do we need publicity?'

So we went to Volvo, who couldn't do enough to help us. Volvo is still going strong ... and Jaguar? Well, they're around.

As 007 I have found myself at the wheel of many modes of vehicular transport; however, as my friend Michael Caine might say 'not a lot of people know that ...' The Bamford & Martin 1.5-litre Side Valve Short Chassis Tourer was James Bond's very first car.

According to the first 'Young Bond' book, *SilverFin*, by Charlie Higson, Jimmy inherited the car at the age of thirteen from his uncle Max, and drove it regularly, even though he was underage. The car was destroyed in the third Young Bond novel, *Double or Die*, leading Bond to replace it with the Bentley Mark IV – as later featured in Fleming's novels, although petrol heads among you will know there has never been a Bentley model known as the 'Mark IV'. That appellation was a creation of Ian Fleming, and erroneously perpetuated ever since.

James Bond's car in the Ian Fleming novels was a grey 1933 Bentley convertible – featuring a 4.5-litre engine with the Amherst Villiers supercharger. Unlike in the films, no gadgets were ever installed in the cars Bond used in Fleming's novels. The only armament mentioned at all was a .45 Colt Army Special revolver that Jim kept in the glove compartment.

The Bentley was actually the very first Bond car seen in the film series, shown briefly during *From Russia With Love* in the scene with Jimmy and Sylvia Trench alongside the River Thames. It featured the added extra of a car phone, which in 1963 was – like many other Bond gadgets – a prototype for future developments.

In *Goldfinger* Bond asks about his Bentley in Q-Branch, only to be told that it has 'had its day' and is instead presented with an

Aston Martin DB5 – perhaps the car most famously associated with the entire 007 series. To date the model has featured in five films – *Goldfinger, Thunderball, GoldenEye, Tomorrow Never Dies* and *Casino Royale*. I'm told it was also due to feature in *The World Is Not Enough*, but the shots of it being driven were cut. The 2006 reboot of the series showed Bond winning it in a game of poker in the Bahamas – without any special extras.

DB OR NOT DB?

Though I never drove an Aston Martin as Bond, I did drive a DB5 in the comedy film *The Cannonball Run*, and a DBS in *The Persuaders!*. The DB5 also popped up in the TV film *The Return of the Man from U.N.C.L.E.*, with George Lazenby playing a character called 'JB'.

The DB5 car as used in *Goldfinger* and *Thunderball* was the prototype model, with another standard car (later modified) used for stunts. Both cars were loaned to Eon Productions for the duration of filmmaking and later for publicity tours. Two further cars were later purchased and 'adapted' for promotional use through to the late 1960s, one of which sold in 2006 for $2,090,000 (approximately £1.4 million); the second is in the Louwman Collection Museum in the Netherlands. The original gadget car, meanwhile, was stripped of its accessories and sold as a standard car, only to be retrofitted by the purchaser. It was mysteriously stolen in 1997 and has never been found. The second 'original'

TOP: Corgi launched its most successful ever film tie-in model with the DB5 and has since sold over seven million units.

ABOVE: And it still sells today!

ABOVE LEFT: Desmond Llewelyn and Honor Blackman at the launch of the new Corgi range of Bond models in the mid-1990s.

ABOVE RIGHT: Prince Andrew was given a fully operational scale model of a DB5 for his sixth birthday.

DB5 was sold in 2010, for £2.6 million.

The famous scene in which Q demonstrates all the car's gadgets to Bond was not originally in the script. Desmond finished his day's filming and returned home. Cubby called him. He'd been thinking: demonstrating the gadgets to Bond would surely heighten the audience's excitement to see them in action. As the set was still in place, would Desmond come in for a second day of filming?

Gadgets fitted for *Goldfinger* include ...

- ⚹ Front-firing Browning .30-calibre machine guns behind the front indicators
- ⚹ Retractable tyre-slashing blades concealed in the rear wheel hub caps
- ⚹ Radio telephone in the driver's door panel
- ⚹ Radar scanner and tracking screen hidden behind car radio speaker
- ⚹ Passenger ejector seat
- ⚹ Oil slick spray hidden within rear light cluster
- ⚹ Caltrop ejector device hidden within rear light cluster
- ⚹ Smoke screen from exhaust pipes
- ⚹ Front and rear extending rams
- ⚹ Gun cabinet under driver's seat
- ⚹ Bulletproof windscreen and rising bulletproof rear screen
- ⚹ Revolving number plates, valid all countries, naturally:
    BMT 216A (UK)   4711-EA-62 (France)   LU 6789 (Switzerland)

Other Astons featured in the series include:

❧ A DBS was used in the pre-credits and closing scenes of *On Her Majesty's Secret Service* as Jim and Tracy's wedding car. It was glimpsed in the subsequent film, *Diamonds Are Forever*, parked up in Q-Branch.

❧ In *The Living Daylights* Timothy Dalton drove a V8 Vantage Volante convertible and its hardtop version. All the usual refinements were in place, including extending side outriggers, spike-producing tyres, missiles, lasers, signal-intercepting smart radio, head-up display and rocket propulsion. It could also self-destruct when primed. Doesn't every car?

❧ Pierce Brosnan's first outing as 007 – *GoldenEye* – brought back the Aston Martin DB5 and this time pitted it against a Ferrari in the hills above Monte Carlo; while in his last outing, *Die Another Day*, the Aston Martin V12 Vanquish (or 'Vanish') was introduced by the new Q. It featured front-firing rockets, hood-mounted target-seeking guns, spike-producing tyres and a passenger ejector seat in homage to the original Aston Martin DB5. This Aston was also equipped with 'adaptive camouflage' – a cloaking device that allowed it to become effectively invisible at the push of a button. Hmmmm. A little far-fetched even for Bond!

❧ When *Casino Royale* hit the screens, we saw the new Aston Martin DBS V1 (right) as Jim's car of choice, although no special gadgets were visible other than the compartments that housed his Walther P99 and an emergency medical kit. It turned up again in *Quantum Of Solace* and was all but destroyed after a chase in Siena, Italy. Nice to know some things don't change.

ABOVE: Special-effects engineer Bert Luxford with his adapted BSA motorcycle for *Thunderball*.

BELOW: The DB5 returns in *Casino Royale*.

TOP LEFT: Little Nellie, the autogyro, held her honour against several SPECTRE airborne thugs in *You Only Live Twice*.

LEFT: And here is her 'Uncle', dear Desmond Llewelyn, describing her operation to 007 – please note he is wearing shorts!

TOP RIGHT: And here she is today, still proudly sporting her 007 weaponry.

ESPRIT DE CORPS!

My own Bondmobile came in the shape of the Lotus Esprit. The story goes that Donovan McLauchlan, public relations manager at Lotus, had been tipped off that the next Bond movie, *The Spy Who Loved Me,* was gearing up for pre-production at Pinewood. It was early 1976, and he drove an Esprit to the studios and parked it right in the path of anyone trying to get in or out of the main admin building entrance. It wasn't long before Cubby saw the car and made a phone call – not to get it towed, but to ask all about it. Their gamble paid off.

Lotus loaned us two production Esprit's, five Esprit body shells and two Lotus personnel for the shoot. The body shells were used to make the underwater car, as adapted by Perry Oceanographics. A full underwater conversion mode with fins, front-mounted rocket launchers, mines, a periscope, a smoke screen and a surface-to-air missile was pretty exciting. There was also a cement sprayer concealed behind the registration plates.

Other body shells were used in various scenes, including the shot of the Esprit driving off the pier into the sea. That one was powered by compressed air, equipped with a space-frame and locked steering wheel … It's nice to know no actors were harmed.

Lotus sales increased dramatically after the film's release, with a

ABOVE: The Corgi model of the Lotus Esprit.

BELOW: Just popping into the cove for its 6,000-mile service.

ABOVE: Always room for a
pretty passenger in the Lotus
Esprit.

three-year waiting list for Esprits in particular. I myself was offered
the opportunity to buy one at a ten per cent discount. Needless
to say, their overwhelming generosity was not something that
particularly excited me.

The cars were problematic in the extreme. During filming,
their engines overheated and batteries ran down quickly. Their low
driving position made elegant exits from the car an issue, and all
this made the action location in Sardinia a little fraught.

When we heard later that publicist John Willis was due to drive
the car from London to the Cannes Film Festival in May 1977, we
took bets on whether he'd make it. He did get as far as Lyon without
issue, before ending up on the back of a tow truck heading for a
local garage. It then limped into Cannes, was positioned outside
the Carlton Hotel and duly refused to move again thanks to a flat
battery. If only the world's press could have snapped the team of
mechanics at work during the dead of night, it would have made
terrific headlines – 'James Bond's car breaks down'.

Though the Lotus transformed into a submarine on screen, a
combination of miniatures and body shells were used to achieve
the effect of the conversion. It could be driven underwater, but only

in a full wetsuit, as the interior was not air-locked. Consequently it was dubbed 'Wet Nellie'.

The scene where the car emerges from the ocean onto a beach, was shot in two parts: with an Esprit shell being pulled on a tow rope to the point at which the car was to emerge, and then a cut to the real car in the surf. The little toddler who watches the car come out of the water and points is Richard Kiel's son, RJ. He's now a thirty-six-year-old doctor.

I thought it might be a giggle to wind down the window and drop a fish out as we drove onto the beach. Cubby wasn't at all happy, and said we should re-shoot; he felt it was a little too flippant and therefore not funny. I said OK, but when we ran both versions in rushes the next day my prank got a huge laugh. Cubby conceded.

In *For Your Eyes Only* the Lotus returned, twice. The first one, a white Esprit Turbo, was destroyed when a thug tripped its self-destruct system by breaking the driver's-side window. The second one, a red version of the same model, was driven by *moi* in Northern Italy, though you didn't get to see many of the gadgets in operation, I'm afraid, as a wonderful scene with John Moreno as Luigi – where he tampered with a few buttons – was unfortunately cut due to time constraints. If you listen carefully, when I leave him in the car to go into the ice rink I tell him not to play with any of the buttons.

BELOW: Cubby really didn't like my little joke of dropping a fish out of the window when we emerged from the sea. However, when it got more laughs than the scripted version in rushes, he conceded it was one of my better ideas.

OVER AIR, LAND AND SEA

ABOVE: The Glastron boat chase in *Live And Let Die* was, thankfully, filmed at the beginning of the production schedule. I'd hurt my leg in rehearsals and could happily sit down for my brave introduction as 007.

The wet bike was another brilliant innovation first seen by the public in a Bond movie – again, in *For Your Eyes Only*. I was given a little time to get used to it on the beach at the Cala di Volpe and, in my bathing trunks, leapt aboard and mastered the controls, swishing around in the surf thinking it was all rather like a jet boat. Then I was told in the scene I'd be wearing full Naval Commander uniform for the ride to Stromberg's lair, and I had to arrive immaculate and dry, without a hair out of place. OK, I thought, I'll give it a whirl.

Fresh from the hair-and-make-up truck, I hopped onto the bike, started her up and made my way out to sea. It was all perfectly fine until I heard the 'chop-chop-chop' of the helicopter above, obviously filming. Just then, a huge downdraft created by its rotors took hold and started pushing the bike down into the sea. I had no way of contacting either the helicopter or the boat behind, but knew if I fell in it would mean a complete wardrobe change, hair, make up, the lot – and that would take a very long time. More by steely determination and grit than anything else I managed to keep the bike going at no more than a forty-five-degree angle to the surface. Sometimes being brave is pretty tough going.

As well as kitting Bond out with the best thing on four wheels, the writers sometimes turn an idea on its head and say, 'Let's try him in a ...' Well, if a Lotus is one of the most powerful cars, the direct opposite would be a Citroën 2CV, with its mere two-horsepower engine, yet another vehicle that featured in *For Your Eyes Only*. It was huge fun to drive down through olive groves in – it just goes to show, it's more about the driver's skill than it is the size of his engine, or so the Bond girls say.

But what on earth could be even less powerful than a 2CV? How about an Indian Tuk-Tuk motorized rickshaw?

With the pull of a lawnmower engine, and manoeuvrability of same, it was used to great effect in *Octopussy* as an escape vehicle.

Oh, and I shouldn't forget the 'Bondola' from *Moonraker*. That was all rather tongue-in-cheek, but why wouldn't Jim have a supercharged gondola? Filming in Venice is never particularly easy, especially with the vast crowds looking on, but shooting around the canals was fairly straightforward as there was nowhere for people to watch – aside from a few bridges – and it all happened so fast, they didn't really know what it was all about anyway as we were there under stealth.

ABOVE LEFT: By land, by sea and then by air ... if I'm not mistaken it was the first time we saw Jimmy hang-glide into the villain's lair. I was so brave.

ABOVE RIGHT: In *The Man With The Golden Gun* it wasn't just Jimmy who had a gadget car. Villain Scaramanga (Christopher Lee) owned a Matador Coupé, which converted into a flying car.

FAR LEFT: Not the most gadget-packed of Bond vehicles ... I think he got the hump with me.

LEFT: The tipping Bondola from *Moonraker*. Lucky I had my little hooter to warn passersby to move out of the way.

Once we reached St Mark's Square for the scene where the gondola converts into a hovercraft, however, we were confronted with 20,000–30,000 tourists, largely Oriental, all armed with Nikon cameras.

There were two gondolas used in the sequence: the first inflated and raised out of the water, then we cut to a second on land, which was built around a Ford chassis. I arrived in my lovely light-grey silk suit for the first take, sat in the boat and the air was switched on – but seemingly only on one side, thus toppling me out and straight into the Grand Canal. Cue much laughter and snapping of Nikons. I trotted off to dry, change, have my hair and make-up done and, thirty minutes later, returned.

'Action!' called Lewis, and I was tipped sideways into the canal yet again. This happened on five takes, where one side inflated faster than the other, tipping me in each time. Each time, the laughter increased, as did the size of the crowds gathered. Take 6 – and my final dry suit. Thankfully, it worked and we wrapped for the day.

Next morning, I hopped inside the Ford-chassis gondola to drive it right the way across the square, which by then was starting to fill with tourists. Rather than attempt to control the crowds, Lewis said we'd just shoot, as they really wouldn't know what we were doing until it was over.

'Fair enough,' I said. 'But I really do feel I need some sort of horn to warn people that there is a motorized gondola approaching

ABOVE: Don't fall off! I knew if I did I'd face a two-mile trip back to shore for make-up, hair and new costume.

BELOW: From the sublime to the ridiculous, a two-horsepower getaway vehicle in *For Your Eyes Only*.

LEFT AND ABOVE: The *Octopussy* Bede Jet folded up into a horse trailer, and could just about accomodate a 6' 2" Bond.

103

them, driven by an English actor, on St Mark's Square as it's not something they'd really expect.' They found some sort of claxon, and I literally beep-beeped my way around unsuspecting tourists, across to a sharp right turn down a narrow road. It was so narrow the F/X boys put Vaseline down the side of the gondola so I could slip down more easily.

Then of course in *Live And Let Die* I took it to another extreme when I drove an AEC Regent RT-type double-decker bus. I remember that day well: it was 7 December 1972, on location in Montego Bay, Jamaica, and I had to drive it under a low bridge, sheering off the top deck. Maurice Patchett from London Transport's Chiswick depot spent three months preparing for the stunt, including taking me on a crash course – forgive the pun – on the Chiswick skid pad. Maurice took over the driving as the bus headed for the bridge; the top deck had been carefully removed and replaced only on rollers, to ensure a relatively clean detachment as it hit at precisely 30 mph.

Maurice said that if the film game didn't work out for me, I'd make a good London bus man. That would have pleased my

ABOVE: On location in Paris for *A View To A Kill*, I had to drive and virtually destroy a Renault taxi in my pursuit of Mayday. I guess it beats having to tip a driver.

mum, who still lived in hope I might one day get a proper job.

I also chopped the top of a car off in a film – a Renault 11 taxi in fact – in the Parisian scenes of *A View To A Kill*, while trying to chase Grace Jones. Wish I hadn't bothered trying, actually. Nevertheless, that was a terrific sequence, all very carefully orchestrated by the superb Remy Julienne. Alas, these days when visiting Paris I have to sit in the traffic just like everyone else.

In my last 007 outing, I found myself at the controls of a San Francisco fire truck. When I heard we were going to be shooting

in the city, I thought, 'Oh, here we go, another attempt at bettering *Bullit* with Steve McQueen,' but when they told me my mode of transport would be somewhat different, I was intrigued. It certainly cleared the traffic off the roads.

And just to prove Q didn't exclusively think of the 00 section in his work, he designed himself a fishing boat – for his retirement. The Q-boat came equipped with submersible capabilities, torpedoes, rocket booster and GPS tracking, though Q was keen to point out it was not properly finished when Jim took off in it during *The World Is Not Enough*.

THE CLASSIC STUNT

I can't end any discussion of Bond cars and assorted vehicles without mentioning the AMC Hornet, can I? The what? Well, if I was to say when Jim is chasing Mary Goodnight in *The Man With The Golden Gun*, he steals a car in which Sheriff J.W. Pepper is about to take a test drive, you'll be with me. During the chase, Jim makes a corkscrew jump over a river. That wasn't just lucky guesswork, but the first case of a computer designing a stunt. Race car driver Jay Milligan, who promoted the American Thrill Show during the 1960s and 1970s, first performed the stunt, known as the Astro Spiral Jump, on 12 January 1972 at the Houston Astrodome. Always keen to hear about anything a bit unusual or daring, Cubby was soon told about the stunt everyone was talking about, and put a call through to Milligan.

Researchers at Cornell University for the National Highway Traffic Safety Administration did a computer simulation of the stunt to calculate the exact angles required, speeds to drive and so forth. These details were passed over to the production team, and the bridge was erected.

With Milligan supervising, the 360-degree spiral was shot in just one take, with British stuntman 'Bumps' Williard at the wheel and with eight cameras simultaneously capturing the action. Meanwhile divers, ambulances and cranes were on standby in case of any unforeseen consequences. The jump was over in a second and to achieve greater screen time is shown in slow motion. Williard was given a large bonus for completing it on the first take, by the way.

ABOVE: The opening of *GoldenEye* saw new 007 Pierce Brosnan chase a plane down a runway on a motorbike. As you do.

BELOW: The AMC Hornet that performed the amazing 360-degree roll in *The Man With The Golden Gun*.

RIGHT: When Q retired, he envisaged a life of fishing. So he built himself a fishing boat – albeit with missiles, GPS and other gadgets. Perhaps to help land those big catches?

MIDDLE RIGHT: Though sometimes, when a BMW or Aston is not available, a smaller mode of transport will suffice.

BELOW: With *Die Another Day* the Aston Martin was back, in the shape of the Vanquish – or Vanish, as 007 dubbed it.

FAR RIGHT TOP: And here is the Vanquish in action!

FAR RIGHT BOTTOM: With Daniel Craig, a new Aston Martin was introduced – the DB9. Something tells me he'll have to go for the expensive valeting option.

BOND
ON
STYLE

BOND ON STYLE

PREVIOUS PAGES: Sharing a glass of bubbly in Chantilly with Tania Roberts.

Once upon a time, heroes wore chainmail and armour, rode around on horses and sat down to an opulent banquet using their bare hands to tear apart their food. That wouldn't do for Jimmy Bond – the quintessential well-dressed English spy who epitomizes style. Old Jimbo has become something of a style icon and the phrase 'living the Bond lifestyle' conjures up images of the very best things life has to offer by way of sharp clothes, expensive champagnes, fast cars, beautiful women, speed boats and fine dining.

Bond preferred Polish or Russian vodka at a time when the only brand available in the West would have been Stolichnaya. Besides his famous 'Martini, shaken, not stirred', Jim often drank

LEFT: The famous vodka Martini, so often stirred instead of being shaken. Although I never ordered one in any of my seven films, here I am with one – though not, I hasten to add, served in a proper Martini glass.

BELOW: Mention the 'Bond lifestyle' and images of casinos, fast cars, speedboats and beautiful girls all come to mind, as is so brilliantly illustrated in this competition flyer from 1989.

ABOVE: Variation on a theme – Daniel Craig enjoys a Vesper Martini with Eva Green – aka Vesper – in *Casino Royale*. When Vesper asks Bond if he named the drink after her because of the bitter aftertaste, 007 replies that he named it for her, 'because once you have tasted it, you won't drink anything else.'

a shot of straight vodka, served with a pinch of black pepper. This was not for the flavour, he explained, 'but because it caused the impurities in cheap vodka to sink to the bottom'. Though I fear that trick wouldn't have improved the Siamese vodka he downed in the film *You Only Live Twice*!

Bond and vodka have gone hand in hand since *Dr. No*, when the titular villain handed 007 a 'Martini, shaken not stirred'. This fleeting moment in the film literally changed the way Martini drinkers made their cocktails from then on, shifting from the traditional gin to a vodka-based drink and popularizing the vodka Martini the world over.

I myself prefer a gin Martini and, in all my years of travelling, believe the best is served in the bar of Maison Pic, in Valence, France. How do they prepare it?

First, the ingredients. My gin of choice is Tanqueray and vermouth has to be Noilly Prat.

Take the glass or cocktail shaker you are using and, for two sensible-sized Martinis, fill ¼ of each glass with Noilly Prat. Swill it around and then discard it. Next, top the glasses up with gin, drop in a zest of lemon, and place the glasses in a freezer or ice-cold fridge until you are – or should I say *she* is – ready.

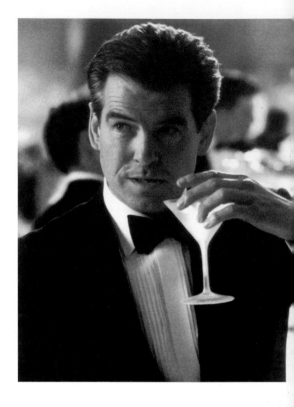

ABOVE AND BELOW: Both Pierce and Timothy were partial to a Martini – but Timothy appears to be mixing his drinks in this shot.

MARTINI IS NOT THE ONLY DRINK ...

Bond appreciates other drinks, too. For instance, when, in my first 007 film, I walked into a Harlem bar, it wasn't a vodka Martini I asked for. Far from it. I requested 'bourbon and water, please – no ice'. In *GoldenEye* Jim drinks a bourbon – Jack Daniel's – with M, while in *The World Is Not Enough* and *Die Another Day* he also enjoys drinking Talisker whisky. M pours Bond a glass of Talisker in *The World Is Not Enough*, into which Bond puts ice – something not at all recommended by the distiller – but his fingers, wet from the ice, exude a fizzing substance, which leads him to realize a bomb had been planted in Sir Robert King's money, money that he'd just been handling. Good old Jim.

But Bond is perhaps more closely associated with the finest champagne – be it served in bed with a delicious girl, in an underwater escape pod or on the way back from the Arctic Circle in a submarine. Most famously Bollinger and Dom Perignon have featured in the movies, though I must admit I have a fondness for Taittinger and am not opposed to Moët & Chandon either.

ABOVE: You can't have a vodka Martini without vodka. Jim preferred Russian. I'm not averse to it, or taking part in a bit of product placement – as seen here in *A View To A Kill*.

Bollinger champagnes used in the movies:

- ❦ *Live And Let Die*: Bollinger
- ❦ Moonraker: Bollinger RD '69
- ❦ *A View To A Kill*: Bollinger '75
- ❦ *Licence To Kill*: Bollinger RD '75
- ❦ *The Living Daylights*: Bollinger ...
- ❦ *GoldenEye*: Bollinger Grande Année 1988
- ❦ *Tomorrow Never Dies*: Bollinger Grande Année 1989
- ❦ *The World Is Not Enough*: Bollinger Grande Année 1990
- ❦ *Die Another Day*: Bollinger '61
- ❦ *Casino Royale*: Bollinger Grande Année 1990

**Dom Pérignon champagnes used
in the movies:**

- *Dr. No*: Dom Pérignon '55 (Bond says he prefers
  the '53)
- *Goldfinger*: Dom Pérignon '53
- *Thunderball*: Dom Pérignon '55
- *You Only Live Twice*: Dom Pérignon '59
- *On Her Majesty's Secret Service*:
  Dom Pérignon '57
- *The Man With The Golden Gun*: Dom Pérignon
  '64 (Bond says he prefers the '62)
- *The Spy Who Loved Me*: Bond mentions a Dom
  Pérignon '52

Man cannot live by bourbon or champagne alone, however, and so there are also some fine wines served and consumed throughout Jim's adventures, along with some less memorable ones – Phuyuck anyone?

In *Goldfinger*, Bond shows off his sommelier skills to M when brandy is served: 'I'd say it was a thirty-year-old fined and indifferently blended, with an overdose of *bon bois*.'

In Japan for *You Only Live Twice* Jim displays his appreciation of the local rice wine drink when Tiger Tanaka offers him the choice of a vodka Martini or sake. 'Oh no, I like sake, especially when it's served at the correct temperature, 98.4 Fahreneit, like this is.' Hang fire, Jimmy!

My wife Kristina and I discovered the true joy of sake when we were in Japan and Korea, where it is, in fact, served cold. There are two basic types of sake: *Futsū-shu*, which is termed 'ordinary' sake, and *Tokutei meishō-shu*, which is 'special-designation' sake. *Futsū-shu* is the equivalent of table wine and accounts for the majority of sake produced, whereas *Tokutei meishō-shu* denotes the premium sakes, distinguished by the degree to which the rice has been polished and the added percentage of brewer's alcohol or the absence of such additives.

I became a bit of an aficionado, as you can tell. And Jimmy, I have to tell you, hot sake is usually only served as a winter drink, and high-grade sake is *never* served hot because the flavours and aromas are lost.

TOP AND ABOVE: Product placement is a big part of the Bond PR machine.

ABOVE: Shirley Eaton enjoys a glass of champers with Sean Connery in *Goldfinger*. Dom Pérignon '53 I believe?

BELOW: Phuyuck – I'll take a case for Christmas.

A couple of films later, in *Diamonds Are Forever*, it is sherry that becomes the talking point of a meal. Bond, M and Sir Donald Munger (played by my old friend Laurence Naismith, from *The Persuaders!*) are being served the Spanish fortified wine.

'Pity about your liver, sir, it's an unusually fine solera. Fifty-one I believe,' says our hero.

'There is no year for sherry, 007,' replies M.

Not to be outdone, Jim retorts, 'I was referring to the original vintage on which the sherry is based: 1851, unless I'm mistaken?'

Of course he wasn't and a decent knowledge of wines can – literally – save your life. Look at how Red Grant gave himself away in *From Russia With Love* by ordering red wine with fish. Unthinkable! (But possible!)

At the climax of *Diamonds Are Forever*, posing as stewards, the limp-wristed Wint and Kidd give themselves away similarly when they offer Bond a Mouton Rothschild '55. The steward uses a gas ejector to remove the cork – they were all the fashion at one point, even on aeroplanes, until the pressurized gas within caused huge problems with exploding champagne bottles at 30,000 feet – and gives it to Bond, who smells the cork and also gets a whiff of the steward's strong

(and familiar) cologne, and realizes it's the bad guy.

Steward: 'A fine selection, if I may say.'

Bond: 'I'll be the judge of that … The wine is quite excellent, although for such a grand meal I had rather expected a claret.'

Steward: 'Of course.Unfortunately, our cellar's rather poorly stocked with clarets.'

Bond: 'Mouton Rothschild *is* a claret.'

They never learn, these ill-educated hoodlums, do they?

Of course, not all villains are ignorant about wine. Take my old adversary Francisco Scaramanga. He had a rather well-stocked wine cellar. When at dinner, Bond remarked on the wine, 'Excellent – slightly reminiscent of a '34 Mouton.'

Scaramanga replied, 'Then I must add it to my cellar!'

Leaving claret aside, I myself prefer a chilled bottle of Sancerre nowadays, a wine I discovered a few years ago when a group of us hired a mini-van to explore the chateaux of the Loire Valley. There, I tasted the wonderful bone-dry, highly aromatic wine with its intense flavours of peaches and gooseberries. The reason we restrict our choice largely to white wines is because, unfortunately, my wife develops terrible migraines if she consumes any red wine or a Chardonnay. Personally, I think a headache is sometimes worthwhile.

ABOVE: With Barbara Bach, or Barbara 'Back-to-Front' as I called her, in *The Spy Who Loved Me*. I'm probably thinking of two good reasons to serve champagne.

UP IN SMOKE

Bond also smokes in the novels, his preference being Morland Specials with their three gold rings, of which he consumes three or more packs a day. He tries other brands on his travels, most notably Shinsei in *You Only Live Twice.* 'He took a cigarette and lit it. It burned rapidly with something of the effect of a slow-burning firework ... it was good and sharp on the lungs with ninety per cent proof spirits. He let the smoke out in a quiet hiss and smiled.'

I didn't smoke cigarettes in my Bond films, as Sean and George had before me, and indeed as Timothy did after me. I gave up cigarettes in 1971 when, just before commencing work on *The Persuaders!*, I, along with my producing partner Bob Baker and script editor Terry Nation, visited Tony Curtis in LA. Tony was head of the anti-smoking lobby (though strangely did not include cannabis in his campaign!) and when, at his home for a meeting, we all lit up, Tony showed me a book with a rather curious photo on the front. It was a cancerous lung. It put me off

BELOW: It was Red Grant's choice of wine that gave him away as a baddie in *From Russia With Love.* Red wine with fish? Honestly!

smoking cigarettes for life, though I must admit I did still smoke cigars into the 1980s.

Contrary to popular myth, it was not part of my Bond contract that I had to be supplied with cigars. Yes, I smoked them on set, but I bought my own – much to the delight of our assistant director Derek Cracknell. Whenever he saw me light up between takes, Derek would call, 'Roger, they're ready for you!' and would offer to hold my cigar for me. Whenever I returned, saying they *weren't* ready, I'd find Derek sitting in a chair puffing away on my Davidoff.

ABOVE: In the bad old days, I smoked Davidoffs, though, contrary to popular myth, they were not supplied as part of my contract. I had to buy them.

SARTORIAL SIMPLICITY

BELOW: Sean at his Savile Row tailors, being outfitted for his Bond debut … and the finished result.

RIGHT: Sean Connery cuts a fine figure in his Conduit Cut suit. His elegantly attired co-star Pedro Armendáriz was terminally ill during filming of *From Russia With Love*, though kept it a secret and completed the film in order to provide income for his family. He took his own life in hospital shortly afterwards.

William Shakespeare wrote 'clothes maketh the man'. If that was the case for the literary James Bond, then I think we'd be a little disappointed in 'the man', to be honest. Contrary to popular thinking, while Ian Fleming had an eye for Savile Row quality, he rarely shopped there, preferring instead the 'off-Row' prices of Benson, Perry and Whitley in Cork Street, just a couple of roads along from the Row. He'd have three suits made at a time, for the princely sum of 58 guineas each.

It was reported by Mr Whitley of said establishment that 'Mr Fleming wore his suits until they were in threads', and, 'He dressed for comfort not for style'. This attitude clearly extended to his hero, as in the books Bond's clothes don't vary a great deal. His look was probably best described in Fleming's last novel, *The Man With The Golden Gun*, where he described Jim's 'dark-blue single-breasted suit, white shirt, thin black knitted silk tie, black casuals' as his 'usual rig'.

In *Moonraker* Fleming had Bond wearing a 'heavy white silk shirt, dark blue trousers of navy serge, dark blue socks and well polished moccasin shoes ... put on a black knitted silk tie and his jacket ...' in readiness for an evening at Blades Club. It was sartorial simplicity.

That didn't stop him noticing other people's wardrobes, though. In the same novel Fleming wrote: 'Bond concluded his inspection with Drax's clothes, which were expensive and in excellent taste, a dark blue pinstripe in lightweight flannel, double-breasted with turn back cuffs, a heavy white silk shirt with a stiff collar, an unobtrusive tie with a small grey and white check, modest cufflinks, which looked like Cartier, and a plain gold Patek Phillippe watch with a black leather strap.'

Despite all of the descriptive detail Fleming wove into his adventures, Bond's wardrobe was by and large indistinct. No shirt maker was ever mentioned; no tailor ever credited. One thing we did garner was he liked 'single-breasted dinner jackets' and a 'heavy silk evening shirt' when it was time to enjoy the 'solid, studied comfort of card rooms and casinos', but that's about as much as Fleming ever enlightened us about his hero's tastes in attire. The films are a very different case.

BELOW: Hey, George! That's how I got into movies.

The New Bond..
GETTING TO THE BOTTOM OF HIS FIRST MYSTERY

JIMBO COMES ALIVE

Bond's on-screen look is credited to Terence Young, the director of *Dr. No.* He brought in his own tailor, Anthony Sinclair of Conduit Street, and shirt maker Turnbull & Asser. Young wanted to achieve the look of a well-dressed man, but one who didn't particularly stand out from the crowd. Sean was not particularly used to wearing suits, and in order for him to feel totally at ease when filming

began, Young asked that he wear suits around the clock, even to the extent of sometimes sleeping in them.

Anthony Sinclair created the classic, pared-down look of Connery's suits that came to be known as the 'Conduit Cut'. They were lightweight, one hundred per cent wool in navy blue, shades of grey and a subtle Glen Urquhart check. They were slim-line, single-breasted, two-button outfits. The Conduit Cut featured in all of Sean's early films, and changed only when Peter Hunt brought in his tailor, Dimi Major of Fulham, for *On Her Majesty's Secret Service*. Peter Hunt and his costume designer Marjory Cornelius came up with a rather timeless three-piece suit for the London scenes, featuring wider lapels and pocket flaps, and more fashionable brighter styles for the overseas settings. It was a marked departure. Bond was now outfitted from a much wider-styled wardrobe, and that gave the feeling of a slightly more casual 007 for the late sixties.

When I stepped into the role, I suggested that my long-time tailor, Cyril Castle (of Mayfair), with whom I had worked on *The Saint* and *The Persuaders!*, would give Jim a more contemporary look for the 1970s. Lots of modern colours, sports jackets and trousers became the new norm. The designs were fashionable, yet also elegant and comfortable. So much so that when Frank Sinatra and Sammy Davis Jr were in London they called to say they thought my clothes in *The Man With The Golden Gun* were very sharp – especially my dinner suits – then took themselves up to Cyril for new outfits.

After *The Spy Who Loved Me* I had, very reluctantly, left the UK due to the 87 per cent income-tax rate imposed by the then Labour government. Cubby also moved out and declared the next Bond film, *Moonraker*, would be shot in France. Initially, I based myself in Italy, at the family holiday home in Castiglione, and, in preparing for the next Bond film, realized it would be impossible

ABOVE: This was one outfit I did not try to steal after production.

ABOVE: With my dear friend Doug Hayward, who supplied my 'Bond look' for many years. I just hope he didn't think I was becoming a big head.

for me to travel back and forward to London for wardrobe fittings. So I suggested to Cubby we could use my Italian tailor, Angelo Litricio. In the month of August it was a joy driving to Rome for fittings – the only sounds I heard on the two-hour journey were burglar alarms. Everyone was on holiday except the thieves!

Meanwhile, back in London, Douglas Hayward had fast established a reputation as a tailor to the stars – and many of my friends. Doug was a real character to say the least. His anecdotage and attitude were the source for the character Harry Pendel in John le Carré's *The Tailor of Panama*; his charming manner was the model for his friend Michael Caine's 1966 performance in *Alfie*. Doug's celebrity client roster included Peter Sellers, Terence Stamp, Richard Burton, Alan Whicker, Michael Parkinson, Rex Harrison, Jackie Stewart and Michael Caine, among many others – whom he often visited in a second-hand Mini, packed full of material. He was so passionate about serving his clients that he'd go wherever they asked. That sounded perfect to me and, apart from becoming a dear friend, he also made all my subsequent suits, right up until his untimely death in 2008.

KEEP IT SIMPLE: MAKE IT CLASSIC

The 1970s were famous for flares and wide collars, and though my Bond's look was contemporary, it was relatively restrained when you look at some of the more outrageous trends in menswear. In the early 1980s a more traditional style was introduced, with classic three-piece suits and blazers, coupled with casual coolness. I've been told – sometimes sneeringly – that nobody can carry off a safari suit quite like me.

At the time, Doug's principle was, 'Keep them as classic as possible, as I believe people will be watching Bond films in twenty years' time … keep noticeable [current fashion] details, such as turnback cuffs, to a minimum. Fred Astaire could walk down the street today in a suit that was made for him in the 1930s and look fabulous. I have always borne that in mind when making clothes for films and I don't think I have ever done work for a film I am now embarrassed by.'

One of the perks of being the so-called star of a film is that you could legitimately steal – or should I say 'request' – items of wardrobe. After all, they are tailor-made for you, so who else can use them? On *The Man With The Golden Gun* I wore a particularly nice suit for what was to be the final scene.

'Hmmm,' I thought, 'must ensure this doesn't get dirty, I'd like this one.' So I did my level best to keep the suit smart, un-creased and unblemished.

As the director called 'Cut!' I smiled widely, stroked my

BELOW: Royal Navy Commander James Bond, CMG, RNVR. Pierce was style personified in uniform.

You too could look like Bond – The Daniel Craig Bond look from *Casino Royale*

❬ Brioni supplied the formal suits and evening wear

❬ Turnbull and Asser are credited with supplying the formal shirts (handmade) and ties

❬ John Lobb supplied many of the shoes from their ready-to-wear collection

❬ La Perla made the blue 'Grigoperla' swimming trunks to costume designer Lindy Hemming's own designs

❬ Sunspel made most of the casual wear including polo shirts, pullovers, T-shirts and underwear

❬ Omega supplied two styles of wristwatch: the Planet Ocean on a black rubber strap (2900.50.91) and the Seamaster on the stainless-steel strap (2220.80)

❬ Persol made the sunglasses, model nos. 2244 & 2720

❬ Converse Jack Purcell OTR ankle boots worn during the Madagascar crane fight sequence

❬ Armani made the leather jacket.

❬ Gieves & Hawkes supplied the white braces (with gold clips) from the Casino scenes

lapels and … a huge bucket of paste came down from above and completely ruined my lovely suit, not to mention my well-groomed hair. I looked up, and saw Cubby Broccoli wetting himself with laughter. He knew I had been admiring it!

In the early 1980s the *Daily Mail* referred to me as one of Britain's best-dressed men. How kind. It's true to say I don't feel particularly comfortable in a pair of jeans and a T-shirt, and I rarely dress down when I'm out and about, except perhaps when on holiday.

If you opened my wardrobe today you'd find shirts made for me by the Swedish company Eton Shirts or perhaps a few from Frank Foster of Pall Mall. For Bond, incidentally, I had my shirts made occasionally by Turnbull and Asser but more often than not by Washington Tremlett. There's also a variety of blazers – as my weight is sometimes a little erratic I have blazers of many sizes – some made to measure and a few 'off the peg'. My shoes are always handmade by Ferragamo.

In fact, I introduced Ferragamo to the Bond films. A neighbour of mine in Italy was married to Salvatore Ferragamo's eldest son, and I took her to a premiere of *Live And Let Die*, where she was horrified to see I was wearing Gucci shoes and belt. From then on Ferragamo supplied shoes, belts and luggage for the films.

BELOW: The Other Fellas and their tuxedos. Latterly, Tom Ford has designed Daniel Craig's. When asked recently whether he still enjoyed taking home some of the costumes, Daniel said, 'When I first did Bond, I was given all these amazing suits and suddenly I've got this huge wardrobe and I'm thinking, "Oh my God, what am I going to wear?" I've kind of flipped the other way now and if I could just wear jeans and T-shirts all the time I would.'

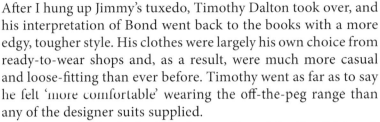

RIGHT: Here I am after my morning swim. Or is it Daniel Craig? We look so alike it's difficult to tell.

BELOW: I'm not sure if blue towelling is still all the rage ... Shirley Eaton and Sean looking 'cool' on set.

After I hung up Jimmy's tuxedo, Timothy Dalton took over, and his interpretation of Bond went back to the books with a more edgy, tougher style. His clothes were largely his own choice from ready-to-wear shops and, as a result, were much more casual and loose-fitting than ever before. Timothy went as far as to say he felt 'more comfortable' wearing the off-the-peg range than any of the designer suits supplied.

Some say he looked a little 'too ordinary' for Her Majesty's Secret Service, with not enough occasions for black tie and more formal outfits. But maybe they miss the point of being a spy in that he should blend into the background and the times.

'I cut the wardrobe down by three-quarters. Bond was never flash or ostentatious. In fact, he really wore a uniform, a dark suit, navy blue. He was very navy blue. He wasn't a wealthy man. He used his money to buy the best that he needed, but then he kept it,' said Timothy in a 1989 interview in *Rolling Stone* magazine.

For his second film, *Licence To Kill*, costume designer Jodie Tillen, who came fresh from the TV series *Miami Vice*, suggested a few ideas, much to the chagrin of her new 007. 'She wanted to put me in pastels,' said Dalton in an interview with Garth Pearce. 'Can you imagine? I thought, "No, we can't have that." The clothes say so much about Bond. He's got a naval background, so he needs a strong, simple colour like dark blue.'

After Timothy's departure, Brioni, an Italian fashion house founded in 1945, was invited to dress the next 007 – in the shape of Pierce Brosnan. With the ability to produce many copies of the same suit, and quickly, to ensure there are numerous intact ones available for action scenes, stunt doubles and so forth, Brioni offered to donate fifty suits for *GoldenEye*. Free of charge, I might add. You see, James Bond must look impeccable at all times. He isn't allowed to get dirty, to sweat or tear his clothes. I remember being on location in India for *Octopussy*. I must have changed my shirt a dozen times one morning as, despite the heat, Jimmy could not have patches of perspiration on his outfit.

The association with Brioni continued into Daniel Craig's first outing as 007, with them making his tuxedo (said to be worth £6,000 alone). However for *Quantum of Solace* designer Tom Ford took over tailoring duties. Daniel was reported to have ruined around forty bespoke suits during filming. 'It really is a crime. It makes me weep every time. They're great suits,' he told the British press.

I just hope he managed to save a few for himself.

BOND
ON
LOCATION

BOND ON LOCATION

PREVIOUS PAGES: At the Berlin Wall in 1983 at the height of the Cold War.

LEFT: Me being brave on the Eiffel Tower. It's a long walk up there, you know, with 347 steps to the first level alone.

BELOW: On location in Jamaica, Sean thought it was time for a beer and a nap. He obviously couldn't get to sleep, and sent for more beer.

It might actually be easier to say where Bond *hasn't* been in the world, though looking at the films, I have so far spotted him travelling to Jamaica, Croatia, Serbia, the UK, the USA, Turkey, Italy, Switzerland, France, Germany, Mexico, Japan, Portugal, Egypt, Lebanon, the Caribbean, Hong Kong, China, Austria, Brazil, Greece, Spain, Russia, Gibraltar, Morocco, Pakistan, Azerbaijan, Monaco, Cuba, South Korea, North Korea, Uganda, Montenegro, Haiti, Bolivia and Madagascar.

HOME OR AWAY?

Of course, the filmmakers didn't actually, or necessarily, visit every country – local locations were often dressed to look like somewhere else. For example, RAF Northolt, the Royal Air Force base near Pinewood Studios, doubled as a Cuban airbase in *Octopussy*, for Blue Grass Kentucky in *Goldfinger* and as an Azerbaijani airbase in *The World Is Not Enough*. The opening scenes of *Casino Royale* were filmed in the same place Sean Connery drove his Aston Martin DB5 in *Goldfinger* – Black Park, near Slough. Then there was Brent Cross shopping centre doubling for a Hamburg hotel car park in *Tomorrow Never Dies*; the Nene Valley Railway in Peterborough doubled for East Germany in *Octopussy* and again in *GoldenEye* for Russia. Amberley Working Museum in West Sussex doubled for Silicon Valley; and the IBM Building in

ABOVE: The height of Bondmania was marked with *Thunderball*. Here Sean arrives for filming in the Bahamas (where he now resides) with Cubby, Terence Young and Kevin McClory.

BELOW: The Peninsula Hotel, Hong Kong, with its trademark green Rolls-Royce cars. Surrounded by press when we filmed there, Britt Ekland smiled at me and said, 'Oh I do like being a film star.'

Staines doubled for the German HQ of Elliot Carver in *Tomorrow Never Dies*.

Typically, when planning 007's travels, a script outline comes together first, then the writer, director and producers explore potential locations in which to set the action, and from there thrash out the story some more. Many stops along the way turn out to be false trails, with nothing visually exciting to offer; others are too difficult to reach, or don't have any local infrastructure; and some are politically dodgy, so they're all ruled out. But once a likely location is confirmed, the whole team of production managers, location managers, production designer and director of photography ship out to lend their thoughts and ideas.

Then there is the important question, 'Where can we find a top class hotel for our beloved star, whom we want to treat royally?'

In the 1960s, there were no such things as economy airlines, cheap all-inclusive package holidays – or even colour television in many homes. The only way people were able to see exotic locations and fancy hotels was by buying a ticket to see a Bond film at the cinema. Nowadays it's harder to find somewhere with which viewers aren't familiar, which is why places like Azerbaijan and Bolivia pop up on the list.

Moving around between countries with a 200+ crew is like a military exercise. Typically, in my day, we started off on location, with the unit going ahead by charter and us swanky stars – who secured a first-class flight from the kindly producers – going in a day or two later. Then, with those location scenes in the can, it was back to the studio for a few weeks before jetting off to location number two, thereby allowing the studio stages to be re-dressed with new sets to await our second coming. One therefore had to be prepared to live out of a suitcase for four or five months. Thankfully, I have a big suitcase.

DOUBLING UP

I can't really go into any great detail on the locations used in the films outside of my seven, as I wasn't there. So let me tell you about me and mine ...

When Live And Let Die was in the planning stage, writer Tom Mankiewicz suggested to Guy Hamilton that they might go to New Orleans. Why? Well, because Guy liked jazz and old Jimbo hadn't been there before. It sounded like a good enough reason for a trip out there at least – not only was there jazz in New Orleans, there were bayous too.

'Wouldn't that give us a great opportunity for a boat chase?'

'Hey and there's this crocodile farm upriver ...'

'How about putting Bond in there on an island surrounded by crocs?'

'Look, there's this low bridge here. How about we put Bond in a vehicle, and have the villain *chase* him here?'

'Yes! How about a double-decker bus?'

... And that's how scripts and set pieces evolve on a Bond film, and in particular this one.

Locations featured include New Orleans, New York, Jamaica (which, of course, was also the setting for *Dr. No*) and Louisiana.

One hotel we used in Jamaica was the Couples Sans Souci,

ABOVE: The majority of *Goldfinger* was set in the USA, including this sequence featuring Honor Blackman and Sean Connery at the villain's Kentucky ranch – though it was all filmed at Pinewood. Sean did not once step foot in America!

in Ocho Rios. It doubled as Bond's San Monique base, and had, incidentally, been used as Miss Taro's home in *Dr. No* a decade earlier. Meanwhile, over at the Half Moon Bay Club in Montego Bay, bungalow 9 was used as Bond's own. The club also featured in *Casino Royale* with Daniel Craig, though it had been extensively remodelled by then – and hopefully without any unwelcome snakes slipping in.

The Man With The Golden Gun was originally planned to shoot in Iran, where part of Fleming's book was set, but the Yom Kippur War broke out. Scouts were sent to Beirut in the Lebanon instead, but declared it 'not particularly interesting' – in the filmic sense, of course. Focus quickly switched to Southeast Asia: Phang Gna Bay, Thailand; Bangkok; Macau; and Hong Kong, where the part-submerged wreck of the RMS

Queen Elizabeth was also used, and written in as a top-secret MI6 base grounded in Victoria Harbour.

From tracking down gunsmith Lazar in Macau, the former Portuguese enclave west of Hong Kong, we visited and filmed on the Floating Macau Palace – a converted vessel moored on the western shore – then took the ferry across the bay to Kowloon (the mainland suburb of Hong Kong), and the Peninsula Hotel, which famously (so Bond was told) runs a fleet of green Rolls-Royce limousines. I thought it seemed more famous for its array of shoes, until I learned Imelda Marcos was in residence.

BOTTOMS UP ...

The Bottoms Up Club, was also found in Kowloon amid the neon dazzle of the Tsim Sha Tsui shopping district. Villain Hai Fat's estate was located at the Dragon Garden on Castle Peak Road, Castle Peak. Once I'd seen him off it was on to Bangkok for a few weeks, and a boat chase through the filthy klongs that criss-cross the city.

'Under no circumstances should a drop of the water touch your lips,' we were all warned. The diseases contained therein were deemed enough to give any chemist nightmares.

Unfortunately, after taking a corner – near an undertaker's – a little too tightly in the boat (a long-tailed sampan) I was driving, I lost my balance and tipped over into the water. I stayed tight-lipped under the water to avoid the rotor blade that was whizzing about overhead, but made the mistake of opening my eyes; and saw what a 'no frills' burial meant in that particular establishment.

Other locations included the karate school in Muang Boran, about twenty miles east of town in Changwat Samut Prakan, which was actually an ancient city and the world's largest outdoor museum, with scaled-down versions of the famous buildings and temples of Bangkok. Most famously, we then moved on to Scaramanga's island hideout on Khow-Ping-Kan – one of a chain of tiny jungle-covered limestone pillars in Phang Nga Bay, Phuket.

It was a remote and undiscovered paradise at the time we filmed there, without even the most basic of facilities. The art department went ahead and built a small six-bedroomed prefabricated billet for myself, Christopher Lee, Guy Hamilton,

ABOVE: This rather odd-shaped mushroom rock is in Thailand, and housed Scaramanga's powerful solar device in *The Man With The Golden Gun.*

BELOW: It pays to advertise. The Bottoms Up Club as seen in my second Bond film. Wonder if I'd get a free drink there?

Maud Adams and Britt Ekland to lodge in. Each room contained a bed, a large circulating ceiling fan and a short step down into a toilet that was 2 foot 6 inches square, with a dripping tap and bucket to slosh out the hole between the footsteps. I worked out I could sit on the steps, do what came naturally, while washing and shaving at the same time. Cubby went one better and said if I could have given him a broom, he could 'shove it up [his] rear end and brush out the room at the same time'.

Today, it's overrun by tourists (and souvenir shops) who take the fifty-four-mile bus journey north from Phuket Town, and a short boat trip out to see 'James Bond Island', as it's now known.

ABOVE: Whilst doing a recce, the crew discovered this terrific crocodile farm entrance and wrote it into the script.

RIGHT: This innocent-looking cave doubled for Scaramanga's lair. I bravely entered with Christopher Lee only for a mass of bats to fly out (past us). I don't think they were vampire bats, though.

GOOD AND BAD

The Spy Who Loved Me started shooting in Sardinia, which became one of my favourite locations of all time, in no small way due to our being based at the Cala di Volpe. It was one of the most luxurious hotels ever, and featured in the film as Bond and Anya's hotel. I was also scheduled time to learn to ride the wet bike (or jet ski, as they are now called) in the beautiful blue sea just outside my room, which was no hardship whatsoever.

Then we set off for Cairo, arriving on my birthday, in fact. I walked onto the location set and couldn't quite understand why there were so many huge tents in the catering area. Catering manager George Crawford walked over, smiling widely, and said it was for my birthday lunch and, what's more, he'd managed to find lobsters for us all. I looked down at these green creatures he proffered – which were still moving despite having been dead for six weeks! The birthday boy did *not* have the lobster for lunch, and lived to see another year.

From Cairo it was on to Luxor, and quite probably the worst hotel in the world. The same menu was presented to us every single night of our two-week stay. It was the only large hotel in Luxor at the time, and guests seemingly only ever stayed for one night when they came to visit the temple of Karnak. My nightly meal consisted of what looked and tasted like a camel's testicle on a bun – it was difficult to figure out which was which.

ABOVE: One of the many, rather polluted, waterways we filmed on in *The Man With The Golden Gun*. We were warned to keep our lips tightly closed if we fell in. I wish I'd kept my eyes closed too, particularly near the undertaker's.

ABOVE: Despite what you may think, the pyramids were not one of Ken Adam's designs! Though they did make a wonderful backdrop for my first encounter with Jaws in *The Spy Who Loved Me*.

BELOW: Rio really is a breathtaking panorama.

I was so pleased when director Lewis Gilbert suggested we take an early plane out on our day of departure, meaning we could have a four-hour stopover in Cairo, before flying back to London. Cubby liked the sound of that. 'We can go to Shepheard's Hotel for a slap-up lunch,' he beamed.

At Cairo airport the customs officials – not realizing how undernourished we were – said we had to remain airside, as we were 'in transit' and could not therefore go into the city. But they told us not to worry, they'd prepared a couple of rooms for us to rest in. I said I'd share with Cubby while Lewis had his own room next door. No sooner had we walked in than Cubby proceeded to take his trousers off.

'I've got the part, Lewis!' I shouted through the wall.

GIDDY HEIGHTS ...

Moonraker decamped from our usual Pinewood base to Paris. Filming with the wonderfully civilized French working hours – long lunches and beautiful architecture – was only slightly frustrated by being split across three separate studios in the city.

It was then on to Venice and the delightful Hotel Danieli (although I prefer the Gritti Palace, personally) for the action sequences, spread between the city's 118 islands. The Venetian glass museum, in which Jimmy and Chang fought it out, was actually shot at Boulogne Studios – in a building that had once been a World War II Luftwaffe factory during the occupation. The sequence still holds the record for the largest amount of breakaway sugar glass used in a single scene.

After spending a family Christmas in Paris, the cast and crew travelled to Rio de Janeiro on Concorde. Unfortunately, I suffered an attack of kidney stones and had to spend a few days in a Parisian hospital before flying down to Rio, where I was immediately whisked off the plane to hair and make-up, before re-boarding to film the sequence of 007 arriving.

It was there one of the most challenging stunts ever took place, atop two cable cars on Table Mountain, two-thousand feet

ABOVE: The famous St Mark's Square in Venice with some old English actor looking lost.

BELOW: And I recommend viewing it by cable car, if there are no steel-toothed hoodlums around.

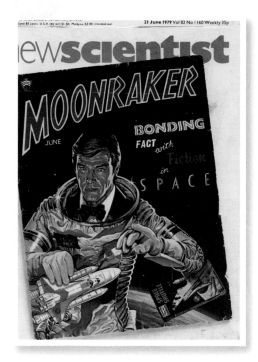

up in the air, with Dickie Graydon and Paul Weston doubling for Jaws and Jim Bond.

No visit to Rio would be complete without seeing the carnival. Scenes were recreated with some 700 extras to cut into footage previously shot by the second unit in the previous summer.

We then travelled inland to film at Iguassu Falls, the second largest waterfalls in the world – and perhaps the toughest of any location I've been on. There was no way of transporting equipment there, apart from carrying it on our backs from the bottom of the valley. The top of the falls was often cloaked by clouds, and Lewis suggested I should follow one of the bevy of Drax's girls across the top of the falls and inside to the hidden HQ. When I looked at the said girl I was rather taken aback – she was totally cross-eyed, and looked to my left as she spoke to me, with her eyes drifting ever further sideward. I had to follow this girl across the top of a sheer drop! I raised my concerns with Lewis that she couldn't even see straight. 'That's OK, dear,' he said. 'We'll tie a rope to your feet.'

The scene culminated in a speedboat plummeting over the top of the falls, but, due to the weather and spray, several attempts failed, so the scene was eventually shot with miniatures at the studio.

Of course it was one film where Jim also left terra firma and headed into space. The hotels there were awful. If I were you I wouldn't bother.

ABOVE: The first and only time I made the cover of *New Scientist*, here flagging up the fact that our next Bond location was going to be in space. I enjoyed the place, but it did lack atmosphere.

TOP RIGHT: When the monks discovered it was a James Bond film they'd given permission to film at their monastery, at Aghia Triatha, Meteora in Greece, they were rather upset and hung out their dirty habits ... along with tarpaulins and anything else they could find to spoil our shots. Thankfully, Cubby managed to smooth things over with a large donation to their charitable fund.

BOTTOM RIGHT: I told our caring director I hated heights. He suggested I take tranquilliser and just get on with climbing the mountain in Meteora to reach the monastery. So I did.

AND *NOT* SO GIDDY ...

From the wondrous scenes of Rio and Venice, the opening sequences of *For Your Eyes Only* took us to Stoke Poges cemetery near Slough and Becton gas works. Very glamorous! The Becton site had previously doubled for Vietnam in Stanley Kubrick's *Full Metal Jacket*, but now my brave stunt double Martin Grace held onto the outside of a helicopter, not trying to evade any military action, but rather that of a crazed bald man with a penchant for white cats.

Fortunately, we then moved on to Corfu, Cortina d'Ampezzo – the latter to film snow scenes, but ended up having to truck the white stuff in after it failed to materialize naturally – and Greece,

which was slightly more exotic than Becton, though none the less problematic.

The mountaintop monastery at Meteora, two kilometres north of Kalambaka in central Greece, was to be the scene of the film's finalé. Like twenty-three other monastries in the area, Aghia Triatha was built in a pretty inaccessible location during the Serbian–Byzantine wars of the fourteenth century, where the only access was by removable wooden ladder.

A deal was done in advance with the monks to allow us to film, though I'm not quite sure our man told them it was going to be a Bond film, as once they realized such a womanizing, gambling and ruthless character was due they protested by hanging out their washing and huge tarpaulin sheets all over the roofs. It was not the panoramic scene our cameraman had envisaged.

I tried to reason with them, saying I'd once been a saint, but that didn't go down too well. Cubby intervened and made a charitable donation, which seemed to placate their worries more readily.

The monastery can be visited today by tourists with a good head for heights, and suitably restrained clothing – but don't worry, it can be hired when you get there. Those enterprising monks think of everything.

ABOVE: The Monsoon Palace, HQ of the evil Kamal Khan. There seem to be more aerials on the roof than anything else these days, maybe all tuned into one of my old TV series?

Cortina was another interesting location we moved on to, chosen primarily for the abundance of snow. The only thing was, there wasn't any when we turned up! However, we had a wonderful stay, and filmed at the Miramonti Majestic Hotel. I remember Jim's room was number 300. It doesn't actually exist, though the balcony he is seen on does and belongs to room 108.

RIGHT: Octopussy made her lair at the Lake Palace Hotel. The crew were warned not to let a drop of river water touch their lips. Many fell in, all survived.

IF YOU KNEW CUBA ...

Octopussy was a lovely shoot. We started on 10 August 1982 at Checkpoint Charlie in West Berlin. The Berlin Wall was still in place and the Cold War had yet to defrost. In the scene, Bond and M are in a car heading to the border, and while M gets out Bond continues across to East Berlin. Of course, we couldn't do it for real and so the car drove a few yards into no man's land before John Glen called, 'Cut!' Happily, the curious East German guards didn't have time to react, as we turned around and drove back quickly.

After six days in Berlin, it was back to Pinewood Studios and UK locations, including Wansford in Cambridgeshire, for the Nene Valley Railway and the majority of the train sequences where Bond infiltrates and faces off against Orlov. The same location doubled for Russia twelve years later, when director Martin Campbell filmed the train-vs-tank sequence in *GoldenEye* along stretches of the six-mile private track.

RAF Upper Heyford, Oxfordshire, doubled for a West German Air Base where a huge circus was staged and, as mentioned earlier, RAF Northolt then doubled for Cuba, with the addition of a few carefully placed palm trees.

We then moved to India, and in particular Udaipur, the city of sunsets. There, the Lake Palace Hotel, which is spread across a four-acre island and constructed from marble on Lake Pichola, became Octopussy's floating palace. The interiors and courtyards of the palace were shot back at Pinewood, much to the relief of cast and crew, who were struggling in the high temperatures; in fact I needed a new shirt and suit jacket almost every take. As you know, of course, James Bond does not sweat, and the wardrobe and make-up department constantly touched me up in order to keep Jim looking cool and collected – no mean feat when temperatures ranged from 48 to 65 degrees Celsius.

At the nearby Shiv Niwas Palace, a team of models were flown from England to partake in the obligatory poolside shoot and when the call went out to recruit some locals for extra work, we were inundated with thousands

ABOVE: I posed outside the Brandenburg Gate with a Walther PPK in *Octopussy*. An understated presence, as always.

BELOW: Not quite California – Amberley Working Museum in West Sussex doubled for the mine where Zorin was going to trigger his dastardly plan of dominating Silicon Valley.

of people. Many had to be paid off just to leave, as we couldn't have shot; in fact it became a daily occurrence for hundreds of onlookers to appear on set. The logistics of organizing crowd control during the stunt and chase sequences proved a bit of a challenge, and not always a successful one: the bicycle rider who broke up the tuk-tuk fight was not intended to be in shot at all, he was merely passing through.

The final Indian location was the Monsoon Palace, a striking building on the hillside of Udaipur, which became the lair of evil Kamal Khan.

Oh! And while we were on location, the first English-language film ever to screen at Udaipur's largest cinema was *Moonraker*. They had good taste, I thought.

RIGHT AND BELOW: Checking the handbrake is on. The Nene Valley Railway stood in for East Germany in an exciting train sequence in *Octopussy*. It also doubled for Russia in *GoldenEye*!

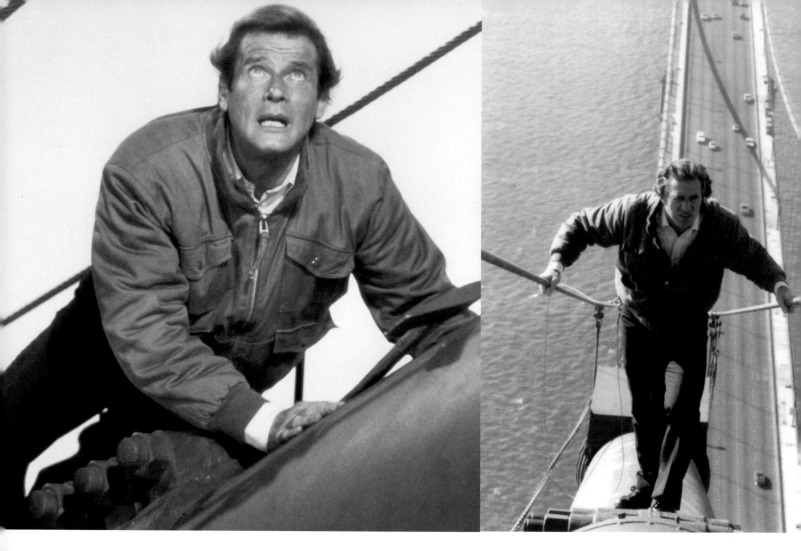

A MAYORAL FAVOURITE

A View To A Kill thankfully avoided the heat of India and Thailand and instead took us to Paris, Chantilly and, of course, San Francisco. At the end of the working day, we had somewhere to go and eat in comfortable surroundings and didn't have to worry about what we were eating!

The snowy opening in Iceland was filmed by the second unit, and I was cut in with pick-up shots at Pinewood before we all headed to Royal Ascot, and then on to Staines for the scene in which Bond and Stacey enter the Zorin mineshaft, along with the Amberley Chalk Pits Museum in West Sussex, which both doubled for California.

When San Francisco was touted as a filming location, Cubby sought the necessary permissions from the Mayor's office – the Mayor at that time being Diane Feinstein – explaining they'd like to set City Hall on fire, stage a chase with a fire engine through the streets, and film the climax on top of the Golden

ABOVE RIGHT: We filmed the climax to *A View To A Kill* on the Golden Gate Bridge. Here my brave stunt double Martin Grace climbs up to the top, some 227 metres above the water.

ABOVE LEFT: Whereas I filmed my close-ups on a Pinewood set out on the backlot, just a few metres above the ground.

ABOVE: City Hall, San Francisco. Our special-effects team carefully laid smoke pots and started controlled fires on parts of the exterior. I believe we were one of the few film crews, if not the only one, ever allowed to wreak such havoc with the full blessing of the Mayor.

Gate Bridge. The response was not particularly positive.

'Who is playing Bond?' Mayor Feinstein asked.

'Roger Moore.'

'Roger Moore? Ah! I like him,' she replied. 'What can I do to help, Mr Broccoli?'

The only caveat to our filming atop the bridge was that there couldn't be any fighting – there could be a bit of a struggle, but no out-and-out fight. My brave stunt double Martin Grace climbed to the top of the bridge – after earlier holding onto the guy rope of the airship as it crossed the harbour – to perform the final tussle, while part of the bridge was then reconstructed on the Pinewood backlot for me to film my close-ups, looking very brave.

There were even mightier heights to climb, as in Paris it was planned that B.J. Worth would film a parachute jump off the Eiffel Tower, after I had chased Grace Jones up most of it. Curiously, while permission had been granted for the jump, as the landing was going to be on a boat cruising down the Seine, that came under a different authority, and at first they refused permission: we could jump, but couldn't land. However, eventually all was smoothed over ...

PINEWOOD BOUND

Of course, I must also pay homage to the home of 007 and indeed my second home, Pinewood Studios. I shot all of my films – except *Moonraker* – out of Pinewood, and have a huge affection and appreciation for the studio. For many years my office was right next door to Cubby's, and I'd like to think we were good neighbours. Now Barbara and Michael occupy Cubby's office and the tradition continues. The studio has featured extensively in the films – Goldfinger's factory was the studio 'covered way' on the lot; the opening shots in *From Russia With Love* were filmed in the gardens; in *The World Is Not Enough* villainous Reynard hid away in the Pinewood pond grotto; the Ice Palace exterior in *Die Another Day* was all built on the backlot; and, of course, the huge volcano set in *You Only Live Twice* stood next to the present site of the 007 stage and could be seen from miles away. Pinewood and Bond are linked very closely, and hopefully will be for many years to come.

Of course, since my time Jimmy has ventured to all manner of new interesting places outside the studio walls; in particular, behind the Iron Curtain and Eastern Blocks. Where will he go next we ask? Well, *Skyfall* was rumoured to be returning to India, but then switched to Turkey instead, where the action sequences could be better accommodated. There were also rumours abound about South Africa and China.

One thing is for sure: when the phone rings next and a voice says, 'I'm working for Eon Productions and would like to talk about shooting the next Bond film in your country ...' they'll be greeted with open arms.

BELOW: On location in Chantilly – it may just be two of us in shot, but a lot goes on behind the camera!

BOND
ON
BONDS

BOND ON BONDS

PREVIOUS PAGE: George Lazenby, Timothy Dalton and me at the BAFTA fortieth anniversary tribute. I guess that makes us 00-21.

BELOW: Harry, Sean, Diane Cilento and Cubby photographed just after Sean signed his multi-picture Bond contract in London.

OPPOSITE TOP: A very youthful looking Sean in one of his first publicity shots for *Dr. No*.

OPPOSITE BOTTOM: Twenty-one years after *Dr. No*, Sean returned in *Never Say Never Again*; a title coined by his wife Micheline after he famously quit the role in 1971, vowing never again.

'm often asked, 'Who is the best Bond?'
'Apart from myself?' I modestly enquire. 'It has to be Sean.'
Sean *was* Bond. He created Bond. He embodied Bond and because of Sean, Bond became an instantly recognizable character the world over – he was rough, tough, mean and witty. Of course, it was an alter ego he didn't always appreciate, but it was one I'd like to think he is ultimately proud of – as he was a bloody good 007.

I first met Sean in the early 1960s at Arlington House in London, at a reception hosted by actress Binnie Barnes and her husband, film producer Mike Frankovich. Sean was there with his then wife Diane Cilento. Apart from his imposing size, the things I remember most from that first meeting were his amazing eyes. I'm happy to say that our meeting at that party

marked the start of a friendship that goes on to this day.

It's no secret that, after *Thunderball*, Sean was becoming disenchanted with the films. He'd helped establish the character internationally and everywhere he went there was merchandise with his image on it. However, he wasn't receiving any extra remuneration and what with that, the constant media attention and the pressure of being Bond causing a rift in his marriage, he obviously felt that no one part was worth all this.

Terence Young told the producers, 'Take Sean as a partner, make it Cubby, Harry and Sean. Sean will stay with you because he's a Scotsman. He likes the sound of gold coins clinking together. He likes the lovely soft rustle of paper. He'll stay with you if he's a partner, but not if you use him as a hired employee.'

Cubby and Harry didn't want another partner at Eon, and so Sean announced *You Only Live Twice* would be his last appearance as 007. At the Royal Charity premiere, even Her Majesty the Queen asked him, 'Is this really your last James Bond film?'

'I'm afraid so, Ma'am,' he told her.

Though Harry and Cubby reportedly offered Sean just under a million dollars to appear in *On Her Majesty's Secret Service*, he turned it down.

Thinking he might take advantage of Sean's disenchantment after *Thunderball* premiered, Charles Feldman, who had acquired the film rights to *Casino Royale*, tried to interest Sean in starring in his movie. Feldman had intended it as a thriller but when Sean declined Feldman abandoned the idea and turned it into a comedy instead. With seven directors and numerous writers, it ended up a confusing mess and a box office disaster, despite featuring David Niven as Sir James Bond and an incredible cast including Ursula Andress, Peter Sellers, Woody Allen, Orson Welles, Deborah Kerr, William Holden and John Huston.

On Her Majesty's Secret Service did respectable business at the box office without Sean, but George Lazenby made it clear that it was his one and only appearance as 007. United Artists were desperate to keep their cash cow on track, and David Picker – president of United Artists – met with Sean to agree a return for *Diamonds Are Forever*. American actor John Gavin had been in the frame and was offered a multi-picture contract, but a week before filming started Sean agreed to take on the role once more and Gavin was paid off.

Sean had been made an offer he simply couldn't refuse: David Picker had guaranteed him $1¾ million, plus a percentage of the profits, and agreed to provide financial backing for two films of Sean's choice.

Sean was then reputedly offered $5 million to return to Bond in *Live And Let Die*, but refused saying, 'Never again'. I'm very grateful to him – and, of course, work cheaper too.

SEAN CONNERY IS JAMES BOND IN NEVER SAY NEVER AGAIN

PG

JACK SCHWARTZMAN & KEVIN McCLORY PRESENT A TALIAFILM HAIR BY CROWN TOPPER. FACIAL WORK BY CEMENTATION. CORSETS BY JANET REGER.

JAK

"They say the wheelchair chase is fantastic."

R THE FIRST TIME ... A HEAD-ON FILM CLASH BE

BATTLE OF THE B

ABOVE: The press like to stir things up, and the 'Battle of the Bonds' was good headline material; that and poking fun at our advancing ages.

NEVER SAY WHAT?

But another story was forming in the wings. With his ten-year restriction over, Kevin McClory began to make plans to rework the *Thunderball* plot for the screen again.

He engaged Len Deighton as his co-writer on the project, *James Bond Of The Secret Service*, and secured backing from Paramount Pictures. Then, in what was to prove a masterstroke, he approached Sean to become involved in the screenplay. Who knew the character better than Sean?

Sean agreed and relished his new creative role.

'The three of us did a screenplay and put all sorts of exotic events in it,' he said. 'You remember the aircraft that were disappearing over the Bermuda Triangle? We had SPECTRE doing that. There was also this fantastic fleet of planes under the sea – and they were going to be used to attack the financial centre of New York by going through the city's sewers – which you can do – right into Wall Street.

'There were going to be mechanical sharks in the bay, a take-over of the Statue of Liberty and the main line of troops on Ellis Island. All that sort of thing.'

The title changed to *Warhead*.

There was a rumour Sean would play Bond, with Orson Welles

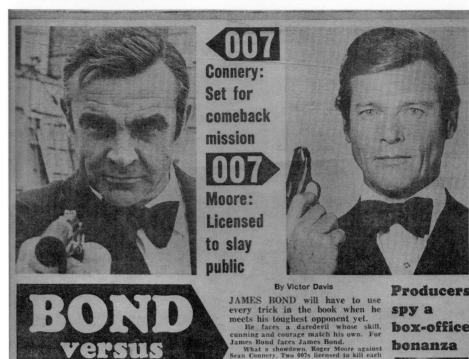

007
Connery: Set for comeback mission

007
Moore: Licensed to slay public

BOND versus BOND

By Victor Davis

JAMES BOND will have to use every trick in the book when he meets his toughest opponent yet.

He faces a daredevil whose skill, cunning and courage match his own. For James Bond faces James Bond.

What a showdown. Roger Moore against Sean Connery. Two 007s licensed to kill each other—at the cinema box office.

Their mission : To pull out all the stops and trap the public.

Moore is making his fourth Bond movie. Connery, the original 007, is almost certain to make a comeback in the role.

The head-on collision is because veteran Bond producer Cubby Broccoli and Irish filmmaker Kevin McClory, now both possess film rights to the late Ian Fleming's stories.

Paramount Pictures announced last night that they are backing McClory to make "James Bond of the Secret Service," next spring.

Rich

The screenplay is the joint work of McClory, Connery and best-selling novelist L e n Deighton. Connery looks set for the part.

Broccoli's next Bond movie is "Moonraker," starring Roger Moore. It

Producers spy a box-office bonanza

Producer Broccoli

goes into production in Paris next month.

The Bond pickings are rich. The Broccoli series—10 so far—are backed by United Artists and have earned more than £200 million at the box office.

McClory was involved in the 1965 production of "Thunderball," starring Connery.

But he then agreed to a 10-year legal freeze on making any more 007 movies.

---

as a villain and Trevor Howard as M, but the Fleming Estate sued and Paramount pulled out of the venture.

The flurry of news as reported in the trade journals brought the fact that Sean was now involved to the attention of Jack Schwartzman, executive vice president of Lorimer and husband of Talia Shire – with whom I made a film called *Bed And Breakfast*.

He raised the money required from twenty-five independent backers and restricted the plot back to that of *Thunderball*, thus avoiding any further legal complications.

Once Sean had written the script, he started to care about the character he'd previously tired of. By this time, Sean had divorced Diane and married his second wife Micheline, who, having heard the rumours of his return as Bond, asked that if he was enjoying it so much, why not play the part again? Adding he should never say never again … which, of course, became the title.

There were various legal issues still to be resolved, not least Cubby Broccoli's lawsuit over the filmic ownership of 007, which was eventually agreed out of court and which gave Cubby a percentage of the *Never Say Never Again* box office.

Sean's film swung into production at Elstree Studios around about the same time as I started shooting *Octopussy* at Pinewood. The press made a splash about our going head to head, with both aiming for a summer 1983 release. *Never Say Never Again* in fact opted for a Christmas release so as not to split the summer audience.

ABOVE: At the Colombe d'Or in St Paul de Vence. Sean and Donald Sutherland stopped by for lunch with me. I'd directed Donald in a *Saint* episode a couple of decades earlier.

I met Sean occasionally for dinner in London during shooting, and still do to this day. He's a very talented actor, and outside of Bond has turned in some fun, impressive and lucrative performances. It's a shame we never got to do one together.

THE OTHER FELLA

When Cubby and Harry told me they'd signed an unknown model and former car salesman to play Bond, I was intrigued.

George Lazenby was incredibly laid back, and the first time I met him – at a cocktail party hosted by Cubby – he greeted me with, 'You all right, mate?'

I've met him several times over the years since, and he's always been equally pleasant and chatty. Though the last time we met in New York a few years ago he was somewhat more subdued, coming to terms with impending divorce and the effect that might have on his relationship with his young children.

I thought his was a great film, with style, energy and a terrific story, though I also felt it was helped along greatly by George Baker's dubbing of the character in a third of the film; something Lazenby wasn't aware of until he went to the premiere.

Of course, Lazenby had announced he was only going to make one movie, on the advice of his friend Ronan O'Rahilly, a music promoter who owned Radio Caroline, the famous pirate radio ship.

'He was introducing me to the Beatles and people like that, y'know …' George said. 'He took me to see them and said, "You know, Bond is over, it's finished." The movie that was out at the time was *Easy Rider*. And, you know, you had to look like one of those guys, a hippie. And so I believed him and he said, "You know, Clint Eastwood's over there doing spaghetti westerns, getting a million bucks a go. You can do those things and make a couple of them in a couple of months and you got the million dollars. Don't worry about the money." I listened to that.'

On Her Majesty's Secret Service director Peter Hunt made a conscious decision not to explain the change from Sean to George in the role of Jimmy Bond; it was just something audiences would (hopefully) accept. And in Maurice Binder's opening credits, scenes from earlier Bond films were incorporated to underline the fact it was the same series. The one nod George gave to Sean was when he delivered the line, 'This never happened to the other fella'.

It actually came about because George, doing his own stunts, said jokingly to the crew, 'The other fella never had to do this!'

Peter Hunt overheard the remark and said, 'Say that line after the opening scene.' So he did.

Fatally, for United Artists, Lazenby never signed a contract. His adviser, O'Rahilly, sent the contract to his lawyer, 'who was a real-estate lawyer', and he kept sending it back. This went on throughout the filming of *On her Majesty's Secret Service*. United Artists, meanwhile, thought he'd signed for seven movies.

George told me he was paid a $50,000 flat fee for the movie. They offered him $1 million to come back for a second, but he refused.

I know after Timothy Dalton had bowed out, George made a call to Cubby saying he was available. It was said half-jokingly, but given the chance I'm sure George would have turned in a good performance. The role went to Pierce, of course, and when we were leaving the *Die Another Day* premiere, I heard someone ask George what he thought of it and Pierce. 'It's made for young folk. It's loud, full of action and doesn't give you a rest. It's one bang after another!'

BELOW: George Lazenby at the Dorchester Hotel in London, having been unveiled as the new 007.

ROUGHER, TOUGHER

Cubby had thought of Timothy as a potential 007 a couple of decades earlier but Timothy, probably very wisely, felt he was too young to play the character: 'There was a time when Sean Connery gave up the role. I guess I, alongside quite a few other actors, was approached about the possibility of playing the part,' he said. 'That was for *On Her Majesty's Secret Service*. I was very flattered, but I think ⹁ ⹁ody would have been off their head to have taken over from Connery. I was also too young, Bond should be a man in his mid-thirties, at least – a mature adult who has been around.'

When I retired from the role in late 1985, Timothy was approached but was then committed to a London theatre production and a film, *Brenda Starr*, with Brooke Shields.

And so Cubby settled on the thirty-three-year-old Pierce Brosnan. As luck had it, with audience figures in decline, NBC had

"THANKS, SIMON, NOW WOULD YOUR GRANDAD SIGN, PLEASE?"

just cancelled Pierce's TV show *Remington Steele*, but as word broke of Eon's interest, NBC suddenly decided to renew the show and exercise their option on Brosnan's contract.

Pierce had no choice but to press on with what was to be the final series of the show. Cubby tried to strike a deal whereby Brosnan could have made a couple of feature-length episodes either side of a Bond film, but NBC and production outfit MTM declined and offered up their own alternative terms – from which Cubby walked away.

Pierce was devastated and Cubby had a production looming without a star attached.

Sam Neill was briefly considered, as was an unknown Australian actor, Finlay Light, but Cubby went back to his first choice, Timothy Dalton, again and told him he was prepared to wait the six weeks until Timothy became available.

On 6 August 1986, Eon Productions announced they had signed their new Bond – Welshman Timothy Dalton. He won both

OPPOSITE TOP: Timothy Dalton was a tougher and younger Bond.

OPPOSITE BOTTOM AND BELOW: Lucky I have a sense of humour! As though I needed reminding I was in my mid-fifties, the British press kindly did so with a couple of newspaper cartoons. Ah to be fifty-six again!

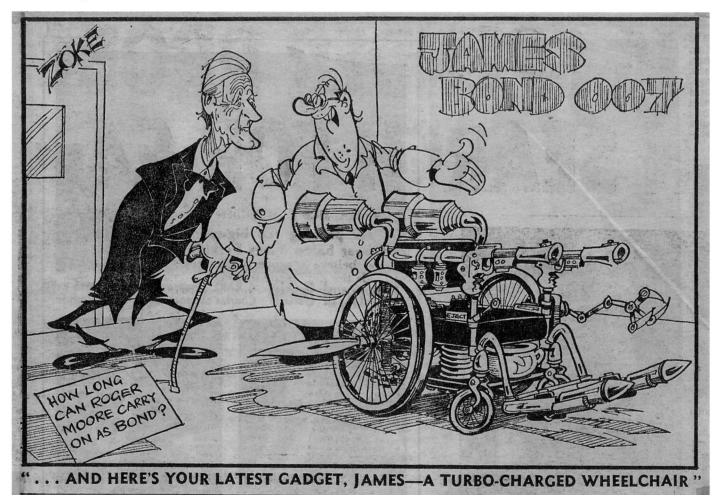

ABOVE: On location with *The Living Daylights*. Michael Wilson, Cubby, Timothy and (far right) director John Glen. Whoever said there was a lot of standing around on film sets?

my and Sean Connery's approval; we both wished Timothy well in the role.

I read there was going to be a change in style with the new Bond: he was going to be less of a womaniser, tougher and closer to the darker character Ian Fleming wrote about. They wanted to get back to 'Fleming's Bond'.

With *The Living Daylights* on release, Eon started planning the next adventure, *Licence Revoked* (the title was later changed to *Licence To Kill* after research suggested a vast number of people didn't know what 'Licence Revoked' meant). As per Timothy's desire to see a darker Bond, the mission centred on a personal vendetta: avenging the brutal attack on Bond's long-time CIA friend, Felix Leiter.

It became the first Bond film to receive a 15 rating in the UK because of 'the level of on-screen violence and realism'.

The film opened in the summer of 1989 and found itself going head to head with other blockbuster action movies, including *Lethal Weapon 2*, *Indiana Jones And The Last Crusade* and *Batman*.

Its lower-than-anticipated worldwide gross caused MGM/ United Artists to get nervous. Cubby began to wonder if the twenty-seven-year-old franchise needed a new captain, and put Eon's parent company, Danjaq, up for sale with an asking price of £200 million.

Timothy was quoted as saying, 'My feeling is this will be the last one. I don't mean my last one. I mean the end of the whole lot. I don't speak with any real authority, but it's sort of a feeling I have. Sorry!'

However, a major spanner was thrown in the works when MGM/United Artists was sold to the Australian-based broadcasting group Qintex, which in turn wanted to merge the company with Pathé. In doing so, the Bond back catalogue was licensed to Pathé for broadcast at sums below what was considered the commercial rate. Danjaq sued.

Eon commenced pre-production of another film in May 1990, and some details were unveiled at the Cannes Film Festival around the same time, mentioning that a detailed story draft had been written by Alfonso Ruggiero Jr and Michael G. Wilson.

However, owing to the ongoing legal disputes, the production of Timothy Dalton's third film was postponed several times. In an interview in 1993, Timothy said Michael France was writing the story for the film, which was 'due to begin production in January or February 1994'.

With continuing delays and uncertainty, Timothy's six-year contract expired in 1993 (which was originally scheduled to be the year of his fourth film), and after he read Michael France's screenplay for Bond 17 he made, and subsequently announced, on

ABOVE: My dear friend David Hedison has the distinction of being the first actor to play Felix Leiter twice, first in *Live And Let Die* and, here, in *Licence To Kill* with the other fella.

BELOW: Press frenzy! Pierce Brosnan was 007 number 005 when he was introduced to the world's press in 1994.

OPPOSITE: A quick brush-up and a shave later, and here he is at the Monte Carlo Casino tables in *GoldenEye*.

12 April 1994, his decision to leave the series. It was now five years since his last outing and he felt the time had come to move on.

It had been reported in the press that the Broccolis were supposedly under pressure from MGM to replace Timothy. Whether that was true or not I don't know, but Eon respected his decision and did not to stand in his way. The search was on for his replacement.

Timothy said at the time of his resignation, 'Even though the [producers] have always made it clear to me that they want me to resume my role in their next James Bond feature, I have now made this difficult decision. As an actor, I believe it is now time to leave that wonderful image behind and accept the challenge of new ones.'

By this time, Cubby's health was suffering and my dear friend could no longer be as active in the new production as he would have liked. When I saw him for one of the last times at his home in California, he told me of his excitement at casting Pierce Brosnan, and that Michael and Barbara would be taking the helm.

Pierce was unveiled as the new 007 on 7 June 1994 in London, while sporting a full beard for an upcoming TV movie of *Robinson*

Crusoe. His first outing was to be called *GoldenEye*, after Ian Fleming's home in Jamaica, and was to be one of a three-film contract (with an option for a fourth). Pierce also separately negotiated a production deal with MGM for his own films, the most successful of which was *The Thomas Crown Affair*.

When that fourth film option was picked up, and a press launch arranged at Pinewood for *Die Another Day* in 2002, Pierce was, of course, asked if he'd be doing any more. He replied that he'd like to do one more, a fifth. Plans swung into action for a fifth film in 2004, and some suggested it might be an adaptation of Ian Fleming's *Casino Royale*. Negotiations stalled, and in July 2004 Pierce announced he was leaving Bond behind him, albeit – from what I saw of him – somewhat reluctantly.

OPPOSITE: They sent for me! It was also my turn to wear the beard we shared.

BELOW: Cool, calculated and too damn handsome!

OPPOSITE: I seemed to be in the minority when I championed Daniel Craig as Bond. Nice to think we proved the doubters wrong!

BELOW: Timothy Dalton with Barbara Broccoli at the tribute to Cubby Broccoli at the Odeon Leicester Square.

The rumour mills swung into overtime on the subject of who would be the next James Bond. Names were bandied around, including Clive Owen, Hugh Jackman, Liam Neeson and Daniel Craig. I personally liked the idea of Daniel Craig, having seen him in *The Mother*, *Munich* and *Layer Cake*. He's a bloody good actor.

The day before Daniel was confirmed as 007, Barbara Broccoli emailed me to tell me of their choice. I was delighted – and it was my birthday too. However, it seemed, at first, that I was in a minority. The British press all but vilified him: too short, too blond, not good-looking enough, and they took great joy in mocking Daniel for wearing a life jacket on board the military launch that brought him speeding up the Thames to a press conference with waiting journalists.

I had never experienced such a massive hate campaign. Websites were set up demanding Pierce Brosnan be reinstated and peddling very negative comments and opinions about Daniel. I felt hugely sorry for Daniel, as, although he would have turned a blind eye to them, he would have been very aware of what was being said. Concentrating on the positive, he confirmed, 'We have got an incredible script, and that is my first line of attack. Once I read it, I knew I did not have any choice, I had to go for it. It is a huge challenge, and I think life is about challenges ... Together with Martin [Campbell, director], I want to make the best film we can, the most entertaining film we can.'

The doubters were soon silenced – and many were converted.

I didn't get to meet Daniel until 5 October 2008. We were both at the London Palladium attending the centenary celebration for Ian Fleming; in fact, we shared a dressing room. I arrived early to ensure I got the best mirror, and when Daniel arrived he grabbed me, hugged me tightly and greeted me like a long-lost friend.

His Bond is terrific, and I hope he'll reign for many years to come.

The only piece of advice I'd offer anyone regarding playing Jimbo is you use what you have in your own personality and be true to yourself, while stealing a bit here and there for added effect.

Nostalgia is quite handy too, as you'll find people who are rather unforgiving at the time often rediscover you in later life. Many is the time I have been stopped by someone who has thanked me for my Bond films, saying they enjoy them for their entertainment value and how well they still stand up.

In closing, my admiration goes to Barbara and Michael above anyone else, for holding this extraordinary franchise – established by Cubby and Harry – together for so many years. I can see it lasting another fifty.

Felix Leiter

Felix Leiter, Bond's brother from Langley, first appeared in Ian Fleming's novel *Casino Royale*. His name originates with two of Fleming's friends: 'Felix' being the middle name of Ivor Bryce, while 'Leiter' was the surname of Marion Oates Leiter Charles, then wife of Thomas Leiter.

On film, the CIA operative was initially portrayed by Jack Lord (left), of *Hawaii Five-O* fame. When the character returned in *Goldfinger*, Lord apparently demanded star billing and a much larger fee, leading to him being re-cast by Cec Linder. Two other actors took the part, Rick Van Nutter in *Thunderball* and Norman Burton in *Diamonds Are Forever* before my great friend David Hedison (right) took the part in *Live And Let Die*. We'd worked together on *The Saint*, and I found David's easy charm, great sense of humour and professionalism to be infectious. He is such a lovely, lovely man. When ideas were passed around about casting Leiter, I suggested David. He went in to see the casting director and the rest is history. We have since worked on two more movies together, so far.

David returned in 1989 for Timothy Dalton's *Licence To Kill* as the story about Bond seeking revenge for his friend's misfortune was felt to work better if the audiences recognized Felix from an earlier adventure. He became the only actor to play the part twice; that is until Daniel Craig's films when Jeffrey Wright (bottom right) appeared in both *Casino Royale* and *Quantum of Solace* as Felix, the second African-American to be cast in the role after Bernie Casey (below) in *Never Say Never Again*. John Terry also played the part in *The Living Daylights*.

BOND
BEHIND
THE
SCENES

PREVIOUS PAGES: Someone
has to make sure the star looks
good and is in focus!

BELOW: Ian Fleming visits the
set of *Dr. No* near his Jamaican
home.

BOND BEHIND THE SCENES

There are a huge number of people involved in each Bond
film, hundreds in fact. From the producers (who raise the
money), directors (who spend it) and writers (who imagine
more elaborate ways to spend it than the director could think of
last time) to the assistant directors, cameramen, sound recordists,
props, continuity, editors, stunt team, production managers, oh
and yes, the actors. We all come together and form one big happy
family for six or seven months, before going our separate ways to
do other things, and await the next Bond a year or so later to bring
us back together.

A FAMILY AFFAIR

With Cubby Broccoli at the helm it became very much a family atmosphere on the movies with a family team – and I think I'm correct in saying that some crew members today are from the second or even third generation to work on a 007 film. Even my sons and daughter have been involved – Geoffrey as a third assistant director on my final Bond; Christian in the location department on *GoldenEye*; and on screen, in Deborah's case, as a 'Bond girl' in *Die Another Day*. She often says to me her small role as an air stewardess still prompts more mail than anything else that hits her doormat, including bills – and you know how thick and fast they arrive.

The established production pattern during my tenure was one film pretty much every two years. They opened in the summer, generally, with a London premiere and a week or two exclusive presentation following, at the Odeon Leicester Square, before a nationwide release. The worldwide release followed with Europe, the USA, Australasia and then – finally – Japan, all involving junkets and promotional events. It could often be a good month or two from the beginning to the end of the PR trail. Needless to say, the questions at these events became a little repetitive, usually starting off with, 'Who is your favourite Bond girl?', 'Who is your favourite villain?' and 'Which is your favourite film?' – 'This one,' I'd reply without hesitation.

I often used to amuse myself by slipping in statements, such as the best thing about location work was that I could steal the hotel towels, or that I did all my own stunts apart from the sex scenes, and that sort of thing. I was often quoted verbatim. Which taught me that some people just don't share my sense of humour.

At the time of a premiere, and with the United Artists executives happy with what they had on their hands, the script for the following Bond film was commissioned and within six months Eon, the production company, would move into pre-production with it – usually for three or four months – in which time they designed sets, brought in the key crew members to scout locations, planned effects, designed and bought costumes, settled camera requirements and so on, ahead of the shoot. So, even though there were two years between films, the time between finishing one and starting another was really quite minimal. Fortunately, we actors tended to bugger off after the last day of shooting and, apart from a bit of dubbing work, didn't really turn up again until premiere time. Then there'd be a break until a few weeks before shooting commenced on the next adventure, allowing time to tackle a couple of other films in between. Make hay while the sun shines, I say.

ABOVE: Dear Barbara Broccoli ... I'd like to play a villain please, Love, Roger Moore.

BELOW: Behind-the-scenes photography.

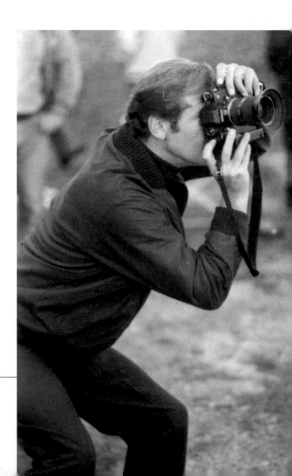

ABOVE: Dear Lewis Gilbert is one of the most gentle gentlemen in the film business, and guided me through two of my adventures.

BELOW: A typical Eon call sheet, this being for *Goldfinger*. I never bothered to keep any of mine – as they'd be on eBay if I had.

AS SEEN ON SCREEN

Of course, several of the other offered projects were very Bondian in style or character. But while there were no contractual restrictions with Eon on my doing anything else, I did feel it would be unwise to prostitute myself in Jimmy Bond rip-offs. It would only serve to damage my credibility – and I didn't want to appear ungrateful to Cubby, either. The odd car commercial in Japan (and only shown in Japan) and an appearance on *The Muppet Show* aside, the nearest I got to playing Jim in another film was in *The Cannonball Run*. In it, I suggested that while I wouldn't appear on screen as JB, I'd happily send myself up; so my character, Seymour Goldfarb Jr, believed he was a daft English actor called Roger Moore. How could I decline a lovely role like that?

Consequently, being away earning a living, I was never closely involved in the 007 scripting process – well, I can hardly act, let alone do anything else creative – though once contracts were agreed, I would have discussions with the writers, directors and producers and go through anything I felt uneasy about: sometimes they asked for one eyebrow too many to be raised, or perhaps there weren't enough love scenes. Then it was into costume fittings, a bit of PR to launch things and learning lines. Unfortunately, being the hero, you're in pretty much every scene, so there's no bunking off.

The first script on a Bond usually bears little resemblance to the final draft. The big set pieces and some important dialogue scenes are always locked, but everything else changed and evolved as we went on, and I'm sure still does to this day with Daniel Craig's adventures. Although only two or three writers are ever credited with the screenplay (due to Writers' Guild rules), there can be a significant number involved in developing story ideas, treatments and on rewrites. The first script is always typed on white pages, and any changes are then slipped in on coloured ones. Each set of changes required new coloured pages, and as there were many drafts of each change there were, accordingly, many different-coloured pages, with script spines resembling a rainbow. It was rare that a final script contained many (if any) white pages.

When I worked with director Lewis Gilbert, I would arrive on set having dutifully learned my pages and Lewis would say, 'OK, dear, what are you going to say today?'

'Well, what's in the script ...' I replied.

'Oh, I think we can improve on that ...' he'd say, in his uniquely vague manner, and put his copy down.

I don't think our screenwriter, Christopher Wood, was particularly enamoured with my playing around with his words after he had wrestled and sweated to craft them, but I hope the pay cheques eased his frustration with this foolish actor. I always made

sure I delivered the lines about how the villain planned to destroy the world, and stuck to the choreographed and rehearsed action and fight scenes. The rest was fair game.

FIRST IMPRESSIONS

On seeing the film of *Dr. No* for the first time, Ian Fleming's verdict was, 'Dreadful. Simply dreadful.' In public he was a little more diplomatic and said, 'Those who have read the books will be disappointed, but those who haven't will find it a wonderful movie. Audiences laugh in all the right places.'

I never met Ian Fleming. However, when I arrived in Jamaica to make *Live And Let Die* I was invited to visit Goldeneye, Fleming's house on the north coast, where he wrote the Bond novels. It was a large sprawling bungalow, occupying a former donkey racecourse and set in fifteen acres of grounds. It was all painted white with large shuttered windows. It looked a bit like a hospital building

BELOW: Tom Mankiewicz (right, with Guy Hamilton centre) worked on three films as screenwriter, and gave me some of my very best lines. Thanks, Tom.

ABOVE: This was lunch
after Harry took away the
tablecloths and silverware.
Guy Hamilton (in the
sunglasses) doesn't look too
impressed, does he?

BELOW: Dear Michael Wilson
... I'd like to play a villain
please. Kind regards, Roger
Moore.

from *Sanders of the River*. It still had his desk in place and various
copies of his books dotted around the shelves. It was quite a
humbling experience walking around and thinking, 'This is where
it all started.'

Incidentally, I did share Fleming's view of *Dr. No* being a film
of laughs. Cubby and Harry were perplexed when I said they had a
fun picture on their hands. They thought it was a dark thriller.

Fleming saw only the first couple of Eon produced films, as
sadly he died during the production of *Goldfinger* in 1964. He
had witnessed only a little of the success his creation was about to
achieve. Cubby Broccoli declared that Fleming's name should be
on the front title of every film, even after they had exhausted his
novels as titles. In my case the above-the-title legend read:

'Albert R. Broccoli presents Roger Moore as Ian Fleming's James
Bond 007 in ...'

When Cubby passed away, his children Barbara and Michael
declared that his name too would still appear above the title, hence
you now see:

'Albert R. Broccoli's Eon Productions presents Daniel Craig as
Ian Fleming's James Bond 007 in ...'

And nobody, but nobody, apart from the actor playing Jim, has
their name above the title. Many have asked, but Cubby always
said, 'nobody is bigger than James Bond'.

There's no arguing with that!

NOT ALWAYS HARMONIOUS

By the time I made my first Bond, the relationship between Cubby and Harry Saltzman was strained. So much so they divided their duties on each film – *Diamonds Are Forever* was largely overseen by Cubby, whereas *Live And Let Die* was, on the whole, Harry's picture, and then Cubby took the main helm of *The Man With The Golden Gun.*

Many newspaper reports had surfaced about the tensions and arguments between the two producers, and Guy Hamilton summed it up well to United Artists' executives visiting the set: 'I can work very happily with Cubby, and I can work very happily with Harry. But working with Cubby and Harry together is a nightmare.'

I liked them both greatly, but sometimes had to dodge the crossfire.

In an interview with the *Daily Mail* in 1973, Harry admitted that, with only five more Fleming stories left, he had every intention of getting out when the going was good. On 11 November that year another story, this time in the London *Evening Standard*, suggested that Harry had engaged lawyers to sell his share in Danjaq, the company he co-owned with Cubby, to Columbia Pictures.

Cubby had approval on any deal, and would have been aghast that his partner was contemplating bailing out and placing him in the hands of a distributor other than UA, who had bankrolled all the films to date.

Harry was undoubtedly in dire financial straits. Two of his more recent films – *The Battle Of Britain* and *Toomorrow* – were not the box office successes he had hoped for. Harry had invested heavily in these projects, as he had in a club in London and in buying Technicolor. He also began mounting a bid to buy Shepperton Studios. He used his collateral in Bond and Danjaq as security against bank loans – something his partnership agreement with Cubby specifically forbade. The banks started foreclosing, and Harry had no option but to sell. But to whom?

Harry started discussions with UA's Arthur Krim. A week after *The*

BELOW: Ian Fleming with his two producers – Harry and Cubby.

Man With The Golden Gun premiered, UA sealed a deal to buy Harry out – for a reported £20 million.

It was a deal – and a new partner – Cubby felt he could live with and he split from Harry, and not on particularly happy terms.

Jacqueline, Harry's wife, sadly succumbed to cancer when we were filming *The Spy Who Loved Me* and Harry seemed to go downhill afterwards. He sold his beloved Buckinghamshire home, moved to the States, and all but withdrew from filmmaking. He did though own a controlling share of H.M. Tennent, the West End theatre company, and eventually made just two more films, *Nijinsky* in 1980 and *Dom Za Vesanje* nine years later.

In 1981, Cubby decided to invite Harry and his family to the premiere of *For Your Eyes Only*. The hatchet was well and truly buried and Harry commented on what a great job Cubby had done with Bond.

Harry passed away in Paris in 1994.

A HOME AT PINEWOOD

I have worked with most of the talented team of Bond production designers including Sir Ken Adam, Syd Cain, Peter Murton and Peter Lamont. They, along with Allan Cameron and Dennis Gassner, have established and developed the look of the movies. Undoubtedly the greatest influence has been that of Ken Adam – his sloping roofs, gigantic sets and wonderful blending of the futuristic and classic was revolutionary. On *Goldfinger*, his fictionalized vision of the interior of Fort Knox caused the American authorities to question their obvious breach of security – even they thought it was real.

Ken also changed the face of Pinewood's lot for ever when he designed and built the huge 007 Stage. He and Cubby scoured the country looking for a facility big enough to house three nuclear submarines. They couldn't find anything, so Cubby said, 'Build it.'

In 1984, just prior to our commencing work on *A View To A Kill*, word came through that the 007 Stage was on fire. But how can a huge steel structure catch fire? It turned out that Tom Cruise's film *Legend* was shooting on there and, during a lunch break, a gas canister exploded. Within minutes, the stage interior was alight and effectively melted.

Cubby later visited the site with production designer Peter Lamont and asked, 'How long and how much to rebuild?' Peter

gave him an answer of sixteen weeks and £1 million. Cubby said, 'OK, do it.' The stage was re-opened and renamed the 'Albert R. Broccoli 007 Stage', in honour of Cubby.

Tragically, on 30 July 2006 during my Sunday lunch, I received a call to say 'Pinewood is on fire'. I dropped my roast parsnips and made a few calls. It turned out to be the 007 Stage (again). During the set dismantling of *Casino Royale*, a blowtorch pilot light was left burning and – over the course of the weekend – a fire broke out and crept towards some gas bottles. In a matter of hours a black, molten mess was all that remained. Six months later, the third incarnation of our stage was opened.

LET THERE BE MUSIC

Another hugely important element of the films is, of course, the music. While Monty Norman wrote the 'James Bond theme', it was really through the efforts of a Yorkshireman by the name of John Barry that its orchestration became the most famous theme music in the world – which still greets me from pianists when I walk into restaurants or hotel bars. Do I mind? Of course not.

John scored eleven of the films, of which four were mine. He was a lovely, intelligent and gentle man, though one who didn't suffer fools in his work. Unfortunately, John suffered a ruptured oesophagus in 1988, following a toxic reaction to a health tonic he consumed, and was unable to tackle his twelfth Bond score for *Licence To Kill*. In fact, he couldn't work for a couple years. When *GoldenEye* came around, different people had different ideas about the music and they didn't coincide with John's thinking. He departed the franchise, but subsequently handed over the baton to a pair of very safe hands in David Arnold.

From my own films, I think the best Bond theme is 'Nobody Does It Better', as performed by Carly Simon. It sums up Jim brilliantly. It might not have charted as high as one or two others, but it's probably (now) the most played Bond song on radio, and to my mind is in the true style of brash, bold and melodic Bond fanfares – you left the cinema humming it. Can that be said of more recent title songs, I wonder?

Going hand in hand with the wonderful title music are the opening titles, and for so very many years they were designed by Maurice Binder, who also created the legendary gun barrel opening sequence that produces goosebumps on the back of all Bond fans'

DIRECTORS ABOVE FROM TOP: Dennis Gassner has designed the sets for the last two Daniel Craig films. Here he is in conversation with director Marc Forster.

Here with Michael Wilson and Barbara Broccoli is the director of *Tomorrow Never Dies*, Roger Spottiswoode.

OPPOSITE FROM TOP: Martin Campbell has directed two in the series so far. Let's hope he returns for the hat trick.

Guy Hamilton was in charge of four Bond films, including two of mine.

Lee Tamahori perhaps directed the most outlandish of all, *Die Another Day*.

John Glen served as second unit diretor, editor and then became director, helming five 007 films, three of which were mine. Thanks, John.

ABOVE: Maurice Binder taught me how to fire right down the barrel of his lens. He created the famous gun barrel opening for the Bond films, and also designed so many of the wonderful opening titles.

BELOW: Long-time Bond composer John Barry with his wife Laurie at the *Licence To Kill* premiere. Sadly ill health had prevented him from scoring the movie.

necks, and I do hope it returns proper with Daniel Craig's third outing.

As the sequence was only ever intended to show Bond in silhouette, Sean Connery's double Bob Simmons was used to film the opening to *Dr. No*. The sequence was used in the next couple of films, but for *Thunderball* – which used the Panavision anamorphic format – it had to be re-shot, and this time they brought Sean in.

I filmed it twice myself: my first two films were shot in 1.85:1 whereas for *Spy* they reverted to the anamorphic format. I know a bit about lenses, having been a director, you see. Not just a pretty face!

Maurice was a perfectionist, and that wasn't without problems. You see, long after we'd wrapped and the release date was announced, he'd be hard at work. As the premiere approached and our PR machine cranked up, he'd still be hard at work. The film was then, and finally, submitted to the BBFC for certification, and Maurice was still hard at work! I often said the titles were still wet when they left Maurice's studio – usually the night before the premiere. But Maurice would never let anyone interfere, and I think that's why he always delivered at the last minute – so nobody had the time to.

He was such a kindly man, and I remember being in LA for his memorial service a couple of months after he died in 1991. Harry's son, Chris Saltzman, spoke with huge fondness of the man who was their Father Christmas. Every year, Harry would ask his slightly rotund friend to don the outfit and play Santa for the children, and every year Maurice did.

M

Bernard Lee – Bernie – played M in eleven of the Bond films. He was asked to appear in *For Your Eyes Only* but his health was waning, and he declined. Cubby pleaded with him to reconsider, and Bernie said, 'I'll come in and test for you,' wanting to prove his point. Sadly, he was very weak, stumbled over his lines and simply couldn't finish the scene. Cubby reluctantly agreed to let his friend stand down, though insisted the part would not be recast immediately. Shortly afterwards, Bernie passed away. A couple of his scenes in the film were given to Desmond Llewelyn, and James Villiers took the others as Chief of Staff, in M's place, saying his boss was on leave.

I had worked with Bernie Lee on a couple of earlier occasions – *Crossplot* and *The Persuaders!* – but very nearly didn't get to work with him on my debut *Live And Let Die* as, just before filming commenced, his wife Gladys tragically died in a house fire. Uncertain as to whether Bernie would be able to reprise his role, the producers suggested I ask Kenneth More if he would be prepared to step in. Kenneth agreed that he could be available on condition his fee be sent to Bernie.

Bernie insisted that he would return, and we filmed our scenes on B-stage at Pinewood, which was dressed as Bond's flat; the only time, I believe, apart from in *Dr. No* that we ever saw Jim's abode, which scholars believe to be in Wellington Square, Chelsea.

Geoffrey Keen was cast as the Defence Minister in *The Spy Who Loved Me* and stayed for five more films. He actually became a bit of a minder to Bernie Lee, particularly when we were on location in Venice filming *Moonraker*. Bernie had a tendency to disappear to a bar, and dear Geoffrey had to keep him out!

When *Octopussy* was gearing up and the question of finding a new M arose, Cubby asked me what I thought. I suggested he might call in Robert Brown for a chat. Bob and I worked on *Ivanhoe* together and I thought he'd be very good as the stoic M. Cubby obviously agreed. Sean, meanwhile, was busy making *Never Say Never Again*, and cast Edward Fox as M.

Of course, in 1995, when Bond returned after the hiatus, the world had changed and Stella Rimmington was head of MI6, prompting the casting of a female M. Who else but the superb Dame Judi Dench?

PULLING STUNTS

Behind every successful action hero lies a talented stunt team. Looking at the closing titles of a Bond film, you might count a hundred or more such folks – from drivers, aerial specialists, skiers, acrobats, horse riders ... and sex doubles. Well, would you expect me to get into bed with Grace Jones?

When I was in *The Saint* and *The Persuaders!* Les Crawford was my brave double. He came with me for the first two Bonds, but then Martin Grace took on the role. Martin became a great friend, and I always enjoyed hanging around with him and the other stunt boys off set, playing cards, chewing the fat and exchanging funny stories.

Martin was terribly brave. He'd think nothing of hanging off the side of a helicopter, a steep cliff, or even a moving train. Sadly, on *Octopussy*, he was doing the latter when the fast moving engine took the train beyond a checked stretch of line at the Nene Valley Railway (doubling for East Germany) and Martin hit a concrete post. He gripped onto the train, refusing to fall and risk going under, but sustained terrible injuries. He was in hospital for months and it was feared he might never walk again, let alone return to work. But such was the stamina of the man that on my next film, *A View To A Kill*, he was back on set.

One of the most talked-about stunts of any Bond film was performed by Rick Sylvester. I am, of course, referring to the pre-title ski-jump in *The Spy Who Loved Me*. I remember the premiere so vividly, when a total hush descended over the auditorium as he, playing me, skied off that perpendicular cliff. The silence was broken by amazing applause when the Union Flag parachute opened. The idea came to Cubby after seeing a magazine advertisement of a similar jump, made by Rick. It was one of the riskiest and most costly sequences ever imagined and if there was ever any doubt in Cubby Broccoli's mind that his first Bond film as a solo producer was going to be anything other than a huge hit, that moment reassured everyone involved.

SAY CHEESE

I must mention my friends in the camera department who made me look so very beautiful on the big screen. Long-time lighting cameraman Ted Moore was on the very first Bond, and worked on my first two before ill health caused him to withdraw from *The Man With The Golden Gun*, and Ossie Morris replaced him. Two very talented Frenchmen, Claude Renoir and Jean Tournier joined Lewis Gilbert and me, before Alan Hume was given the opportunity to lens *For Your Eyes Only*, *Octopussy* and *A View To A Kill* with my old mate from *The Saint* Alec Mills as his operator. I used to tease young Alec relentlessly, and I remember when we were working on *The Spy Who Loved Me* Lewis suggested it would be an idea to film the inside of a submarine missile tube, to give the impression of a missile loading. Alec refused, unless he was given a guarantee I was not on board. He reckoned I'd hit the 'fire' button. Me? Would I?!

We were on location somewhere or other and I remember Alec coming down for breakfast in the hotel, looking rather ashen faced. He explained that half way through the night his door opened and a big burly guy came in and climbed into bed with him and fell asleep. Alec said, in a state of semi-sleep, he was quite terrified.

Elaine Shreyeck, our wonderful continuity supervisor, asked 'Was he tight? [meaning drunk]'

I couldn't help myself, and called out, 'Only the first time!'

Alan and Alec took great trouble to make the leading ladies look good, and as a result made me look less pretty. But I don't bear a grudge.

ABOVE LEFT: Special-effects pioneer John Stears (centre), with his right hand men Burt Luxford (left) and Joe Fitt, was one of only two people to ever win an Oscar for a Bond film.

ABOVE RIGHT: Alec Mills on set with Cubby Broccoli, probably complaining he couldn't see me and wanted to know where I was as he never trusted me outside his eye line!

FAR LEFT: A brave bunch of boys made me look so good on screen – be it hanging from a helicopter or skiing off a mountain.

BELOW LEFT: Here is my stunt dream team: George Leech, Paul Weston, Martin Grace, Richard Graydon.

BOND
ON
SCREEN

BOND ON SCREEN

PREVIOUS PAGES: Daniel Craig was presented to Her Majesty at the premiere of *Casino Royale* in 2006.

TOP RIGHT: *From Russia With Love* didn't have a premiere, but its opening was big news.

RIGHT: Cover stories – being Jim Bond could never be described as a low-key occupation.

BELOW: Sean gets in the swing of things during the *Thunderball* post-premiere party.

A vital part of making any Bond film is promotion, publicity and premieres. It's all very well having made a film, but people need to know about it and want to go and see it; only then will its success be judged at the box office. Personally, I don't like to bring up the subject of money, but you can find the budgets and worldwide gross takings of each film towards the back of the book – it makes for interesting reading.

CAUGHT IN THE WEB

There is always a huge press and public interest when a new Bond film is announced. At the time of writing, for example, Daniel Craig's third 007 adventure, *Skyfall*, is in pre-production just a few doors down the corridor from my office at Pinewood Studios. The Art Department has all manner of sketches, models and storyboards laid out; the runner's office is bursting with mail, coffee machines and baskets of fruit and snacks; the executives, accountants and producers are ensconced in suites a few doors further along and everybody who walks down the corridor is fascinated by the names on the doors and asks, 'So what's this one about?'

During my tenure as Bond, there was no such thing as the Internet. Any titbits of information and production stills were released to the media through the Unit Publicist's office, and they'd

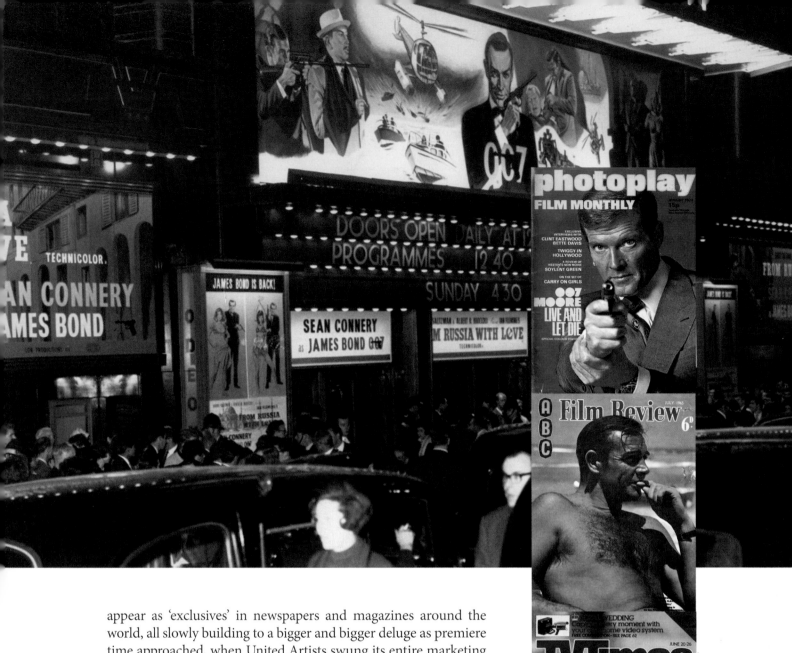

appear as 'exclusives' in newspapers and magazines around the world, all slowly building to a bigger and bigger deluge as premiere time approached, when United Artists swung its entire marketing team behind us. Back then, the various fan club publications carried the odd rumour, early photographs and potential storylines. Now all of that is on the Web, with daily updates and interactive forums where anybody can post just about anything – and they are no doubt frustrated by the huge secrecy surrounding a production. Well, if you were spending $100 million+ the last thing you'd want is everybody to know everything about a film before you even make it.

By the way, everyone – but everyone – on the film is sworn to secrecy and has to sign a confidentiality agreement. Scripts are kept under lock and key and all are watermarked. But let me tell you all you need to know: it's going to be a great film, with lots of action, wonderful gadgets and rather beautiful leading ladies – the rest is to be discovered and enjoyed in a darkened room with 350 of your local neighbours.

TALKING THE TALK

Product placement and tie-ins have always been a big part of the 007 movies. Sean promoted Smirnoff Vodka way back in *Dr. No* and mentioned a certain brand of champagne too. That wasn't just by chance – that was paid for by the manufacturer. Bond tie-ins over the years have featured everything from the drinks, watches and cars I've written about elsewhere in this book, to things like airlines (Richard Branson's Virgin), toys, clocks, soft drinks – Coke, 7Up, Perrier – Easter eggs, sweets, stickers, dolls, stationery, mugs, T-shirts, lighters and so very much more. I haven't been surprised to see my face on ties or underpants either.

The exploitation of Bond is really all controlled by Eon, Danjaq and their marketing departments, as once run by Jerry Juroe, John Parkinson and Anne Bennett, and now Keith Snelgrove and Stephanie Wenborn. I am fortunate in that a few pennies occasionally find their way to me from my little involvement. It keeps an old actor in baked beans, y'know.

Ahead of any premiere, out-of-town journalists converge on London for a press junket. United Artists would take four or five rooms at one of the big hotels, set up TV cameras and wheel in the TV journalists one by one. I'd be in situ and they'd get a few minutes with me, before being given a tape of what we'd just recorded, and waved goodbye. This would go on all morning, then they'd call lunch ... and I'd move into a dining room full of tables of twelve print journalists, all waiting to interview me. I'd spend three or four hours, shifting between tables while trying to eat the odd mouthful of food. It was always quite an exhausting couple of days – and one that was repeated in each major city we visited overseas.

Then there are the film festivals, the most famous and important of which is Cannes each May. There Jimmy usually graces the front of the Carlton Hotel on La Croisette. I must admit, when promoting *The Spy Who Loved Me*, it was rather intimidating to drive up and see my face all over the famous building. Okay, I admit there is a fizzy thrill the first time you see it, but after that passes, it becomes a little embarrassing. As a rule I always try to avoid festivals, as they're simply too terrifying for modest actors such as I.

As for the previews and premieres, I could have quite probably seen any one of my Bond films twenty times over. Imagine having to endure that! After the Royal premiere, where, of course, I sat with the Royal Party, I'd then avoid sitting through the film again. Sure, I'd walk the red carpet of whatever city we were premiering in, but then Cubby and I would sneak out and head off for dinner.

These premieres are always very glamorous occasions, where the stars and principals of the movie, plus a few other stars from TV and film, come together to unveil the movie to world audiences.

ABOVE LEFT: I'm never late for an audition, thanks to my trusted Zeon alarm clock.

ABOVE RIGHT: A few of these gold-plated Lotus Esprit models were made for presentation to the Royal party, stars and a few other folks during the premiere of *The Spy Who Loved Me*.

ABOVE: Another close shave averted!

THE PREMIERE EVENT

Although the first two Bond films were just screened at the Pavilion Cinemas in Piccadilly Circus, from *Goldfinger* onwards there were premieres, usually at the Odeon Leicester Square. With its 2,000 seats (now reduced to 1,683), it really is the cathedral of British cinema, and helps launch each film with style, excitement and fanfare.

On the evening of the *Goldfinger* premiere, 5,000 fans gathered outside the Odeon Leicester Square to watch the cans of film being delivered by armoured truck, but little did they know that Guy Hamilton was still shooting the final scenes in those cans in America just a few days earlier.

'The first thing to be locked on any Bond film is the premiere,' Guy told me. 'And that date is set in stone – you have to hit it. No excuses.'

Sean didn't attend the opening, as he was in Spain shooting *The Hill*. However, all his co-stars were there, including Honor Blackman, who wore a diamond ring worth £10,000.

ABOVE: Paul and Linda McCartney, who sang the theme tune, attending the premiere of *Live And Let Die*.

LEFT: As did I and Jane Seymour, where we were presented to Her Majesty The Queen Mother. Jean-Pierre Cassel (with whom I was filming *That Lucky Touch*), looks on.

ABOVE AND BELOW:
A miniature Bonding session.
And a fan magazine.

When *Thunderball* premiered in December 1965 at the Hibiya Cinema in Tokyo, Japan had become the epicentre of Bondmania and old Jim was dubbed 'Mr Kiss Kiss Bang Bang'. How appropriate.

At the New York premiere a few days later, United Artists arranged for one of the Bell Jet-Pack pilots to fly off the marquee of the Paramount Theatre at 1501 Broadway, Manhattan, as a promotion at the launch. A number of United Artists publicity personnel and the pilot were arrested as no one had sought permission from the authorities. The UK hosted dual premieres in London on 29 December 1965 at the Rialto Theatre and Pavilion Theatre, Piccadilly Circus.

You Only Live Twice premiered on 12 June 1967 at the Odeon Leicester Square, and marked Sean's first attendance at a Bond opening since *From Russia With Love*. The unofficial spoof version of *Casino Royale* also opened the same year, and United Artists pulled out all the stops to ensure *You Only Live Twice* scored bigger at the box office, and insisted that posters read Sean Connery IS James Bond.

To mark the event, two television specials were broadcast. The first, on BBC1 in the UK, was a special edition of *Whicker's World* with a behind-the-scenes look at the film. NBC in the USA meanwhile broadcast *Welcome To Japan, Mr Bond*, featuring skits by M, Q and Moneypenny.

The premiere was graced by the appearance of Her Majesty Queen Elizabeth II and her husband Prince Philip – their first James Bond premiere – and it broke the opening-day record at the Odeon and instantly became the number one film in the USA when it opened there the following day.

By the premiere of *On Her Majesty's Secret Service* in December 1969, the new 007, George Lazenby, had already decided to quit when he attended the event. Against the wishes of the producers,

he arrived sporting long hair and a bushy beard, looking nothing like his on-screen persona. Although profits were down compared with earlier films, *On Her Majesty's Secret Service* has since been regarded by critics and fans as one of the best Bond films, outside of my own, of course.

Diamonds Are Forever premiered on 17 December 1971 at the DeMille Theatre in New York, followed by a British premiere on 30 December at the Odeon Leicester Square, London. The film broke records again at the Odeon, taking £35,000 in its first week (£13,500 more than the previous high).

Unlike *On Her Majesty's Secret Service*, which overshot by two months, principal photography on *Diamonds Are Forever* wrapped on Friday, 13 August, bang on time, and no doubt in part due to Sean's contract adding an additional $145,000 on top of his salary of $1.25 million for every week the production overran.

ABOVE: Although there was no premiere for *Dr. No*, the first-night opening was attended by cast and crew at the London Pavilion followed by a dinner. Sean was accompanied by Zena Marshall.

NERVOUS, JIMMY?

I can honestly say that the only time I was nervous about being the new James Bond was on the way to the premiere of *Live And Let Die*. We'd been shooting for months, I'd attended countless press conferences and interviews, but in the car on the way to the Odeon Leicester Square on 5 July 1973, the labour pains started. 'The baby is coming out and it's too late to do anything about it,' I told myself.

HRH Princess Anne graced the event, and thankfully the audience didn't all get up and walk out halfway through. They asked me back for a second film, so all was not lost.

The Man With The Golden Gun premiered on 18 December 1974, at the Odeon Leicester Square in the presence of HRH Prince Philip.

Incidentally, this was the first James Bond movie to be shown at the Kremlin. When the movie had finished, one Russian official

LEFT: Director Guy Hamilton and his wife Keri are presented to HRH the Duke of Edinburgh in the Royal line up at the Odeon Leicester Square for *The Man With The Golden Gun*.

ABOVE: *For Your Eyes Only* was HRH Princess Diana's first Royal Premiere, which she attended with HRH Prince Charles and HRH Princess Margaret.

turned around to Cubby and said, 'We didn't train Scaramanga very well, did we?'

The Spy Who Loved Me premiered on 7 July 1977. The date on the posters read 07/07/77. Jim's lucky numbers. This was Cubby's first solo Bond production, and he was obviously anxious it was a success. After Rick Sylvester (doubling for me in the ski stunt) launched himself off the snowy cliff top to reveal a Union Jack parachute, the audience leapt to their feet and cheered – and Cubby smiled widely. 007 was back!

A limited number of gold Lotus Esprit models were produced for the evening, and presented to the Royal Party, myself and one or two other notables.

The post-premiere party was held at the InterContinental Hotel in Park Lane and cost £143,000 – the budget of a small British film.

When *Moonraker* premiered, the original plan was to do it in

Houston, to coincide with the first launch of NASA's new space shuttle. However, the space shuttle was delayed for two years, and we returned to the Odeon Leicester Square on 26 June 1979 instead.

A large model Moonraker space shuttle was driven around the square, accompanied by two extras in space suits and greeting celebrity guests including Richard Kiel, Michael Lonsdale, Corinne Clery, Blanche Ravalec, Bernard Lee, Toshiro Suga, former Bond girl Britt Ekland, along with big names of the day Joan Collins, Dodi Fayed, Dino De Laurentis, Michael Winner and Richard Johnson.

A post-premiere party was held at the London Playboy Club with the bunny girls dressed in space outfits. The Odeon took £86,084 in its first week, breaking records once again.

For Your Eyes Only premiered on 24 June 1981 at the Odeon Leicester Square in the presence of Prince Charles and (the then) Lady Diana Spencer. It was the first ever premiere they'd attended together, and my daughter Deborah was asked to travel to Kensington Palace to meet and escort them. Thousands of fans waited hours for the Royal couple, who were also accompanied by Princess Margaret.

I presented the Prince of Wales with a solid-gold version of a 007 Seiko digital watch, which played the James Bond theme at the touch of a button.

I then sat next to Lady Diana during the screening and, being conscious of having had a Jack Daniel's or two in the run-up to the evening, I acquired a little spray to freshen my breath, and kept it in my hand throughout. Apparently, this amused Diana, as she reported back to the Palace that I must have thought my halitosis would bother her.

Topol, who played Columbo in the film, suggested to Cubby he should invite his former producing partner Harry Saltzman to the event. Their split had been acrimonious, but time is a great healer and the reunion was a happy one.

Unbeknown to us all, there was also a future James Bond in the audience that night, as Pierce Brosnan accompanied his wife Cassandra Harris.

Their Royal Highnesses the Prince and Princess of Wales joined us once again for the premiere of *Octopussy* on 6 June 1981 at the Odeon Leicester Square. By this time, United Artists had all but collapsed after

ABOVE: The *Moonraker* post-premiere party was at the Playboy Club in Park Lane.

BELOW: Richard Kiel is presented to HRH Princess Anne.

ABOVE: Marvel produced this *Octopussy* special annual.

TOP RIGHT: Diana Rigg and George Lazenby at the *On Her Majesty's Secret Service* premiere at the Odeon Leicester Square. Cubby and Harry were not best pleased when their star turned up with a beard and long hair, looking quite unlike his screen image.

BOTTOM RIGHT: Pierce Brosnan and Halle Berry at the Royal Albert Hall for *Die Another Day*.

the disastrous financial problems *Heaven's Gate* had left in its wake. However, MGM structured a merger/buy-out deal and swung behind the thirteenth Bond adventure (particularly with Sean's unofficial *Never Say Never Again* lurking on the release schedule) with a huge marketing campaign.

Never Say Never Again premiered on 7 October 1983 in the USA, before a Royal Premiere on 14 December at the Warner West End cinema in the presence of HRH Prince Andrew. The film drew largely positive reviews, though the lack of familiar 007 elements such as the music, gun barrel opening and MI6 staff disappointed some fans. Originally, Peter Hunt had been offered the chance to direct, though declined, as did Richard Donner. Irvin Kershner ultimately took the helm. Incidentally, MGM acquired the distribution rights to the movie in 1997 after its acquisition of Orion Pictures.

I never saw it myself. I probably never will. But, then again, never say never, eh?

It was San Francisco's Palace of Fine Arts that welcomed the world premiere of *A View To A Kill* in May 1985. Given the overwhelming cooperation the city had offered us during filming, Cubby decided they should benefit from hosting the event. It was followed a few weeks later with a UK premiere, on 12 June, at the Odeon Leicester Square in the presence of TRH The Prince and Princess of Wales.

Of course, all the press asked me if I'd do another Bond, to which I replied, 'I wouldn't be a bit surprised.' I knew I wouldn't do any more, but the last thing you do at a film opening is announce you're retiring!

THE NEW BOYS

By the time the premiere of *The Living Daylights* rolled around in June 1987, Timothy Dalton's debut opened to positive press and a healthy box office and people were saying, 'Roger who?'

Pierce Brosnan's debut film *GoldenEye* launched in New York City on 17 November 1995. Five days later, on 22 November, in the presence of HRH the Prince of Wales, it premiered at the Odeon Leicester Square. After a six-year absence from the screen, the newspapers declared 007 was well and truly back. The movie smashed records, and overtook *Moonraker* in the box-office stakes.

After my retirement I purposely avoided attending any of the premieres, though I did attend the premiere for *Die Another Day*

at the Royal Albert Hall in 2002, which celebrated the fortieth anniversary of 007 in film. Timothy Dalton was there, along with Pierce and George Lazenby – who admitted it was the first Bond film he'd seen since 1969. 'Maybe I'll start getting into them,' he quipped. Just then he exited and bumped into Dana Broccoli.

'Hello, George,' she said. 'I'm so pleased to see you have finally grown up.'

For once, George was speechless.

For the premiere of *Die Another Day* the Royal Albert Hall was transformed into a giant ice palace, and welcomed Her Majesty the Queen and HRH Prince Philip. It was Her Majesty's first Bond premiere since 1967, and my first one since 1985.

I agreed to attend because my daughter Deborah had a small part in the film, plus, of course, it was the fortieth anniversary, and a few of us former 007s were invited to be in the Royal line-up. We were also introduced on stage prior to Pierce welcoming the audience to what was to be his last Bond film.

Then Daniel Craig took over the helm and, after some uncertainty, much negative press and nervous anticipation, *Casino Royale* premiered in Leicester Square in the presence of HM the Queen on 14 November 2006. It was the first film to simultaneously premiere in three cinemas across the square: the Odeon Leicester Square, Odeon West End and Empire Leicester Square – accommodating over 5,000 people.

For *Quantum Of Solace* they went even bigger, premiering across three cinemas again and with Leicester Square itself totally given over to a 007 theme. It had the biggest budget of all the Bond films to date and to my mind only proves that there is still huge and genuine love for this incredible series. It's hard to see how much bigger it can get – but you can bet your bottom dollar they'll think of something. James Bond will return …

SEAN CONNERY IS JAMES BOND

IAN FLEMING'S

"YOU ONLY LIVE TWICE"

...and "TWICE" is

Presented by

HARRY SALTZMAN and ALB

Produced by

HARRY SALTZMAN and ALBERT R. BF

TECHNICOLOR

BOND
ON
FILMS

the only way to live!

T R. BROCCOLI · Directed by LEWIS GILBERT · Screenplay by ROALD DAHL

Music by OLI · JOHN BARRY · Production designed by KEN ADAM · PANAVISION

Released through UNITED ARTISTS

Dr. No (1962)

Producers: Albert R. Broccoli, Harry Saltzman
Director: Terence Young
Director of Photography: Ted Moore
Screenwriters: Richard Maibaum, Johanna Harwood and Berkely Mather; based on the book by Ian Fleming
Leading Players: Sean Connery, Ursula Andress, Joseph Wiseman
Opened on 5 October 1962 at the London Pavilion, Piccadilly Circus

Budget: $1,000,000
Worldwide gross: $59,567,035

FROM RUSSIA WITH LOVE (1963)

Producers: Albert R. Broccoli, Harry Saltzman
Director: Terence Young
Director of Photography: Ted Moore
Screenwriters: Richard Maibaum and Johanna Harwood; based on the book by Ian Fleming
Leading Players: Sean Connery, Daniela Bianchi, Robert Shaw, Lotte Lenya
Opened on 10 October 1963 at the London Pavilion, Piccadilly Circus

Budget: $2,000,000
Worldwide gross: $78,900,000

Previous pages:
YOU ONLY LIVE TWICE (1967)

Producers: Albert R. Broccoli, Harry Saltzman
Director: Lewis Gilbert
Director of Photography: Freddie Young
Screenwriter: Roald Dahl; based on the book by Ian Fleming

Leading Players: Sean Connery, Akiko Wakabayashi, Mie Hama, Tetsuro Tamba, Donald Pleasence
Premiered on 12 June 1967 at the Odeon Leicester Square

Budget: $9,500,000
Worldwide gross: $111,600,000

Meet James Bond,

secret agent **007**

His new incredible women...

His new incredible enemies...

His new incredible adventures...

HARRY SALTZMAN AND ALBERT R. BROCCOLI PRESENT

IAN FLEMING'S

FROM RUSSIA WITH LOVE

STARRING

SEAN CONNERY AS JAMES BOND

Also starring
PEDRO ARMENDARIZ · LOTTE LENYA
ROBERT SHAW · BERNARD LEE AS "M"

And
introducing DANIELA BIANCHI

Screenplay by RICHARD MAIBAUM · Adapted by JOHANNA HARWOOD · Title Song Written by LIONEL BART · Orchestral Music Composed and Conducted by JOHN BARRY

Produced by HARRY SALTZMAN AND ALBERT R. BROCCOLI · Directed by TERENCE YOUNG

TECHNICOLOR EON PRODUCTIONS LTD. Released thru **UNITED ARTISTS**

GOLDFINGER (1964)
Producers: Albert R. Broccoli,
 Harry Saltzman
Director: Guy Hamilton
Director of Photography:
 Ted Moore
Screenwriters: Richard
 Maibaum and Paul Dehn;
 based on the book by Ian
 Fleming
Leading Players: Sean
 Connery, Gert Fröbe,
 Honor Blackman
Opened on 17 September
 1964 at the Odeon
 Leicester Square

BUDGET: $3,000,000
WORLDWIDE GROSS:
$124,900,000

THUNDERBALL (1965)
Producer: Kevin McClory
Executive Producers:
 Albert R. Broccoli,
 Harry Saltzman
Director: Terence Young
Director of Photography:
 Ted Moore
Screenwriters: Richard
 Maibaum and John
 Hopkins; based on an
 original story by Jack
 Whittingham, Kevin
 McClory and Ian Fleming
Leading Players: Sean
 Connery, Claudine Auger,
 Adolfo Celi
The UK hosted dual premieres
 in London on 29 December
 1965 at the Rialto Theatre
 and Pavilion Theatre,
 Piccadilly Circus

BUDGET: $9,000,000
WORLDWIDE GROSS:
$141,200,000

L007 UP!

L007 DOWN!

L007 OUT!

HERE COMES THE BIGGEST BOND OF ALL!

ALBERT R. BROCCOLI and HARRY SALTZMAN present SEAN CONNERY as JAMES BOND 007 in IAN FLEMING's

THUNDERBALL

CHARLES K. FELDMAN
presents
A FAMOUS ARTISTS PRODUCTIONS LTD.
CASINO ROYALE
Starring
PETER SELLERS
URSULA ANDRESS
DAVID NIVEN
WOODY ALLEN
JOANNA PETTET
ORSON WELLES
DALIAH LAVI
Guest Stars
DEBORAH KERR
WILLIAM HOLDEN
CHARLES BOYER
JEAN PAUL BELMONDO
GEORGE RAFT
JOHN HUSTON
and Co-Starring
TERENCE COOPER
BARBARA BOUCHET
With
GABRIELLA LICUDI
TRACY REED
TRACEY CRISP
KURT KASZNAR
ELAINE TAYLOR
ANGELA SCOULAR

plus a Bondwagon full of the most beautiful and talented girls you ever saw!

Produced by CHARLES K. FELDMAN and JERRY BRESLER
Directed by JOHN HUSTON, KEN HUGHES, ROBERT PARRISH, JOE McGRATH, VAL GUEST
Screenplay by WOLF MANKOWITZ, JOHN LAW, MICHAEL SAYERS
Suggested by the Ian Fleming novel
Music by BURT BACHARACH
PANAVISION® TECHNICOLOR®
A COLUMBIA PICTURES RELEASE

CHARLES K. FELDMAN'S
CASINO ROYALE
IS **TOO MUCH...** FOR ONE JAMES BOND!

JAMES BOND 007
CASINO ROYALE
007

CASINO ROYALE (1967)

Producer: Charles K. Feldman
Director: Val Guest, Ken Hughes, John Huston, Joseph McGrath, Robert Parrish, Richard Talmadge
Director of Photography: Jack Hildyard
Screenwriters: Wolf Mankowitz, John Law, Michael Sayers; based on the book by Ian Fleming
Leading Players: David Niven, Peter Sellers, Woody Allen, Ursula Andress, Orson Welles
Opened on 30 December 1967

BUDGET: $12,000,000
WORLDWIDE GROSS: $41,744,718

ON HER MAJESTY'S SECRET SERVICE (1969)

Producer: Albert R. Broccoli, Harry Saltzman
Director: Peter Hunt
Director of Photography: Michael Reed
Screenwriter: Richard Maibaum; based on the book by Ian Fleming
Leading Players: George Lazenby, Diana Rigg, Telly Savalas
Premiered on 18 December 1969, at the Odeon Leicester Square

BUDGET: $8,000,000
WORLDWIDE GROSS: $82,000,000

DIAMONDS ARE FOREVER (1971)

Producers: Albert R. Broccoli, Harry Saltzman
Director: Guy Hamilton
Director of Photography: Ted Moore
Screenwriters: Richard Maibaum and Tom Mankiewicz; based on the book by Ian Fleming
Leading Players: Sean Connery, Jill St John, Charles Gray
Premiered on 17 December 1971 at the DeMille Theatre in New York, followed by a British premiere on 30 December at the Odeon Leicester Square

BUDGET: $7,200,000
WORLDWIDE GROSS: $116,000,000

LIVE AND LET DIE (1973)

Producers: Albert R. Broccoli, Harry Saltzman
Director: Guy Hamilton
Director of Photography: Ted Moore
Screenwriter: Tom Mankiewicz; based on the book by Ian Fleming
Leading Players: Roger Moore, Jane Seymour, Yaphet Kotto
Opened on 5 July 1973 at the Odeon Leicester Square

BUDGET: $7,000,000
WORLDWIDE GROSS: $161,800,000

HARRY SALTZMAN and ALBERT R. BROCCOLI present

ROGER MOORE as JAMES BOND

7

in IAN FLEMING'S

"LIVE AND LET DIE"

with

YAPHET KOTTO · JANE SEYMOUR · Produced by HARRY SALTZMAN and ALBERT R. BROCCOLI · Directed by GUY HAMILTON

Screenplay by TOM MANKIEWICZ · Title Song Composed by PAUL and LINDA McCARTNEY and Sung by PAUL McCARTNEY and WINGS

Music Score by GEORGE MARTIN · COLOR   Original Motion Picture Soundtrack Available on United Artists Records and Tapes

MGM/UA
Entertainment Co

The Man With The Golden Gun (1974)

Producers: Albert R. Broccoli, Harry Saltzman
Director: Guy Hamilton
Directors of Photography: Ted Moore and Oswald Morris
Screenwriter: Tom Mankiewicz; based on the book by Ian Fleming
Leading Players: Roger Moore, Christopher Lee, Britt Ekland, Maud Adams
Premiered on 18 December 1974 at the Odeon Leicester Square

Budget: $7,000,000
Worldwide gross: $97,600,000

The Spy Who Loved Me (1977)

Producer: Albert R. Broccoli
Director: Lewis Gilbert
Director of Photography: Claude Renoir
Screenwriters: Richard Maibaum and Christopher Wood; based on a title and characters by Ian Fleming
Leading Players: Roger Moore, Curt Jurgens, Barbara Bach, Richard Kiel
Premiered on 7 July 1977 at the Odeon Leicester Square

Budget: $14,000,000
Worldwide gross: $185,400,000

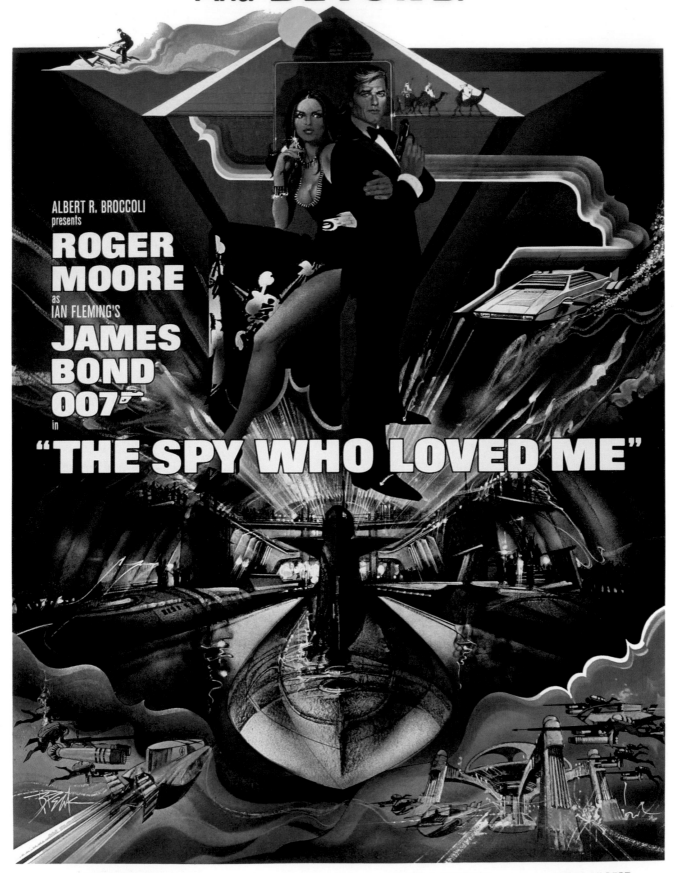

Outer space now belongs to 007.

Albert R. Broccoli
presents

ROGER MOORE

is

JAMES BOND 007

in Ian Fleming's

MOONRAKER

Co-Starring **Lois Chiles** **Richard Kiel** as 'Jaws' **Michael Lonsdale** as 'Drax'
'roduced by **Albert R. Broccoli** Directed by **Lewis Gilbert** Screenplay by **Christopher Wood**
Music by **John Barry** Production Design by **Ken Adam**

Blasting Off Next Summer.

MOONRAKER (1979)
Producer: Albert R. Broccoli
Director: Lewis Gilbert
Director of Photography: Jean Tournier
Screenwriter: Christopher Wood; based on the book by Ian Fleming
Leading Players: Roger Moore, Lois Chiles, Michael Lonsdale, Richard Kiel
Premiered on June 26 1979 at the Odeon Leicester Square

BUDGET: $31,000,000
WORLDWIDE GROSS: $210,300,000
(NOT IMPROVED ON UNTIL GOLDENEYE IN 1995)

FOR YOUR EYES ONLY (1981)
Producer: Albert R. Broccoli
Director: John Glen
Director of Photography: Alan Hume
Screenwriters: Richard Maibaum and Michael G. Wilson; based on the book by Ian Fleming
Leading Players: Roger Moore, Julian Glover, Topol, Carole Bouquet, Lynn-Holly Johnson
Premiered on 24 June 1981 at the Odeon Leicester Square

BUDGET: $28,000,000
WORLDWIDE GROSS: $195,300,000

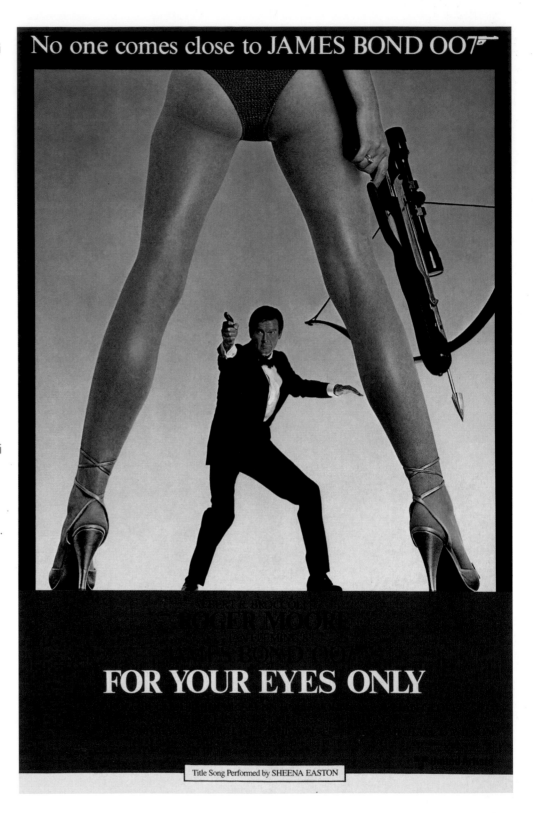

OCTOPUSSY (1983)

Producer: Albert R. Broccoli
Director: John Glen
Director of Photography:
 Alan Hume
Screenwriters: Richard
 Maibaum and Michael G.
 Wilson; based on a story
 by George MacDonald
 Fraser and short stories
 by Ian Fleming
Leading Players: Roger
 Moore, Maud Adams,
 Louis Jourdan, Steven
 Berkoff
Premiered on 6 June 1983
 at the Odeon Leicester
 Square

**BUDGET: $27,500,000
WORLDWIDE GROSS:
$187,500,000**

NEVER SAY NEVER
AGAIN (1983)

Producer: Jack Schwartzman
Executive Producer: Kevin
 McClory
Director: Irvin Kershner
Director of Photography:
 Douglas Slocombe
Screenwriter: Lorenzo
 Semple Jr; based on a
 story by Ian Fleming, Jack
 Whittingham and Kevin
 McClory
Leading Players: Sean
 Connery, Kim Basinger,
 Klaus Maria Brandauer,
 Barbara Carrera
Premiered on 7 October
 1983 in the USA, before
 a Royal Premiere on 14
 December at the Warner
 West End cinema

**BUDGET: $36,000,000
WORLDWIDE GROSS:
$160,000,000**

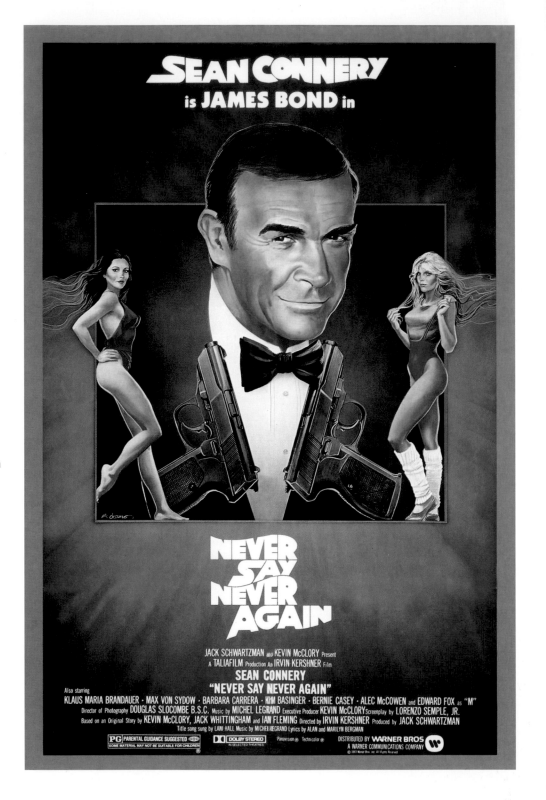

A VIEW TO A KILL (1985)

Producers: Albert R. Broccoli, Michael G. Wilson
Director: John Glen
Director of Photography: Alan Hume
Screenwriters: Richard Maibaum and Michael G. Wilson; based on the short story by Ian Fleming
Leading Players: Roger Moore, Christopher Walken, Tanya Roberts, Grace Jones
Premiered in California on 24 May 1985 at San Francisco's Palace of Fine Arts

BUDGET: $30,000,000
WORLDWIDE GROSS: $152,627,960

THE LIVING DAYLIGHTS (1987)

Producers: Albert R. Broccoli, Michael G. Wilson
Director: John Glen
Director of Photography: Alec Mills
Screenwriters: Richard Maibaum and Michael G. Wilson; based on the short story by Ian Fleming
Leading Players: Timothy Dalton, Maryam d'Abo, Jeroen Krabbé
Premiered on 29 June 1987 at the Odeon Leicester Square

BUDGET: $40,000,000
WORLDWIDE GROSS: $191,200,000

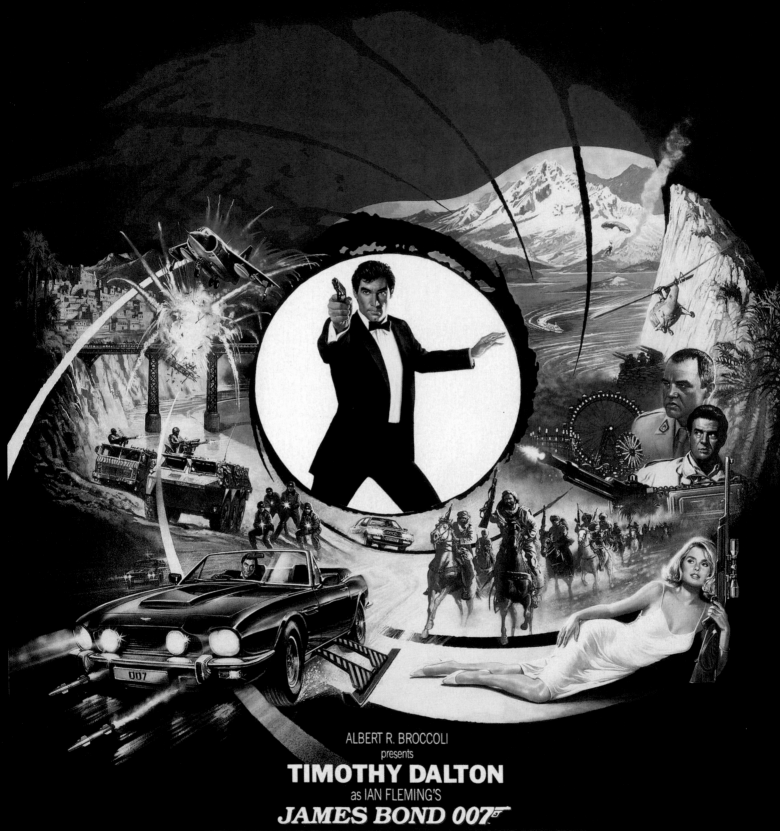

LICENCE TO KILL (1989)

Producers: Albert R. Broccoli, Michael G. Wilson
Director: John Glen
Director of Photography: Alec Mills
Screenwriters: Richard Maibaum and Michael G. Wilson
Leading Players: Timothy Dalton, Robert Davi, Carey Lowell
Premiered on 13 June 1989 at the Odeon Leicester Square

BUDGET: $42,000,000
WORLDWIDE GROSS: $156,200,000

GOLDENEYE (1995)

Producers: Barbara Broccoli, Michael G. Wilson
Director: Martin Campbell
Director of Photography: Phil Meheux
Screenwriters: Bruce Feirstein, Jeffrey Caine; based on a story by Michael France
Leading Players: Pierce Brosnan, Sean Bean, Izabella Scorupco, Famke Janssen
Premiered at the Odeon Leicester Square

BUDGET: $60,000,000
WORLDWIDE GROSS: $350,731,227

ALBERT R. BROCCOLI PRESENTA A PIERCE BROSNAN COMO JAMES BOND 007 DE IAN FLEMING EN

GOLDENEYE

ALBERT R. BROCCOLI'S EON PRODUCTIONS PRESENTS PIERCE BROSNAN AS IAN FLEMING'S JAMES BOND 007 in

007
Tomorrow Never Dies

ALBERT R. BROCCOLI'S EON PRODUCTIONS PRESENTS PIERCE BROSNAN AS IAN FLEMING'S JAMES BOND 007 IN "TOMORROW NEVER DIES"

JONATHAN PRYCE MICHELLE YEOH TERI HATCHER JOE DON BAKER AND JUDI DENCH COSTUME DESIGNER LINDY HEMMING MUSIC BY DAVID ARNOLD DIRECTOR OF PHOTOGRAPHY ROBERT ELSWIT PRODUCTION DESIGNER ALLAN CAMERON LINE PRODUCER ANTHONY WAYE

WRITTEN BY BRUCE FEIRSTEIN PRODUCED BY MICHAEL G. WILSON AND BARBARA BROCCOLI DIRECTED BY ROGER SPOTTISWOODE

TOMORROW NEVER DIES (1997)

Producers: Barbara Broccoli, Michael G. Wilson
Director: Roger Spottiswoode
Director of Photography: Robert Elswit
Screenwriter: Bruce Feirstein
Leading Players: Pierce Brosnan, Michele Yeoh, Jonathan Pryce
Premiered on 9 December 1997 at the Odeon Leicester Square

BUDGET: $110,000,000
WORLDWIDE GROSS: $339,504,276

THE WORLD IS NOT ENOUGH (1999)

Producers: Barbara Broccoli, Michael G. Wilson
Director: Michael Apted
Director of Photography: Adrian Biddle
Screenwriters: Neal Purvis, Robert Wade, Bruce Feirstein
Leading Players: Pierce Brosnan, Sophie Marceau, Robert Carlyle, Denise Richards
Premiered on 9 November 1999 in LA

BUDGET: $135,000,000
WORLDWIDE GROSS: $361,730,660

DIE ANOTHER DAY (2002)
Producers: Barbara Broccoli,
  Michael G. Wilson
Director: Lee Tamahori
Director of Photography:
  David Tattersall
Screenwriters: Neal Purvis,
  Robert Wade
Leading Players: Pierce Brosnan,
  Halle Berry, Toby Stephens
Premiered on 18 November
  2002 at the Royal Albert Hall

BUDGET: $142,000,000
WORLDWIDE GROSS:
$431,942,139

CASINO ROYALE (2006)
Producers: Barbara Broccoli,
  Michael G. Wilson
Director: Martin Campbell
Director of Photography:
  Phil Meheux
Screenwriters: Neal Purvis,
  Robert Wade, Paul Haggis;
  based on the book by Ian
  Fleming
Leading Players: Daniel Craig,
  Eva Green, Mads Mikklesen
Premiered in Leicester Square
  on 14 November 2006.

BUDGET: $102,000,000
WORLDWIDE GROSS:
$596,365,000

QUANTUM OF SOLACE (2008)

Producers: Barbara Broccoli, Michael G. Wilson
Director: Marc Forster
Director of Photography: Roberto Schaefer
Screenwriters: Paul Haggis, Neal Purvis, Robert Wade
Leading Players: Daniel Craig, Olga Kurylenko, Mathieu Amalric
Premiered on 29 October 2008 at the Odeon Leicester Square.

**BUDGET: $230,000,000
WORLDWIDE GROSS: $576,368,427**

SKYFALL (2012)

Producers: Barbara Broccoli, Michael G. Wilson
Director: Sam Mendes
Director of Photography: Roger Deakin
Screenwriters: Neal Purvis, Robert Wade, John Logan
Leading Players: Daniel Craig, Javier Bardem, Ralph Fiennes, Albert Finney

INDEX

Cracknell, Derek 118
Craig, Daniel 61, 77, *87*, *107*, 166–7, *167*, *168*, *184–5*
   and Bond's clothes 126, 128
   in *Casino Royale* 112
   takes over as Bond 128, 166, 195
Crawford, George 139
Crawford, Les 182
Crossplot 16
Curtis, Tony 54, 118

d'Abo, Maryam 58, *62*
Dahl, Roald 52
Dalton, Timothy 58, 85, *86*, 159–62, *160*, *166*
   Bond debut launch of 194
   and Bond's clothes 128
   CB signs 25, 159
   in *Licence To Kill* 161
Davi, Robert *44*
Deighton, Len 154
Dench, Judi 50, 181
Diamonds Are Forever 33, 49, 191, *204*
   and Bond's car 95
   and Bond's drinks 115–16
   SC returns for 81, 153
Diana, Princess of Wales, *see* Spencer
Die Another Day 45, 61, 173, 194, 195, *218*
   and Bond's car 95, *106*
   and Bond's drinks 113, *114*
Dr. No 6, 21, *28*, 48, *77*, *172*, 180, *198*
   and Bond's drinks 112, 115
   budget of 22
   Fleming's verdict on 175
   futuristic set for 34
   locations for 136
   metal hands from *29*
   Q character in 69
Donner, Richard 194

Eaton, Shirley *46–7*, *50*, *116*, *128*
Ekland, Britt 57, *57*, 138
Elizabeth II 190, 195
Eon Productions:
   formation of 24
   and McClory 30

firearms, *see under* gadgets and equipment
Fleming, Ian *172*
   clothes preferred by 120
   death of 176

Dr. No verdict of 175
Largo described by 37
and origin of Bond name 6
and *Thunderball* film-rights wrangle 30
For Your Eyes Only 43, 83, 100, 193, *209*
   and Bond's car 99, *102*
   locations for 142–4, *143*
   pre-title sequence of 33
Ford, Tom 128
Fox, Edward 181
Frears, Stephen 61
Fröbe, Gert 35, *35*, 36–7, *36*
From Russia With Love 29–30, 78, *118*, 199
   Bond's first car seen in 92
   Klebb's lethal shoe 34
Fullerton, Fiona 58, *59*

gadgets and equipment:
   attaché case *70*, 78
   auto-gyro 81, *96*
   billfold 85
   binoculars *80*
   bug detector *72*, 85
   cable-containing belt 87
   in car *90*
   clothes brush communicator 82
   credit card *83*
   crocodile boat 85
   Esprit 82
   exploding clock 87
   Fabergé egg *84*
   finger trap *72*, *73*
   firearms *69*, 75–7, *76*
   golden gun *75*, 82
   gondola 101–2, *101*, 104
   hairbrush radio transmitter *72*
   homing beacons 80
   Identigraph *84*
   jackpot-winning ring 81
   key finder *86*
   laser gun 83
   lighter 82
   mini-camera 83
   phones *79*, 87
   radio transmitter *68*
   ring camera *80*, 85
   rocket belt 80
   rocket-firing cigarette *71*
   rocket-firing plaster cast 78
   safe-cracking device 83
   Shark gun 82
   shaver 85, *85*

SNOOPER *80*, 85
spectacles 85, *85*
spy camera *70*
toothpaste *87*
tracking devices *71*, *72*
travel kit 77
underwater breather *72*
underwater camera *72*
underwater car *97*
underwater jet pack 80
watches *74*, 82–3, *82*, *83*, 87, *87*
wet bike/jet ski 100, *102*, 139–40
see also cars
Gayson, Eunice *49*
Gilbert, Lewis 31, 41, 55, 72, 140, 174, 183
Glen, John 72, 145
Glover, Julian 43
GoldenEye 44, *105*, 163, 165, 179, 194, *215*
   and Bond's car 93, 95
   and Bond's drinks 113, 114
   locations for 133, 145
Goldfinger 7, 35–7, *35*, *36*, *46–7*, *50*, *51*, 80, 189, *200*
   and Bond's car 92–3
   and Bond's car, gadgets fitted to 94
   and Bond's drinks 115, *116*
   lethal laser *36*
   locations for 133, *136*
   Oddjob's hat *34*
   realistic set on 178
Goldfinger, Ernö 35–6
Goldstein, Bob 23
Goodman, Johnny 91
Grace, Martin 41, 142, 148
   injured 182
Grade, Lew 19
Grant, Cary 18
Gray, Charles 33, *33*
Graydon, Dickie 142
Green, Eva *60*, 61, *112*
guns, *see under* gadgets and equipment

Hamilton, Guy 22, 36–7, 135, 137, 177, 189
Harris, Cassandra *56*
Hatcher, Teri *60*, 61
Hayward, Douglas 124
Hedison, David *151*, 169
Higson, Charlie 92

Mountain rifle lost by Mosby during the heavy fighting.

**Englishman Charles Green, owner of "The Lawn",
who assisted the wounded following the fighting.**

Courtesy Mr. James Cooke

Early photograph of "The Lawn". It was destroyed by fire.

Courtesy Mr. James Cooke

**Grave of Captain Hoskins, an Englishman serving
with Mosby, who was mortally wounded during
the fighting around Greenwich.**

Highway Marker relates Mosby's and Stuart's actions here.

The "Mosby crowbar" used to remove spikes holding the railroad rails and wreck the Union
supply train near Catlett's Station.

Warrenton Junction. Here Mosby attacked a home occupied by Union cavalry
located inside the Y-angle formed by the railroad tracks.

dismounted West Virginia cavalry fortified in a home and out-buildings located inside the forks of the tracks. Mosby set fire to the main buildings and finally forced the surrender of the Union troops. A large force of the 5th New York Cavalry suddenly appeared from the north in the direction of the Cedar Run Bridge and attacked Mosby. Mosby was forced to retreat leaving behind 23 captured Rangers, 17 of whom were wounded, as well as the recently captured prisoners. Mosby later stated he should have avoided this fight and should have instead attempted to disrupt the rear communications lines of Union General Joseph Hooker at Chancellorsville.

THIS IS THE END OF THIS TOUR.

(Return on Rt 616 to Rt 28, turn right and retrace path back to Rt 29 or continue on Rt 28 to Manassas. Or turn left on Rt 28 and take an immediate right on Rt 616 traveling 4 miles to the intersection with Rt 643 [Meetze Road]. Turn right and go 5.2 miles to Warrenton.)

MOSBY RODE HERE

HERNDON — LEESBURG — BERRYVILLE — FRONT ROYAL

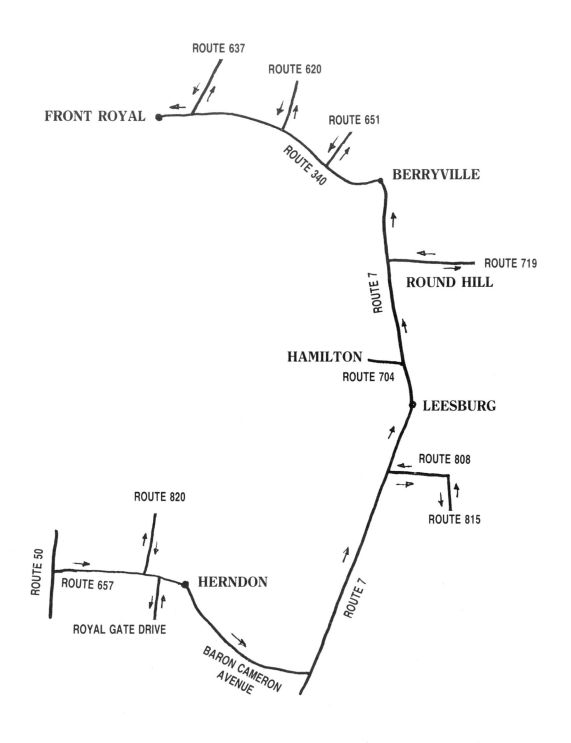

TOUR TWO

HERNDON — LEESBURG — BERRYVILLE — FRONT ROYAL

THIS TOUR identifies the homes of spy Laura Radcliffe and visits her grave. Numerous skirmish sites and homes are identified and the tour passes through the battlefield of Dranesville. No efforts have been made to save this site and it will soon disappear as construction continues in the area. The skirmish at Miskel's Farm clearly reflects the leadership shown by Mosby and is an indication of the fighting ability of the Rangers. Visit the cemetery in Leesburg where several Rangers are buried and see the monument to Colonel Elijah Veirs White, a great Southern partisan leader, who became a Baptist minister following the war. Visit Berryville where Mosby hanged and shot five Union soldiers in retaliation for the execution of his men and where Union Lieutenant Ferris shot it out with five of Mosby's Rangers and won the Medal of Honor. End the tour at Front Royal where six of Mosby's Rangers were hanged and shot following a raid, and take time to visit the museum there containing numerous relics of Mosby and his Rangers.

Tour begins at the junction of Rt 50 and Rt 657 (Centerville Road).

#1 LAURA RADCLIFFE'S CHILDHOOD HOME. *
Drive north on Rt 657 for 2.3 miles.

Known locally as "The Old Peck Home", the house on the left side of the highway in front of the old silo is the childhood home of Laura Radcliffe. Here she spent many happy years before the war. Devoted to the cause, she was a friend of Colonel Mosby and General Jeb Stuart. She supplied Mosby with much valuable information about Union Army activities.

#2 FRYING PAN CHURCH. *Continue north on Rt 657 for 1.5 miles and park in the church lot on the right side of the highway.*

According to the *"History of Fairfax County"*, this area received its unusual name when early settlers discovered a large iron frying pan left behind by Indians. War records indicate the following actions occurred here:

August 31, 1862. The cavalry of Union Army Brigadier General Jacob D. Cox made a reconnaissance of the area but encountered no Confederate forces. He noted in his report that General Jeb Stuart had on the previous Wednesday eaten dinner at Benson's (The Robertson House). His source was a Mrs. Butler who he described as, "an intelligent and apparently candid woman, about thirty years of age, resides at Bull Run, near Blackburn's Ford.

December 29, 1862. Late in December General Robert E. Lee wrote to General Jeb Stuart: "General: You are desired to proceed with a portion of the cavalry across the Rappahannock, penetrate the enemy's rear, ascertain, if possible, his position and movements, and inflict upon him such damage

Frying Pan Church. Ranger Mortimer Lane is buried here in an unmarked grave.

as circumstances will permit. This action became known as the "Christmas Raid".

Major General Heintzelman of the Union Army reported, "On the 28th cavalry passed through Vienna to Hunter's Mill, and from there to Frying Pan. Had 5 guns, 25 wagons, and 40 prisoners." He also wrote, "The small cavalry force I had at Dranesville, under Major Taggert, I ordered to move on Fairfax Court-House. It came in contact with the enemy at Frying Pan, and drove in their advance, but could make no impression on their main body.

Stuart reported of the raid, "The rear of the column, turning to the right, continued its march by way of Vienna, toward Frying Pan, near which latter point I halted about dawn and fed and rested some hours. Stuart moved on towards Middlesburg and the Christmas Raid became history.

June 4, 1863. A skirmish occurred at/near Frying Pan on this date but no reports were received from either side and the details are unknown.

October 17, 1863. On this date a sharp engagement occurred at the Frying Pan Church. Reported Confederate Major D. G. McIntosh, "Passing through Gum Springs reached Frying Pan Church, near which point a squadron of Young's Brigade, which was in our front, charged and captured a number of the enemy's picket; and our sharpshooters being thrown forward a brisk engagement ensued with a regiment of the Sixth Army Corps, MG Sedgwick, which was posted at this place."

Mosby used this church as a meeting point and often visited the nearby residence of Laura Radcliffe. At least one of his Rangers, Mortimer Lane, is buried in the cemetery in an unmarked grave. Brothers Mortimer and Joe Lane both rode with Mosby, and Mortimer was captured at a house still standing today near Arcola when they rode there to seek food. Mortimer was imprisoned at Point Lookout, Maryland for nearly a year, then released when it was discovered he had contacted tuberculosis. He died shortly after his parole.

Mosby's Rock. A rendezvous point for the Rangers.

#3   MOSBY'S ROCK.   *Continue north on Rt 657 for 1.5 miles, turn left on Squirrel Hill Road (Rt 820), and go .1 mile.*

Mosby's Rock, now almost completely covered by overgrowth and silt, is on the left. It is a large rock formation lying partially in the road and outside of the roadbed at the intersection of Squirrel Hill Road and an old road from the Frying Pan Church area. The readily identifiable features of this rock made it a rendezvous point for Mosby Rangers in this neighborhood.

#4   BROOKSIDE. *   *Return on Squirrel Hill Road to Rt 657, turn left, and drive .6 mile.*

Now called "Merrybrook", this is the post war home of Laura Radcliffe, Mosby's spy in this area. Mosby credited her with saving her life from a Union Army ambush near Frying Pan Church.

#5   LAURA RADCLIFFE'S GRAVE.   *Continue north on Rt 657 for .5 mile and turn right on Royal Gate Drive and then into the Marriott Hotel. Drive to the front of the hotel and park.*

At the southern edge of the road surrounded by a metal fence is the grave of Laura Radcliffe.

#6   COLEMAN HOUSE.   *Return to Rt 657.*

On the right formerly stood the Coleman House. Here Colonel Mosby captured two Union Army soldiers up in a cherry tree eating the ripe fruit. The tree stood in the yard of the house.

#7   HERNDON RAILROAD STATION AND SAWMILL.
Turn right on Rt 657 (which becomes Elden Street in Herndon), travel 1.3 miles and park.

Mosby frequently raided picket post and sutler's wagons in this area. On St. Patrick's Day, March 17, 1863 he attacked the Vermont Cavalry picket post at the railroad station and the nearby sawmill located on Folly Lick Run and now in the middle of town. The attack was a complete surprise and the entire 30-40 man picket post was captured. Mosby threatened to burn the sawmill unless soldiers taking shelter there surrendered.

The Railroad Station is now a museum and stands beside a regional jogging and bicycle pathway on the old railroad roadbed.

#8   HANNAH HOUSE. *   Across from the Railroad Station at 727 Elden Street (known as the Printz House), is the former residence of Union sympathizer Nat Hannah. At the time of Mosby's attack, his wife was entertaining four Union Army officers. As the Rangers were leaving town, Mosby noticed four well equipped horses tied in front of this house. He sent "Big Yankee" Ames and several men to the house, but the officers had taken refuge in the attic. Ames fired a pistol shot through the ceiling calling for their immediate surrender and they promptly did so. In the rush to climb down, one officer, Major (later General) William Wells, fell through the plaster ceiling. General Wells became a friend of Colonel Mosby after the war.

Brookside. Home of Laura Radcliffe after the war.

Laura Radcliffe. She provided information about Union Army activities to Mosby and Stuart.

Courtesy Mrs. Jeanne Rust

Coleman House. No longer standing. In the yard of this house Mosby surprised 2 Union soldiers in a cherry tree.

Herndon Railroad Station. Scene of a skirmish between the Rangers and Vermont cavalry.

#9 DARLINGTON GROVE. *Continue north on Elden Street for .2 mile to the intersection with Van Buren Street.*

To the right formerly stood Darlington Grove, the site of reunion gatherings by Mosby's Rangers.

Skirmish at Dranesville.
Courtesy MUNSEY'S MAGAZINE

#10 BATTLE OF DRANESVILLE. *Continue north on Elden Street (which becomes Barron Cameron Drive) for 1 mile to the intersection of Rt 657 and Rt 7 (Leesburg Pike). Turn left on Rt 7 and travel 2.1 miles to Virginia Highway Historical Marker on left side of the highway.*

In this area was fought the Battle of Dranesville on December 20, 1861. The Census of 1860 identified Loudoun County as the major producer of wheat and corn in Virginia. Taking the supply wagons of the Confederate Army, General Jeb Stuart moved into the Leesburg area. Guarding the wagon train were the: 6th South Carolina Regiment; 1st Kentucky Regiment; 10th Alabama Regiment; 11th Virginia Regiment; Cutts' Georgia Battery (4 guns); and 150 cavalry all totalling 2,500 men.

Moving on Dranesville from their camps near Langley were 10,000 men the 3rd Brigade, Pennsylvania Reserves under the command of Union General Ord seeking Confederate pickets and guerillas operating in the area. Ord marched down the Alexandria-Leesburg Turnpike pausing to leave General Reynolds with 5,000 men at Colvin Mill (Difficult Run Creek) to protect his rear and prevent his being cut off from the camp at Langley.

Approaching Dranesville, General Ord had the: 6th, 9th, 10th, and 12th Pennsylvania Regiments; Lt. Colonel Kane's "Bucktail Regiment"; Battery "A", (Easton's) 1st PA Artillery (4 guns); and two squadrons of the first PA Cavalry. His forces totaled 5,000 men.

Arriving at the heights overlooking Dranesville, General Ord saw the dust from the wagon trains and marching Confederate troops and assumed Stuart was moving to get between his force and Langley. On the other hand, Stuart observing Ord's guns on the heights, assumed an attempt was underway to capture the wagon train. Accordingly, both made ready to fight what was to become widely known as the "Battle Of The Hay Wagons".

Ord deployed his regiments along the right side of the Leesburg Turnpike, moving his guns back from the heights to the junction of the Georgetown Turnpike and the Alexandria-Leesburg Turnpike. Stuart moved his regiments into a front on the left of the turnpike. While doing so, the 6th South Carolina mistakenly thought the 1st Kentucky to be a Union Army regiment and opened a brisk fire that was returned by the Kentuckians.

Approximately half of the Confederate casualties occurred before the Union troops had a chance to fire their guns. Hearing the shooting, the 9th Pennsylvania charged across the turnpike and were promptly driven back. A general engagement then occurred along the line with the Union artillery destroying the Confederate guns. Finding his wagons had safely left the valley, Stuart disengaged and dropped back to Frying Pan Church. Ord, feeling he was in danger of being bottled up, promptly fell back to Langley. Both sides claimed victory. Union Army casualties were 7 killed, 61 wounded, for a total of 68. Confederate casualties were 43 killed, 143 wounded, and 8 missing in action, for a total of 194. The losses were small compared with what would come to both sides in the future in battles at Sharpsburg and Gettysburg.

Stuart returned the following day reinforced with the 9th Georgia and 8th Virginia Regiments. However, he discovered the Union Army was gone and the conflict could not be renewed.

The battlefield is not preserved. The Union guns were first positioned at the Methodist Church, then relocated to where the service station now stands in the road junction. The 9th and 10th PA Regs were located near the traffic light. The 1st KY and 6th SC Regs were behind the open air market. Cutts' GA Battery straddled the Centerville Road below where the 7-11 Store now stand. The other Union and Confederate units were along this line, both sides facing Route 7.

The George Town Pike connects with the Leesburg Pike in about the middle of the battlefield. Mosby and his Rangers continuously made raids on Union picket posts along this road during the war.

#11 DRANESVILLE TAVERN.   *Continue west on Rt 7 for 1.2 miles.*

Mosby made numerous forays into this area attacking picket posts. This early tavern was a one day trip to Georgetown or Alexandria. Drovers ate here preferring to sleep outside in the yard to escape bed bugs and other vermin. The tavern was not located here during the war. It formerly stood on the left side of the highway about one eighth of a mile away from Dranesville. On the march to Sharpsburg, Jackson's troops camped in the field across the road from the tavern.

#12 SUGARLAND RUN.   *Continue west on Rt 7 for .5 mile to the bridge over Sugarland Run.*

Mosby Ranger Baron Von Massow was seriously wounded here, removed to Oatlands near Leesburg, and from there to the William Chapman home Edgehill from where he returned to Germany.

Green Home. No longer standing. From here Ranger Dick Moran rode across country to alert Mosby that cavalry was heading towards Miskel's Farm.

#13 GREEN HOME.   *Continue west on Rt 7 for 1.8 miles.*

Where the gazebo building now stands on the right side of the highway at the entrance to the shopping center stood the home of the Green Family. Ranger Dick Moran, a family friend, stayed here overnight on March 31, 1863. Colonel Mosby and the rest of a group of Rangers, who had unsuccessfully been seeking picket posts around Dranesville, continued on to the Miskel Farm for food and forage for their horses. Early the next morning Moran was awakened by Union Cavalry moving rapidly west on the Leesburg turnpike. Suspecting that they were seeking the Rangers, Moran rode swiftly through the fields to warn of their approach.

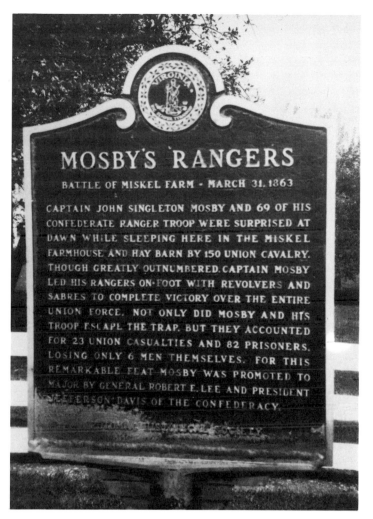

Marker. Provides information about the battle. The bottom is corroded.

#14 THE BATTLE OF MISKEL'S FARM. *   Continue west on Rt 7 for 2.8 miles. Turn right on Rt 808 (Broad Run Drive), travel 1 mile and turn right on Rt 815 (Daisy Lane). Proceed .1 mile to the marker on left side of the highway.*

On a cold March 31, 1863, Captain John S. Mosby called a gathering of his men at Rector's Crossroads in Loudoun County. Their ranks swelled by local soldiers at home on furlough from winter camp, he discovered he had 69 men ready to do battle with the Union forces stationed on the fringes of Fairfax County. Mosby led the group to Dranesville expecting to find some 300 men of a Vermont cavalry company, but he soon discovered there were no Federals there due to the lack of forage and grazing for horses.

Disappointed, the group turned towards Leesburg. As darkness approached, Ranger Dick Moran dropped off to spend the night with the Green Family who lived on the Leesburg Turnpike while the rest of the force moved on to the former home of George Miskel where it was known there

Battle of Miskel's Farm.
Williamson, MOSBY'S RANGERS

Miskel's Farm House. Mosby knew he would be welcomed here with food and forage for his horses.

Miskel's Barn. The Rangers slept here in the hay. Barn is no longer standing.

Mosby slept on the floor in front of this fireplace on the night before the battle.

was feed for their horses. Arriving at nearly 10 p.m., most of the men took shelter in the barn loft for the night. Mosby and several others slept in the front room of the house near the large fireplace.

Miskel's Farm, as it was known locally, was one of the largest and well run in that section. It had formerly belonged to George Miskel and his wife, and upon their death during 1860, their daughter Anna had sold it to Robert Bently, Jr. The entire outer boundary was fenced, and the house and barn were inside a second and higher fence that separated the pasture and crop land from the farmhouse area. The farm sat on high ground and was itself overlooked by a Federal signal station on the other side of the Potomac River. This station had been unusually active that evening, all would later remember.

Sentinels had been posted to guard the horses; however, none were posted on the lane into the farm from the Leesburg Pike. "The men had been marching all day, and were cold and tired. The enemy's camps were about 15 miles below, and I did not think they could possibly hear of us before the next morning," Mosby later wrote.

While Mosby and his men slept, Captain Henry C. Flint, with more than 150 men of the First Vermont, was on the move. A Union sympathizer from Dranesville had reported Mosby was in the area and provided an accurate count of his men. The signal station was able to pinpoint their location. For once, Union intelligence was ahead of Mosby.

Mosby arose at sunrise and noted the Union signal station across the river was again active. Before anything was suspicioned, Dick Moran, a trusted regular, came riding across the fields shouting, "The Yankees are coming!" Moran had seen the Vermont cavalry pass the house where he was staying and had cut across the fields to give a warning. All ran for their horses, but the Union troopers were already passing through a gate a scant 200 yards away. The last troopers through closed the gate in the outer fence so that no Confederates would escape.

Wrote Mosby of the scene, "In every sense, things looked rather blue for us." Captain Flint divided his troopers to attack from both sides, a fact that encouraged Mosby who noted, "I knew that my chances had improved at least 50 per cent." As the Union troopers rode in Mosby stood alone in the yard, then noting most of his men had saddled their mounts, he ran and opened the barnyard gate, waving his shouting men forward to attack the surprised Federals. Harry Hatcher was the first through the gate and gallantly gave his horse to Mosby. The battle was on!

The first volley from the Federals was ineffective, and they soon received a storm of pistol bullets in return. Captain Flint was the first to fall dead, a half dozen bullets in his body. The Union troopers froze in surprise, and their initiative was lost. They they turned to flee only to find they were now trapped by the gate they had recently closed. A crowd gathered helplessly as Mosby's men emptied their pistols into the mass.

Finally, the gate broke and the Federals retreated, pursued by the yelling Rangers. As Mosby rode by, one dismounted and dejected Vermonter shouted, "You have played us a nice April fool, boys!" The fight at Miskel's Farm was quickly ended.

Mosby's men captured 82 prisoners and 95 excellent cavalry horses. They paroled 15 Vermonters too badly wounded to move and left behind 9 dead Union troopers. Mosby's loss was one man killed and three wounded. Mosby had set the example by standing alone in the yard and opening the gate for his men. He asked them only to follow — his leadership was established!

#15 LEESBURG COURTHOUSE. *Return to Rt 7, turn right and continue west for 8.6 miles to the courthouse on the right side of the street.*

On April 28, 1864 Mosby sent several wagons to Leesburg to secure grain from the Exter Plantation. Eighteen Mosby Rangers were sent along to guard the wagons. In this group was John DeButts, a fearless and hard-riding fighter. Following the First Manassas Battle a neighbor had written: "I met Mr. DeButts yesterday going home from Manassas, one finger shot to pieces and his right hand otherwise injured". Later joining the Rangers, DeButts had participated in the Fairfax Courthouse Raid helping capture General Stoughton, and in the fight at Miskel's Farm as well as other skirmishes.

Without warning a squadron of Colonel Charles R. Lowell's 2nd Massachusetts Cavalry swept into town from the east catching the Rangers by surprise. John DeButts had tied his horse to the courthouse fence, and it began to rear and plunge about wildly as shooting commenced. John, unable to mount and escape, stood his ground firing at the Union cavalrymen until severely wounded in the shoulder and arm. He was captured and sent to the Old Capitol Prison and from there to Fort Delaware where he was paroled on April 23, 1865, having served only four days short of four years in the Confederate service.

The bullet removed from John DeButts is now in the possession of his kinsman, Arthur DeButts.

There is a museum in town containing relics from the closeby Battle of Ball's Bluff. This impressive small battleground and related National Cemetery are a short drive away.

#16 LEESBURG CEMETERY. *Turn right on East Market Street for .4 mile, turn right on South King Street, left on Union Street and enter the cemetery. Proceed .1 mile to the tall monument of Colonel E. V. White.*

Colonel White's Monument. Elijah Viers White rode away from his Leesburg, Virginia home at the beginning of the war to serve as a private in the Confederate Army. Following distinguished service during the Battle of Ball's Bluff, he was commissioned to raise a border company of cavalry. Their wild charges, together with their blood chilling yells when they encountered any Union forces, prompted General Tom Rosser to give them their everlasting nickname of "Comanches". Always in the front of his hard riding command, "Lige" was wounded seven times during the war. "I never called on White when he did not ride over everything in sight," stated General Wade Hampton.

When brigaded, the Comanches became part of the famous "Laurel Brigade" which Lige White would ultimately command. The unit fought through the mountains of West Virginia with General "Grumble" Jones, then suffered their heaviest losses during the great cavalry battle at Brandy Station. Always where the fighting was thickest, they were first in and last out at Gettysburg, serving as Lee's eyes and ears during that historic engagement. When the war ended at Appomattox Court House the Comanches never surrendered. They charged and escaped through the Union Army lines with the expectations of fighting another day — but that day never came for the Comanches or their brilliant leader.

Following the war Colonel White became a Baptist minister.

Ball's Bluff Monument. Near here occurred the Battle of Ball's Bluff early in the war. Confederate dead where removed and buried in this cemetery. The Union dead are buried in a small National Cemetery located on the battlefield.

Mosby Rangers. A number of Mosby Rangers are buried throughout this cemetery.

#17 HAMILTON. *Exit the cemetery, and drive on Wirt Street turning right on Market Street (Rt 7). Travel approximately 6 miles west and exit off Rt 7. Turn south on Hamilton Station Road (Rt 704), go .3 mile, then turn right on East Colonial Highway (Rt 7 Business). Drive .5 mile west to St. Paul Street in Hamilton.*

On March 20, 1865 Union Army Colonel Marcus Reno, in command of a force of about one thousand men (1st US Veteran Infantry, 12th Penn. Cavalry, and the Loudoun Rangers), marched from Harpers Ferry through Hillsboro to Purcellville in search of the Mosby Rangers. They then marched towards Hamilton (also known as Harmony) encountering harassing sniper fire on the way as the Rangers followed their line of march. Mosby, with one hundred men, contended the Union advance here at Hamilton. He withdrew one mile south on what is now Sands Road and sent six riders toward Hamilton to lure the Union force in his direction. The Union cavalry dashed after the riders south along the road to where Mosby had his Rangers hidden in ambush in Katy Hollow. He then struck the Union cavalry force hard on both the front and flank, killing 15 and wounding 12. The Union cavalry, pursued by the Rangers, retreated rapidly to the safety of the infantry who had moved into the woods near Hamilton. The Rangers then rode into an ambush themselves as the Union infantry opened a tremendous rifle fire, killing 2 and wounding 7. Both sides pulled back to safer areas and the skirmish was ended.

#18 PURCELLVILLE. *Go south on St. Paul Street-Sands Road for 1 mile, turn around and drive back to Hamilton. Return to Rt 7, turn left and drive 3.6 miles.*

In this area Union General Wesley Merritt initiated operations on November 28, 1864 to drive out all of the Mosby Rangers. His cavalry commenced what became known the "Great Burning Raid" as they torched houses, barns, mills, and outbuildings throughout "Mosby's Confederacy". They did not succeed and Colonel Mosby and his Rangers survived to fight another day.

#19 ROUND HILL. *Continue west on Rt 7 for 3.2 miles.*

Riding from Upperville, Mosby and one hundred-six Rangers crossed Rt 7 on their way to Loudoun Heights at Harpers Ferry to make a surprise night attack on Cole's Cavalry.

#20 WOOD GROVE. * *In the center of Round Hill, turn right on Rt 719 and travel 1.3 miles to Wood Grove on the right side of the highway.*

This stone house in Loudoun County was the home of Mosby Ranger Henry Heaton. Mosby and his one hundred-six Rangers stopped here on their way to Loudoun Heights and on their return. January 9, 1864, the night of the raid, was bitterly cold with a foot of snow on the ground. The opportunity to warm by the fire and to eat was welcomed by the Rangers.

#21 CHEW'S BOYHOOD HOME. * *Return to Round Hill, turn right on Rt 7, and continue west for 3 miles.*

The house on the right was the boyhood home of Roger Preston Chew, an outstanding Confederate artillery officer. Chew's battery could always be found where the fighting was thickest. The present owners have the Mosby family dining room table and the sword of Amos Benson, the farmer who nursed Pvt. John Rice to health. Benson was called into the Confederate service at a later date.

#22 MT. AIRY. *Continue west on Rt 7 for 1.6 miles to the top of the mountain. On the right side of the highway is a granite marker commemorating a skirmish here on September 16, 1864 between Mosby's Rangers and New York Cavalry.*

Union General George H. Chapman with a brigade of cavalry, seeking Mosby and burning and looting as they rode, crossed the Shenandoah River at Castleman's Ferry and rode into Loudoun County. After going to Paris, Chapman returned through Upperville to Bluemont where he paused to rest his command. A company was sent to the top of the mountain to keep watch and to meet with a company of the 8th New York Cavalry which had been detached after crossing the river with orders to scout along the banks up-river.

Typical granite marker commemorates Ranger skirmish.

Captain William Chapman had been alerted to the movements of the 8th NYC and followed them along the mountain to the gap. Finding a company resting here, he attacked, taking 18 prisoners and 40 horses, and releasing some 12 Confederate prisoners who had been captured during the raid. Captain Chapman was gone before the main Federal force at Bluemont could come to the assistance of their comrades.

Wagon Raid near Berryville.
Williamson, MOSBY'S RANGERS

#23 WAGON TRAIN RAID. *Continue west on Rt 7 for 7.9 miles, cross over the Shenandoah River (Castleman's Ferry) to intersection with Rt 340, turn right taking the first cross-over and park on the right of the highway where the granite marker stands.*

The date on the marker for the raid is incorrect: it is August 13, 1864.

General Sheridan began moving down the valley on August 10th. At 10:30 a.m. on the 12th, the vanguard of a train of 525 wagons departed from Harpers Ferry. It was guarded by 3,000 men — three small regiments of the Third Maryland and the 144th and 149th Ohio National Guard.

The wagon train moved in five sections and took two and a half hours to pass a given point. At 11 o'clock that night, Brigadier General John R. Kenly, in charge of the train, ordered it into park at Buck Marsh Creek long enough to water the horses and mules.

Before 1 a.m. the first section moved out. By 2 a.m., the second section was gone and the third starting to move. At dawn, just as the last of the train was preparing to start moving, Mosby struck with a light howitzer from the brow of a nearby hill. He fired three shots from the gun and then charged, and the train guard was panicked.

The Rangers burned 75 wagons, captured more than 200 prisoners, including 7 officers, carried off between 500 and 600 mules and horses, and nearly 200 beef cattle and quantities of supplies.

The Federals tried to minimize this attack, but Sheridan himself set the record straight, admitting in official reports that the losses had been heavy. In a matter of hours, he was turned about and on his way back to Harper's Ferry. Word was received Longstreet had been detached from Lee's army and been sent by the way of Culpeper and now was in the rear of Sheridan's troops. This upset the high command to such an extent that Sheridan's march down the Valley was delayed.

#24 GRINDSTONE HILL HANGING SITE. *Continue south on Rt 340 and turn right on Rt 7. Continue west for 2.7 miles and turn left on Business Rt 7 going east into Berryville. Travel .9 mile to Grindstone Hill.*

On November 6th, Mosby ordered twenty-seven captured Union prisoners, some from Custer's and Powell's Brigades and a few from other units, lined up at a store building in Rectortown. He had decided, and received permission from the Confederate Government, to execute seven Union soldiers following the execution of six of his men at Front Royal and one at Flint Hill. The twenty-seven men drew marked pieces of paper from a hat and seven were selected. One happened to be a very young drummer boy, James A. Daley, and Mosby ordered a second drawing to select a substitute for him.

Mosby ordered Lt. Ed Thomson to carry the seven Union prisoners west to the Valley Turnpike near Winchester

Grindstone Hill hanging site, scene of the execution of the selected Union soldiers from General Custer's command.

Colonel Bonham's House. Stable is the small shed in the rear.

and hang them. Ranger Thomson moved the prisoners as far as Grindstone Hill near Beamer's woods. It was a dark and rainy night and Union forces were near. Thomson made the decision to go no further and to execute the prisoners in the early hours of November 7, 1864.

During the journey from Rectortown, one Union soldier, Private George H. Sowle, 5th Michigan Cavalry Regiment, slipped unnoticed away from the party and escaped. As the group passed westward through Ashby's Gap, they encountered Captain R. P. Mountjoy guarding a party of Union soldiers recently captured in the Valley. Among the condemned Union prisoners Mountjoy recognized a fellow Freemason and artillery officer, Lieutenant (later Captain) Israel C. Disosway and one other member of that order. Mountjoy proceeded to substitute two of his own prisoners for these two condemned prisoners. (Mountjoy was later chastised by Mosby who reminded him the Ranger command was not a Masonic Lodge.) These two new prisoners were Corporals James Bennett and Charles E. Marvin, both members of the 2nd New York ("Harris Light") Cavalry Regiment, a part of Custer's 3rd Division.

Three unidentified Union prisoners were hanged on a large red oak tree standing beside the road here. Two other prisoners were shot at this spot. They were Corporal James Bennett of the 2nd New York Cavalry and Private Melchoir H. Hoffnagle of the 153rd New York Infantry Regiment. Miraculously, both of these men survived, although each suffered life-long injuries.

On one of the bodies of the three hanged Union prisoners was placed a note reading: "These men have been hung in retaliation for an equal number of Colonel Mosby's men, hung by order of General Custer at Front Royal. Measure for measure."

Colonel Mosby then sent a message, delivered by scout John Russell to General Philip Sheridan at Winchester, stating that from then on Union prisoners would be treated accordingly and not harmed as long as Mosby's Rangers were treated likewise.

(See Appendix H for information about the Hanging Tree.)

#25 COLONEL BONHAM'S HOUSE. *

Through the Grindstone Hill entrance .4 mile down the gravel road stands the former home of Colonel Bonham and behind it is the old wood building used as a stable.

Returning from a scout in Leesburg on April 1, 1865 Ranger Charles B. Wiltshire was met by Col. Mosby who informed him he was being promoted to a Lieutenant in Company H. Mosby also ordered him to take a party and scout in the vicinity of Stevenson's depot on the Winchester and Potomac Railroad. Wiltshire selected Rangers John C. Orrick, Bartlett Boling, Pomroy Gill, and Robert W. Eastham (Bob Ridley) for the party and proceeded towards Berryville. Wiltshire chose to take the road past the home of Col. Daniel Bonham who had a comely daughter that he was interested in.

Visiting Col. Bonham was Lieutenant Eugene W. Ferris, 30th Massachusetts Infantry and his orderly, Private McLaughlin. They had ridden from their camp and placed their horses out of sight in a shed in the rear of the residence. Lt. Ferris was inside talking with the family and his orderly walked outside in the front yard.

Wiltshire riding at the head of the group of Rangers spied the orderly and shouting, "Come on boys", spurred his horse foward. One of Col. Bonham's small daughters, observing what was happening, ran into the house and alerted Ferris. Ferris and the orderly made their way to the shed when Wiltshire and Gill were upon them before they could mount.

"Good Day, Surrender!" exclaimed Wiltshire.

"Good Day, but I never surrender with life," replied Ferris.

Ferris drew his revolver and shot Wiltshire off of his horse. Gill returned his fire until Ferris shot him through the neck and his horse bolted carrying him away from the firing. The orderly had managed to free Ferris' horse while Ferris moved forward taking both of Wiltshire's pistols from their holsters. Both Orrick and Bolling had ridden into the yard and were busily shooting at Ferris. Ferris, now well armed with extra pistols, shot Orrick in the chest, and Orrick was unhorsed when his mount was also struck by a pistol bullet and reared wildly. Ferris next wounded Bolling, and he and Eastman fled down the lane pursued by Ferris who had mounted Wiltshire's horse. Neither the orderly or Eastman had fired a shot.

Orrick regained control of his wounded horse and set out in pursuit of Ferris and his orderly. Bolling had secured a second pistol from Eastman and with Orrick attacked Ferris and the orderly who now turned and fled towards the Union Army lines. The orderly was overtaken and captured but as soon as the Rangers moved on he escaped. Ferris was slightly wounded but rode into the lines to safety.

Wiltshire, mortally wounded, was moved to the Bonham porch. Lt. Ferris removed him to the Federal camp where he died a few days later. Gill, also mortally wounded, managed to ride to a cabin in the nearby mountains where he died in a few days.

It was not a good day for the Rangers.

On reading the description of the action in John Scott's *Partisan Life with Mosby*, Dr. Lawrence Wilson was of the opinion Lt. Ferris was entitled to the Medal of Honor for his bravery during the action. He collected statements from all of the witnesses available and persuaded Ferris to file for the medal with the War Department. It was awarded October 4, 1897, nearly 32 years after the incident. (See Appendix I.)

#26 BERRYVILLE.   *Continue on Business Rt 7 for .8 mile and enter the town of Berryville.*

Colonel Mosby made many raids on picket posts and wagon trains in this area. Ranger John Russell lived close by.

Ranger John Russell, scout and fierce fighter.
Courtesy Dr. Kenneth McAtee

#27 GREEN HILL CEMETERY.   *Turn left on Rt 340 and travel .6 mile to the church cemetery on the right side of the highway. Enter and park.*

The grave of Ranger John "Mosby" Russell, one of Mosby's most famous scouts and fighters, is located near the center of the cemetery.

From the low heights on the left Mosby posted his howitzer and shelled Union General Sheridan's wagon train on his August 13, 1864 raid. Buck Marsh Creek is just north of here.

#28 MOSBY MUSEUM — COURTHOUSE.   *Exit cemetery and return to Berryville on Rt 340. At the intersection with Rt 7 (Main Street), turn left, go 1 block and turn left on Church Street. The Courthouse is on the right.*

The museum contains a number of Mosby items. A piece of the Oak Hanging Tree is on display. The museum is open 2 p.m.-4 p.m. on Wednesday: 10 a.m.-4 p.m. on Tuesday, Friday, and Saturday.

#29 GOLD'S FARM FIGHT.   *Return to Main Street, turn right, go 1 block and turn left on Rt 340 South. Travel 1.1 miles and stop at the granite marker on right side of the highway.*

This commemorates a skirmish on September 3, 1864 between Mosby's Rangers and the 6th New York Cavalry.

Early September brought greatly heightened military activity to the Berryville area. The main body of General Sheridan's Union Army was camped north of town and General Early's Confederate forces were marching east from Winchester toward Berryville. Their encounter was unexpected and the Union Artillery positions on Grindstone Hill opened fire on Early's forces. Union General Torbert, on hearing the firing, turned his command towards Berryville, and it was this advanced unit of his force that the Southerners attacked. A unit of Mosby's Rangers, commanded by Captain Sam Chapman, was concealed in the woods at Possum Hollow across from the Gold Farm. As the 6th New York Cavalry rode alongside of Mr. Gold's fields, Chapman and two companies of his men charged the column, putting it to flight. The officers were heard shouting: "Fall back, fall back to the woods. We'll give them hell there." The Rangers drove the Union forces across the farm until their flight was stopped by a locked gate. Several Rangers who dismounted to open the gate were killed in their attempt. Finally spilling through the gate, the chase neared the Golds house. The Union soldiers fell wounded or dead in the oak grove near the house and still others in the woods beyond.

The Rangers lost Robert Jarman and Benjamin Iden killed while attempting to open the gate, and Rangers Frank Fox and Henry Clay Adams would later die from wounds received during the fighting. As the main body of Torbert's force came in sight, the Rangers escaped across the fields towards the river, taking 40 horses and 30 prisoners with them. The Battle of Gold's Farm typified the opportune tactics used by Mosby and his men so successfully in the Confederate cause.

#30 AVENEL. * *Go a short distance on Rt 340 and turn right on Rt 651. Drive .9 mile and Avenel is on the right side of the highway.*

At the outbreak of the Civil War, Thomas Gold and his family lived peacefully in their large home, Elwood (Avenel). Early in the war, the Golds' only son, sixteen year old Thomas, left home to join the Stonewall Brigade and to fight for the Southern cause. He was wounded, captured, and imprisoned at the infamous Elmira military prison. Surviving the war, he became active in veteran's organizations and is responsible for placement of many of the granite markers on Civil War sites in the county.

#31 PAGEBROOK. * *Turn right on Rt 340 South, go 6.1 miles to Rt 620, turn right and travel 1.9 miles to the entrance of Pagebrook. The old house has partially fallen down. It sits .4 mile from the highway and is not visible from the road entrance.*

Following the execution of Custer's men on Grindstone Hill, Mosby sent his scout John Russell from Rectortown to Winchester carrying a message to General Sheridan. The message stated that hereafter all Union prisoners would be respected as prisoners of war if Sheridan did likewise. On his way to Winchester Russell stopped here. Judge Page, fearful that his home would be burned if Russell was caught here by the Union troops, made Russell sleep in the nearby barn.

The Briars. Home of John Esten Cooke, a Captain on General Jeb Stuart's staff. An author, he wrote many of his books at his home.

#32 THE BRIARS. * *Continue on Rt 620 for .8 mile to the entrance of The Briars on the left side of the highway.*

The Briars was the T-shaped home of John Esten Cooke, a Captain on General Jeb Stuart's staff who served as Ordnance Officer early in the war. A noted author, many of his books were written here. Colonel Mosby was portrayed in several of his novels and was described in Cooke's *Wearing of the Gray.* In this book he also mentions having to ride close

to the exhausted Stuart during a raid to keep him from falling from his horse. It was to Cooke the "Gallant Pelham" confided that he never felt that he was destined to be killed in the war, and it was Cooke who wrote memorial verses upon Pelham's death. Following the war Cooke wrote about both Lee and Jackson, and his books were widely acclaimed.

#33 GUARD HILL. *Return to Rt 340, turn right and drive south until reaching the small village of Cedarville about 3 miles north of Front Royal. Travel .2 mile past the Cedarville store. On the right are an old barn and three small huts in a grove of trees. Here formerly stood the brick home of a Dr. Melton.*

Mosby, with a hundred men, left Paris on May 19, 1864 to attack the large Union Army picket post on Guard Hill. This is the high hill just after crossing the North Fork of the Shenandoah River traveling north. The river was flooded causing the Rangers to wait until the morning of May 20th. They then crossed the river at Berry's Farm using small boats and also swam their horses to the far side. They rode to Cedarville, arriving about dark, and stayed at Antrim Farm, the home of Mrs. Joshua McKay, where they received food and forage for their horses. Mrs. McKay informed Mosby that the picket post on Guard Hill had been reinforced, but Mosby decided to attack anyway stating: "So much the better, now we will get two horses apiece instead of one."

The next morning, May 21st, Mosby led his Rangers around Cedarville to the home of Dr. Melton. Here they waited while Mosby and four men reconnoitered the Union lines. Upon returning, Mosby led the entire force along the road to the crest of the ridge on Pine Hills to approach the Union picket post from the rear. Sam Chapman and fifteen dismounted Rangers went ahead of the remaining eighty-five mounted Mosby men. Challenged by a sentry, the entire Ranger force charged the picket post on the top of Guard Hill. The garrison was surprised and overrun. However, it was discovered the guard force was split with half of the guard, mostly officers, staying in the Stinson House located at the base of the hill.

The attack was successful, Mosby captured 16 prisoners and 66 horses. Hearing the shooting, the post commander, Captain Michael Auer, 15th New York Cavalry, hurried to the scene in time to be captured by the departing Rangers.

The Stinson House was not attacked. The Rangers suffered no casualties; the Union, 1 killed and 1 wounded. The attack had been a complete surprise. The Rangers returned to Fauquier and Loudoun Counties.

#34 VIRGINIA HIGHWAY HISTORICAL MARKER.
Continue south on Rt 340 a distance of 2.5 miles.

On the left side of the highway formerly stood a wayside park containing a highway marker entitled "Mosby's Men" indicating several had been executed nearby by order of General Custer on September 23, 1864. Other markers in this popular tour stop provided information about the Civil War in this area. The wayside was destroyed during road construction in the summer of 1992.

#35 GUARD HILL HOUSE. * (Stinson House.) *Continue south on Rt 340 for .1 mile, turn right on Rt. 637 (Guard Hill Road) for .8 mile, and go .1 mile to the Stinson House.*

The Guard Hill House is on the first road to the left and is not visible from the entrance. The Union Army officers and half of the picket guard were here during Mosby's surprise attack on the picket post on May 21, 1864. Continue for .8 mile to where Mosby attacked and routed the picket post.

#36 FRONT ROYAL. *Return to Rt 340, turn right, and cross over both forks of the Shenandoah River into Front Royal.*

The scene of many Ranger actions throughout the war, this town is remembered as the execution site of six Mosby Rangers.

Hanging Site — Two Rangers. *After crossing the second bridge, go .3 mile and turn left on Rt 340 (North Royal Avenue). Travel .2 mile to the 14th Street intersection where the road curves to the right.*

On the opposite side of the road on the left formerly stood a large walnut tree from which Ranger William Thomas Overby and Ranger Carter (his first name was never identified) were hanged on September 23, 1864. Around Overby's neck was placed a placard reading: "This will be the fate of Mosby and his men." This tree was later cut down and small pieces sold as mementos to raise funds for the monument to Mosby's Rangers erected in Prospect Cemetery here in the city.

Rose Hill. * *Continue south on North Royal Avenue for .4 mile to the intersection with 8th Street.*

The old home standing on the hill to the right was owned by the Richardson Family who witnessed the shooting of young Henry C. Rhodes in a nearby field.

Shooting Site — One Ranger. *Turn left and drive 2 blocks to the intersection with Commerce Street.*

The young seventeen year old Henry C. Rhodes, a Front Royal native who was riding on his first raid with the Rangers, was shot in the field close to the ball park stadium.

Dragging Location. *Return .4 mile to North Royal Avenue and turn left on Chester Street.*

Following his capture, Henry Rhodes was dragged down this street roped between two Union cavalrymen prior to being shot.

Warren Rifles Confederate Museum. *Continue on .3 mile to 95 Chester Street to museum on the left of the street.*

Museum contains many historical relics of Mosby and his men. A pair of Colonel Mosby's spurs and the pistol and powder horn belonging to Ranger John Mason Lawrence, who participated in the "No Prisoners" fight at Colonel Morgan's Lane, are on display. The Sons of Confederate Veterans Medal of Honor awarded Mosby is also here. The museum is open 9 a.m.-5 p.m. Monday through Saturday and 12 noon-5 p.m. on Sundays.

Warren Rifles Confederate Museum, Front Royal, Va. The museum has interesting collection of memorabilia of Mosby and his Rangers.

Warren Rifles Confederate Museum

Monument to Mosby's Rangers executed in Front Royal, Va.

Confederate Veterans Monument. *Continue south on Chester Street to Main Street. Turn right on Main Street and go 3 blocks to the Courthouse.*

The Confederate Monument on the courthouse lawn contains the names of thirty-one Mosby Rangers from Warren County.

Shooting Site — Two Rangers. *Turn around and return 6 blocks to Blue Ridge Avenue, turn right and go 3 blocks to Short Street and turn left.*

In this Brookside Section of Front Royal in the back yard of the Methodist Church were shot to death Rangers David L. Jones and Lucian Love.

Prospect Cemetery. *Continue on Short Street to Front Street, turn left and follow Prospect Street to Prospect Cemetery.*

Directly on entering the cemetery on the hillside is a monument to Mosby's men, dedicated on September 23, 1899. The speaker was ex-Ranger "Dolly" Richards. Continue on the road to the right and drive to the top of the hill to the Soldier's Circle. Three of the executed rangers; Henry C. Rhodes, Lucian Love, and David Jones are buried here. A number of Mosby Rangers are buried throughout the cemetery.

Attack on Ambulance Train. *Return to South Royal Avenue (Rt 340), turn right and drive .4 mile to Criser Road. Turn left.*

In this area, the Mosby Rangers, led by Sam Chapman, attacked a Union Army ambulance train traveling into Front Royal from the south.

Shooting Site — One Ranger. *Continue on for .6 mile and stop at the side of the road.*

Ranger Thomas E. Anderson was shot in this area at the foot of the hill leading to the Perry Criser House, Oak Hill.

Skirmish Area. Here in Criser's Bottom occurred much of the fighting when Ranger Sam Chapman and his men attacked a Union Army ambulance train on September 23, 1864. Through this area Mosby's men fought desperately to escape from a large Union Cavalry force which moved up to defend the ambulance train guard detail.

Killing of Lieutenant McMaster. *Continue on Criser Road to Rt 522 (Remount Road), turn right and go .5 mile.*

In their attempt to escape, Mosby's men mortally wounded Lieutenant Charles McMaster of the 2nd U.S. Cavalry. Comrades of McMaster claimed he was shot after he attempted to surrender. Mosby's men stated he was shot during the heat of combat. Bitterness over this incident only aided in the drama about to befall in Front Royal, the execution of six of Mosby's Rangers. Four were to be shot and two to be hanged.

Who gave the order for their execution? General George Custer, General Alfred Torbert, General Wesley Merritt, or Colonel Charles R. Lowell, Jr.? Union Army records provide no evidence as to this order which continues to be a matter of controversy. Custer has long been blamed for the death of Mosby's men. It was a tragic day in the history of this Shenandoah town.

THIS IS THE END OF THE TOUR.

MOSBY RODE HERE

OAKTON — HUNTER'S MILL — FREEDOM HILL

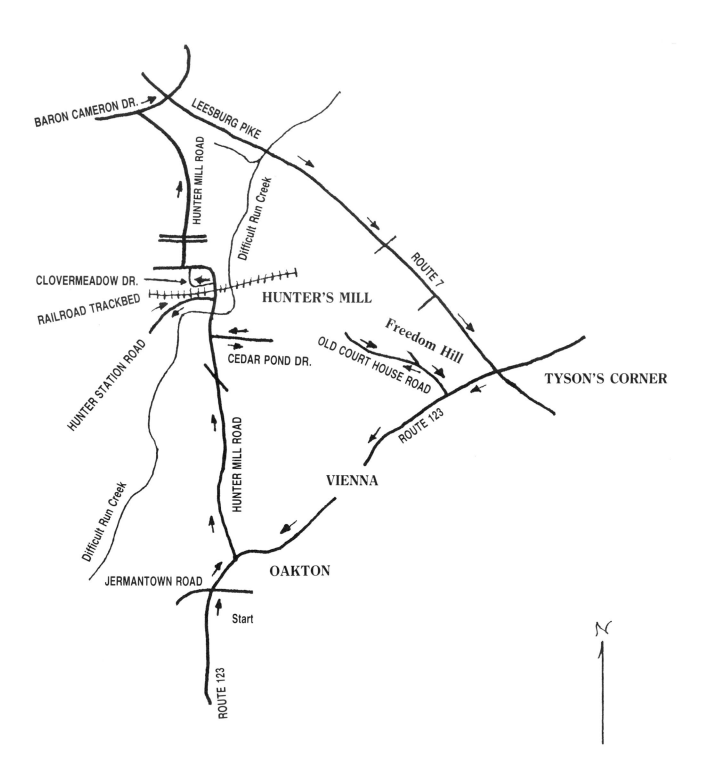

(This area lies in the middle of Northern Virginia; Maryland and Pennsylvania are to the north; south is the Shenandoah Valley; and west is West Virginia.)

TOUR TWO — OPTION A

OAKTON — HUNTER'S MILL — FREEDOM HILL

THIS TOUR permits driving through an area frequented by Mosby and his Rangers. A photograph of the Mosby Oak is a must as no expense has been spared to save this beautiful tree. See the home of Mrs. Brooke, frequently identified in army dispatches. Cross Difficult Run Creek where Union Army soldiers drank on the way to Gettysburg and where Confederate Jeb Stuart's command paused to drink and water their mounts as they too rode to that bloody battlefield. See the former location of old Hunter's Station and note the list of actions that occurred in this immediate area. A visit to the fort or picket post on Freedom Hill will provide some good pictures of an earthwork built solely to guard against the Rangers who made an attack on Union cavalry well within sight of this fortification.

Tour starts at Chain Bridge Road (Route 123) and Jermantown Road.

Flint Hill School.

#1 CHAIN BRIDGE ROAD.
On July 16th, 1861 Union Army General David V. Tyler marched his division from Vienna to Fairfax Courthouse enroute to Centerville to participate in the First Battle of Bull Run. Later during the war as Union forces garrisoned this area, supply wagons routinely traveled this road from the railhead at Vienna. The railroad bridges beyond Vienna towards Leesburg were burned by the Confederates early in the war, leaving Vienna as the last major point that could be reached by railroad.

#2 CONFEDERATE CAMP.   *To the immediate right.*
Following the Confederate victory at the first Battle of Bull Run, many Confederate units moved into this area and camped during July-October 1861. South Carolina troops were located where the large telephone company building now stands.

#3 FLINT HILL SCHOOL.   *To the left.*
Some 75,000 bricks in the Flint Hill School came from the old Wilcoxon Inn that originally stood across from the Fairfax Courthouse. Confederate General Jeb Stuart used the Inn as a Headquarters early in the war. Colonel Mosby used the Inn to hold prisoners for a short time.

#4 CONFEDERATE CAMP.   *To the left.*
The Washington Artillery from Louisiana camped in the area behind the school. They constructed a target range for artillery practice and pieces of cannon balls and shrapnel may still be found throughout the area.

#5 OLD METHODIST CHURCH.   *Drive .3 mile. Old church sits on the right of the highway.*
In the fields behind this church on March 7, 1865, a Union Army Lieutenant, Sergeant, and 20 troopers from the 16th New

York Cavalry were ambushed by 30 of Mosby's men as the troop carried daily dispatches to Fairfax Courthouse. 2 were killed, 1 wounded, and 3 captured as were several horses with arms and equipment. There were no losses to the Rangers.

#6 HUNTER MILL ROAD.   *Go .1 mile and turn left.*

This road follows the same path as during the war and saw the movement of large numbers of troops from both Armies. Following the Battle of Chantilly, elements of General Robert E. Lee's Army used this road in early September 1861 to move to Sharpsburg, Maryland and fight in the Battle of Antietam Creek. On June 17, 1863 Union General William's Division of the 12th Corps marched on this road to reach the Battle of Gettysburg, Pennsylvania. General Jeb Stuart's Cavalry followed on the 27th of June, also seeking to reach Gettysburg and join General Lee.

The Mosby Oak. Efforts continue to keep this beautiful ancient tree alive and growing.

#7   THE MOSBY OAK TREE.   *Continue for .1 mile. Tree stands close to the right side of the highway.*

During the Civil War Mosby laid a trap for a Union sympathizer, New York born Quaker Alexander Haight under this 400 year old, 100 foot high oak tree. Haight escaped the trap, survived the war, and lived to see his grandchildren play with the grandchildren of Confederate veterans. To his annoyance they would yell and clap as loudly as their playmates when some aged Confederate veteran related how he had whipped the Yankees!

Recognized as a historical landmark, the tree was saved during development related construction at the cost of $8,000. Yearly maintenance and decoration with lights during the Christmas season costs another $5,000 annually.

#8   FLINT HILL RIDGE.   *Drive .6 mile and the ridge is the high ground on the left.*

During the September 1, 1862 Battle of Chantilly, Mosby, serving as a scout for General Jeb Stuart, led cavalry to this ridge searching for a way to get into the rear of Union General Pope's army. Encountering heavy resistance from Union forces, they withdrew back towards Chantilly.

#9   PROVOST MARSHAL OFFICE.   *Continue for .1 mile. The former house site is in the vicinity of the large Mormon Church on the right side of the highway.*

The home of James LaRue Smith, located in this area, became Headquarters and the Provost Marshal's Office for Confederate forces camped in this area following the Battle of Bull Run. Confederate Generals Bonham and Longstreet had their brigades bivouacked in the surrounding countryside. Scouting for General Bonham was Frank Williams, who later became a Mosby Ranger and participated in the capture of General Stoughton at Fairfax Courthouse. There was a $2,000 reward for his capture early in the war. Also scouting for General Bonham was C. H. Jackson, whose brother James W. Jackson shot Union Colonel Ellsworth in the Marshall House at Alexandria.

Mr. Smith, a Quaker, did not take sides during the conflict. He was arrested by General Jeb Stuart's cavalry following the Battle of Chantilly and held prisoner until exchanged for a prominent civilian.

Mrs. Brooke's House. Frequently mentioned in the Official Records, War of the Rebellion. A skirmish started here early in the war.

#10   MRS. BROOKE'S HOUSE. *   *Continue west on Hunter Mill Road for 1.8 miles. The large white house is on the left on top of the hill.*

On October 20, 1862 Union forces scouting down the railroad discovered the Confederate pickets from the 1st North Carolina Cavalry guarding Hunter's Mill enjoying themselves at the home of Mrs. Brooke. A running fight occurred with no losses to either side. On February 7, 1862 Union General

William F. "Baldy" Smith sent 5 squadrons of the 5th Pennsylvania Cavalry to raid Flint Hill (Oakton) and reassemble at "Mrs. Brooke's House". This house became known as "Mrs. Brooke's" and is so shown on Army maps and mentioned in dispatches, although this was not accurate.

Inheriting the house from her father, Margret Adams married Marine Corps officer Benjamin E. Brooke in 1844. Following his death, she remarried Horatio P. Lanham in 1861. Accordingly, the proper designation should have been the "Lanham House".

#11 LAWYERS ROAD.   *Continue .2 mile to intersection with Lawyers Road.*

While riding near the Thompson farm in this area, Mosby paused to talk with Jeremiah Thompson and made him the present of a cavalry sword. Thompson passed it to his nephew saying, "Pete, Colonel Mosby rode by one day and gave me that sword. You take it home and keep it, and when you marry, give it to your children". Pete kept the sword for 84 years before passing it on. The sword remains in the possession of the family.

#12 HIDDEN VALLEY.   *Continue on Hunter Mill Road for .2 mile, turn right on Cedar Pond Drive and travel .1 mile to tennis courts on the right.*

A Union Army message dated August 10, 1863 states: "It is reported that one of our cavalry pickets was fired on last night while on duty near Falls Church. A Mr. Reed (Read), resident of that place, says he knows that Mosby's headquarters are only about 5 miles from Falls Church, where he has about 40 men." Here in this secluded area Mosby hid horses for use during raids.

At a nearby farm house, Mosby stopped for meals several times, always paying cash. He would take the small children, mount them in the saddle of his horse, and lead the horse around the yard. It was an event they remembered all of their lives.

#13 HORSE PASTURE.   *Return to Hunter Mill Road, turn right and go .1 mile west. Field is on the right.*

Colonel E. V. White's "Comanches" grazed 64 captured horses here on October 1, 1863 following his raid on the Union Army garrison at Lewinsville Station. Union casualties in the raid were 4 killed and 20 soldiers captured. Bypassing the Leesburg Turnpike where he would be expected to travel, White evaded pursuit by coming here and then following the railroad tracks to Leesburg. Horses still graze in this field.

#14 DIFFICULT RUN CREEK.   *Continue .1 mile to the bridge over the creek.*

The large supply of fresh water in this creek resulted in many Civil War troop units camping here and on the nearby hills. The 6th Michigan Cavalry Provost Guard occupied this site during June 15-17, 1863. They provided William's Division with road guides to speed the march to Gettysburg. Pausing to eat at the creek, William's troops emptied their cartridge boxes of bullets that had become loose from the paper covering. Road construction during 1988 uncovered many of these .58 caliber lead "Minie Balls". Near here the 1st Virginia Cavalry skirmished with the 14th New York Zouaves on December 11, 1861.

#15 UNRECORDED SKIRMISH.   *The site lies about 1 mile down this creek.*

The late Stuart Evans, a member of the Mosby Society and the Northern Virginia Relic Hunters' Association, discovered the site of an unrecorded skirmish while metal detecting on Difficult Run Creek near here. His major find was a large metal halberd from the top of a flag staff of a type known to be used by Massachusetts troops. It is believed to belong to the 2nd Massachusetts Cavalry stationed in Vienna and manning picket posts throughout the area. Fired and dropped pistol bullets, Spencer cartridges, brass from a lost cap, buttons, and a broken sword scabbard gave evidence of an ambush with the Union Cavalry retreating towards Vienna.

The late Stuart A. Evans displays a flag staff tip metal detected at the scene of a cavalry ambush near Hunter's Mill.

Because loss of a flag would have been a serious incident to the Union Cavalry, and capture of a flag would have been a major triumph for the Confederates, it is believed that only the halberd was lost from the tip of the flag staff or the skirmish would have been reported by one side or the other. Many such small skirmishes went unreported.

#16 MILL RACE. *About 25 yards from the bridge lies the old mill race.*

The mill race from Hunter's Mill is visible on the side of the road. The mill race was greatly damaged by soldiers draining it to catch fish to supplement their rations.

#17 HUNTER'S MILL. *Continue west for .2 mile, turn right on Hunter Station Road, drive .1 mile. The mill sat in the valley on the left behind the "New" Miller's House.*

Established prior to the 1830s, this was both a saw and grist mill. Many maps of the period identify it as Hunter's Saw Mill. Burned during the war, it was rebuilt. It has since been demolished.

#18 "NEW" MILLER'S HOUSE. * On June 15, 1862 following heavy fighting around New Market, severe casualties were received by the 1st Pennsylvania Reserve Rifles (Pennsylvania Bucktails). The Bucktails had skirmished here on October 20th, 1861 and recognized the "new" Miller's house was suitable for a hospital. Captain Tailor, Captain Blanchard, and Lieutenant Swayne were moved here. Lieutenant Colonel Thomas L. Kane, commander of the Bucktails, was wounded and captured during the fighting. He was paroled and returned here to convalesce. He was exchanged for Lieutenant Colonel W. C. Wickham of the 4th Virginia Cavalry on August 16th and was in a skirmish at Catlett's Station on August 23rd. During December, 1862 he was promoted to Brigadier General of Volunteers.

#19 ALEXANDRIA, LOUDOUN, AND HAMPSHIRE RAILROAD TRACKS. *Return to Hunter Mill Road and turn left. The bicycle path immediately in the front is the old trackbed.*

Early in the war on October 20, 1861 a reconnaissance was made down the tracks from Dranesville by a company of Pennsylvania "Bucktail Rangers". A skirmish developed with the 1st North Carolina Cavalry. The Union report notes the Confederates had burned all of the railroad bridges as far south as Vienna, and had also burned several box cars near Hunter's Mill. This was the first fighting in this area. The rails were removed for use elsewhere; however, the roadbed offered an excellent path between Vienna, Dranesville and Leesburg and it was in continuous use by both sides throughout the war.

On December 28, 1862 Mosby, scouting for Confederate General Jeb Stuart, guided the Confederate cavalry up this track from Vienna on what became known as the "Christmas Raid". Reaching Dranesville, Stuart turned and camped at Frying Pan Church before returning to Confederate territory. Herman Melville, who would become famous as the author of *Moby Dick*, accompanied the 2nd Massachusetts Cavalry on April 28, 1864 in following these tracks on a scouting mission to Leesburg. Melville later wrote a poem about searching for Mosby, "The Scout Towards Aldie".

On February 22, 1862 the 5th Pennsylvania Cavalry seeking Confederate pickets in the neighborhood, met the 6th Maine Infantry Regiment here. The anticipated heavy fighting did not occur.

#20 HUNTER'S STATION. The railroad station stood immediately on the right side of the road and is considered the "heart" of Hunter's Mill. A summary of military actions here follows:

Aug 10, 1861.	Confederates occupy Hunter's Mill.
Oct 20, 1861.	Skirmish, 1st N.C. Cav *vs* Pennsylvania Bucktails.
Dec 11, 1861.	Skirmish, 1st Va. Cav *vs* 14th N.Y. Zouaves.
Feb 7, 1862.	Skirmish, 1st N.C. Cav *vs* 5th Penn Cav.
Feb 22, 1862.	5th Penn Cav and 6th Maine Inf reconnaissance.
Mar 10, 1862.	Penn Reserve Corps camp — Peninsula Campaign.
Jun 15, 1862.	1st Penn Rifles (Penn Bucktails) establish hospital.
Dec 28, 1862.	Mosby here as scout on Gen Jeb Stuart's Christmas Raid.
Jun 15, 1863.	6th Mich Cav Provost Guard road guides arrive.
Jun 17, 1863.	Gen Williams' Div, 12th Corps route to Gettysburg.
Jun 27, 1863.	Gen Jeb Stuart's cavalry route to Gettysburg.
Oct 1, 1863.	Col E. V. White's route from Lewinsville Station raid.
Dec 21, 1863.	Col Mosby attacks 2nd Mass Cav picket post.
Apr 23, 1864.	Col Mosby attacks 2nd Mass Cav picket post.
Apr 28, 1864.	2nd Mass Cav with Herman Melville raid route to Leesburg.
Oct 18, 1864.	Col Mosby's cavalry execute the Rev. John D. Read.

#21 EXECUTION OF REVEREND READ. *Approximately 1.5 miles to the right near these railroad tracks.*

On October 18, 1864 the Reverend John D. Read was executed near here. The Reverend Read was pastor of the First Baptist Church at Falls Church. A known Federal spy, he

**Reverend John D. Read.
Executed by the Rangers near Hunter's Mill.**

received much information from the students of a black school run by his daughter. His fate is stated in the following Union Army message:

"About 2 a.m. on the morning of October 18, a force of Mosby's men estimated at 75, entered Falls Church village, halted at the church (brigade hospital), and after breaking open the barn of Mr. Sines, a citizen who lives opposite, and taking therefrom 5 valuable horses, passed up the Alexandria and Lewinsville pike towards Vienna. The post at the junction of the Lewinsville road with the pike, consisting of one Corporal and three men of the Sixteenth New York Cavalry, was captured, with one horse. A Negro named Frank Brooks, belonging to the citizen's home guard of the village, was shot dead while attempting to assist the picket in making defense. Mr. J. B. Reed, a citizen and a member of the same guard, with one of his Negro employees, were taken prisoner at the same time. Mr. Reed was afterwards brutally murdered by the party who captured him, in a dense pine wood near Hunter's Mill, and his body has been found and brought into his house. An attempt to kill the Negro taken with Mr. Reed was also made, and the Rebels, supposing him dead, left him in the woods. He escaped afterwards, however, and has but a slight wound to the head, with the loss of an ear, blown off by a pistol shot. There is no doubt concerning the murder of Mr. Reed, as the surgeon, who has made an examina-

tion of the body, states that the skull at the base of the brain is blown to atoms, and the flesh about the wound is filled with powder, as if the pistol had been placed close to the head."

As a result of this unfortunate incident, for many years after the war children jumping rope would chant:

> Isn't any school,
> Isn't any teacher;
> Isn't any church,
> Mosby shot the preacher.

#22 UNION ARMY PICKET POST. *Continue .1 mile to Hunter Mill Road.*

On the hill to the left is the site of the picket post overlooking the junction of the railroad, Hunter Mill Road, and Hunter Station Road. This was a strategic position. It was manned by the 2nd Massachusetts Cavalry whose headquarters was in Vienna. On December 21, 1863 Mosby attacked this post manned by a Corporal and 5 Privates, wounding 2 men and capturing 4 horses. It was estimated 20-30 guerillas were present in the attacking force. Again, on April 23, 1864 pickets here were attacked at 4 a.m. with one man wounded, 3 men captured and 9 horses lost. It was reported to Union Army Headquarters that Mosby with 50 men crossed Difficult Run where several of the group dismounted and attacked the picket post.

#23 WARREN'S HEADQUARTERS. * *Immediately on the right side of the road on top of the hill.*

During the period around March 10, 1862 the Pennsylvania Reserve Corps camped here while marching to participate in the Peninsular Campaign. General Gouverneur K. Warren, later to become known as the "Savior of Gettysburg", from recognizing the need for the Union Army to hold Little Roundtop Mountain, made his headquarters here. Local legend indicates Warren's headquarter's tent was erected in the yard of the "old" Miller's house at the top of the hill overlooking Difficult Run Creek. This house is the original Miller's house and dates back to the eighteenth century.

#24 HOSPITAL HILL. *Continue .2 mile on Hunter Mill Road, turn left on Clovermeadow Drive and drive .2 mile. Site is on the right on top of the hill.*

Measles and other diseases struck the Southern troops who fortified this area. A hospital was located in the area marked by the tall trees. Those who died were buried in a mass grave in the rear of a family cemetery in the Wayside Subdivision. Their bodies were reinterred and buried under the Confederate Monument in the Fairfax Cemetery after the war. The black servants who died from disease while accompanying their masters here are buried on what is known locally as "Dead Man's Hill". Across from the hospital is a large spring known as "Hospital Spring". Metal detecting in this location revealed uniform buttons and a "CS" belt buckle that showed signs of being burned. Possibly uniforms were burned should the owner have contacted a contagious disease.

#25 CONFEDERATE TRENCHES.   *On the hills to the left along the railroad tracks remain a few of these early works.*

Confederates moving into this area during August, 1861 fortified the nearby ridge with trenches and artillery positions. They were in a position to halt Union troops entering the area following the tracks from Dranesville, and to control Hunter Mill Road with artillery fire. Uniform brass buttons detected in this location indicate these works were also used by Union troops at some later period during the war. Construction has since destroyed most of the fortifications.

#26 LEESBURG PIKE.   *Continue .1 mile on Clover-meadow Drive, turn left on Hunter Mill Road, then right at the traffic signal following Hunter Mill Road for 3 miles. Turn right at the intersection with Baron Cameron Drive (Rt 606) and travel .3 mile to the intersection with the Leesburg Pike (Rt 7). Turn right and proceed on Rt 7.*

Troops from both sides continually marched down this road throughout the war. It provided a straight route between Langley, Dranesville, and Leesburg.

#27 COLVIN MILL.   *Continue on Rt 7 for 1.3 miles and the mill is on the left side of the highway.*

The fresh water in Difficult Run Creek and Colvin Run made this a stop for thirsty troops and cavalry horses. General Reynolds stopped here with 5,000 troops guarding the way back to Langley for General Ord's command during the Battle of Dranesville. Near here is the home of Mosby Ranger John Nelson Follin. When Union soldiers came looking for him one night, he hid under the house so close to their horses' hoofs that he could have reached out and touched them.

The mill had difficult times during the war as it was located in "no Man's land" with farmer's bound here with grain for milling subject to capture by either side.

#28 ANDREWS CHAPEL.   *Continue on Rt 7 for 2.1 miles. The church is on the right of the highway.*

This church was severely damaged during the war by Union soldiers and the Government later paid a claim to permit renovation. Here in the cemetery are the well marked graves of Ranger John Nelson Follin and his brother who both initially joined Col. White's "Comanches" when John was only 15. Follin's horse was shot out from under him at the Battle of Bull Run resulting in his joining an infantry unit. Wounded at Petersburg, he returned home to ride with Mosby's Rangers. One of 30 children, all of the same father, but 21 by one mother and 9 by a second, Follin fathered a child at the age of 71 who provided the above information during a 1989 interview. Ranger Follin died in 1939 at the age of 91.

#29 PEACH GROVE STOCKADE AND SIGNAL TOWER.   *Continue east on Rt 7 for 2.6 miles. The signal tower and stockade were located on the left at the same site as the modern signal tower.*

This high ground enabled the construction of a Union signal tower permitting contact with the defenses of Washington and surrounding Union strong points. Peach Grove was a staging area for Union troops. It was used to maneuver troops along the strategically important Chain Bridge Road between Fort Marcy and Vienna. Fort Marcy was part of the defensive forts surrounding Washington. Dense pine woods in this area were burned early in the war because Mosby's men were hiding in the neighborhood.

Freedom Hill Picket Post.
Built solely to protect the area from Mosby's Rangers.

#30 FREEDOM HILL FORT OR PICKET POST.   *Turn right on Rt 123 (Chain Bridge Road), go south for .4 mile, then turn right on Old Courthouse Road. Follow this road for .3 mile (turning left at the first traffic signal) and then turn left into the parking lot. Walk to the restored fortification.*

This defensive position was constructed solely in an attempt to halt Mosby's activities in this area. During the winter of 1864-1865, the 5th Pennsylvania Heavy Artillery was ordered to Vienna with the mission of halting Mosby's marauding in this area considered well behind the Union lines. The soldiers constructed a fort on this rise that commanded an excellent view of the surrounding countryside for many miles. At that time all of the trees in this area had been cut by the troops for use as firewood, and the view was unobstructed. Construction was finished on January 11, 1865 and it was fully manned by a battery of artillery. There was no halt to Mosby's actions.

#31 MOSBY SKIRMISH. *Return to Rt 123, turn right and drive .3 mile.*

On March 12, 1865 Mosby ignored the nearby fort and attacked an Officer, Sergeant, and 20 men of the 13th New York Cavalry near here on the Chain Bridge Road. Union casualties were 2 killed; 5 wounded; and 6 horses killed. The survivors fled into Vienna. Mosby suffered no casualties. One Union cavalryman whose horse was killed was Russel A. Alger who hid in the cellar of a nearby house until Mosby and his Rangers were gone. Alger later became Governor and Senator from Michigan. He served as Secretary of War with distinction and Camp Alger, the Spanish-American War camp established in Dunn Loring, was named for him.

#32 VIENNA. *Continue south on Chain Bridge Road for .7 mile.*

While stationed here, Private William E. "Pony" Ormsley deserted the 2nd Massachusetts Cavalry on January 24, 1864 to join Mosby's Rangers. He took with him two cavalry horses and six pistols. Drinking heavily, he and eight Mosby Rangers attacked his former regiment at Aldie Mill on February 5, 1864. His misfortune was to be captured by his old comrades who were highly displeased with his performance. He was tied to his horse and returned to Vienna. On February 6 he was court-martialed, found guilty of desertion to the enemy, and sentenced to be executed by musketry the following day.

February 7, 1864 was a chilly, cloudy day as the regiments of cavalry camped at Vienna slowly filled three sides of a vacant field. A regimental band playing a dirge led a firing squad pulling an ambulance. Sitting on his crude coffin was Pony Ormsley who, when the procession halted, jumped out and helped unload the pine box.

"William E. Ormsley, do you have anything to say to your fellow soldiers at this moment of your last day on earth?" asked Colonel Charles Russel Lowell.

"This box is mighty hard, men. Hope you put shavings or something inside", said Ormsley.

He then apologized to the group admitting his guilt and stating his punishment was just. He then sat on his coffin and a white paper heart was pinned to his jacket. "Farewell, comrades!" were the last words he spoke. Twenty rifles roared and Ormsley fell backwards over his coffin.

"May God have mercy on his soul", prayed a chaplain. The execution was over, and the remains of William E. Ormsley were buried in an unmarked grave.

Mosby's Rangers were active around Vienna, attracted by the fine horses stabled here by the Federal cavalry. In an early morning raid, fifteen Rangers slipped to the edge of one camp, and three times entered the unguarded stables and brought out horses.

First Lieutenant Frank Williams, a Mosby Ranger who accompanied Mosby in the abduction of General Stoughton during the Fairfax Courthouse raid, lived here after the war. He is buried in the family cemetery at 8501 Electric Avenue. There is a trail angling to the left on this property leading to the cemetery which lies behind the homes on 2222 and 2224 Benedictine Court.

Headquarters, Independent Cavalry Brigade XXII, commanded by Colonel Charles Russel Lowell, was located here during 1863-64. The regiments of this organization continually clashed with Mosby's Rangers.

The First Ohio Infantry Brigade, riding flat cars on the railroad, were ambushed here on June 17, 1861. The first Ohio troops killed during the Civil War were casualties of this skirmish. When the Union Army controlled this area, the railroad resulted in Vienna becoming a supply depot for food and ammunition. The railroad bridges towards Hunter's Mill had been burned by the Confederates early in the war and were never rebuilt leaving Vienna the end of the line.

#33 FLINT HILL CHURCH. *Continue 2.8 miles south on Rt 123. Church is on the left side of the highway.*

A large Confederate fort was constructed where the church now stands following the Union defeat at the First Manassas Battle. The high location provided an excellent view of the roads and the surrounding countryside in that period. When the Confederates withdrew to Centerville from this area during the Fall of 1861, the fort was used as an advanced picket post until the Union Army occupied the area.

THIS IS THE END OF THIS TOUR.

(Continue on Rt 123 and return to Oakton where the tour originally started.)

MOSBY RODE HERE

DELAPLANE — PARIS — UPPERVILLE

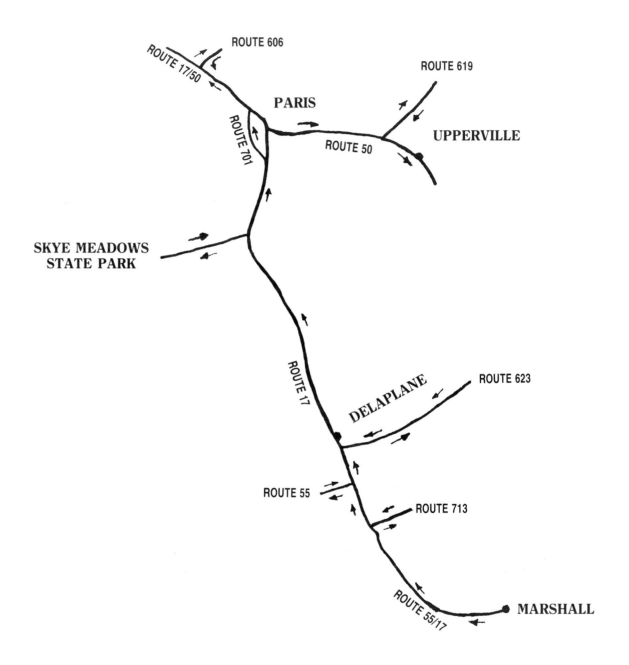

TOUR TWO — OPTION B

Delaplane — Paris — Upperville

THIS TOUR passes through some of the most beautiful countryside in Virginia. A number of historic Mosby related houses are included on this tour including Yew Hill, where "Big Yankee" Ames was killed; Highfield, where Mosby lost his horse and commission to an escaping Union prisoner; Belle Grove, home of Amanda Edmonds whose diary reveals much about Ranger activities in this area; and Mount Bleak, home of Ranger Captain George Slater after the war. Mount Bleak is located in Skye Meadows State Park and a picnic lunch makes a welcome addition to this tour. Visit Mt. Carmel Church where Major "Dolly" Richards severely defeated a Union cavalry force, and the Oakley area where the Rangers lost a sharp skirmish. Heartland, the home of Ranger Joe Blackwell and used as a headquarters by Mosby, was burned to the ground with only a chimney remaining while nearby Brookside, next used as a headquarters, was untouched and remains standing today. There exist many opportunities for photographs on this tour, especially when the leaves are turning colors in the fall.

Tour begins at Marshall (old Salem).

#1 EMMANUEL EPISCOPAL CHURCH. *Continue west on Rts 55 & 17 for 2.1 miles to intersection of Rt 713. Turn right and immediately turn left into the church parking lot.*

In the church cemetery near the front is the grave of Channing Smith, one of Mosby's most able scouts. Following Lee's surrender at Appomattox, it was Smith who Mosby sent into Richmond to see their ex-commander and determine a course of action. General Lee advised Smith to tell the Rangers to return to their homes and help rebuild Virginia.

#2 ASHLEIGH. * *Exit the cemetery and turn right on 713 followed by an immediate right on Rt 55 & 17. Drive .5 mile and Ashleigh is on the left side of the highway.*

Mosby was a visitor here when he was in the neighborhood. Miss Kitty Shacklett of nearby Yew Hill would warn of Union cavalry approaching from the north by waving her apron from her bedroom window where it could be observed from Ashleigh.

Yew Hill. "Big Yankee" Ames was killed near this home where Mosby and Stuart met, June 17, 1863, less than one month before the Battle of Gettysburg.

#3 YEW HILL. * *Continue .1 mile north on Rt 17, turn left on Rt 55, and immediately on the right is Yew Hill.*

"Big Yankee" Ames, a Union deserter who rode with Mosby, was killed here. Ranger Ludwell Lake, Jr., riding on the road, discovered a Yankee going through the pockets of a dead Confederate. He killed the Yankee and discovered the dead Confederate was Big Ames.

Here lived Miss Kitty Shacklett during the war, and she would warn Mosby of the approach of Union troops by waving her apron from an upstairs window towards Ashleigh.

Her brother Hezekiah was threatened with hanging for not taking the Oath of Allegiance to the Federal Government. His arms were bound and he was raised from the ground by a rope over a tree limb in the front yard of the house. He was let down periodically, but refused to take the oath. He recovered from the experience.

Pat Jones writes in *Ranger Mosby*:

"On the 16th of June, 1863, General Jeb Stuart drew up at the house of Miss Kitty Shacklett, near Delaplane in Fauquier and pitched his headquarters tent in the front yard near the road. Next morning, early, a dusty horseman followed by a small entourage of roughly dressed men rode up and dismounted. It was Mosby, ready to join forces with his superior, whom he had not seen since the day General Stoughton was paroled at Culpeper."

George Washington stayed here while surveying his Ashby Bent Gap Run Tract.

To the southeast is Little Cobbler Mountain where Mosby hid several of his artillery pieces. However, an informer told Union soldiers of their location and a Union force captured the cannon during mid-October 1864.

#5 PIEDMONT RAILROAD STATION MARKER.
Return to Rt 17, turn left and drive .1 mile, then turn right on Rt 623.

The Virginia Highway Historical Marker provides information about the Piedmont Railroad Station. The station formerly stood on the right near the warehouse buildings located along the side tracks. From here General "Stonewall" Jackson's troops were transported by rail to the First Manassas Battle.

#6 HEARTLAND.
Continue east on Rt 623 (becoming the dirt road, Chapplear Lane) for 1.4 miles and stop.

One mile to the south are the remains of Heartland (not visible from the road), the home of Mosby Ranger Joseph Blackwell. Blackwell was affectionately known as "The Chief" to the young Rangers in Mosby's command, and his home served as the unofficial headquarters of Mosby and his Rangers when in this neighborhood. Mosby stored records, guns, powder and other supplies here until the "black day" of September 26, 1864 when Union cavalry burned down the house, barns, and outbuildings. Following the fire, Joe Blackwell went to live temporarily at Rosenvix. Mosby turned to Brookside as a new meeting place for his Rangers.

Heartland. A Mosby headquarters.
Union cavalry burned the house.

Following the war a new home, renamed Heartland, was rebuilt on the old foundation, but it also burned. Today only a stone chimney and stone spring house mark the former site of Heartland.

#7 ROSENVIX.
Continue east on Chapplear Lane (Rt 623) for .4 mile.

On the left side of the lane formerly stood Rosenvix, the home of Miss Clotilda Carter. Ranger Joe Blackwell stayed at this house following the destruction of Heartland. On the afternoon of December 21, 1864 Colonel Mosby attended the wedding here of his Ordnance Sergeant, Jake Lavender, and Judith Edmonds, a niece of Miss Carter. Mosby, informed that Union cavalry was leaving Salem and advancing towards Rectortown, left this house with Ranger Tom Love to investigate. Finding the Union troops camped around Rectortown, Mosby and Love scouted towards Rector's Cross-Roads and stopped to eat at Lakeland, the home of Ludwell Lake. Mosby was seriously wounded at Lakeland later that evening.

The site, about .4 mile north of this lane, contains only the rock foundation walls of the old house, all that remains.

#8 BROOKSIDE. * *Continue down the lane 1.2 miles to Brookside.*

After the burning of Heartland, Colonel Mosby often met with his Rangers here in this house and used it as his headquarters. The Holland Mill located here was burned by Union troops.

#9 HIGHFIELD. * *Return to Rt 17, turn right and drive 4.4 miles. Highfield is on the left side of the highway.*

This house was formerly called Hill and Dale by owner Benjamin Triplett during the war.

On March 25, 1864 Mosby and five Rangers crossed the Shenandoah River on a raid and captured four Union Army troopers. He successfully returned arriving here at Triplett's late in the evening. The raiders went into the house leaving the prisoners with one guard at the stile. The guard ordered the prisoners to dismount and secure their horses. One of the prisoners, Corporal Simpson, Company H, Griswald's Light Cavalry, 21st New York Cavalry, pretended to be tying his horse at the same time he was untying Mosby's horse. This he swiftly mounted, and with Mosby's pistols strapped to the fine saddle, galloped off with great speed. One of the other prisoners who had not yet dismounted seized this opportunity to escape, and both managed to evade recapture although vigorously pursued for some distance. Mosby greatly regretted the loss of his fine horse, and his captain's commission carried in the saddle bags of his horse along with other important documents.

The Wrenn brothers, members of Mosby's command, boarded here when in the area. A detachment of Federal cavalry arrived at the house during February, 1864, but before they could surround the house, the Wrenn brothers left it dressed only in their night clothes, and went barefoot over the frozen ground and a creek to Mt. Edie. Here they stayed until the Yankees left, taking all of the horses in the Triplett stables.

#10 BELLE GROVE. * *Continue north on Rt 17 for .4 mile. The house stands on the left side of the highway.*

This is the home of Amanda Virginia Edmonds, whose published diary provided insight into the operations of Mosby's command in this area. Amanda's brothers rode with Mosby and maintained a hideout on the mountains in back of the residence. Several of Mosby's men stayed here at various times during the war. Amanda is buried in the family cemetery near the house.

#11 MT. BLEAK. *Continue for .5 mile on Rt 17 and turn left onto the road leading to Skye Meadows State Park ($1.50 entrance fee). Proceed 1.2 miles to the house called Mt. Bleak.*

This was the home of Dr. Thomas Settle and family during the war. Dr. Settle checked the pulse of the hanged John Brown and officially pronounced him dead following

the execution in Charles Town, West Virginia. Five Mosby Rangers stayed in the attic of this house, a common practice of boarding with friendly local families. Following the war, this was the home of Ranger George Slater. John Mosby, Jr. lived with Slater during several post-war periods.

#12 PARIS. *Return to Rt 17, turn left and drive .8 mile to junction with Rt 701, turn left and go .7 mile to the Ashby Inn located on the left of the highway. Turn left on Rt 659 (Main Street) and go .2 mile.*

Here is the home and office (right on the front lawn) of Dr. Albin Payne. A Mosby Ranger, Lewis Thornton Powell stayed with Dr. Payne while in Mosby's command during 1864-1865. Powell assumed the Payne last name at times due to his friendship with one of Dr. Payne's sons. When Union cavalry patrols made this location dangerous, Powell would evade capture by moving to the Payne home on the side of a mountain on Rt 688.

Powell left Mosby's Rangers in early January, 1865 and became allied with John Wilkes Booth. It was Powell who attacked Secretary of State William H. Seward during the plot to assassinate President Lincoln. Powell was hanged with the other conspirators for his part in the assassination.

An Irishman, Mosby Ranger John Atkins, is buried in the Paris Cemetery on Republican Street. He was killed in a skirmish with the 8th Illinois Cavalry at Dulaney's Farm (Oakley) near Upperville. The cemetery is now overgrown and no headstones may be seen.

#13 HISTORICAL MARKER. *Continue on Main Street to Rt 50, turn left, and note the Virginia Highway Historical Marker just on the right as you enter Rt 50.*

The Virginia Highway Historical Marker denotes the site of a Union Army Signal Station. The movement of Confederate troops was tracked from stations of this type. Confederate General Jackson also bivouacked here.

#14 MT. CARMEL CHURCH. *Continue west on Rt 50 for 1.6 miles and turn right on Rt 606. The church is .1 mile on the right side of the highway and has a parking lot in the front and on the side.*

On February 19, 1865, led by a Southern deserter named Spotts, Major Thomas Gibson crossed the river at Berry's Ferry with 125 troopers from the 14th Pa. Cavalry and 100 from the 21st New York Cavalry seeking Mosby's men who sometimes stayed in homes in that neighborhood. In particular, they were searching for Major Adolphus "Dolly" Richards believed to be at his father's home. Dividing into two groups, one led by Captain Henry Snow and the other by Major Gibson, they searched the area and captured about 25 prisoners. Capt. Snow's men discovered a large cache of whiskey, became drunk, and he was forced to abandon the search.

Belle Grove. Home of Amanda Virginia Edmonds who compiled a diary of life during the war. Her brothers rode with Mosby.

Amanda Virginia "Tee" Edmonds

Courtesy Nancy C. Baird

Dr. Albin Payne's home and office building.
Mosby Ranger Lewis Thornton Powell stayed here.

Lewis Thornton Powell Payne (also spelled "Paine").
Executed for conspiracy in the Lincoln assassination.

National Archives

70

Mt. Carmel Church. Scene of a major Ranger victory when Major "Dolly" Richards struck the rear of a large Union cavalry raiding party. There is a marker nearby.

By now Dolly Richards had become aware of the Federal raid, and fell in behind Major Gibson gathering strength as more and more of Mosby's men joined him. At Mt. Carmel Church the road was narrow and made a sharp bend. Here Richards attacked throwing the Federals into a panic. They were armed with carbines which were no match for pistols at close quarters. The Federals retreated towards the river abandoning their weapons, prisoners, and the loot gathered during the day. Of the Federals, 13 were killed, 63 captured, and 90 horses taken; the Rangers had 1 man wounded. Spotts made good his escape, much to the sorrow of Mosby's men.

There is a granite marker along the highway commemorating the skirmish.

#15 AYRESHIRE FARM. *   *Return to Rt 50, turn left and drive east to the village of Upperville. Just before entering Upperville, turn left on Rt 619 (Trappe Road) and go 2.5 miles.*

Ayreshire Farm on the right side of the highway was frequently visited by Mosby while he was conducting operations in this neighborhood.

#16 STONEHOUSE. *   *Return to Rt 50, turn left and enter the village. From the Post Office on the left, drive .2 mile.*

Heros Von Borcke, a German Officer serving on the staff of General Jeb Stuart, was wounded east of Upperville in a cavalry skirmish. He was brought to the low stone house on the left of the highway to recover.

#17 HIGHWAY MARKER.   *Continue east on Rt 50 for .6 mile.*

This Virginia Highway Historical Marker provides information about the cavalry battle here between the forces of Generals Stuart and Gregg.

#18 OAKLEY. *   *Continue on Rt 50 for .2 mile. House is located on the right side of the highway but is not visible from the entrance.*

The 8th Illinois Cavalry here defeated Mosby's Rangers in a skirmish. The fighting occurred in these fields and around the mansion house of Henry Dulaney. Captain Walter Franklin, with one hundred Rangers under his command, divided his force into two groups. His strategy was to have one group under command of Lieutenant Albert Wrenn attack the enemy in the front, while the second group, led by Lieutenant Charlie Grogan, would make a surprise flank attack.

The Union Cavalry formed in three squadrons to receive the frontal attack which they halted with a steady stream of carbine fire. Grogan, attempting to attack the flank, was slowed by a fence and gate that prevented him from uniting his force with Wrenn. The Rangers lost 4 killed, 4 wounded, and 5 captured. Mosby's Rangers did not always win the day!

THIS IS THE END OF THE TOUR.

MOSBY RODE HERE

MILLWOOD — CHARLES TOWN — HARPERS FERRY

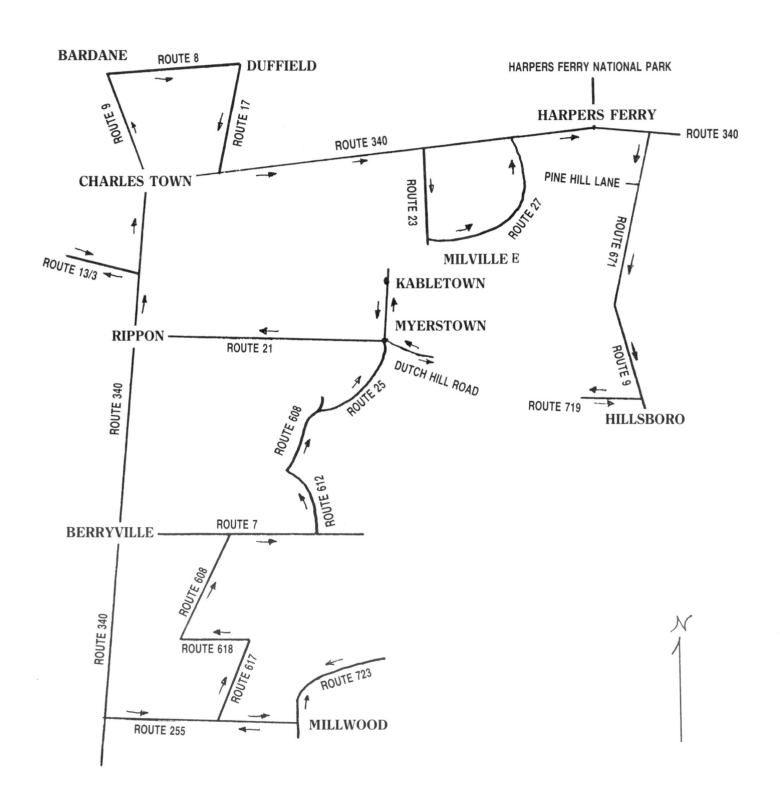

(Middleburg is east; Winchester is to the west.)

TOUR THREE

MILLWOOD — CHARLES TOWN — HARPERS FERRY

THIS TOUR visits some remote areas and takes in a number of skirmish sites. Old Chapel, at the beginning, has a most interesting cemetery and a walk through it with its acrid smell of the boxwood is highly recommended. The Clarke Hotel building still stands, and it was here Mosby met unsuccessfully with Union officers to determine the terms of surrender for the Rangers. On the tour are skirmish sites for the Vinyard, Colonel Morgan's Lane, and Myerstown. The site of the "Greenback Raid" where the Rangers took $173,000 is included. Harpers Ferry National Park is on the edge of this tour and it is recommended time be taken to visit the old armory and museum. There are picnic facilities along the banks of the Potomac River offering a pause for relaxation. Also on this tour is the Headquarters of Cole's Cavalry where Mosby's Rangers suffered a heavy loss in officers during a night attack. The Rangers did not always win their engagements.

Begin the Tour at the intersection of Rt 340 and Rt 255 south of Berryville.

Old Chapel. Contains a monument to local Confederate veterans. Many prominent Civil War veterans are buried here. There is a monument to black servants buried in the cemetery.

Grave of Stuart's aide and author Captain John Esten Cooke.

#1 OLD CHAPEL.   *Turn left on Rt 255 and the chapel is on your immediate right. Parking space is available on both sides of the highway.*

Lord Fairfax worshipped here in the Old Chapel of colonial Fredrick Parish established 1738. This stone building dates from 1790 and witnessed the early ministry (1810-1835) of Bishop Meade. "Governor Edmond Randolph and Colonel Nathaniel Burwell lie in this burying ground with relatives, friends, and neighbors," reads the plaque at this historical building. The acrid smell of the boxwood permeates this beautiful cemetery with its Confederate monument located by the side of the chapel. Here are buried veterans of numerous wars, from early times to the present.

During the latter days of the Civil War, a number of burials of Confederates were conducted during the night when Union Army forces were in the area. Civil War veterans who are buried here include: John Esten Cooke, Stuart's aide and author; Major Hugh M. Nelson, General Ewell's aide; Richard Kidder Meade, Jackson's Ordnance Officer who lost an arm at First Manassas; Francis Key Meade, Richard's brother who served with the Clarke Cavalry; Nathanial Burwell, a private in the 2nd Va. Regiment, "Stonewall Brigade", who died of wounds received at 2nd Battle of Manassas; William Hay, M.D., Surgeon in charge of General Hospital, Staunton, Va. and a 1st Lt. in the "Stonewall Brigade"; and many others. 'Capit' Robert Carter Randolph's stone is written only in Latin; and Lieut. J. L. Vandiver was a Partisan Ranger in McNeil's West Virginia force. Of interest is the area devoted to former slaves and the tombstone of Joanna Throckmorton, "Mammy", who died in 1864 may be seen. Also located here is a monument dedicated in 1957 that reads:

"To the glory of God and in remembrance of the many personal servants buried here before 1865. Faithful and devoted in life, their friends and masters laid them near them in death, with affection and gratitude. Their memory remains, though their wooden markers, like the way of life of that day, are gone forever."

#2 CARTER HALL. *   *Continue east on Rt 255 for 2.8 miles. Not visible from the highway, the mansion is on the left.*

Colonel Mosby ate breakfast here before going to the nearby Clarke's Hotel in Millwood on April 20, 1865. Mosby met there with Union Army officers to discuss surrender terms for himself and the Rangers.

#3 CLARKE HOTEL. *   *Continue on Rt 255 for .2 mile to Millwood. The old Clarke's Hotel is directly in the front of the intersection of Rt 255 with Rt 723.*

This old hotel is where Mosby met with Union Army officers on April 18 and April 20, 1865 to discuss the terms of surrender for himself and his Rangers. It was owned by J. H. Clarke at that time who may have been related to Mosby's

Clarke Hotel. Mosby met here with Union representatives at the end of the war to discuss surrender terms.

wife who was also a Clarke. It was Clarke who let the Federals know that he would contact Mosby, and it was for this reason the hotel was chosen for a meeting place.

Lee's surrender at Appomattox was announced to the people in the area on April 10th, and a move was made with Grant's approval, to have Mosby included in the terms of the surrender. Accordingly, a message to that effect was sent to Clarke. It was the 15th before Mosby replied. He said in effect that the only notice of the surrender he had received had come through the enemy, and he didn't know whether to believe it or not, but that he would agree to a suspension of hostilities until he could decide upon his future action. Some of the men wanted to keep the command intact and go to Mexico, while others wanted to join Joe Johnson still fighting farther south.

General Hancock, in command in this area, agreed to the truce until noon of the following Tuesday, April the 18th. He gave notice that at that date an officer of equal rank would meet Mosby at Millwood to talk terms of surrender.

Mosby ordered a few selected Rangers to meet him at Paris at 10 a.m. on the 18th. When the hour of the meeting scheduled at Millwood arrived, two Rangers came in to announce that Mosby was on his way. Waiting there to meet him was General George H. Chapman, who was thoroughly familiar, by experience, with Mosby's activities. When the meeting began, Mosby asked for an extension of the truce, explaining that he still had not been able to get word from Johnson's army. He also announced he intended to disband his command rather than surrender, and already had told his men that they could give parole if they so desired. As for himself, he didn't intend to stay in the country.

Chapman proposed a 10-day extension of the truce, from April 20th to 30th, provided General Hancock would agree. Mosby was to be notified at Millwood on the 20th of Hancock's decision. Chapman reported the meeting to Hancock, and Hancock informed General Grant who immediately sent back this terse order: "If Mosby does not avail himself of the present truce, end it and hunt him and his men down. Guerillas will not be entitled to quarter."

One reason for Grant's decision may have been the report that Mosby had taken part in the assassination of President Lincoln on the 14th. Actually he hadn't, but one of his men, Louis Thornton Powell (Payne) Paine, was involved. It was he who stabbed the bedridden Secretary of State Seward. Chapman sent Mosby word that the truce would end at noon of the 20th and that an officer would be at Clarke's Hotel to talk terms at that time.

Mosby was at Millwood on the 20th, but still refused to surrender. While he was conferring with Chapman, one of his men, John Hearn, rushed in and excitedly reported that a trap had been set for them. Hearn had been on the outside racing horses with some of Chapman's soldiers and came suddenly upon a Yankee column moving up the road. He got the idea that Mosby had been tricked. At any rate, Mosby immediately broke off the meeting and marched out of the room saying, "Sir, if we are no longer under the protection of our truce, we are, of course, at the mercy of your men. We shall protect ourselves." Outside he said to his men, "Mount and follow me," and rode away. The truce had failed.

On November 11, 1864 Scout John Russell of Mosby's command stopped here on his way from Rectortown to Winchester to deliver a message from Mosby to Sheridan explaining that the soldiers hung and shot at Grindstone Hill were in retaliation for General Custer's misconduct. Russell was successful in delivering the message.

#5 VINEYARD FIGHT. *Turn left on Rt 723 and continue east for 2 miles to the granite marker on the left side of the highway.*

On December 15, 1864 Captain Sam Chapman crossed the river at Berry's Ferry with the objective of attacking a Federal cavalry force that habitually rode down to check the river by way of either Millwood or Bethel roads. He split his command giving about 60 men to Lt. John Russell to make an ambush in the woods on Millwood road in case the Federals came that way. About noon of the 16th Russell observed Captain William H. Miles and 100 troopers of the 14th Pa. Cavalry cautiously approaching. They had been warned by a black man living in the area that Mosby's men were about. Lt. Russell told his men, "We can't get back across the river without being butchered, so the only safe thing to do is whip them. Don't fire a shot until you are within 40 steps of them and we will whip them." The Federals fought valiantly, but Capt. Miles was killed along with 9 of his men. 20 Union troopers were wounded, 68 were taken prisoner, and 60 horses captured. Lt. Russell's tactics had saved the day for his men who suffered not a single casualty.

Clarke Store. Scout John Russell paused here for information enroute to deliver a message from Mosby to General Sheridan.

#4 CLARKE STORE. *Directly on the left is the old store building.*

Skirmish in Colonel Morgan's Lane.
Williamson, MOSBY'S RANGERS

#6 COLONEL MORGAN'S LANE. *Turn around and return on Rt 723 to Millwood, turn right on Rt 255, and go to the intersection with Rt 617 at the railroad overpass. Turn right on Rt 617 and drive .9 mile to Rt 618, turn left and go 2.1 miles to Rt 608. Drive 1.9 miles on Rt 608 to the granite marker at the left side of the highway.*

Mosby's scouts, on the night of the 18th, attacked a picket post of the 5th Michigan Cavalry at Castleman's Ferry, killing one soldier, wounding one, and taking 2 prisoners. In retaliation for this act, General Custer ordered the burning of houses in the neighborhood. This was done on August 19th by a detachment of 50 men; however, in several instances the arrival of Mosby's men prevented loss of some residences.

The raiders had burned Colonel Benjamin Morgan's house and were leaving when they were attacked by Captain William Chapman and his company of Rangers. Enraged by the burning, Chapman vowed "no prisoners" and his men killed 30 of the party in and around the lane. All were members of the 5th Michigan Cavalry.

This lane was the entrance to Hill and Dale, the estate of Colonel Benjamin Morgan during the war.

#7 MYERSTOWN.
Continue north on Rt 608 for 1.6 miles to Rt 7, turn right and travel 2.3 miles to Rt 612 on the left. Turn left on Rt 612 and go 1.9 miles to Rt 608. Drive on Rt 608 for 2.5 miles to Rt 25 (Kabletown Road). Turn right on Rt 25 and go 2.9 miles to the intersection with Rt 21 (Rippon Road).

On the left on the porch of the house is stone marker number fifteen (Slaughter and Capture of Blazer's Men at Myerstown).

Skirmish site near Kabletown. Major "Dolly" Richards lured Captain Blazer's Scouts into an ambush here.

#8 SKIRMISH SITE.
Turn right on Dutch Hill-Avon Bend Road and go .4 mile.

In the depression and low hills to the right was fought a skirmish between one hundred picked men from the Union cavalry under command of Captain Richard Blazer, and an equal number of Mosby's Rangers under the command of "Dolly" Richards. This area was known as "Betheny". After searching for each other for two days, Richards discovered Blazer camped at Kabletown on the early morning of

November 18, 1864. Richards quickly withdrew south on the Kablestown-Myerstown Road and then east on the river road with his Rangers. Blazer's scouts quickly discovered the movement and followed.

Concealing one-half of his men in the woods behind a small hill, he used the other body of Rangers to appear to be rapidly retreating from the scene. Blazer took the bait and was lured into a deadly trap when the concealed Rangers hit his flank. Mosby's men completely routed the enemy, killing 22, wounding an undetermined number, and capturing Blazer and all but 2 of the group. Blazer's Scouts ceased to exist!

#9 KABLETOWN.
Turn around and return to the Myersville-Kabletown Road, turn right and drive .7 mile.

Marker. Note stone marker number 17 (General Bradley T. Johnson Repulses the Enemy Near Kabletown).

Blacksmith's Shop. Continue .1 mile over the bridge into Kabletown. On the left side of the road formerly stood the Blacksmith's Shop where 22 of Blazer's dead were laid in a row on the floor following the skirmish.

Ruins of Union Church used as a hospital for Blazer's wounded following the skirmish.

Union Church. Continue for .4 mile to the ruins of the church standing on the left side of the road in undergrowth.

Blazer's wounded used this church as a hospital, leaving blood stains on the floor that were visible for years afterwards.

Blazer's Camp. Turn around and return on the Kabletown-Myersville road towards Myersville.

As you leave town Blazer's Camp was in the field on the left when Richards discovered him.

Puryear's Revenge. On the day before the skirmish, Ranger John Puryear had been taken prisoner, and in an effort to force information from him, Lieutenant Cole of Blazer's Scouts had a rope placed around Puryear's neck and thrown over a tree limb. He was then pulled up several times while threatened to be hanged if he didn't provide information about the Rangers. Puryear would not speak. The threat was not carried out, but Puryear was left with rope burns on his neck for the rest of his life. During the skirmish Puryear escaped from his captors, found a pistol, and sought out Lieutenant Cole. Cole had surrendered, however Puryear killed him on the spot.

#10 HEFFLEBOWER HOUSE. * *At Myerstown, turn right on Rt 21 (Myerstown-Rippon Road) and drive 3.6 miles.*

On the right side of the road is the Hefflebower House. During the confusion of the skirmish at Myerstown, Captain Richard Blazer, commander of the one hundred men picked to destroy the Rangers, attempted to escape up this road from Myerstown to Rippon. Four Mosby Rangers, Sam Alexander, Cab Maddux, Lewis Thornton Powell (known as ''Powell The Terrible'' for his fighting demeanor), and Syd Ferguson gave chase. Ferguson, on his swift horse ''Fashion'', finally caught up with Blazer, knocked him from his horse, and took him prisoner in front of this house.

#11 CLAYMONT. * *Continue west on Rt 21 for .3 mile to Rippon, turn right on Rt 340, and travel 4.5 miles to Rt 13/3. Turn left and go 2.2 miles west.*

The lane on the right leads into Claymont, a former home of the Washington Family and now used as a school. Here in 1864 the Union cavalry captured two youthful Mosby Rangers, James Washington and Herbert Alexander. Sent to prison at Point Lookout, Maryland both boys died from the harsh prison conditions. The Union cavalry destroyed and burned Claymont's fences, and drove off all of the livestock but one milk cow, as the penalty for harboring guerillas.

#12 CHARLES TOWN. *Return to Rt 340, turn left and drive 1.9 miles to Charles Town.*

Mosby's Rangers constantly made forays into this area to attack Union Army picket posts.

Courthouse. *Turn right on East Washington Street and go to the intersection with South George Street (intersection of Rt 340 and Rt 9).*

On the left is the Charles Town Courthouse where the trial of John Brown was conducted.

Jefferson County Museum. *Continue north on Washington Street (340) to the intersection with South Samuel Street. Turn left and park on the street or in the nearby lot.*

The Jefferson County Museum is located in the basement of the library and contains many interesting exhibits.

John Brown Scaffold. *Turn around and return on Samuel Street across Rt 340 (Washington Street) for .4 mile.*

In the yard of the Perkins House on the left is the site of the scaffold where John Brown was hanged. A marker provides information.

#13 GREENBACK RAID. *Return to Rt 340 (Washington Street), and turn right on Rt 9 at the Charles Town Courthouse. Follow Rt 9 west for 5.5 miles through Ranson to Bardane.*

Turn right on Rt 8 which immediately crosses the Baltimore and Ohio Railroad tracks. This was known as Brown's Crossing during the war. Park at the side of the road and walk west for about 200 yards alongside of the tracks around the curve where there is a track siding. This was Quincy's Siding.

Mosby's famous Greenback Raid took place here on October 13, 1864 in a deep cut now leveled in areas along the track. Mosby and eighty-three Rangers conducted this raid during the dark hours of the autumn night on a B & O passenger express train coming west from Harpers Ferry and passing through Kearneysville two miles further along the track. The train consisted of a locomotive, tender, an Adams Express Company car, and nine coaches filled with passengers. After derailing the train, Mosby's Rangers emptied the cars, damaged the locomotive, and set the train afire. Two Army Paymasters among the passengers were found to be carrying $173,000. The money was taken back to Loudoun County and divided next day between the Rangers at Ebenezer Chapel near Bloomfield. Each Ranger who participated in the raid received nearly $2100 apiece. Mosby, as was his custom, refused his share and had it distributed among his men. Each of the Rangers chipped in and purchased the horse ''Croquette'' for him. This was a horse he had admired at ''Oatlands'' near Leesburg and which later became his favorite horse.

Duffield Station. Typical Jefferson County Marker identifies location where Mosby captured the entire Union garrison guarding the railroad.

Wreck of B & O express train following the Greenback Raid.
Smithsonian Institution

#14 DUFFIELD STATION. *Continue north on Rt 8 for 2.4 miles to intersection with Rt 17, turn right and drive .1 mile. Stone marker number 9 (Capture by Mosby) is on the left in the yard next to the railroad tracks.*

During July, 1864 Mosby surprised and captured the entire garrison of 100 Union soldiers at this location. The station and log guard house formerly stood on the right beside the tracks.

#15 MILVILLE. *Continue on Rt 17 for 5.1 miles to Rt 340, turn left and go 2.5 miles to Rt 23 (Blair Road). Turn right on Rt 23 and go 1.5 miles to Rt 27, turn left and go .3 mile to the railroad crossing.*

Directly in front in the yard wall is stone marker number 23 (Surprise for Loudoun Rangers at Keye's Switch).

On April 5, 1865 the newly formed Company H of Mosby's Rangers under command of Captain George Baylor, made a surprise attack upon their old adversaries, the Loudoun Rangers, the only unit from Virginia to fight in the Union Army. The Loudoun Rangers were camped here at Keye's Switch (Milville). Passing the Union infantry camp at nearby Halltown, the Rangers charged into this camp, killing 2, wounding 4, and capturing 65 prisoners. The Rangers had only 1 man wounded.

#16 HARPERS FERRY. *Continue on Rt 27 a distance of 2.2 miles to Rt 340, turn right and continue to the bridge over the Potomac River.*

To the left is Harpers Ferry and a National Park that is well worth a visit. The firehouse where John Brown made his final stand and was captured is located here. There is a museum with Civil War exhibits and an excavation where the arsenal formerly stood before being destroyed during the war. Rifle barrels are still visible in the pit. Harpers Ferry changed hands several times during the war. The nearby Potomac River was an attraction to the soldiers who constantly sought bathing facilities. For an episode about the dangers of swimming see Appendix J.

#17 LOUDOUN HEIGHTS AND COLE'S HEADQUARTERS. * *Cross over the bridge and follow Rt 340 to the intersection with Rt 671 on the right. The distance from the intersection of Rt 27 and Rt 340 with Rt 671 is 3.5 miles. Turn right on Rt 671 and go .5 mile to the top of the hill.*

Mosby's January 9, 1864 night attack here on the camp of Union Major Henry Cole was a disaster. Mosby suffered his most serious defeat of the war at this location across from the Union garrison at Harpers Ferry.

January 9th was a bitter cold day with a foot of snow on the ground when Major Mosby and scout Frank Stringfellow made a joint attack on Cole's camp. Cole had his headquarters in this house on the right and about two hundred of his command were camped in tents in the surrounding fields. Mosby and one hundred-six Rangers left Upperville around 3 p.m., moved through Round Hill, stopped, rested, and ate at Wood Grove before riding to the base of Loudoun Heights to join Frank Stringfellow and ten of his men.

It was decided Stringfellow and his men would attack Cole's headquarters on top of the mountain while Mosby and his Rangers would climb the mountain by a little used pathway and attack the camp of the cavalrymen. A Union sentry heard the approach of Mosby's men up the mountain, fired his carbine, and all coordination between Mosby and Stringfellow was lost as the two attacking groups mistakenly exchanged gun fire. Cole's cavalry, awakened by the shooting and shouting of the attackers, learned a basic fact — a man sitting on horseback makes a better target at night than does a man on the ground. Cole's cavalrymen rallied and fought back, quickly driving the attackers back towards Hillsboro.

Mosby's six dead included several of his most able officers, Captain William R. Smith and Charlie Paxton. Lieutenant Tom Turner was mortally wounded and several other Rangers suffered wounds. Cole's casualties were 4 dead and 16 wounded. Learning from this failed attack, Mosby was reluctant to make further night attacks.

#18 LEVI WALTERS HOUSE. * *Continue south on Rt 671 for 1.5 miles to the intersection with Pine Hill Lane.*

This is the home where Mosby was forced to leave the mortally wounded Lieutenant Tom Turner. Turner died a week later from his wound.

#19 JOHN MOBBERLY GRAVE. *Continue south on Rt 671 for .5 mile to the cemetery of the Old Salem Church. Park at the gate on the right side of the highway.*

Serving early in Lige White's cavalry, a scout and a guerilla, John Mobberly joined with whatever Confederate forces offered him an opportunity to strike at the Union forces. Guerilla actions along the Potomac River were brutal, leading Union General E. B. Tyler to send his headquarters the following message:

"These men are supposed to belong to a Lieutenant Mobberly's gang of outlaws. I have instructed my command not to bring any of them to my headquarters except for interment".

Mobberly's end came as the result of an engagement with The Independent Loudoun (VA) Rangers (Union Army) near Waterford when Mobberly rode his horse over the wounded Sergeant Charles B. Stewart as he lay helpless on the ground. Mobberly then leaned over the fallen Stewart and fired his pistol into Stewart's face, inflicting a bloody and painful wound that was nearly fatal. He then dismounted and stole Stewart's new boots.

Headquarters of Cole's Cavalry. Attacking here during the night, the Rangers suffered their most serious defeat of the war.

Frank Stringfellow. Scouted Cole's Cavalry camp and located the headquarters for Mosby's attack.

Courtesy Mrs. Roger Boyle

Levi Walters House. Mosby Ranger Lieutenant Tom Turner died here from a wound received during the attack on Cole's Cavalry.

Guerilla John W. Mobberly.
Shot by the Loudoun Rangers.

Courtesy Horace Mewborn

Sergeant Stewart had time to think about Mobberly during his convalescence. On April 3, 1865 Stewart and two hand-picked Loudoun Rangers crossed the Potomac River and made their way to the barn on the Luther Potterfield farm. Word had been spread that a prize horse was there that would benefit the hard-riding Mobberly. Early on the morning of April 5th, Mobberly rode into the farm yard and directly to the barn. He stopped in dismay when he recognized Sergeant Stewart standing in the dark entrance way pistols on the ready. "Oh Lord, I'm gone!" were Mobberly's last prophetic words. When his bullet-riddled body was delivered to Union headquarters at Harpers Ferry, it was noticed he was not wearing boots!

Mobberly's gravestone is deserving of a photograph. It reads:

> JOHN W. MOBBERLY
> Member of Company A, White's
> Battalion of Va Cavl'y,
> was born June 1, 1844,
> was assassinated
> April 5th 1865
> Aged 20 years 10
> mo's & 4 days.

**Grave of John W. Mobberly.
Verses on the back are
badly weathered.**

Legend states the verses on the back were added by Mobberly's lady friends, of whom it is rumored, several existed.

God bless thee, brave soldier,
Thy life dream is o're;
For country and freedom,
Thou will battle no more.

To the land of the blessed,
Thou has gone to depart;
With a smile on thy face,
And a joy in thy heart.

Thrice hallowed the green spot,
There our hero is laid:
His deeds from our memory,
Shall never more fade.

The stranger will say,
As he lingers around;
'Tis the grave of a hero,
'Tis liberty's mound.

#20 HILLSBORO. *Continue south for .6 mile, then turn left and drive east towards Hillsboro. Just prior to entering the town, turn right on Stoney Point Road (Rt 719) and go 1.4 miles to the intersection with Woodgrove Road. When finished, return to Rt 9.*

The "Great Burning Raid" was a major effort to clear the valley of food and forage for Mosby's Rangers and to hinder their activities. Everything that could aid Mosby was put to the torch between November 28 through December 2, 1864. To the right side of the highway stand the remains of Pott's Mill, a woolen mill, burned during the raid. Most of the damage from the raid was either rebuilt or razed. This is believed to be the sole remaining evidence of the raid now remaining in the county.

**Pott's Mill. Burned by Union cavalry seeking to clear
Mosby from the valley. This is believed to be the
only remaining ruin in the county.**

THIS IS THE END OF THE TOUR.

MOSBY RODE HERE

RICHMOND — CENTRAL VIRGINIA — CHARLOTTESVILLE

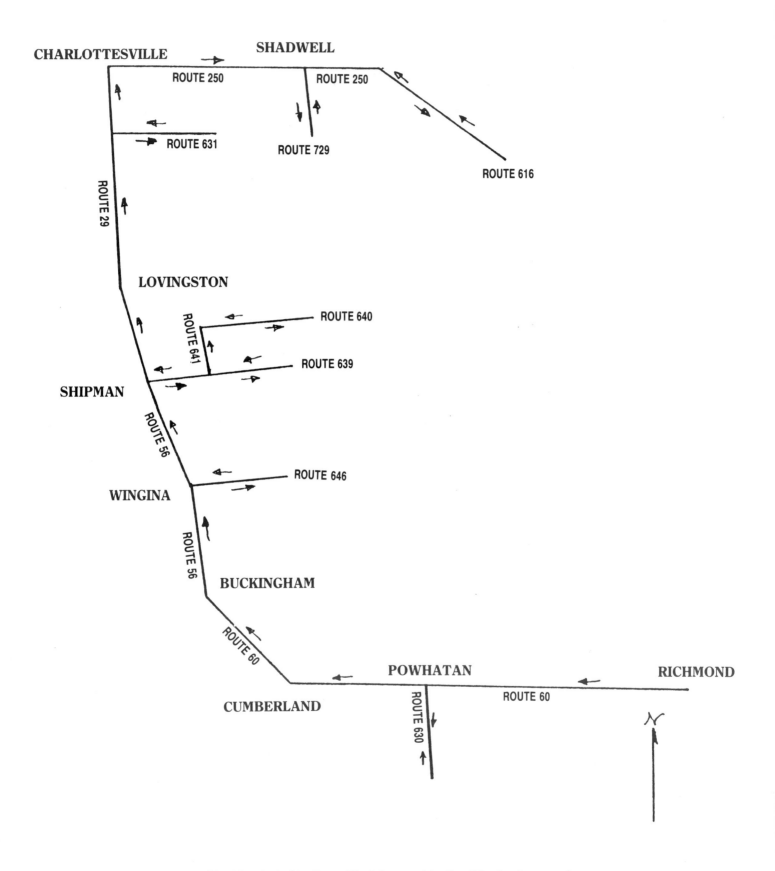

(East leads to Northern Virginia; west to the Winchester area.)

TOUR FOUR

RICHMOND — CENTRAL VIRGINIA — CHARLOTTESVILLE

THIS TOUR is through central Virginia and starts at the American Historical Foundation Museum in Richmond. There are many interesting displays here beside Mosby articles. Hollywood cemetery contains the graves of several Mosby Rangers as well as a monument to "Big Yankee" Ames. Many of the well known Confederate generals are buried here as is President of the Confederacy Jefferson Davis. Several Mosby homes and home sites are on this tour. Mosby attended the University of Virginia until he shot George Turpin in a dispute. The Albermarle Courthouse and jail still stand as does the law office of Judge Robertson who encouraged Mosby to enter the study of law. Mosby remained friends with the Judge throughout his life.

**American Historical Foundation Museum.
Displays memorabilia of Mosby and General Jeb Stuart.**

#1 AMERICAN HISTORICAL FOUNDATION MUSEUM.
1142 West Grace Street.

This historic old building offers the Stuart-Mosby Room containing personal and war mementoes of both men. The museum is open from 8:30 a.m.-5 p.m. Monday through Friday.

**#2 VIRGIL C. JONES HOUSE. ** *Continue east on Grace Street to 1106 West Grace Street on the left side of the street.*

In this apartment building was conceived the idea of writing a biography of Colonel John S. Mosby. The first twelve chapters of *Ranger Mosby* were written here by noted Civil War historian and author Virgil Carrington Jones. An explosion and fire that killed the building custodian almost destroyed the manuscript.

#3 HOLLYWOOD CEMETERY. *Continue east on Grace Street to Belvedere Boulevard, turn right and enter the Downtown Expressway. Drive to the second traffic signal and turn right on Albemarle Street. Proceed to the intersection with Cherry Avenue and turn into the cemetery.*

A number of Mosby Rangers are buried within this cemetery. A marker to James F. "Big Yankee" Ames stands beside the tall Confederate pyramid monument in the Confederate Soldier's section of the cemetery. Mosby's friend and commanding officer, General Jeb Stuart is buried here.

Confederate generals and President Jefferson Davis are buried here because of the location of the former capital of the Confederacy.

Monument to James F. "Big Yankee" Ames.

#4 EDGEMONT. * (Mosby's birthplace.) *Exit from the cemetery onto Cherry Avenue and continue north over the Downtown Expressway. Turn left on Cumberland Avenue and enter the exit ramp onto the Downtown Expressway West. Follow the expressway and exit onto the Powhite Parkway West. Continue over the James River and exit west on the Midlothian Turnpike (Rt 60). Continue west until the dual highway decreases into two lane traffic in Powhatan County. Continue 8.3 miles and turn left on Rt 630 (Ballsville Road). Travel .5 mile to 2211 Ballsville Road. You are approximately 35 miles west of Richmond and 10 miles east of Cumberland Courthouse.*

The large two story house on the right is Edgemont, now the home of the gracious Mr. and Mrs. Warren C. West and their family. The Wests purchased this deteriorated home in 1978 and have beautifully restored it. It was moved about two-thirds of a mile from its original location.

Edgemont was built by William Chamberlayne in 1764; it was purchased by James McLaurine in 1794. James McLaurine's daughter Virginia married Colonel Mosby's father, Alfred Daniel Mosby here. Virginia Mosby returned to give birth to her son John in a second story bedroom. Colonel Mosby visited here several times during the war.

Following the end of the war, General Robert E. Lee lived for a brief period at Derwent, a short drive from here.

#5 VALLEY FARM * *Return to Rt 60 and turn left traveling through Cumberland and Buckingham Counties. Shortly before Buckingham Courthouse, turn right on Rt 56 and drive west crossing the James River into Nelson County at Wingina. Drive 4.5 miles and turn right on Rt 646. Travel 1 mile and Valley Farm is on the left side of the highway.*

This house was used as a hideout by Colonel Mosby due to its remoteness and "the worst roads ever inflicted on mankind by God". It was the home of John Ware Mosby, Colonel Mosby's uncle and the person for which he was named. Colonel Mosby narrowly escaped capture here by a Union Army patrol near the end of the war. Following the end of hostilities, Colonel Mosby was here and his uncle thought it wise to send Ranger John Hipkins, Co. H, into Richmond to determine the Federal attitude towards a parole for his nephew.

Several members of General Longstreet's staff stayed here briefly following the surrender at nearby Appomattox.

#6 BOYHOOD HOME. * *Return to Rt 646 and turn right. Continue west on Rt 56 10 miles to Shipman. Cross the railroad tracks and turn right on Rt 639. Travel 3.6 miles to Rt 641, turn left and proceed .5 mile. Turn right on Rt 640 for 2.1 miles.*

200 yards on the left is the site of Colonel Mosby's boyhood home which was located in a clearing on a hill about one fourth mile from the road at the foot of Mosby's (Helm) Mountain. The only remains of the home are three rows of foundation stones. There is a cemetery west containing three fieldstone markers. The spring used by the family still flows from the roots of a beech tree located near the house site. The foundation stones are behind a weatherboard building with a rusted tin roof. The house either fell down or was demolished around 1940.

The WPA Historical Houses Inventory of 1937 for Nelson County describes the home as a plain one and one-half story, five room frame building with a steeped roof. All the timbers were hewn by hand and held together with locust pins and shop-made nails. The flooring was constructed of wide planks. The fireplaces were very large and had plain mantels over them. There was a chimney at each end of the house and a small one story porch in front.

There is a Virginia Historical Marker on Rt 29 near Woods Mill in Nelson County recognizing this home. The Mosby Family moved from here to Albermarle County around 1841.

#7 MURRELL'S SHOP SCHOOL. *Return to Rt 640, turn left on Rt 641 and return to Rt 639. Turn left on Rt 639 and proceed 1.3 miles to where the old wagon road crosses Rt 639. This is now a narrow two-track lane into the woods. Park on Rt 639 and walk up this lane about 50 yards.*

This overgrown area was formerly Murrell's Shop having a wheelwright's and a blacksmith shop. A home and several

The Homes of Mosby

Edgemont, the birthplace of Mosby.
The house was restored by Mr. and Mrs. Warren C. West.

Valley Farm. A hideout of Colonel Mosby and
the home of his uncle John Ware Mosby.

The Boyhood Home stood behind this farm house.

Mosby's Boyhood Home. These foundation rocks are all that
remain of the house which stood in Nelson County.

other buildings were once in this small settlement but are long vanished. The old log school house stood on the south side of the old road that ran from Warminster on the James River to the stagecoach road in Throughfare Gap.

Mosby attended this school when he was six - seven years old and here encountered his first drunken man, his schoolmaster. It so impressed his memory that he later gave it as the main reason why he never took freely of strong drink and why he prohibited the use of liquor among his Rangers.

Tudor Grove. Owned by the Mosby Family from 1841-1857. Remarks by a fellow student about a party Mosby held here led to the shooting incident. An early photograph.

Tudor Grove as it appears today.

#8 TUDOR GROVE. * *Return (Ebenezer Baptist Church is on your right) on Rt 639 to Shipman. Turn right and go west to Rt 29 at Lovingston. Turn right on Rt 29 and drive north crossing the Rockfish River at Woods Mills. About 2.5 miles is a Virginia Highway Historical Marker on the*

Marker on the right. Continue on Rt 29 approaching Charlottesville and exit onto Business Rt 29 (Fountaine Avenue). Travel .7 mile to Jefferson Park Avenue, turn right and go .5 mile. Exit right on the Old Lynchburg Road (Rt 631) and drive 2.1 miles to the bottom of the hill. The stone entrance to Tudor Grove is on the right. Unfortunately, the house is not visible from the road.

The Mosby Family owned Tudor Grove with its surrounding 395 acres from 1841-1857. John S. Mosby was eight years old when his family moved here. The original brick home has been altered extensively and enlarged. Following a party here George Turpin made slurring remarks that resulted in his wounding by Mosby. Mosby hunted and rode horses regularly while living here, creating a solid basis for his shooting ability while riding during the war.

Mosby attended school at nearby Frye's Woods and Charlottesville. He later entered the University of Virginia.

#9 UNIVERSITY OF VIRGINIA.   *Return on Old Lynchburg Road to Jefferson Park Avenue, turn left and drive to the intersection with Emmet Street. The University of Virginia "grounds" are directly ahead. Turn left on Emmet Street and drive to Main Street, turn right and school grounds are on both sides of the street. After passing Rugby Street the Rotunda Building is on the right.*

John S. Mosby entered the University in 1850 and had an excellent scholastic record during his first two years. He was expelled following the shooting of George Turpin which occurred at Brock's Boarding House where Mosby was living while a student.

In 1915 the eighty-two year old Mosby was invited to return to the University to be honored with a medal and scroll during a ceremony. A painting of Mosby now hangs on the wall of Alderman Library.

#10 ALBERMARLE COUNTY COURTHOUSE.   *Drive east on Main Street to the intersection with McIntyre Road in downtown Charlottesville, turn left for one block, then right on Preston Avenue. Keep left and go east on East Market Street. Turn left on North 5th Street, go one block and face the old Albermarle County Courthouse in Court Square.*

This is where Mosby was tried for the shooting of fellow student George Turpin. The prosecuting attorney for Albermarle County was the outstanding lawyer, and later judge, William Joseph Robertson with whom Mosby became life-long friends. Mosby always had a photograph of Judge Robertson on the wall of his law office.

Mosby was convicted of unlawful shooting, fined $500, and sentenced to one year in jail. With the aid of a petition signed by 298 individuals, Mosby shortly received a pardon from the Governor of Virginia.

Mosby and The University of Virginia

Albermarle County Courthouse. Mosby was tried here while a student at the University of Virginia when he shot a fellow student.

Jailor's House and Jail. Mosby was confined here following his conviction for wounding a fellow student.

Judge William J. Robertson. Prosecutor of Mosby for the shooting of a fellow student, he became a life-long friend.

Courtesy Lindsay Robertson

Judge Robertson's Law Office. Mosby studied law in this office.

Medal awarded Mosby by the University of Virginia. Mosby greatly treasured this award and recognition by the University.

Courtesy Admiral Beverly Mosby Coleman

88

More Mosby Homes

Clifton. Mosby's wife and children "refugeed" here late in the war.

Cumber. (Dancing Hall.) Home owned by Mosby's father, Alfred Daniel Mosby, from 1854-1862.

#11   JUDGE ROBERTSON'S LAW OFFICE.   *At 220 Court Square, just to the right of the courthouse, stands the former law office of Judge William J. Robertson who prosecuted Mosby.*

Judge Robertson became friends with the young Mosby, permitted him to borrow his law books while he was in jail, and encouraged him to undertake the study of law. Later Mosby would study here in this office and discuss issues with the judge. The building now houses the Albermarle County Historical Society.

#12   ALBERMARLE COUNTY JAIL.   *Drive left of Court Square, turn right on North Fourth Street and go one block and turn right on East High Street. Travel one-half block and turn into 409 East High Street.*

Here stands the old jail with its stone walls and barred windows. Mosby was a prisoner here following his trial, and it was here that he first studied law.

The brick jailor's house is now municipal offices.

#13   WILLIAM J. ROBERTSON HOUSE. *   *Return to East High Street, turn left and go one-half block to Park Street. Turn left on Park Street and drive north to 705 Park Street, the former home of Judge Robertson.*

Mosby was a welcome visitor in this home when he was in the Charlottesville area. On April 23, 1896 while riding with Judge Robertson's daughter in a buggy, he was kicked in the face by the horse resulting in the loss of the sight in his left eye.

#14   CLIFTON. *   *Continue north on Park Street to the Rt 250 By-Pass, turn right and follow Rt 250 east 4 miles to Shadwell. At the intersection with Rt 279 turn right and drive .2 mile. Clifton is on the left of the highway.*

Here is the home where Mosby's wife Pauline, with their children May and Beverly (and later a baby — John Mosby, Jr.), "refugeed" during the later part of the war upon being forced to abandon the Hathaway House near Middleburg. They remained for the duration of the war. Mosby visited his family here and sent medicines to his family and other scarce necessities captured in Northern Virginia. When Union Army patrols were roving about, these were left in a hollow depression in an old pine tree near the entrance to the house. This tree was afterwards known as the "Mosby Pine".

#15   CUMBER. *   (Dancing Hall.)   *Return on Rt 729 to Rt 250, turn right and travel east 3.6 miles to the intersection of Rt 250 and Rt 616. Turn right and drive 3.2 miles and Cumber is located to the right of the highway.*

Colonel Mosby's father, Alfred Daniel Mosby, owned this farm from 1854-1862. Accordingly, from 1854-1857 the older Mosby had dual responsibility for two farms: Tudor Grove in Albermarle County and Dancing Hall in Fluvanna County. The Mosby Family moved to McIvor's Station in Arnherst County north of Lynchburg. William Mosby, Colonel Mosby's younger brother, spent his childhood here at Dancing Hall. He later joined his brother's command as adjutant and served with distinction throughout the war.

THIS IS THE END OF THIS TOUR.

(Return to Rt 50. From here east will lead to Richmond, west to Charlottesville.)

Artifacts of Mosby's Confederacy

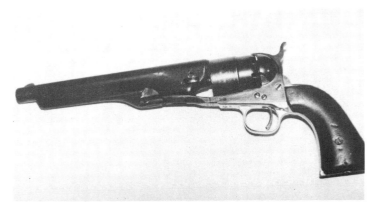

Ranger Ned Hurst's revolver.
He killed 18 Union cavalrymen with this gun during the war.
Old Gaol Museum

Bullet removed from the wounded
Ranger John P. DeButts.
Courtesy Arthur DeButts

Ranger John M. Lawrence's pistol and powder horn.
Warren Rifles Confederate Museum

Stick pin owned by Ranger Ludwell Lake, Jr. made
from a Union uniform button of a cavalryman Lake
killed when he discovered him rifling the uniform
pockets of the dead "Big Yankee" Ames.
Courtesy John K. Gott

Colonel Mosby's spurs
Warren Rifles Confederate Museum

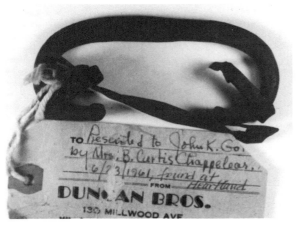

Handle from an ammunition chest found in the
ruins of Heartland, burned by Union cavalry
when they discovered it was being used
by Mosby as a headquarters.
Courtesy John K. Gott

ADDITIONAL TOURING INFORMATION

THERE ARE a number of sites that can not be conveniently added to a tour due to their out of the way locations. Because many of these are referenced in publications about Colonel Mosby and the Rangers, we have collected them in this chapter and have provided directions for driving there. It is regrettable that many of the structures no longer stand, having given way to modern requirements. Unfortunately, historic significance is not always given much consideration when present day needs arise and when building maintenance costs increase so dramatically with age.

Ewell's Chapel. No longer standing. A skirmish occurred here when a Union spy reported the Rangers were in the area.

EWELL'S CHAPEL. A skirmish occurred here on June 22, 1864, when a spy reported Mosby and his Rangers would be riding through this area, and an ambush was planned by Federal forces. Forty cavalry and one hundred of the Seventeenth Pennsylvania Volunteer Infantry under command of Captain Harvey Brown hurriedly marched to the chapel. Captain Brown posted his men around the chapel area and sent a small detachment of cavalry out as bait to lure Mosby into an attack. A sergeant with s spy glass was posted in a tall tree near the lane to the Ewell home to provide information about Mosby's maneuvers. Two local lads and a black boy searching for cattle were apprehended and locked in the chapel to prevent their spreading word of the presence of the Federal force.

Mosby and thirty Rangers arrived, attacked the small band of cavalry and chased them towards the chapel. Suspecting a trap, the Rangers suddenly broke off the chase and departed back into the mountains from where they had come. Mosby, detecting the sergeant in the tree, personally shot him from his perch and he was the only casualty of the conflict. The infantry's long range rifle fire was not effective, and the cavalry pursued for over a mile before they lost the trail of the Rangers. The sergeant from the Seventeenth Pennsylvania killed during the skirmish was left behind, much to the disgust of the Ewell family, and had to be buried by a neighbor.

Reporting the incident to headquarters, Major General George G. Meade stated: "I came near catching our friend Mosby this morning." But the plan had failed, and Mosby captured four wagons and six mules a short distance from the chapel later in the day.

Dr. Jesse Ewell was the brother of Confederate General Richard S. Ewell. Following the wounding and amputation of his leg during the Second Battle of Bull Run, General Ewell was brought to Dunblane to recuperate and receive an artificial leg. During the Battle of Gettysburg, Ewell's staff were startled when a bullet struck Ewell with a resounding crack. Looking over the hole in his trousers, Ewell announced: "It doesn't hurt a bit to be shot in a wooden leg."

Nearby is "Dunblane", the home of Dr. Jesse Ewell. Two sons served the Confederacy, one who was killed early in the war at the Battle of Williamsburg.

Also known as Grace Chapel, the chapel was located just west of Rt 15 on Rt 615 in Prince William County. The chapel was demolished and the former site is now a grass covered area at the entrance to a subdivision.

ODD FELLOWS HALL. *218 North Columbus Street, Alexandria, Virginia.*

On January 16, 1895 this hall hosted the first reunion of Mosby's Rangers. It was the only reunion attended by Colonel Mosby; many of his men took exception to his politics and he refused to attend any future reunions. Members of his family would represent him at future reunions.

Following an evening of exchanging war stories and singing Mosby made an highly emotional speech that brought tears to the eyes of many of the veterans attending the gathering. Part of what he said on that occasion was a tribute to his last meeting at Marshall and to some of the men who died as a part of the 43rd Battalion. He stated:

"Your presence here this evening recalls our last parting. I see the line drawn up to hear the last order I ever gave you. I see the moistened eyes and quivering lips. I hear the command break ranks. I feel the grasp of the hands and see the tears on the cheeks of men who had dared death so long it had lost its terror. And I know now, as I knew then, that each heart suffered with mine the agony of the Titan in his resignation to fate.

Modern skepticism has destroyed one of the most beautiful creations of Epic ages, the belief that the spirits of dead warriors meet daily in the halls of Valhalla, and there around the festive board recount the deeds they did in the other world. For this evening, at least, let us adopt the ancient superstition, if superstition it be. It may seem presumptuous of me, but a man who belonged to my command may be forgiven for thinking that, in the assembly of heroes, when the feast of the wild boar is spread, Smith and Turner, Mountjoy and Glascock, Fox and Whitescarver, and all their comrades, will not be unnoticed in the mighty throng.

I must soon say to you again farewell, a word that must be and hath been. I shall come back to my home by the Golden Gate with proud recollections of this evening. And I shall still feel, as I have always felt, that life cannot offer a more difficult cup than the one I drained when we parted at Salem nor any higher reward to ambition than that I received as commander of the Forty-third Virginia Battalion of Cavalry."

ROSE HILL. *Sometimes called Chestnut Hill, Rose Hill formerly stood on the west side of Old Telegraph Road, four miles south of Alexandria.*

Using the same method he used to capture General Edward Stoughton at Fairfax Courthouse, Major Mosby, with five of his Rangers, slipped into this area on the night of September 28, 1863 and captured Colonel D. H. Dulaney, aide to Francis H. Pierpont, governor of the "pretend State Government" formed in the northern counties of Western Virginia. This organization was in sympathy with the Federal Government and moved to Alexandria when Federal troops occupied this area.

Rose Hill. No longer standing. Ranger French Dulaney assisted Mosby in the capture of his father, Colonel D. H. Delaney who was staying in this house on September 28, 1863.
Fairfax County Public Library Photographic Archive

Among the Rangers was French Dulaney, the son of Colonel Dulaney. Accordingly, the father suffered the embarrassment of being captured and spirited away from this house by his own son. This house was demolished around 1960, but an elementary school and a subdivision still bear its name.

IDLE WILDE. Colonel Mosby's parents moved from their farms in Albermarle and Fluvanna Counties to McIvor's Station in Amherst County, about twelve miles north of Lynchburg. Their home, Idle Wilde, stood across the railroad tracks from McIvor's Station (now Monroe) on the Orange and Alexandria Railroad. The home was later demolished by the Southern Railroad and a roundtable built on the site. The Norfolk Southern has since demolished all of the buildings that formerly stood on the site.

Whenever wounded, Mosby was transported to his parents' home at McIvor Station for convalescence.

To reach the site of Idle Wilde, drive on Rt 29 south from Amherst or north from Lynchburg to Monroe. Turn on Rt 1202 and go .4 mile to the railroad tracks. Idle Wilde stood on the left diagonally across the tracks.

MT. SAN ANGELO. *This was the home of William Hamilton Mosby, a relative of Colonel Mosby's, and it stood on the east side of Rt 29 about 3.5 miles south of Amherst Courthouse, directly across from Sweet Briar College.*

William H. Mosby built a large mansion here in 1870 which burned to the ground on July 17, 1979. Before the large mansion house was constructed, a smaller house stood nearby. It is this house Colonel Mosby writes about in his letters just after the Confederate surrender at Appomattox. Colonel Mosby would stay in his parents' home at McIvor Station, switch to his uncle's Valley Farm near Winginia, and then relocate here to avoid Union cavalry scouring the countryside searching for him. Mosby was unsure how the Federal officials would treat him if he surrendered.

ARUNDEL'S TAVERN. * The last official skirmish of Mosby's Rangers during the Civil War occurred here on April 10, 1865. Companies D and H of the Rangers, about one hundred-fifteen men under the command of Captain George Baylor, had ridden to this area from Marshall (old Salem), and camped here on the evening of April 9th. Some Rangers stayed with the Arundel Family and others camped around the house. The next morning they rode to attack Burke Station hoping to capture the mule teams working there.

About two hundred-fifty men of the 8th Illinois Cavalry, forewarned of the Rangers' plan, met them at Burke Station and forced them to retreat towards this location. The Rangers attempted to make a stand here at Arundel's Tavern, but the superior numbers of the Union cavalry soon forced them to retreat across the Wolf Run Shoals of the Occoquan River. The Rangers suffered 1 man wounded and 5 captured; the Union reported 7 wounded in the skirmish.

Arundel's Tavern is located at the intersection of Rt 123 (Ox Road) and Burke Lake Road, about 5 miles east of Fairfax. The home with the columned porch in the northeast corner of the intersection is the old Arundel's Tavern. The area is known as Brimstone Hill.

Green Spring Farm. Home of Ranger Fount Beattie following the war. The Mosby Family frequently visited here.

GREEN SPRING FARM. This was the home of Mosby Ranger Fount Beattie and his large family following the Civil War. Beattie had married Anne Hathaway. They sold West View near Middleburg, and purchased this farm. Beattie, Colonel Mosby's closest friend during and after the war, often had the Mosby Family here as guests.

The farm is located just north of Annandale on Rt 236 (Little River Turnpike). Drive north from Annandale or south from Alexandria and turn on Green Spring Road. Go .2 mile and the driveway to the house is on the right. The estate is now a farm park.

ROCK GRAVE MARKER — RECTORTOWN.
On the large rock just inside of a fence near Rectortown are carved two grave inscriptions of Union soldiers, however only one is now legible. It reads:

"Chn. Wall, Z.d.A., died May 8, 1862."

Christian Wall, born in Germany, came to America and lived in Philadelphia. He first joined the 21st Penn. on April 29, 1861 and was discharged on August 8, 1861. He then reenlisted in Captain Collis' Company of Independent Zouaves d'Afrique on August 17, 1861. This unit later became Co. A, 114th Penn. Infantry. On May 1, 1862 Private Wall was admitted to the regimental hospital located here at Rectortown. He was suffering from severe diarrhea. He died of "congestion of the bowels" on May 8, 1862 and was buried here.

Rawlingsdale. (Flint Hill Farm.) The Rangers often used this high location for observation posts. John Rawlings, then a small boy, served as a messenger for the Rangers.

The farm on which this rock grave marker is located is called Flint Hill Farm, Rawlingsdale, or Eshton. The property was once owned by George Washington. Because of its height in relation to the surrounding area, the farm was often used as an observation post by Mosby and the Rangers. It was here in early October, 1864 that Mosby mounted his two howitzers to shell Union cavalry and railroad workers attempting to rebuild the Manassas Gap Railroad around Rectortown. Three unsuspecting Mosby Rangers were captured in Rawlingsdale by Union cavalry. A small boy living here, John Rawlings, would always remember the sight of looking out to see Heartland burning on September 26, 1864. Rawlings himself served as a messenger boy for Mosby and the Rangers.

This rock lies just west of Rectortown on Rt 713. Drive west on Rt 713, cross the railroad tracks, and proceed .2 mile. On the left across the fence is a large tree with a large boulder at its base. On this boulder are the two inscriptions.

HOPE PARK, HOPE PARK MILL, AND JACK BARNES. * This was the home of Jack Barnes and his family who operated the Hope Park Mill. Barnes lived here prior to, and following, the Civil War until financial difficulties forced him to sell the home and mill.

With the onset of hostilities, Jack Barnes and two younger brothers, William and Samuel, enlisted in the "Fairfax Rifles". Jack Barnes was captured near Fairfax courthouse on June 9, 1861 and taken to Old Capitol Prison in Washington, D.C. Eventually exchanged and paroled in January, 1861, he walked to Upperville during early March and joined Mosby's Rangers. He next saw action on March 8-9, 1863 when he was one of the 29 men who rode with Mosby on the famous Fairfax Courthouse Raid resulting in the capture of Union General Stoughton.

Jack Barnes returned to Hope Park following the raid and had the misfortune to again be captured by a Union cavalry patrol. He was returned to the Old Capitol Prison, and the following message accompanied him:

"Provost Marshal's Office
Fairfax C. House, Va.
March 13th, 1863

H. H. Wells
Provost Marshal Gen'l.
Alexandria, Va.

Sir:

I have the Honor to forward to you under Guard J. H. Barnes a Resedint of this County, and a man who I am told Piloted captain Mosby & Command into this town on the night of the 8th Inst. and Entertained them at his House. He bears a hard name.

Very Respectfully Yours
Lt. L. L. O'Conner
Provost Marshal"

Again Barnes was released and reenlisted with Mosby on June 10, 1863 at Rector's Cross-Roads. He accompanied Major Mosby on a daring 2-man raid on a Union train of thirty wagons near Fairfax Courthouse in the summer of 1863. Barnes captured the first in line of the wagons, the others followed the leader, and Mosby captured the last in line. Barnes led them on a winding course to a secluded spot near Fairfax where other Rangers were awaiting their arrival.

For this accomplishment Barnes became known to the enemy as "the celebrated Guerilla", but he had the misfortune to be captured for the third time. He and fellow Ranger Phillip Trammel were tried and sent to the penitentiary at Albany, New York. Mosby, outraged at the treatment of his men, sent two Union prisoners, Major Forbes and Captain Manning to the penitentiary at Richmond, Virginia.

Family tradition states Mosby once hid in the attic in an open space in the huge chimney to escape from a Union cavalry patrol who stopped here.

To visit this location, follow Rt 123 (Chain Bridge Road) south from Fairfax, and turn left on Popes Head Road. Go .5 mile to where the road forks in three directions. Straight ahead is Hope Park.

Return to Popes Head Road, turn left and go .7 mile to Hope Park Mill on the right, next to the miller's house. Return to Rt 123.

**Beaver Dam Railroad Station.
Mosby was surprised and captured here.**

BEAVER DAM RAILROAD STATION. It was here that Mosby was captured for the first and only time during his military career. Mosby, wishing to operate independently behind Union lines, had obtained General Jeb Stuart's permission to see General "Stonewall" Jackson about obtaining men for such an action. Mosby started from Gordonsville on July 19, 1862 and arrived here on the 20th. The Harris Light Cavalry, sweeping in from Fredericksburg to strike against the Virginia Central Railroad on that day, captured Mosby at this station. He was sent to Old Capitol Prison in Washington, D.C. and confined for ten days before he was exchanged.

The station is located northwest of Ashland on the Chesapeake and Ohio Railroad (the old Virginia Central Railroad). To visit the station, now under renovation, exit Interstate 95 at Doswell, cross over Rt 1, and take Rt 684 for sixteen miles to Beaver Dam.

MYER'S FORD. On the morning of September 5, 1864 Mosby and six Rangers crossed the river here to scout around Charles Town. He left Lieutenant Joe Nelson in charge of the eighty men in the raiding party to await their return. Many of the Rangers unsaddled their horses and rested.

Unknown to the Rangers, Captain Richard Blazer with his selected command of one hundred Independent Scouts

Myer's Ford. Captain Richard Blazer's Scouts attacked and defated the Rangers as they rested along the river.

all armed with repeating rifles, had fallen in behind them near Hillsboro and was on their trail. He struck unexpectedly at the Rangers, completely surprising them. Some of the Rangers led by Nelson fought savagely; however, many were forced to scatter. Ranger losses were 1 killed, 3 wounded, and 3 captured; Union losses were about the same.

The Rangers would gain revenge on November 18, 1864 when under the command of Major "Dolly" Richards, the entire command of Blazer's was destroyed and he captured.

This ford was a favorite crossing place for Mosby's Rangers traveling between Hillsboro in Loudoun County, and what is today Jefferson County in West Virginia.

To visit the ford, drive west from Hillsboro on Rt 9 (Charles Town Turnpike), or east on Rt 9 from Charles Town. Drive to the top of the mountain and turn on Mountain Mission Road. Travel 1 mile and note marker number 16 (Engagement at Myer's Ford, Sunday, Sept. 5, 1864 - Blazer's and Mosby's men).

PAYNE MOUNTAIN HOUSE AND SYD FERGUSON HOUSE. *

About two miles south of the intersection with Rt 50 on Rt 17, exit on Rt 688 and travel .9 mile. Turn right on Rt 711, go .2 mile, and stop at the forks in the road. On top of the hill straight ahead is the Nalley-Strother Cemetery. 100 feet to the west are the chimney remains from the Payne House which stood high on the mountainside in what was then a deserted part of the county.

Dr. Albin Payne's house was used by Ranger Louis Thornton Powell as a hideout while fighting with Mosby during 1864-65.

Turn left at the forks of the road and go .7 mile to the house on the left side of the road. This was the home of Ranger Syd Ferguson who captured Captain Richard Blazer following the skirmish at Kabletown.

SHERIDAN'S HEADQUARTERS.

Located at 135 North Braddock Street (intersection with Picadilly Street), Winchester stands the building used by General Sheridan as a headquarters in late 1864.

It was to this building Ranger John Russell was brought to deliver Colonel Mosby's message following the hangings at Berryville. Russell rode from Rectortown to Millwood where he stopped at Clarke's Store, then spent the night in the barn at Pagebrook before riding to Winchester.

At 415 North Braddock Street are the "Stonewall" Jackson Headquarters and a museum.

Mosby Home. No longer standing. The Mosby Family lived here when he started to practice law in 1858.

Courtesy Mr. & Mrs. Harry R. Jones

BRISTOL, VIRGINIA.

John S. Mosby began his law practice here in November, 1858. He and his new wife, Pauline (Clarke of Kentucky) settled in a home at the corner of Scott and Moore Streets. This home was demolished, and a dentist's office now stands in its place. A historical marker recognizing the location of the home stands a few hundred feet away at the intersection of Scott and Rebecca Streets and Piedmont Avenue. Mosby's law office stood at the corner of State and Lee Streets and a bank building now occupies the site.

The young lawyer began his military training in this area as he rode to Abingdon to join the Washington Mounted Rifles under the command of William E. "Grumble" Jones.

CHAPMAN'S MILL.

A familiar landmark for Mosby and the Rangers as they passed through Thoroughfare Gap was the six-story Chapman's Mill standing on the north side of the road. Partially burned by the Confederates in 1862, the mill was rebuilt after the war by Robert and William Beverly and became known as Beverly's Mill. In the nearby Bull Run Mountains, Mosby kept Union Army prisoners and captured horses at "Camp Spindle" until they could be moved elsewhere. This camp was north of Hopewell Gap about 7 miles east of The Plains.

**Chapman's Mill. A familiar landmark.
Mosby held prisoners and horses near here.**

Green Gardens. Home of Ranger Major "Dolly" Richards.

The home is located on Rt 719 (Green Gardens Road), just east of Upperville, and .7 mile north of Rt 50.

OATLANDS. This is the farm where Mosby first spotted a thoroughbred horse that was later purchased by his Rangers and presented him following the Greenback Raid. Also to this home was brought the seriously wounded Baron Von Massow after he was seriously wounded near Dranesville in February, 1864. The Baron was later moved to Edgehill for safety. He returned to Germany due to the serious nature of his wounds and fought no more during the war.

The home is located on the east side of Rt 15 about 5 miles south of Leesburg.

OLD CAPITOL PRISON, WASHINGTON, D.C.

Mosby was imprisoned here for ten days after being captured by Union Cavalry at Beaver Dam Railroad Station on the Virginia Central Railroad on July 20, 1862. He was exchanged and later passed on important information he had observed to General Robert E. Lee concerning the movement north of Union troops to reinforce General Pope. The prison has since been destroyed.

A plaque at the visitor's entrance to the Supreme Court Building in Washington, D.C. marks the site of the Old Capitol Prison.

GREEN GARDENS. This is the home of Ranger Major "Dolly" Richards. During the dark morning hours on February 19, 1865 Richards was surprised here by a surprise raid of two hundred twenty-five Union cavalry. He managed to hide underneath the house and evade capture; however, many Rangers living in the area were not so lucky. Quickly gathering up a force of Rangers, Richards charged the rear of the Union cavalry at Mt. Carmel Church near Ashby Gap. The Union forces beat a panicky retreat with heavy casualties and the loss of the captured Rangers.

**Ebenezer Chapel. The Rangers met here to divide
the $173,000 captured in the Greenback Raid.**

EBENEZER CHAPEL. Here the $173,000 captured during the Greenback Raid was divided on October 14, 1864. Each Ranger received about $2,100. Some of the Rangers wasted their share foolishly while others saved their share to purchase farms following the end of the war.

To reach the chapel take Green Garden Road (Rt 719, which becomes Ebenezer Road) off of Rt 50 just east of Upperville. Travel 6.1 miles and turn left into the church yard. Ebenezer Chapel is the older building on the left.

ANDERSON FAMILY CEMETERY — MARKHAM, VA.

Here are buried Rangers Thomas E. Anderson and William Thomas Overby, executed at Front Royal on September 23, 1864. Both men were returned here for burial.

Anderson Family Cemetery. Historian Nancy Baird holds back brush to permit a photograph of the grave markers of Mosby Rangers Thomas E. Anderson and William Thomas Overby. Both were executed at Front Royal.

Although buried here, Overby, a native of Georgia, is remembered in his home state with a seven foot tall, four foot wide monument on the courthouse lawn in Newnan, Georgia. Erected in 1956, the monument proclaims Overby as the "Nathan Hale of the Confederacy".

To reach the cemetery take Exit 4 off Interstate 66 for Markham. Turn left on Rt 688 and go to Rt 55. Turn left (east) and travel .5 mile. The cemetery is in the rear sideyard to the right of the house now having a green roof and shutters.

JOSEPH HANCOCK BLACKWELL — "THE CHIEF". John S. Mosby first met Joe Blackwell in the summer of 1863 following the organization of his Partisan Rangers. Blackwell, whose family had deep roots in the Piedmont area of Fauquier County, lived in a home overlooking the Manassas Gap Railroad whose Piedmont Station lay only a mile and a half to the southwest. Blackwell's home and hospitality made it a focal point for both friend and foe. Mosby often met with

his Rangers there, stored arms and ammunition for their use, and often partook of the freely offered food. Due to Blackwell's being ten to twelve years older than most of the young Rangers, he was respectfully referred to as "The Chief". He rarely took part in raids and narrowly escaped capture by Union cavalry at Glen Welby near Salem.

The Union forces, trying to open the Manassas Gap Railroad, were not long in determining that Blackwell's home was being used as Mosby's headquarters. On September 26, 1864 the 13th New York Cavalry burned Blackwell's home, barn, and outbuildings leaving only the stone springhouse standing. Blackwell moved his family to nearby Rosenvix and Mosby relocated his headquarters to Brookside. Blackwell and his family had paid the price for loyalty to the Rangers.

Grave of Mosby Ranger Joseph Hancock Blackwell

Following the war, Blackwell moved to Ivy in Albermarle County where Colonel Mosby had used his influence to obtain him a position as a mail agent. Joseph Blackwell died March 14, 1905 and is buried in a private cemetery at The Meadows, the ancestral home of the Blackwell Family. This is located on Rt 628 about 2 miles east of Bethel.

Colonel Murry F. Rose (Ret), grandnephew of Blackwell, diligently searched out his grave and secured a Government marker that has been installed in the cemetery. It was dedicated in a ceremony honoring "The Chief".

BLAKLEY GROVE SKIRMISH. Several skirmishes occurred in this area, the most notable taking place in a two day period, February 20-21, 1864 between Mosby's Rangers and Cole's Maryland Cavalry. Cole, with two hundred-fifty troopers, rode to Piedmont and made a surprise attack on the Rangers, taking several as prisoners. Cole then drew back towards Upperville where he paused to feed his horses. Mosby, with a force of fifty Rangers, struck Cole causing him to retreat towards Blakely Grove. The two groups skirmished back and forth as Cole withdrew. At the Schoolhouse here on February 21, 1864 Cole decided to make a stand behind the rock walls that line the crossroads. The Rangers flanked Cole's troopers and put them to flight pursuing them about two miles to Bloomfield where the affair ended. Union losses were 7 killed, 8 captured, and several wounded; the Rangers suffered 3 wounded.

To visit the skirmish site drive east from Upperville on Rt 50 for 2 miles and turn left on Rt 623. The horse show grounds will be on the right. Continue for 2.3 miles and pass the Blakely Grove estate on the right. Travel .7 mile to the intersection of Rt 623 and Rt 719. This is Blakely Grove School House Crossroads.

BEDFORD, VA. Here lived William H. Mosby, adjutant of the Rangers and brother to Colonel Mosby. He served as postmaster and also operated several other businesses. His home was in the small settlement of Thaxton's Switch just outside the town. He is buried in Longwood Cemetery here.

OAK HILL. * Oak Hill was the home of the Fairfax Family and was a familiar sight to Mosby and his men in this area. Colonel John Fairfax was a staff officer of General James Longstreet. Mosby was a frequent visitor here during and following the war. In 1863 Union General George G. Meade made this house his headquarters. He was standing with Mrs. John Fairfax on the south patio facing Aldie when he mentioned how much he wanted to catch the elusive Mosby. Mrs. Fairfax pointed to a lone horseman cutting across the property and informed him he had just missed his chance.

Oak Hill is located on Rt 15 two miles north of Rt 50. The house is on a hill and visible from the highway. There is a Virginia Highway Historical Marker one mile north of Rt 50 (Gilbert's Corner) on Rt 15 on the right side of the highway. It provides information about Oak Hill.

CAPTAIN SAMUEL CARRINGTON MEANS.
A Quaker by birth with anti-slavery sentiments, Samuel Means had his flour mill, crops, and livestock (including 42 hogs) confiscated by the Confederate government at the beginning of the war. He was forced to flee from his home in Waterford, Virginia to Point Of Rocks, Maryland where he owned and operated a store. Means' fiery speeches in favor of the Union caught the attention of the Secretary of War, Edwin M. Stanton, who summoned him to Washington, D.C. and offered him a commission as a Captain of cavalry.

Captain Samuel Carrington Means. Headed the only organized military unit from Virginia to fight in the Union Army. His unit fought numerous skirmishes with the Rangers.
Courtesy John E. Divine

Means promptly raised Company A, Independent Loudoun (Virginia) Rangers, the only organized military unit from Virginia to fight in the Union Army. He fought Elijah V. White's Comanches and Mosby's Rangers until relieved from command on April 18, 1864. He then moved to Washington, D.C. where he established a boarding house. He had sacrificed his wealth and religion for the Union. He contacted cancer, died March 2, 1884, and is buried in an unmarked grave in Rock Creek Cemetery in the District of Columbia.

Mean's residence and mill are still standing in Waterford, a historic old village. A number of Loudoun Rangers are buried in the village cemetery. There are "Waterford Days" held during the fall that are well worthwhile to attend. Waterford is northwest of Leesburg, and assessable from Rt 9 by either Rt 662 or Rt 704.

SCUFFLEBURG. Company B of Mosby's Rangers was organized here on October 1, 1863. As was his practice, Mosby personally selected the officers for the company. William R. Smith, formerly of the Black Horse Troop, was named captain. The small hamlet at that time consisted of a blacksmith shop, a wheelwright shop, and a home. It was also known as Mechanicsville at that time, and it is located not

Pleasant Vale Baptist Church.
Company B of Mosby's Rangers was organized in this neighborhood and the church was an assembly point.

far from Pleasant Vale Baptist Church where the Rangers would assemble from time to time. The Rangers liked to mingle here due to the isolated location, and the Union Army viewed the tiny hamlet as a "second Gibralter".

To visit the area take Rt 17 about 2 miles north of Delaplane, turn on Rt 724 and travel 1 mile to Pleasant Vale Church. Turn right on Rt 826 (Scuffleburg Road) and drive to the small settlement.

OLD VERDIERSVILLE HOUSE. * On the late evening of August 17, 1862 General Jeb Stuart, Heros Von Borcke, Mosby, a friend named Gibson, and several other members of Stuart's staff stopped at this house to sleep in the yard and on the porch. About 4 a.m. the next morning cavalry rode into Verdiersville. Mosby awoke Stuart, then taking Gibson, went to investigate whether the cavalry was friend or foe. It was Union cavalry whose charge almost captured Stuart, Mosby and the others. The Confederates narrowly escaped, and Stuart left behind his plumed hat, cloak, and haversack.

This house stands about 12 miles east of Orange just north of the small village of Verdiersville. From Rt 20 (the Old Plank Road) exit on Rt 621, go north .8 mile, and the house stands on the right side of the highway.

WOODBURY FORREST. * A private college preparatory college, the headmaster here after the war was Ranger Robert Walker. Frank Stringfellow, "The Scout", served as chaplain. Colonel Mosby, always greatly interested in the field of education, visited here following the end of the war until his death.

This school is located about 2 miles north of Orange. Exit Rt 15 onto Rt 634 and continue 2 miles to the school grounds.

SEDGELEY. * Several Mosby Rangers boarded here during their winter stay in the Northern Neck region of Virginia. A lack of forage for horses forced Companies C, E, F and G of the Rangers to move to this area during late December, 1864 to mid-April 1865. Commanded by William H. Chapman, the Rangers continued their attacks in this area including a daring night raid on Williamsburg.

The home of the Smith and Settle Family, the house is located near Ethel in Richmond County, Virginia.

AVENEL. * (The Plains.) *Located on Rt 55 1½ miles east of The Plains in Fauquier County,* Avenel was the home of the Beverly Family during the Civil War era. Mosby was a frequent visitor here during and after the war. Another visitor during the war was Ranger Nick Carter. The home is not visible from the highway.

BURKE STATION. This was the site of an attack during General Jeb Stuart's Christmas Raid. Guided by Mosby, Stuart with 1800 cavalry left camp in the Fredricksburg area on Christmas Day, 1862. Broken into three attack groups commanded by Fitz Lee, Roney Lee and Wade Hampton, the cavalry struck Union Army outposts in Stafford, Prince William and Fairfax Counties. After successfully raiding Burke Station, Stuart skirted around Fairfax Courthouse, through Vienna to Dranesville, and camped that night at Frying Pan Church. Proceeding westward, Stuart and Mosby stayed overnight at the Hamilton Rogers' home, Oakham, at Dover on December 29, 1862. The following morning Mosby secured permission from Stuart to remain behind with nine men to initiate his independent fighting career.

Nothing remains of the former depot. A highway marker located on the corner of Rt 236 (Little River Turnpike) and Burke Station Road reads:

"Burke Station was raided in December, 1862 by Confederate General J.E.B. Stuart. It was from this site, originally the Burke Station Depot, that he sent his famous telegram to Union Quartermaster General Meigs complaining of the poor quality of the Union mules he had just captured."

POINT OF ROCKS, MARYLAND. Located where Rt 15 crosses the Potomac River, Mosby raided this important town at various times during the war striking the boats, barges and locks of the Chesapeake and Ohio Canal and the Baltimore and Ohio Railroad. Captain Samuel Means owned a store in the town before the war and frequently brought his Loudoun Rangers to camp here between skirmishes. This was a favorite place for Union Army spies to come by train from Washington, D.C. to cross the river and enter the Confederacy.

Appendix A

ON MOSBY'S CHARACTER

Courtesy John E. Divine

Ball's Bluff near Leesburg is naturally one of my favorite battles, and I do everything that I can to preserve bits of human interest, not only in the participants there that day, but also into their later war experiences during the conflict. Lieutenant Colonel Isaac Jones Wistar led the so called 1st California Regiment on the bluffs above the Potomac River that day, suffered a grievous wound there, but recovered and continued in service.

About 1892, when writing his memoirs of the war, he remembered in particular an experience during the Battle of Antietam Creek. Wistar, now a Colonel of the 71st Pennsylvania Regiment, was leading his men as they charged across the open ground past the Dunkard Church and into the West Woods. Colonel Wistar was again seriously wounded. As Stonewall Jackson threw back the Federal lines, Wistar was left lying wounded on the field.

There congregated at this point at this time Confederate Generals Layfette McLaws, John G. Gordon, and Jeb Stuart who came to watch the action, and with them came their staffs. Wistar was lying there in pain and was being harassed by a young Confederate lieutenant, trying first to take his sword, and then trying to get his parole. Jeb Stuart ordered the lieutenant away, and then one of Stuart's couriers came over, lifted his head, gave him a drink of water, and eased his position before moving off.

Colonel Wistar, later General Wistar by the end of the war, went on to a distinguished career, both in war and in peace. It was many years later before he discovered who his benefactor was that day. It was John Singleton Mosby of Jeb Stuart's staff who had been serving as a courier that day who had eased the pain of a wounded foe. This to me adds another dimension to Colonel Mosby.

(An excerpt from John Divine's address to the Stuart-Mosby Society during their annual meeting on June 29, 1985.)

Appendix B

JAMES F. "BIG YANKEE" AMES

One of the qualities which made Colonel John S. Mosby an outstanding leader, military or otherwise, was his ability to judge his fellow men. Nowhere was his judgement placed to a more stern test than that of the Union Army deserter James F. Ames, who was to be given the epithet "Big Yankee" by Mosby's men. Strongly distrusted at first contact with Mosby and his small command at that time, Ames was to prove himself an invaluable, able, and worthy fighter.

A native of Bangor, Maine, Ames was a large, physically imposing man with piercing black eyes. Before the war he had made his living as a seaman, however, at the time of his desertion he was a sergeant with the Fifth New York Cavalry stationed at Fairfax Courthouse, Virginia. Ames was well acquainted with this town occupied by the Federal forces as well as with the surrounding area, a knowledge which was to prove very helpful to Mosby at a later date.

About February 1st, 1863, Ames deserted his unit then in winter quarters at Fairfax Courthouse and walked unarmed to Rector's Cross Roads to meet with Mosby and his small command of about a dozen troopers. When he expressed his desire to join Mosby's command, Ames was not initially trusted by the partisans who felt he was a spy of some type or that he would prove to be a betrayer.

Ames stated that he had deserted because of the Emancipation Proclamation which he believed indicated the war had changed to become a war for the black man instead a war for the Union.[1] Mosby never questioned Ames' motive for deserting and instinctively accepted this new recruit who was to supply him with information needed about the Union picket lines in and around Fairfax Courthouse.

At this same meeting also appeared an additional new unmounted recruit named Walter F. Franklin. Informing both men that their first task would be to find mounts for themselves, Mosby left on a raid with his men leaving the two new recruits to accomplish this difficult mission. However, both passed their first assignment as they walked through the snow the entire 25 mile distance back to the stables of the Fifth New York Cavalry at Germantown, two miles west of Fairfax Courthouse. Here Ames used his acquired knowledge of Union Army procedures to steal two fine horses. Unchallenged by the pickets guarding the stable and nearby camp, he and Franklin mounted the stolen horses and quietly rode away to join Mosby.

On February 26, 1863, Ames agreed to his second test of fidelity consisting of riding unarmed with Mosby during an attack on a Union picket post located at Thompson's Corner near Germantown. The unarmed Ames rushed a mounted Union soldier, seized him by the collar, and threatened him into surrendering his arms. From this time on Ames was an accepted member of Mosby's command and proved himself to be as faithful and courageous as any of Mosby's brave followers.

During the first week of March, 1863, Ames secretly scouted the area around Fairfax Courthouse for up to date information about Union picket posts, living accommodations, and other military matters. Mosby used this knowledge on his famous night raid of March 8-9, 1863, which resulted in the capture of the Union General Edwin H. Stoughton. In fact, Ames was the only member of the raiding party whom Mosby had informed of their destination. In the center of the small village, Mosby selected Ames and a few companions to go to the house where a major enemy, Colonel Percy Wyndham, was staying and capture him. Unfortunately, Wyndham had been ordered into Washington, D.C., earlier in the day and was not home. Ames did, however, capture his former commanding officer, Captain Barker of the Fifth New York Cavalry, who was staying in the house that night. Mosby commended Ames for his part in this famous and successful raid.

Ames was also cited for his aggressive fighting tactics during the next few weeks of skirmishing at Chantilly, Herndon Station, Dranesville, Miskel's Farm and other locations within Mosby's Confederacy.

During the March 17th, 1863 skirmish at Herndon Station, Ames was one of Mosby's raiders who successfully defeated the Union picket post at that location. As the raiders were leaving the area they noticed four officers' horses tethered outside the Herndon home of Nat Hanna, a known Union sympathizer. Stopping at the house, Mosby's men conducted a thorough search and discovered a large dinner on the dining room table but no apparent diners. Ames finally located a small door off the second floor which evidently led to an overhead garret. He kicked the door open and demanded for anyone above to come out. Receiving no reply, he fired a shot into the darkness resulting in three Union officers quickly appearing and surrendering. These were soon joined by a fourth companion who managed to fall through the plaster ceiling in his haste to surrender. All four prisoners were added to the total captured that day. Ames and the other Mosby men then ate the prepared meal before leaving the house which is known to the older residents today as the Prinz Home.[2]

About mid-April of 1863, "Big Yankee" was out of action for a short period of time from a shoulder wound received in a skirmish with five Union cavalrymen just west of Middleberg. He was fighting alongside the two Hatcher brothers, Dan and Harry, at the time. Ames speedily recovered and in late June of that year rode with Mosby's command as they crossed the Potomac River into Maryland and Pennsylvania (going as far north as Mercersburg) during the Gettysburg campaign.

As Mosby's group crossed the boundary into Pennsylvania Ames stated to his companions: "Well, I am going with you, but I will not fire a shot. When the Emancipation Proclamation was issued and I saw it was a war for the black man and not for the Union, I joined the South and am willing to fight to repel the invasion of her soil, and am willing to give my life in her defense, but I will not fight on Northern soil."[3]

Returning from the Gettysburg campaign, Ames continued his aggressive fighting style throughout Northern Virginia, and in September, 1864, he was elected Second Lieutenant of the newly formed Company F of Mosby's Rangers.

On Sunday, October 9th, 1864, as Ames was riding along the road in front of "Yew Hill", the residence of Miss Kitty Shacklett, near Piedmont in Fauquier County, he stopped and dismounted, presumably to get a drink of water at a roadside spring flowing there. He was shot and killed by a Union soldier, who was in the process of rifling Ames' pockets and removing his pistols, when he, in turn, was shot and killed by Mosby Ranger Lud Lake, Jr. who happened to ride upon the scene. Young Lake removed an eagle button from the blouse of the

Union soldier's uniform, and later had it made into a stick pin. It is now in the possession of Mr. John Gott, noted author and Fauquier County historian, who is a Lake descendant.[4]

"Big Yankee" Ames, the eighth officer of the 43rd Battalion to be overtaken by death, was buried in a clump of trees near where he was shot at Yew Hill.

After the war Colonel Mosby wrote of Ames, "Since the war I have often passed his lonely grave, and remember this prominent figure in the history of my command."[5]

An entirely different view of Ames was taken by a Union soldier, Cornelious Raver. Writing home to his wife in Pennsylvania, Raver stated (original spelling):

Elexanfre October the 16 1864

Mrs Elizabeth Raver
   Cavettsville PO
      Westmoreland Co.
         Penna.

dear Wife and dear little Babie after my love to you all I informe you that I am well and hartey I hope you are all the same Well i will informe you that we have had some Big times since I rote Before on the night of the (?) at half past nine oclock we marched about nine miles and Captured 9 Rebels and then we heard that the Rebels had hid 4 pieces of artillery and then Company E ower one Company started up the mountain about 2 miles than We Poot out a skirmish lien and surcled the Woods till we found them fore pieses of artillery that they had bin pepering us with all the time so We took it and did not fier a gun to take it Before We Started the mager told us if we Captured it We should have a bib Bounty for it so We will look for it We hulled them 4 pieses of artillery 10 mile by hand Back to Camp and did not git back till about 7 oclock the next morning then we poot them on the cars ans We sent Back Flexander along to gard them so we are hear this the morning of the 16 I expect we will go Back today We are all Well and hartey Conner and me stick together like two ticks Well I must tell you that We had the pleasure of bering Mosbeys first liutenant he went by the name of yankey Ames one of our Boys shot him on last monday throu the hart he was the sunofa bitch that cut so many of ower mens throats so he is gon up the spout at last Well i wish you Would send me some money Please send it in Shin Plasters We cant git iy chainged hear Well this aboutall at present Please Right Soon direct as Before goog by for this time
                                 Cornelious Raver"[6]

Raver and his Union comrades had received much satisfaction in bringing an end to the exploits of "Big Yankee" Ames and sending him "up the spout".

Although believed to be buried by the spring at Yew Hill, Ames has a grave marker besides the tall Confederate pyramid monument in Hollywood Cemetery in Richmond. His mystique lives on.

FOOTNOTES

1. Williamson, James J., *Mosby's Rangers*, Ralph B. Kenyon, Publisher, New York, 1896, p 29.

2. Interview with Mrs. Virginia Greear, 93 year old Herndon historian, on March 30, 1985.

3. Williamson, op. cit., p 80.

4. Information supplied by Mr. John Gott of Arlington, VA.

5. Mosby, Col. John S., *Mosby's War Reminiscences and Stuart's Cavalry Campaigns*, Pageant Book Company, New York, 1958, p 68.

6. Stackpole, Edward J., *Sheridan in the Shenandoah, Jubal Early's Nemesis*, Bonanza Books, New York, 1956, pp 372-73.

Appendix C

COLONEL MOSBY'S CANE

Courtesy Admiral Beverly Mosby Coleman (Ret)

"During mid-September, 1864 Union General Philip Sheridan was skirmishing with Confederate General Jubal Early's men around Fisher's Hill, Virginia. Part of Sheridan's cavalry met Fitz Lee's cavalry in a sharp fight and chased them to Milford where the Confederate troopers made a highly successful stand. The Union cavalry then fell back with Custer's and Merritt's brigades retreating through Front Royal, Virginia on the 23rd of September.

The Colonel's men had been watching the Union forces and waiting for a chance to make a successful attack. As Merritt's supply and ambulance train neared the town, it became known it was guarded by only a small cavalry escort, and there was a good possibility it could be captured. It was not recognized that the train was part of general retreat and that there were large bodies of Union cavalry passing nearby throughout the area.

Sam Chapman, William's brother, was leading the Colonel's men in that particular area. Sam was a ministerial student, and during the Spanish-American War, served as a US Army chaplain in Cuba. A large number of the Colonel's men became ministers after the war. The Colonel once told a group of them, 'Well, boys, if you fight the devil like you fought the Yankees, there will be something to record Judgement Day!'

Well, Sam Chapman and the men attacked the wagon train, and it didn't take them long to realize it was a big mistake. Large bodies of Union Cavalry were attracted to the scene of the shooting, and Sam's route for retreat was blocked. He adopted the Colonel's tactics of riding right into the enemy, shooting and yelling, and creating a general panic. Most of the Colonel's men escaped; however, when the fighting was over and the dust had all settled down, the Yankees had captured six of the Confederates.

General George A. Custer was the ranking senior Union officer then in Front Royal, and he ordered the execution of the Colonel's men who had taken prisoners. Some were hanged from a tree just outside of town. One of these was hanged with a sign saying, 'This will be the fate of Mosby and all his men.'

Now the members of the Colonel's command over in the Shenandoah Valley were pretty bitter over the matter. Some of them wanted to fight under the Black Flag which meant no prisoners would be taken. I think some of the older members prevailed, and they said nobody should do anything until the Colonel came back to duty. He was recovering from a serious wound during that period, and he had to ride around in a buggy for some time after he returned. In the meantime, Union Army Colonel Powell captured and hung another one of the Colonel's men.

The Colonel continued business as usual, sending captured Union Army prisoners back to Richmond. He waited until his men could capture some prisoners from Custer's Michigan Brigade, and they finally brought in thirty of them. These were lined up and a hat passed containing seven marked ballots. Whoever drew a market ballot was to be executed because of what was happening to the Colonel's men who were captured. After the hat had been fully passed and everyone had drawn a ballot, one of the members of the Federal group, a young lieutenant who had not drawn a marked ballot, asked to speak to the Colonel. He explained that a young fellow who had drawn a marked ballot was a drummer boy. He had never carried a weapon, and had never fired a shot, and it seemed too hard for a young fellow of sixteen to be among the others to be executed.

The Colonel agreed and gave orders to put the drummer boy's ballot back in the hat and pass it among the remaining prisoners. The young lieutenant who had interceded on behalf of the drummer boy drew the remaining marked ballot.

Well, the seven unlucky Yankee prisoners were tied up and started down to the Valley pike to be executed. On the way the group met Captain Mountjoy of the Colonel's command, and the young lieutenant gave him a Masonic sign. Mountjoy was a Mason, so he took one of a group of Custer's men he had just captured and substituted him for the lieutenant. The Colonel didn't hear about it for some time later and told Mountjoy he wasn't interested in opening up any Masonic Lodges in the Valley. While the group was traveling to the pike, one of the Union soldiers managed to untie himself and escape in the darkness. The other six were shot and hung there beside the pike where the Union forces were sure to find them.

Following the execution the Colonel wrote to General Sheridan. I have often thought the text of his letter was something that, under the tragic and delicate circumstances, comprised a rather forthright and matter of fact, not too strong statement, and I would like to read it:

'Major General P. H. Sheridan,
Commanding US Forces in the Valley.

General:

Some time in the month of September during my absence from my command, six of my men who had been captured by your forces, were hung and shot in the streets of Front Royal by the order and in the presence of Brigadier General Custer. Since then another, captured by a Colonel Powell on a plundering expedition into Rappahannock, shared a similar fate. A label affixed to the coat of one of the murdered men declared that, quote: "This will be the fate of Mosby and all his men."

Since the murder of my men not less than 700 prisoners, including many officers of high rank, captured from your army by this command, have been forwarded to Richmond. But the execution of my purpose of retaliation was deferred in order as far as possible, to confine its operation to the men of Custer and Powell. Accordingly, on the sixth instant, seven of your men were by my order executed on the Valley pike, your highway of travel.

Hereafter, any prisoners falling into my hands will be treated with the kindness due to their condition, unless some new act of barbarity shall compel me, reluctantly, to adopt a line of policy repugnant to humanity.'

In closing, of course, was the customary winding up of a letter, 'Very Respectfully, Your Obedient Servant, John S. Mosby, Lieutenant Colonel.'

This was a proper manner of ending a letter for a gentleman, no matter which side he fought on.

Now, the Colonel lived with our family in the District of Columbia for the last eight or ten years of his life. When I was fairly young various people would come to call on the Colonel, and they would get into a huddle. If it was some of his men in their conversation they might make some allusion to the war. Generally, politics were discussed, they were hot then, even hotter than now. Of course, the Colonel had become a Republican after the war, and many of his men were Democrats, with almost a religious fervor, so the discussions were friendly, but warm. Before they left he usually introduced me to his callers.

I remember one day a distinguished old gentleman came to call on the Colonel. They had quite a close conversation for some time, and as the gentleman was leaving, the Colonel called me out and introduced him as the drummer boy whose life he had spared many years previously during the war. Well, the drummer boy had brought the Colonel a fine cane, and he was quite pleased with it. It has a silver plate reading:

'To Colonel John S. Mosby, with the profound regards of James A. Daley, the Drummer Boy, captured by Mosby's command near Newtown, Virginia, 16 April 1864.'

The Colonel used this cane a great deal, and it is pretty well worn. It was used regularly until his death on Memorial Day, 1916 when he died on the operating table during surgery.

At the time of his death the Colonel was in Garfield Hospital, and my mother, my sister, myself, and my two aunts, (his daughters from Baltimore) came over. We were all in his room when the attendants brought in the wheeled table on which he was placed to be taken to the operating room. Well, as he was taken down the corridor my mother and I were standing outside watching. He was attended by his nurse, and they came to the door of the operating room which was closed. They had to wait, I guess, until the preceding operation was finished. While they were waiting there were three very nice looking gentlemen engaged in conversation nearby. One of them went over and exchanged a few words with the nurse and then returned.

After the Colonel had been delivered to the operating room staff, and the nurse came back to where we were all

Admiral Beverly Mosby Coleman (Ret), Mosby's grandson, displays the walking cane presented the Colonel by the drummer boy for sparing his life.

waiting, my mother asked, 'Who was that very fine looking gentleman who spoke to you while you were waiting?'

'He came over and asked me who the patient was, and I told him,' the nurse replied, 'He then said, ''I am Colonel Ulysses S. Grant III. If there is anything Colonel Mosby needs, please be sure and let me know.'' '

So it seems there at the very end was the grandson of General Grant extending a kind offering to the Colonel minutes before his death. As I mentioned, the Colonel died on the operating table, so Colonel Grant was one of the last people he saw.''

(A special presentation by Admiral Beverly Mosby Coleman [Ret], grandson of Colonel Mosby, at the conclusion of the October 14, 1984 field trip of the Stuart-Mosby Historical Society. Sitting in the parlor of what is today the Truro Episcopal Rectory where Colonel Mosby captured Union General Stoughton, Admiral Coleman displayed a cane owned by Colonel Mosby and related the above story.)

Appendix D

LAKELAND

Courtesy Virgil Carrington Jones

This is the home at which on December 21, 1864 at least one chapter of history of the Civil War was greatly changed. Mosby was summoned to Richmond in December, 1864 only a few months before the end of the war. On his return, he reported that he had gone there to get authority to divide his command, at this period numbering 800, into two battalions. He had been made a full colonel and returned wearing a new uniform, complete even to a scarlet-lined cape.

Records indicate that Mosby was called to Richmond for a more important purpose. It seems that the South was in a desperate plight. Lee was defending Richmond and the South with his back against the wall. A solution was for the South to begin wholesale guerilla warfare. Mosby and the other Partisan leaders, in blocking Sheridan in his Valley campaign, had shown how valuable it was, and the Rebel high command looked upon it as a way to hold on.

So Mosby was called to Richmond by Jefferson Davis to talk about reorganizing the guerilla bands in the area. Fauquier County was to be the principal point of rendezvous. There were to be eight battalions of four companies each, and these were to be divided as the necessities of the service required. All of the gaps in the Blue Ridge, Bull Run, and Catoctin Mountains were to be guarded by picked men, with fleet horses, to herald the approach of the enemy and to give the signal for a concentration of forces. A few detachments were to be set up as a mobile force, to move from point to point, gathering conscripts and arming old men, who were to be local guerillas. There was to be a system of mountain signal stations for quick communication. The overall leader of this force of eight battalions was to be Mosby, who would be promoted to the rank of brigadier-general at the proper time.

But what happened here in this house on the night of December 21st definitely spelled the end of any plans for guerilla warfare.

On this day, Mosby attended the afternoon wedding of his ordnance sergeant, Jake Lavender to Catherine Edmonds. He had scarcely reached the Edmonds home where the marriage was to take place before someone brought him word that a body of Union cavalry was advancing on the Salem road. Motioning to one of his men, Tom Love, he slipped away. A cold drizzling rain had started earlier in the day and by this time it was a solid coating of sleet. Mosby found the enemy cavalry and watched it go into camp near Rectortown, not far from here, and he was confident all the Federals in the neighborhood had gone into bivouac for the night.

Mosby planned an attack on the camp at dawn. Finding a Ranger at a neighboring home, he sent him back to the command with word to be prepared for this attack, and then he and Love rode in this direction, on a sweep designed to round up additional men for the raid. From the road down at Atoka, he spied the lights of this home here, which he recognized as that of Ludwell Lake, whose sons rode with Mosby's Rangers. So they rode here for dinner, finding the old man, a short, fat, balding farmer with his two daughters. Love wanted to stay outside as a guard, but Mosby insisted that he come inside out of the weather.

Inside the home, Mosby and Love took off their heavy coats, Mosby dropping his, along with his cape and plumed hat, in one corner of the dining room. Then they sat down to a pleasant meal near the fireplace on which there was a blazing fire.

About 9 o'clock, after most of the food had disappeared from the table, they heard horses outside in the yard and Mosby slipped to the door and peeped out. When he saw what was going on, he motioned for the candle on the table to be snuffed, and this was quickly done. Then he tiptoed toward the door of the bedroom on that side, forgetting the reflection of the fireplace. And it was from this light that Corporal Kane of the 13th New York Cavalry was able to see him and fire through the window. Mosby turned just as Kane fired and the bullet struck him just left of the navel.

When the Yankees entered, they found the two women, Old Man Lake, and Love gathered in the dining room. In the opposite room, in a pool of blood, they found a coatless Confederate wearing long cavalry boots. He lay on the floor, bloody saliva running out of his mouth and apparently dying. What they didn't know was that Mosby had the presence of mind to take off his uniform coat and shove it under the bureau, after which he collected some of the blood from his wound and put it in his mouth.

The Federals, who were returning from a scout after Mosby that had started on the 17th, were drinking heavily, and that may have been responsible for what happened next. They asked Mosby his name, and he groaned faintly it was Lt. Johnson of the Sixth Virginia Cavalry. Major Douglass Frazer, in command of the Union party, was a bit tipsy himself, and he looked Mosby over and decided he was dying, and since he was just a lieutenant, according to his word, they didn't worry about him.

So they rode away, leaving him lying on the floor. With them they took his cavalry boots and Tom Love, and somewhere in the dark a trooper was carrying a plumed hat, a gray overcoat and a scarlet-lined cape he had picked up from one corner of the dining room. It was some hours before the latter came to light, and then they were identified as Mosby's. But by the time they had got back here, Mosby had been taken by oxcart to a neighboring home and soon was on his way to his parents' home near Lynchburg. Desperately wounded, he remained until the latter part of February, and by that time the war was nearing a close, so the plans for wholesale guerilla warfare never were actually carried out, thanks to Corporal Kane.

And here's an odd detail; when the Yankees rode away they overlooked the fine horses of Mosby and Love, tied at the gate, and left them standing there, where they were later found by Mosby's men.

The Shooting of Mosby

An early picture of Lakeland.
Courtesy John K. Gott

An early picture of the back of Lakeland.
Mosby was shot through a window of the back dining room.
Courtesy John K. Gott

Mosby was critically wounded by
Corporal Kane of the 13th New York
Cavalry who shot through this
window pane. Two bullet holes can be
seen in the glass.
Courtesy John K. Gott

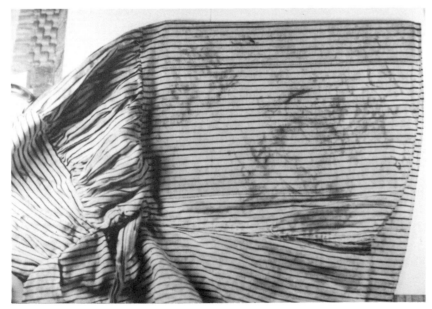

Blood stains from Mosby's wound can be seen as dark areas on Sarah Lake's
bonnet. Mosby quickly grabbed this up and briefly held it to his wound.
Courtesy John K. Gott

Sarah Lake's bonnet is modeled by Sarah E. Evans.
The blood stains can be seen on the
outside of the bonnet.

Ludwell Lake, owner of Lakeland.
Two sons served with Mosby.
Courtesy John K. Gott

Sarah Lake in later life. She slipped her
only shoes on Mosby's feet and stood
barefooted in the sleet the next day
denying to the Union cavalry that
she knew anything about Mosby.
Courtesy John K. Gott

Landonia Lake Skinner who was present in
the room when Mosby was wounded. She had
recently smuggled her captured husband
a $20 gold piece hidden in an apple.
Courtesy John K. Gott

Oxcart used by Uncle Daniel Strother
to move the wounded Mosby.
Courtesy John K. Gott

This is the picture Mosby gave Sarah Lake.
"If you have any varmints at home, they
will all leave," he commented.
Courtesy John K. Gott

Appendix E

SARAH LAKE'S SHOES

(Mr. John Gott is the great-grandson of Sarah Lake who was present when Colonel John S. Mosby was wounded at Lakeland, her home. Mosby and Ranger Tom Love had stopped here to eat and visit the Lake family. Mr. Gott kindly told the following information to the authors.)

"Ludwell Lake, who owned Lakeland, was a big man — he weighed over 300 pounds — never saw his feet after he was 30 years old. He had two daughters living at home at that time during the war, Sarah, who was my great-grandmother, and Landonia, who they called 'Doanie' (pronounced dough-knee). Both of those sisters were present the night Mosby was wounded. They all just finished a meal of ribs, vegetables, and buttermilk. Doanie was married and may have had a child there, I am not sure, and she had just come back from the prisoner of war camp at Point Lookout, Maryland where her husband was being held. He was riding with Mosby when he was captured. They would not allow her to take him any money, only fruit and things to eat, and she had stuffed a $20 gold piece in an apple and slipped it to him. Anyway, Mosby was talking to them about her husband when the bullet came, so the story goes.

Well, the Yankees rushed in and moved all but Mosby to another room. He told them he was someone else and smeared blood from his wound on his mouth like he was dying. The Yankees figured he was dying also, and went on their way taking the other Ranger prisoner.

Lud Lake was scared to death. He was an old man, although even with his great weight he lived to be 78 years old. He slipped getting into a buggy and struck his leg on the iron step, and this developed into blood poisoning that killed him. Well, he always swore that bullet had taken a button off of his vest. They were dancing around trying to figure what to do when Mosby walked out of the room, and they nearly all fainted from surprise. 'Doanie swooned when he walked out,' is the way Sarah wrote about it afterwards.

'We have to get Mosby out of here. I don't want my house burned down and that is what they will do if they come back and catch him here,' Ludwell Lake said. He wasn't going to have his house burned down, he was too old for that. Colonel Mosby was welcome, as was anybody with him, but when it came between a half dead man and his home, Ludwell Lake had a hard choice to make. His choice was that Mosby would be better off further south.

Now Colonel Mosby didn't want to go — it was cold, and raining and sleeting — and he thought Lud was sending him off to die at someone else's place. There were some hard feelings about this later.

There wasn't anybody there to move Mosby but this slave, Daniel Strother was his name. I remember him well, he was still living when I was a boy. Uncle Daniel lived outside of Marshall, and every time he came to town he stopped by our house. Lud called Uncle Daniel in and told him to get the oxcart ready, to fill it with straw, and yoke up the oxen for they were going to move Mosby. Mosby was sure they were going to take him right to the Yankees!

They took Mosby and wrapped him in quilts and put him in the ox cart. The Yankees had taken his hat and boots and his feet were sticking out from under the quilts. Sarah had just had a new pair of shoes made — they were rough — someone there in the neighborhood had made them. She took off those shoes and put them on Colonel Mosby's feet — he was a small man — and he had small hands and feet. Then Uncle Daniel took Mosby to Aquilla Glascock's place near Rectortown —

114

he was a cousin of the Lakes — and they operated on him and removed the pistol bullet. Then they moved him on to another Lake brother at Wheatland, down on Carter's Run, and from there on the back roads to Culpeper.

The Yankees returned the next morning and tried to get them to admit it was Mosby who they had shot, but the family wouldn't say. They made everyone go out in the yard and stand in the sleet for a half day while they questioned them. My great-grandmother was barefooted — the only pair of shoes she had she gave to Colonel Mosby — and she stood in that sleet and never said a thing. The Yankees threatened to burn down the house — they even had the firebrands ready — but they wouldn't tell them anything. 'No, we do not know who it was — if that was Colonel Mosby, he had changed from the last time we had seen him — it wasn't him,' is what they said.

Sarah was always fond of Mosby and his men and she clipped out everything from the paper about any of them or any event. When Mosby was shot he had grabbed her bonnet and stuck it on his wound to stop the bleeding. It was all blood stained, but she never washed it. I have it now and the glass panes from the window with the bullet holes in it.

After the war Mosby practiced law in Warrenton. Sarah was over there sitting in a buggy when he happened to pass by. He tipped his hat, and when he recognized her he came over and talked for some time about the war days. She asked him for his picture, and his disposition changed immediately — he became quite cold — said he didn't know why anyone would want his picture. She said she just thought it would be nice to have. He said he didn't have one and walked away. In a few minutes he was back and threw a picture in her lap. She thanked him and said she would value it. 'It is not worth thanking for — if you have any varmints at home, they will all leave,' Mosby said.

That became a family saying — if anyone saw a picture in the newspaper, engagement announcements and such — and it was not a striking person — they would say, ' That picture is for scaring away varmints.'

Times changed in the South, and the next generation of Lakes, my Grandmother, was not as fond of Mosby. He had become a 'Black Republican' and was a traitor to his fine battalion — a turncoat! When Pat (Virgil Carrington) Jones was secretary to the governor, he started writing his book *Ranger Mosby*. A cousin of ours, Lake Triplett is his name, lived right outside of Marshall here and heard about the book.

'Why don't you come and go to Marshall with me and I'll show you around and introduce you to the daughter of one of the two ladies who was at Lakeland the night Mosby was shot, and you can see what she has gleaned,' he said to Pat.

So Lake brought Pat around — it must have been in the early 40s — I was 10 or 12 years old. I knew Lake and was sitting there on the front porch with my Grandmother. Pat told her what he was doing and that he was going to write a book about Colonel Mosby and would like to know what she had heard about the incident at Lakeland.

'That is the greatest waste of time I have ever heard — I don't know why anyone would want to write about that old Devil! Yes, Maw used to talk about it all the time, and it was a pity he wasn't killed when that bullet came through the window,' my Grandmother told him.

Well, Pat was a little startled, and he saw she really despised Mosby for his politics — she had got this from the family over the years. He didn't ask her anything more so the story of her mother giving Mosby her only pair of shoes never appeared in any of Pat's books. I believe Sarah's obituary is the only place mention was ever made of it.''

Appendix F

A CIVIL WAR LETTER

Courtesy John E. Divine

On July 6, 1864, Col. John S. Mosby was raiding near Point of Rocks, Maryland. Hearing a party of 150 Union Cavalry was scouting for his command, he returned and attacked them at Mt. Zion Church, killing, wounding, or capturing 80. Following the fighting, "Yankee" Davis, Union sympathizer and scout, roamed the area collecting the wounded and burying the dead. These are the dead mentioned in the following letter from his wife.

Feb. the _____

Dear Mother, It is a long time since I have seen or heard anything particularly from you. I sometimes hear from Henry that you are well. How are you enjoying yourself in your old age. I hope that you are getting along comfortably in these times of War and Calamity that you know of in the land but you can only know War by rumor. I have lived on the battlefield for the last four years, have seen the dead and dying all around me, the wounded brought in numbers to die or with amputated limbs to recover crippled for life. Just as the all wise Providence should see fit our barn on one side and the church on the other for as hospitals both been full of wounded, dead and dying at the same time. An army of men encamped about on every side in every direction as far as eye could see — now at the present time while I am writing everything is quite. But it may be in less than an hour a band of guerillas or Squad of Yankees may come in large numbers perhaps both meet in a few yards of the house and if they happen so to meet a skirmish must ensue and some wounded and killed. Both horses and men are left on the side. It has often been the case under my own eyes. One that died in the barn said when he was dying, Oh my poor wife and child. I don't know who he was or where his wife and child are but his body is buried in a grave with two others just back of our barn, all three buried without coffins, two more are buried the same way back of the house so you see I live along on a battlefield with the Brave and Dead around me. Ellen saw eleven all buried in one grave last summer without coffins. They are buried a little over a mile from here where they fell. They belonged to Col. Lowell's Command, fellow soldiers in the same Reg. with your son and my husband that was a skirmish with Mosby's guerilas. Alexander was not out at that time. I have seen of places in Fairfax where 37 soldiers lie in one grave, Yankee and Rebel both lie side by side just about as their animosity and hatred are over and Bayonets and sabers laid aside and they sleep the quiet sleep of Death that knows no waking. Four soldiers came here the other night and said they were going to drive off my cows and burn the barn. They did not scare or frighten me much. I am too much accustomed to such threats. They did not put their threat in execution.

116

You would ask perhaps if I am not afraid. I was at the beginning of the War as timid and nervous as most people but know since I have seen and realize so much of War I have become hardened and almost fearless — I am not much afraid of anything. I have an opportunity of seeing and knowing more of War living here on the border and amongst _____ and guerillas than the soldiers in the field the art and deception and intrigue that is practiced. None but an eye witness has any idea — I have been writing about War. I suppose you would like to know of the health of the family. Ellen has been sick for the last four weeks. She is better now but not well. Able to be about the house again. Josie is staying with her. Alexander I suppose you hear from him nearly as often as I do. The Command that he is with are stationed at Fairfax Court House and now I intend to go down and to see him in a day or so and then I will carry this letter and mail it. We have no mail here and I seldom hear from any of my relatives in the North. I have generally found enough to eat in Dixie and learned to be content as anyone could expect. More so than I would have believed four years ago. If the War should end perhaps I should see you once more. I don't know when or where it will end. The South will hold out four years longer if it can I am satisfied of that. Jeff will never give up if he can help it so long as he can find man to fight for him.

From your daughter Eliza
to Mother

Appendix H

THE HANGING TREE

Courtesy Dr. Kenneth McAtee

I well remember Lt. John Russell of Mosby's Rangers, and will never forget when he pointed out the Hanging Tree to me. It was a tall white oak tree with many large limbs growing parallel to the ground and located close to the road. I was but a small lad, and he took me for rides in his "buggy" drawn by his favorite horse. He had such a relationship with the horse that I'm sure the horse would take him home without any guidance. Of the experiences that stood out most in my mind was that of the location of the "hanging tree" where Mosby ordered Custer's men hung in retaliation for those Mosby men executed in Front Royal by Custer's troops.

I can remember how "majestic" the old tree was in the sight of a young boy's eyes as it stood at the right of the entrance to Beemer's Woods on Grindstone Hill. This was a short distance from the Berryville Raceway to the west while the entrance to Rosemont was a short distance to the east. After his vivid explanation of the action there, I was frightened by its sight. This was especially true at night. I remember riding my bicycle down the hill at night at great speed as I heard the leaves rustle in the woods. This noise was in all probability caused by a dead branch falling or the movement of some small animal, however I would imagine that those people that John Russell had called "Yankees" were going to capture me at any moment.

As to the various statements and experiences explained to me by John, my memories were so vivid that I visited the old tree often. Years later the tree died and I cut sections of it and saved it for posterity. The American Historical Museum in Richmond and the Clark County Museum in Berryville have samples of the tree presented to them by me.

Knowing John Russell has been one of the highlights of my life, as it has afforded me an interest in the study of John Mosby in my retirement years.

Doctor Kenneth McAtee holds a section of wood from the "Hanging Tree".

Appendix I

MEDAL OF HONOR

Letter from former Captain Eugene W. Ferris:

Albany, Ind. August 7th, 1897

To the Hon Secretary of War, Washington, D.C.

Sir -

I hereby make application for a Medal of Honor — and respectfully submit the following sworn statement —

"On or about April 1st 1865, while in camp at Opequan Crossing, Va., near Berryville, I applied to the commanding officer of the regiment — the 30th Mass Vet Vols — Capt. Shipley now dead. The Lt. Col. Whittier since dead being absent on court martial duty and the Col. N.A.M. Dudley — now Col. U.S. Army retired — being on detached service, for permission to go outside the lines attended by an orderly. I was adjutant of the regiment at the time and was granted the desired request. I proceeded as far as the residence of Col. Danl. Bonham — about three miles from camp — where I halted and had our horses put in the stable in the rear of the yard, a short distance from the house.

After being seated for a short time in the house, a little girl came running in and excitedly exclaimed: "Oh, adjutant there is a whole squad of rebs coming down the road — what will you do?"

I walked out, looked down the road coming from Berryville and saw five of Mosby's men coming towards the house. I told the orderly to get the horses ready and walked to the stable, walked in, and as I did so they galloped into the yard. I turned about, came to the doorway when they were onto me.

Wiltshire was in the advance and as he came towards me he said: "Good Day, Surrender!"

I said: "Good Day, but I never surrender with life!"

With this I fired, wounding him in the neck (he afterwards died in our camp). The man to the left I unhorsed, and wounded two others, when I seemed to have them paralyzed, I mounted Wiltshire's horse, told the orderly to mount mine and chased them in the direction of Berryville, wounding another on the run. I then turned towards camp and they after me. I took the orderly's revolver and shortly after he was thrown from his horse. I stopped for and protected him until I had to get to camp for my pistols were empty — but one shot left. They left the orderly telling him to stay there until they caught that adjutant. While they were following me to the picket line the orderly made his escape and reached the camp. The last shot fired at me struck me in my left thigh. My coat was bored through in several places, my pants legs also, but I was uninjured except from the last shot fired at me."

On reaching camp and having reported the facts to the Comd'g Officer — (Shipley) I was ordered to take a company to the scene of the action and bring in the wounded. Wiltshire was the only one remaining. I took him to Camp and he died there in a very few days. The name of the Orderly was McLaughlin — since dead — during the melee he did not fire a shot. He was a member of Co "I". The first shot fired was from the stable door — and I did not fire one shot from under cover. I never entered the stable after firing the first shot.

Respectfully submitted — the forgoing for your consideration — Knowing that if I am considered entitled to the Medal of Honor — I will receive it.

I am sir -
Very respectfully Yours
Eugene W. Ferris
late Capt "E" Company
30th Mass V. Vols
Albany, Ind   Deleware P.O.

Excerpts from supporting statements in the files of the National Archives:

"His conduct in the affair of, about, April 12, 1865, near Berryville, Va., when his regiment was stationed at Opequan Crossing, was as reported to me, one of the most brave and gallant exhibitions of courage that I can recall during the war."
Col. N.A.M. Dudley, 30th Mass Inf Vols.

"Lieut. Ferris reached the Camp with but a slight wound but his clothes were riddled with bullet holes, he had one charge left in his pistol, this he told me he was saving for himself as he said he knew that if he was captured that they would murder him and that he had made up his mind to die by his own hand rather than have them take him."
First Lieutenant J. H. Burnham, Company D, 30th Mass Inf Vols.

"Wiltshire passed through the gate first, followed by Orrick, Gill, and myself. The gallant Wiltshire fell from his horse a few feet from the stable door, he got up, reeled, and fell again. Gill was shot in the gate way, he reeled but did not fall, but he was mortally wounded, and in consequence, unable to control his horse, which ran back into the public road, and he (Gill) poor fellow, took to some mountain home near by where he lingered for a few days and died. Eastham did not enter the yard, considering perhaps that, 'discretion was the better part of valor.'"
Mosby Ranger Bartlett Boling.

"I was an eyewitness to the whole affair. Orrick and Gill both met Boling and myself at the gate both shot. While there Boling was shot, then the two Yankees inside the barn ran out and got both of Wiltshire's pistols, mounted Wiltshire's horse, then nothing but a running chase after the two Yankees began resulted in our getting one Yankee and horse while the officer got safe to his camp."
Mosby Ranger Robert W. Eastham.

"I am a daughter of Col Daniel S. Bonham deceased who formerly resided near Berryville, Va., and was present on or about April 1, 1865 when Lt. Eugene. W. Ferris, then adjutant of the 30th Mass Inf resisted capture by a squad of Mosby's Rangers. In about an hour after the fight the Union Soldiers came and moved Wiltshire to their camp on the Opequan 2½ miles from our house where he was treated with the greatest kindness by his late foe Lt. Ferris. His Mother was sent for and remained with her boy until he died and took his remains with her to near Charlestown, W. Va. Wiltshire was a brave gallant soldier and died not fearing death.

If you are permitted to issue a Medal of Honor for true courage and gallant defense in the face of the enemy, I sincerely hope you will issue one to Lt. Ferris than whom a braver Officer never wore uniform."
Mrs. Emma Bonham Perry.

"I cannot possibly reply to your request in response to the distinguished courage exhibited on the Ocoquan mentioned in *Partisan Life with Mosby* for I have forgotten all about the affair except the fact of the brilliant display of bravery on the part of Captain Ferris."
Mosby Ranger John Scott of Fauquier.

"Since your letter of the 2nd inst., I have written to some ten or better of my friends, as to John Orrick, and he cannot be traced. I rather think that he is dead, or else we would have heard from him."
Mosby Ranger W. Ben Palmer.

"I have searched far and near for Orrick and Col. Mosby says he is dead."
Laurence Wilson, M.D., Co. "D", Ohio Inf.

Authors' Note. The search for Orrick was not successful at the time in spite of Dr. Wilson's determined efforts. On April 29, 1865 Orrick was paroled by Gen. Chapman, USA, near Berryville, Clark County, VA and headed back to his home in Greensboro, Alabama. His hometown soon became a haven for carpetbaggers. On June 13, 1867, Orrick shot and killed Alex Webb, a black man who was serving as registrar for Hale and Green Counties. He then disappeared until changing his name to George Washington Arrington (his mother's name and one used when spying in Maryland for Mosby), he enlisted in Co. E of the Texas Rangers on September 1, 1875 with a monthly salary of $120. He became First Sergeant in 1876. On December 25, 1877, he was promoted to First Lieutenant, Co. C., and to Captain of Co. C in 1880. He resigned from the Texas Rangers on 1 July, 1882 and was elected sheriff of Wheeler County, Texas for 2 four year terms. He is buried in Mobeetie, Texas. His tombstone reads as follows:

ARRINGTON
Capt. G.W. Arrington
Dec. 23, 1844 -- Mar. 31, 1923

A daring scout in Col. Mosby's command during the Civil War.

Captain of Company "C" of the Texas Rangers.
Sheriff of Wheeler and attached counties for eight years.
A fearless officer to whom the frontier of Texas
owes a debt of gratitude.

Appendix J

A MOSBY LEGEND

(Oral history — as told after the war by Pvt. Thomas Evans, Co. D, 54th Regiment Pennsylvania Volunteer Infantry. Pvt. Evans was unable to read or write his name, and the receipt for a Medal of Honor he won in battle is signed:

his

Thomas   X   Evans.)

mark

"It was a fall day, just the kind of warm day makes a fellow think he was a child again. Me and three other boys was doing picket duty way off from the Regiment. Things was quiet and had been for some time. Right next to us was this stream and it was deep enough in spots for a good swim. I said to the boys we should go swimming since there wasn't anything going on and nobody would be the wiser anyway. We needed a bath for the graybacks (lice) was starting to act up again like they could feel cold weather coming.

We had one boy to stand guard and the rest of us stripped off and went in. We were frolicking around and all and finally called the boy on guard to come on in. Well, he done it, and we were having a good old time when I noticed the other boys got quiet all of a sudden. I looked up and three Rebels in gray uniforms was just sitting on their horses there on the bank enjoying watching us.

'Boys, you are having a good time and I don't want to spoil it for you,' said a wiry little Confederate Officer. Says, 'But I am going to take these nice rifles and cartridge boxes you have stacked here for me. If I was a mean man I would take your uniforms, too, but I reckon you will have need for them.'

And that is what they did do, and then they all just rode off slowly, carrying our rifles and equipment.

'That's Mosby,' said one of the boys. Says, 'We are sure lucky he didn't take us prisoner.'

Well, there wasn't a thing to do but go on back to camp and confess to being the fool. The Captain took on something awful and the old Colonel Jakey Campbell got red as a beet and jumped around.

'You idiots are going to pay for those rifles and that equipment,' shouted the Colonel. Says, 'Expected more from you, Tommy Evans, you hard-headed Welshman. Serve you right if some Rebel shoots you with your own gun.'

Now we had a bad time out of it and had to pay up. I was sure sorry to lose that rifle. It was a good English made one I used down in the Shenandoah Valley when I won the Medal of Honor. But we could have been taken prisoner or killed by Mosby while acting the fool, and I still don't enjoy swimming as much as I used to before that day."

(Pay Records in the National Archives show that during September-October, 1864 Pvt. Thomas Evans was charged $15.32 for losing an Enfield Rifle and belt.)

123

MOSBY'S OFFICERS AND MEN

Mosby's personal exploits often overshadowed the abilities of the outstanding officers and men that served in his command. Several of the officers and one of the enlisted men mentioned in this book are shown below.

Major Adolphus E. Richards.
Williamson, MOSBY'S RANGERS

Captain Willie Mosby.
Courtesy Admiral Coleman

Captain Mountjoy.
Courtesy Admiral Coleman

Charles H. Dear, Co. E., Enlisted Man From a Photograph taken during the War.
Williamson, MOSBY'S RANGERS

Lieutenant Frank Fox, Co. C.
Williamson, MOSBY'S RANGERS

Lieutenant Ed. F. Thomson, Co. H.
Williamson, MOSBY'S RANGERS

BIBLIOGRAPHY

Alexander, John H. *Mosby's Men*. New York: Neale Publishing Co., 1907.

Baird, Nancy C. *Fauquier County, Virginia Tombstone Inscriptions*. Delaplane: Privately Printed, 1970.

Baird, Nancy C. *Journals of Amanda Virginia Edmonds, Lass of the Mosby Confederacy, 1859-1867*. Stephens City: Commercial Press, 1984.

Bakeless, John. *Spies of the Confederacy*. Philadelphia and New York: J. B. Lippincott Co., 1970.

Baker, La Fayette C. *Secret Service*. Washington, D.C.: The National Tribune, 1898.

Baylor, George. *Bull Run to Bull Run*. Richmond: B. F. Johnson Publishing Co., 1900.

Blackford, W. W. *War Years with JEB Stuart*. New York: Charles Scribner's Sons, 1945.

Brewster, Charles. *Captured By Mosby's Guerillas*. Suffolk: Robert Hardy Publications, 1988.

Brown, R. Shepard. *Stringfellow of the Fourth*. New York: Crown Publishers, Inc., 1960.

Brown, Stuart E., Jr. *Annals of Clarke County, Virginia*. Berryville: Virginia Book Co., 1983.

Bruce, Philip A. *Brave Deeds of Confederate Soldiers*. Philadelphia: George W. Jacobs and Co., 1916.

Bryan, John S. *Joseph Bryan, His Times, His Family, His Friends*. Richmond: Privately Printed, 1935.

Bryan, Thomas Joseph, III. *The Sword Over The Mantle*. New York: McGraw-Hill Book Co., Inc., 1960.

Bushong, Millard K. *Historic Jefferson County*. Boyce: Carr Publishing Co., 1972.

Bushong, Millard K. and Dean M. *Fightin' Tom Rosser, C.S.A.* Shippensburg: Beidel Printing House, Inc., 1983.

Carter, Samuel, III. *The Last Cavaliers*. New York: St. Martin's Press, 1979.

Castleman, Virginia C. *Reminiscences of an Oldest Inhabitant*. Herndon: Herndon Historical Society, 1976.

Chappelear, B. Curtis. *Maps and Notes Pertaining to the Upper Section of Fauquier County, Virginia*. Warrenton: Warrenton Antiquarian Society, 1954.

City of Fairfax Historical Sites. Fairfax: City of Fairfax Public Information Office, 1988.

City of Fairfax Public Information Office. *A Walking Tour of the Historical City of Fairfax, Virginia*. Fairfax: Colorcraft Litho, Inc., 1986.

Cooke, John E. *Outlines From the Outpost*. Chicago: The Lakeside Press, 1961.

Cooke, John E. *Wearing of the Gray*. Millwood: Kraus Reprint Co., 1977.

Cooling, B. F. *Symbol, Sword, & Shield*: Defending Washington During The Civil War. Hamden: Anchor Book, 1975.

Couper, William. *History of the Shenandoah Valley*, 3 vols. New York: Lewis Historical Publishing Co., Inc., 1952.

Couture, Richard T. *Powhatan: A Bicentennial History*. Richmond: The Dietz Press, Inc., 1980.

Crawford, J. Marshall. *Mosby and His Men: A record of the Adventures of that Renowned Partisan Ranger, John S. Mosby*. New York: G. W. Carleton & Co., 1867.

Curran, Louise C. *McLean Remembers Again*. McLean: The Sound Publication, 1976.

Daniels, Jonathan. *Mosby, Gray Ghost of the Confederacy*. New York and Philadelphia: J. B. Lippincott Co., 1959.

Danett, Sylvia G. L. and Burkat, Rosamond H. *Confederate Surgeon Aristideo Monteiro*. New York: Dodd, Meade, & Co., 1969.

Day, Annie G. *Warrenton and Fauquier County, Virginia*. Warrenton: Fauquier County Library, 1970.

Drickamer, Lee C. and Karen D. *Fort Lyon To Harpers Ferry*. Shippensburg: White Mane Publishing Co., Inc., 1987.

Editor, Time - Life Books. *Spies, Scouts and Raiders. Irregular Operations*. Alexandria: Time - Life Books, 1985.

Editor, Time - Life Books. *The Shenandoah in Flames. The Valley Campaign of 1864*. Alexandria: Time - Life Books, 1987.

Engle, Stephen D. *Thunder in the Hills, A History of the Civil War in Jefferson County, West Virginia*. Charleston: Mountain State Press, The University of Charleston, West Virginia, 1989.

Eskew, Garnett, L. *Willards of Washington*. New York: Coward-McCann, Inc, 1954.

Evans, D'Anne A. *The Story of Oakton, Virginia: 1758-1982*. Oakton: Greater Oakton Citizens Association, 1982.

Evans, D'Anne A. *Prince William County. A Pictorial History*. Norfolk: The Danning Co., 1989.

Evans, M. Louise. *An Old Timer In Warrenton and Fauquier County*. Warrenton: Virginia Publishing Inc., 1955.

Ewell, Alice M. *A Virginia Scene*. Lynchburg: J. P. Bell Co., Inc., 1931.

Fairfax County Civil War Centennial Commission. *Fairfax County and the War Between the States*. Vienna: Stenger Typographic Service, 1961.

Famous Adventures and Prison Escapes of the Civil War. New York: The Century Co., 1917.

Fauquier County, Virginia. Warrenton: Fauquier County Bicentennial Committee, 1959.

Fellman, Michael. *Inside War*. New York: Oxford University Press, 1989.

Forsythe, John W. *Guerilla Warfare and Life in Libby Prison*. Annandale: Turnpike Press, 1967.

Freeman, Douglas Southall. *Lee's Lieutenants: A Study in Command*. 3 vols., New York: Charles Scribner's Sons, 1942.

Frost, Lawrence A. *The Phil Sheridan Album*. Seattle: Superior Publishing Co., 1968.

Gamble, Robert S. *Sully, The Biography of a House*. Falls Church: United Litho, Inc., 1973.

Garrett, Richard. *The Raider*. New York: Norstrand Reinhold Co., 1980.

Glasgow, W. M., Jr. *Northern Virginia's Own*. Alexandria: Gobill Press, 1989.

Geddes, Jean. *Fairfax County Historical Highlights From 1607*. Middleburg: Denlinger's, 1967.

Gold, Thomas D. *History of Clarke County, Virginia*. Berryville: Chesapeake Book Co., 1962.

Goodhart, Briscoe. *History of the Independent Loudoun Virginia Rangers, 1862-1865*. Gaithersburg: Butternut Press, Inc., 1985.

Gott, John K. *A History of Marshall (formerly Salem), Fauquier County, Virginia*. Middleburg: Denlinger's, 1959.

Gott, John K. *High in Old Virginia's Piedmont. A History of Marshall (formerly Salem), Fauquier County, Virginia*. Marshall: Marshall National Bank & Trust Co., 1987.

Grant, U.S. *Personal Memoirs*, 2 vols., 1885. 2 vols. in 1, edited by E. B. Long. Cleveland: World Publishing Co., 1952.

Green, Anne. *With Much Love*. New York: Harper and Brothers, Publishers, 1948.

Guy, Anne W. *John Mosby, Rebel Raider of the Civil War*. New York: Abelord-Schuman, 1965.

Hale, Laura V. *Four Valient Years in the Lower Shenandoah Valley*. Strausburg: Shenandoah Publishing House, Inc., 1968.

Hale, Laura V. *On Chester Street ... Presence of the Past, Patterns of the Future*. Stephens City: Commercial Press, 1985.

Hale, Laura V. *Memories in Marble. The Story of the Four Confederate Monuments at Front Royal, Virginia*. Front Royal: Warren Rifle Chapter, U.D.C., 1956.

Heblich, F. T. and Elwood, M. A. *Charlottesville and the University of Virginia, a Pictorial History*. Norfolk: The Donning Company, 1982.

Herbert, Robert B. *Life On A Virginia Farm*. Warrenton: The Fauquier Democrat, 1968.

Hillsboro, Memories of a Milltown. Hillsboro: Hillsboro Bi-Centennial Commission, 1976.

Hite, Mary E. *My Rappahannock Story Book*. Richmond: The Dietz Press, Inc., 1950.

Hopkins, G. M. *Atlas of Fifteen Miles Around Washington Including the Counties of Fairfax and Alexandria, Virginia*. Philadelphia: G. M. Hopkins, 1879.

Hunter, Alexander. *The Women of the Debatable Land*. Port Washington, Kennikat Press, 1912.

Hutchison, Louis. *Come America To a Land of Simple Pleasures. The Story of Loudoun: Land of Contrast - Land of Beauty*. Leesburg: Potomac Press, 1983.

Janney, Asa M. and Werner L. *The Composition Book. Stories From the Old Days in Lincoln, Virginia*. Privately Printed.

Janney, Samuel M. *Memories of Samuel M. Janney*. Philadelphia: Friends Book Association, 1881.

Jefferson County Camp, U.C.V. *Military Operations in Jefferson County, Virginia (and West Virginia), 1861-1865*. Charles Town: Farmers Advocate Printers, 1911.

Jefferson County Historical Society. *The Washington Homes of Jefferson County, West Virginia*. Private Printing, 1975. Revised 1988.

Johnson, Elizabeth B. and C. E., Jr. *Rappahannock County, Virginia, A History*. Orange: Green Publishing Co., 1981.

Johnston, Angus J., II. *Virginia Railroads in the Civil War*. Chapel Hill: University of North Carolina Press, 1961.

Jones, Virgil C. *Gray Ghosts and Rebel Raiders*. New York: Henry Holt & Co., 1956.

Jones, Virgil C. *Ranger Mosby*. Chapel Hill: University of North Carolina Press, 1944.

Jordan, Ervin L., Jr. *Charlottesville and the University of Virginia in the Civil War*. Lynchburg: H. E. Howard, Inc., 1988.

Kane, Harnett, T. *Spies for the Blue and Gray*. Garden City: Hanover House, 1954.

Kinsley, D. A. *Favor the Bold, Custer, The Civil War Years*. New York: Promontory Press, 1967.

Kirkland, Alberta C. *They Came To Kentucky*. Baltimore: Gateway Press, Inc., 1976.

Klitch, Helen J. *Joseph Arthur Jeffries' Fauquier County, 1840-1919*. San Antonio: Phil Bate Associates, 1989.

Lancaster, Mary H. and Dallas M. *The Civil War Diary of Anne S. Frobel of Wilton Hill in Virginia*. Birmingham: Birmingham Printing & Publishing Co., 1986.

Leech, Margret. *Reville in Washington*. New York: Harper & Brothers, 1941.

Little Big Horn Associates, Inc. *Custer and His Times, Book Three*, edited by Gregory J. W. Urwin. Albertville: Private Printing, 1987.

Long, E. B. *The Civil War Day by Day. An Almanac 1861-1865*. New York: Doubleday & Co., 1971.

Loudoun County Civil War Centennial Commission. *Loudoun County and the Civil War*. Leesburg: Potomac Press, 1961.

McCarty, Clara S. *The Foothills of the Blue Ridge in Fauquier County, Virginia*. Berryville: Chesapeake Book Co., 1974.

McGriffin, Lee. *Swords, Stars, and Bars*. New York: E. P. Dutton & Co., 1958.

McKim, Randolph H. *A Soldier's Recollections*. Washington, D.C.: Zenger Publishing Co., 1983.

McMillin, Loyal. *A Walk With History*. Middleburg: Privately Printed, 1987.

Moffet, Lee. *The Diary of Court House Square, Warrenton, Virginia. From Early Times Through 1986*. Stephens City: Commercial Press, 1988.

Mogelever, Jacob. *Death To Traitors*. Garden City: Doubleday & Co., 1960.

Monteiro, Aristides. *War Reminiscences by the Surgeon of Mosby's Command*. Gaithersburg: Reprinted by the Butternut Press, 1983.

Moore, John H. *Albermarle, Jefferson's County, 1727-1976*. Charlottesville: University Press of Virginia, 1976.

Moore, Robert H., III. *The Danville, Eight Star New Market and Dixie Artillery*. Lynchburg; H. E. Howard, Inc., 1989.

Mosby, John S. *Mosby's War Reminiscences and Stuart's Cavalry Campaign*. New York: Pagent Book Co., 1958.

Mosby, John S. *The Memoirs of Colonel John S. Mosby*, edited by Charles Wells Russel, 1917. Bloomington: Indiana University Press, 1959.

Munson, John W. *Reminiscences of a Mosby Guerilla*. New York: Moffat, Yard, and Co., 1906.

National Archives, Washington, D.C., Records of Captain E. F. Ferris; 493, 029-2,3,5,6,7,9.

Neff, Ray A. *Valley of the Shadow*, second edition. Terre Haute: Rana Publications, 1989.

Nelson, Alice Jean. *Virginia Lineage, Letters & Memories*. Sarasota: Privately Published, 1984.

Nelson, Robert F. *Thrilling Legends of Virginia*. Richmond: Whittet & Shepperson, 1971.

Netherton, Ross and Nan. *Fairfax County in Virginia: A Pictorial History*. Norfolk/Virginia Beach: The Donning Company Publishers, 1986.

Netherton, Ross and Nan. *Green Spring Farm, Fairfax County, Virginia*. Fairfax: Fairfax County Board of Supervisors, 1970.

Netherton, Nan and Rose, Ruth. *Memories of Beautiful Burke, Virginia*. Burke: Burke Historical Society, 1988.

Newcomer, C. Armour. *Cole's Cavalry: Three Years in the Saddle in the Shenandoah Valley*. Books for Libraries Press, 1970.

Nichols, James L. *General Fitzhugh Lee, A Biography*. Lynchburg: H. E. Howard, Inc., 1989.

Northern Virginia History Officials Advisory Committee. *Historic Northern Virginia*. Falls Church: Northern Virginia Planning District Commission, 1981.

Peters, Margret T. *A Guidebook to Virginia Historical Markers*. Charlottesville: University Press of Virginia,. 1985.

Petersilia, Martin and Wright, Russel. *Hope Park and the Hope Park Mill*. Fairfax: County Office of Comprehensive Planning, 1978.

Poland, Charles P., Jr. *From Frontier To Suburbia*. Marceline: Walsworth Publishing Co., 1976.

Prince William County Historical Commission. *Prince William; A Past To Preserve*. Manassas: Private Printing, 1982.

Proceedings of the Clarke County Historical Association, vol. XV. Berryville: Clarke County Historical Association, 1964.

Rahm, Frank H. *Reminiscences of Frank H. Rahm of Mosby's Command*. Suffolk: Robert Hardy Publications, 1989.

Ramey, Emily G. and Gott, John K. *The Years of Anguish, Fauquier County Virginia, 1861-1865*. Warrenton: Fauquier Democrat, 1965.

Ratcliffe, R. Jackson. *This Was Prince William*. Leesburg: Potomac Press, 1978.

Reeder, Colonel Red. *Heros and Leaders of West Point*. New York: Thomas Nelson, Inc., 1970.

Rodenbough, Theo. F. *The Photographic History of the Civil War: The Cavalry*. New York: The Fairfax Press, 1983.

Rust, Jeanne, J. *A History of the Town of Fairfax*. Washington, D.C.: Moore & Moore, Inc., 1960.

Saegesser, Lee and Ruth. *A History of Dunn Loring, Virginia*. Privately Printed, 1986.

Scheel, Eugene M. *The Civil War in Fauquier*. Warrenton: Fauquier National Bank, 1985.

Scheel, Eugene M. *The Guide to Fauquier*. Warrenton: Warrenton Printing & Publishing, 1976.

Scheel, Eugene M. *The Guide to Loudoun*. Leesburg: Potomac Press, 1975.

Scheel, Eugene M. *The History of Middleburg and Vicinity*. Warrenton: Piedmont Press, 1987.

Schuyler, Colfax. *A Day With Mosby's Men*. Suffolk: Robert Hardy Publications, 1989.

Scott, John. *Partisan Life with Col. John S. Mosby*. New York: Harper & Bros., 1867.

Sergent, Mary E. *They Lie Forgotten*. Middletown: The Prior King Press, 1986.

Sheridan, Philip H. *Personal Memoirs*. 2 vols., 1888. St. Clair Shores: Scholarly Press, 1977.

Siepel, Kevin H. *Rebel: The Life and Times of John Singleton Mosby*. New York: St. Martin's Press, 1983.

Sinise, Jerry. *George Washington Arrington, Civil War Spy, Texas Ranger, Sheriff and Rancher*. Bunnet: Eakin Press, 1979.

Slater, Kitty. *The Hunt Country of America Revisited*. New York: Cornwell Books, 1987.

Smallwood, Marianna. *Something About Kabletown*. Kabletown: Privately Printed, 1983.

Smallwood, Marianna. *Lost Treasures*. Kabletown: Privately Printed, 1928.

Smith, P.A.L. *Boyhood Memories of Fauquier*. Owensburg: Cook & McDowell Publications, 1980.

Smith, V. E. *Middleburg and Nearby*. Leesburg: Potomac Press, 1986.

Stackpole, Edward J. *Sheridan in the Shenandoah, Jubal Early's Nemesis*. New York: Bonanza Books, 1956.

Stem, Philip V.D. *Secret Missions of the Civil War*. New York: Bonanza Books, 1959.

Stevens, William T. *Virginia House Tour*. Charlottesville: Stevenpost Publications, 1962.

Stover, John F. *History of the Baltimore and Ohio Railroad*. Lafayette: Purdue University Press, 1987.

Stuntz, Connie P. and Mayo S. *This Was Tysons Corner, Virginia: Facts and Photos*. Vienna: Privately Printed, 1990.

Stuntz, Connie P. and Mayo S. *This Was Vienna: Facts and Photos*. Vienna: Privately Printed, 1987.

Taylor, James E. *With Sheridan Up The Shenandoah Valley in 1864: Leaves From A Special Artist's Sketchbook and Diary*. Dayton: Morningside House, Inc., 1989.

Templeman, Eleanor L. *Arlington Heritage, Vignettes of a Virginia County*. Arlington: Privately Printed, 1959.

Templeman, Eleanor L. and Netherton, Nan. *Northern Virginia Heritage*. Arlington: Privately Printed, 1966.

The Letters of John S. Mosby, second edition. Carlisle: Stuart-Mosby Historical Society, 1986.

Thomason, John W., Jr. *Jeb Stuart*. New York: Charles Scribner's Sons, 1930.

Tidwell, William A. Hall, James O., and Gaddy, David W. *Come Retribution*. Jackson and London: University Press of Mississippi, 1988.

U.S. Government. *The War of the Rebellion: A Compilation of the Official Records of the Union and Confederate Armies*. Washington, D.C.: U.S. Government Printing Office, 1884.

U.S. Government. *The Medical and Surgical History of the War of the Rebellion*, vol. I. Washington, D.C.: U.S. Government Printing Office, 1870-88.

Valentine, Elizabeth G. *Dawn to Twilight*. Richmond: William Byrd Press, Inc., 1929.

Van De Water, Frederic F. *Glory-Hunter: A Life of General Custer*. Indianapolis: Bobbs-Merrill, 1934.

Wallace, Robert C. *A Few Memories of a Long Life*. Fairfield: Ye Golden Press, 1988.

Wayland, John W. *Historic Homes of Northern Virginia and the Eastern Panhandle of West Virginia*. Staunton: McClure Co., Inc., 1937.

Weichmann, Louis J. *A True History of the Assassination of Abraham Lincoln and of the Conspiracy of 1865*. New York: Alfred A. Knopf, 1975.

Went, Jeffery D. *From Winchester to Cedar Creek: The Shenandoah Campaign of 1864*. Carlisle: South Mountain Press, Inc., 1987.

Whitt, James C. *Elephants and Quaker Guns*. New York: Vantage Press, 1966.

Williams, Harrison. *Legends of Loudoun*. Richmond: Garrett and Massie, Inc., 1938.

Williamson, James J. *Mosby's Rangers*. 2d ed. New York: The Macmillian Co., 1909.

Willis, Connie H. and Ealker, Etta B. *Legends of the Skyline Drive and the Great Valley of Virginia*. Richmond: The Dietz Press, 1940.

Wintz, William D. *Civil War Memories of Two Rebel Sisters*. Charlestown: Pictorial Histories Publishing Co., 1989.

Newspapers:

Alexandria Gazette	*New York Times*
Clarke Courier	*Northern Virginia Daily*
Fauquier Democrat	*Richmond Times-Dispatch*
Herndon Observer	*Warrenton Sentinel*
Herndon Times	*Washington Evening Star*
Loudoun Times Mirror	*Washington Post*
New York Herald	

Interviews:

Mr. Ted Ballard	Mr. Hugh Keen
Mrs. Nancy C. Baird	Mr. Lewis Leigh, Jr.
Mr. Paul Brown, Jr.	Dr. Kenneth S. McAtee
Mr. William S. Burrell	Mr. Horace Mewborn
Mr. Randy Carter	Mr. Walter Minnick
Admiral Beverly Mosby Coleman (Ret)	Mrs. Ralph Mitchell
Mr. Jim Davis	Mrs. Marion Ralph
Mr. Arthur DeButts	Mr. Ripley Robertson
Mr. John E. Divine	Colonel Murray F. Rose (Ret)
Mr. Robert W. Eastham	Mrs. Jeanne Rust
Mr. J. Walton Follin	Mr. Whynne Saffer
Mr. John K. Gott	Mrs. Marianna Smallwood
Mrs. Virginia Greear	Colonel Don Stumbo
Mr. Kim B. Holien	Mr. Dewey Vaughn
Mr. Lee Hubbard	Mrs. Lola Wood
Ms. Marsha Hyde	
Mr. Virgil Carrington Jones	

INDEX